Fourth Edition

Teaching Students with Special Needs in Inclusive Settings

Tom E. C. Smith
University of Arkansas

Edward A. Polloway
Lynchburg College

James R. Patton
University of Texas

Carol A. Dowdy
University of Alabama at Birmingham

D0219299

PEARSON

A and B

Boston New York San Francisco
Mexico City Montreal Toronto London Madrid Munich Paris
Hong Kong Singapore Tokyo Cape Town Sydney

Executive Editor:	Virginia Lanigan
Developmental Editor:	Sonny Regelman
Executive Marketing Manager:	Amy Cronin Jordan
Associate Editor:	Tom Jefferies
Editorial Assistant:	Robert Champagne
Senior Production Administrator:	Deborah Brown
Editorial-Production Service:	PM Gordon Associates
Photo Researcher:	Laurie Frankenthaler
Manufacturing Buyer:	Andrew Turso
Text Designer:	Glenna Collett
Electronic Composition:	Shelley Smigelski
Cover Administrator:	Linda Knowles

Between the time Web site information is gathered and published, some sites may have closed. Also, the transcription of URLs can result in typographical errors. The publisher would appreciate notification where these occur so that they may be corrected in subsequent editions.

Library of Congress Cataloging-in-Publication Data

Teaching students with special needs in inclusive settings / Tom E.C. Smith . . . [et al.].—4th ed.

    p. cm.

    Includes bibliographical references and index.

    ISBN 0-205-37349-6

    1. Inclusive education—United States. 2. Special education—United States.

  3. Handicapped children—Education—United States.—4. Classroom management—United States. I. Smith, Tom E. C.

LC1201.T43 2003

371.9'046—dc21   02-043884

Printed in the United States of America

10 9 8 7 6 5 4 3 2   [WC]   07 06 05 04 03

Photo credits appear on page 570, which constitutes a continuation of the copyright page.

For
Debi, Jake, Alex, Suni
Carolyn and Lyndsay
Joy and Kimi
Jim, Cameron, and Meredith

Brief Contents

Contents

7 Teaching Students with Emotional and Behavioral Disorders   200

8 Teaching Students with Mental Retardation   228

9 Teaching Students with Sensory Impairments   256

Special Features

Rights & Responsibilities

TECHNOLOGY TODAY

Personal Spotlight

Preface

The fourth edition of *Teaching Students with Special Needs in Inclusive Settings* comes almost 10 years after we wrote the first edition. In that time, the field of special education has evolved significantly. The movement to include students with disabilities has taken hold; the debate is far less about whether inclusion should be used and more about how we can use it better and more effectively.

Most recently, the discussion and debate about how we educate all students who differ in their learning and behavior has come to the national forefront. The White House Commission on Special Education issued a report that has resulted in a healthy discussion and debate about the role of special education in the future. Section 504 and the Americans with Disabilities Act, as they relate to school age children, are receiving more attention than ever before. The prospects for "full funding" for special education seem to be getting closer to the promise that the original PL 94-142 envisioned. And once again, the re-authorization of IDEA is approaching, a process which could significantly alter the nature of special education.

While professionals, advocates, parents, and individuals with disabilities may disagree over some issues, the one thing that will remain constant is the commitment to provide all students, regardless of their abilities or disabilities, with an equal opportunity to receive an appropriate education.

Making the Links

A key priority in our approach to this fourth edition was to help our readers make the necessary, practical, and satisfying "links" involved in successful inclusive teaching. These links are between: (1) understanding the nature and characteristics of the learning and behavior problems, struggles, and challenges students face; and (2) the practical (and required) procedures, collaborative practices, and instructional strategies educators will employ to help their students learn well, be accepted within their school community, and ultimately achieve their fullest academic and social potential.

Inclusive education is an evolving, problem solving, and recursive process, and as educators, we need to ask ourselves, "How is my plan working for this child? What changes do I need to make going forward? How are these changes working?" To that end, each chapter begins with a story related to the chapter topic through an introductory vignette, and then we revisit this same student and/or teacher throughout the chapter in the "Goals and Objectives" and "Tips for Adapting a Lesson" features (both detailed in a later section of this preface). Complete IEPs for two students with specific disabilities are also addressed in the new appendixes. These added features help you link the needs of your students with specific interventions intended to help them become more successful in school and afterwards.

ew and Expanded in This Edition

▶ **Increased coverage of professional collaboration in Chapter 2.** Collaboration among school professionals is a critical aspect of successful inclusion of students with disabilities. Therefore, our discussion of this topic is increased early in the book so that readers will be aware of its critical nature.

▶ **Increased coverage of IEP programming in Chapter 4.** The IEP continues to be the basis for meeting the needs of students. As more attention is paid to the role of general education teachers in this process, they must understand their role and have the skills to perform it.

▶ **Increased focus on family collaboration in Chapter 3.** The importance of families in the education of children with special needs becomes clearer every day. Teachers and other school personnel must work closely with family members and empower them to be active participants in the education of their children.

▶ **Increased coverage of cultural and linguistic diversity throughout all chapters.** As linguistic and cultural diversity increases in U.S. society, it becomes critical that school personnel possess a thorough understanding of this diversity and how to use it to enhance the education of all students.

pecial Features and Pedagogy in the Fourth Edition

▶ **Chapter-opening Vignettes**   These mini case studies present the story of a student or teacher who exemplifies the topic of the chapter. The students profiled in the chapter-opening vignettes are spotlighted in the new features "IEP Goals and Objectives" and "Tips for Adapting a Lesson" in Chapters 6–11.

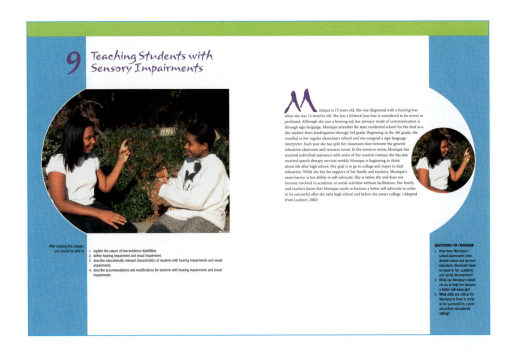

▶ **NEW! IEP Goals and Objectives** This feature presents sample goals and objectives for the IEP of the student highlighted in the chapter-opening vignettes. This feature allows students to become familiar with the IEP process, in which they will play an important part, and to see what the IEP goals and objectives might be when planning the educational strategy for a child with a particular disability. The specific goals and objectives are good examples of what an IEP might look like for a particular child; they provide a realistic view of how to turn a child's characteristics into IEP goals and objectives.

▶ **NEW! Tips for Adapting a Lesson** This feature presents concrete suggestions for lesson adaptations for the student highlighted in the chapter-opening vignette and the IEP Goals and Objectives features. This practical information will show readers how their knowledge of effective adaptations can greatly enhance the learning of students with disabilities in their classrooms. As students with special needs spend more time in general classrooms, the adaptations made by classroom teachers become the basis of success for those students.

▶ **Inclusion Strategies** Teachers who have more ideas and strategies will be better prepared to meet the needs of students. This feature provides practical ideas for implementing instructional adaptations and curricular modifications in the general education classroom.

▶ **Diversity Forum** This fully revised feature, contributed by our colleagues Shernaz García and Gwen Webb-Johnson from the University of Texas at Austin, provides practical, research-proven information that will help teachers in inclusive classrooms meet the needs of culturally diverse students.

▶ **Technology Today**   This fully revised feature provides clear and practical information about the ever-changing technology available to help all students learn in today's inclusive classrooms.

Technology applications can reduce the chance of failure for some at risk students.

▶ **Personal Spotlight**   This feature profiles teachers, parents of children with special needs, and individuals with special needs, bringing reality to the text discussions and providing insight into the multifaceted experiences of people most affected by the challenges of inclusion.

▶ **Rights & Responsibilities**   This feature examines legal cases and issues to illustrate the many laws that affect students with disabilities and their teachers.

▶ **Margin Notes**   These notes throughout the chapters present three themes: *Teaching Tip* provides brief, specific suggestions related to the content; *Cross-Reference* points out related information found in other parts of the text; and *Consider This* presents issues that require problem-solving or creative thinking related to a challenging topic.

▶ **NEW! Appendixes**   These appendixes present sample IEPs for an elementary student and for a secondary student. In order to help readers understand the underlying issues reflected in the IEPs, running *Take Note* margin notes point out the central concepts of the IEP, and *Cross-Reference* margin notes state where additional and related information is found in the chapters.

General Organization and Content of the Fourth Edition

The fourth edition focuses on **comprehensive information** and **practical suggestions** for classroom teachers, including topics such as **professional and family collaboration, understanding the IEP process, cultural and linguistic diversity,** and **technology.**

Chapters 1 and 2 present a **complete explanation of inclusion** so that general education teachers learn how to meet student needs and why it's necessary to do so. **Chapter 3** explains how **families** influence the implementation of inclusion and how teachers and parents can work together to increase the success of their children. **Chapter 4** explains the **steps in the IEP process,** including referral, assessment, and development of individual programs for students.

Chapters 5–11 each focus on **specific categories of disabilities and exceptionalities** to help teachers identify and teach students with special needs who are included in their general education classrooms. These chapters include practical strategies, adaptations, and interventions for teaching these students.

Chapters on students with **ADHD (Chapter 5), gifted and talented students (Chapter 12),** and **students at risk for school failure (Chapter 13)** address common student needs beyond the clinical categories of special education.

Chapter 14 presents the basics of **classroom organization and management** and their influence on inclusion. **Chapters 15 and 16** provide specific coverage of inclusion as it relates to **elementary and secondary curriculum and instruction,** including **preschool** and **transition from high school,** to help teachers at all levels create inclusive classrooms.

Supplements for Instructors and Students

Instructor Supplements

▶ **Instructor's Resource Manual and Test Bank**   Fully revised for this edition, the Instructor's Resource Manual includes ideas and activities to help instructors teach the course. It provides goals and objectives; classroom discussion topics and activities; student assignments and classroom handouts; and video resources for each chapter. The Test Bank contains hundreds of challenging questions in multiple-choice, true/false, and essay formats, along with an answer key.

▶ **Computerized Test Bank**   The printed Test Bank is also available electronically through our computerized testing system: TestGen EQ. Instructors can use TestGen EQ to create exams in just minutes by selecting from the existing database of questions, editing questions, or writing original questions.

▶ **PowerPoint™ Presentation**   Ideal for lecture presentations or student handouts, the PowerPoint™ presentation created for this text provides dozens of ready-to-use graphic and text images (available on the Web at ablongman.com/ppt).

▶ **Videos**   Allyn and Bacon provides several choices of videos for special education. Please contact your publisher's representative for additional information about our videos.

▶ **VideoWorkshop for Special Education CD-ROM**   Available free when packaged with *Teaching Students with Special Needs in Inclusive Settings,* fourth edition, this CD-ROM contains digitized video footage. An Instructor's Teaching Guide is also available to provide ideas and exercises to assist faculty in incorporating this convenient supplement into course assignments and assessments. (Visit ablongman.com/videoworkshop for more details.)

▶ **Allyn & Bacon Transparencies for Special Education 2002**   This package includes 100 full-color acetates.

▶ **Digital Media Archive for Special Education**   This CD-ROM contains a variety of media elements that instructors can use to create electronic presentations in the classroom. It includes hundreds of original images, as well as selected art from Allyn and Bacon special education texts, providing instructors with a broad selection of graphs, charts, and tables. For classrooms with full multimedia capability, it also contains video segments and Web links.

Student Supplements

▶ **VideoWorkshop for Special Education CD-ROM**   This exciting new supplement puts digitized video footage of children and classrooms, organized into 3- to 5-minute clips, covering several categories and topics, directly into the hands of students. The VideoWorkshop Extra! feature at the end of each chapter relates the video clips to the chapter's contents. The VideoWorkshop CD also comes with a Student Learning Guide, containing all the materials needed to help students get started. With questions for reflection before, during, and after viewing, this guide extends classroom discussion and allows for more in-class time spent on analysis of material.

▶ **"What's Best for Matthew?" Interactive CD-ROM Case Study for Learning to Develop IEPs, Version 2.0**   This CD-ROM helps pre-service and in-service teachers develop their IEP writing skills through the case study of Matthew, a nine-year-old boy with autism. It is sold separately and is also available at a reduced price as a "value package" with the textbook.

▶ **Companion Website**   Students who visit the Companion Website for *Teaching Students with Special Needs in Inclusive Settings* (ablongman.com/sppd4e) will find many features and activities to help them in their studies:

- web links and learning activities
- practice tests
- text correlations to national and state professional standards and the Praxis II exams
- an interactive glossary
- vocabulary flash cards

The website also features an interactive Special Education Timeline that highlights the people and events that have shaped special education through history. In addition, adopting instructors may use the website's convenient **Syllabus Manager,** an online syllabus creation and management tool. Instructors can easily create syllabi with direct links to the companion website, links to other online resources, and student assignments. Students may access the syllabus at any time to help them with research projects and to complete the assignments.

▶ **Research Navigator™ (with ContentSelect Research Database)** (Access Code Required)   Research Navigator™ is the easiest way for students to start a research assignment or research paper. Complete with extensive help on the research process and three exclusive online databases of credible and reliable source material including EBSCO's ContentSelect™ Academic Journal Database, *New York Times* Search by Subject Archive, and "Best of the Web" Link Library, Research Navigator™ helps students quickly and efficiently make the most of their research time. Research Navigator™ is free when packaged with the textbook and requires an Access Code.

▶ **iSearch Guide for Special Education (with access code to Research Navigator™)** This free reference guide includes tips, resources, activities, and URLs to help students use the Internet for their research projects. Part One introduces students to the basics of the Internet and the World Wide Web. Part Two includes over thirty Net activities that tie into the content of the text. Part Three lists hundreds of special education Internet resources. The guide also includes information on how to correctly cite research and a guide to building an online glossary.

Acknowledgments

The fourth edition of *Teaching Students with Special Needs in Inclusive Settings* is the result of a great deal of effort on the part of many people. We would like to acknowledge the significant contribution made by numerous professionals in the field of special and general education whose daily jobs give us information to share in this textbook, and we also acknowledge those authors whose works we cite regularly, who make a real contribution to the education of children with special needs. We would also like to thank every member of our families who put up with our time away from them, whether it is physically or just mentally away while we ponder permissions, references, or the changes we need to make in that one last chapter. Especially we thank our spouses, Debi, Carolyn, Joy, and Jim. And, we could never have the energy to write about children without having the wonderful opportunity presented by the children in our own lives, namely Jake, Alex, Suni, Lyndsay, Kimi, Cameron, and Meredith.

We wish to thank Peggy Kipping and Kathleen McConnell Fad for the contribution of Chapter 11, "Teaching Students with Communication Disorders." We are also especially grateful to Dr. Shernaz B. García and Dr. Gwen Webb-Johnson at the University of Texas at Austin, who coordinated and edited the contribution of the new Diversity Forum features. Their writing team included Sandra Valle (Ch. 2), Suzette Whitehead-Anderson (Ch. 2, 6), Barbara Dray (Ch. 3, 9), Mary Ellen Alsobrook (Ch. 3, 8), Lee Ming Tan (Ch. 4), Audrey Trainor (Ch. 5), Peggy Hickman (Ch. 6, 13), Satasha Green (Ch. 7, 10), Jessica Ross (Ch. 8), and Rocio Delgado (Ch. 7, 9, 11). Further, we appreciate the support of Amy Smith-Thomas in the revision process of a number of chapters. We also thank Rebecca B. Evers of Winthrop University for contributing the VideoWorkshop Extra! questions.

As always, our extended family at Allyn and Bacon deserve thanks. We acknowledge, in particular, Virginia Lanigan, our editor, and Sonny Regelman, our developmental editor, Tom Jefferies, our supplements editor, Deborah Brown, our production editor, and Amy Cronin Jordan, our marketing manager. We also owe a great deal of thanks to the production people at PM Gordon Associates—especially to Nancy Lombardi, who once more kept this book on track, and to Peter Reinhart, our copyeditor.

Finally, we want to thank those persons who reviewed our third edition and gave us some wonderful ideas for this fourth edition. These individuals include: Mitra Fallahi,

Saint Xavier University; Jennifer Buie Hune, University of Arkansas at Little Rock; Karen L. Kelly, University of Montana, Missoula; Kevin A. Koury, California University of Pennsylvania; Loretta Salas, New Mexico State University; Qaisar Sultana, Eastern Kentucky University.

About the Authors

Tom E. C. Smith is currently Professor and Head, Department of Curriculum and Instruction, University of Arkansas. He has been on the faculties of the University of Arkansas at Little Rock, University of Alabama at Birmingham, and the University of Arkansas for Medical Sciences. Prior to receiving his EdD from Texas Tech University, he taught children with mental retardation, learning disabilities, and autism at the elementary and secondary levels. President Clinton appointed him to three terms on the President's Committee on Mental Retardation. He has served as the Executive Director of the Division on Developmental Disabilities of the Council for Exceptional Children since 1996. His current professional interests focus on legal issues and special education.

Edward A. Polloway is a Professor of Education and Human Development at Lynchburg College in Virginia, where he has taught since 1976. He also serves as Vice President for Graduate Studies and Community Advancement. He received his doctoral degree from the University of Virginia and his undergraduate degree from Dickinson College in Pennsylvania. He has served twice as president of the Division on Developmental Disabilities of the Council for Exceptional Children and on the board of directors of the Council for Learning Disabilities. He also served on the committee that developed the 1992 definition of mental retardation for the American Association on Mental Retardation. He is the author of 12 books and 100 articles in the field of special education with primary interests in the areas of learning disabilities and mental retardation.

James R. Patton is an Educational Consultant and Adjunct Associate Professor at the University of Texas at Austin. He received his EdD from the University of Virginia. He is a former high school biology teacher and elementary-level special education resource teacher. He has also taught students who were gifted and those who were gifted/learning disabled. His professional interests include transition, life skills instruction, adult issues related to individuals with special needs, behavioral intervention planning, and classroom accommodations. He has served on national boards of the Division on Developmental Disabilities, the Council for Learning Disabilities, and the National Joint Committee on Learning Disabilities.

Carol A. Dowdy is Professor of Special Education at the University of Alabama at Birmingham, where she has taught since receiving her EdD degree from the University of Alabama, Tuscaloosa. She was written eight books on special education and published 34 articles on learning disabilities. She has served on the national board of the Council for Learning Disabilities and the Professional Advisory Board for the Learning Disabilities Association of America, and she has worked closely with the federal department of Vocational Rehabilitation to assist in their efforts to better serve adults with learning disabilities.

Teaching Students with Special Needs in Inclusive Settings

1 Inclusive Education: An Introduction

After reading this chapter, you should be able to

1. describe the evolution of services for students with special needs.
2. describe different disabilities served in public schools.
3. describe the key components of IDEA, Section 504, and the ADA.
4. describe the advantages and disadvantages of different service delivery models for students with special needs.
5. discuss methods that enhance the inclusion of students with disabilities.
6. discuss the role of school personnel in inclusion.
7. describe issues facing special education.
8. describe the role of philosophy and ethics in serving children with disabilities.

Annalee has Down syndrome, and she has had many problems in school. When she started in kindergarten, she did not have many of the readiness skills that other students had. In first grade, after Annalee continued to fall behind, her teacher, Mrs. Jenkins, referred her for an evaluation. It was found that even though she had Down syndrome, her IQ score was a little too high for her to be classified as having mental retardation, and since she did not have any other recognized disability, she was not eligible for special education. She continued to fall behind her peers, and by the middle of the second grade, she was referred for special education again. This time her test scores indicated mild mental retardation. An individualized education program (IEP) was developed, and she was placed in a self-contained special education classroom for the remainder of the school year. She appeared to improve in this setting. She was again placed in the self-contained classroom for the third grade. However, by the middle of that year, she began to display behavior problems. While her academic work continued to improve, her social skills and behavior control were deteriorating. At an IEP meeting it was decided by committee members, including Annalee's parents, to try a more inclusive setting. Annalee was placed half-time in the third grade and half-time in a resource room. She immediately began to do better with this change of placement. Her academic skills, social skills, and behavior all improved. When asked about what she likes about school, she readily states that she likes to be in her classroom with her friends and also likes to go to the resource room for extra help in areas where she has difficulties. For Annalee, the change of placement to a more inclusive setting appears to have met her academic, social, and behavior needs.

QUESTIONS TO CONSIDER

1. Why did Annalee initially do better when she was placed in a special education classroom?

2. Why did Annalee begin to develop behavior problems in the self-contained classroom?

3. Why did Annalee begin to improve in the more inclusive setting?

The public education system in the United States continues to be unequaled in the world. Rather than serving the needs of certain groups of students, such as those who are wealthy, those with certain academic potential, or those of certain genders, the U.S. education system is for all children. It attempts to offer 13 years of free, equal educational opportunities to all children, including those with parents who are not educated and those from families without financial means. Children with *disabilities* and those who have learning or behavior problems are included in this educational system. Students do not have to pass certain tests to attend various schools, nor do their families need to pay for a comprehensive educational program. Students do not have to choose, early in their school years, the school track that they will follow.

The U.S. Constitution, which guarantees equal opportunities for all citizens, is the basis for the free public educational system. Since their beginning in the mid-1800s, public schools have evolved into a system that provides educational opportunities for all students. Initially that was not the case. Girls did not secure their right to equal educational opportunities until the early 1900s, racial minorities not until the 1950s and 1960s, and students with disabilities not until the 1970s and 1980s. Litigation and legislation played important roles as each group secured the right to participate in public educational programs (Lipsky & Gartner, 1996).

History of Education for Students with Disabilities

Prior to federal legislation passed in the mid-1970s, many schools did not provide any programs for students with disabilities, or the programs they provided were very minimal (Yell, Rogers, & Rogers, 1998). Until the 1970s, it was estimated that 3 million children with disabilities received inappropriate or inadequate services, while up to 1 million were totally excluded from the educational system (U.S. Department of Education, 2000). It was estimated that only 20% of students with disabilities were educated in the early 1970s (Katsiyannis, Yell, & Bradley, 2001). The only recourses available for most parents were private educational programs or programs specifically designed for "handicapped" students. In many cases, parents paid for these educational programs out of their own resources. And in many situations, students with disabilities stayed home and received no formal education (Katsiyannis et al., 2001).

In a few schools, students with *physical disabilities* or *mental retardation* were provided with services; however, these services were nearly always in self-contained, isolated classrooms, and the students rarely interacted with nondisabled students. Services for this group of children were simply slow to develop because of limited financial resources and public apathy (Alexander & Alexander, 2001).

Some children with disabilities received services in *residential programs*. Typically, children with mental retardation and with sensory deficits were placed in these settings (Crane, 2002). In 1965 approximately 100,000 children, from birth to 21 years old, lived in institutions for persons with mental retardation in the United States (White, Lakin, Bruininks, & Li, 1991). The first school for children with deafness in the United States was established in 1817 as the American Asylum for the Education of the Deaf and Dumb (now the American School for the Deaf) (Stewart & Kluwin, 2000). The first school for children with visual problems, the New England Asylum for the Blind, was founded in 1832. In 1963 nearly 50% of children classified as legally blind in the United States lived in residential schools for the blind. These residential programs offered daily living support as well as some education and training.

Since the mid-1970s services to students with disabilities have changed dramatically. Not only are more appropriate services provided by schools, but also they are frequently provided in both *resource rooms* and general education classrooms with collaboration between special education and general classroom teachers. Many different developments brought about this change, including parental advocacy, legislation, and litigation. The federal government played a major part in the evolution of special education services, primarily through legislation, litigation, and funding.

Services for students with disabilities evolved in three distinct phases: *relative isolation, integration (mainstreaming),* and *inclusion.* In the **relative isolation** phase, which included the first 60–70 years in the 20th century, students were either denied access to public schools or only permitted to attend in isolated settings. In the **integration** phase, which began in the 1970s, students with disabilities were mainstreamed, or integrated, into general education programs when appropriate. Finally, the **inclusion** phase, starting in the mid-1980s, emphasized that students with disabilities should be included in all school programs and activities. This phase differed from the integration phase in a minor but very significant way.

Although students with disabilities were in general classrooms under both integration and inclusion, in the inclusion phase it was assumed that these students belonged in general classrooms, whereas in the integration phase they were considered to be special education students who were simply placed in the general classroom part of the time, primarily for socialization. Most recently, empowerment and self-determination for students with disabilities have been the focus of inclusion efforts, to better prepare students for the highest degree of independence possible (Field, Hoffman, & Spezia, 1998; Polloway, Smith, Patton, & Smith, 1996). The idea of student-led conferences is a prime example of the focus on self-determination (Conderman, Ikan, & Hatcher, 2000). Figure 1.1 depicts the historical changes in the education of students with disabilities in public education. While the changes in special education over the past 25 years have been dramatic, probably the most significant change has been acceptance of the idea that special education is a service, not a place. In other words, special education is not a classroom in a building; rather, it is the specialized instruction and services provided for students with disabilities (Implementing IDEA, 2001).

Because all children are entitled to a public education in the United States, teachers in today's public schools must provide instruction and other educational services that meet the needs of a very diverse student population. In fact, the diversity of students in today's schools is far greater than in the past. Traditionally, teacher education programs have focused on teaching students who learn in similar ways and at similar levels. However, today's teachers do not have the luxury of teaching only students who learn easily and behave in a manner the teachers deem appropriate based on their own standards. They must be prepared to deal effectively with all kinds of students. The Inclusion Strategies feature shows a positive result of the inclusion movement—a change in the way individuals with disabilities are labeled.

CONSIDER THIS

Should all children, even those with very different learning needs, have access to free educational services in public schools? Why or why not? What about the high costs that may be incurred?

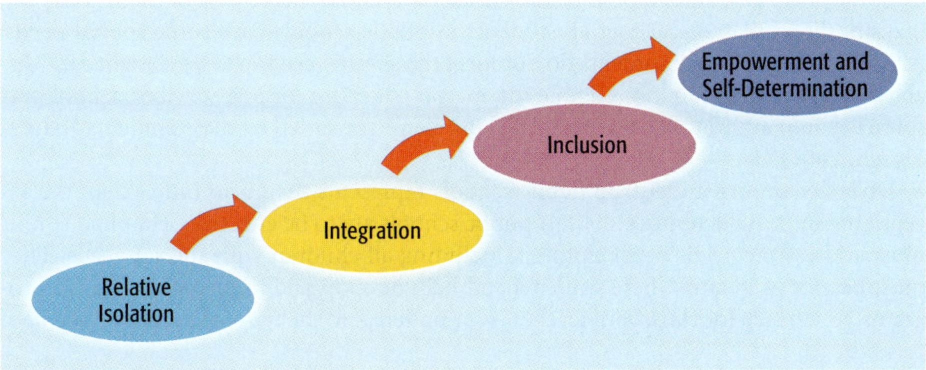

FIGURE 1.1

Historical Changes in Education for Students with Disabilities

From "Historic Changes in Mental Retardation and Developmental Disabilities" by E. A. Polloway, J. D. Smith, J. R. Patton, and T. E. C. Smith, 1996, *Education and Training in Mental Retardation and Developmental Disabilities, 31,* p. 9. Used by permission.

Using "People-First" Language

One of the results of the inclusion movement has been a change in the way individuals with disabilities are labeled. "People first" language has become the appropriate nomenclature for individuals with disabilities. The following list provides examples of using "people first" language:

Say	Do Not Say
Person with a disability	The disabled person
Billy with mental retardation	Mentally retarded Billy
Children with autism	The autistic children
Classroom for students with mental retardation	The mentally retarded classroom
Students with visual impairments	The blind students
Bus for students with disabilities	The special education bus
Individuals with disabilities	Disabled individuals
Disability or disabled	Handicap or handicapped
The boy with cerebral palsy	The cerebral palsied boy
The girl with a hearing impairment	The deaf girl
Mary with a learning disability	The learning disabled girl

Companion Website

For follow-up questions about "people first" language, go to Chapter 1 of the Companion Website (ablongman.com/sppd4e) and click on Inclusion Strategies.

Students with Special Needs

CONSIDER THIS

What is a typical child? Is there such a thing as an average child or person? Can schools afford to look at each child as a unique learner?

Many students do not fit the mold of the "typical" student. They include those with identified disabilities, those who are classified as gifted and talented, and those who are "at risk" for developing problems. It has been estimated that 11% of school-age children, or approximately 5.5 million students, are classified as disabled (U.S. Department of Education, 2000). Another group of students experience a degree of disability that is not significant enough to result in special education eligibility. Many of these students, approximately 1–3% of the student population, are eligible for certain services and protections under Section 504 and the Americans with Disabilities Act (Smith, 2001; Smith, 2002; Zirkell, 1999). Still other students need special attention because of poverty, difficulties with language, or other at-risk factors. These students exhibit various characteristics that often result in school problems (Morgan, 1994a). Adding all these students together, plus gifted students, who are considered to be another 3–5% of the school population, shows that 20–30% of all students in public schools have some special needs. Although many of these students do not meet the specific criteria to be classified as "disabled" and are therefore not eligible for special education or 504 services, school personnel cannot afford to ignore the special problems presented by these students (Barr & Parrett, 2001).

Diversity among students in public schools represents the norm rather than the exception (Anton-Oldenburg, 2000). If public schools are to be effective, school personnel must address the needs of all children, including all children with special needs. They must be able to identify these students and help develop and implement effective programs. A first step for classroom teachers is to understand the types of students they need to serve.

Students with Disabilities Served Under IDEA

One of the largest and most visible groups of students with special needs in the public school system includes those formally classified as having disabilities as defined by the **Individuals with Disabilities Education Act (IDEA)**. Students with disabilities are defined as those who exhibit one of several specific conditions that result in their need for special education and related services. The number of children with disabilities has grown significantly since the mid-1970s (U.S. Department of Education, 2001). Table 1.1 shows the number of children, by disability, served during the 1989–1990 and 1999–2000 school years.

Many different types of students are found in these 13 categories. For example, the broad area of **other health impairments** includes hemophilia, diabetes, epilepsy, and sickle-cell anemia. Even the category of learning disabilities comprises an extremely heterogeneous group of students. The fact that disability categories are composed of different types of students makes it impossible to draw simple conclusions about them. The following paragraphs provide a general description of the categories of disabilities recognized in IDEA.

Mental Retardation   The disability category that has been recognized for the longest time in most school districts is mental retardation (Crane, 2002). Students with mental retardation are usually identified through intelligence tests and measures of adaptive behavior, which indicate a person's ability to perform functional activities expected of age and cultural norms. By definition, individuals with mental retardation score less than 70–75 on individual intelligence tests and have concurrent deficits in adaptive behavior (American Association on Mental Retardation, 2002). Their general characteristics include problems in learning, memory, problem solving, and social skills (Beirne-Smith, Patton, & Ittenbach, 2000).

Learning Disabilities   The learning disabilities category accounts for more than 50% of all students served in special education (U.S. Department of Education, 2000). This category is beset with problems of definition and programming, but it continues to include

TABLE 1.1   **Number of Students Ages 6–21 Served Under IDEA in the 1989–1990 and 1999–2000 School Years**

	1989–1990	1999–2000
Specific learning disabilities	2,062,076	2,871,966
Speech and language impairments	974,256	1,086,964
Mental retardation	563,902	614,433
Emotional disturbance	381,639	470,111
Multiple disabilities	87,957	112,993
Hearing impairments	57,906	71,671
Orthopedic impairments	48,050	71,422
Other health impairments	52,733	254,110
Visual impairments	22,866	26,590
Autism	NA	65,424
Deaf-blindness	1,633	1,845
Traumatic brain injury	NA	13,874
Developmental delay	NA	19,304
All disabilities	4,253,018	5,683,707

From U.S. Department of Education, 2001

more children than all other special education categories combined (Lyon et al., 2001; Smith, Dowdy, Polloway, & Blalock, 1997). In general, the achievements of students with learning disabilities are not proportionate with their abilities. Although the cause of learning disabilities is unclear, the controversial assumption is that a neurological dysfunction causes the learning disability (Lyon et al., 2001).

Emotional Disturbance   Students with emotional disturbance exhibit inappropriate behaviors or emotions that result in disruptions for themselves or others in their environment. Whereas the federal government uses the term *emotional disturbance*, specifically eliminating from the category children and youth who are *socially maladjusted*, other groups prefer the terms *emotional and behavior disorders* or *behavior disorders*. Mental health professionals use still other terms, such as *conduct disorder* and *depression*. In addition to differing on terminology, professionals serving children with these problems also differ on definitions of the problems and the types of services they provide (Coleman & Webber, 2002).

Deafness/Hearing Impairments   Students with hearing impairment include those whose permanent or fluctuating impairments in hearing adversely affect their educational performance. Those considered deaf have impairments that result in difficulties in processing linguistic information through hearing, with or without amplification (Final Regulations, IDEA, 1999). Students classified as hard of hearing can process linguistic information through hearing with assistance (Stewart & Kluwin, 2001).

Visual Impairments   Students' educational performance may be adversely affected because of impairments in vision, even with correction. This category includes both students who are partially sighted and those who are blind (Final Regulations, IDEA, 1999). Students who are partially sighted can generally read print, whereas those classified as blind cannot (Sacks & Silberman, 1998).

Orthopedic Impairments   Many students experience problems related to their physical abilities. Students with cerebral palsy, spina bifida, amputations, and muscular dystrophy are a few examples. For these students, physical access to educational facilities and problems with writing and manipulation are important concerns.

Other Health Impairments   Students are classified as having other health impairments when they have limited strength, vitality, or alertness due to chronic or acute health problems. Examples of such problems include asthma, diabetes, epilepsy, hemophilia, and leukemia. Attention deficit disorder (ADD) or attention deficit hyperactivity disorder (ADHD) may be included in this category (Final Regulations, IDEA, 1999). As with orthopedic impairment, this category includes a wide variety of disabling conditions.

Autism   In the 1990 reauthorization of Public Law (PL) 94–142, Congress added autism as a separate disability category. Autism is a lifelong disability that primarily affects communication and social interactions. Children with autism typically relate to people, objects, and events in abnormal ways; they insist on structured environments and display many self-stimulating behaviors (Scheuermann & Webber, 2002).

Traumatic Brain Injury   In 1990, Congress also added traumatic brain injury (TBI) as a separate disability category. TBI "means an acquired injury to the brain caused by an external physical force, resulting in total or partial functional disability or psychosocial impairment, or both, that adversely affects a child's educational performance" (Final Regulations, IDEA, 1999). The regulations note that TBI applies to both open or closed head injuries that affect a variety of areas, including cognition, memory, attention, judgment, and problem solving.

Speech or Language Impairments   For some children, speech difficulties are a serious problem. When the impairment results in a need for special education and related services, children are considered eligible for services under IDEA. Most of these children need speech therapy (Polloway, Miller, & Smith, 2003). Teachers need to work closely with speech and language specialists when dealing with this group of students.

Students Eligible for Section 504 and the ADA

Students who need special assistance do not all fit neatly into disability categories defined by IDEA. Other federal statutes, namely, Section 504 of the Rehabilitation Act and the Americans with Disabilities Act (ADA), use a very different definition of disability, employing a functional, not a categorical, model. Under Section 504 and the ADA, a person is considered to have a disability if that individual (1) has a physical or mental impairment that substantially limits one or more major life activities, (2) has a record of such an impairment, or (3) is regarded as having such an impairment. The acts do not provide an exhaustive list of such impairments but require the functional criterion of "substantial limitation" to be the qualifying element (Smith, 2001; Smith & Patton, 1998).

As previously noted, many students not eligible for IDEA services may have disabilities that are covered under Section 504, because the definition of disability in Section 504 and the ADA is broader than the definition used in IDEA. Eligibility for Section 504 and the ADA is based on impairments that result in substantial limitations on such major life activities as breathing, walking, seeing, hearing, and learning. Schools are required to refer students who are thought to be eligible for services and protections under Section 504 and the ADA for evaluation. If students are determined eligible, schools must provide accommodations for them in academic and nonacademic areas that enable them to receive a free appropriate public education (Smith, 2002; Smith & Patton, 1998).

Students Classified as Gifted and Talented

Some students differ from their peers by having above-average intelligence and learning abilities. These students, classified as gifted and talented, were traditionally defined and identified using intelligence quotient (IQ) test scores. IQ scores of 120 or higher were the primary criterion, but current criteria are much broader. Although no single definition is accepted by all groups, most focus on students who are capable of making significant contributions to society in a variety of areas, including academic endeavors and creative, mechanical, motor, or fine arts skills.

Students at Risk for School Problems

Some students who do not have a specific disability category and do not have an above-average capacity to achieve also present problems for the educational system. These students, considered to be **at risk** for developing problems, manifest characteristics that could easily lead to learning and behavior problems (Barr & Parrett, 2001). Some of these students considered at risk include the following:

▶ Drug and alcohol abusers
▶ Students from minority cultures
▶ Students from low-income homes
▶ Teenagers who become pregnant
▶ Students who speak English as a second language
▶ Students who are in trouble with the legal system

These students may present unique problems for teachers who attempt to meet their educational needs in general education classrooms. Since students in the at-risk group are

Teenage girls who have babies are at risk for dropping out of school.

not eligible for special education services, classroom teachers bear the primary responsibility for their educational programs, which may need to be modified to meet these students' needs.

Current Services for Students with Special Needs

Most students with special needs receive a portion of their education from classroom teachers in general education classrooms. In 2000 the U.S. Department of Education predicted that 50% of all students with disabilities, ages 6–21, would be educated in general education settings at least 80% of each school day by the 2000–2001 school year (U.S. Department of Education, 2000). For students who are gifted or at risk, this has always been the norm. Students in these two groups have always remained in general education classes for most, if not all, of their instruction. Similarly, students who are eligible for services under Section 504 and the ADA are served in general classrooms because they are not eligible for IDEA services.

Since the mid-1980s, however, students with disabilities have been served more and more in general classrooms with their nondisabled peers (U.S. Department of Education, 2000). In fact, "one of the most significant changes that has occurred in public education in the United States over the past 15 years has been the movement toward inclusion—that is, educating students with disabilities for increasingly more of the school day in general education classrooms" (McLeskey, Henry, & Hodges, 1998, p. 4). This expansion of inclusion entails more than merely physically locating students with special needs in classrooms with their chronological-age peers; it requires that they be included in all aspects of the classroom and their educational needs met through services provided within the general education classroom. The Personal Spotlight highlights a school principal's experiences in moving from segregated to inclusive classrooms.

Personal Spotlight

A Principal's Perspective on Education

John Colbert has been an elementary principal for more than 20 years. During that time he has witnessed major changes in the way students with disabilities are taught. For the most part, John thinks these changes have been very positive. For example, he says that "having students with disabilities in our school building, and indeed, our regular classrooms, has done more than anything else in getting these students accepted by their classmates." John notes that while the movement to include students with disabilities has been mostly positive, there have been some bumps in the road. Dealing with teachers who have not wanted these students in their rooms has been one of the most difficult barriers to successful inclusion. He says that the best way to deal with teachers who have reservations about inclusion is to talk to teachers who have been successful. "I can talk to them all day long, but they really don't think I know the problems created by some of these students. On the other hand, when they talk to other teachers who have had success, they tend to believe them."

John Colbert
Principal

Holcomb Elementary School, Fayetteville, AR

John thinks that full inclusion is not an appropriate solution for many students who need to be pulled out periodically for special instruction. He is a strong supporter of the resource room model where students spend most of their days in regular classes but are pulled out into the resource room for specialized instruction. John believes that this model provides the best of all worlds—opportunities to be with peers for socialization purposes and opportunities for specialized instruction by special education teachers. John believes that one of the easiest groups to deal with regarding inclusion is students. He says that students, in general, think that including students with disabilities is not a problem at all. His view is that barriers to this movement, while very fixable, are primarily adult based, not child based.

For follow-up questions about this Personal Spotlight, go to Chapter 1 of the Companion Website (ablongman. com/sppd4e) and click on Personal Spotlight.

Actions Leading to Inclusion of Students with Disabilities

From 1950 to 1970 the self-contained classroom was the primary setting for serving students with disabilities. This service model greatly limited the interaction between students with disabilities and general education teachers and students, thus isolating these students. In the late 1970s this segregated service approach gave way to mainstreaming students with disabilities into general education classrooms, either full-time or for part of each school day. The process of mainstreaming did not just happen but came about as a result of several factors. These included the civil rights movement, federal and state legislation, litigation, actions by advocacy groups, and actions by professionals.

The Civil Rights Movement   Prior to the 1950s many students from minority racial groups were educated in "separate but equal" schools. Most communities had separate schools for African American children and separate schools for white children. Often, Mexican American and Asian children were educated in the "white" schools. The civil rights movement to eliminate discrimination based on racial differences emerged as a significant social force in the 1950s. It culminated in the 1960s with the dismantling of the system of school segregation on the basis of race. State and federal court cases and legislation mandated equal access to all schools by children from all backgrounds, including all races.

The critical event in the civil rights movement that supported the education of students with disabilities was the *Brown v. Board of Education* court case in 1954. In this case, the United States Supreme Court "maintained that state-required or state-sanctioned segregation solely because of a person's unalterable characteristics (e.g., race or disability) was unconstitutional" (Yell, Rogers, & Rogers, 1998, p. 221). Parents of students with disabilities soon realized that they could emulate the successful actions of civil rights groups and gain better services for their children. Using legislation, litigation, and advocacy, they sought to gain equal opportunities for their children, who had been denied access to public education solely on the basis of having a disability.

Legislation   Probably the factor most responsible for the inclusion of students with disabilities was legislation, which was often enacted in response to litigation. Parents of students with disabilities noted that the civil rights legislation passed in the 1960s helped break down racial segregation barriers in schools. Therefore, they advocated for legislation that would have the same result for their children. In advocating for appropriate legislation, parents also noted that funds needed to be provided and teachers appropriately trained to meet the needs of students with disabilities. The most important legislation to help students with disabilities access general education programs was PL 94–142, which was passed in 1975 and implemented in 1978. However, prior to its passage, several other legislative acts helped pave the way. These included the following (Smith, Marsh, & Price, 1986):

▶ *PL 83–531* (1954), which provided funding for research into mental retardation
▶ *PL 89–313* (1965), which provided funds for children in hospitals and institutions
▶ *PL 93–380* (1973), the precursor to PL 94–142

An in-depth discussion of PL 94–142/IDEA, Section 504, and the ADA will be presented in a later section.

Litigation   In addition to legislation, litigation has played a major role in the development of current services to students with disabilities. The *Brown v. Board of Education* case set the stage by supporting the notion that equal opportunities in education were just as applicable to students with disabilities as to students from racial minorities (Yell et al., 1998). Important litigation has focused on numerous issues, including (1) the right to education for students with disabilities, (2) nonbiased assessment for students, (3) procedural safeguards for students with disabilities, (4) the right to an extended school year at public

CONSIDER THIS

How available do you think services for students with disabilities would be today were it not for the civil rights movement of the 1960s? Would services be better or worse for these students?

CONSIDER THIS

How are students with disabilities similar to students from racial minorities? Are similar educational services being offered to both groups of students?

TABLE 1.2   Key Court Cases Related to Special Education

Case	Description
PARC v. Pennsylvania, 1972	Considered the first right-to-education case for students with disabilities. Consent agreement resulted in students with disabilities gaining access to public education.
Mills v. Board of Education of District of Columbia, 1972	Court ruled that school district cannot exclude any child eligible for a publicly supported education by a rule or policy and cannot use limited funds as an excuse for not providing services. Also outlined procedural due process rights of students with disabilities.
Board of Education of Hendrick Hudson Central School District v. Rowley, 1982	First case dealing with PL 94–142 to reach the U.S. Supreme Court. Noted that PL 94–142 requires schools to provide adequate educational services and not services designed to maximize performance.
Honig v. Doe, 1988	U.S. Supreme Court ruled that schools must determine if inappropriate behavior is related to the disability before taking disciplinary actions that result in excluding the student from the school for more than 10 days.
Timothy W. v. Rochester, New Hampshire School District, 1989	Federal appeals court overturned a district court and noted that PL 94–142 requires schools to provide services to all children and that no child is too severely disabled to receive services.
Oberti v. Board of Education 1993	Supported the family preference that a child with Down syndrone be educated in the general education classroom
Foley v. Special School District of St. Louis County, 1998	Federal court of appeals affirmed a district court's decision that a public school was not obligated to provide special education services to a child placed by his parents in a private school.
Cedar Rapids Community School District v. Garret F., 1999	U.S. Supreme Court ruled that providing nursing services to a student with extensive medical needs is required under IDEA.

From *American Public School Law,* 5th ed., by K. Alexander and M. D. Alexander, 2001, Belmont, CA: West/Thomson Learning.

CONSIDER THIS

How can schools deal with the financial impact of special services for students with disabilities? Is there a limit to how much should be spent on a single child?

expense for some students, (5) related services for students, (6) the right to be educated in general education classrooms, and (7) the interpretation by the U.S. Supreme Court of the intent of Congress in PL 94–142 (Turnbull & Turnbull, 2000). Several landmark court cases from the 1970s, 1980s, and 1990s helped shape current special education services by setting legal precedents and encouraging Congress to act to pass critical federal legislation (Alexander & Alexander, 2001). These cases are summarized in Table 1.2.

Parental Advocacy   The third primary force that facilitated the inclusion of students with disabilities in general classrooms was parental advocacy. Parents not only encouraged schools to integrate students with disabilities, but they were also directly involved with the legislation and litigation that broke down barriers for these students. Without them, Congress would not have passed PL 94–142. Also, parental advocacy was directly responsible for litigation that forced many schools to include students with disabilities in general education classrooms. The result was a powerful coalition that targeted discriminatory practices that excluded students with disabilities from public education.

Parents have unified their efforts and maximized their influence by forming advocacy groups. The power of such organizations frequently results in changes in educational systems. The **Arc** (formerly the Association for Retarded Citizens), formed in 1950 as the National Association of Retarded Children, played a major role in getting local school districts, state education agencies, and the federal government to require the inclusion of students with disabilities in general education classrooms (Yell et al., 1998). Following the lead of the Arc, other groups, such as the Association for Children with Learning Disabilities (ACLD) (now the Learning Disabilities Association), continued to pressure schools to provide appropriate educational services in the least restrictive setting.

PL 94–142/IDEA

Public Law 94–142, the Education for All Handicapped Children Act (EHA), literally opened the doors of public schools and general education classrooms to students with disabilities (Katsiyannis et al., 2001). It was the result of much debate that followed the *PARC* and *Mills* cases (Yell et al., 1998). Under PL 94–142, schools are required to seek out and implement appropriate educational services for all students with disabilities, regardless of the severity, to provide appropriate, individualized services to students with disabilities, and to actively involve parents in the educational process. For general education teachers, the most important part of the legislation is the requirement that students with disabilities be educated with their nondisabled peers as much as possible.

Since its original passage in 1975, PL 94–142 has been reauthorized by Congress several times. Though each reauthorization has made changes in the original law, the basic requirements have remained relatively intact. The 1986 reauthorization mandated services for children with disabilities ages 3–5. In the 1990 reauthorization, the legislation was renamed the Individuals with Disabilities Education Act (IDEA), and the word *handicap* was replaced throughout with the word *disability*. In addition, two new separate categories of disabilities were added—autism and TBI—and schools were required to develop transition planning for students when they turned 16 years old (Katsiyannis et al., 2001). The most recent reauthorization of the act was in 1997. Table 1.3 summarizes some of the key components of the legislation, including the most recent reauthorization. The following paragraphs describe some of the most important elements found in IDEA.

Child Find   IDEA requires schools to seek out students with disabilities. This provision was a "hallmark of the 1975 statute and subsequent amendments" because so many children had been excluded from services before the legislation was passed (U. S. Department

---

TABLE 1.3   **Key Components of the Individuals with Disabilities Education Act (IDEA) (1997)**

Provisions	Description
Least restrictive environment	Children with disabilities are educated with nondisabled children as much as possible.
Individualized education program	All children served in special education must have an individualized education program (IEP).
Due-process rights	Children and their parents must be involved in decisions about special education.
Due-process hearing	Parents and schools can request an impartial hearing if there is a conflict over special education services.
Nondiscriminatory assessment	Students must be given a comprehensive assessment that is nondiscriminatory in nature.
Related services	Schools must provide related services, such as physical therapy, counseling, and transportation, if needed.
Free appropriate public education	The primary requirement of IDEA is the provision of a free appropriate public education to all school-age children with disabilities.
Mediation	Parents have a right, if they choose, to have a qualified mediator attempt to resolve differences with the school. Using mediation should not deny or delay a parent's request for a due-process hearing.
Transfer of rights	When the student reaches the age of majority, as defined by the state, the school shall notify both the parents and the student and transfer all rights of the parents to the child.
Discipline	A child with a disability cannot be expelled or suspended for 10 or more cumulative days in a school year without a manifest determination as to whether the child's disability is related to the inappropriate behavior.
State assessments	Children with disabilities must be included in districtwide and statewide assessment programs with appropriate accommodations. Alternative assessment programs must be developed for children who cannot participate in districtwide or statewide assessment programs.
Transition	Transition planning and programming must begin when students with disabilities reach age 14.

of Education, 2000, p. vii). In order to meet this mandate, schools have conducted a number of activities, including the dissemination of "child find" posters, commercial and public television announcements, newspaper articles, and other widespread public relations campaigns. IDEA requires schools to identify highly mobile children, such as homeless children and migrant children, who may qualify for special education.

Nondiscriminatory Assessment   Before students can be classified as disabled and determined to be eligible for special education services, they must receive a comprehensive evaluation. The evaluation must not discriminate against students from minority cultural groups. The requirement for **nondiscriminatory assessment** resulted from evidence that certain norm-referenced standardized tests are inherently discriminatory toward students from minority racial and disadvantaged socioeconomic groups. Teachers and other school personnel must be extremely cautious when interpreting standardized test scores for their students. The scores may not reflect an accurate estimate of the student's abilities.

Individualized Education Program (IEP)   A key requirement of IDEA is that all students with disabilities have an **individualized education program (IEP).** The IEP, based on information collected during the comprehensive assessment, is developed by a group of individuals knowledgeable about the student (Drasgow, Yell, & Robinson, 2001). For students who are 16 years old who have transition plans, additional individuals should attend the IEP/transition planning meeting. The participation of parents is critical (Lytle & Bordin, 2001), although schools may proceed to develop and implement an IEP if a parent simply does not wish to meet with the team. However, parents are uniquely qualified to provide important information during the development of an appropriate program for their child (Drasgow et al., 2001).

Another key requirement related to the IEP is access to the general curriculum. The 1997 reauthorization of IDEA requires that students with disabilities have access to the general education curriculum. This requirement means that "outcomes linked to the general education program have become the optimal target of special education programs" (Pugach & Warger, 2001, p. 194)

CONSIDER THIS

Should students without disabilities have an IEP? What would be the advantages, disadvantages, and impact of such a requirement?

Least Restrictive Environment   IDEA also requires that a student's education take place in the **least restrictive environment (LRE).** The law further states that special classes, separate schooling, or other removal of students with disabilities from general educational settings should be used only when students cannot succeed in general education classrooms, even with supplementary aids and services. "In the 1997 Amendments to the IDEA, for the first time supplementary aids and services were expressly defined as 'aids, services, and other supports that are provided in regular education classes or other education-related settings to enable children with disabilities to be educated with nondisabled children to the maximum extent appropriate'" (Etscheidt & Bartlett, 1999, p. 164). This definition adds emphasis and clarification to the purpose of supplementary aids and services.

The least-restrictive-environment requirement obviously results in the inclusion of many students with disabilities in general education classrooms. Exactly how much each student is included depends on the student's IEP. Some students are able to benefit from full-time inclusion, whereas others may be able to benefit from minimal placement in general education classrooms. IDEA requires that schools provide a continuum of placement options for students, with the IEP determining the most appropriate placement. Therefore, if the IEP committee determines that the least restrictive environment for a particular child is a special classroom, then for that child, that is the LRE. The decision about how much to include students with disabilities in general education settings is complex; it is based on family variables, school variables, and individual student variables (Hanson et al., 2001).

For the majority of students with disabilities and other special needs, placement in general education classrooms for at least a portion of each school day is the appropriate option. Students with more severe disabilities may be less likely to benefit from inclusion and will generally spend less time with their peers. The implementation of the least-restrictive-environment concept means that all classroom teachers will become more involved with students with special needs. General education teachers and special education teachers must share in the responsibility for educating students with disabilities. Close communication among all teachers involved with specific students is required (Cramer, 1998; Walther-Thomas, Korinek, McLaughlin, & Williams, 2000).

Due-Process Safeguards   Providing **due-process safeguards** to students with disabilities and their parents is another requirement of IDEA. Prior to this legislation, school personnel often made unilateral decisions about a student's education, including placement and specific components of the educational program; parents had little input and little recourse if they disagreed with the school. Due-process safeguards make parents and schools equal partners in the educational process. Parents must be notified and give their consent before schools can take certain actions that affect their child.

When the school and parents do not agree on the educational program, either party can request a due-process hearing. In this administrative appeals process, parents and schools present evidence and testimony to an impartial hearing officer who decides on the appropriateness of an educational program. The decision of the hearing officer is final and must be implemented unless it is appealed to state or federal court. Table 1.4 provides a brief description of the due-process safeguards provided by IDEA.

> **CONSIDER THIS**
>
> Why should students with severe disabilities not be served in institutional or other segregated services? Are there some children who you think should be placed in these types of settings? Why or why not?

TABLE 1.4   **Due-Process Requirements of IDEA**

Requirement	Explanation	Reference
Opportunity to examine records	Parents have a right to inspect and review all educational records.	300.501
Independent evaluation	Parents have a right to obtain an independent evaluation of their child at their expense or the school's expense. The school pays only if it agrees to the evaluation or if it is required by a hearing officer.	300.502
Prior notice; parental consent	Schools must provide written notice to parents before the school initiates or changes the identification, evaluation, or placement of a child. Consent must be obtained before conducting the evaluation and before initial placement.	300.503 300.505
Contents of notice	Parental notice must provide a description of the proposed actions in the written native language of the home. If the communication is not written, oral notification must be given. The notice must be understandable to the parents.	300.504
Impartial due-process hearing	A parent or school may initiate a due-process hearing if there is a dispute over the identification, evaluation, or placement of the child.	300.507

From *Final Regulations, IDEA 1999,* Washington, DC: U.S. Government Printing Office.

Functional Behavior Assessment and Behavior Intervention Planning   Discipline is a controversial area of PL 94–142 and the IDEA. Advocates for children with disabilities are adamant that a child's disability should not be the cause of punitive actions. In other words, if a student's inappropriate behaviors are related to his or her disabilities, then any punitive actions must take into consideration the role played by the disability.

The 1997 reauthorization of IDEA requires that schools conduct a functional behavior analysis and develop behavior intervention plans for students with disabilities who have behavior problems (Gartin & Murdick, 2001). A complete description of the requirements and best practices for behavior intervention planning is in Chapter 14.

Transition   "By 1990, researchers and practitioners had recognized the importance of careful planning to help students with disabilities move from school to adult life" (U.S. Department of Education, 2000, p. xi). The result was that IDEA was amended to require transition planning and programming. When students with disabilities reach the age of 14, a statement of each student's transition-service needs must be included in the IEP. When the student reaches age 16, the IEP must include a statement of needed transition services, including interagency responsibilities and actions.

Section 504 and the Americans with Disabilities Act

In addition to IDEA, Section 504 of the Rehabilitation Act of 1973 and the Americans with Disabilities Act (ADA), passed in 1990, provide a strong legal base of appropriate educational services for students with disabilities. Unlike IDEA, which is an entitlement, funding program, 504 and the ADA are both civil rights statutes. These laws ensure that individuals with disabilities are not discriminated against on the basis of disability (Smith, 2001; Smith, 2002).

Section 504 and the ADA extend coverage to individuals who meet the definition of disability, in the laws, who are "otherwise qualified." Section 504 states: "No otherwise qualified individual with a disability, shall solely by reason of her or his disability, be excluded from participation in, be denied the benefits of, or be subjected to discrimination under any program or activity receiving federal financial assistance" (29 U.S.C.A. § 794). "In other words, if a person with a disability wants to participate in some activity in which he or she is not *otherwise qualified* to participate, not allowing the person to participate would not be considered discrimination" (Smith, 2001, p. 336). Discrimination is only a factor if the person with the disability is qualified to engage in the activity.

Section 504 applies to programs and institutions that receive federal funds. The ADA, on the other hand, applies to just about everything except churches and private clubs. As a result, virtually every public accommodation and governmental agency must comply with the ADA, regardless of whether it receives federal funds or not. Private schools that do not receive federal funds do not have to comply with Section 504, but unless they are associated with a church, they do have to comply with the ADA.

Section 504 and the ADA use a very different approach to defining disability than the IDEA. Under the IDEA, individuals are considered eligible for services if they have one of the recognized disabilities and need special education. Under 504 and the ADA, a person must have a mental or physical impairment that substantially limits a major life activity. The definition of disability under 504 and the ADA is presented in Table 1.5. Because the definition is broadly stated, some individuals who are classified as disabled under 504 and the ADA do not meet the eligibility criteria of the IDEA.

Section 504 and the ADA, like IDEA, require schools to provide students with disabilities with a free appropriate public education (FAPE). FAPE, under 504 and the ADA, is defined as "the provision of regular or special education, related aids and services, designed to meet the individual needs of students with disabilities as well as the needs of individuals without disabilities are met." Remember, 504 and the ADA are both civil rights statutes. Equal opportunity is a key factor in these two laws (Smith, 2002).

TABLE 1.5   **Definition of Disability Under Section 504 and the ADA**

Under 504 and the ADA, a person is considered to have a disability if that person

(1) has a physical or mental impairment which substantially limits one or more of such person's major life activities,

(2) has a record of such an impairment, or

(3) is regarded as having such an impairment.

Section 504 and the ADA define a physical or mental impairment as

(A) any physiological disorder or condition, cosmetic disfigurement, or anatomical loss affecting one or more of the following body systems: neurological; musculoskeletal; special sense organs; respiratory, including speech organs; cardiovascular; reproductive; digestive; genito-urinary; hemic and lymphatic; skin; and endocrine; or

(B) any mental or psychological disorder, such as mental retardation, organic brain syndrome, emotional or mental illness, and specific learning disabilities.

There are many similarities and differences between IDEA and 504/ADA. The Rights & Responsibilities feature on pages 18 and 19 compares the elements of IDEA, Section 504, and the ADA. Although school personnel must adhere to the requirements and criteria established by the U.S. Department of Education, they must also remember that many students who are ineligible for classification as disabled still need assistance if they are to succeed in educational programs.

Where Should Students with Disabilities Be Educated?

The setting in which students with disabilities should receive educational and related services is a much-discussed, much-debated topic. In fact, as early as 1989, Jenkins and Heinen wrote that the issue has "received more attention, undergone more modifications, and generated even more controversy than have decisions about how or what these students are taught" (p. 516). The topic has continued to be much discussed and remains one of the key issues in the field of education for children with disabilities. Simply saying the word *inclusion* "is likely to engender fervent debate" (Kavale & Forness, 2000, p. 279).

Most students with disabilities experience mild disabilities and are included in general education classrooms for at least a portion of each school day. A smaller number of students, with more severe disabilities, are more typically educated in segregated special education environments (McLeskey, Henry, & Hodges, 1999). However, even some students with more severe disabilities are included in general education classrooms part of the time (Hobbs & Westling, 1998).

Approximately 75% of all students with disabilities are included for at least 40% of each day in general education classrooms and taught by general education classroom teachers (U.S. Department of Education, 2000). They spend at least a portion of each school day with their chronological-age peers. In addition to these students, many students continue to spend a large portion of their school days outside general education settings. Table 1.6 provides the percentage of students, by disability category, and their school placement.

While still raging, the debate about where students should be educated has shifted in favor of more inclusion, which can be implemented in many different ways. Students can be placed in general education classrooms for a majority of the school day and "pulled

Rights & Responsibilities   **Comparison of IDEA, Section 504, and ADA**

Area	IDEA	504	ADA
Who is covered?	All children ages 3–21 who have one of the designated disability areas who need special education.	All individuals who have a disability as defined; no age restrictions.	Same as 504
Who must comply?	All public schools in states that participate in IDEA.	An entity that receives federal funds of any kind or amount.	Any business, governmental agency, or public accommodation other than churches or private clubs.
What is the basic requirement?	Provide eligible children with a free appropriate public education.	Do not discriminate against any individual because of a disability.	Same as 504
Due-process requirements	Provide notice and gain consent before taking specific actions with a child.	Provide notice.	Same as 504
Specific requirements	IEP Nondiscriminatory assessment Least restrictive environment	Accommodation plan Same as IDEA Same as IDEA	Same as 504 Same as IDEA Same as IDEA
Definition of free appropriate public education (FAPE)	A student's individual program determined by an IEP.	An individual program designed to meet the disabled student's educational needs as well as the needs of nondisabled students are met.	Same as 504
Transition requirements	Begin transition planning at age 14.	No requirement	No requirement
Assessment	Nondiscriminatory comprehensive assessment before determining eligibility and developing an IEP; required every 3 years unless determined not needed.	Nondiscriminatory preplacement assessment before determining eligibility for 504 services and protections; required before any significant change of placement.	Same as 504
Complaints	Administrative appeals process must be available and mediation must be offered. Attorney's fees may be required if parents prevail.	Administrative appeals must be offered; parents may go straight to federal court or file complaint with the Office of Civil Rights.	Same as 504; may file complaint with Department of Justice.
Designated coordinator	No requirement	At least one person in each district must be designated in writing as the district 504 coordinator.	Same as 504 (ADA coordinator)

Area	IDEA	504	ADA
Self-study	No requirement	Each district must form a committee and do a self-study to determine any areas where physical or program discrimination occurs. A plan to correct deficiencies must be developed.	Same as 504. Only areas added since 504 self-study must be reviewed.
Monitoring agency	U.S. Department of Education—Office of Special Education	Office for Civil Rights	Department of Justice

For follow-up questions about IDEA, ADA, and Section 504, go to Chapter 1 of the Companion Website (ablongman.com/sppd4e) and click on Rights & Responsibilities.

out" periodically and provided instruction in resource settings by special education teachers. Or they can be placed full-time in general education classrooms. In this latter model, special education teachers may go into general education classrooms and work with students who are experiencing difficulties or collaborate directly with classroom teachers to develop and implement methods and materials that will meet the needs of

T ABLE 1.6   **Percentage of Students with Disabilities, Ages 6–21, Served in Different Educational Environments During the 1998–1999 School Year**

	Served Outside the Regular Classroom					
	0–21% of the Day	21–60% of the Day	>60% of the Day	Separate Facilities	Residential Facilities	Home/ Hospital
All disabilities	47.43	28.44	20.07	2.91	0.68	0.48
Specific learning disabilities	45.11	38.43	15.49	0.64	0.15	0.17
Speech or language impairments	88.5	6.64	4.46	0.29	0.04	0.07
Mental retardation	13.76	29.25	51.07	5.04	0.49	0.39
Emotional disturbance	25.5	23.04	33.18	13.3	3.59	1.36
Multiple disabilities	10.5	16.6	44.8	22.9	2.87	2.26
Hearing impairments	39.63	18.7	25.3	7.12	8.99	0.21
Orthopedic impairments	45.56	20.55	27.29	4.54	0.19	1.87
Other health impairments	44.34	33.18	17.23	1.63	0.27	3.35
Visual impairments	49.65	19.39	16.52	6.78	7.10	0.56
Autism	20.32	13.15	51.13	13.53	1.42	0.45
Deaf-blindness	14.09	9.38	34.33	21.5	17.3	1.75
Traumatic brain injury	31.23	26.29	29.85	9.01	1.36	2.26

From U.S. Department of Education, 2001

many students. Schools use the model that best meets the individual's needs, developed through the IEP process.

The specific placement of students with disabilities falls along a continuum of options. This **continuum-of-services model** provides a range of placements, from institutions to full-time general education classrooms (Deno, 1970). The 1997 reauthorization of IDEA requires schools to have a continuum of alternative placements available "to meet the needs of children with disabilities for special education and related services" (IDEA Final Regulations, 1999, 300.551). The regulations specifically include instruction in regular classes, special classes, special schools, home instruction, and instruction in hospitals and institutions. Therefore, while IDEA mandates that services be provided in the least restrictive environment, it also acknowledges that schools should have options available along a continuum of placement options.

The Special Education Classroom Approach

Traditionally, students with disabilities received their educational programs in specialized classrooms, typically called self-contained classrooms. Serving students with disabilities in special programs was based on the presumption that general educators did not have the skills necessary to meet the needs of all students representing different learning needs (Shanker, 1994–1995). This placement option has been considered a "stage" in the movement from isolation for students with disabilities to inclusion (Safford & Safford, 1998). The result was the removal of students from the general education environment and an education provided by specialists. In the special education classroom approach, students receive the majority of their educational program from a special education teacher specifically trained to serve the population of students with mental retardation, learning disabilities, or some other specific disability.

Self-contained special education classes were the preferred and dominant service model between 1950 and 1970 (Podemski et al., 1995; Smith, 1990; Smith et al., 1986). Special education teachers were trained to teach students with disabilities, but usually only students with one kind of disability, in all subject areas. However, the primary focus was on a functional curriculum. Students placed in self-contained special education classrooms rarely interacted with their nondisabled peers, often even eating lunch alone. Likewise, the special education teacher interacted very little with nondisabled students or general classroom teachers.

Many general education teachers liked the self-contained special class model because they did not have to deal with students who differed from their view of "typical" children. The role of classroom teachers in the self-contained model was extremely limited. They might have indirect contact with students with disabilities but rarely had to instruct them. The primary role of general education teachers in the self-contained model was to refer students to the special education program. This assignment primarily occurred in lower elementary grades, where the majority of students with disabilities are identified.

During the late 1960s and early 1970s, parents and professionals began questioning the efficacy of the self-contained model (Smith et al., 1986). Indeed, Dunn's classic 1968 article concluded that segregated classes did not result in improved academic performance for students with mental retardation. With the passage of PL 94–142 and the requirement to serve students with disabilities in the least restrictive environment, the special class model was doomed as the preferred service model (Blackman, 1989). In the 1997-1998 school year, only 20.4% of all students with disabilities were served outside the general education classroom, in separate classes, compared to nearly 100% of students with disabilities prior to passage of PL 94–142 (U.S. Department of Education, 2000).

The movement away from special class programs has not been without dissent. Advocates for special classes have noted several problems with inclusion. Arguing against in-

CONSIDER THIS

Think about services for students with disabilities when you were in school. Did you have much contact and interaction with students with disabilities? Why or why not?

cluding all students with disabilities in general education classes, Fuchs and Fuchs (1994–1995) note that separate settings have several advantages:

▶ Education is provided by well-trained special educators.
▶ Education is selected from a variety of instructional methods, curriculums, and motivational strategies.
▶ The system monitors student growth and progress.

Regardless of these advantages, the self-contained model has had many critics. The movement away from self-contained classrooms was sparked by several factors, including the following:

▶ Students served in special classes are isolated from their nondisabled peers.
▶ Students do not have "typical" role models.
▶ Students may be isolated from many of the activities that are engaged in by nondisabled students.
▶ Special education teachers in special class models have limited interaction with general education teachers.
▶ Special education students are considered to "belong" to the special education teacher and program.
▶ Nondisabled students do not have the opportunity to interact with students with disabilities.
▶ Teachers are required to teach all areas rather than relying on colleagues with specialized expertise in selected areas.

One final reason for the demise of the self-contained special class model was a growing awareness of the diversity of students with disabilities. Although the special class was the predominant model, the majority of students with disabilities served in special education were those with mild mental retardation. As exceptional populations, such as students with learning disabilities and emotional problems were recognized, the number of students needing special education grew significantly. Serving all these students in isolated special classes became less attractive and less feasible.

The Resource Room Model

As a result of PL 94–142 and its LRE requirement, as well as the growing criticism of the self-contained model, the primary service delivery option used for most students with disabilities (except for those with speech impairments) became the resource room (U.S. Department of Education, 1995). Unlike the self-contained special class, where students spend their entire day, students go to the resource room only for special instruction. Students who use resource rooms spend part of each school day with their nondisabled, chronological-age peers and attend resource rooms for special assistance in deficit areas (Friend & Bursuck, 2002).

Advantages of the Resource Room Model   Several obvious advantages make the resource room model preferable to the self-contained special class. Most important, students with disabilities have an opportunity to interact with their chronological age peers. Other advantages include these:

▶ Students are more visible throughout the school and are more likely considered to be a part of the school.
▶ Students have the opportunity to receive instruction from more than one person.
▶ Students have the opportunity to receive instruction from "specialists" in specific academic areas.
▶ Special education teachers have the opportunity to interact with general education teachers and be an active part of the school staff.

CONSIDER THIS

Public Law 94–142 (IDEA) greatly changed services for students with disabilities. Was such change good or bad? Why or why not?

CONSIDER THIS

What problems are created by students coming and going from general education classrooms? How can teachers deal with some of these problems?

CROSS-REFERENCE

Chapter 2 focuses extensively on creating environments for successfully including students in general education classrooms.

Disadvantages of the Resource Room Model   Despite the numerous advantages of the resource room model, this approach does not offer the ultimate answer to the complex question of where students with disabilities should be educated. Identifying students as needing special education and requiring them to leave the general education classroom, even for only part of the day, can be detrimental. Guterman (1995) found this concern to be one "unifying element" among students interviewed about their special education placement.

Dunn's article in 1968 questioned the efficacy of serving students with disabilities in separate classes. His article, along with others, helped move the field from segregated to integrated services. Research currently being reported is similarly questioning the efficacy of resource room services. While there are many advantages to serving students with disabilities in resource rooms, there are some obvious disadvantages, including these:

▶ Pull-out programs are disruptive to the routine of the general classroom.
▶ Students who exit the classroom to receive specialized services are ostracized.
▶ Communication between the resource room teacher and general classroom teachers, which must be mandatory for programs to be successful, is often difficult.
▶ Students may become confused if teachers use different strategies to teach similar content.
▶ Students may miss some favorite activities when they are pulled out for resource room time.

CROSS-REFERENCE

Read Chapter 7 on serious emotional disturbance to see how modeling appropriate behaviors can impact students with this type of disability.

Role of Special Education Personnel   In the resource room model, a key role of special education personnel is to collaborate with classroom teachers to deliver appropriate programs to students with disabilities. Resource room teachers cannot simply focus on their students only when they are in the special education classroom. Close collaboration between the resource room teacher and the classroom teacher must occur to ensure that students receiving instruction in the special education room and general education classroom are not becoming confused by contradictory methods, assignments, curricula, and so on. The special education teacher should take the lead in opening up lines of communication and facilitating collaborative efforts.

Role of Classroom Teachers   Unlike the special class model, the resource room model requires that classroom teachers play numerous roles related to students with disabilities. One primary role is referral. The majority of students with mild disabilities and other special needs are referred for services by classroom teachers. Students with mild mental retardation, learning disabilities, and mild behavior problems are usually in elementary classrooms before their problems become apparent enough to warrant a referral for special education. General education teachers are often the first to recognize that a student is experiencing problems that could require special education services.

Classroom teachers also play the important role of implementing interventions that can bring improvement in problem areas and thereby prevent unnecessary referrals, with the result that fewer students will be labeled with a disability and served in special education programs. Many states and local school districts actually require classroom teachers to implement and document intervention strategies prior to a formal referral (Smith et al., 1997). These strategies, called prereferral interventions, will be discussed in Chapter 4.

Inclusive Education Programs

Just as full-time special class placement of students with disabilities received criticism in the early 1970s, resource room programs began to be criticized in the 1980s. Madeline Will, formerly assistant secretary of the U.S. Department of Education, helped formulate the criticism of the resource room model and spur the movement toward inclusion. In 1986 she stated, "Although well-intentioned, this so-called 'pull-out' approach to the educational difficulties of students with learning problems has failed in many instances to meet the educational needs of these students and has created, however unwittingly, barriers to their successful education" (p. 412).

Since the mid-1980s there has been a call for dismantling the dual education system (general and special) in favor of a unified system that attempts to meet the needs of all students. Rather than spend a great deal of time and effort identifying students with special problems and determining whether they are eligible for special education services, proponents of a single educational system suggest that efforts be expended on providing appropriate services to all students. In the early 1980s this model was advocated for students classified as gifted and talented by Renzulli and Reis (1985). Their model, called **schoolwide enrichment,** offered gifted programming services to all students without their having to meet restrictive eligibility criteria.

The model for more fully including students with special needs in general education programs was originally called the **Regular Education Initiative (REI).** More recently, the term *inclusion* has been used to identify this program model. Inclusion has been defined in many different ways. Unfortunately, the term **full inclusion** was originally used, suggesting that all students with disabilities, regardless of the severity of the disability, be included full-time in general education classes (Kavale & Forness, 2000). This approach was advocated by several professional and advocacy groups, most notably **The Association for the Severely Handicapped (TASH)** and the Arc. Their encouragement of full-time general education classroom placement for all students was met with a great deal of criticism and skepticism. In advocating such an approach, proponents basically asserted that there was no need for a continuum of placement options for students, since the least restrictive environment was always the general education classroom for all students (Kavale & Forness, 2000).

Currently, the terms *inclusion* and *responsible inclusion* are used to identify the movement to provide services to students with disabilities in general education settings (Smith & Dowdy, 1998). It is acknowledged that within the context of inclusion, some services to students may be necessary outside the general education classroom. While acknowledging that some students with disabilities may need some services outside the general classroom, proponents suggest that all students with disabilities *belong* with their nondisabled peers. Smith (1995) states that inclusion means "(1) that every child should be included in a regular classroom to the optimum extent appropriate to the needs of that child while preserving the placements and services that special education can provide; (2) that the education of children with disabilities is viewed by all educators as a shared responsi-

CONSIDER THIS

Why are some people opposed to merging special education and general education into one system?

Children with disabilities were often educated in isolated, self-contained classes between 1950 and 1970.

bility and privilege; (3) that there is a commitment to include students with disabilities in every facet of school; (4) that every child must have a place and be welcome in a regular classroom" (p. 1).

As early as 1984, Stainback and Stainback suggested the following reasons to support inclusion:

CONSIDER THIS

How can terms such as *mainstreaming, inclusion,* and *full inclusion* complicate services for students with disabilities? What could be done to clarify terminology?

1. *"Special" and "regular" students:* The current dual system of general and special education assumes that there are two distinct types of children, special and regular. In reality, all students display a variety of characteristics along a continuum; there simply is no way to divide all students into two groups. All students exhibit strengths and weaknesses that make them unique.

2. *Individualized services:* There is no single group of children who can benefit from individualized educational programming. The dual system of special and general education adopts the notion that students with disabilities require individual education, whereas other students do not. In fact, some research suggests that students with diverse characteristics do not benefit from different instructional techniques. If future research concludes that individualized instruction does indeed result in improved education, then all students should be afforded the opportunity.

3. *Instructional methods:* Contrary to many beliefs, there are no special teaching methods that are effective only with students who have disabilities. Good, basic instructional programs can be effective for all students.

4. *Classification:* A dual system of education, general and special, requires extensive, time-consuming, and costly efforts to determine which system students fit into and, in the case of those students determined to be eligible for special education, which disability category they fit into. Unfortunately, classification often is unreliable, results in stigma, and does not lead to better educational programming.

5. *Competition and duplication:* Perpetuating the general and special systems has resulted in competition between professionals as well as duplication of effort. If the educational system is to improve, all educators must work together, sharing expertise, effective methods, and educational goals.

CONSIDER THIS

How can serving students based on their individual needs benefit all students, not just those fitting into certain disability categories? Do the benefits outweigh the disadvantages?

6. *Eligibility by category:* The dual system results in extensive effort being spent on determining who is eligible for special services. The programs for students are often based on which category they are placed in, not on their specific needs. Placements and even curricular options are often restricted on the basis of clinical classification. For example, students classified as having mental retardation may be placed in work-study programs without having the opportunity to participate in regular vocational education.

7. *"Deviant" label:* A major negative result of the dual system is the requirement to place "deviant" labels on students. In order to determine that a student is eligible for the special system, a clinical label must be attached to him or her. Few, if any, would argue that clinical labels result in positive reactions. The routine reaction to the labels "mental retardation," "emotionally disturbed," and even "learning disabled" is an assumption that the student is not capable of functioning as well as other students.

Although proponents of inclusion have articulated numerous reasons to support the model, many oppose its implementation (Fuchs & Fuchs, 1994–1995). Al Shanker, past president of the American Federation of Teachers, noted that "we need to discard the ideology that inclusion in a regular classroom is the only appropriate placement for a disabled child and get back to the idea of a 'continuum of placements,' based on the nature and severity of the handicap" (1994–1995, p. 20).

Several professional and advocacy groups also support the continued use of a continuum of placement options. These include the Council for Exceptional Children (CEC), American Council on the Blind, Commission on the Education of the Deaf, the Division on Mental Retardation and Developmental Disabilities of CEC, and the Council for Children with Behavior Disorders of CEC. It also should be noted that the U.S. Department of Education does not mandate inclusion. Rather, the most recent reauthorization of IDEA in 1997 continues to require that schools provide a continuum of alternative placement options for students (Final Regulations, IDEA, 1999). If an IEP committee determines that a child needs a self-contained placement in order to receive an appropriate education, then failing to provide such an opportunity would be a violation of IDEA.

Advantages of Inclusion   There are many different advantages to inclusion, including opportunities for social interaction (Hunt et al., 2000), ease in accessing the general curriculum (King-Sears, 2001; Wehmeyer, Lattin, & Agran, 2001), academic improvement (Hunt et al., 2001), and positive outcomes for students with and without disabilities (Federico, Herrold, & Venn, 1999; Rieck & Wadsworth, 1999; Salend & Duhaney, 1999).

Although not mandatory, parental and teacher support for inclusion is very important. Hobbs and Westling (1998) note that many parents have mixed views. While they believe that inclusion has some obvious benefits for their children, they also worry about their children being in integrated placements. The concept has simply "not been embraced by all parents" (Palmer, Fuller, Arora, & Nelson, 2001, p. 481).

Teachers, for the most part, have expressed support for inclusion. After reviewing several studies, Scruggs and Mastropieri (1996) noted that most teachers support inclusion, are willing to teach students in their classrooms (although those who respond in this way are fewer than those who support the concept), and believe that inclusion results in positive benefits for students with disabilities and does not harm other students or the instructional process. In a recent study it was determined that both teachers and parents of children with and without disabilities generally supported inclusion both at the beginning and at the end of a school year in which inclusive practices were utilized. However, there were some differences in the support of these two groups, and both groups had a variety of concerns related to inclusion (Seery, Davis, & Johnson, 2000).

Disadvantages of Inclusion   Just as there are many supporters of inclusion and reasons for its implementation, there are also professionals and parents who decry the movement. Among the reasons they oppose inclusion are the following:

1. General educators have not been involved sufficiently and are therefore not likely to support the model.
2. General educators as well as special educators do not have the collaboration skills necessary to make inclusion successful.
3. There are limited empirical data to support the model. Therefore, full implementation should be put on hold until sound research supports the effort.
4. Full inclusion of students with disabilities into general education classrooms may take away from students without disabilities and lessen their quality of education.
5. Current funding, teacher training, and teacher certification are based on separate educational systems.
6. Some students with disabilities do better when served in special education classes by special education teachers.

Although some of these criticisms may have merit, others have been discounted. For example, research indicates that the education of nondisabled students is not negatively affected by inclusion (*National Study on Inclusion*, 1995). Therefore, though the movement has its critics, research on inclusion provides support for its continuation.

Role of Special Education Personnel   In the inclusion model, special education personnel become much more integral to the broad educational efforts of the school. In the dual system, special education teachers provide instructional programming only to students

CONSIDER THIS

How can some of the problems caused by inclusion be addressed in order to facilitate success in school for all students?

identified as disabled and determined eligible for special education programs under state and federal guidelines. In inclusive schools, these teachers work with a variety of students, including those having difficulties but not identified specifically as having a disability. The special education teacher works much more closely with classroom teachers in the inclusion model, with the result being increased opportunities for all students.

CONSIDER THIS

How would you feel if you were a classroom teacher who was suddenly asked to teach a student with a disability and you did not have any skills in special education?

Role of Classroom Teachers   Teachers must develop strategies to facilitate the successful inclusion of students with disabilities in general education classrooms. Neither classroom teachers nor special education teachers want students with disabilities simply "dumped" into general education classes (Banks, 1992), and the successful inclusion of students does not normally happen without assistance. School personnel must work on effective, cooperative methods to provide appropriate programs to all students.

Two methods are generally used to implement inclusion: facilitating the acceptance of the students with disabilities and providing services to support their academic success. Chapter 2 provides extensive information on creating classroom environments to enhance acceptance and provide academic support; later chapters provide specific, practical suggestions for providing academic support.

King-Sears and Cummings (1996) note seven different practices that teachers can use to help students succeed in inclusive settings. These include (1) curriculum-based assessment, (2) cooperative learning, (3) self-management, (4) peer tutoring, (5) strategy instruction, (6) direct instruction, and (7) goal setting. Figure 1.2 depicts the comfort of teachers in using these seven different methods. Clearly, some practices are only moderately or slightly comfortable, suggesting that in order for inclusion to be successful, teacher training and preparation need to be modified.

FIGURE 1.2   **Comfort Level of Implementing Various Strategies**

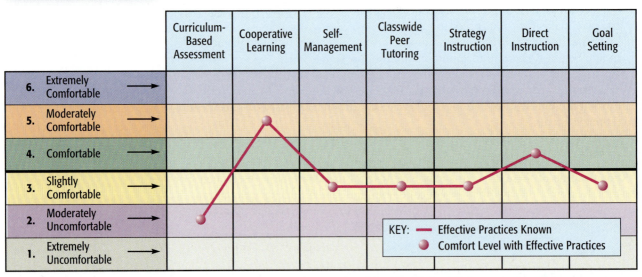

From "Inclusive Practices of Classroom Teachers" by M. E. King-Sears and C. S. Cummings, 1996, *Remedial and Special Education, 17*, p. 218. Used by permission.

Classroom teachers play a vital role in the education of students with disabilities. As noted by Hobbs and Westling (1998), teachers possibly play the most important role in the success of inclusion. Classroom teachers must be able to perform many different functions, such as the following:

▶ Acting as a team member on assessment and IEP committees
▶ Advocating for children with disabilities when they are in general education classrooms and in special programs
▶ Counseling and interacting with parents of students with disabilities
▶ Individualizing instruction for students with disabilities
▶ Understanding and abiding by due-process procedures required by federal and state regulations
▶ Being innovative in providing equal educational opportunities for all students, including those with disabilities

Sharing responsibility among classroom teachers, special education teachers, and other specialists, such as reading teachers, is the key to providing effective educational programs for all students (Voltz, Brazil, & Ford, 2001).

In general, the classroom teacher controls the educational programs for all students in the classroom, including students with disabilities, students at risk for developing problems, and those classified as gifted and talented. The attitude of the teacher toward students and the general climate the teacher establishes in the classroom have a major impact on the success of all students, particularly those with disabilities.

Classroom teachers need to be able to use a variety of techniques when meeting the needs of students included in their classes. Technology can be a great asset. The Technology Today feature provides examples of technology-based applications. The primary

CONSIDER THIS

What tips would you give teachers to enhance the inclusion of students with special needs in general education classrooms?

Examples of Technology-Based Applications for Special Education

Type of Technology	Applications
Word processing software	Assists students who have problems with written expression
Oral reading software	Assists students who have reading problems
Instructional technology	Drill and practice for students with deficits or problems in basic skill areas and students with motivational problems
Gamelike software	Assists students with attention problems
Databases	Data collection; IEP development
IEP software	IEP development and monitoring
Assistive technology	Assists students with a wide variety of disabilities, particularly those with physical limitations and visual and hearing problems
Medical technology	Supports students with medical needs
Augmentative technology	Assists students with oral language problems

For follow-up questions about technology-based applications for special education, go to Chapter 1 of the Companion Website (ablongman.com/sppd4e) and click on Technology Today.

From *Special Education in Contemporary Society: An Introduction to Exceptionality,* by R. Gargiullo, 2003, Belmont, CA: Wadsworth/Thomson Learning; and "Computers and Individuals with Mild Disabilities" by C. M. Okolo, 1993, in J. D. Lindsey (Ed.), *Computers and Exceptional Individuals,* Austin, TX: Pro-Ed.

function of teachers, both general education and special education teachers, is to teach. Good teaching has been described in many different ways. Researchers have attempted to define good teaching based on student outcomes, parental opinions, peers, supervisor ratings, and self-evaluations.

Conclusions Concerning Where Students with Disabilities Should Be Educated

Because of the limitations of empirical research, it is difficult if not impossible to say that inclusion always works and results in appropriate educational opportunities for students with disabilities. The debate about placement remains volatile, and will likely continue to be so until sufficient data have been collected to enable one side or the other to conclusively state that inclusion is or is not effective.

While generalizations about inclusion cannot be made, it can be stated that inclusion is a very effective model for serving some students with disabilities. However, to indiscriminately implement such an educational model without adequate preparation is definitely not recommended and could result in placing students with disabilities "at risk for adverse consequences" (Kavale & Forness, 2000, p. 287).

In light of the limited empirical information and the emotional nature of the debate, it is currently recommended that the inclusion movement proceed slowly. Because "requisite attitudes, accommodations, and adaptations for students with disabilities" are not yet in place, "a more tempered approach that formulates and implements policy on the basis of research and evaluation findings as well as ideological and political considerations is necessary" (Kavale & Forness, 2000, p. 290). In the meantime, using the least-restrictive-environment approach appears to be the prudent means of providing services to students with disabilities.

Philosophical and Ethical Issues in Special Education

School personnel involved in the education of students with disabilities must have a positive attitude about serving this group of students. If teachers feel that they are being asked to do things that are unnecessary, the entire classroom climate may be affected. Teachers set the example for students in their classrooms by either accepting and supporting students with disabilities or rejecting them. Therefore, the philosophy of educators regarding special education is critical to the success of these students.

All educational personnel need to be able to articulate their philosophy of education in general, as well as the way in which it relates to children with special needs. A philosophy should include the purposes of general education, the purposes of special education, characteristics of educational programs that meet the needs of all children, and a personal vision translated into practical applications (Bates, 2000). In order to incorporate these ideas into a philosophy of education, Bates (2000) suggests teachers answer the following questions:

1. Who am I?
2. What do I value?
3. How do I define myself as an educator?
4. What is my vision of education?
5. How does education serve individuals and society?
6. How might my vision of education be implemented?

FIGURE 1.3   Code of Ethics for Educators of Persons with Exceptionalities

We declare the following principles to be the Code of Ethics for educators of persons with exceptionalities. Members of the special education profession are responsible for upholding and advancing these principles. Members of the Council for Exceptional Children agree to judge and be judged by them in accordance with the spirit and provisions of this code.

A. Special education professionals are committed to developing the highest educational and quality of life potential of individuals with exceptionalities.

B. Special education professionals promote and maintain a high level of competence and integrity in practicing their profession.

C. Special education professionals engage in professional activities which benefit individuals with exceptionalities, their families, other colleagues, students, or research subjects.

D. Special education professionals exercise objective professional judgment in the practice of their profession.

E. Special education professionals strive to advance their knowledge and skills regarding the education of individuals with exceptionalities.

F. Special education professionals work within the standards and policies of their profession.

G. Special education professionals seek to uphold and improve where necessary the laws, regulations, and policies governing the delivery of special education and related services and the practice of their profession.

H. Special education professionals do not condone or participate in unethical or illegal acts, nor violate professional standards adopted by the Delegate Assembly of CEC.

http://cec.sped.org/ps/code.html

These questions can be answered as they relate to education in general and to serving children with special needs in particular.

In addition to having a personal philosophy of education that forms the basis for meeting the needs of all children, including those with special needs, educators must be aware of the code of ethics that is used to govern meeting the needs of students with special needs. The Council for Exceptional Children (CEC), the primary professional group of special education personnel, has a code of ethics that could be adopted by all educators serving this group of students. Figure 1.3 presents their code of ethics. All educators should adhere to professional ethics in meeting the needs of the diverse group of students in our schools, including those with special needs.

Summary

Students with Special Needs

▶ The public school system in the United States attempts to provide 13 years of equal educational opportunity to all its citizens.

▶ Today's student population is very diverse and includes students with a variety of disabilities.

▶ During the 1950s and 1960s, students from minority cultures won the right to equal educational opportunities.

▶ Many students in today's schools have specific special needs.

▶ A sizable percentage of students are at risk for developing problems, present learning or behavior problems, or may be classified as having a disability.

▶ The largest group of students with special needs in the public school system consists of those formally classified as having disabilities.

▶ Although there are 13 recognized categories of disabilities in schools, many students do not fit neatly into a specific category.

▶ Mental retardation, learning disabilities, and emotional and behavior disorders make up the majority of student disabilities.

▶ Students who are at risk for developing problems, as well as those considered gifted and talented, also require special attention from school personnel.

Current Services for Students with Special Needs

▶ Services for students with disabilities have evolved significantly over the past 20 years.

▶ Services for students with disabilities focus on inclusion—including students in general education classroom situations as much as possible.

▶ The civil rights movement, legislation, litigation, and parental advocacy all helped shape the service system for students with disabilities.

▶ Public Law 94–142, now the IDEA, provides the framework for services to students with disabilities in school settings.

▶ IDEA requires that students with disabilities be educated in the least restrictive environment, using an IEP.

Where Should Students with Special Needs Be Educated?

▶ About 70% of all students with disabilities spend a substantial portion of each school day in general education classrooms.

▶ The preferred service model for students with disabilities between 1950 and 1970 was segregated classroom settings.

▶ In the self-contained model, special education teachers were trained to teach specific types of students, primarily based on clinical labels.

▶ Classroom teachers had a very limited role in special education in the self-contained classroom model.

▶ Many parents advocated more inclusion of their students than was possible in the self-contained model.

▶ The least-restrictive-environment mandate of PL 94–142 was the impetus for the development of the resource room model.

Classroom Teachers and Students with Disabilities

▶ General education teachers play a very critical role in providing services to students with disabilities.

▶ The attitudes of classroom teachers are extremely important in the quality of services rendered to students with disabilities.

Further Readings

Alexander, K., & Alexander, M. D. (2001). *American public school law* (5th ed.). Belmont, CA: Wadsworth/Thomson Learning.

Coleman, M. C., & Webber, J. (2002). *Emotional and behavioral disorders: Theory and practice* (4th ed.). Boston: Allyn & Bacon.

Elksnin, L. K., Bryant, D. P., Gartland, D., King-Sears, M., Rosenberg, M. S., Scanlon, D., Strosnider, R., & Wilson, R. (2001). LD summit: Important issues for the field of learning disabilities. *Learning Disability Quarterly, 24,* 297–305.

Halvorsen, A. T., & Neary, T. (2001). *Building inclusive schools: Tools and strategies for success.* Boston: Allyn & Bacon.

Katsiyananis, A., Yell, M. L., & Bradley, R. (2001). Reflections on the 25th anniversary of the Individuals with Disabilities Education Act. *Remedial and Special Education, 22,* 324–334.

Kavale, K. A., & Forness, S. R. (2000). History, rhetoric, and reality: Analysis of the inclusion debate. *Remedial and Special Education, 21,* 279–296.

King-Sears, M. E. (2001). Three steps for gaining access to the general education curriculum for learners with disabilities. *Intervention in School and Clinic, 37,* 67–76.

Lyon, G. R., Fletcher, J. M., Shaywitz, S. E., Shaywitz, B. A., Torgesen, J. K., Wood, F. B., Schulte, A., & Olson, R. (2001). Rethinking learning disabilities. In C. E. Finn, A. J. Rotherham, & C. R. Hokanson, Jr. (Eds.), *Rethinking special education for a new century.* Washington, DC: Thomas B. Fordham Foundation.

Scheuermann, B., & Webber, J. (2002). *Autism: Teaching does make a difference.* Belmont, CA: Wadsworth/Thomson.

Smith, T. E. C. (2001). Section 504, the ADA, and public schools: What educators need to know. *Remedial and Special Education, 22,* 335–343.

Voltz, D. L., Brazil, N., & Ford, A. (2001). What matters most in inclusive education: A practical guide for moving forward. *Intervention in School and Clinic, 37,* 3–8.

Yell, M. L., Rogers, D., & Rogers, E. L. (1998). The legal history of special education: What a long, strange trip it's been! *Remedial and Special Education, 19,* 219–228.

VideoWorkshop Extra!

If the VideoWorkshop package was included with your text-book, go to Chapter 1 of the Companion Website (www. ablongman.com/sppd4e) and click on the VideoWorkshop button. Follow the instructions for viewing video clip 2. Then consider this information along with what you've read in Chapter 1 while answering the following questions.

1. This chapter notes that research data about inclusion suggests that student outcomes are positive. How does Lily benefit from inclusion in this class? How do the other students, but specifically the peer tutors Anita and Amy, benefit from working with Lily?

2. Ms. Roberts uses learning centers and supports Lily's use of assistive technology in her classroom. How do these strategies support Lily's inclusion overall?

2 Effective Inclusion Practices and Professional Collaboration

After reading this chapter, you should be able to

1. discuss the concept of diversity.
2. explain different perceptions among teachers, students, and parents regarding inclusion.
3. delineate critical dimensions of inclusive classrooms.
4. describe the role of classroom management, curricular options, and accommodative practices in inclusive classrooms.
5. discuss the range of personnel supports in inclusive classrooms.
6. create and maintain successful inclusive classrooms.
7. describe different methods of maintaining inclusive programs after they are initiated.
8. describe the consultation-collaboration and co-teaching strategies used in inclusive classrooms.

Libby is one of the favorites in Ms. Jordan's third grade class. She is popular among her peers and an excellent student, and she never gets into trouble. At the beginning of this school year, a new student was placed in her classroom. This student, Rhonda, has cerebral palsy and mild mental retardation. At first Libby was sort of afraid of Rhonda. Rhonda rarely talked, did not follow Ms. Jordan's directions very well, and could read hardly anything. All of the class thought Rhonda was really dumb. Libby, and all the other students in the class, did not want anything to do with Rhonda in the classroom, on the playground, or in the lunchroom.

After Rhonda had been in the class for about a week, a new teacher came into the room. Ms. Baker, the special education teacher, started working with Rhonda on some specific activities, such as reading at a much lower level than third graders were reading. Libby and all her friends thought this proved that Rhonda was dumb and really did not belong in the class. About two weeks later, Ms. Baker asked if any of the students in Ms. Jordan's class wanted to be a peer tutor. None of the students knew what a peer tutor was, but it sounded pretty important. Libby, of course, volunteered, and was chosen, partly because she was doing so well in all her subjects. When Ms. Baker and Ms. Jordan met with Libby and talked to her about being a peer tutor, they explained that Rhonda had some learning problems and needed some extra help in the classroom. Libby didn't know she would have to work with Rhonda when she volunteered, but she hated to back out, so she decided to go ahead for a little while. Ms. Baker and Ms. Jordan talked to Libby a long time about what it means to be a peer tutor.

Finally, the day to begin tutoring came, and Libby discovered that she loved helping others. She also learned a very important fact that she quickly spread to all her classmates—Rhonda was okay. In fact, Rhonda was pretty cool. Getting to know Rhonda made Libby stop and think about people's differences. From then on, Rhonda was considered by all the students in Ms. Jordan's class as an equal. The big step in getting her to be accepted was to get one of the most popular students in the room to accept her as a fellow classmate.

QUESTIONS TO CONSIDER

1. Do you think that Ms. Jordan and Ms. Baker planned for this result?
2. Can events be planned to orchestrate social interactions among students with and without disabilities in the classroom?
3. Who is responsible for facilitating the acceptance of students with disabilities into general education classrooms?
4. What are some other ways that Ms. Jordan could have encouraged the students in the class to accept Rhonda?

*I*ncluding students with special needs in general education classrooms continues to receive significant attention on a philosophical level. It is implemented for a variety of reasons; chief reasons are to improve educational opportunities and social development (Salend, 2000) and to give all students equal opportunities. However, too little discussion has focused on specific ways to implement inclusion successfully. Addressing the needs of a growing, diverse student population is a daunting challenge for today's schools. Adding students with disabilities to the mix only increases the challenges faced by general educators. This chapter discusses some of the key features of sound inclusive settings. It also addresses how to create and maintain these settings and the collaborative relationships that are critical to help them function well.

Accepting Diversity

*T*he most important issue underlying successful inclusion is the acceptance of diversity. Students often do not befriend each other because of perceived differences (Salend, 1999). These differences can be based on racial, socioeconomic, gender, or disability factors. Unfortunately, acceptance of diverse students is not likely to happen easily or without major changes in the way many schools operate. The complexity of the challenge is explained by Ferguson (1995):

> The real challenge is a lot harder and more complicated than we thought. Neither special or general education alone has either the capacity or the vision to challenge and change the deep-rooted assumptions that separate and track children and youths according to presumptions about ability, achievement, and eventual social contribution. Meaningful change will require nothing less than a joint effort to reinvent schools to be more accommodating to all dimensions of human diversity. (p. 285)

Although Ferguson's admonition is accurate and perhaps overwhelming, positive steps toward successful inclusion can be taken on classroom-by-classroom and school-by-school bases. It is important to remember that one teacher can have a dramatic effect on the lives of students who are different and who have learning challenges. Through their own actions and attitudes, teachers can have a profound influence on the acceptance of students by their peers and their ultimate success in school (Salend, 1999).

While the merits of inclusion have been debated, the reality is that the movement has taken hold. A comparison of national placement figures from the early 1980s to the present reveals a significant increase in the number of students with disabilities educated in general classrooms at least part of the day. The U.S. Department of Education (2001) estimated that approximately 75% of all students with disabilities were served in general education settings at least 40% of every school day.

The discussion of inclusion and how to make it work has focused mostly on students with disabilities. However, gifted students, at-risk students, and students from diverse backgrounds often face the same obstacles to acceptance and the same problems gaining access to appropriate educational programming. Consequently, the ideas in this chapter apply to students with all sorts of special needs.

Developing effective inclusive classrooms has relevance for students' immediate needs as well as their long-term needs. In the short term, students need to learn in settings along with their peers (that is, inclusive schools). Extensive research findings show that students with disabilities in inclusive settings learn as well as or better than they do in segregated settings, while enjoying opportunities for social interactions that they do not have in segregated settings (Rea, McLaughlin, & Walther-Thomas, 2002). In the long term, we want these students, as adults, to live, work, and play along with their peers in their home communities (i.e., inclusive living). Without the opportunity to grow and

CONSIDER THIS

What does the term *diversity* include? Is our society becoming more or less diverse?

CROSS-REFERENCE

Refer to Chapters 5 and 13 on gifted students and students at risk to determine how inclusion applies to these groups of students.

learn with nondisabled peers throughout their lives, individuals with disabilities will not be able to accomplish these goals as adults. Inclusion must begin in the early years. Expecting students with disabilities who have been isolated in segregated settings the first 18 to 20 years of their lives to assimilate into society is unrealistic.

Perceptions of Inclusion

A significant amount of discussion has surrounded the movement toward inclusion. On the philosophical level, only a few arguments have been levied against this movement. Who, for example, would argue against the idea of educating students together and giving all students equal opportunities? It is, however, primarily on the implementation level that concerns have arisen. Although most teachers and administrators agree that inclusion is a good thing, making decisions about how to achieve it is often problematic. Studies focusing on attitudes toward inclusion have involved two primary groups: general education teachers and parents.

Scruggs and Mastropieri (1996) studied teacher perceptions of inclusion by analyzing research that had been conducted on this topic between 1958 and 1995. Their results reflect many current issues related to responsibly including students with special needs in general education settings. Overall, they found that nearly two-thirds of general education classroom teachers support, for the most part, the concept of inclusion. However, when asked whether they were willing to teach students with disabilities in their own classes, many teachers expressed concerns or a lack of willingness to do so. This response was affected by the type of disability and the perceived impact on the teacher. A relatively low percentage of teachers (33% or less) felt that they had sufficient time, expertise, training, and resources (material support and support personnel) to enable them to work successfully with students with special needs (Scruggs & Mastropieri, 1996). These findings coincide with Roach's (1995) comment: "Teachers' fears seem to arise not so much from concerns about the philosophy of inclusion as from concerns and doubts about teachers' own teaching abilities as they relate to specific students" (p. 298).

These findings have a direct impact on teacher education. Teacher education programs must do a better job of preparing teachers, both general and special education, to work together to effectively implement inclusion in their schools. The inclusion movement has dimmed the line between general education and special education. The nearby Rights & Responsibilities feature addresses this issue.

The support of parents in the inclusion of their children with disabilities in general education settings has a great deal to do with the ultimate success the child experiences (Duhaney & Salend, 2000). Some parents support inclusion, while others are opposed (Palmer, Borthwick-Duffy, & Widaman, 1998). For parents of students with disabilities, the reaction to the inclusion movement is mixed, ranging from complete support of the idea (i.e., as propounded by the Arc) to skepticism, especially concerning the concept of full-time inclusion. This latter orientation is reflected in the position statements of various parent organizations, most notably the Learning Disabilities Association of America.

One national survey of parents of students with learning disabilities (Elam & Rose, 1995) found that they supported federal funding for services to students with disabilities. However, only about one-fourth of these parents thought that students with learning problems should be included in the same classes with nondisabled students. Duhaney and Salend (2000) did a literature review of parental perceptions of inclusive educational settings. After reviewing 17 studies published since 1985, they concluded that "parents of children with disabilities have mixed but generally positive perceptions toward inclusive educational placements" (p. 125)

Many parents who oppose inclusion are concerned that their children will simply not receive the amount of attention they would in a special education setting, or they are worried about the fact that many general education teachers need additional training (Strong

CONSIDER THIS

What factors would make teachers who support inclusion more willing to accept students with disabilities into their classrooms?

Where Does General Education Stop and Special Education Begin?

The distinction between regular education and special education has become increasingly less clear over time. In the mid 1970s, when special education laws were first enacted, the special education and "regular" education domains were very distinct. Increased inclusion means that many special education students now spend most or all of their day in the regular education setting. This means that both regular and special education teachers must be fully involved in programming for these students.

Identification, Referral and Evaluation

Through the "child find" process, as defined in the Individuals with Disabilities Education Act, 20 U.S.C. § 1400 *et seq.,* students are referred for special education assessment to determine if services are needed. In Minnesota, before being referred, a district must conduct and document at least two instructional strategies, alternatives, or interventions that were implemented while the student was in the regular classroom. The student's teacher must provide this documentation, unless the assessment team determines that there is an urgent need for assessment. After a referral is submitted to the assessment team, but before conducting the assessment, the team must review the student's performance, including prereferral interventions. Districts must use alternative intervention services to serve at-risk students who demonstrate a need for alternative instruction strategies.

When it is determined that a child initially qualifies for special education services, at least one regular education teacher must be a member of the individualized education program team. A representative of the district who is knowledgeable about the school's general curriculum must also participate in the IEP team. In developing an IEP for a child with a disability, districts are required to take steps to ensure that the disabled child has access to the same services that are available to nondisabled peers. These services may include various programs such as music, industrial arts, consumer and homemaking education, and vocational education.

Planning and Implementation

The child's IEP should be accessible to each regular education teacher, special education teacher, related service provider, and any other service provider who is responsible for implementation of the goals, objectives or adaptations contained in the IEP. Each teacher and service provider must be informed of his or her specific responsibilities related to the implementation of the IEP. Further, all specific accommodations, modifications and support services should be communicated to the appropriate parties and monitored to ensure compliance with the IEP.

Coordination of Responsibilities

The coordination of regular and special education requires that teachers and service providers understand how the child's services will be delivered. In order to accomplish this goal, administrators, teachers, service providers and counselors should be well trained. Service coordinators should carefully monitor the delivery of services. This can be done through regular contact with teachers and other providers to confirm that the child is receiving the services delineated in the IEP.

Documentation of Progress or Lack of Progress

The IEP team should track student progress to ensure that the current program is providing meaningful benefit to the child. Teachers and service providers should maintain accurate, logically compiled data regarding progress in regular classes and on IEP goals. The student's progress, or lack thereof, should be communicated to all team members, including the parents. Similarly, specific information about progress is important where the team wants to support a proposed action or discontinue service based on a student's success or lack of progress.

Discipline

Applying disciplinary standards to students with disabilities can be a challenge for districts. According to 34 C.F.R. § 300.527, "a child who has not been deemed eligible for special education may assert any of the protections provided for under the IDEA, if the district had knowledge that the child was a child with a disability *before* the behavior that precipitated the disciplinary action occurred." (emphasis added)

A district is deemed to have knowledge that a child is a child with a disability if:

▶ The parent of the child has expressed concern in writing, or orally to personnel of the district that the child is in need of special education and related services;

▶ The behavior or performance of a child demonstrates the need for special education services;

▶ The parent of the child has requested an evaluation of the child; or

▶ The child's teacher or other district personnel has expressed concern about the behavior or performance of the child to the director of special education or to other personnel in accordance with the district's established child-find or special education referral system.

When a child with a disability engages in conduct that violates district policies, a manifestation determination must be made by a team knowledgeable about the student. If the team determines that the behavior is a manifestation of the child's disabling condition, the student is not subject to standard disciplinary procedures regarding expulsion. If the team determines that the behavior is not a manifestation of the child's behavior, and the district initiates disciplinary procedures applicable to all children, including exclusion or expulsion, the district must ensure that the special education and disciplinary records of the child with a disability are transmitted for consideration by the person making the final determination regarding disciplinary action.

Records

Critical stages of educational planning should include a review of records and information. The records review should include the child's cumulative file, attendance data, grades, discipline records, counselor information, child study, nurse's files, health records, parent notes and communications, e-mails, teacher files, and information regarding any past services and referrals. A careful review of

current information can help in avoiding overlooking factors that may be critical to legal compliance.

 For follow-up questions about the distinction between general education and special education, go to Chapter 2 of the Companion Website (ablongman.com/sppd4e) and click on Rights & Responsibilities.

From "Where Does General Education Stop and Special Education Begin?" by S. E. Torgerson & K. H. Boyd, 2001, *Special Education Law Update, 10(4)*, p. 1+. Used with permission. Susan E. Torgerson and Kimberly H. Boyd are education-law attorneys with the Minneapolis law firm Rider, Bennett, Egan and Arundel LLP. They can be reached via e-mail at *setorgerson@riderlaw.com* and *khboyd@riderlaw.com*, respectively. The firm's Web site is *www.riderlaw.com*. The foregoing article was based on their presentation "Where Does General Education Stop and Special Education Begin?" as part of Rider, Bennett, Egan and Arundel's first annual "Back to School Legal Seminar," held in Bloomington, MN on August 17, 2001.

& Sandoval, 1999). These results were confirmed in the literature review by Duhaney and Salend (2000). As a result of these concerns, school personnel should assess the impact on individual children with disabilities to insure that inclusion does not have a negative impact.

Attitudinal research provides a glimpse of the task faced by professionals who support teaching students with special needs in inclusive settings. First, accurate information about inclusion in general and about individuals who need to be included must be distributed to teachers, parents, and the general public. Yet the greatest challenge will be changing an educational system that presents great barriers to inclusion, since teachers' perceptions, attitudes, and opportunities for collaboration are directly related to the success of inclusion. There is reason to believe that these changes can occur (Hobbs & Westling, 1998).

CONSIDER THIS

Often parents of students with mental retardation are more supportive of inclusion than parents of students with less severe disabilities. Why do you think this is the case?

Critical Dimensions of Inclusive Classrooms

The concept of inclusion purports that students with special needs can be active, valued, fully participating members of a school community in which diversity is viewed as the norm and high-quality education is provided through a combination of meaningful curriculum, effective teaching, and necessary supports (Halvorsen & Neary, 2001). Anything less is unacceptable. Inclusion is distinctly different from the notion of integration or mainstreaming, in which students with special needs are educated in physical proximity to their age peers, yet without significant attention paid to the qualitative features of this arrangement. Both integration and mainstreaming begin with the notion that students with disabilities belong in special classes and should be integrated as much as possible in general classrooms. Inclusion, on the other hand, assumes that all students *belong* in the general education classroom and should be pulled out only when appropriate services cannot be provided in the inclusive setting. While seemingly a simple difference, these two approaches vary significantly (Halvorsen & Neary, 2001). Several key structural and philosophical differences distinguish the inclusive model and more traditional special education models. Figure 2.1 depicts some of these differences.

Many different factors are critical to the success of inclusion. Webber (1997) identified five essential features that characterize successful inclusion of students with special needs. They are (1) a sense of community and social acceptance, (2) an appreciation of student diversity, (3) attention to curricular needs, (4) effective management and instruction, and

Traditional Models	*Inclusive Educational Models*
1. Some students do not "fit" in general education classes.	1. All students "fit" in general education classrooms.
2. The teacher is the instructional leader.	2. Collaborative teams share leadership responsibilities.
3. Students learn from teachers and teachers solve the problems.	3. Students and teachers learn from each other and solve problems together.
4. Students are purposely grouped by similar ability.	4. Students are purposely grouped by differing abilities.
5. Instruction is geared toward middle-achieving students.	5. Instruction is geared to match students at all levels of achievement.
6. Grade-level placement is considered synonymous with curricular content.	6. Grade-level placement and individual curricular content are independent of each other.
7. Instruction is often passive, competitive, didactic, and/or teacher-directed.	7. Instruction is active, creative, and collaborative among members of the classroom.
8. Most instructional supports are provided outside the classroom.	8. Most instructional supports are provided within the classroom.
9. Students who do not "fit in" are excluded from general classes and/or activities.	9. Activities are designed to include students though participation levels may vary.
10. The classroom teacher assumes ownership for the education of general education students, and special education staff assume ownership for the education of students with special needs.	10. The classroom teacher, special educators, related service staff, and families assume shared ownership for educating all students.
11. Students are evaluated by common standards.	11. Students are evaluated by individually appropriate standards.
12. Students' success is achieved by meeting common standards.	12. The system of education is considered successful when it strives to meet each student's needs. Students' success is achieved when both individual and group goals are met.

(5) personnel support and collaboration. Voltz, Brazil, and Ford (2001) list three critical elements—(1) active, meaningful participation in the mainstream, (2) sense of belonging, and (3) shared ownership among faculty. Finally, Mastropieri and Scruggs (2001) add administrative support to the list.

When in place, the features noted by Webber (1997), Voltz et al. (2001), and Mastropieri and Scruggs (2001) make the general education classroom the best possible placement option for many students with disabilities. If these features are not present, however, the likelihood of inclusion being successful is significantly limited. The five dimensions for successful inclusion are discussed in the following sections.

Sense of Community and Social Acceptance

In desirable inclusive settings, every student is valued and nurtured. Such settings promote an environment in which all members are seen as equal, all have the opportunity

If students with special needs are to enjoy a sense of acceptance in general classrooms, teachers must play a critical role.

to contribute, and all contributions are respected. Deno, Foegen, Robinson, and Espin (1996) describe the ideal school settings as "caring and nurturant places with a strong sense of community where all children and youth belong, where diversity is valued, and where the needs of all students are addressed" (p. 350).

Students with special needs are truly included in their classroom communities only when they are appreciated by their teachers and socially accepted by their classmates. An understanding teacher more effectively meets students' instructional and curricular needs, and social acceptance among classmates contributes to students' self-perception of value. Both these goals are equally critical to creating effective inclusive settings and responsible learning environments. It is imperative that we address the need for acceptance, belonging, and friendship (Voltz et al., 2001); Lang and Berberich (1995) suggest that inclusive classrooms should be characterized as settings where basic human needs are met. Figure 2.2 highlights critical needs that should be prominent in an inclusive classroom community.

Teachers play a very critical role in creating a positive classroom environment (Favazza, Phillipsen, & Kumar, 2000). Several factors controlled by teachers are essential to establishing a successful inclusive setting. These factors include teacher attitude, teacher expectations, teacher competence, teacher collaborative skills, and teacher support (Mastropieri & Scruggs, 2001; Salend, 1999).

CONSIDER THIS

How are the attitudes of administrators linked to the attitudes of teachers regarding inclusion? Is this linkage important or not?

FIGURE 2.2

The Basic Needs of Children in a Learning Environment

From *All Children Are Special: Creating an Inclusive Classroom* (p. 73), by G. Lang and C. Berberich, 1995, York, ME: Stenhouse Publishers. Used by permission.

Belonging

Freedom

Enjoyment

Valuing

Safety

Teachers must have a positive attitude about students with special needs being in their classrooms. Students are aware of the support given by their teachers to students with disabilities, and they have a tendency to model these attitudes and behaviors. As a result, teachers "need to examine their own attitudes and behaviors as they relate to interactions with students and the acceptance of individual differences" (Salend, 1999, p. 10). If they are not supportive of the inclusion of these students, other students will detect this attitude and be less likely to accept the students (Salend, 1999).

Teachers also have to expect students with special needs to perform at a high level. Students often achieve at a level that is expected of them; if teachers expect less, they get less. A great deal of research has shown that teachers actually treat students whom they consider underachievers differently than they treat other students (Jones & Jones, 2001).

Teachers also need to have the skills necessary to meet the instructional needs of students with special needs (Mastropieri & Scruggs, 2001). Teaching all students the same way will not be effective for many students with special needs. Teachers also must prepare students to interact with others whose physical characteristics, behaviors, or learning-related needs require special consideration. Sometimes students need to be educated about diversity and disabilities to reduce the fear of differences. While teachers can serve as excellent role models for acceptance of diversity, they can also facilitate interactions and acceptance by orchestrating situations where students with and without disabilities interact. Remember the chapter-opening vignette, where the teacher's actions resulted in a student without a disability interacting positively with a student with a disability.

When determining if the school does promote a sense of community and social acceptance, school personnel can ask the following questions (Voltz et al., 2001):

▶ Are students with disabilities disproportionately teased by other students?
▶ Do students with disabilities seem to enjoy being in the general education classroom?
▶ Do students without disabilities voluntarily include students with disabilities in various activities?
▶ Do students without disabilities seem to value the ideas and opinions of students with disabilities? Do students with disabilities seem to value the ideas and opinions of nondisabled students?
▶ Do students with disabilities consider the general education classroom to be their "real class"? Do they consider the general education teacher to be one of their "real teachers"? (p. 25)

In addition to teachers, students also play a critical role in the success of inclusion. Both students with disabilities and students without disabilities need to understand and accept diversity. Because attitudes begin to develop in young children (Favazza et al., 2000), it is critical that teachers of young children create a positive, accepting attitude and model acceptance to their young students.

Students must also achieve a level of interaction that leads to classroom communities where peer understanding and support are the norm. "The more consistently students receive the message that school is a place where everyone belongs and is cared for, will get needed support, and has something to contribute, the more likely it is that classroom programs will be effective" (Korinek et al., 1999, p. 5). Though 100% success cannot be guaranteed in making inclusion work in every classroom, well-prepared students and capable, optimistic, caring teachers can set the stage for a positive educational experience for each person in the class.

While students may develop friendships and a classroom community naturally, teachers can do some things to facilitate the process. Friendship facilitation should be an integral part of both special education and general education teachers' roles in inclusive settings (Turnbull, Pereira, & Blue-Banning, 2000). Facilitation can occur through organized group activities, pairing students for various tasks, seating arrangements, buddy systems, and other methods. The Inclusion Strategies feature provides some examples of how music and art can be used to promote friendships.

CONSIDER THIS

How likely is it that students with special needs will be successfully included if teachers leave peer acceptance of these students to chance? Why?

Music and Art Activities to Promote Friendships

▸ Teach students songs that deal with the theme of friendship, including recorded songs such as "Friends" (Linhart & Klingman, 1976), "You've Got a Friend" (Taylor, 1971), "That's What Friends Are For" (Bayer Sager & Bacharach, 1985), and "A Little Help from My Friends" (Lennon & McCartney, 1967), and nonrecorded songs that appear in music books, such as "All I Need Is a Friend" (Worsley, 1995), "Best of Friends" (Fidel & Hohnston, 1986), and "Best Friends" (Ravosa & Jones, 1981).

▸ Teach students group sing-along songs.
▸ Teach students songs that require two or more students to perform accompanying physical gestures and movements.
▸ Teach students humorous songs.
▸ Ask students to draw pictures of scenes depicting friendships.
▸ Have students work on group art projects such as a friendship mural, a friendship book with illustrations, and a friendship bulletin board.
▸ Have students make silhouettes and collages of their friends.

▸ Have students make friendship posters that include the qualities that contribute to making someone a good friend.

 For follow-up questions about music and art activities that promote friendships, go to Chapter 2 of the Companion Website (ablongman.com/sppd4e) and click Inclusion Strategies.

From "Facilitating Friendships Among Diverse Students" (p. 11) by S. J. Salend, 1999, *Intervention in School and Clinic, 35.* Used with permission.

Appreciation of Student Diversity

To maximize learning, a teacher needs to understand each individual in the classroom as well as possible. The increasing diversity of today's classrooms makes teaching a very complex activity that will likely only get more complex in the future as our culture becomes more diverse (Maheady, Harper, & Mallette, 2001). In addition to recognizing and responding to each student's educational needs, teachers must be sensitive to the cultural, community, and family values that can have an impact on a student's educational experience. For instance, the nature of teacher–student interactions may be directly affected by certain cultural factors, or the type of home–school contact will be dictated by how the family wants to interact with the school.

Different types of diversity exist within classroom settings. It is important to recognize and celebrate each one. Schwartz and Karge (1996) have identified the following types of differences: racial and ethnic diversity; gender and sexual orientation; religious diversity; physical, learning, and intellectual differences; linguistic differences; and behavior and personality diversity. Although the following chapters focus on areas of exceptionality, and to a lesser extent cultural diversity, teachers should consider the much broader range of individual variance.

Diversity is enriching. All students can flourish in an atmosphere in which diversity is recognized, opportunities exist to better understand its various forms, and differences are appreciated. Clearly, a classroom setting that champions differences provides a welcoming environment for students whose learning, physical, emotional, and social needs vary from those of their classmates. All students benefit from being in an inclusive classroom (Voltz et al., 2001). Students learn tolerance and the ability to accept differences in each other, as well as having opportunities to benefit from cooperative learning and other alternative instructional strategies.

Attention to Curricular Needs

Many discussions of inclusion lose track of an important consideration: what the student needs to learn. Teachers must seriously look at the curriculum and ask what students are learning and how students with disabilities can access the curriculum (Pugach & Warger, 2001). If the individual curricular needs of a student are not being met, the curriculum

CONSIDER THIS

Describe the ways in which today's school population can be diverse. What kinds of actions can school personnel take to show sensitivity to this diversity?

CONSIDER THIS

Can you imagine a situation in which a student with special needs cannot be taught in a general education classroom? What would be an appropriate action if this were the case?

must be modified or the educational placement must be reexamined. Not meeting the curricular needs of students will definitely make it difficult for the student to learn, but it will also likely lead to behavior problems (Jones & Jones, 2001). A student's learning and life needs should always be the driving force in programmatic efforts and decisions (Smith & Hilton, 1994). Good teachers vary their curricula to meet the needs of the students (Walther-Thomas, Korinek, McLaughlin, & Williams, 2000). While some students with disabilities included in general classrooms may be able to deal effectively with the curricula, many need substantial modifications (Van Laarhoven, Coutinho, Van Laarhoven-Myers, & Repp, 1999). Fortunately, most curricular needs can usually be addressed within the context of the general educational classroom.

Curricular concerns include two issues: (1) content that is meaningful to students in a current and future sense, and (2) approaches and materials that work best for them. Dealing with the first issue helps ensure that what students need to learn (i.e., knowledge and skills acquisition) is provided within the inclusive setting. The second issue involves choosing how to teach relevant content. Scruggs and Mastropieri (1994) found that the provision of appropriate curriculum appeared to be meaningfully associated with success in general education classes. Teachers can modify the academic level of the content and focus more on functional objectives, reduce the content to a manageable amount, and change how students are asked to demonstrate mastery of the content.

Effective Management and Instruction

Another essential component of successful inclusive settings is the effective management of the classroom and effective instruction provided by the teacher to meet the wide range of needs of students (Voltz et al., 2001). These practices include four elements: successful classroom management, effective instructional techniques, appropriate accommodative practices, and instructional flexibility. Without effective practices in these areas, successful inclusion is improbable.

CROSS-REFERENCE

For more information on appropriate classroom management techniques for inclusive settings, see Chapter 14.

Successful Classroom Management   Classrooms that encourage learning are characterized by sound organizational and management systems. Classroom management—including physical, procedural, instructional, and behavior management—sets the stage for the smooth delivery of instruction. Effective classroom management is required if students are to benefit from any form of instruction, especially in inclusive classrooms where students display a wide range of diversity (Jones & Jones, 2001). Without effective classroom organization and management, learning will not be optimal for any student.

Effective Instructional Techniques   Teachers must feel comfortable using a wide variety of instructional techniques to meet the needs of diverse classrooms (Voltz et al., 2001). An impressive body of research validates the effectiveness of certain instructional practices (Brody & Good, 1986; Rosenshine & Stevens, 1986). Obviously, when instructional techniques are ineffective, successful inclusion will not occur. Students with disabilities, especially those eligible for special education services, by definition, have learning problems. As a result, effective instructional techniques must be used if these students will be successful. Mastropieri and Scruggs (1993) have summarized key elements of effective instructional practice: daily review, specific techniques for presenting new information, guided practice, independent practice, and formative evaluation. These concepts are addressed throughout this book as they apply to children with various special needs. Chapters 15 and 16 specifically address instructional concerns in elementary and secondary classes, respectively.

Appropriate Accommodative Practices   Some students require special adaptations to the physical environment, the curriculum, the way instruction is provided, or the assignments given to them. Scruggs and Mastropieri (1994) note that instructional supports are a key variable in classrooms where inclusion is successful. Chapters 5–11 provide examples of disability-specific accommodations that might be needed.

The concept of supports within classrooms is a particularly critical one and refashions inclusion as "supported education" (Snell & Drake, 1994). Supports include accommodations and modifications to enhance learning and acceptance in the general education curriculum. Accommodations consist of changes in the manner in which students are taught, including changes in instruction, assignments and homework, and testing. Modifications, on the other hand, generally refer to changes in policies that may affect students with disabilities. Altering the school curriculum or attendance policy would be an example of a modification.

Whenever possible, accommodative supports should be designed so that they benefit not only students with special needs, but also other students in the class as well (Stainback, Stainback, & Wehman, 1997). The idea has merit for three primary reasons. First, it provides support to other students who will find the accommodations helpful. Second, this approach can minimize overt attention to the fact that a certain student needs special adaptations. Third, it enhances the likelihood of treatment acceptance, that is, the likelihood that teachers will see the specific strategy as feasible, desirable, helpful, and fair.

One support that can have a significant impact on the success of inclusion efforts is the use of assistive technology. Ranging from low-tech applications (e.g., optical devices) to high-tech ones (e.g., computer-based augmentative communication systems), assistive technology can allow students with specific disabilities to participate more fully in ongoing classroom activities. Moreover, as Woronov (1996) acknowledges, nondisabled students can benefit from assistive technology as well. Technology Today lists special education Websites that can support inclusion.

Instructional Flexibility   The ability to respond to unexpected and changing situations to support students with special needs is a key characteristic of responsible inclusive settings. As Schaffner and Buswell (1996) note, classroom teachers need to develop the capabilities that families have acquired to react successfully and spontaneously to challenges

CONSIDER THIS

How can appropriate accommodative practices benefit all students, including those without special needs?

Web Resources on Inclusion and Disability

Inclusion	Disability Resources
www.ici.coled.umn.edu/ici	www.iser.com
www.asri.edu/cfsp/brochure/abtcons.htm	www.ed.gov/offices/OSERS/OSEP/index.html
www.tash.org	www.schwablearning.org
interwork.sdsu.edu	www.mankato.msus.edu/dept/comdis/kuster2/welcome.html
www.nyise.org/college.htm	www.ldonline.org
www.ldonline.org	www.downsyndrome.com
	www.iltech.org
	www.hsdc.org
	www.ncld.org

For follow-up questions about web resources for inclusion and disability, go to Chapter 2 of the Companion Website (ablongman.com/sppd4e) and click Technology Today.

From *Quick Guide to the Internet for Special Education 2000 Edition* (p. 13) by M. Male and D. Gotthoffer, 2000, Boston: Allyn and Bacon.

that arise on a day-to-day basis. Teachers must be flexible; they must be able to handle behavior problems, provide extra support during instruction, modify assessment techniques, and orchestrate social interactions (Jones & Jones, 2001).

Personnel Support and Collaboration

Students with special needs require personnel supports to allow them to benefit from placement in inclusive settings, in addition to the instructional supports noted earlier (accommodative practices and assistive technology). Special education teachers, **para-educators** (teacher aides), and other related service professionals such as speech and language pathologists, occupational and physical therapists, and audiologists are typically involved in providing supports to students with disabilities. They also assist general education teachers in inclusive settings through a variety of collaborative models, including collaboration-consultation, peer support systems, teacher assistance teams, and co-teaching. Table 2.1 summarizes these approaches. A more in-depth discussion of these approaches will be presented in the following section. Equally important is administrative support for inclusion, as reflected by attitudes, policies, and practices at the district and individual school level (Podemski et al., 1995; Mastropieri & Scruggs, 2001). The next section focuses on collaboration as a critical element in successful inclusive practices.

The use of teams to provide services to students with disabilities, especially students included in general education classrooms, has grown significantly over the past several years. A primary reason for this growth is the realization that it takes a creative use of manpower to effectively implement an inclusion teaching model. As one study found, "Working as a team enables teachers to plan more effectively, to problem-solve more efficiently, and to intervene with a student throughout the school day" (Allsop, Santos, & Linn, 2000, p. 142).

Several critical variables must be in place for these teams to be successful. These include many factors, ranging from knowing the purpose of the team to making sure that the team appreciates disagreement. Table 2.2 lists variables for success determined by Fleming and Monda-Amaya (2001) in a recent study. Cooperative teams should be evaluated periodically to ensure their effectiveness. Salend, Gordon, and Lopez-Vona (2002) recommend that in order to review their effectiveness, teams should be evaluated using information on team member experiences and their reactions to working together.

T ABLE 2.1   Types of Collaborative Efforts

Approach	Nature of Contact with Student	Description
Collaboration–Consultation	Indirect	General education teacher requests the services of the special education teacher (i.e., consultant) to help generate ideas for addressing an ongoing situation. The approach is interactive.
Peer Support Systems	Indirect	Two general education teachers work together to identify effective solutions to classroom situations. The approach emphasizes the balance of the relationship.
Teacher Assistance Teams	Indirect	Teams provide support to general education teachers. Made up of core members plus the teacher seeking assistance, it emphasizes analyzing the problem situation and developing potential solutions.
Co-Teaching	Direct	General and special education teachers work together in providing direct service to students. Employing joint planning and teaching, the approach emphasizes the joint responsibilities of instruction.

From *Cooperative Teaching: Rebuilding the Schoolhouse for All Students* (p. 74) by J. Bauwens and J. J. Hourcade, 1995, Austin, TX: Pro-Ed. Used by permission.

TABLE 2.2	Critical Variables for Team Efforts and Effectiveness, Ranked by Categories

Team Goals
  Purpose of the team is clear.
  Team goals are understood by all members.
  Team goals are regularly reviewed.
  Team goals are established by team members.
  Team goals are clearly stated.
  Team goals are modified by team members.
  Team goals are supported by the family.
  Team goals are attainable.
  Team goals are prioritized.
  Members anticipate both positive and negative outcomes.
  Members are satisfied with goals that have been selected.

Team Roles and Team Membership
  Team members are committed to the team process.
  The team has a leader.
  Members are accountable to the team.
  Team roles are clearly understood.
  Team roles are perceived by members as being important.
  New team members are added when practical.
  The team leader is unbiased.

Team Communication
  Decisions are made for the good of the student.
  Team members have adequate listening time.
  Decisions are alterable.
  Team members have equal opportunities to speak.
  Decisions are reached by consensus.

Team Cohesion
  Members feel safe sharing ideas.
  The team has trust among members.

Members (especially parents) feel equally empowered.
The team has a unified goal.
The team has time to celebrate.
The team has support from superiors.
Members have respect for each other.
The has recognition for efforts.
The team has autonomy for decision making.
The team has a healthy regard for disagreement.

Team Logistics
  Progress is evaluated internally, by members.
  Team procedures are clearly understood.

Team Outcomes
  Team makes modifications to the plan as needed.
  Members are clear about their responsibilities for the plan.
  Members are committed to implementing the plan.
  Solutions are practical.
  A plan was implemented.
  Team reviews the impact of the plan.
  A plan was developed.
  Parent satisfaction is part of the evaluation.
  Outcomes are evaluated internally, by members.
  The family is generally feeling better.
  A plan was agreed on.
  A decision was made.
  Outcomes are evaluated at regularly scheduled times.
  Members are satisfied with the plan.

From "Process Variables Critical for Team Effectiveness" (p. 168) by J. L. Fleming & L. E. Monda-Amaya, 2001, *Remedial and Special Education, 22.* Used with permission.

Professional Collaboration

Collaboration among professionals has been discussed in the social services research since the early 1900s; it is not a new concept. In the field of special education, collaboration has been studied since 1960. Collaboration in schools for serving children with special needs occurs both formally, when teams are formed around a particular child, and informally, when two teachers get together and discuss how to meet a child's specific need (Friend, 2000). Collaboration occurs when more than one person works voluntarily toward a common goal, frequently related to the success of students (Halvorsen & Neary, 2001).

Professional collaboration has become a key component of effective schools and a necessity for successful inclusion. Collaboration can occur in a variety of settings and activities, including prereferral efforts and IEP meetings (see Chapter 4), consulting and cooperative teaching arrangements, and teacher assistance teams. Still another form of collaboration is peer tutoring or some other peer support framework.

Collaboration is not successful without a great deal of planning and effort (Clark, 2000). It "requires commitment on the part of each individual to a shared goal, demands careful attention to communication skills, and obliges participants to maintain parity throughout their interactions" (Friend, 2000, p. 131). In general, collaboration should be accomplished to ensure (1) natural inclusion of students in all activities of the general education classroom; (2) appropriate specialized instruction of students; and (3) adaptations of curriculum and materials necessary for each student (Halvorsen & Neary, 2001).

Unfortunately, many schools implement collaborative models because "everyone else is doing it." In order to make it work effectively, "collaboration should become a topic for study and staff development that is addressed as regularly as are approaches for teaching language arts, classroom discipline, and drug and alcohol awareness" (Friend, 2000, p. 160). Schools can use several different models that rely on collaboration among school staff. One particular model is not better than others. Schools need to understand the variations that are possible and implement the approach that best meets their needs and the needs of their students.

Collaboration-Consultation

Collaboration-consultation is a model that emphasizes a close working relationship between general and special educators. "Effective collaboration consists of designing and using a sequence of goal-oriented activities that result in improved working relationships between professional colleagues. The responsibility for collaborating can either be the sole responsibility of one individual who seeks to improve a professional relationship, or a joint commitment of two or more people who wish to improve their working relationship" (Cramer, 1998, p. 3).

There are several benefits of collaboration (Mundschenk & Foley, 1997):

1. Collaboration facilitates the ongoing planning, evaluation, and modification necessary to ensure the success of included placements.
2. Collaboration enables general education classrooms to meet the needs of students with and without disabilities in new and exciting ways.
3. Collaboration can provide the personal and professional support of highly skilled colleagues.
4. Collaboration can result in personal and professional growth for all participants.
5. Collaboration helps teachers identify ways to access the skills, knowledge, and expertise of other teachers. (p. 58)

*T*EACHING TIP

Teachers who use the collaboration-consultation model should spend time together socially in order to better understand each other.

Teachers often need to work together to solve some of the challenges created by inclusion.

Diversity Forum

Planning as a Team, Learning from Each Other

I just received a new student in my second grade class. Her name is Eun-Ja Kim, and she is from Korea. In addition to speaking only Korean she also has some developmental delays. Our school is inclusive, so the special education teacher comes in to work with Eun-Ja during reading and math, and Eun-Ja also gets 45 minutes a day of ESL [English as a second language] instruction, since our school doesn't have a Korean-English bilingual program. But that's really not enough, so this child is sitting in all her classes, probably bored out of her mind! I wish I knew how to help her!

Providing appropriate services to English language learners (ELLs) with disabilities requires many teachers to collaborate to make sure that the students' educational needs are addressed in the context of their disability, culture, and language (Yates & Ortiz, 1995). Each team member provides expertise and experience related to his or her own role, and they have opportunities to learn from each other in this process.

▶ General education teachers contribute their expertise related to the general education curriculum.

▶ Bilingual education and ESL teachers bring expertise related to culture, as well as English language modifications for instruction in general and special education. Both professionals can promote their colleagues' understanding of bilingualism, second-language acquisition, and language modifications for ELLs.

▶ The special education teacher shares knowledge of appropriate modifications with other team members that can facilitate accommodations related to the student's disability-related needs.

▶ Parents and other significant family members not only contribute their knowledge about their child's abilities and educational needs, but also are instrumental in identifying appropriate goals and objectives, providing relevant cultural information to team members, and offering native language development and support for their child.

For follow-up questions about ELLs with disabilities, go to Chapter 2 of the Companion Website (ablongman.com/sppd4e) and click Diversity Forum.

Through collaborating with each other, general education and special education teachers can bring more ideas and experiences to help students achieve success. Through consultation, teachers can assist each other in utilizing skills that also result in positive outcomes for students.

A critical skill in collaboration is effective communication. Without the ability to communicate with each other, school personnel will not be able to collaborate effectively (Hollingsworth, 2001). The more individuals involved in a child's educational program, the more effective communication must be. Communication allows the sharing of information about a student, expertise, perceptions, concerns, ideas, and questions (Halvorsen & Neary, 2001).

In order to facilitate communication, school staff must have time for planning. Regardless of the collaboration approach used, planning time is critical. Unfortunately, the logistics of arranging planning time is often complicated. Teachers may not share planning periods, and in elementary schools teachers may not even have planning periods. Also, students with disabilities included in secondary schools may have six or seven general classroom teachers. Trying to sit down and plan with so many players is extremely difficult (Halvorsen & Neary, 2001).

Making planning time available for school staff requires the support of school administrators. If school administrators support inclusion, they generally find a way to arrange for planning opportunities for professionals and paraprofessionals. On the other hand, if they are not supportive of inclusion or do not see the need for planning time, then they are less likely to make the time available.

Making time for teachers and other staff members to plan for specific students can be accomplished in several ways. Arranging for team members to have the same planning periods, having split schedules for teachers, utilizing roving aides to cover classes, and providing financial incentives are only a few methods for finding planning time. Regardless of how it is accomplished, the fact remains that without time to plan, many attempts to provide supports for students with disabilities in general education classes

CONSIDER THIS

How can administrators make time available for teams of teachers to plan? Why is it important for administrators to support this planning effort?

Personal Spotlight

Two Teachers on Collaboration

Betty Bolte and **Debi Smith** teach at Harp Elementary School in Springdale, Arkansas. Betty has taught special education for more than 15 years, while Debi has taught more than 10 years as a special education teacher in both self-contained and resource rooms, and regular education. Currently she is teaching in a first grade classroom. While both Betty and Debi believe strongly in the inclusive educational model, they are adamant that inclusion will not work without extensive collaboration among general educators and special educators. Notes Betty, "Inclusion will simply not work at all if special education and general education teachers are not able to work together to meet the needs of these students." Unfortunately, they see many barriers to this collaboration. These include attitudes of teachers, involvement of parents, lack of knowledge about students with disabilities, and time.

Lack of time for collaboration is one of the barriers that often results in ineffective inclusive classrooms. Unless special education teachers and general classroom teachers have an opportunity to plan together, educational opportunities for stu-

Debi Smith and Betty Bolte

Co-Teachers, Harp Elementary School, Springdale, AR

dents will not be optimal. Debi says that after teaching in both special and general education she can better understand the frustrations of teachers from both areas when students are included in general classrooms but need some special education services. "Although it is easy to think that the special education teacher is not doing her job, it is a very different story when you are in the special education teacher's shoes. I used to think that having only five or six students at a time was an easy load until I was a resource room teacher. Although you might only have five students each period, that turns out to be 25 or 30 individual teaching assignments over the day." Adds Betty, "I know that when I have a student for one or two periods each day I am not really helping that student unless I have had a chance to talk with his or her regular classroom teacher to find out how I can really help the student."

For follow-up questions about this Personal Spotlight, go to Chapter 2 of the Companion Website (ablongman.com/sppd4e) and click Personal Spotlight.

will be unsuccessful. The Personal Spotlight provides a glimpse of a general and a special education teacher and their thoughts on collaboration.

Co-Teaching

Another model to provide support for students in general education classrooms is **co-teaching**. Cooperative teaching or co-teaching can be defined as

> a restructuring of teaching procedures in which two or more educators possessing distinct sets of skills work in a co-active and coordinated fashion to jointly teach academically and behaviorally heterogeneous groups of students in educationally integrated settings, that is, in general [education] classrooms. (Bauwens & Hourcade, 1995, p. 46)

Co-teaching is an arrangement of two or more teachers or other school staff who collectively assume the responsibilities for the same group of students on a regular basis (Thousand & Villa, 1990). This model "provides students with an educational environment that lends itself to an increased potential for individualized instruction to meet the needs of all students" (Van Laarhoven, 1999, p. 170). Like all collaborative models, it requires extensive planning (Lanagerock, 2000).

Cooperative teaching is a logical outgrowth of collaborative efforts between teachers that include consultative arrangements, additional help given by special education teachers to children not identified as eligible for special services, and the sharing of teaching assistants, especially to accompany students who are disabled in the general education classroom. Cooperative teaching involves a team approach to supporting students within the general classroom, combining the content expertise of the classroom teacher with the pedagogical skills of the special education teacher. Perhaps the best vehicle for attaining successful inclusive classrooms, it truly provides supported education, the school-based equivalent of supported work in which students are placed in the least restrictive environment and provided the necessary support (e.g., by the special educator) to be successful.

Co-teaching usually occurs at set times, such as during second period every day or certain days of each week. When students with disabilities are included in general education classrooms, the special education teacher, who becomes a co-teacher, is usually present (Friend & Bursuck, 1999). Co-teachers perform many tasks jointly, including planning and teaching, developing instructional accommodations, monitoring and evaluating students, and communicating student progress (Walther-Thomas et al., 2000). Co-teaching can take the form of one teaching, one supporting; station teaching; parallel teaching; team teaching; complementary teaching; supportive learning activities; and alternative teaching (Halvorsen & Neary, 2001). Figure 2.3 summarizes the advantages and disadvantages of several variations.

Austin (2001) studied 139 co-teachers from nine school districts, kindergarten through 12th grade. He found that although the majority of co-teachers had not volunteered for the role, "a major percentage indicated that they considered co-teaching worthwhile" (p. 252). Also, the majority felt that co-teaching actually contributed to academic gains made by all students in their classrooms. Austin's study (2001) found that the important co-teaching activities included providing feedback to each other, sharing classroom management, having daily planning time, and using cooperative learning techniques.

Cooperative teaching is not a simple solution for the many challenges of accommodating a broad range of students with disabilities. There are difficulties that may create barriers for effective co-teaching (Langerock, 2000). Bauwens et al. (1989) and Harris (1998) have identified obstacles that must be overcome including limitations of time, cooperation with others, and workload. Time problems can be alleviated through careful planning, regularly scheduled discussions on teaching, and support for planning periods from administrators. The issue of cooperation is best addressed through training in the use of cooperative teaching, experience with the process, development of guidelines specific to the program, and attention to effective communication accompanied, as needed, by conflict resolution. The concern for workload should be addressed as the team relationship develops, delegating tasks in a way that allows each individual to focus on areas of expertise and interests. Evaluation should be a component of the workload as well.

Another critical issue regarding cooperative teaching is voluntary involvement. Setting up cooperative teaching arrangements without regard to input from the teachers themselves will not set the stage for success for teachers or ultimately for the students. Teachers should be given some choice and flexibility—for example, allowing general and special education teachers to select partners with whom to collaborate has worked well.

Teachers, both general and special education, involved in co-teaching activities rated having scheduled planning time and administrative support as either very important or important (Austin, 2001). Figure 2.4 reflects the ratings of other areas by co-teachers.

One of the obvious difficulties in implementing the co-teaching model is insuring the compatibility of the individuals working together. Co-teaching requires individuals who are willing to give up some control and accept positive, constructive criticism from colleagues. Common characteristics of successful co-teachers include the following (Walther-Thomas et al., 2000):

- Professional competence
- Personal confidence
- Respect of colleagues
- Professional enthusiasm
- Respect for colleagues' skills and contributions
- Good communication and problem-solving skills
- Personal interest in professional growth
- Flexibility and openness to new ideas
- Effective organizational skills

FIGURE 2.3   Variations of Co-Teaching: Advantages and Disadvantages

Variation	▶ Advantages	▶ Disadvantages
Interactive Teaching (Whole group) Partners alternate roles presenting new concepts, reviewing, demonstrating, role playing, and monitoring.	▶ Provides systematic observation/ data collection ▶ Promotes role/content sharing ▶ Facilitates individual assistance ▶ Models appropriate academic, social, and help-seeking behaviors ▶ Teaches question asking ▶ Provides clarification (e.g., concepts, rules, vocabulary)	▶ May be job sharing, not learning enriching ▶ Requires considerable planning ▶ Requires modeling and role-playing skills ▶ Becomes easy to "typecast" specialist with this role
Station Teaching (Small group) Students in groups of three or more rotate to various teacher-led and independent work stations where new instruction, review, and/or practice is provided. Students may work at all stations during the rotation.	▶ Provides active learning format ▶ Increases small-group attention ▶ Encourages cooperation and independence ▶ Allows strategic grouping ▶ Increases response rate	▶ Requires considerable planning and preparation ▶ Increases noise level ▶ Requires goup and independent work skills ▶ Is difficult to monitor
Parallel Teaching (Small group) Students are divided into mixed-ability groups, then each partner teaches a group. The same material is presented in each group.	▶ Provides effective review format ▶ Encourages student responses ▶ Reduces pupil–teacher ratio for group instruction/review	▶ Not easy to achieve equal depth of content coverage ▶ May be difficult to coordinate ▶ Requires monitoring of partner pacing ▶ Increases noise level ▶ Encourages some teacher–student competition
Alternative Teaching (Big group; small group) One partner teaches an enrichment lesson or reteaches a concept for the benefit of a small group, while the other partner teaches and/or monitors the remaining members of the class.	▶ Facilitates enrichment opportunities ▶ Offers absent students "catch up" time ▶ Keeps individuals and class on pace ▶ Offers time to develop missing skills	▶ May be easy to select the same low-achieving students for help ▶ Creates segregated learning environments ▶ Is difficult to coordinate ▶ May single out students

From *Collaboration for Inclusive Education* (p. 190) by C. Walther-Thomas, L. Korinek, V. L. McLaughlin, and B. T. Williams, 2000, Boston: Allyn and Bacon. Used by permission.

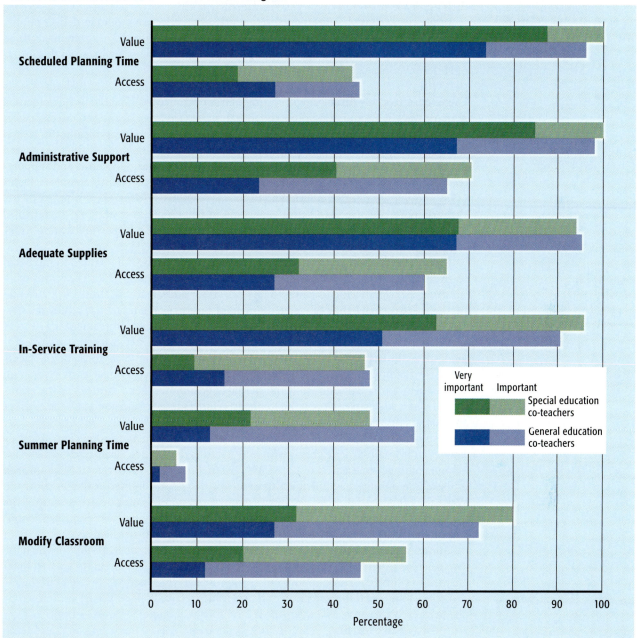

FIGURE 2.4   Comparison of Percentages of Very Important and Important Responses of Co-teachers in Value Versus Access Categories

From Austin, *Remedial and Special Education 4*(22). July/August 2001.

▶ Previous experience teaming with others
▶ Willingness to invest extra time in the process as needed
▶ Commitment to planning weekly with partner
▶ Voluntary participation in co-teaching

Still another characteristic of effective co-teaching teams is a shared work ethic (Mc-Cormick, Noonan, Ogata, & Heck, 2001). Co-teaching works extremely well when the co-teachers are committed to the success of students and find a common ground for working together. Since it requires the development of a unique relationship, it will not work in all situations. In a recent study by McCormick et al. (2001), it was concluded that "the extent to which co-teachers perceive themselves to be similar to one another in personal characteristics and traits, professional style, and philosophical beliefs and biases may affect their ability to provide a quality environment" (p. 128).

While co-teaching has been cited frequently as an effective model to deliver appropriate educational services to students with disabilities, additional research needs to be conducted before this model can be considered a valid method of educating this group of children (Murawski & Swanson, 2001).

Cooperative Teaching Arrangements   Although cooperative teaching can be implemented in many ways, it essentially involves collaboration between special and general education teachers in the environment of the general education classroom, typically for several periods per day. Bauwens, Hourcade, and Friend (1989) discuss three distinct yet related forms of cooperative teaching: complementary instruction, team teaching, and supportive learning activities. These options and the work of Vaughn, Schumm, and Arguelles (1997) outline a strategy for designing effective programs. Further, they foster strategies that are more effective than simply engaging in what Vaughn et al. (1997) refer to as "grazing" (unstructured roaming around to monitor work) or "tag team teaching" (taking turns being active/passive instructors).

Complementary instruction involves teaching students the skills related to success in learning. Bauwens and Hourcade (1995) define these as thinking skills (i.e., processing information cognitively), learning skills (e.g., study skills, learning strategies), and acting skills (i.e., social behaviors related to school success). One teacher, typically the special education teacher, can provide instruction on these skills to complement the content instruction taught by the partner teacher. In this example, the two teachers can work collaboratively to ensure that information is presented clearly and that learning is facilitated. For example, in social studies, the general education teacher may teach a lesson on the Kennedy administration while the special education teacher provides specific examples of personal perspectives on the Kennedy White House ("Camelot") and the spirit of the early 1960s.

In **team teaching,** the general and special education teachers plan one lesson jointly and teach it to all students, both with and without disabilities. Each teacher may take responsibility for one aspect of the teaching. Vaughn et al. (1997) refer to this approach as "teaching on purpose," in which one teacher has responsibility for the larger group while the other teacher provides short lessons (e.g., two minutes or five minutes) to a small group, student pairs, or individual students—to provide follow-up to previous instruction, for example, or to check for understanding by the students.

Another team teaching option is one described by Vaughn et al. (1997) in which the two teachers teach the same content to two smaller groups. The intent of this arrangement is to provide further opportunities for students to be actively involved in the instruction, to respond to the teacher and peers, and to have their responses monitored by the teacher. It can serve as a wrap-up session for the larger group instruction.

In **supportive learning activities,** the general and special educators plan and teach the lesson to the whole class. The general educator typically delivers the main content; the special educator then plans and implements activities that reinforce the learning of the content material (e.g., cooperative learning groups, tutoring, reciprocal teaching, or simulations). Figure 2.5 shows how the different types of cooperative teaching might be combined in an instructional lesson at the upper elementary level.

Unfortunately, although the use of co-teaching and other collaborative staffing patterns is increasing along with inclusive programs, preservice programs have not kept up with preparing teachers for their new roles. These programs must develop curricula and activities that better prepare both special education teachers and general education teachers for their roles in collaborative teaching models (Austin, 2001).

Teacher Assistance Teams   Another collaborative model to provide support to students in general education classrooms is the use of **teacher assistance teams**. Teacher assistance

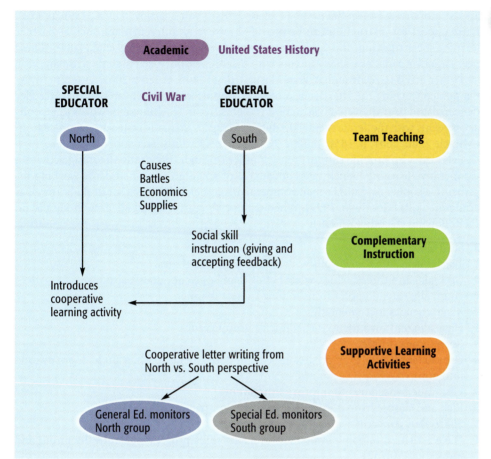

FIGURE 2.5

Variations of Cooperative Teaching: U.S. History

From *Cooperative Teaching* (p. 64), by J. Bauwens and J. Hourcade, 1995, Austin, TX: Pro-Ed. Used by permission.

teams can be defined as "school-based, problem-solving teams designed to enable all teachers to meet the needs of their students demonstrating difficulties" (Walther-Thomas et al., 2000, p. 140). These teams comprise teachers and other instructional support personnel, either elected or voluntary; they provide a forum where problems are raised and discussed, and solutions are developed. The use of teacher assistance teams enables educators to bring a diverse set of skills and experience to bear on specific problems.

While the specific composition of teacher assistance teams should not be prescribed, members of these teams should have experience and knowledge that would be helpful in solving specific student problems. Members of the team should also not be overcommitted and should be willing to serve (McCullough, 1992). Forcing teachers to serve on assistance teams leads to problems. Since administrative support is important for the success of teams, it is recommended that administrators either participate as team members or designate a team member to represent the administration.

Peer Support Systems   Educators must realize that the staffing needed to successfully support students with disabilities in inclusive settings is increasing, and one way to help meet that growing need is through **peer support systems** (Maheady, Harper, & Mallette, 2001). In this model, students with disabilities in general education classrooms receive social or instructional help from their nondisabled peers. While not the same as professional collaboration, peer support systems do result in collaborative efforts on behalf of students with disabilities. Peer support systems are some of the best means of providing support to students with disabilities in general education classrooms because students rely on the natural support of other students. "Students learn a lot from one another—particularly about things that matter to them in their world" (Collins, Hendricks, Fetko, & Land, 2002, p. 56). These student supports "fit well with the current movement to individualize instruction and to support and meet the needs of all students" (Van Laarhoven et al., 1999, p. 172). Peer support for instruction can be provided in several different ways, such as partner learning, peer tutoring, and cooperative learning (Walther-Thomas et al., 2000). These peer supports assist not only students with disabilities, but also students with language and other needs (Greenwood, Arrega-Mayer, Utley, Gavin, & Terry, 2001). A recent investigation concerning the effectiveness of peer support systems determined that "teacher delivered and peer-delivered instruction was effective in teaching sight words to secondary students with moderate mental disabilities using a systematic instructional procedure" (Miracle et al., 2001, p. 383). Table 2.3 summarizes various peer support models.

Peers can also provide support to each other through cooperative learning activities. Cooperative learning, which takes advantage of small groups of students working together in a cooperative rather than competitive manner, helps teach social skills as well as academic skills (Goodwin, 1999). When using cooperative learning, teachers should do the following (Goodwin, 1999):

> ▶ Start slowly.
> ▶ Teach beginning social skills with nonacademic activities.
> ▶ Use pairs and threes, which work better than large cooperative groups.
> ▶ Gradually extend applications to new subject manner.
> ▶ Make changes incrementally.
> ▶ Have a parent meeting to dispel fear of group grades.
> ▶ Keep things simple.
> ▶ Use old tennis balls to fit on desk legs to cut down on noise when students are moving into groups.
> ▶ Fine-tune procedures to improve functioning.
> ▶ Pick and choose from a variety of cooperative structures.
> ▶ Share your concerns with a "veteran" teacher.
> ▶ Have a written ongoing evaluation of social skills progress for both the group and individuals. (p. 32)

TEACHING TIP

When selecting students to be part of a peer support system, teachers must consider the student's maturity level as well as his or her ability level.

TABLE 2.3   **Description of Various Peer Support Systems**

Partner Learning
Students work in pairs to practice skills
Examples include peer modeling and paired reading
Behaviors include completing various academic tasks, following routines, or engaging in social activities

Peer Tutoring
More structured and ongoing than partner learning
Offers an alternative to one-on-one instruction
Enhances social skills
Provides opportunities for correction and feedback
Can be beneficial for both tutors and tutees
Best results when tutoring sessions are regularly scheduled

Cooperative Learning
Utilizes peer discussion groups and projects
Promotes improved academic achievement and classroom climate
Enhances interactions among diverse students
Facilitates social skill development
More structured cooperative activities are recommended for less experienced learners
Requires carefully planned and monitored learning experiences

From *Collaboration for Inclusive Education* (p. 11) by C. Walther-Thomas, L. Korinek, V. L. McLaughlin, & B. T. Williams, 2000, Boston: Allyn and Bacon. Used by permission.

$\mathbf{T}$ABLE 2.4	Implementation Guidelines for Peer Tutoring Programs

1. Explain the purpose and rationale for the technique. Stress the idea of increased opportunities for practice and "on-task" behavior.
2. Stress collaboration and cooperation rather than competition.
3. Select the content and instructional materials for tutoring sessions.
4. Train students in the roles of tutor and tutee. Include specific procedures for (a) feedback for correct responses, (b) error correction procedures, and (c) score-keeping.
5. Model appropriate behaviors for tutor and tutee. Demonstrate acceptable ways to give and accept corrective feedback.
6. Provide sample scripts for student practice of roles. Divide the class into practice pairs and teams.
7. Let pairs practice roles of tutor as teacher circulates, provides feedback, and reinforcement.
8. Conduct further discussion regarding constructive and nonconstructive pair behavior. Answer questions and problem-solve as needed.
9. Let pairs switch roles and practice new roles as teacher circulates and provides feedback, and reinforcement. Repeat Step 8.

From "Classwide Peer Tutoring at Work" (p. 49) by B. M. Fulk and K. King, 2001, *Teaching Exceptional Children, 34.* Used with permission.

Peer-mediated instruction and interventions can successfully support inclusion. Teacher educators need to include training in how to use these support systems (King-Sears, 2001).

When implementing any peer support system, school personnel must always remember that while these approaches may work extremely well in some situations, the peers providing the support are also students. They may provide a great deal of help, but providing the necessary support to enable students to be successful remains a professional responsibility. Nine guidelines should be considered before implementing a peer tutoring system (Table 2.4). These guidelines emphasize the importance of planning before implementing any peer support system.

There are benefits to both the peers receiving supports and the peers providing the supports (Hughes et al., 2001). Peer support networks enhance a sense of classroom community, student motivation, and student learning (Korinek et al., 1999). One way of implementing a peer support system is through service learning activities. "Service learning experiences allow students to extend their learning by applying their knowledge and skills to actual problems outside their classroom environments" (Hughes et al., 2001, p. 343). When implementing a peer buddy system using service learning, the general education students would receive academic credit for their work. Activities that could easily be included in a service learning, peer support program could include (Hughes et al., 2001)

▶ accompanying their special education peers to general education classes and activities.
▶ helping their peers become included in the mainstream of everyday high school life.
▶ assisting their peers in performing activities in the community or at employment training sites.
▶ providing friendship.

In a study of peer buddy systems implemented through service learning, nearly 50% of all peer buddies felt that the program resulted in their providing assistance to their buddies, while enabling them to perform service activities (Hughes et al., 2001).

Establishing a circle of friends for students can assist the development of a peer support network. This is particularly important for students who are different and who are new to a classroom situation. As Pearpoint, Forest, and O'Brien (1996) assert:

> In the absence of a natural circle of friends, educators can facilitate a circle process, which
> can be used to enlist the involvement and commitment of peers around an individual

student. For a student who is not well connected or does not have an extensive network of friends, a circle of friends process can be useful. (p. 74)

The use of a circle of friends is further discussed in Chapter 8.

Using Paraprofessionals

The use of paraprofessionals to provide direct support to students with significant learning problems is occurring more commonly (Giangreco et al., 2001). The most recent IDEA amendments specifically note that "paraprofessionals who are adequately trained and supervised may assist in the delivery of special education and related services" [Part B, Sec. 612 (a) (15)]. This regulation provides regulatory support for using paraprofessionals in a direct support role for students with disabilities (Carroll, 2001) and indicates that paraprofessionals should have adequate training. Carroll (2001) suggests that this training should be in professional interaction, communication, and conflict-management skills. The U.S. Department of Education (2000) noted that in the 1996–1997 school year, 203,672 paraprofessionals were involved in providing education services to children with disabilities.

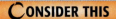

CONSIDER THIS

How could the use of paraprofessionals be a detriment to the successful inclusion of students with special needs in a general education classroom?

However, the mere presence of paraprofessionals in inclusive classrooms is not positive. "Whether willingly or reluctantly, many classroom teachers relinquish primary responsibility for the education of students with disabilities to paraprofessionals" (Giangreco et al., 2001, p. 59). If their knowledge of working with students with disabilities is minimal, paraprofessionals must be trained and supervised carefully if they are to provide critical assistance to students in inclusive classrooms. The practice could have great potential as long as proper safeguards ensure that paraprofessionals implement support services effectively.

The role of paraprofessionals is often unclear. Whereas sometimes they take a major responsibility for the education of some students with disabilities, in other settings they function primarily as clerical aides. Still, their role in providing instruction appears to be increasing. As a result, they must be familiar with students' IEP goals and objectives (Carroll, 2001).

Once roles are determined, regardless of what those roles are, then appropriate training must be afforded paraprofessionals to enable them to be prepared to successfully implement those roles (Giangreco et al., 2001)

The five critical dimensions we have discussed—(1) a sense of community and social acceptance, (2) an appreciation of student diversity, (3) attention to curricular needs, (4) effective management and instruction, and (5) personnel support and collaboration—are essential to making inclusive settings effective. Appropriate programming for students

Paraeducators can provide direct services to some students with special needs in general classrooms.

with disabilities should always be based on an "individual student's needs as determined by an interdisciplinary team and represented by the student's IEP" (Smith & Hilton, 1994, p. 8). Just as important, however, is the need to evaluate those instructional settings on the basis of the five critical dimensions.

Creating and Maintaining Inclusive Classrooms

This section presents practical ways to establish responsible inclusive classrooms and to ensure that they continue to provide appropriate educational programs to students. Specific ideas for preparing staff and students who do not have special needs as well as mechanisms for developing collaborative relationships are discussed.

Preparing Staff for Inclusion

A comprehensive program for preparing a school setting for inclusion must consider the involvement of all staff members. As Roach (1995) points out, "Successful planning models ensure that all teachers, paraprofessionals, and related service personnel are included in the process" (p. 298). Although many preservice training programs acquaint teachers-in-training with working with students with diverse needs, the nature of this preparation varies greatly. Moreover, many teachers who are already in the field have not been exposed to information important for implementing good inclusive practices. This conclusion is supported by the data discussed earlier in this chapter.

The primary goals of all preservice and in-service training of general education teachers include creating positive attitudes about working with students with diverse needs and allaying apprehensions and concerns teachers might have about their competence to address the needs of these students. These goals are achieved by three major training-related activities: (1) opportunities to see good examples of inclusion, (2) provision of information about inclusion, student diversity, and inclusion-related practices, together with the development of skills that a teacher needs to feel comfortable and competent when working with students with special needs, and (3) time to plan with team members.

Exposure to Good Inclusive Classrooms   Nothing is more encouraging and motivating than to see wonderful examples of what one wants to achieve. It is essential that teachers have opportunities to visit schools or classrooms that demonstrate the five critical dimensions of inclusion discussed earlier in this chapter. It is one thing to talk about these practices, and yet another thing to see them being implemented. A number of projects in the United States have developed model inclusion classrooms. These settings can serve as demonstration sites that teachers can observe and imitate.

Information and Skills Needed   Teachers regularly express a desire to know more about the inclusion process, the needs of students with learning-related challenges, and ways to address these needs. Teachers must find practical ways of matching individual needs with sound instructional practices. For teachers to become comfortable in making and implementing such decisions, they must have sufficient training in management techniques, instructional strategies, and curriculum adaptation tactics.

Teachers can also benefit from instruction in topics such as social skills, self-determination, learning strategies, and study skills. From time to time, updates and new ideas in these important areas can be offered to teaching staff to spark strategies and deepen knowledge. In turn, teachers can enhance the social acceptance of students with special needs by instructing their classes in social skills, such as how to make and keep friends.

Other skills are also needed in most inclusive arrangements. First and foremost are skills in collaboration. General education teachers will need to work collaboratively with other professionals within the school setting, especially special education staff, and with parents or other individuals who are responsible for students at home.

CONSIDER THIS

Why is preparing school staff for inclusion important? How could a prepared staff make a difference in the success of inclusion?

CONSIDER THIS

If examples of good inclusion classrooms are unavailable in a school district, how can teachers in that district be exposed to such examples?

Preparing Students for Inclusion

Like those for staff, the goals for preparing students for inclusion focus on developing positive attitudes and allaying concerns. Ultimately, we want students to understand the needs of others who are different and to welcome them into the classroom community as valued members. Many nondisabled students have not been involved with students with special needs. As a result, the movement to inclusive schools often results in students being unprepared for dealing with such diverse classrooms. While nondisabled students are generally supportive of inclusion, they need to be prepared for the changes that accompany this educational model. Awareness programs, class discussions, simulations, guest speakers, and social interactions can pave the way for inclusion.

Awareness Programs   Over the years, an assortment of formal programs has emerged to help change the attitudes of nondisabled students toward their classmates who have special needs. Tovey (1995) describes three programs that promote this type of awareness: Friends Who Care, New Friends, and Kids on the Block. These programs are highlighted in Table 2.5.

> ### ᴛEACHING TIP
>
> When attempting to prepare students for the inclusion of students with special needs, teachers should use a variety of techniques and not rely on only one method.

Discussions   In-class discussion is a good way to address topics related to students with special needs. Topics for discussion can be found in a variety of sources, including books and films about disabilities or famous people with special needs who have been successful in a variety of fields. Guest speakers can also be effective. Schulz and Carpenter (1995) warn, however, that "caution must be taken to ensure that the discussions are based on accurate information, avoiding the possibility that uninformed biases would form the core of the exchanges" (p. 400).

Imaginative literature offers many examples of characters with special needs. A great source of information for elementary students is children's literature. A number of books have been written about disabilities or conditions that might directly relate to students who are about to be included in a general education class.

For secondary level students, films can stimulate discussion about people with special needs. A listing of such films can be found in Table 2.6. However, a note of caution is warranted, as this table includes some films containing characterizations that are "dis-

ᴛABLE 2.5   Disability Awareness Programs

Program	Description
Friends Who Care (National Easter Seals Society)	▷ Elementary level curriculum. ▷ Information about major types of disabilities. ▷ Hands-on activities. ▷ Recommends inviting guest speakers. ▷ Package contains teacher's guide, videotape, worksheet activities, guest speaker guidelines, posters, etiquette bookmarks, and attitude survey.
New Friends (Chapel Hill Training Outreach Project)	▷ Goal—to promote awareness and understanding of disabilities. ▷ Parents and children make dolls out of cloth patterns—the dolls are used for instructional purposes.
Kids on the Block	▷ Lifesize puppets include disabled and nondisabled. ▷ Skits are scripted—puppeteers follow the scripts. ▷ Presents various situations in which certain information is discussed. ▷ Audience is given an opportunity to ask the puppets questions after the skit is over. ▷ Uses volunteers as puppeteers.

From "Awareness Programs Help Change Students' Attitudes Toward Their Disabled Peers" (pp. 7–8), by R. Tovey, 1995, *Harvard Educational Letter, 11*(6). Used by permission.

T ABLE 2.6		**Motion Pictures with Characters Who Are Disabled or Gifted**	
Title	Identifier	Title	Identifier
KEY		King of Hearts	BD
Behavior Disorder	BD	La Strada	MR
Gifted	G	Last Picture Show, The	MR
Hearing Impairment	HI	Little Man Tate	G
Learning Disability	LD	Lorenzo's Oil	PHI
Mental Retardation	MR	Man Without a Face, The	PHI
Physical or Health Impairment	PHI	Mash	VI, PHI (H)
Traumatic Brain Injury	TBI	Miracle Worker, The	VI, PHI (H)
Visual Impairment	VI	Moby Dick	PHI
		My Left Foot	PHI
Awakenings	BD	Of Mice and Men	MR
Bedlam	MR	One Flew Over the Cuckoo's Nest	BD
Being There	MR	Ordinary People	BD
Benny and Joon	BD	Other Side of the Mountain, The	PHI
Best Boy	MR	Patch of Blue, A	VI
Bill	MR	Philadelphia	PHI
Blackboard Jungle	At Risk	Places in the Heart	VI
Born on the Fourth of July	PHI	Rain Man	Autism
Butterflies Are Free	VI	Regarding Henry	TBI
Camille Claudel	BD	Rudy	LD
Charley	MR	Scent of a Woman	VI
Children of a Lesser God	PHI (H)	See No Evil, Hear No Evil	VI
Coming Home	PHI	Sneakers	VI
Deliverance	MR	Stand and Deliver	At Risk
Dr. Strangelove	PHI	Sting, The	PHI
Dream Team	BD	Sybil	BD
Edward Scissorhands	PHI	Tim	MR
Elephant Man, The	PHI	Tin Man	PHI (H)
Fisher King, The	BD	To Kill a Mockingbird	MR
Forrest Gump	MR	To Sir with Love	At Risk
Gaby: A True Story	PHI (P)	Wait Until Dark	VI
Hand That Rocks the Cradle, The	MR	Whatever Happened to Baby Jane?	PHI
Heart Is a Lonely Hunter, The	PHI (H)	What's Eating Gilbert Grape?	PHI
I Never Promised You a Rose Garden	BD	Young Frankenstein	PHI
If You Could See What I Hear	VI	Zelly and Me	BD

ablist" (an updated term for "handicapist"). This means that they may make generalizations about individuals with disabilities that relate to their inability to do things that nondisabled persons can do.

Salend (1994) recommends the development of lessons about successful individuals with disabilities, focusing on their achievements and the ways they were able to deal with the challenges their disabilities have presented. Teachers can generally find successful individuals with disabilities in their own communities. These persons, plus famous people with disabilities, such as Tom Cruise (learning disabilities) and Christopher Reeve (physical disabilities), can be the focus of lessons that can help nondisabled students understand the capabilities of individuals with disabilities.

Guest speakers with disabilities provide positive role models for students with disabilities, give all students exposure to individuals who are different in some way, and generate meaningful class discussion. However, the choice of guest speakers must match the intended purposes of the teacher. For example, securing a guest speaker who is in a wheelchair and who has a negative attitude about his or her condition may not serve a positive purpose for the class. Advance planning and communication ensure that maximum benefit is achieved from this type of experience and avoid inappropriate presentations. Guest speakers who are comfortable and effective when talking with students usually can be identified through local agencies and organizations.

Simulations   Simulating a specific condition, to give students the opportunity to feel what it might be like to have the condition, is a common practice. For example, visual impairment is often simulated by blindfolding sighted students and having them perform activities that they typically use their vision to perform. In another simulation, students can use a wheelchair for a period of time to experience this type of mobility.

Although simulations can be effective in engendering positive attitudes toward individuals with special needs, this technique should be used with caution. Bittner (cited in Tovey, 1995) warns that "it is impossible to pretend to have a disability. An able-bodied kid sitting in a wheelchair knows he can get up and walk away" (p. 8). Also, some simulation activities seem to be amusing, rather than meaningful, to students. Therefore, teachers must use caution when simulations are conducted to ensure that they serve their intended purpose.

Maintaining Effective Inclusive Classrooms

Setting up a responsible inclusive classroom does not guarantee that it will remain effective over time. Constant vigilance concerning the critical dimensions of inclusive settings and ongoing reevaluation of standard operating procedures can ensure continued success. Blenk (1995) describes an effective process for ongoing evaluation:

> On a daily basis, teaching colleagues should be observing inclusive procedures and educational techniques. These observations need to be shared among the teacher group to decide whether the practice achieved its intended outcomes, and if not, what changes could occur. Individual staff conferences and meetings, even if they are only two minutes long, need to happen on an ongoing basis to maintain communication in the teaching staff and to share experiences and impressions, sometimes *at that moment!* (p. 71)

A related method of dealing with ongoing issues is the use of problem-solving sessions (Roach, 1995). With this strategy, teachers meet and work together to find ways to handle specific inclusion-related situations that have become problematic. In addition to identifying resources that might be helpful, the teachers also generate new strategies to try out.

Maintaining flexibility contributes to long-term success; rigid procedures cannot adequately address the unpredictable situations that arise as challenges to management and instruction. Unforeseen problems will inevitably surface as a result of including students with special needs in general education classrooms. The more flexible a school can be in dealing with new challenges, the more likely it is that responsible inclusion will continue.

Planning for Successful Inclusion One Student at a Time

Regardless of how much time and effort have been expended to create an environment that is conducive for students with disabilities to achieve success in general education classrooms, the fact remains that planning must be accomplished for students on an individual basis. Students with disabilities cannot simply be placed in a school regardless of the supports provided or teaching methods used and be expected to succeed. School personnel must develop a planning model that provides opportunities for school staff to develop supportive, individualized inclusive environments for each student.

Van Laarhoven et al. (1999) provide a planning model for determining the support needed for each student prior to implementing inclusion. The model, depicted in Figure 2.6, includes both a list of possible environments for a student and steps to ensure an inclusive environment that is geared to each student. When determining the least re-

---

CONSIDER THIS

How could having a guest speaker with a disability backfire on a teacher's effort to prepare the class for the inclusion of students with special needs?

CONSIDER THIS

Why is ongoing monitoring of the effectiveness of an inclusion program necessary? Why not evaluate effectiveness only every five years?

FIGURE 2.6   **Steps in the Development of a Plan to Support Successful Inclusion of Students with Disabilities**

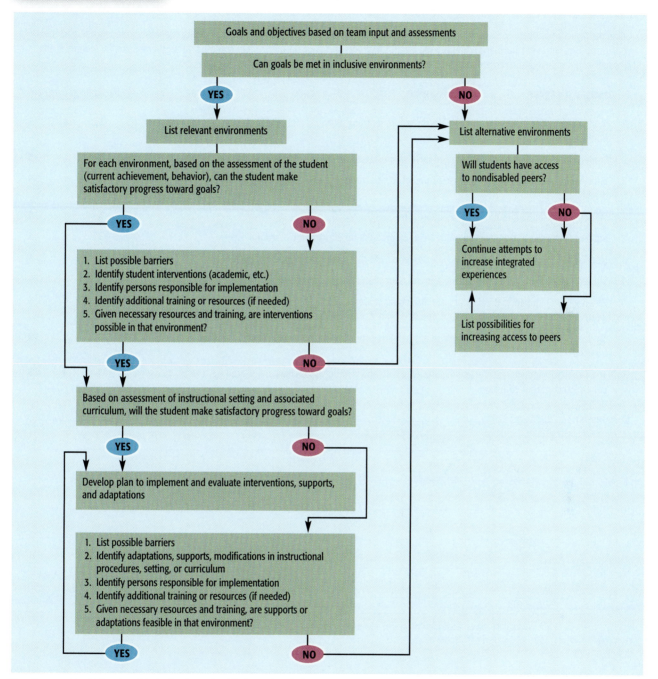

From "Assessment and Adaptation of the Student, Instructional Setting, and Curriculum to Support Successful Integration" by T. Van Laarhoven, M. Coutinho, T. Van Laarhoven-Myers, and A. C. Repp (p. 163), in *Inclusion: The Integration of Students with Disabilities*, edited by M. J. Coutinho and A. C. Repp, 1999, Belmont, CA: Wadsworth Publishing. Used by permission.

strictive environment for an individual student during the IEP process, school personnel should be sure that each student's unique characteristics have been considered in the planning process.

School personnel must routinely review their programs to ensure that their buildings, programs, and instructional techniques support the inclusion of students with disabilities and other special needs. Figure 2.7 includes ten questions that can facilitate a discussion among school personnel around reviewing school programs and inclusion.

FIGURE 2.7   **Ten Discussion Questions Related to Inclusion**

Using the scale below, rate the extent to which you agree or disagree with each statement. After rating the items independently, discuss your responses with your partner(s). Identify the area(s) that you and your partner(s) feel could be strengthened. Jointly identify strategies that could be used to strengthen these areas.

1—strongly disagree	2—disagree	3—unsure	4—agree			5—strongly agree		

1.	Students with disabilities are engaged in classroom learning activities along with their nondisabled peers.	1	2	3	4	5
2.	Students with disabilities participate productively in classroom learning activities.	1	2	3	4	5
3.	Effective instruction strategies are used to meet the educational needs of students with disabilities.	1	2	3	4	5
4.	Students with and without disabilities interact frequently.	1	2	3	4	5
5.	Students with disabilities seem to enjoy being in the general education classroom.	1	2	3	4	5
6.	Nondisabled students voluntarily include students with disabilities in various activities.	1	2	3	4	5
7.	Students with disabilities consider the general education classroom to be their "real" class.	1	2	3	4	5
8.	When general and special educators are discussing students with and without disabilities, words like "our" and "we" are used more often than words like "your" or "you."	1	2	3	4	5
9.	Students with disabilities are included in any school accountability system that may be used.	1	2	3	4	5
10.	The problems and successes involving students with and without disabilities are shared by general and special educators.	1	2	3	4	5

Comments: _____

_____

_____

_____

_____

_____

_____

From D. L. Voltz, N. Brazil, & A. Ford (2001). What matters most in inclusive education: A practical guide for moving forward. *Intervention in School and Clinic, 37,* 28. Used with permission.

Final Thought

The concept of inclusion and its practical applications keeps evolving as just one of the changing dynamics in the schools today. According to Ferguson (1995), "The new challenge of inclusion is to create schools in which our day-to-day efforts no longer assume that a particular text, activity, or teaching mode will 'work' to support any particular student's learning" (p. 287). Because the inclusive classroom contains many students with diverse needs, teachers must be equipped to address an array of challenges. To do so effectively, teachers need to create classroom communities that embrace diversity and that are responsive to individual needs.

Summary

Perceptions of Inclusion

- Inclusion of students with special needs in general education classes has received more attention on a philosophical level than on a practical level.
- The critical issue of successful inclusion is the acceptance of diversity.
- Effective inclusive settings have an impact on the student's immediate as well as long-range needs.
- On a philosophical level, there are few arguments against inclusion.
- Although many teachers support the concept of inclusion, a large percentage are uncomfortable about teaching students with special needs in their own classrooms.
- The opinions of parents regarding inclusion vary greatly.

Critical Dimensions of Inclusive Classrooms

- Five essential features must be in place to ensure maximum success of inclusion, including creating a sense of community and social acceptance, appreciating student diversity, attending to curricular needs, effectively managing and instructing students, and offering access to adequate personnel supports.
- The concept of inclusion affirms that students with special needs can be active, valued, and fully participating members of the school community.

- Students with special needs will be truly included in their classrooms only when they are appreciated by their teachers and socially accepted by their classmates.
- Teachers play a critical role in the success of inclusion.
- The curricular needs of students cannot be lost in the philosophical and political debate on inclusion.
- Effective classroom management is an important component in a successful inclusive classroom.
- Accommodative practices that are good for students with special needs are usually good for all students.

Creating and Maintaining Inclusive Classrooms

- Appropriately trained personnel, in adequate numbers, are a major factor in successful inclusion programs.
- Both staff and students must be prepared for inclusion.
- Once inclusion is initiated, its effectiveness must be monitored to ensure its ongoing success.

Planning for Successful Inclusion One Student at a Time

- In order to be effective, planning an appropriate environment for students with disabilities must be carried out one student at a time.
- School personnel must develop supports that provide each student with the least restrictive environments possible that still meet the individual needs of each student.

Further Readings

Cramer, S. (1998). *Collaboration: A successful strategy for special education.* Boston: Allyn & Bacon.

Deno, S. L., Foegen, A., Robinson, S., & Espin, C. (1996). Commentary: Facing the realities of inclusion for students with mild disabilities. *Journal of Special Education, 30,* 345–357.

Fox, T., & Williams, W. (1991). *Implementing best practices for all students in their local school.* Burlington: University of Vermont.

National Association of State Boards of Education. (1992). *Winners all: A call for inclusive schools* (chapter 5). Alexandria, VA: Author.

Schwartz, S. E., & Karge, B. D. (1996). *Human diversity: A guide for understanding* (2nd ed.). New York: McGraw-Hill.

VideoWorkshop Extra!

If the VideoWorkshop package was included with your textbook, then answer the following questions by going to Chapter 2 of the Companion Website (www.ablongman.com/sppd4e) and clicking on VideoWorkshop. Follow the instructions for viewing video clip 3. Then consider this information along with what you've read in Chapter 2 to answer the following questions.

1. Based on information in this chapter, what characteristics of successful co-teaching do these two teachers exhibit? Provide specific examples from the videoclip.
2. The form of co-teaching shown in this video is: one teach, one drift. Other methods of co-teaching are noted in this chapter. Which method might you select to replace the co-teaching in the video? Why?

3 Home-School Collaboration: Working with Families

After reading this chapter, you should be able to

1. discuss the particular challenges experienced by parents of individuals with disabilities.
2. discuss effective ways to involve the family in educational programs.
3. understand the perspectives of parents of children with special needs.
4. list principles of effective communication with parents.
5. delineate support roles that parents and family members can play.

The authors acknowledge the significant assistance provided by G. Kenneth West of the Center for Family Studies and Educational Advancement at Lynchburg College in the development of this chapter.

J ody Alvarez, a primary school educator, was approached by Josh and Sally Williams with their concerns.

Sally spoke first: "One month ago, Josh and I were told by our family doctor that our four-year-old daughter, Susie, has autism. Needless to say, this information came to us as a total shock. Since then, we have gone over and over how this could have happened, why this happened, and what we should do about it. We have also struggled with how we should share information with our older children, Tiffany, who is eight, and Benjamin, who's ten."

Josh added, "We still really haven't adjusted to the news that our doctor gave us, and I guess we both would admit that our concerns as well as our disappointments have been a real problem for us. Our biggest worry now is, What lies ahead? We would be very grateful for any help with our own concerns and, most important, anything that can help Susie. Thank you very much."

QUESTIONS TO CONSIDER

1. Analyze Josh and Sally's potential feelings and possible reactions upon learning that Susie has a disability.
2. What advice, recommendations, and help would you provide for these parents?
3. What would you tell them about the advantages and challenges of inclusive school programs?
4. What influence could Susie's condition have on her siblings and Josh and Sally's marriage?

CONSIDER THIS

The enactment of federal laws mandating special education ended a laissez-faire period of home-school relationships. What do you think the situation would be like today without these federal laws mandating parental involvement?

*P*rior to the enactment of Public Law 94–142 (later the Individuals with Disabilities Education Act, or IDEA), schools frequently did not encourage parents of children with special needs to actively participate in the education of their children. However, given the numerous concerns that parents may have (such as those mentioned in the chapter-opening vignette) and given the value of family input into educational programs, increasing parental involvement is a welcome trend. This chapter highlights the challenges facing parents, examples of perspectives provided by parents, and strategies for collaboration between educators and parents. The chapter also discusses the potential influences on marriage and siblings of raising a child with disabilities.

Federal law formally established the role of parents relative to students with special needs through IDEA, which requires schools to

▶ involve parents in decision-making activities regarding the education of their child.
▶ inform parents of impending actions regarding their child.
▶ provide information to parents in a form that can be easily understood.
▶ make available due-process rights for parents and their child.
▶ enable parents to request a due-process hearing if the disagreement with school personnel cannot be resolved.

Legislation and parental advocacy have established an increasingly higher degree of family involvement in the education of students with disabilities. School personnel acknowledge the merit of having parents actively participate in the educational process, including identification, referral, assessment, program planning, and implementation. Comprehensive programs of family involvement begin when children with disabilities are young and continue through the transition process out of school and into adulthood.

CROSS-REFERENCE

See Chapter 8 to review how supports have been provided to families of students with mental retardation.

The challenge for educators is to consider effective ways to involve families in the education of children with disabilities. Table 3.1 describes six categories of **family support** principles.

Family participation can and should occur in many areas. These include involvement with the student's assessment and development of the individualized education program (IEP), involvement with parent groups (e.g., for education and support), observation of the student in the school setting, and communication with educators. Participation in developing the IEP process typically occurs the most frequently. Some families are very involved in their child's special education program, while others have limited involvement. Professionals can satisfy the law by simply inviting parental participation; however, school personnel should develop strategies to facilitate parental involvement or, more appropriately, family involvement. Although some parents create challenges for the school because of their intense level of involvement, for the most part educational programs are greatly strengthened by parental support.

CONSIDER THIS

Not unexpectedly, the degree of parental participation in the IEP process is correlated with socioeconomic level. Why do you think this is the case?

*T*he Family

*T*he viewpoint of what constitutes a family has changed dramatically in recent decades. Traditionally, a *family* was thought of as a group of individuals who live together that includes a mother, a father, and one or more children. However, this stereotypical picture has been challenged by the reality that many, perhaps most, families do not resemble this model. "The idealized *nuclear family* of yesteryear with the stay-at-home, take-care-of-the-children mother and the outside-the-home breadwinner father no longer represents the typical American family" (Allen, 1992, p. 319). Thus, the "Leave It to Beaver" or "Ozzie and Harriet" family of the 1950s has given way to the diversity of the twenty-first-century family (Hanson & Carta, 1996), which can more simply be defined as a group of individuals who live together and care for each others' needs.

TABLE 3.1	**Major Categories and Examples of Family Support Principles**

Category/Characteristic	*Examples of Principles*
1. **Enhancing a Sense of Community** Promoting the coming together of people around shared values and common needs in ways that create mutually beneficial interdependencies	▶ Interventions should focus on the building of interdependencies between members of the community and the family unit. ▶ Interventions should emphasize the common needs and supports of all people and base intervention actions on those commonalities.
2. **Mobilizing Resources and Supports** Building support systems that enhance the flow of resources in ways that assist families with parenting responsibilities	▶ Interventions should focus on building and strengthening informal support networks for families rather than depending solely on professionals' support systems. ▶ Resources and supports should be made available to families in ways that are flexible, individualized, and responsive to the needs of the entire family unit.
3. **Shared Responsibility and Collaboration** Sharing of ideas and skills by parents and professionals in ways that build and strengthen collaborative arrangements	▶ Interventions should employ partnerships between parents and professionals as a primary mechanism for supporting and strengthening family functioning. ▶ Resources and support mobilization interactions between families and service providers should be based on mutual respect and sharing of unbiased information.
4. **Protecting Family Integrity** Respecting the family's beliefs and values and protecting the family from intrusion upon its beliefs by outsiders	▶ Resources and supports should be provided to families in ways that encourage, develop, and maintain healthy, stable relationships among all family members. ▶ Interventions should be conducted in ways that accept, value, and protect a family's personal and cultural values and beliefs.
5. **Strengthening Family Functioning** Promoting the capabilities and competencies of families necessary to mobilize resources and perform parenting responsibilities in ways that have empowering consequences	▶ Interventions should build on family strengths rather than correct weaknesses or deficits as a primary way of supporting and strengthening family functioning. ▶ Resources and supports should be made available to families in ways that maximize the family's control over and decision-making power regarding services they receive.
6. **Proactive Human Service Practices** Adoption of consumer-driven human service delivery models and practices that support and strengthen family functioning	▶ Service-delivery programs should employ promotion rather than treatment approaches as the framework for strengthening family functioning. ▶ Resource and support mobilization should be consumer-driven rather than service provider–driven or professionally prescribed.

From "Family-Oriented Early Intervention Policies and Practices: Family-Centered or Not?" by C. J. Dunst, C. Johanson, C. M. Trivette, and D. Hamby, 1991, *Exceptional Children, 58,* p. 117. Copyright 1991 by the Council for Exceptional Children. Used by permission.

Numerous family arrangements exist. For example, many families are single-parent families, most frequently with the father absent. A growing number of families are now headed by grandparents, with the children's parents unable or unwilling to accept parental responsibility. And, although not as common as they once were, some families constitute extended family units, with grandparents living with parents and children. Some children also live in foster homes, wherein foster parents fill all legal parental roles Finally, school personnel must also be able to interact with families headed by parents living in gay or lesbian relationships.

An additional twenty-first-century challenge to the family is the increase in both younger and older parents, the increase in the number of families living below the poverty line, the realities of substance abuse, the permeation of violence throughout society, and the move away from state residential care for children with serious support needs (see Agosta & Melda, 1996; Hanson & Carta, 1996; Lesar, Gerber, & Semmel, 1996; Simpson,

1996). There may never have been a time when family changes and challenges have more clearly called for understanding and support.

Cultural Considerations

The success of parent-professional partnerships often hinges on the ability of professionals to develop a level of cultural competence. Wehmeyer, Morningstar, and Husted (1999) summarized thirteen key steps for educators in this process:

1. Ask, rather than assume, what language is spoken at home and by which members.
2. Set goals that take into account the cultural and family norms for personal and social development; this is particularly important with regard to employment and independent living goals.
3. Develop a clear understanding of the cultural interpretations of the disability. Many cultures differ in this aspect, and these views may affect how the family copes.
4. Respect the child-rearing practices of the culture and do not place blame on the family for ways in which those practices differ from those in the mainstream.
5. Ensure that parents have access to all sources of information, including advocacy groups, and ensure that materials explaining rights and responsibilities are available in the native language or through personalized explanations by speakers of the family's language.
6. Enhance self-awareness by understanding who you are from a variety of perspectives, including your family origins and your beliefs, biases, and behaviors. Be aware that your beliefs and values may be different from those of the families you work with.
7. Enhance culture-specific awareness by learning about different cultural groups in terms of child-rearing practices and family patterns. Be careful not to stereotype, but become familiar with the general traditions, customs, and values of the families in your community.
8. Enhance culture-generic awareness by identifying values and practices found in all cultures. This is a way to develop common ground when working with families from different cultures.
9. Enhance cultural issues related to the disability by understanding how cultural views influence the definition and meaning of the disability and therefore the family-professional roles, communication patterns, and expectations and anticipated outcomes.
10. Establish alliances with culturally diverse families by taking a personalized approach to working with the family.
11. Develop outcomes and strategies for facilitating transition to adulthood that promote self-esteem, community interdependence, and inclusion.
12. Improve the multicultural competence of [educational staff]:
    - Provide opportunities to learn how the world views and values of other cultures might differ from their own.
    - Provide opportunities to learn about intercultural communication, including nonverbal communication.
    - Subscribe to resources that focus on multicultural issues, including journals and Internet discussion groups . . .
13. Expose culturally diverse students and families to a variety of role models and resources:
    - Subscribe to magazines that highlight culturally diverse role models and use these in various content areas.
    - Develop mentor programs with role models of color in the community. (pp. 17–18)

Despite undergoing major changes in its structure, the family remains the basic unit of American society. It is a dynamic, evolving social force that remains the key ingredient in a child's life. Teachers must be sensitive to the background of the family to ensure that cultural differences do not interfere with school-family relationships. In addition, school personnel must remember that students' parents or guardians should be involved in educational programs regardless of the specific composition of the family. School per-

Diversity Forum

Working Toward Cultural Reciprocity

Brianna is a kindergartner with ADHD. During story time she regularly interrupts her teacher, Ms. Alvarez, with numerous questions and comments about the story. Ms. Alvarez has tried to modify this disruptive behavior, but with little success. When she calls Brianna's parents to discuss this problem, they reply, "Oh yes, that's the Hawai'ian way. It's part of our storytelling tradition."

How should Ms. Alvarez deal with Brianna's behavior without offending her family or disregarding their cultural traditions? Kalyanpur and Harry (1999) offer a four-step process that can help teachers to build relationships with families through cultural reciprocity.

1. We must identify our own beliefs, values, and expectations that lead us to view the behavior as problematic. By doing so, Ms. Alvarez would realize that, like many teachers, she expects students to remain quiet during teacher-directed activities and that she views interruptions as inappropriate and off-task behavior.
2. We need to establish whether the family shares these values and expectations, and how their views may be different from our own. Ms. Alvarez would realize that the parents do not share her concern. She would also be sure to find out how they feel about her classroom expectations for Brianna.
3. We should make sure that parents understand the underlying cultural basis for our perspective, while honoring and respecting the cultural differences that have been identified. Ms. Alvarez would recognize that Brianna's interruptions demonstrate that she is paying attention. She would explain that students are expected to demon-strate that they are paying attention by listening quietly, and to wait to be called on to participate.
4. Through dialogue and collaboration with the family, we should identify ways to adapt our interpretations to accommodate the value system of the home. Ms. Alvarez might decide that she will accept a few interjections during storytelling. Similarly, Brianna's parents may be willing to set aside time to practice the story-time routines of school with their daughter while maintaining their tradition at other times.

For follow-up questions about understanding disabilities and cultural reciprocity, go to Chapter 3 of the Companion Website (ablongman.com/sppd4e) and click Diversity Forum.

---

sonnel must put aside any preconceived notions they may have about various lifestyles and work with students' families to develop and implement the most effective programs for the students. Finally, professionals should adopt a family systems perspective to involve the whole family—rather than just the child—in efforts to enhance programs (Wehmeyer et al., 1999).

Families and Children with Disabilities

The arrival of any child results in changes in family structure and dynamics. Obviously, children change the lives of the mother and father, and each child alters the dynamics of the family unit, including finances, the amount and quality of time parents can devote to individual children, the relationship between the husband and wife, and family's future goals.

The arrival of a child with a disability exacerbates the challenges that such changes bring. When a child with a disability becomes a member of the family, whether through birth, adoption, or later onset of the disability, the entire family must make adjustments. The almost immediate financial and emotional impact can create major problems for family members, including siblings.

While all children present challenges to parents, a number of critical problems may face families when the child has a severe disability. These include such challenges as expensive medical treatment, expensive equipment, recurring crisis situations, stress on marriages, and limited respite care services (Allen, 1992).

In addition to these problems, a primary difficulty may be accepting and understanding the child and the disability. Parents with a limited understanding of a diagnosis will probably have difficulty in developing realistic expectations of the child, possibly creating major problems within the family. On one hand, parents might not understand the

CONSIDER THIS

What are some problems faced by families following the birth of a child with a disability or the identification of a child's disability?

nature of a learning disability and therefore accuse the child of being lazy and not trying. On the other hand, parents may overlook the potential of students with mental retardation and develop low expectations that will limit the child's success. For example, parents of adolescents might not support a school-work program for their son or daughter because they believe that adults with retardation are not capable of holding a job.

Families who discover that their child has a disability may have a variety of reactions. These responses may include the following (adapted from Smith, 1997):

▶ *denial:* "This cannot be happening to me, to my child, to our family."
▶ *anger:* An emotion that may be directed toward the medical personnel involved in providing the information about the child's problem or at a spouse because of the tendency to assign blame.
▶ *grief:* An inexplicable loss that one does not know how to explain or deal with.
▶ *fear:* People often fear the unknown more than they fear the known. Having the complete diagnosis and some knowledge of the child's future prospects can be easier than uncertainty.
▶ *guilt:* Concern about whether the parents themselves have caused the problem.
▶ *confusion:* As a result of not fully understanding what is happening and what will happen, confusion [may reveal] itself in sleeplessness, inability to make decisions, and mental overload.
▶ *powerlessness:* [The feeling may relate to the parents' inability to] change the fact that their child has a disability, yet parents want to feel competent and capable of handling their own life situations.
▶ *disappointment:* [The fact that] a child is not perfect may pose a threat to many parents' egos and a challenge to their value system.
▶ *acceptance:* The child has needs to be met and has value as a member of the family. (pp. 2–3)

Although it cannot be assumed that all or even most parents have these particular reactions, many must deal with complicated emotions, often experienced as a "bombardment of feelings" that may recur over many years (Hilton, 1990). Sileo, Sileo, and Prater (1996) refer to the "shattering of dreams" that underlies many of these feelings. School personnel, including teachers, school social workers, counselors, and administrators, need to be aware of these dynamics and be prepared to deal with family members who are experiencing various feelings. For example, when parents say that they feel guilt after learning that their child has a disability, school personnel should listen with acceptance to the parents and help them understand the nature of the disability and the fact that they are not responsible for it. The Personal Spotlight provides a vivid portrait of the reactions of one family to these emotions.

CROSS-REFERENCE

Review Chapters 5–11, which discuss specific disabilities that can affect children. Then reflect on how different types of problems can cause different reactions in parents.

CONSIDER THIS

As a teacher, how could you deal with families experiencing various reactions to a child with a disability? What role, if any, should a teacher play in helping parents work through their reactions?

TEACHING TIP

Teachers need to be aware of the different reactions that parents may have and know some specific strategies for dealing with these reactions.

Many parents of students with special needs require assistance in their acceptance of their child's problems.

A Mother's Perspective

We have a beautiful, vibrant, intelligent, and mischievous 6-year-old little girl, Kayla, who is a big sister to our 19-month-old son, Joey, a boy who lights up the room with his blond hair, blue eyes, and brilliant smile. When I was pregnant with Joey, the doctors grew concerned about his prenatal growth and delivered him three weeks early. The delivery was uneventful, and I held my 4-pound 15-ounce baby boy in my arms as my husband and I decided upon a name. When it came time to visit my son in the nursery, however, he was not there and had been transferred to the neonatal intensive care unit (NICU). And so begins our "story." He stayed in the NICU for one week. Leaving the hospital without my son was the beginning of the emotional roller coaster on which I have found myself a passenger.

Joey was released with a clean bill of health and a huge sigh of relief; however, I noticed a difference in my son as compared to my daughter. His arm had a tendency to arbitrarily jerk, and he didn't move quite as fluently as other babies. Because of time spent in the NICU, coupled with his prematurity, Joey was scheduled for a three-month checkup at the neonatal clinic. It was there that my suspicions were confirmed —Joey showed signs of developmental delay, and as he grew older, the gap between his chronological and developmental age widened.

Tracey Corriveau and Family

Lynchburg, VA

Sixteen months and what seems like a million tests after his first check up, the doctors remain unable to determine what caused his delays, so they have labeled him with a mild form of cerebral palsy. To me this means that Joey will have to work harder to do what comes naturally to many others. It took my son 10 months to learn to sit, 14 months to stand, and 16 months to crawl. Now, at 19 months, he is able to walk behind an object while pushing it across the floor. Joey cannot speak, but he babbles incessantly and loudly! Kayla has sisterly intuition; she dotes on her baby brother and always seems to understand what he is communicating. She realizes that her brother is different, although she does not fully comprehend why he cannot do the things that the other children his age can do. When Joey reaches a milestone, Kayla is equally as excited as we are, as each milestone reached brings him one step closer to playing with her as a toddler who is not disabled might.

Accepting that my son is different has been both easy and difficult. There are moments when I look at him and forget that he has a disability, yet there are times when his imperfections glare at me from behind his sweet smile. My heart aches when I think of the teasing he will encounter from the mouths of unmerciful children who know no better. I worry about how my daughter has been affected by her brother's disability; have I been remiss in showing an equal amount of attention to both children?

I have learned a great deal from my son. I detect a sense of determination that is not often found in people. It is at these moments that I mentally pledge to do everything in my power to foster this determination and optimism, as these are the qualities that will assist him in overcoming any obstacles, whether physical, mental, or emotional. It is because of my son that I have converted from a "glass half-empty" point of view to a "glass half-full" approach.

I also have learned how to be a better friend, knowing when to keep quiet and when to offer advice. I have become more patient and tolerant of others, although I continue to find myself becoming frustrated with the endless questions and constant probing into my personal life—it is not easy to open your heart and your home to strangers (e.g., doctors, therapists, early intervention personnel).

Raising a child with a disability has also strengthened my marriage. My husband and I have leaned on each other for emotional support on numerous occasions. He has validated my feelings, assuring me that he, too, feels the same myriad of emotions. One of the hardest aspects of dealing with Joey's disability is believing that I am a bad parent for feeling certain emotions (e.g., anger, disappointment). Understanding that these emotions are normal, and even acceptable, and felt by others brings a great sense of relief.

I thank God every day for the life and the family he has given me. I love my husband more than I can express, yet somehow, some way, I love my children even deeper. Where others may feel sorry for my family or my son, I feel proud that I have two children who will understand firsthand that being different is not something of which to be ashamed but rather to embrace. Thank you for allowing me to share my story with you.

Companion Website

For follow-up questions about this Personal Spotlight, go to Chapter 3 of the Companion Website (ablongman.com/sppd4e) and click Personal Spotlight.

Some models of potential parental reactions reflect a **stage theory** approach to understanding these responses (i.e., a series of presumed phases in response to learning that a child has a disability). However, parental responses rarely follow any formal stage process (e.g., shock-denial-anger-rejection-acceptance). Rather, the preceding reactions more often reflect responses that individual parents *may* experience when accepting the fact that they have a child with a disability and that they need to meet that child's needs. For example, Elisabeth Kubler-Ross, who originated the stage theory in her book *On Death and Dying* (1969), discovered that stages can be skipped or a person can become "stuck" in a single stage.

School personnel need to support family members' acceptance of children with disabilities. This effort begins with assisting parents in understanding the needs of their child; at the same time, the educator should listen to the parents in order to better understand the child from their perspective. Further, teachers must be sensitive to the fact that many parents do not see the school as a welcoming place for various reasons (e.g., problems the parents experienced as students themselves, negative responses communicated to them as advocates for their child).

Summarizing previous research on the topic of support for parents, Wilson (1995) lists the following guidelines regarding what parents want and need from professionals:

▶ To communicate without jargon or to have terms explained
▶ Conferences to be held so both parents can attend
▶ To receive written materials that provide information to assist them in understanding their child's problem
▶ To receive a copy of a written report about their child
▶ Specific advice on how to manage the specific behavior problems of their children or how to teach them needed skills
▶ Information on their child's social as well as academic behavior (p. 31)

Parents' Views on Inclusion

Many parents struggle with the issue of school inclusion. Educators remain divided on the implementation aspects of school inclusion, as do parents and parents' groups. On the one hand, some parents of students with learning disabilities (such as those represented by the Learning Disabilities Association) have remained cautious about inclusion; on the other hand, the Arc (1995) (formerly the Association for Retarded Citizens) has actively favored it. Fisher, Pumpian, and Sax (1998) noted, "The success and enhancement of any educational program depends on the attitude and involvement of many stakeholders, including parents, in its design and renewal" (p. 179).

In an enlightening study of parental views of inclusion, Palmer, Fuller, Arora, and Nelson (2001) surveyed 460 parents of children with severe disabilities. The comments of the parents are quite informative. (Selected comments are included in Table 3.2.) Overall, they show that teachers should be sensitive to the fact that individual parents and groups of parents may have quite different views of the benefits of inclusionary educational practices, and teachers should involve these parents in discussions related to the development of the most effective programs for their children. When inclusion is perceived as successful by parents, a strong working relationship can be created.

Involvement of Fathers

Frequently when people say that families should be involved in a child's education, the "family" is defined as the child's mother. The involvement of the entire family should be the primary goal, but the father is often left out of the planning process. Governmental research indicates that fathers are only half as likely to be highly involved in their child's special education program (U.S. Department of Education, 1997). This report also concluded (U.S. Department of Education, 1997):

▶ Children are more likely to get [good grades] and are less likely to repeat a grade if their fathers are involved in their schools.

▶ Children do better in school when their fathers are involved, regardless of whether their fathers live with them and whether their mothers are also involved.

▶ Many fathers in two-parent families, as well as fathers not living with their children, have low involvement.

▶ The relationship between fathers' involvement and children's success in school is important, regardless of income, race/ethnicity, or the parent's education. (p. 3)

Hietsch (1986) described a program to encourage fathers to get involved in the educational program of their child. The program focuses on Father's Day, when the fathers of children in the class are invited to participate in a specific activity. However, teachers need to be sensitive to single-parent (i.e., mother only) homes in arranging such events. The inclusion of a grandfather or an uncle may be a good alternative.

TABLE 3.2   **Written Statements by Parents Explaining Why They Are or Are Not Supportive of Inclusive Placement**

1. Statements reflecting parental support for inclusion:
   - The "special education" program is very limiting and acts to confine people to "expected limitations" closing the door to the ability or opportunity to learn because they are not expected to or thought able.
   - My son has recently in the past 6 months improved his language, and he's using more words, and I know he will do better mainstreamed in a "regular" classroom.
   - I also feel the program she is in through the county isn't enough, she isn't challenged . . . she is in a class with others that have such low skills that she is bored or ignored.
   - Lots of kids I see are working down to someone's level when they would blossom in a more demanding environment.
   - Teaches nondisabled children to be sensitive to other children who do not have the same capabilities.
   - I see mainstreaming as a plus, and both sides benefit—besides getting a great education in the triumphs and difficulties of life.
   - I am adamantly opposed to any segregation by disability or ability because the situation created . . . is not representative of the society their children will live to grow up and eventually work in.

2. Statements reflecting parental rejection of inclusion.
   - Jennifer has many medical conditions that I feel need a special classroom and teacher. She will never learn to take care of herself. I feel she needs to be in a protective class.
   - My child would be stuck in her wheelchair most of the day, unless the classroom were completely modified with carpet, and room to move. A lot of special equipment would be needed.
   - Until she can communicate expressively, she does not need inclusion. She has cerebral palsy and can't verbalize or sign so others can understand.
   - It would be extremely difficult for a teacher to take care of regular students, let alone students with severe disabilities, even with help.
   - Regular classrooms are so overbooked with students already that are struggling to learn, that neither the student nor the teacher needs the additional . . . diversion of a severely disabled child.
   - Our 13-year-old is attention deficit. His teachers have been at their wit's end with him year after year. How will they help my autistic son?
   - This has got to be an expense that most parents of regular schoolchildren would resent.
   - Most severely disabled children . . . need to learn living skills so as to survive in the outside world. Vocational training and independent living training are more necessary than what is taught in the regular classroom.
   - My child is 14 years old, and I don't think he is capable of learning academic subjects at a 9th grade level, nor would that be particularly helpful. He needs to learn to behave appropriately, speak as much as possible, get along with others, and be as independent as possible.
   - I also think that she needs to see other children that are having the same level of instruction so that she won't feel that she is the only one that needs special attention, and she needs to be around children that can relate to what she is dealing with.

Adapted from "Taking Sides: Parent Views on Inclusion for Their Children with Severe Disabilities" by D. S., Palmer, K., Fuller, T., Arora, & M. Nelson, 2001, *Exceptional Children, 67,* pp. 474–479.

A father's direct involvement with his child with disabilities increases the child's chance for success in school and in the community.

Involvement of Siblings

Like adults, siblings are important in developing and implementing appropriate educational programs. Because over 10% of the school population is identified as disabled, the number of children with siblings who are disabled is significant: a working estimate of 15–20% or more seems realistic. Although not all siblings experience adjustment problems, some doubtlessly have significant difficulties responding to the disability. Nevertheless, these siblings have a unique opportunity to learn about the diversity of individual needs.

Meyer (2001) summarized the literature and noted these areas of concern expressed by siblings:

▶ A lifelong and ever-changing need for information about the disability or illness.
▶ Feelings of isolation when siblings are excluded from information available to other family members, ignored by service providers, or denied access to peers who share their often ambivalent feelings about their siblings.
▶ Feelings of guilt about having caused the illness or disability, or being spared having the condition.
▶ Feelings of resentment when the child with special needs becomes the focus of the family's attention or when the child with special needs is indulged, overprotected, or permitted to engage in behaviors unacceptable by other family members.
▶ A perceived pressure to achieve in academics, sports, or behavior.
▶ Increased caregiving demands, especially for older sisters.
▶ Concerns about their role in their sibling's future. (p. 30)

One way some schools involve siblings of children with disabilities is through **sibling support groups** (Summers, Bridge, & Summers, 1991). In addition to disseminating basic information about disabilities, these groups provide a forum in which children share experiences with other children who have siblings with disabilities. Like parent support groups, sibling groups help children cope with having a brother or sister with a disability. Understanding that similar problems exist in other families, as well as learning new ways to deal with them, helps siblings.

CONSIDER THIS

The recent emphasis on family (rather than parental) involvement reflects the importance of siblings and others in supporting the child. Is it a good idea to include siblings in the education of a brother or sister with a disability? Why or why not?

> ▶ Parents and service providers have an obligation to proactively provide brothers and sisters with helpful, age-appropriate information.

> ▶ Provide siblings with opportunities to meet other siblings of children with special needs. For most parents, "going it alone" without the benefit of knowing another parent in a similar situation is unthinkable. Yet, this happens routinely to brothers and sisters. Sibshops (workshops for siblings) and similar efforts offer siblings the same common-sense support that parents value.

> ▶ Encourage good communication with typically developing children. Good communication between parent and child is especially important in families where there is a child with special needs.

> ▶ Encourage parents to set aside special time to spend with the typically developing children. Children need to know from their parents' deeds and words that their parents care about them as individuals.

> ▶ Parents and service providers need to learn more about siblings' experiences. Sibling panels, books, newsletters, and videos are all excellent means of learning more about sibling issues.

FIGURE 3.1

Recommendations for Siblings

Adapted from "Meeting the Unique Concerns of Brothers and Sisters of Children with Special Needs" by D. Meyer, 2001, *Insight, 51*(4), p. 31.

Building on his analysis of the challenges, concerns, and opportunities for siblings of a child with a disability, Meyer (2001) provided a series of recommendations to alleviate concerns and to enhance opportunities; these are presented in Figure 3.1.

Several additional suggestions can enhance the positive benefits of involving siblings:

1. Inform siblings of the nature and cause of the disability.
2. Allow siblings to attend conferences with school personnel.
3. Openly discuss the disability with all family members.

Parent Education

Many educators believe parents of children with disabilities benefit tremendously by attending parent education classes. One reason is that parents too frequently attribute normal and predictable misbehavior to a child's disability rather than to the age and stage of a child. Seeing that all parents face similar challenges with their children can be both comforting and empowering to parents (West, 2002). Some helpful hints parents learn through parent education include the following (from West, 2002):

1. Never compare children.
2. Notice the improvements and accomplishments of each child in the family, and always reinforce the positive.
3. Hold family meetings that allow children a weekly opportunity to voice their concerns, accept chores, and plan enjoyable family nights and outings.
4. Learn to help children become responsible by the use of logical and natural consequences rather than using punishment or becoming permissive.
5. Spend special time alone with each child in the family. Be sure that no child feels lost or left out because others require more attention.
6. Plan family events that allow children to enjoy being together.
7. Reduce criticism and increase encouragement.
8. Be sensitive to the possibility that children functioning at a higher academic level in the family may be finding their place through perfectionism and a need to excel at all costs.
9. Invest time in your marriage. A strong marriage is important to your children's sense of well-being.
10. All families experience stress. The more stress is encountered, the more time they need together to share their feelings, plan ahead, solve problems mutually, and plan time to enrich relationships.

Home-School Collaboration

TEACHING TIP

Teachers and other school personnel must keep in mind that parents are the senior partners in the education of their children and should be involved in all major decisions.

Educators and parents of children with disabilities must be partners in ensuring that appropriate education is available to children. In reality, parents should be seen as the "senior partners" because they are responsible for their child every day. In order to best meet the child's needs, classroom teachers, special education teachers, administrators, and support personnel need to be actively involved with families.

In working with parents of students with special needs, educators find that parents vary tremendously in knowledge and expertise about disabilities. Some parents may be well-versed in special education laws and practices and may have informed opinions that must be considered in effective instructional planning. Other parents may be limited in their knowledge and their understanding of special education law. In this case, educators are responsible to inform parents so that they can become effective advocates for their child and partners in educational programming. See the Rights & Responsibilities feature.

Although effective collaboration cannot be based on professionals' presumptions that they understand the way a parent feels, it is useful to consider the advice that parents give other parents in learning how to respond effectively to the needs of their child and also of themselves. Table 3.3 provides a summary of some parent-to-parent suggestions.

Communicating with Parents

TEACHING TIP

When communicating with parents, avoid using educational jargon, including acronyms, that might be meaningless to parents.

Many parents feel that too little communication takes place between themselves and the school. Perhaps this response is to be expected—approximately 50% of both general and special education teachers indicate that they have received no training in this area and consequently rate themselves as only moderately skilled (e.g., Buck et al., 1996; Epstein et al., 1996). This deficiency is particularly unfortunate because problems between parents and school personnel often can be avoided with proper communication by school

Rights & Responsibilities

Recommendations for Parental Involvement

In 2002 the President's Commission on Excellence in Special Education released a report entitled "A New Era" that included two recommendations related directly to parents and family:

1. **Increase parental empowerment and school choice:**
   Parents should be provided with meaningful information about their children's progress, based on objective assessment results, and with educational options. The majority of special education students will continue to be in the regular public school system. In that context, IDEA should allow state use of federal special education funds to enable students with disabilities to attend schools or to access services of their family's choosing, provided states measure and report outcomes for all students benefiting from IDEA funds. IDEA should increase informed opportunities for parents to make choices about their children's education. Consistent with the No Child Left Behind Act, IDEA funds should be available for parents to choose services or schools, particularly for parents whose children are in schools that have not made adequate yearly progress under IDEA for three consecutive years.

2. **Prevent disputes and improve dispute resolution:**
   IDEA should empower parents as key players and decision-makers in their children's education. IDEA should require states to develop early processes that avoid conflict and promote individualized education program (IEP) agreements, such as IEP facilitators. Require states to make mediation available anytime it is requested and not only when a request for a hearing has been made. Permit parents and schools to enter binding arbitration and ensure that mediators, arbitrators, and hearing officers are trained in conflict resolution and negotiation.

For follow-up questions about this report, go to Chapter 3 of the Companion Website (ablongman.com/sppd4e) and click Rights & Responsibilities.

From "A New Era: Revitalizing Special Education for Children and Their Families" by the President's Commission on Excellence in Special Education, 2002, retrieved from www.ed.gov/inits /commissionboards/whspecialeducation/reports/intro.html

TABLE 3.3   **Parent-to-Parent Suggestions**

- Seek the assistance of another parent of a child with a disability.
- Communicate feelings with spouse, family members, and significant others.
- Rely on positive sources in your life (e.g., minister, priest, rabbi, counselor).
- Take one day at a time.
- Learn the key terminology.
- Seek accurate information.
- Do not be intimidated by medical or educational professionals.
- Do not be afraid to show emotion.
- Learn how to deal with natural feelings of bitterness and anger.
- Maintain a positive outlook.
- Keep in touch with reality (e.g., there are some things that can be changed and others that cannot be changed).
- Find effective programs for your child.
- Take care of yourself.
- Avoid pity.
- Keep daily routines as normal as possible.
- Remember that this is your child.
- Recognize that you are not alone.

Adapted from "You Are Not Alone: For Parents When They Learn That Their Child Has a Disability," by P. M. Smith, 1997, *NICHY News Digest, 2,* pp. 3–5.

professionals. They should make a conscious effort to begin the year with a discussion of roles and responsibilities in terms of communication (Munk et al., 2001).

Wilson (1995) outlined the following principles of effective communication with the parents of students with disabilities:

- *Accept*: Show respect for the parents' knowledge and understanding, and convey a language of acceptance.
- *Listen*: Actively listen and make an effort to confirm the perceptions of the speaker's intent and meaning.

Teachers must communicate regularly with parents to keep them informed about their child's progress and needs.

▶ *Question*: Probe to solicit parents' perspectives. Often questions will generate helpful illustrations.

▶ *Encourage*: Stress students' strengths along with weaknesses. Find positive aspects to share, and end meetings or conversations on an encouraging note.

▶ *Stay directed*: Keep the discussions focused on the issues being discussed, and direct the parents to resources regarding concerns that lie beyond the teacher's scope.

▶ *Develop an alliance*: Stress that the parents and teachers share a common goal: to help the child. (pp. 31–32)

One additional recommendation complements these points:

▶ *Avoid defensiveness*: Because of life stresses, many parents may become frustrated with school personnel. Sometimes parents may without justification unload on teachers or administrators. Listen carefully. Avoid being defensive. Then assure parents that "we are all in this together."

TABLE 3.4 — Making Positive Word Choices

▶ Avoid	▶ Use Instead
Must	Needs to
Lazy	Is motivated toward less helpful interests
Culturally deprived	Culturally different, diverse
Troublemaker	Disturbs class
Uncooperative	Needs to work more with others
Below average	Works at his (her) own level
Truant	Absent without permission
Impertinent	Disrespectful
Steals	Takes things without permission
Dirty	Has poor grooming habits
Disinterested	Complacent, not challenged
Stubborn	Has a mind of his or her own
Wastes time	Could make better use of time
Sloppy	Could be neater
Mean	Has difficulty getting along with others
Time and time again	Usually, repeatedly
Poor grade or work	Works below his (her) usual standard

Adapted from *Parents and Teachers of Children with Exceptionalities: A Handbook for Collaboration* (2nd ed., p. 82), by T. M. Shea and A. M. Bauer, 1991, Boston: Allyn and Bacon. Used by permission.

Effective communication must be regular and useful. Communicating with parents only once or twice per year, such as with IEP conferences, or communicating with parents regularly but with information that is not useful, will not facilitate meeting educational goals.

Communication between school personnel and parents does not have to be formal written communication. Effective communication can be informal, including telephone calls, written notes, e-mail, or newsletters. When communicating with parents, school personnel should be aware of how they convey messages. For example, they should never "talk down" to parents. They should also choose their words thoughtfully. Some words convey very negative meanings, while other words are just as useful in transmitting the message and are more positive. Table 3.4 lists words that should be avoided along with preferred alternatives.

When communicating with parents, school personnel should also be aware of cultural and language differences. Taking these factors into consideration enhances the quality of communication with family members.

Informal Exchanges Informal exchanges can take place without preparation. Teachers may see a parent in the community and stop to talk momentarily about the student. Teachers should always be prepared to talk briefly to parents about their children but should avoid talking about confidential information, particularly in the presence of individuals who do not need to know about it. If the conversation becomes too involved, the teacher should request that it be continued later, in a more appropriate setting.

TEACHING TIP

When talking with parents outside the school in an informal manner, avoid discussing items that are related to due-process requirements—they require that several individuals be present, and formal documents must validate the meeting.

Parent Observations Parents should be encouraged to visit the school to observe their children in the classroom. Although the parents' presence could cause some disruption in the daily routine, school personnel need to keep in mind that parents have a critical stake in the success of the educational efforts. Therefore, they should always feel welcome. If the teacher feels that one time would be better than another, this information should be conveyed to the parent. Also, both teacher and parents should realize that children tend to behave differently when being observed by parents.

Telephone Calls Many teachers use telephone calls effectively to communicate with parents. Parents feel that teachers are interested in their child if the teacher takes the time to call and discuss the child's progress with the parent. Teachers should remember to call when there is good news about the child as well as to report problems the child is experiencing. For example, teachers can make notes of positive behaviors and follow through with a call. Again, understanding the language and culture of the home is important when making telephone calls. Giving parents your home telephone number is an option that may reassure parents. Used appropriately, voice mail may enhance ongoing communication, especially when contact times are not mutually convenient.

Written Notes   Written communication to parents is also an effective method of communication. Teachers should consider the literacy level of the parents and use words and phrases that will be readily understandable. They should also be aware of the primary language of the home. Written communications that are not understood can be intimidating for parents. When using written communication, teachers should provide an opportunity for parents to respond, either in writing or through a telephone call.

Increasingly, e-mail offers opportunities for ongoing communication. The Technology Today feature provides some websites to use as a starting point. However, as Patton, Jayanthi, and Polloway (2001, p. 228) noted, "Although the use of new technologies [is] attractive in terms of their immediacy and efficiency, such use poses a dilemma, as a significant number of families may not have access to technology."

Home Visits   A home visit is the best way to get an understanding of the family. When possible, school personnel should consider making the extra effort required to arrange

> **CONSIDER THIS**
>
> Some teachers think that daily written communication with parents is too much for them to do. When might this form of communication be necessary, and is it a legitimate responsibility for teachers?

Websites for Families of Children with Disabilities

The Alliance	www.taalliance.org
Federation of Families for Children's Mental Health	www.ffcmh.org
The Center for Law and Education	www.cleweb.org
Family Voices	www.familyvoices.org
National Down Syndrome Congress	www.ndsccenter.org
National Council on Independent Living	www.ncil.org
National Indian Child Welfare Association	www.nicwa.org
National Coalition for Parent Involvement in Education	www.ncpie.org
Fiesta Educativa	www.fiestaeducativa.org
National Association for Parents of Children with Visual Impairments	www.spedex.com/napvi/
The Arc of the United States	www.thearc.org
Autism Society of America, Inc.	www.autism-society.org
Brain Injury Association of America	www.biausa.org
Epilepsy Foundation of America	www.efa.org
Learning Disabilities Association of America	www.ldanatl.org
Spina Bifida Association of America	www.sbaa.org
UCP national (aka United Cerebral Palsy)	www.ucpa.org

Companion Website

For follow-up questions about the websites of organizations for families with disabilities, go to Chapter 3 of the Companion Website (ablongman.com/sppd4e) and click Technology Today.

and make home visits. When visiting homes, school personnel need to follow certain procedures, including the following:

▶ Have specific information to deliver or obtain.
▶ If you need to meet with parents alone, find out if it is possible for the child to be elsewhere during the visit.
▶ Keep visits to an hour or less.
▶ Arrive at the scheduled time.
▶ Dress appropriately, but be sensitive to cultural variance (e.g., formal, professional dress may distance yourself from the family in some homes).
▶ Plan visits with another school system resource person.
▶ Be prepared to join the parents (or family) for something to eat if offered (declining may be perceived as an insult).
▶ Be sure to do as much listening as talking.
▶ Leave on a positive note. (adapted from Westling & Koorland, 1988)

Although home visits are an important option, there is a low "teacher acceptability" of this practice. General education teachers report that they consider home visits the least effective (and perhaps least desirable) alternative available to them in terms of home-school collaborations (Polloway et al., 1996). Among other possible concerns, home visits for a potentially large number of children simply may be unrealistic. They tend to be more common, and perhaps more effective, at the preschool level. However, this form of communication can be essential in some instances and can take on greater significance when parents decline invitations to visit the school.

Formal Meetings Parent-teacher meetings and conferences provide an important opportunity for collaboration. As Patton et al. (2001, p. 228) indicated, "Conferences are called for one of three primary reasons: administrative purposes (e.g., assessment or eligibility issues); crisis situations (e.g., disciplinary actions); and routine progress reporting, which is typically held at the end of grading periods."

Under federal special education law, formal meetings include conferences to develop the individualized educational program (IEP), the individualized family service plan (IFSP), the individualized transitional plan (ITP) (see Chapter 16), and, as applicable, behavioral intervention plans (BIPs) (see Chapter 14). Regardless of the purpose of the meeting, school personnel should focus attention on the topics at hand. They should send advance information home (e.g., a week before the meeting) to parents and make them feel at ease about their participation. Directing their attention to academic, social, and transitional goals before such meetings enhances their participation.

When preparing to meet with parents to discuss children who are experiencing problems, school personnel need to anticipate the components of the discussion in order to have a successful meeting. Figure 3.2 provides typical questions raised at such conferences.

School personnel must take steps to ensure parental involvement in their children's education program.

FIGURE 3.2   Common Questions Asked by Parents and Teachers

QUESTIONS PARENTS MAY ASK TEACHERS

- What is normal for a child this age?
- What is the most important subject or area for my child to learn?
- What can I work on at home?
- How can I manage her behavior?
- Should I spank?
- When will my child be ready for community living?
- Should I plan on her learning to drive?
- Will you just listen to what my child did the other day and tell me what you think?
- What is a learning disability?
- My child has emotional problems; is it my fault?
- The doctor said my child will grow out of this. What do you think?
- Will physical therapy make a big difference in my child's control of his hands and arms?
- Have you become harder on our child? Her behavior has changed at home.
- Can I call you at home if I have a question?
- What is the difference between delayed, retarded, and learning disabled?
- What kind of after-school activities can I get my child involved in?
- Can my child live on his own?
- What should I do about sexual activity?
- What's he going to be like in five years?
- Will she have a job?
- Who takes care of him when I can no longer care for him?
- What happens if she doesn't make her IEP goals?

QUESTIONS TEACHERS SHOULD ASK PARENTS

- What activities at home could you provide as a reward?
- What particular skill areas concern you most for inclusion on the IEP?
- What behavior at home do you feel needs to improve?
- Would you be interested in coming to a parent group with other parents of my students?
- When is a good time to call you at home?
- May I call you at work? What is the best time?
- Is there someone at home who can pick the child up during the day if necessary?
- Would you be interested in volunteering in our school?
- What is the most difficult problem you face in rearing your child?
- What are your expectations for your child?
- How can I help you the most?
- What is your home routine in the evenings? Is there a quiet place for your child to study?
- Can you or your spouse do some special activity with your child if he or she earns it at school?
- Can you spend some time tutoring your child in the evening?
- Would you like to have a conference with your child participating?
- When is the best time to meet?

Adapted from *The Special Educator's Handbook* (pp. 208–209), by D. L. Westling and M. A. Koorland, 1988, Boston: Allyn and Bacon. Used by permission.

To increase parental participation in formal conferences, school personnel may wish to consider whether parents should have an advocate present at formal conferences. The advocate could be a member of the school staff or, in some cases, will be privately contracted by the parents. An advocate can facilitate parental participation by enhancing communication, encouraging parental participation, and providing them a summary of the discussions and decisions at the end of the conference. State regulations govern this practice; teachers should consult with administrative colleagues concerning this practice.

CROSS-REFERENCE

For more information on the IDEA requirements for family involvement, see Chapter 2.

IEP Meetings   Parents should be involved in the development of students' individualized education programs for two reasons. First, IDEA requires that parents be invited to participate in the development of the child's IEP and must "sign off" on the completed IEP (see Chapter 4 for information on the IEP content and process).

The more important reason for involvement, however, is to gain the input of parents. Parents know more about their children than school personnel do. They have been involved with the child longer, and beyond the hours of a school day. Schools need to take advantage of this knowledge about the child in the development of the IEP.

In facilitating exchanges between school personnel and parents, deBettencourt (1987) suggests the following:

1. Hold conferences in a small location that is free from external distractions (e.g., student or staff interruption, cell phones).
2. Hold conferences on time and maintain the schedule; do not let conferences start late or run late because many parents may be taking time off from work to attend.
3. Arrange the room so that parents and school personnel are comfortable and can look at one another without barriers.
4. Present information clearly, concisely, and in a way that parents can understand.

IFSP Meetings   Public Law 99–457 significantly altered the relationship between families and agencies serving young children with disabilities. The law required that agencies serving preschool children develop an IFSP for each child and his/her family. The IFSP requirement is based on the assumption that families cannot be as effective in a child's intervention program if their own needs are not being met. Thus the IFSP takes family needs (e.g., respite care, transportation) into consideration and provides strategies that can help solve some of the family's problems while delivering services to children with disabilities.

Mediation   The legal requirements concerning the involvement of parents in their child's education provide a foundation for appropriate practices in home-school collaboration. Nevertheless, even when careful efforts at compliance are made by school personnel and when educators attempt to fulfill both the letter and spirit of the law, some conflicts are inevitable in such an emotionally charged area as the determination of an appropriate education for a student with a disability. Many state and local education agencies use **mediation** to resolve disagreements between parents and school personnel. In mediation, the parties both share their concerns and then work to develop a solution that is mutually acceptable, typically through the facilitation of a third party.

Mediation can be a common-sense method of working through conflicts by establishing an environment in which parents and educators can develop a consensus regarding a child's educational program (Dobbs, Primm, & Primm, 1991). If effective, a mediation process can also result in the avoidance of the active involvement of legal representation, the subsequent cost of attorney fees, and the potential for an adversarial relationship developing as a result of due-process hearings.

Cross-Cultural Considerations   A particularly sensitive area for teachers is working with families from another cultural background. Parents, for example, may have a different view than the teacher about issues such as the nature of a presenting problem or the preferred solution. One suggestion for dealing with these challenges is a four step, two-way communicative process to share information and establish reciprocity across cultures.

Step 1: Identify the cultural values that are embedded in your interpretation of a student's difficulties or in the recommendation for service. Ask yourself which values underlie your recommendation. For many of us, the values of equity, independence, and individuality are central to our recommendation. Next, analyze your experiences that contributed to these values. Consider the roles of nationality, culture, socioeconomic status, and professional education in shaping your values. (Note that within some cultures, families may perceive relationships as more important than school achievement.)

Step 2: Find out whether the family being served recognizes and values your assumptions, and if not, how their view differs from yours.

Step 3: Acknowledge and give explicit respect to any cultural differences identified, and fully explain the cultural basis of your assumptions.

Step 4: Through discussion and collaboration, set about determining the most effective way of adapting your professional interpretations or recommendations to the value system of this family. (Harry, cited in *Research Connections*, 2001, p. 4)

Common Concerns   The preceding discussion highlighted vehicles for effective communication between teachers, other school personnel, parents, and other family members. Note the value for teachers in anticipating possible concerns that parents may express about their child's education. Table 3.5 identifies three domains of possible concerns of

---

TABLE 3.5   What Do Parents Want?

What Do Parents Want for Their Children?	What Do Parents Expect of Teachers?	What Do Parents Expect of Schools?
Personal and Social Adjustment "To belong to more groups." "More socialization." "To open up a little bit so he can learn to mix and mingle more." **Accommodation and Adaptation** "One-to-one learning environment for academics." "More hands-on learning." "Sometimes the test should be given verbally." **Responsibility and Independence** "To buckle down and study [to get better grades]." "To learn to finish his tasks." "To be able to set limits with people she goes out with [when she is on her own]." **Academic and Functional Literacy** "To read better." "To get every opportunity to learn what he should know . . . and continue to progress every year." **Supportive Environment** "A sense of accomplishment, success." "A positive environment." "Constant encouragement to stick to the tasks he is [working] on."	**Personal Characteristics** "Enjoy what they are teaching." "Love what they are doing." "Be enthusiastic." "Be open-minded, friendly, and down-to-earth." "Be caring and patient." **Accountability and Instructional Skills** "Evaluate themselves instead of turning to outside sources to evaluate what they are doing." "Direct the students toward resources and information that can further their studies." **Management Skills** "Make [students] follow through with assignments." "Be very well-organized." "Be fair in remediating disputes between students." **Communication** "Consider parents as part of a team for learning." "Keep in touch with parents at times other than IEP meetings."	**Responsibility and Independence** "Help them make decisions." "Train them to be self-sufficient." "[Help] them handle a checking and savings account." **Academic and Functional Literacy** "[Help them] meet certain proficiency requirements to get their high school degree or whatever." "Prepare him to go on to [further education]." **Supportive Environment** "Keep kids interested [in learning]." "Provide an atmosphere for learning." "[Provide an environment] where they feel safe and respected. . . . Warmth is important."

Adapted from "Parents' Perspectives on School Choice," by C. M. Lange, J. E. Ysseldyke, and C. A. Lehr, 1997, *Teaching Exceptional Children, 30*(1), pp. 17–19.

parents: expectations for their child, expectations of schools, and expectations of teachers. These examples provide a picture of ways in which teachers can anticipate and respond to parents effectively.

Home-Based Intervention

Families can become involved with the education of a family member with a disability through home-based intervention. For preschool children, home-based services are fairly common; however, parents less frequently provide instruction at home for older students. Nevertheless, such support can be very beneficial to all students with disabilities.

Parents and other family members at home can get involved in the student's educational program by providing reinforcement and instructional support, as well as by facilitating homework efforts. At the same time, teachers should be sensitive to the numerous roles parents must play in addition to supporting their child with special needs. The purpose of this section is to briefly outline some considerations in each of these three areas; elements of each are discussed further in Chapters 14, 15, and 16.

Providing Reinforcement and Encouragement

CROSS-REFERENCE

A description of the principles of reinforcement is presented in Chapter 14.

Most students with disabilities experience some failure and related frustration. This failure cycle becomes difficult to break, especially after it becomes established over several years. Reinforcing success is an important strategy to interrupt the failure cycle. Parents can work with school personnel to provide positive reinforcement and encourage students to strive for school success.

Parents are in an excellent position to provide reinforcement. They are with the child more than school personnel and are involved in all aspects of the child's life. As a result, parents can provide reinforcement in areas where a child most desires rewards, such as time with friends, money, toys, or trips. For many students, simply allowing them to have a friend over or stay up late at night on a weekend may prove reinforcing. School personnel do not have this range of reinforcers available to them; therefore, parents should take advantage of their repertoire of rewards to reinforce the positive efforts of students.

TEACHING TIP

Regardless of the format, the key element in home-school contingencies is ongoing, effective communication between school personnel and parents.

A special example of reinforcement is home-school contingencies, which typically involve providing reinforcement in the home that is based on the documentation of learning or behavioral reports from school. The basic mechanism for home-school contingencies is written reports that highlight a student's behavior with regard to particular targets or objectives. Two popular forms are daily report cards and passports.

Daily report cards give feedback on schoolwork, homework, and behavior. They range in complexity from forms calling for responses to simple rating scales to more precisely designed behavioral instruments with direct, daily behavioral measures of target behaviors. *Passports* typically take the form of notebooks, which students bring to each class and then take home daily. Individual teachers (or all of a student's teachers) and parents can make regular notations. Reinforcement is based both on carrying the passport and on meeting the specific target behaviors that are indicated on it (Walker & Shea, 1988). A comprehensive discussion of other specific reinforcement strategies is presented in Chapter 14.

Some overarching considerations will enhance reinforcement programs in the home. Discipline in the home involves two types of parental action: (1) imposing consequences for misbehavior and (2) reinforcement of positive behavior. Rushed and stressed parents frequently are better in one area than another. School personnel need to let parents understand that reinforcement of positive behaviors is crucial to a child's self-esteem and growth. To see a new positive behavior or achievement and fail to reinforce it is a form of neglect that is unintentional but damaging. Parents need to train themselves to see and to reinforce positive behaviors, attitudes, and achievements.

Providing Instructional Support

Parents and other family members may become directly involved with instructional programs at home, which can be critical to student success. Unfortunately, many family members provide less direct instruction as the child gets older, assuming that the student is capable of doing the work alone. Too often, the reverse is true; students may need more assistance at home as they progress through the grades. While older children sometimes resist their parents' attempts to help, parents nevertheless should endeavor to remain involved at an appropriate level.

Since parents are generally with the child more than school personnel, it is logical to involve them in selected instructional activities. Advocates for expanding the role of parents in educating their children adhere to the following assumptions:

◗ Parents are the first and most important teachers of their children.
◗ The home is the child's first schoolhouse.
◗ Children will learn more during the early years than at any other time in life.
◗ All parents want to be good parents and care about their child's development.
    (Ehlers & Ruffin, 1990, p. 1)

Although the final assumption may not always be reflected in practice, it provides a positive foundation for building home programs.

One effective intervention is a systematic home tutoring program. Thurston (1989) describes an effective program that includes four steps.

Step 1: The parents and teachers discuss the area in which home tutoring would be most helpful. Many parents will feel more comfortable with helping their children "practice" skills than with teaching them new skills.
Step 2: Family members implement home tutoring procedures: selecting the location for the tutoring and deciding on a time.
Step 3: The family member who provides the tutoring uses techniques for encouragement, reinforcement, and error correction.
Step 4: Family members complete the tutoring session and make a record of the student's accomplishments. Tutoring periods should be short, probably no more than 15 minutes, and should end with a record of the day's activities. A visual chart, on which the student can actually see progress, is often reinforcing to the student.

Providing Homework Support

We conclude this chapter with the topic of homework, an area that may be in many ways the most problematic for successful home-school collaboration. As Polloway, Bursuck, and Epstein (2001, p. 196) noted, "The challenge of homework for students with special needs who are served in inclusive settings remains a significant concern for American education, one that tends to escalate as more students are educated in these settings."

Jayanthi, Nelson, Sawyer, Bursuck, and Epstein's (1995) report on communication problems within the homework process reveals significant misunderstandings among general and special education teachers and parents regarding the development, implementation, and coordination of homework practices for students with disabilities in inclusive settings. Teachers and parents indicated concerns about failures to initiate communication (in terms of informing the other of a student's learning and behavior characteristics as well as the delineation of roles and responsibilities) and to provide follow-up communications, especially early on, when problems first become evident. In addition, respondents identified several variables that they believed influence the severity of these problems (e.g., lack of time, student-to-teacher ratio, student interference, not knowing whom to contact). Munk et al.'s (2001) survey research on 348 parents confirmed this pattern of findings.

As Epstein et al. (1996) reviewed these problem areas, they found that general education teachers reported the following key communication problems: lack of follow-through

CONSIDER THIS

Parents generally know more about their children than school personnel. In what ways can this knowledge be used to develop programs that meet the needs of children?

CROSS-REFERENCE

School-based aspects of homework are discussed in Chapters 15 and 16.

by parents, lateness of communication, the relative lack of importance placed on homework, parental defensiveness, and denial of problems. These concerns were generally consistent with the reports of special education teachers in a parallel study (Buck et al., 1996). However, these data are open to interpretation because they are survey responses by teachers about parents.

The concerns raised in these two studies focus primarily on underinvolved parents. Teachers should also be sensitive to overinvolved parents and, when appropriate, encourage them to "not do for children what [they] can do for themselves."

Despite the numerous problems associated with homework, solutions can be found. Based on their study, Bursuck et al. (1999) found that special education teachers indicated the following recommendations:

▶ General educators and parents need to take an active and daily role in monitoring and communicating with students about homework.
▶ Schools should find ways to provide teachers with the time to engage in regular communication with parents and should provide students with increased opportunities to complete homework after school.
▶ Teachers need assistance in taking advantage of technological innovations (e.g., homework hotlines, computerized student progress records).
▶ Students need to be held responsible for keeping up with their homework.
▶ Special educators need to share with general educators more information about the needs of students with disabilities and appropriate instructional accommodations.

Examples of strategies that general education teachers ranked most effective in resolving homework dilemmas are provided in Figure 3.3. Note that many of these strategies have validity for all students, not only those with special needs.

Callahan, Redemacher, and Hildreth (1998) developed an intensive program that included parent training sessions, student training, systematic homework procedures, and self-management strategies followed by home- and school-based positive reinforcement

FIGURE 3.3   **Effective Strategies Relative to Homework**

Parents' Efforts to Communicate

Parents should
▶ check with their child about homework daily.
▶ regularly attend parent–teacher conferences.
▶ sign their child's assignment book daily.

Adopting Policies to Facilitate Communication

Schools should
▶ provide release time for teachers to communicate with parents on a regular basis.
▶ require frequent written communication from teachers to parents about homework (e.g., monthly progress reports).
▶ schedule conferences in the evenings for working parents.

General Education Teachers' Roles

Teachers should
▶ require that students keep a daily assignment book.
▶ provide parents at the start of school with a list of suggestions on how parents can assist with homework.
▶ remind students of due dates on a regular basis.

Technologies to Enhance Communication

Schools should
▶ establish telephone hotlines so that parents can call when questions or problems arise.
▶ regularly provide computerized student progress reports for parents.
▶ establish systems that enable teachers to place homework assignments on audiotapes so that parents can gain access by telephone or voice mail.

From "Strategies for Improving Home–School Communication Problems about Homework for Students with Disabilities," by M. H. Epstein, D. D. Munk, W. D. Bursuck, E. A. Polloway, and M. M. Jayanthi, 1999, *Journal of Special Education, 33,* pp. 166–176.

Facilitating Family Involvement

When she was a child, Mary Russo knew that going to school was her job. The time used to complete homework assignments was considered sacred. "There was always a place in our home for homework," Russo recalls. "My grandmother . . . would bring me and my brother sandwiches and milk while we studied." And, says Russo, her actions "showed us the value of what we were doing."

Russo, now the principal at Samuel Mason Elementary School in Roxbury, Massachusetts, regularly stresses the importance of homework to parents. "Children have to understand that their work—schoolwork—is important," she asserts, and they get that message when families make homework a priority. What's more, says Russo, making homework a priority gives children more opportunities to learn. "We want children to continue learning beyond the school day," she explains. "Homework is a powerful way to extend learning."

What [too often] isn't taught [to teachers] says Russo, is the power homework has to engage parents in school life. "Teachers

need to consider how parents can contribute to a child's development," she contends. The homework policy at Samuel Mason Elementary School requires teachers to create homework assignments that are "interactive" and to include activities children can do with their parents or older siblings.

"We call our homework Homelinks because it's the link between home and school," says Peg Sands, a kindergarten teacher. "Throughout Homelinks, parents have an opportunity to reinforce learning, to become involved in their child's education."

The program asks parents to guide students through the 30 minutes of homework assigned each night, except Friday. Each night's homework focuses on a different content area: On Monday, students take a book home, read it with a family member, and then do a short book report. On Tuesday, the homework focuses on math. Wednesday's homework is connected to themes, such as bus safety or holidays. On Thursday, the homework involves practicing a writing skill—letter,

word, or sentence recognition, or differentiating between uppercase and lowercase letters, for example. Parents then sign the completed homework.

The Homelinks program also features parenting workshops that teach parents how to best help their children complete homework assignments. When the homework requires parents and children to read together, for example, Sands and her colleagues share with parents "the kinds of questions to ask to help develop early literacy skills." When parents ask children such questions as "What is the title of this book?" or " Who is the author?" children learn to "examine books and understand a book's parts."

For follow-up questions about homework and Homelinks, go to Chapter 3 of the Companion Website (ablongman.com/sppd4e) and click Inclusion Strategies.

Adapted from "Homework: A New Look at an Age-Old Practice," by ASCD, 1997, *Education Update, 39*(7), pp. 1, 5.

---

programs. They reported that homework completion as well as the quality of homework significantly increased for children of those parents who were able to follow the homework program and that significant increases in achievement in mathematics also were the result. See Inclusion Strategies for a further strategy of how parents and educators can work together to solve the homework dilemma.

As Patton et al. (2001, p. 240) noted, "Even conscientious parents who understand the significance of homework in their children's lives and the importance of their own role in supporting, nurturing, and helping their children have successful homework experiences sometimes simply fail at their daily responsibilities of checking the assignment book or asking 'What homework did you get today?' and 'Have you completed it?'" Thus, teachers should reflect an understanding in communication with parents that homework may be a lower priority for families when compared with other issues (e.g., school attendance, family illness) and respond accordingly by helping to address these other issues first.

In Chapters 15 and 16 strategies for use by elementary and secondary teachers in the area of homework are explored in further detail. Although calls for an end to, or a reform of, homework are increasing (e.g., Kralovec & Buell, 2000), the coincidental trend toward testing of students for accountability purposes is likely to have the effect of increasing homework. Therefore, until such time occurs (if ever) that homework's role in education is diminished, concerns in this area will greatly influence home-school partnerships.

Final Thoughts

Establishing good working relationships with parents and families enhances the school experience of their children. Thus an important objective for the schools should be to achieve and maintain such relationships. Most professionals acknowledge the importance of the involvement of families in the schooling of their children, and this importance can be especially critical for students with disabilities. However, programs that promote home-school collaboration must aim for more than students' classroom success. Often, parental involvement has been focused on children's goals (i.e., student progress), with less attention given to parental outcomes (i.e., their particular needs). Teachers and family members all should gain from cooperative relationships that flow in both directions and are concerned with success in both home and school settings. Both general and special education teachers need to help family members understand the importance of their involvement, give them suggestions for how to get involved, and empower them with the skills and confidence they will need. Students with disabilities, and those at risk for developing problems, require assistance from all parties in order to maximize success. Family members are critical components of the educational team.

Summary

The Family

▶ A major change in the past several decades in provision of educational services to students with special needs is the active involvement of families.

▶ Encouraging parents to participate in school decisions is essential.

▶ Schools need to take proactive steps to ensure the involvement of families of students with disabilities. Regardless of their own values, school personnel must involve all family members of a student with special needs, regardless of the type of family.

▶ All family members must make adjustments when a child with a disability becomes a family member.

▶ Siblings of students with disabilities may experience special problems and challenges.

▶ Overriding attention needs to be given to cultural differences in families as a basis for collaborative programs.

Home-School Collaboration

▶ Families and schools must collaborate to ensure appropriate educational programs for students with disabilities. IDEA requires that schools involve families in educational decisions for students with disabilities.

▶ A critical component in any collaboration between school personnel and family members is effective communication. All types of communication, formal and informal, between school and families are important.

Home-Based Intervention

▶ Family members should be encouraged and taught how to become involved in the educational programs implemented in the school. A variety of strategies are available to facilitate successful home intervention programs (i.e., reinforcement, instruction, homework support).

Further Readings

Darling, R. B., & Baxter, C. (1996). *Families in focus: Sociological methods in early intervention.* Austin, TX: Pro-Ed.

Hanson, M. J., & Carter, J. J. (1996). Addressing the challenges of families with multiple risks. *Exceptional Children 62,* 201–211.

Klein, S. D., & Schive, K. (Eds.). (2001). *You will dream new dreams: Inspiring personal stories by parents of children with disabilities.* New York: Kensington Books.

Palmer, D. S., Fuller, K., Arora, T., & Nelson, M. (2001). Taking sides: Parent views on inclusion for their children with severe disabilities. *Exceptional Children, 67,* 467–484.

Rosenkoetter, S. E., Hains, A. H., & Fowler, S. A. (1994). *Bridging early services for children with special needs and their families.* Baltimore: Brookes.

Turnbull, A. P., & Turnbull, H. R. (1997). *Families, professionals, and exceptionality: A special partnership.* Columbus, OH: Merrill.

Welch, M., & Sheridan, S. M. (1995). *Educational partnerships: Serving students at risk.* Fort Worth, TX: Harcourt Brace.

West, K. (2000). *The Shelbys need help: A choose-your-own solutions guidebook for parents.* Atascadero, CA: Impact.

VideoWorkshop Extra!

If the VideoWorkshop package was included with your textbook, go to Chapter 3 of the Companion Website (www. ablongman.com/sppd4e) and click on the VideoWorkshop button. Follow the instructions for viewing the video clip 13. Then consider this information along with what you've read in Chapter 3 while answering the following questions.

1. When they have a relative with a disability, family members often must wear many hats, including parent, teacher, medical caregiver, therapist, friend, and comforter. In the videoclip one parent explains that she spends hours each evening helping her daughter with homework. According to this chapter, what are some ways in which teachers can help and support the caregiving family members?

2. Both parents in the videoclip discussed the need for families to collaborate with teachers. Based on this comment, class discussions, and this chapter, what would you say parents want from teachers?

4 Identifying and Programming for Student Needs

After reading this chapter, you should be able to

1. describe the steps in the special education process, including due-process procedures.
2. identify the rights and responsibilities of students with disabilities and their parents in the special education process.
3. explain the prereferral intervention process and identify successful strategies in the general education classroom.
4. discuss the uses of assessment throughout the special education process.
5. list the major components of an IEP.
6. highlight the major elements of behavioral intervention planning.
7. discuss the intent and recommended practices associated with transition services.
8. identify the key components of Section 504.
9. describe the role of the general education teacher in the various services and programs provided to students with special needs.

Last year was my first year to teach! I was so happy to be assigned a fourth-grade class of 25 students. My class had children from several cultures; I met with parents and planned activities to expose the class to these rich cultural differences. The special education teachers contacted me about the needs of several children who were in my class for some or all of a day.

My lack of experience was balanced by my eagerness and enthusiasm. Each day I spent several hours planning exciting learning experiences. I was so caught up in the process of teaching that it took me a couple of months to realize that one of my students was floundering, despite my efforts. Jessica was new to our school, so I could not consult with other teachers to gain insight. She was a puzzle. Some days were better than others. She had difficulty following directions, seldom finished her work or handed in homework; her desk and papers were a mess, and she spent too much time looking for pencils and supplies needed to complete an activity. She read slowly and laboriously and had problems decoding and predicting unknown words. I tried to talk to her, but she had little to say. She was a loner with only one or two friends with whom she seemed comfortable.

The school had a child study team that met weekly to discuss children like Jessica who were experiencing problems. I didn't like admitting that I needed help, but I was glad that the resource was available. I let Jessica's parents know I was concerned about her progress and was seeking help within the school. I filled out the required form requesting a brief summary of the problems and attached examples of Jessica's work.

The child study team meeting, held at 7:00 A.M., gave us uninterrupted time. The team was composed of an experienced teacher from each grade, the assistant principal, the counselor, and a special education teacher. Other teachers were there to discuss children having difficulties in their classrooms. When Jessica's case was discussed, I came up with some strategies, and the team agreed they would be appropriate. I guess I just needed the peer support to give me ideas and confidence to help Jessica. Thanks to intervention strategies developed by this team, Jessica finished fourth grade. I never had to refer her for additional testing. Both she and her parents were pleased. I think she will be successful in fifth grade. I'm glad the child study team is in place so that Jessica and others like her will have help if problems arise.

QUESTIONS TO CONSIDER
1. What suggestions can you make to help Jessica?
2. How would you feel about making accommodations to keep Jessica in a general education classroom?
3. Do you think treating Jessica differently was fair to the other students?

*I*n the preceding vignette, a concerned teacher identified Jessica's needs and reached out for resources that would help keep her successfully learning in the general education classroom. This chapter focuses on identifying the needs of students like Jessica and programming for those needs in an inclusive classroom whenever possible.

For a student who needs to be evaluated to determine if he or she is eligible for special educational services, a comprehensive process should be in place in every school system. This process is governed by the Education for All Handicapped Children Act (PL 94–142) and its successor, the Individuals with Disabilities Education Act (IDEA; PL 101–476) (1990, 1997), as well as by regulations developed in each state. This chapter reviews key steps in the process: prereferral/child study, referral, assessment, and the development and implementation of individualized education programs (IEPs). In addition, the chapter examines other services that are mandated under IDEA and Section 504 of the Rehabilitation Act.

All educational procedures must be consistent with the due-process clause under the U.S. Constitution, which ensures that no person will be deprived of legal rights or privileges without appropriate established procedures being followed. The implications of the due-process clause have resulted in regulations in IDEA (1997) that give parents and students with disabilities significant rights throughout the special education process. These are listed in the Rights & Responsibilities feature. While these basic rights are guaran-

CROSS-REFERENCE

Refer to Chapter 1 for a comprehensive summary of the provisions of IDEA.

Rights & Responsibilities

IDEA Regulations

According to the 1999 Rules and Regulations for Parent Participation under IDEA (1997), school personnel must

▶ make reasonable efforts to ensure parental participation in group discussions relating to the educational placement of their child.

▶ notify parents of meetings early enough to ensure they will have an opportunity to attend and use conference or individual calls if they cannot attend.

▶ inform parents of the purpose, time, and location of a meeting and who will attend it.

▶ notify parents that they, or school personnel, may invite individuals with special knowledge or expertise to IEP meetings.

▶ schedule the meetings at a mutually agreed upon time and place.

▶ provide written notification (in the parent or guardian's native language) before any changes are initiated or refused in the identification, evaluation, educational placement, or provision of a free, appropriate public education.

▶ obtain written consent from parents before the initial evaluation, preceding initial provisions of special education and related services, or before conducting a new test as part of a reevaluation. Parents have a right to question any educational decision through due-process procedures.

▶ inform parents that they have the right to an independent educational evaluation that may be provided at pub-

lic expense if the evaluation provided by the education agency is determined to be inappropriate.

▶ inform parents of requirements for membership on the IEP committee, including an invitation to the student to attend beginning at age 14 or younger if appropriate.

▶ use interpreters or take other action to ensure that the parents understand the proceedings of the IEP meetings.

▶ notify parents of the need to develop a statement regarding transition services at age 14.

▶ inform parents of requirement to consider transition services needed for students by age 16.

▶ consider the student's strengths and the parental concerns in all decisions.

▶ provide the parents with a copy of the IEP at no cost.

▶ help parents acquire skills necessary to support implementation of their child's IFSP or IEP.

▶ inform parents of their right to ask for revisions to the IEP or invoke due-process procedures if they are not satisfied.

▶ allow parents to review all records and request amendments if deemed appropriate.

Companion Website

For follow-up questions about the 1999 Rules and Regulations for Parent Participation under IDEA, go to Chapter 4 of the Companion Website (ablongman.com/sppd4e) and click Rights & Responsibilities.

teed nationwide, procedures guiding the special education process may vary from state to state.

The process for addressing the classroom challenges presented by students with special needs is discussed throughout this chapter. The flowchart provided in Figure 4.1 shows that procedures begin with efforts to address student issues that are focused on keeping the student in the general education classroom. If these are ineffective, a formal referral to evaluate the eligibility for special education services results. Based on the eligibility determination, either special education–related services, along with the various services specified by IDEA, are provided, or other considerations such as Section 504 eligibility are pursued.

The key players in the process include special and general education teachers, administrative staff, other professional staff (e.g., school psychologists; various therapists, including speech/language, occupational, and physical; school social workers; and school nurse), parents, and the student. Even though teamwork is required by IDEA (1997), involving many people should not be simply an issue of compliance or happenstance. Many people should have a vested interest in the educational program for a student, and consideration of a student's needs is best accomplished by a team approach. Thus, a team, representing various disciplines and relationships with the student, makes key decisions

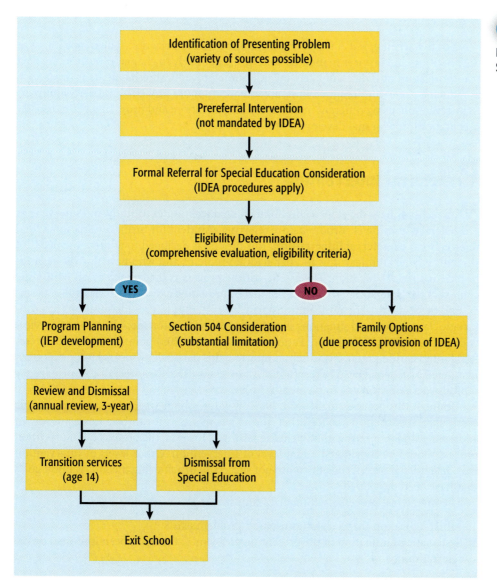

FIGURE 4.1

Flowchart of Services for Students with Special Needs

in regard to the student. Important decisions that have to be made include eligibility for special services, design of the IEP, evaluation of annual progress made on implementation of the IEP, and reevaluation of eligibility.

All teams, when dealing with the important issue of a student's educational program, must keep in mind certain guidelines during this process. Doing so will increase the chances that positive outcomes will be realized. Some of the most crucial guidelines are the following:

1. The best interests of the student should dictate all aspects of the decision-making process.
2. Sensitivity to family values and cultural differences must pervade all activities.
3. Ongoing and effective home-school collaboration efforts should be established.
4. Parents and students have a right to and should be given information about the educational performance of the student, the special education programs and services to which the student is entitled and from which the student may receive benefit, and what will happen after formal schooling ends.
5. Each student should be taught and encouraged to participate as an active, contributing member of the team.
6. Programs and services, including the rules and regulations that apply, should be reviewed regularly, and improvements should be made whenever possible and allowable under the law.

As of this writing, IDEA is undergoing another reauthorization. The major intent of the programs and services mandated by IDEA is not likely to change. However, the next reauthorization of IDEA will likely include some procedural refinements in areas such as reducing paperwork requirements, accentuating a more proactive and early approach to intervention, using different methods for identification, and providing better teacher preparation/professional development.

Prereferral Intervention

Most schools have developed and implemented techniques to study and intervene in the general education classroom before referring a student for formal evaluation. Often referred to as **prereferral intervention,** this process is designed to address the needs of students who exhibit learning and behavioral problems and who have not yet been referred for special education. The essence of the process is that intervention within the context of the general classroom is facilitated by providing assistance to classroom teachers and the students. The interventions primarily attempt to provide solutions to problematic classroom-based situations so that a formal referral for special education services will not be needed. As Buck, Fad, Patton, and Polloway (2003) point out, while the prereferral intervention practice is widely supported, this particular process has not yet been mandated by federal law. As a result, if this process is used, the local educational agency typically develops ways to implement it.

Although this process might seem like a way for school systems to avoid providing costly special education services, the process has merit, as it can be a powerful way of addressing student needs within inclusive settings. However, the prereferral intervention process should be considered a first level of intervention. Other levels of intervention may be needed if prereferral efforts are not successful in achieving the intervention goals that have been developed.

The prereferral process itself involves four major phases:

1. Initial indication that a classroom-based problem exists
2. Systematic examination of the presenting problem(s) that have been indicated by the referral source

CONSIDER THIS

The three-year reevaluation is a good time to update our levels of knowledge about students and make adjustments to their program of studies if the decision is to continue providing special education services.

CONSIDER THIS

IDEA is reviewed and amended on a regular basis.

3. Development of an intervention plan that contains strategies and other suggestions for addressing the presenting problem
4. Evaluation of the effectiveness of the interventions and decision on what to do next if the interventions have not yielded the outcomes originally desired

The prereferral intervention process ordinarily begins with concerns voiced by a classroom teacher about the performance, progress, or behavior(s) of a student. Other sources for a referral could be parents, end-of-year reviews of student progress, or an external service provider. Most schools provide a form for teachers and others to use when making a referral. Figure 4.2 shows an example of a referral form, which is simple to complete, asks for critical initial information, and provides a starting point for the next phase.

After a referral has been made, a group of school-based personnel, often referred to as the **child study team,** reviews available information provided in the initial referral. Depending upon geographical location, other terms may be used to refer to the team, such as *child assistance team, teacher intervention team, teacher assistance team, support team,* or *prereferral intervention team* (Buck, Wilcox-Cook, Polloway, & Smith-Thomas,

CONSIDER THIS

Estimate the elapsed time from a teacher's initial concern about a student to implementation of special education services. Is this time frame reasonable from the perspective of the student? the parent? the teacher?

FIGURE 4.2

Child Study Request for Review Form

From *The Prereferral Resource Guide* by G. Buck, E. A. Polloway, J. R. Patton, and K. McConnell, in press, Austin, TX: Pro-Ed.

Student Name: _____

Age: _____ DOB __/__/__ Grade: _____ School: _____

Referred by: _____ Date: _____

1. **Presenting Problems:** (Briefly describe using clear and observable terms.)

2. **Support Services:** (Check any support services the student currently receives.)
   ___ remedial reading–Chapter 1   ___ outside agency:
   ___ speech/language therapy   Specify: _____
   ___ tutorial assistance   ___ other:
   ___ school guidance service   Specify: _____

3. **Intervention(s) Attempted:** (List interventions that have been implemented to date along with how long the interventions were tried.)

   Intervention(s)   Duration of Intervention

4. **Student Strengths:** (Indicate areas where student shows strengths.)

Members of a child study team may help develop pre-referral interventions for students having problems

2002). Frequently, the team will need more in-depth information on the student and will seek information in the following areas:

▶ Student's school history
▶ Previous evaluations performed: psychological, educational, speech/language, functional behavioral assessments, outside agency evaluations
▶ Observations (previous and new)
▶ Interviews (previous and new): teachers, family, student

Once the team has sufficient information to understand the nature of the presenting problem(s), it will attempt to generate suggestions to address the student's difficulties. At the outset, the team attempts to assist the teacher in targeting the most significant problems in the classroom by identifying intervention goals. Then, the task is to identify strategies to address the intervention goals, such as alternative teaching methods, modifications of task requirements, or behavioral interventions. Emphasis should be placed on choosing positive interventions that rely on the natural support systems within a classroom. Figure 4.3 shows an example of a form that can be used to document a prereferral intervention plan.

Prereferral intervention techniques are generally implemented for at least one grading period, typically six to nine weeks; however, the teacher and the team may be flexible and specify a different time period, according to the needs of the individual student. Contact with the classroom teachers should be an ongoing part of the child study team activities in order to determine whether the recommended interventions are being implemented properly and whether they are successful. However, at the end of the agreed-upon period, the team more formally evaluates the success of the prereferral intervention to determine whether the intervention goals have been met and whether a formal referral for a comprehensive special education evaluation is warranted. Note that the purpose of the prereferral team is to review concerns and design interventions, rather than to pass cases on for special education consideration. The prereferral process appears to be both effective in helping teachers and students and efficient in generally forwarding referrals of only those students who need specialized services (Safran & Safran, 1996).

Prereferral intervention is not a brand-new concept. Certain professionals (such as Chalfant, Pysh, & Moultrie, 1979) have championed this idea for a number of years. The value of intervening early and within the context of the general education classroom is heightened by the ongoing discussions regarding the reauthorization of IDEA. Far too often in the past, the easy action to take for a student who exhibited learning or behavioral problems was to refer him or her immediately to special education. The learning and behavioral needs of many students can, and should, be handled in the general education classroom. To do so, however, requires a system (i.e., prereferral) that is respon-

**G
O
A
L**

Student: _____ Grade: _____ Teacher: _____

Intervention Goal #____

What observable, measurable changes do we want to see in the student?

_____

_____

What criteria for success will be used? _____

_____

**I
N
T
E
R
V
E
N
T
I
O
N**

Curricular Changes	Environmental Adjustments
Instructional Adaptations	Behavioral Strategies

**F
O
L
L
O
W

U
P**

Who is responsible for implementing the plan? _____

What supports will be available? _____

_____

How will effectiveness be evaluated? _____

When will the team reconvene to review intervention? _____

FIGURE 4.3

Child Study Intervention Plan

From *The Prereferral Resource Guide* by G. Buck, E. A. Polloway, J. R. Patton, & K. McConnell, in press, Austin, TX: Pro-Ed.

sive to teachers' dilemmas and timely and that is able to provide the requisite supports to achieve the intervention goals laid out.

The Special Education Process

Unfortunately, prereferral intervention sometimes is not able to achieve the goals that were set by the child study team after reasonable and robust interventions have been tried. Moreover, in some instances in which students display significant learning and behavioral problems, prereferral intervention was never attempted. Regardless of how a student gets to this particular stage, a referral for special education consideration marks the official beginning of the special education process.

FIGURE 4.4   Special Education Process

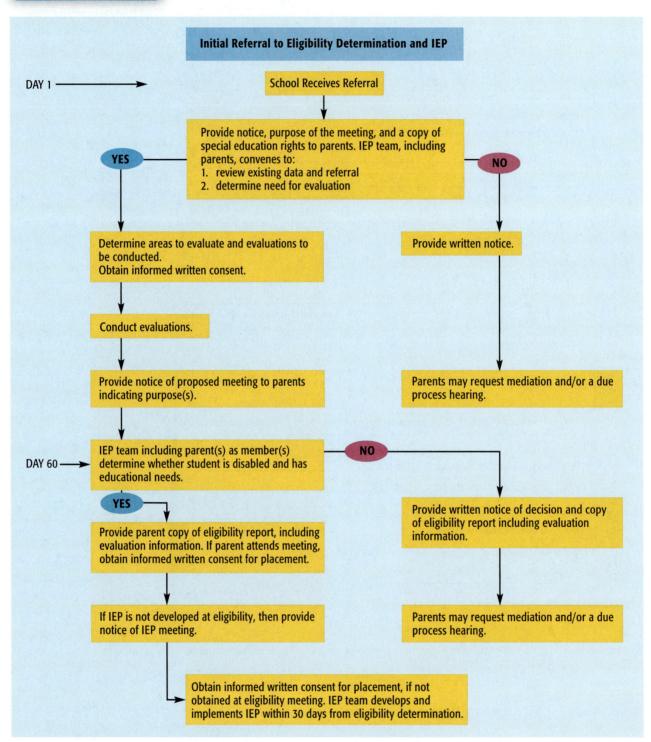

Figure 4.4 provides a flowchart of how the special education process works. Inherent in this process are specific timelines and actions that must be followed to be compliant with federal and state law. This figure relates closely to the major elements presented in Figure 4.1 (see page 93) and provides more detail of the formal special education process.

TEACHING TIP

Be very specific when describing a student's problem in the classroom.

Formal Referral

Submitting a **referral** to a designated school official initiates a set of formal activities. First and foremost, a decision is made as to whether a comprehensive evaluation should be undertaken (i.e., whether the referral has merit). If the decision is yes, then data are gathered to determine whether a student meets the criteria for a particular disability as developed within a given state and whether the student needs special education and/or related services. The initial referral process invokes the involvement of various school-based professionals and likely requires collaboration between general education teachers.

Figure 4.5 shows a completed referral form for a student who was evaluated by an in-school team. Notice the documentation of the prereferral interventions that were implemented for Frank and the additional information that will be included for consideration. As noted earlier (see Figure 4.4), the referral is submitted to the designated school official who provides written notice to the parents, documenting the time, purpose of the meeting, and the parents' rights in the special education process. The IEP team, including the parents and the student, when appropriate, convenes to review the existing data and to determine whether the referral will be accepted for a formal evaluation to decide eligibility for special education services. The Personal Spotlight on page 102 highlights how the team approach contributed to one student's improvement. As might be expected, the ramifications of this decision to proceed with an evaluation for a student and his or her family are great.

CONSIDER THIS

A comprehensive evaluation implies that information is gathered from a variety of sources using a number of techniques, and is conducted by several individuals.

Determination of Eligibility

If the decision to proceed with a **comprehensive evaluation** is affirmed, then the eligibility phase commences. The specific assessment instruments and techniques selected for use, along with the personnel who will administer them, will vary greatly within and across states. Nevertheless, the evaluation process and any assessment battery chosen must be sensitive to age, grade level, and culture, and must be comprehensive and flexible enough to address the learning and behavioral difficulties of any student referred. Because the vast majority of students who are disabled are referred during the elementary years, the process is often less visible at the secondary level. However, since the demands of the middle school and high school settings are more complex, child study and referral must be available and operative at these levels as well, as indicated in the case study of Jessica.

FIGURE 4.5

Student Referral Form (page 1)

From N. Dunavant, 1996, Homewood
School System, Birmingham, AL.

Referral was made by
Phone _____
Mail _____
Conference _____
Referral Form _____
on _____ (date). THE
90-DAY TIME LINE BEGINS WITH
THE DATE IN THIS BOX.

Student's Complete Legal Name ___Frank P._____
Person Referring ___Mrs. Sally P._____ Position ___2nd teacher___
Social Security No. _____ Sex ___M___ Grade ___2nd___ Race ___W___
Date of Birth ___9-10-86___ School/Service Provider ___Hunter School___
Parent's Name(s) ___Mr. & Mrs. Frank P._____
Address ___100 Oak Street_____ Home Phone ___555-9097___
_____ Work Phone ___555-8335___
Primary Language in Home ___English_____ Work Phone _____
Reason for Referral (List specific concerns)
Frank has difficulty decoding words in text using phonics. He avoids text with multi-syllable
words. Directions have to be repeated frequently. He is not completing reading work. He is
becoming quite frustrated. He can't spell multi-syllable words in his writing.
_____
_____

Have the parents been informed of the reason for this referral? ___yes___ If no, please explain. __
_____
_____
_____

PREREFERRAL INTERVENTIONS WITHIN THE REGULAR PROGRAM

For school-based referrals only, indicate below, or briefly describe the interventions you
have used over a six-week period of time in response to this student's problem(s).

TEACHING STRATEGIES	No. of Days Attempted	Problem Better	No Change	Problem Worse
Taped or oral presentation/testing				
Modeling				
Preteach vocabulary				
Slower pace	30+	✓		
Alternative/additional materials	30+		✓	
Tutoring—peers, volunteers, paraprofessionals	30+		✓	
Guided practice	30+			
Special grouping				

TASK REQUIREMENTS

Change criteria for success				
Break into smaller steps				
Provide prompts				
Clarify directions (restate)	30+	✓		

Name ___*Frank P.*___   School Year __*95*__ Page __*2*__

PREREFERRAL INTERVENTIONS WITHIN THE REGULAR PROGRAM (CON'T)

BEHAVIOR TECHNIQUES	No. of Days Attempted	Problem Better	No Change	Problem Worse
Behavior management (attach explanation)				
Student contract				
Consultation with _____				
Sessions with school counselor	2	✓		
Other (describe) _____				
_____				
_____				
_____				
_____				

ADDITIONAL INFORMATION

1. Attach copies of relevant evaluations.
2. Attach the most recent BCT, HSBSE (Exit Exam), Stanford Achievement Test, and/or Otis Lennon results.
3. Attach copies of cumulative records containing grades and attendance.
4. Has the student ever repeated a grade? ___*no**___ If so, which one(s)? _____ How many times? __**late birthday—Frank didn't start until he was 6.*__
5. Attach current work samples.
6. Attach current report card.
7. Has the student received other services? ___*no*___ If so, what? _____
8. Does the student wear glasses?   Yes _____ No ✓
9. Does the student wear a hearing aid?   Yes _____ No ✓
10. Does the student have a health problem?   Yes _____ No ✓ If yes, what? _____
11. Does the student have an orthopedic problem?   Yes _____ No ✓ If yes, what? _____
12. Does the student take any medication regularly?   Yes _____ No ✓ If yes, what? _____
13. Other relevant information. _____
            new to Hunter School _____
_____

MULTIDISCIPLINARY EVALUATION TEAM (MET) RECOMMENDATIONS

Date
3-21-95 ✓ ACCEPTED FOR EVALUATION. Send *Notice and Consent for Initial Evaluation/Large Print Rights/Parents–Partners in Special Education.*
_____ NOT ACCEPTED FOR EVALUATION. Send *Notice of Intent Not to Evaluate/Large Print Rights/Parents–Partners in Special Education.*

MET MEMBERS	POSITION	DATE
Mrs. Sally Principi	Teacher	4-25-95
Lydia Williams	principal	4-25-95
Ms D Castre	counselor	4-25-95
Nancy Agincourt	special ed	4-25-95
Mrs Lee Brown	psychometrist	4-25-95

FIGURE 4.5

Student Referral Form (page 2)

From N. Dunavant, 1996, Homewood School System, Birmingham, AL.

CROSS-REFERENCE

Methods for modifying the curriculum and instruction in elementary and secondary general education settings are described in Chapters 15 and 16. Many of these techniques are appropriate at the prereferral stage.

Personal Spotlight

Mother and Daughter Team

After **Lauren** suffered a stroke as a complication of open heart surgery at 8 months, her parents were given an uncertain prognosis for her recovery. As developmental milestones began to emerge slowly, it was evident that Lauren had cognitive and physical disabilities, as well as speech and language deficits. During her earlier years, she received physical and speech therapy in her home with visiting specialists. When it was time to enroll in the public schools her parents and teacher decided to begin her education in a self-contained class with other children with severe disabilities. There Lauren received intense remediation by a physical therapist and a speech therapist. She also learned many self-help skills such as potty training and self-feeding. Lauren met many of her learning goals through the help of an intense program implemented by the special education teacher. It was soon evident that Lauren would benefit from an experience in an inclusive classroom. She joined a class of students in kindergarten and made tremendous improvements.

At first it was considered a challenge for Lauren to use her walker daily on the long walk required to get to the general education kindergarten class. Soon, this strengthened her legs, and

Susan and Lauren Parrish

her walking skills were greatly improved. Three years later, she threw away her walker! The increased verbal interactions with her peers greatly enhanced her language and speech abilities. She had always been able to listen and understand most of what was said to her, but now others were able to understand what she wanted to say. Lauren continues to work hard and is making progress both socially and academically. However, her mother says that every year she goes to the IEP team hoping that these same services will be available for her in the next grade. She doesn't know what the future holds for Lauren, but because of the great improvements that have been made during her three years of inclusion, the future looks bright. Susan believes that it took a team approach and experience in both a self-contained and inclusive setting to increase Lauren's chances for a productive future.

Companion Website

For follow-up questions about this Personal Spotlight, go to Chapter 4 of the Companion Website (ablongman.com/sppd4e) and click Personal Spotlight.

During the eligibility determination phase, the general education teacher will likely be called upon to provide background information on the student. The teacher might be interviewed or asked to complete rating scales or checklists. On occasion, the teacher will be asked to conduct some observations of a student. The teacher will likely be asked to provide samples of the student's academic work.

Ultimately, the team responsible for making the eligibility decision compiles all the pertinent information on a student. The team examines the data to determine whether a disability exists, whether the student meets the state eligibility guidelines for the particular disability, and whether, even if the student has a disability, the student needs special education. At this point, a determination of whether a student qualifies for special education is made, and the decision is conveyed to the family according to procedural guidelines (see Figure 4.4).

If a student does qualify for special education, then an individualized education program (IEP) must be developed for the student. Some of the data collected during the eligibility determination phase can be useful for generating instructional programs; however, typically, additional assessments will have to be conducted to determine actual present levels of performance upon which goals are developed.

Individualized Education Programs (IEPs)

The individualized education program is a description of services planned for students with disabilities and is a requirement under IDEA. This document is developed after a student becomes eligible for special education and related services and is reviewed at least once annually thereafter. The overriding concept behind the IEP is that all educational programming should be driven by the needs of the student. If academic, behavioral, or social needs are identified, then goals need to be written to address these needs. In other words, services are determined by individual need, not by availability.

IEP Team   The educational program is developed by the IEP team. The federal regulations of IDEA stress that every school district should ensure that the IEP team assembled for each student with a disability includes the following:

1. The parents of the student
2. At least one general education teacher of the student (if the student is in general education classrooms)
3. At least one special education teacher
4. A representative of the school district who is
   a. qualified to provide or supervise the provision of specially designed instruction to meet the unique need of students with disabilities
   b. knowledgeable about the general education curriculum
   c. knowledgeable about the availability of resources of the school district
   d. an individual who can interpret the instructional implications of evaluation results
5. Other individuals who have knowledge or special expertise regarding the student, including related service personnel as appropriate (at the discretion of the parent or the school district)
6. The student, if appropriate

Federal Regulations for IEPs   The IDEA Amendments of 1997 and the accompanying final regulations (*Federal Register,* 1999) specify the content for IEPs in general, the content for transition services for students beginning no later than age 14, and the special requirements for plans for young children from birth to age 3. The law also requires that a student be notified of the transfer of his or her rights at least one year prior to reaching the **age of majority** specified by law in his or her state. For example, in many states, the age of majority is 18; so, by this age, the student must sign the IEP verifying that this right has been explained. After this birthday, students can make decisions regarding school, independent living, and work. In extreme cases, when students are judged incapable of making their own decisions and protecting their own rights, the courts will award guardianship to parents or another advocate.

The general requirements of an IEP for students between ages 3 and 21 are as follows:

▶ A statement of present levels of performance and how the disability affects the student's progress in the general education curriculum (or appropriate activities for preschoolers).
▶ Measurable annual goals including short-term benchmarks or objectives enabling the student to be involved in and to progress in the regular curriculum (as appropriate) and meet the annual goals.
▶ Special education and related services for the student and supplemental aids.
▶ Program modifications or supports for school personnel to help the student be involved in and progress in both the curriculum and extracurricular and nonacademic activities.
▶ An explanation of the extent, if any, to which the student will not participate in regular education classes.
▶ Modifications to be used in statewide or districtwide assessment of student achievement or an explanation of how the student is to be assessed if different from nondisabled peers.

CROSS-REFERENCE

Transition for adolescents from school to life after school is discussed again in Chapter 16.

▶ Projected dates for beginning of services and the frequency, location, and duration of services and modifications.

▶ How progress toward annual goals and modifications is to be measured.

▶ How parents will be regularly informed, at least as often as parents of nondisabled students, of progress toward the annual goals and whether progress will enable the student to meet goals by year-end.

▶ For students age 14 or younger, if appropriate, a statement of transition needs that focuses on the student's course of study (e.g., advanced classes or a vocational program).

▶ Beginning at age 16 or younger, if appropriate, in addition to the preceding information, a statement of interagency responsibilities or linkages if needed.

Other special considerations include these:

▶ For students whose behavior impedes their learning or that of others, behavior strategy supports and interventions, when appropriate.

▶ For students whose English proficiency is limited, language needs as they relate to the IEP.

▶ For children who are blind or visually impaired, Braille instruction, unless the IEP team determines that use of Braille is not appropriate.

▶ For students with hearing impairments or language and communication needs, opportunities for communication with peers and teachers in each student's language and communication mode, including direct instruction in the mode.

▶ Assistive technology devices and services for eligible students.

The written plan for children from birth to age three and their families, the **individualized family service plan** (IFSP), serves as a guide for available early intervention services. The basic philosophy underlying the IFSP is that infants and toddlers with known or suspected disabilities, medical conditions, or other development issues are uniquely dependent on their families and can best be understood within the context of their families. Thus, the intent of the IFSP is to focus on the family unit and to support the natural caregiving role of families. Many of the components of the IFSP are the same as those of the IEP; however, they have several important differences. For example, the goals in the IFSP are called outcome statements, which reflects changes that families want to see for their child and for themselves. The outcome statements on the IFSP are family-centered rather than child-centered, as they are on the IEP. In addition, a service coordinator must be identified for each family, who is responsible for the implementation of the IFSP and coordination with other agencies and persons. Finally, a transition plan must be included to support the child and family when moving to the next stage of services at age three.

Three Key Components of an IEP   The major components in the IEP document that guide intervention are (1) present levels of educational performance, (2) measurable annual goals, and (3) short-term objectives, or benchmarks. Other elements of the IEP are important, as cited previously; however, these three elements provide the foundation that directs the services that will be implemented.

The first component, **present level of educational performance,** provides a summary of assessment data on a student's current functioning, which subsequently serves as the basis for establishing annual goals. Therefore, the information should include data for each priority area in which instructional support is needed. Depending on the individual student, consideration might be given to reading, math, and other academic skills, written and oral communication skills, vocational talents and needs, social skills, behavioral patterns, study skills, self-help skills and other life skills, and motor skills.

Performance levels can be provided in various forms, such as formal and informal assessment data, behavioral descriptions, and specific abilities delineated by checklists or skill sequences. Functional summary statements of an individual's strengths and weak-

---

CONSIDER THIS

Some individuals are negative about the use and value of IEPs. Do you see a purpose in their development? How would you improve the process?

CONSIDER THIS

The IFSP is driven by the needs of the very young child and his family—this document is very family-considerate.

CONSIDER THIS

Writing good present-levels-of-educational-performance statements is often overlooked.

nesses draw on information from a variety of sources rather than relying on a single source. Test scores in math, for example, might be combined with a description of how the child performed on a curriculum-based measure such as a computational checklist. In general, the phrasing used to define levels of performance should be positive and describe things the child can do. For example, the same information is conveyed by the two following statements, but the former demonstrates the more positive approach: "The student can identify 50% of the most frequently used occupational vocabulary words," versus "The student does not know half of the most frequently-used occupational vocabulary words." Appropriately written performance levels provide a broad range of data in order to help generate relevant and appropriate annual goals. In addition, Gibb and Dyches (2000) recommend that present levels of educational performance include some sense of how the disability affects the student's involvement and progress in the general curriculum and logical cues for writing the accompanying goals. An example of a present-level-of-educational-performance statement that conforms to these criteria is presented in Figure 4.6.

The second, and central, IEP instructional component is **annual goals.** Each student's goals should be individually determined to address unique needs and abilities. Since it is obviously impossible to predict the precise amount of progress a student will make in a year, goals should be reasonable projections of what the student will accomplish. To develop realistic expectations, teachers can consider a number of variables, including the chronological age of the child, the expected rate of learning, and past and current learning profiles.

Sammy is a seventh grade student whose disability inhibits his ability to understand vocabulary associated with occupations and employment. Sammy can define orally 37 out of 52 words correctly from a list of the most frequently used occupational vocabulary words.

FIGURE 4.6

Example of a Present-Level-of-Educational-Performance Statement

From *Understanding Occupational Vocabulary* by S. Fisher, G. M. Clark, & J. R. Patton, 2003, Austin, TX: Pro-Ed.

Annual goals should be measurable, positive, student-oriented, and relevant (Polloway, Patton, & Serna, 2001). *Measurable* goals provide a basis for evaluation. Statements should use terms that denote action and can therefore be operationally defined (e.g., *pronounce, write*), rather than vague, general language that confounds evaluation and observer agreement (e.g., *know, understand*). *Positive* goals provide an appropriate direction for instruction. Avoiding negative goals creates an atmosphere conducive to good home-school relationships and makes it easier to chart student progress. Goals should also be *oriented to the student.* Developing students' skills is the intent, and the only measure of effectiveness should be what is learned, rather than what is taught. Finally, goals must be *relevant* to the individual's actual needs in terms of remediation and other desirable skills.

Annual goals should subsequently be broken down into **short-term objectives,** given in a logical and sequential series to provide a general plan for instruction. Short-term objectives, the third major IEP component, can be derived only after annual goals are written. They should be based on a task analysis process; skill sequences and checklists can be used to divide an annual goal into components that can be shaped into precise objectives. Each broad goal will generate a cluster of objectives. The four criteria applied to annual goals are also appropriate to short-term objectives. Since objectives are narrower in focus, an objective's measurability should be enhanced with a criterion for mastery. For example, a math short-term objective might read, "Given 20 multiplication facts using numbers 1–5, John will give correct answers for 90%." These benchmarks should be obtained from the general education curriculum being used by the student's nondisabled peers. A portion of an IEP containing annual goals, short-term objectives, and method of evaluation is presented in Table 4.1. Throughout Chapters 6–11, the IEP Goals and Objectives feature will illustrate this portion of the IEP for the students featured in the chapter-opening vignettes.

Role of the General Education Teacher in the IEP Although IEPs are supposed to be jointly developed by the whole IEP team, in practice the task has often largely fallen to special education teachers. Some abuses of the system have been common. Instances in

*T*ABLE 4.1   Examples of Lark's IEP Goals and Objectives

Goal 2: Lark will follow school and team rules.

Objectives	Criteria	Evaluation Procedures
Lark will wear appropriate clothing to school	0 occurrences per week of being sent home for dress code violations	Teacher observation using school dress code requirements
Lark will use appropriate language on the bus and at school	0 occurrences per week of inappropriate language	Number of referrals to office or disciplinary actions for inappropriate language
Lark will talk respectfully to teachers and other school personnel	0 referrals for inappropriate language per week	Number of referrals to office or disciplinary actions for inappropriate language

Goal 4: Lark will develop effective organizational and study skills.

Objectives	Criteria	Evaluation Procedures
Lark will record all class assignments in a daily planner	90%	Daily checks by teacher and grandmother
Lark will complete and submit assignments	4 of 5 days (80%) with 80% accuracy	Daily records in teacher grade books
Lark will attend and participate in the student homework support group	6 of 8 times/month (75%)	Student self-evaluation and peer evaluations of participation

Adapted from *Collaboration for Inclusive Education: Developing Successful Programs* (p. 226) by C. Walther-Thomas, L. Korinek, V. McLaughlin, & B. T. Williams, 2000, Boston: Allyn and Bacon.

which general education classroom teachers ask if they were "allowed to see the IEP" and of parents being asked to copy over the IEP in their handwriting so they "would be involved in its 'writing'" (Turnbull & Turnbull, 1986) have been too frequent.

The final regulations for the IDEA Amendments of 1997 state that the extent of involvement of the general education teacher in the developing, reviewing, and revising of IEPs will be determined on a case-by-case basis. However, as a member of the IEP team, the general education teacher must, to an appropriate extent, participate in the development, review, and revision of the student's IEP. This participation includes assisting in developing positive behavioral intervention and strategies (discussed in the next section), determining supplemental aids and services needed, and identifying program modifications.

Ideally, the classroom teacher is very involved in the IEP meeting. If this involvement does not occur, a different means of teacher input should be developed (e.g., a pre-IEP informal meeting); otherwise, the document may not reflect the student's needs in the inclusive classroom. Furthermore, a copy of the IEP itself should be readily available as a reference tool throughout the year. In particular, the teacher should keep the goals and benchmarks at hand so that the IEP can influence instructional programs.

An IEP's annual goals and short-term objectives ultimately should be reflected in instructional plans in the classroom; however, short-term objectives are not intended to be used as weekly plans, let alone daily plans. Teachers should refer to the document periodically to ensure that instruction is consistent with the long-term needs of the student. When significant variance is noted, it may become the basis for a correction in instruction or perhaps a rationale for a change in the goals or objectives of the IEP.

Epstein et al. (1992) indicate that teachers must not lose sight of the spirit of individualization that should guide the IEP process. Teachers need to view the documents not just as a process of legal compliance but as a tool for meeting students' individual needs. Unless guided by the rationale and spirit that informed the original development of the IEP concept, the process can degenerate into a mere bookkeeping activity. Instead, well-thought-out IEPs should form the foundation for individually designed educational programs for students with disabilities. The teacher should continue to include parents in the implementation and evaluation of the IEP. Extra effort is required, especially if the parents have limited English skills, but the effect on outcomes is significant.

Behavioral Intervention Planning

The behavioral intervention planning (BIP) requirement was introduced in the 1997 Amendments to IDEA. Although the fundamental concept is not new and has been used in various settings previously, especially settings that included students with severe behavioral difficulties, the fact that BIPs were required stunned many school-based professionals.

In general, behavioral intervention plans are required for (1) students whose behaviors impede their learning or that of others, (2) students who put peers at risk because of their behaviors, and (3) students with disabilities for whom serious disciplinary action is being taken. The major assumptions underlying the development of behavioral intervention plans include the following points:

▶ Behavior problems are best addressed when the causes (i.e., function) of the behaviors are known.
▶ Interventions that are based on positive intervention strategies are more effective than punitive ones.
▶ Dealing with difficult behaviors demands a team approach.

Many teachers reacted negatively to the notion of having to develop behavioral plans, citing the lack of time as the leading reason for their lack of enthusiasm. However, students with behavior problems require some time and effort. Dedicating time and effort to understanding the true function of a behavior and then intervening appropriately seems like a better way to expend effort than reacting to inappropriate behavior on an ongoing basis.

TEACHING TIP

As a general education teacher, you should be invited to participate in the IEP meeting of any child in your class. If you were not present, ask the special education teacher to give you documentation of the child's strengths, weaknesses, and goals to incorporate into your daily planning.

TEACHING TIP

The IEP is a plan, not a contract. If teachers are making a good faith effort to implement the IEP, they cannot be held responsible for lack of progress. Ongoing communication with the IEP team is critical, and a revision of the IEP may be necessary.

CONSIDER THIS

It is important to note that behavioral intervention planning is useful for any student with challenging behaviors.

The BIP Process   The behavioral intervention planning process typically includes the following specific steps (Fad et al., 2000):

▶ Collect background information to provide context for the presenting problems.
▶ Conduct a functional behavioral assessment (FBA), where you analyze the relationship of the target behavior to environmental antecedents and consequences and you explore the purpose of the behavior.
▶ Determine whether the behavior in question is directly related to the student's disability (i.e., whether the behavior is a manifestation of the disability).
▶ Determine specific goals that involve either increasing or decreasing the target behavior.
▶ Develop intervention strategies, preferably of a positive nature, that will be used and identify the person(s) who will be responsible for implementation.
▶ Implement the plan and evaluate its effectiveness.
▶ Use information from the implementation of the intervention to revisit the assessment information as a basis for further intervention efforts.

The topic of behavioral intervention planning is revisited in Chapters 7 and 14. A sample of a completed BIP is shown in Figure 4.7.

Role of the General Education Teacher in the BIP Process   General education teachers can be involved in all aspects of the BIP process. During the first stage of collecting background information, the general education teacher plays a crucial role in supplying classroom-related information about the behaviors under review. Although the FBA is likely to be conducted by someone other than the classroom teacher, on occasion the general education teacher might be asked to be involved in generating it. Classroom teachers are quite likely to be involved in the various interventions that are identified, for the simple reason that many students requiring a BIP will receive their education in a general education classroom. Last, classroom teachers will be intricately involved in monitoring the effectiveness of the interventions when students with BIPs are in their classes.

Transition Services

The 1990 amendments to the Education for All Handicapped Children Act of 1975, which changed the name of the law to the Individuals with Disabilities Education Act (IDEA), had a significant effect on transition services. Up to this point, no federal mandate had existed for implementing transition planning. Under the amendments of 1990, one of the purposes of the annual IEP meeting for students with disabilities, upon reaching 16 years of age, is to plan for necessary transition services.

Definition of Transition Services   The 1990 amendments to IDEA provided a definition of transition services that was retained in the 1997 amendments. IDEA defines transition services as

> a coordinated set of activities for a student, designed within an outcome-oriented process, which promotes movement from school to postschool activities, including postsecondary education, vocational training, integrated employment (including supported employment), continuing and adult education, adult services, independent living or community participation.
>
> The coordinated set of activities shall be based upon the individual student's needs, taking into account student preferences and interests, and shall include instruction, community experiences, and the development of employment and other postschool objectives, and if appropriate, acquisition of daily living skills and functional vocational evaluation. (§300.18)

Essential Elements   Individual planning for transition services, as prescribed in the legislation and accompanying regulations, stresses a number of critical concepts. First, the

FIGURE 4.7　　**Behavioral Intervention Plan (BIP)**

Specific Goal(s)	Proposed Intervention(s)	Person(s) Responsible	Methods	Criterion	Schedule Date	Code
					Evaluation	
					Progress Codes: / = ongoing X = mastered D = discontinued	
1. Casey will increase respectful language in class, including saying "yes, sir" or "yes, ma'am" when requested to do something.	1. Contract for • positive comments • saying "yes, ma'am" or "yes, sir" • refrain from verbal threats	1. Student Teachers Counselor	–Contract forms –Discipline referrals	1. Respectful language 90% of time	9/1/99 10/15/99 12/1/99 1/15/00 3/1/00 4/15/00 6/1/00	
2. Casey will decrease verbal threats and teasing.	2. Delay release from classroom to hallway by 5 minutes	2. Teachers		2. Contract • positive comments: 5 per day • "yes" responses: 80% of time • verbal threats: fewer than 8 per 6 weeks		
3. Casey will decrease aggressive incidents toward peers (fighting, hitting, tripping).	3. Continuum of responses to aggression: • Parent–Asst. Principal conference and suspension to AEP for 3 days • Go to antiaggression classes • Notify probation officer	3. Parents Assistant Principal Counselor		3. Aggression: No incidents in next 6 weeks		

These goals were developed with consideration of the following information:

☐ Parent concerns regarding special circumstances: _____ _____

☐ Teacher/administrator concerns regarding special circumstances: _____ _____

☑ Outside agency/professional concerns regarding special circumstances: _____ Probation officer requires notification. _____

From *Behavioral Intervention Planning: Completing a Functional Behavioral Assessment and Developing a Behavioral Intervention Plan* (p. 21), by K. Fad, J. R. Patton, & E. A. Polloway, 2000, Austin, TX: Pro-Ed.

student and his or her family need to be actively involved in the process. Second, planning activities, including assessing transition needs, must begin early in a student's school career. Third, the complexity of adult life needs to be recognized and planned for. Fourth, in keeping with ongoing discussions related to transition, a closer link between transition services and the goals in a student's IEP should be made. Unfortunately, the nature and quality of transition services vary widely from one school district to another across the country, ranging from minimal compliance activities to what could be considered best practices in transition (Patton, 2001).

When examined closely, the transition planning process is found to be a multifaceted series of events. Ultimately, all transitions, if approached systematically, are composed of comprehensive planning, follow-through, and coordination among various agencies.

The 1997 reauthorization of IDEA further refined the nature of mandated transition practice. Transition planning activities now have to begin sooner: a statement of transition needs, which integrates transition planning within the process of educational planning, must be in a student's IEP by age 14. The 1997 amendments made it very clear that a student's program of study must be related to the general education curriculum as well.

Role of the General Education Teacher in the Transition Process   The general education teacher can contribute to the transition process in two primary ways. First, the classroom teacher, mindful of adult outcomes (i.e., the demands of everyday living) can integrate real-life topics of current or future importance into the existing curriculum, as a way of covering topics that will be relevant and meaningful to students in their classes (see Patton, Cronin, & Wood, 1999). Second, classroom teachers can participate by contributing information to the transition assessment phase. Here, teachers who know the academic, social, and behavioral competence of their students can provide valuable information to the transition planning process.

Extended School Year Services

Another service to which some students with disabilities are entitled is "summer school," or, more appropriately, "the extended school year." The provision of services beyond the normal school year emerged as a way of ensuring that a natural disruption of services (i.e., summer) did not interfere with a student's continued educational progress. The IEP team determines whether summer programming is necessary for the provision of a "free, appropriate public education."

Review and Dismissal

Two additional critical features of the special education process are (1) the ongoing monitoring of a student's progress in special education and (2) continued need for special education services. By law, a student's IEP must be reviewed and revised on an annual basis. A comprehensive reevaluation must be undertaken every three years. In Texas the term used to refer to IEP-related meetings is "admission, review, and dismissal" (ARD) meetings, clearly indicating that attention should be given to the monitoring of a student's program and possible exit from special education.

The annual review of the IEP is essential for updating the student's goals. The IEP meeting when this topic is discussed should not only look closely at existing goals but also be open to the development of new goals in areas of need. For example, new goals may need to be written into the IEP during the transition assessment process. Further, the IEP team can identify areas needing instructional attention after examining a student's competence across a range of transition areas.

Although being admitted to special education is too frequently a one-way street, many students can and should reach levels of academic competence whereby they will no longer need special education or related services. The process to dismiss students from special education can be politically charged. Some parents may not want the cessation of services for their son or daughter; some school-based professionals do not like to see services cease when a student reaches a plateau—a situation in which a student may still be skill-deficient but has not shown any progress after robust interventions have been utilized.

Section 504 Eligibility and Planning

CONSIDER THIS

A relatively small number of people even know that Section 504 applies to students, and even fewer know what it means.

As noted in Chapter 1, Section 504 is an antidiscrimination statute. It prohibits discrimination against any individual because of a disability. It applies to any organization that receives federal monies and includes public schools.

Eligibility

Eligibility is based on a student having a physical or mental impairment that results in a substantial limitation in one or more major life activities (e.g., seeing, hearing, learning). A "substantial limitation" is related to two primary factors: severity of the impairment and duration (i.e., permanence of the condition).

As previously suggested, Section 504 consideration should be given to any student who is referred for special education services but does not qualify under IDEA. Even though

FIGURE 4.8

Section 504 Eligibility Determination Form

From *Section 504 and Public Schools: A Practical Guide for Determining Eligibility, Developing Accommodation Plans, and Documenting Compliance* (p. 34) by T. E. C. Smith & J. R. Patton, 1998, Austin, TX: Pro-Ed.

I. General Information

Student Name _____   Today's Date _____

Address _____ City _____   State _____ ZIP _____

School _____ Home Phone _____   Work Phone _____

District 504 Coordinator _____   Phone _____

II. Reason for Meeting

☐ initial evaluation

☐ periodic reevalutaion

☐ reevaluation before significant change in placement

III. Eligibility Criteria and Determination

☐ yes ☐ no   1. Student has a mental or physical impairment.

☐ yes ☐ no   2. Student's impairment substantially limits a major life activity.

Area(s) where substantial limitation exists (see other side):

*_____   *_____

*_____   *_____

☐ yes ☐ no   3. Student meets 504 committee eligibility criteria.

IV. Placement

☐ regular classes

☐ regular classes with use of supplementary services

☐ special education and related services

V. Committee Members

_____   _____

_____   _____

_____   _____

VI. Record of Action

Date   *Action*

____/____/____   Parents/guardians provided written notice of rights

____/____/____   Notice of 504 evaluation and committee meeting

____/____/____   Accommodation plan developed

VII. Projected Review/Reevaluation Date: _____

this procedure makes sense, few school systems include it as part of the overall umbrella of service coverage.

Every public school should have a committee and process for handling 504 eligibility and planning activities. Schools should document that a logical and reasonable process for determining eligibility is used. A good plan is to have someone on staff who is knowledgeable about 504 and to develop a coherent system for addressing 504 queries. Figure 4.8 provides a sample of a 504 eligibility determination form.

Reasonable Accommodations

If a student is determined to be eligible for services under 504, schools are required to provide reasonable accommodations for the student in academic and nonacademic areas.

Technological Applications in the Special Education Process

Without question, technology pervades the full spectrum of the education in schools today. Significant changes can be seen in the curriculum (e.g., teaching keyboarding in grade 6 versus teaching it at the beginning of high school, as in previous times) and instruction (e.g., the large number of multimedia materials that are available commercially). Technology has had an impact on the various elements of the special education process, as discussed in this chapter and highlighted in Figure 4.1. Some selected examples of what is available today to improve the efficiency of requisite activities in the special education process are the following:

Identification of the Presenting Problem

1. Videotaping capabilities to provide observational data.
2. Computerized assessment systems for collecting and graphing student performance.

Prereferral Intervention

1. Sophisticated school record management systems.
2. Software programs that assist in the compilation of data.

Formal Referral and Eligibility Determination

1. Systems for submitting referrals electronically.
2. Assessment instruments that can now be given using a computer.
3. Many assessment instruments that have computer scoring software.

Program Planning and Delivery

1. Computer-based IEP systems.
2. Vast array of teacher utilities (grade books, activity-generating software— e.g., crossword puzzles, calendars).
3. Lesson plans and ideas available on-line.
4. Computer-based instruction systems (e.g., reading programs, brainstorming).

5. Innovative curricular programs that incorporate extensive use of the Internet.
6. Availability of easy-to-use multimedia devices and delivery systems (e.g., digital photography and video).
7. Use of personal digital assistants in instruction.
8. Various assistive technology devices for use with students with specific needs.
9. Curriculum-based assessment systems for monitoring student progress.

Review and Dismissal

See ideas under "Formal Referral and Eligibility Determination."

Transition Services

1. Computer-based systems for determining occupational interests and transition needs.
2. Curricular materials on CD for addressing real-world topics.
3. Individual transition portfolios.

 For follow-up questions about technological applications in the special education process, go to Chapter 4 of the Companion Website (ablongman.com/sppd4e) and click Technology Today.

Accommodations may range from providing extended time on tests for a student with attention deficit/hyperactivity disorder (ADHD) to providing dry marker boards for a student with severe allergies to chalk dust. Most accommodations are easy to implement and do not cost much money. Some accommodations that require the use of technology may be more costly. See the Technology Today feature for some forms of technology that are inexpensive and some that would be expensive.

Typically, a written accommodation plan is developed that specifies the nature and scope of the accommodations to be implemented. This document differs greatly from an IEP because it has no specifically mandated components. As a result, many accommodation plan formats have emerged, ranging from very basic to semielaborate. Figure 4.9 is an example of a basic accommodation plan.

CONSIDER THIS

The main intent of a written accommodation plan is to furnish a record of what is to be provided.

Role of the General Education Teacher in Section 504 Activities

General education teachers play a crucial role in identifying students who might qualify for services under Section 504. Being knowledgeable about what Section 504 provides and how one qualifies for services contributes to a classroom teacher's resourcefulness. Classroom teachers may be contacted during the eligibility determination phase to provide information to the committee to assist with the decision-making task. Teachers may also be required to monitor the effectiveness of the accommodations that are suggested.

Name: _Ricky Rives_

School/Class: _Mablevale Junior High—7th grade_

Teacher: _Mr. Barnes; Ms. Johns_   Date: _10/8/96_

General Strengths: _Ricky wants very much to be successful in his classes. He tries very hard and wants to please his parents. His motivation is strong._

General Weaknesses: _Ricky has a learning disability. Although his discrepancy was not significant enough to make him eligible for special education, he still has major problems in reading. Recently his behavior has become problematic due to his being frustrated in classes._

Specific Accommodations:

Accommodation #1

Class: _Science_   Accommodation(s): _Mr. Barnes will give Ricky a note-taking guide before he lectures. He will also allow Ricky to use a tape recorder in class._

Person Responsible for Accommodation #1: _Mr. Barnes—teacher_

Accommodation #2

Class: _Science_   Addommodation(s): _Mr. Barnes will have Ricky's test read orally to him and give him extra time to complete the examination._

Person Responsible for Accommodation #2: _Mr. Barnes—teacher_

Accommodation #3

Class: _Social Studies_   Accommodation(s): _Ms. Johns will allow Ricky to use a tape recorder during class. She will also highlight Ricky's textbook, pointing out the important facts for each chapter._

Person Responsible for Accommodation #1: _Ms. Johns—teacher_

Accommodation #4

Class: _Social Studies_   Accommodation(s): _Ms. Johns will give Ricky extra time on written assignments and provide feedback and allow Ricky to redo work that needs improvement._

Person Responsible for Accommodation #1: _Ms. Johns—teacher_

Accommodation #5

Class: _All classes_   Accommodation(s): _A behavior management plan will be developed and used in all of Ricky's classes. The plan will focus on positive reinforcement of appropriate behaviors._

Person Responsible for Accommodation #5: _Mr. Frank—asst. prin._

General Comments:

Ricky's plan will be reviewed at the end of the fall term to determine if additional modifications are required.

Individuals Participating in Development of Accommodation Plan:

John Barnes—teacher   _Ralph Frank—asst. prin. and 504 coor._

Linda Johns—teacher

Darlene Rives—mother

FIGURE 4.9

A Section 504 Accommodation Plan

Assessment Practices Throughout the Special Education Process

Assessment is the process of gathering relevant information to use in making decisions about students (Salvia & Ysseldyke, 2001). It is a dynamic, continuous process that guides and directs decisions about students with suspected or known disabilities. Assessment is so integral to the special education process that much of what educators do is addressed in regulations. However, the states still vary in the types of procedures used, the specific approaches to assessment, and the criteria used to determine student eligibility.

Teachers play four major roles in regard to school-based assessment and, as a result, need to have skills in all four areas.

1. Teachers are *consumers* of assessment information—in this role, they must be able to understand assessment information.
2. Teachers are *producers* of assessment information—they must be able to generate assessment information by administering tests, conducting observations, and so on.
3. Teachers are *communicators* of assessment information—by virtue of the fact that much of what we do in schools today is team-based, teachers must be able to share assessment information with others (professionals, parents, students).
4. Teachers are *developers* of assessment instruments—most teachers will find that they have to create assessment techniques to accomplish some education-related tasks.

Purpose of Assessment

Assessment is critical in each of the major phases of the special education process. During the **screening** phase, including the steps of prereferral and referral discussed previously, the concerns expressed by teachers and parents are the result of their informal "assessment" of the student's lack of progress. Their concern comes from their observations and interactions with the student in the natural environment. When parents and teachers get concerned, they may consult others who have worked with the child or review previous records or current work. At this point these students are at risk for failure, and the first level of assessment for special education services has begun.

If a referral is made and the IEP team accepts the referral, the identification and **eligibility** phase of assessment begins. During this phase the child is formally evaluated to determine if he or she has a disability and is eligible for special education services. The student's intellectual ability, strengths, and limitations are evaluated individually by trained professionals. These results are studied by the IEP team along with the information gathered during the screening, prereferral, and referral phases.

If the student is determined to be eligible, assessment data are needed for **program planning.** Existing data are studied further, and new data may be collected to help the IEP team select goals and objectives or benchmarks, as well as identify the most effective methods of instruction to include in the IEP. After the IEP has been implemented, assessment is conducted to **monitor** and **evaluate** the student's progress. The student is assessed annually to evaluate the outcome of the IEP and provide a measure of accountability. In addition, the student's eligibility or need for services is reconsidered by the IEP team every three years, and additional assessments may be required to make decisions at that time. The results of each phase of this assessment determine which of several approaches to assessment are used.

Approaches to Assessment

Salvia and Ysseldyke (2001) identified four approaches used to gather information on students: (1) observation, (2) recollection (by means of interview or rating scale), (3) record or portfolio review, and (4) testing. Data collected through naturalistic **observation** can be highly accurate and provide detailed, relevant information on how the student performs in the natural environment. The observer may be systematically looking for one or more specific behaviors, such as inattention or inappropriate comments. In this approach, the frequency, duration, and intensity of the behavior(s) are usually recorded for study. The student's behavior can then be compared to normal standards of his or her peers or to the individual's previous behavior. Another method of collecting observational data is more anecdotal, in which case the observer records any behavior that seems significant. This type of data may be more subjective than the systematic recordings and harder to validate. Observational data may also be collected using audiotape or videotape.

In data collection involving **recollection,** individuals familiar with the student are asked to recall events and interpret the behaviors. The most commonly used are interviews or ratings scales that can be obtained from the students through a self-report or from peers, family members, teachers, counselors, or others. Through interviews, parents' concerns and preferences can be determined. Since interviews are generally held in person, reactions to questions can be observed and, when appropriate, questions can be explored more thoroughly. **Ratings scales** offer a structured method of data collection involving asking the rater to respond to a statement by indicating the degree to which an item describes an individual. When using rating-scale data, care should be taken to confirm the rater's ability to understand the scale and determine the possibility of bias in reporting.

Another important component of assessment is record or **portfolio review.** Existing information such as school cumulative records, databases, anecdotal records, nonschool records, or student products (often found in a student's portfolio) should be reviewed carefully for insight into the student's needs and strengths. Usually a school will consider the same kinds of records for each child being considered to maintain consistency.

The most common method of gathering information on students is through **testing. Testing,** formal or informal, is the process of presenting challenges or problems to students and measuring the student's competency, attitude, or behavior by evaluating his or her responses (Ysseldyke & Olsen, 1999).

Formal assessment instruments are generally available commercially. They typically contain detailed guidelines for administration, scoring, and interpretation as well as statistical data regarding **validity,** reliability, and **standardization procedures.** They are most often **norm-referenced;** that is, the tests provide quantitative information comparing the performance of an individual student to others in his or her norm group (determined, for example, by age, grade, or gender). Test results are usually reported in the form of test quotients, percentiles, and age or grade equivalents. These tools are most useful early in an assessment procedure, when relatively little is known of a student's strengths and weaknesses, and thus they may help identify areas in which informal assessment can begin. The ability to compare the student to his or her age and grade peers is also an advantage in making eligibility and placement decisions and fulfilling related administrative requirements. Table 4.2 is a useful assessment resource that shows the relationship across various types of scores obtained through standardized testing.

Professionals can make more informed decisions about the use of formal instruments if they study the instrument and become familiar with its features, benefits, and possible liabilities. One way to do so is to consult one or more of the excellent resources on tests.

Although formal testing provides quantitative and sometimes qualitative data based on student performance, tests can only obtain a measure of a student's best performance in a contrived situation; they cannot broadly represent a student's typical performance under natural conditions. When considered in isolation, the results of formal tests can also result in lost data that can lead to poor decisions in placement and instructional planning. Rigid administration and interpretation of test results can obscure, rather than reveal, a student's strengths and weaknesses. It has become increasingly apparent that traditional, formal approaches must be augmented with assessment techniques that more accurately represent a student's typical skills.

Informal tests and measurements are usually more loosely structured than formal instruments and are more closely tied to teaching. Such tools are typically devised by teachers to determine what skills or knowledge a child possesses. Their key advantage

CONSIDER THIS

Test scores often confuse and concern parents. The information in Table 4.2 will help you convey students' scores more accurately to parents. Notice that the 50th percentile rank is in the non-deficit range. A score indicating a mild disability begins with a score of 16th percentile, and a moderate deficit begins with a score of 5th percentile.

TEACHING TIP

When the results of standardized tests differ significantly from your observations and experiences with a student, consult the examiner. Additional assessment may be necessary.

TABLE 4.2   **Relation of Various Standard Scores to Percentile Rank and to Each Other**

| Percentile Rank | Standard Scores | | | | | Deficit |
	Quotients	NCE Scores	T-scores	Z-scores	Stanines	
99	150	99	83	+3.33	9	
99	145	99	80	+3.00	9	
99	140	99	77	+2.67	9	
99	135	99	73	+2.33	9	
98	130	92	70	+2.00	9	
95	125	85	67	+1.67	8	
91	120	78	63	+1.34	8	None
84	115	71	60	+1.00	7	
75	110	64	57	+0.67	6	
63	105	57	53	+0.33	6	
50	100	50	50	+0.00	5	
37	95	43	47	−0.33	4	
25	90	36	43	−0.67	4	
16	85	29	40	−1.00	3	
9	80	22	37	−1.34	2	Mild
5	75	15	33	−1.67	2	
2	70	8	30	−2.00	1	Moderate
1	65	1	27	−2.33	1	
1	60	1	23	−2.67	1	Severe
1	55	1	20	−3.00	1	

From "The Role of Standardized Tests in Planning Academic Instruction" (p. 377) by D. D. Hammill and B. R. Bryant, in *Handbook on the Assessment of Learning Disabilities,* edited by H. L. Swanson, 1991, Austin, TX: Pro-Ed. Copyright 1991 by Pro-Ed, Inc. Used by permission.

Curriculum-based assessment can focus attention on changes in a student's academic behavior.

is the direct application of assessment data to instructional programs. By incorporating informal tests and measurements and by monitoring students' responses each day, teachers can achieve a more accurate assessment of growth in learning or behavioral change. Following is a brief discussion of general types of informal assessment procedures.

Criterion-referenced testing (CRT) compares a student's performance with a criterion of mastery for a specific task, disregarding his or her relative standing in a group. This form of informal assessment can be especially useful when documentation of progress is needed for accountability because the acquisition of skills can be clearly demonstrated. As Taylor (2000) stresses, CRTs are quite popular because they focus attention on specific skills in the curriculum, provide measures of progress toward mastery, and assist teachers in designing instructional strategies. Traditionally, teachers have developed most criterion-referenced instruments, but publishers have begun to produce assessment tools of this type.

One important and popular form of criterion-referenced assessment is **curriculum-based assessment,** which, unlike norm-referenced tools, uses the actual curriculum as the standard and thus provides a basis for evaluating and modifying the curriculum for an individual student (McLoughlin & Lewis, 1999). This type of assessment can have a role in many important tasks: identification, eligibility, instructional grouping, program planning, progress monitoring, and program evaluation. Curriculum-based assessment can focus attention on changes in academic behavior within the context of the curriculum being used, thus enhancing the relationship between assessment and teaching (Deno & Fuchs, 1987).

Alternative assessment procedures have emerged as dissatisfaction with group-administered standardized tests has increased. Two terms commonly used to describe these procedures are **authentic assessment** and portfolio assessment. These assessment methods use similar techniques such as requiring students to construct, produce, perform, or demonstrate a task. These types of student responses are considered alternatives to typical testing responses, such as selecting from multiple-choice items, a technique commonly used on standardized, formal tests. An example of an authentic assessment would be assigning a student the task of asking an individual whom he or she does not know for help. The individual being asked would be trained to evaluate the quality of the interaction and recommend the supports or accommodations that a student might need to improve the interaction (Ysseldyke & Olsen, 1999). Portfolio assessment was described in the previous section on assessment approaches.

Ecological assessment is another approach used with many types of informal assessment. As educational assessment has increasingly begun to reflect a trend toward appreciating the ecology of the student, data obtained are now more frequently analyzed in relation to the child's functioning in his or her various environments. Although a full discussion of ecological assessment is beyond the scope of this chapter, the following information highlights some basic considerations, and the nearby Inclusion Strategies feature provides an example of a classroom ecological inventory.

The focus of ecological assessment is to place the evaluation process within the context of the student's environment. Its central element is *functionality*—how well the student operates in the current environment or the one into which he or she will be moving. This focus shifts a program's emphasis from correcting deficits toward determining how to build on strengths and interests. This type of assessment is particularly useful in early childhood.

Legal Requirements for Assessment

PL 94–142, the first major law dealing with special education policy, introduced many of the assessment mandates that still exist today. The final regulations for the IDEA Amendments of 1997 continue to address and refine the assessment process. The law specifically addresses the concept of nondiscriminatory evaluations. Only tests that are not racially or culturally biased can be used to determine a disability and the extent of special education and related services that the student needs. If possible, the tests are to be administered in the student's native language or with other means of communication. Those professionals using assessment procedures for a student with limited English proficiency have to ensure that they are measuring the disability and the need for special education, not the student's English language skills. Eligibility also cannot be determined if the deficits are found to be a reflection of a lack of instruction in reading or math.

Any assessment measures must be validated for the specific purpose for which they are used and administered by an individual trained to give the test. No single procedure or test can be the sole criterion for determining eligibility for special education. The student must be assessed in all areas of suspected disability. These areas might include health, vision, hearing, social and emotional status, intelligence, academic performance, communication status, and motor abilities. The variety of assessment tools and strategies used must provide relevant, functional information to directly assist in determining the needs of the student. Information provided by parents must also be considered. Finally, the information must address how to enable the student to participate and progress in the general education curriculum (or for a preschool student, to participate in appropriate activities).

Significant trends in the area of assessment include a focus on the informal assessment procedures that produce more relevant, functional information, as described in the previous section. This type of assessment offers information helpful in eligibility determination as well as IEP development. The increase of the importance of parental input is apparent in the IDEA Amendments of 1997, as is the focus on increasing the student's chances for

TEACHING TIP

When entering a new school system, ask the principal or lead teachers to describe the assessment instruments typically used. If curriculum-based assessment has not been developed, organize a grade level team to begin this important process.

CONSIDER THIS

Access to the general education curriculum is a major theme of IDEA.

Classroom Ecological Inventory

Special Education Teacher _____   Grade _____ Date _____

General Education Teacher _____   Number of Students in General Class _____

Student _____

PART 1: CLASSROOM OBSERVATION

Physical Environment

Directions: Please circle or provide the appropriate answer.

1. Is there an area for small groups?	Yes	No
2. Are partitions used in the room?	Yes	No
3. Is there a computer in the classroom?	Yes	No

4. Where is the student's desk located? (for example, front of room, back, middle, away from other students, etc.) _____

Teacher/Student Behavior

Directions for #1–#4: Please circle the appropriate answer.

1. How much movement or activity is tolerated by the teacher?	Much	Average	Little	Unclear
2. How much talking among students is tolerated?	Much	Average	Little	Unclear
3. Does the teacher use praise?	Much	Average	Little	Unclear
4. Was subject taught to the entire group or to small groups?		Entire	Small	

Directions for #5–#7: Please provide an appropriate answer.

5. During the observation, where did the teacher spend most of the time? (for example, at the board, at teacher's desk, at student's desk) _____

6. What teaching methods did you observe while in the classroom? (for example, teacher modeled the lesson, asked students to work at board, helped small groups, helped individual students) _____

7. How did the teacher interact with students who appeared to be low achieving or slower than their classmates? (for example, helped them individually, talked to them in the large group) _____

Posted Classroom Rules
If classroom rules are posted, what are they?

Special Education	*General Education*
_____	_____
_____	_____
_____	_____

Is there any other pertinent information you observed about this classroom that would be helpful in reintegrating the student? (for example, crowded classroom)

PART 2: TEACHER INTERVIEW

Classroom Rules

	Special Ed	General Ed
1. During class are there important rules? (Yes or No)	_____	_____
2. If yes, how are they communicated? (for example, written or oral)	_____	_____
3. If class rules are *not* posted, what are they?	_____	_____
	_____	_____
	_____	_____

Classroom Rules   *Special Ed*   *General Ed*
4. If a rule is broken, what happens? What is the typical consequence?   _____   _____
5. Who enforces the rules? (teacher, aide, students)   _____   _____

Teacher Behavior
1. a. Is homework assigned? (Yes or No)   _____   _____
    b. If so, indicate approximate amount (minutes) of homework, and   _____   _____
    c. the frequency with which it is given.   _____   _____

Directions for #2–#4: Using a 3-point scale (1 = Often, 2 = Sometimes, 3 = Never), rate each item according to frequency of occurrence in class. Place an asterisk (*) in the right-hand margin to indicate important differences between the special and regular education classrooms.

	Special Ed	General Ed		Special Ed	General Ed
2. Assignments in Class			**4. Academic/Social Rewards**		
a. Students are given assignments:			a. Classroom rewards or reinforcement include:		
• that are the same for all	___	___	• material rewards (example, stars)	___	___
• that differ in amount or type	___	___	b. Classroom punishment includes:		
• to complete in school at a specified time	___	___	• time out	___	___
• that, if unfinished in school, are assigned as homework	___	___	• loss of activity-related privileges	___	___
b. Evaluation of assignment:			• (example, loss of free time)	___	___
• teacher evaluation	___	___	• teacher ignoring	___	___
• student self-evaluation	___	___	• reprimands	___	___
• peer evaluation	___	___	• poorer grade, loss of star, etc.	___	___
3. Tests			• extra work	___	___
a. Tests are			• staying after school	___	___
• presented orally	___	___	• physical punishment (cxample, paddling)	___	___
• copied from board	___	___	**5. To what extent does each of the following contribute to an overall grade?** *Estimate the percentage for each so that the total sums to 100%.*		
• timed	___	___	• homework	___	___
• based on study guides given to students prior to test	___	___	• daily work	___	___
• administered by resource teacher	___	___	• tests	___	___
b. Grades are:			• class participation	___	___
• percentages (example, 75%)	___	___	**6. Please list skills that have been taught since the beginning of the school year (general education teacher only):**		
• letter grades (example, B+	___	___			
• both	___	___			

6. Please list skills that have been taught since the beginning of the school year (general education teacher only):

Skill	Will Reteach Later? (Yes or No)
_____	_____

For follow-up questions about the Classroom Ecological Inventory, go to Chapter 4 of the Companion Website (ablongman.com/sppd4e) and click Inclusion Strategies.

From "Classroom Ecological Inventory" by D. Fuchs, P. Fernstrom, S. Scott, L. Fuchs, and L. Vandermeer, 1994, *Teaching Exceptional Children, 26*, pp. 14–15.

successful participation in the general education classroom. This includes participation in statewide or districtwide assessments given to all students. The increased emphasis on participation in the general education curriculum is not useful without a measure of the student's progress in the curriculum. The IEP team may decide that the student with a disability should not participate in the traditional testing program without accommodations. Table 4.3 provides a checklist of recommended adaptations for test taking that may be considered by the IEP team for a student. The team also may decide that participation in standardized testing is not appropriate even with accommodations. In this case, the team must identify an alternate assessment procedure that allows the student to demonstrate

TABLE 4.3   **Suggested Adaptations for Test Taking: Checklist**

Behavioral and Environmental Adaptations

Distracted/off task
- ❏ Provide both written and verbal instructions
- ❏ Provide additional space between work areas
- ❏ Place student near teacher and/or in the front of the class
- ❏ Develop a secret signal for on-task behavior
- ❏ Keep work area free from unnecessary materials (e.g., books, pencils)
- ❏ Provide positive feedback
- ❏ Enforce behavior management system
- ❏ Seat apart from others

Completion of Task-Related Adaptations

Getting started and completing tasks
- ❏ Reduce length of test (e.g., select questions to be answered)
- ❏ Allow additional time
- ❏ Break test into shorter tasks (e.g., break every 10 minutes)
- ❏ Establish a reward system
- ❏ Set timer for designated amount of work time and allow student to take a one-minute break after the timer is complete
- ❏ Provide checklist of appropriate behaviors

Processing difficulties
- ❏ Allow use of manipulatives (e.g., counting blocks)
- ❏ Provide both written and verbal instructions

- ❏ Take frequent breaks
- ❏ Break test into shorter tasks
- ❏ Provide list of things to do

Difficulty keeping place when reading
- ❏ Provide large-print version
- ❏ Allow use of place keeper (e.g., bookmark, paper)
- ❏ Create version of test with fewer questions per page

Academic Adaptations

Difficulty with reading comprehension
- ❏ Identify key vocabulary (e.g., highlight or underline)
- ❏ Review key vocabulary
- ❏ Read questions or passages to student

Difficulty with writing
- ❏ Allow oral response
- ❏ Have proctor or teacher write student response
- ❏ Allow the use of computer or word processor

Difficulty with mathematics
- ❏ Have calculation read to student
- ❏ Allow the use of a calculator
- ❏ Break task into smaller parts
- ❏ Reduce the number of questions to be answered (e.g., answer only even-numbered questions)

From *Step-by-Step Guide: For Including Students with Disabilities in State and District-wide Assessments* (p. 29) by D. P. Bryant, J. R. Patton, & S. Vaughn, 2000, Austin, TX: Pro-Ed.

what he or she has learned. Alternate assessment activities may encompass a variety of activities, including authentic assessment or portfolio assessment (Yell & Shriner, 1997).

Issues of Bias in Assessment

By the year 2010 in the United States, the number of K–12 students from diverse cultures is expected to increase by 37%, rising to approximately 24 million students. This trend will present one of the greatest challenges for special educators—accurately assessing culturally and linguistically diverse students for disabilities (CEC, 1997).

The importance of ensuring fair and equitable assessment procedures clearly was emphasized in IDEA. This basic assumption of the law stated that assessment procedures must be established to make sure

> that testing and evaluation materials and procedures utilized for the purposes of evaluation and placement of handicapped children will be selected and administered so as not to be racially or culturally discriminatory. Such material or procedures shall be provided and administered in the child's native language or mode of communication, unless it is clearly not feasible to do so, and no single procedure shall be the sole criterion for determining an appropriate educational program for a child.

As Waterman (1994) notes, this regulation within IDEA stemmed directly from court cases that served as legal precursors to this federal legislation. For example, these cases related to the use of IQ in the placement of minority children into classes for students with mental retardation (e.g., *Larry P. v. Riles*, 1972; *Diana v. State Board of Education*, 1970) and "tracking systems" in the public schools (e.g., *Hobson v. Hansen*, 1967). The decision in *Hobson v. Hansen* stipulated that tests standardized on a white middle-class

Diversity Forum

Child Study Teams and Cultural Differences

Han is an English language learner (ELL), and his limited fluency in English often leads to frustration and disruptive behavior. Because he is the only Chinese American in class, the perceptions of others often accelerate his aggressiveness toward his peers. He is the only boy at home, with three older sisters. As a member of a traditional Chinese family, where males hold an honored status because of their ability to pass on the family name, Han often has his way at home.

As discussed in this chapter, child study teams can support teachers in designing appropriate classroom interventions . For students like Han, though, team members must also have the background knowledge to help the teacher distinguish between cultural differences and behavior disorders (Ortiz, 1997).

Specifically, Han's teacher would be asked to document his behavior problem; in reviewing the situation, the team would compare this information with profiles of peers and others who have similar cultural, linguistic, and socioeconomic backgrounds. Significant events in Han's medical, family, and school histories would also be considered, and interventions recommended by the team would be responsive to his sociocultural and linguistic experience.

When designing interventions for Han, his teacher and the team should find ways to incorporate the following components (Cartledge & Milburn, 1996):

▶ Direct instruction through role-playing, modeling, and feedback

▶ English as a second language (ESL) lessons focused specifically on language conventions used during play time
▶ Implementing instruction through literature to foster cultural identity
▶ Cooperative learning experiences that enhance respect and positive interactions among peers
▶ Engaging parents in the school socialization process

For follow-up questions about child study teams and cultural differences, go to Chapter 4 of the Companion Website (ablongman.com/sppd4e) and click Diversity Forum.

---

population were used to effectively classify students by socioeconomic status rather than by ability. As Wallace et al. (1992) stress,

> It is clear that bias in the evaluation of students, particularly those from a minority background, can and will significantly affect the educational opportunities afforded these youngsters. To minimize the effects of bias in the evaluation, it is absolutely essential that every [professional] . . . be aware of the various ways in which bias is exhibited and take steps to minimize its effects when making educational decisions. (p. 473)

In addition to racial or cultural bias in assessment, a separate concern is the accurate assessment of individuals who experience sensory or motor disabilities. For example, individuals who have hearing impairments may require a nonverbal test, whereas persons who have visual impairments require measures that do not rely on object manipulation and do not include cards or pictures (Hoy & Gregg, 1994). An individual with a severe motor impairment may have limited voluntary responses and may need to respond using an eye scan or blink. Other students may have limited receptive or expressive language capabilities.

Students who have multiple disabilities compound the difficulties of administering the assessment task. Browder and Snell (1988) note that some individuals simply lack "test behaviors." For example, they may refuse to stay seated for an assessment session or may exhibit interfering self-stimulatory behavior (e.g., hand flapping, rocking). Such disabilities or behaviors may cause the test to measure problems rather than assess functioning. Considered collectively, these problems can make traditional testing procedures ineffective, resulting in discriminatory practices despite the best intentions of the tester (Luckasson et al., 1992). Implementation of accommodations appropriate for the needs of each student with a disability greatly reduces this type of test bias. Refer to Table 4.3 for a list of commonly used adaptations.

Role of the General Education Teacher in Assessment

The list that follows suggests ways in which the general education professional can take an active role in the assessment process.

CONSIDER THIS

Do you feel that the role of the classroom teacher in the assessment process is realistic? In what areas do you feel comfortable participating? In what areas are you uncomfortable?

▶ Ask questions about the assessment process. Special education teachers and school psychologists should be committed to clarifying the nature of the assessments used and the interpretation of the results.

▶ Seek help as needed in conveying information to parents. Special education teachers may offer the support you need during a conference.

▶ Provide input. Formal test data should not be allowed to contradict observations in the classroom about a student's ability, achievement, and learning patterns. A valid diagnostic picture should bring together multiple sources of data.

▶ Observe assessment procedures. If time and facilities are available (e.g., a one-way mirror), observing the testing process can be educational and can enhance your ability to take part in decision making.

▶ Consider issues of possible bias. Since formal assessments are often administered by an individual relatively unknown to the child (e.g., a psychologist), inadvertent bias factors between examiner and examinee may be more likely to creep into the results. Work with other staff to ensure an unbiased process.

▶ Avoid viewing assessment as a means of confirming a set of observations or conclusions about a student's difficulties. Assessment is exploratory and may not lead to expected results. Too often, after a student is not judged eligible for special services, various parties feel resentment toward the assessment process. However, the key commitment should be to elicit useful information to help the student, not to arrive at a foregone eligibility decision that may please the student, parent, or teacher.

Final Thoughts

The intent of this chapter is to provide an overview of the special education programs and services that are available in schools today. Despite the availability of services, certain conditions must exist for teachers to address the needs of students with challenging characteristics who are placed in inclusive classrooms. Five basic teacher needs can be identified:

1. Teachers need comprehensive training in how to work with these students.
2. Teachers need certain knowledge and skills to be successful with these students.
3. Teachers need a wealth of information about the students they teach.
4. Teachers need adequate time to collaborate with other teachers within the school.
5. Teachers need appropriate supports to be successful—it requires a "village" approach.

The special education process discussed in this chapter provides essential services to students who need them. This process does require that efficient and effective procedures are in place in schools. More importantly, for this process to work, the dedication of administration and staff to fulfilling the goals of providing an appropriate education to students with special needs is essential.

Summary

Prereferral Intervention

▶ All procedures associated with special education programs must be consistent with due-process requirements.

▶ Each state provides timelines that govern the referral, assessment, and IEP processes.

▶ Prereferral intervention is a process of assisting students in the general education classroom prior to referral for full assessment.

▶ Child study or teacher assistance committees are responsible for helping teachers modify instruction for a student experiencing learning difficulties.

▶ Well-trained child study teams can assist teachers and limit referrals.

The Special Education Process

▶ The formal referral process initiates a series of activities.

▶ Not all referrals have merit and therefore require evaluation.

▶ A comprehensive evaluation precedes eligibility determination.

▶ The IEP includes many required components.

▶ The three essential elements of the IEP document are present levels of educational performance, measurable annual goals, and short-term objectives/benchmarks.

▶ Behavioral intervention plans (BIPs) are required for certain students.

▶ Transition services are mandated for all students with IEPs who are age 14.

- Some students can qualify for extended school year services.
- Goals within the IEP are reviewed annually, and a comprehensive reevaluation is conducted every three years.
- The final regulations of the IDEA Amendments of 1997 contain very specific mandates for assessment, developing the IEP or IFSP, and ensuring parental involvement throughout the special education process.

Section 504 Eligibility and Planning
- Some students who do not qualify under IDEA may qualify for services under Section 504.
- Eligibility is determined by whether a person has a physical or mental impairment that results in a substantial limitation in one or more major life activities.
- If a student qualifies under 504, an accommodation plan is typically developed.

Assessment Practices Throughout the Special Education Process
- Assessment includes testing and a broader range of methods that help define a student's strengths and problems leading to the development of educational interventions.

- Formal assessment is based on the administration of commercial instruments, typically for survey or diagnostic purposes.
- Informal assessment includes a variety of tools that can enhance a teacher's knowledge of students' learning needs.
- Curriculum-based measures are tied to the class curriculum and assess a student within this context.
- Ecological assessment places the evaluative data within the context of a student's environment.
- Authentic and portfolio assessment documents a student's ability to construct, perform, produce, or demonstrate a task.
- The control of bias in assessment is not only essential to accurate and fair evaluation, but is also a legal requirement.
- Classroom teachers may not administer the formal assessments but nevertheless are important members of any assessment process and should be informed about the assessment process and the IEP.

Further Readings

Bedard, E. (1995). Collaboration in educational planning: A parent's perspective. *LD Forum, 20,* 23–25.

Bauevens, J., & Hourcade, J. (1995). *Cooperative teaching: Rebuilding the schoolhouse for all students.* Austin, TX: Pro-Ed.

Blalock, G., & Patton, J. R. (1996). Transition and students with learning disabilities. *Journal of Learning Disability, 29,* 7–16.

Cummings, R., & Fishers, G. (1993). *The survival guide for teenagers with LD.* Minneapolis, MN: Free Spirit.

Dowdy, C. A. (1996). Vocational rehabilitation and special education. *Journal of Learning Disabilities, 2*(9), 137–147.

Dunn, K., & Dunn, K. (1993). *Trouble with school: A family story about LD.* Rockville, MD: Woodbine House.

Gehret, J. (1990). *The don't-give-up kid and learning disabilities.* Fairport, NY: Verbal Images.

Gehret, J. (1993). *Before the well runs dry: Taking care of yourself as a parent of an LD/ADD child.* Springville, VA: EDRS. (For information on ordering, write to EDRS, 7420 Fullerton Road, Suite 110, Springville, VA, 22153-2852.)

Gersten, R. (1998). Recent advances in instructional research for students with learning disabilities: An overview. *Learning Disabilities Research & Practice, 13*(3), 162–170.

Gregg, N., Heggoy, S. J., Stapleton, M., Jackson, R. S., & Morris, R. (1996). Eligibility for college learning disability services. *Learning Disabilities: A Multidisciplinary Journal, 1,* 29–36.

Hadden, S., & Fowler, S. A. (1997). Preschool: A new beginning for children and parents. *The Council for Exceptional Children, 30*(1), 36–39.

Hammill, D. D. (1993). A brief look at the learning disabilities movement in the United States. *Journal of Learning Disabilities, 2,* 295–310.

Janover, C. (1988). *A boy with dyslexia.* Burlington, VT: Waterfront Books.

Latham, P., & Latham, P. (1993). *Learning disabilities and the law.* Washington, DC: JKL Communication.

Meese, R. (1992). Adapting textbooks for children in mainstreamed classrooms. *Teaching Exceptional Children, 24,* pp. 49–51.

Michaels, C. A. (1994). Employment issues: Transition from school to work. In C. A. Michaels (Ed.), *Transition, strategies for persons with learning disabilities* (pp. 119–152). San Diego: Singular Publishing.

Smith, T. E., Dowdy, C., Polloway, E., & Blalock, G. (1997). *Children and adults with learning disabilities.* Boston: Allyn and Bacon.

 # VideoWorkshop Extra!

If the VideoWorkshop package was included with your textbook, go to Chapter 4 of the Companion Website (www.ablongman.com/sppd4e) and click on the VideoWorkshop button. Follow the instructions for viewing video clip 1. Then consider this information along with what you've read in Chapter 4 while answering the following questions.

1. In the video clip, Dr. Denti explains what information a general education teacher should bring to an IEP meeting.

This chapter also discusses the role of general education teachers in the development of an IEP. Based on these two sources, develop a checklist that general educators can use to prepare for IEP meetings.

2. After an IEP meeting has occurred, what is a classroom teacher's obligation during implementation of the IEP? Support your answer with information from the video clip and the chapter.

5 Teaching Students with Attention Deficit/Hyperactivity Disorder

After reading this chapter, you should be able to

1. discuss the legal basis for services to students with attention deficit/hyperactivity disorder (ADHD).
2. describe the characteristics and identification process for students with ADHD, including the impact of cultural diversity.
3. discuss educational, technological, and medical intervention.
4. design strategies to enhance instruction and classroom adaptations.
5. develop methods for promoting a sense of community and social acceptance.

Jake was always described as a "handful." He was the second son, so his mom was used to lots of noise and activity, but nothing prepared her for Jake. He was always into something, he climbed everything, he pulled all the toys out at once, and he was fussy and seldom slept. As he entered school, his mom hoped that the scheduled day would help, but his teachers complained and called her often to discuss how difficult Jake was to manage. He was held back in kindergarten to allow him an extra year to mature, but he didn't make the progress that was hoped for. He was still disruptive and frequently in trouble with teachers.

At the same time, everyone else seemed to love Jake. He talked all the time and could really entertain a group. From the beginning, he was an excellent athlete. Baseball, swimming, football, wrestling, and basketball kept him busy but didn't really leave enough time for homework to be completed properly. He was described as "all boy!" Because he was so intelligent, he was able to make passing grades without much effort, but he never excelled in school. Teachers always called him an underachiever and told his parents frequently that he just wasn't trying. He tried medication for one year for his hyperactivity, but that was dropped over the summer and never started again.

During high school Jake was state heavyweight champion and placed fourth in the nation in wrestling. He made the regional all-star football team, but his teachers still complained about his attitude and commitment to his studies; he had a short attention span and was easily distracted. Jake became frustrated as more effort was needed to pass all his subjects. He wanted to go to a good college and expected a scholarship, but he had to graduate with a grade point average that met the college standards. With this goal in mind, he agreed to begin taking medication, and he and his mom met with his teachers to develop a plan to improve his grades and behavior. Jake also met with a psychologist several times to discuss strategies that would make him more independent. The plan worked, and Jake got his scholarship. Without the adaptations, strategy training, and medication, Jake and his parents wonder how different his life would be.

QUESTIONS TO CONSIDER

1. How could Jake's early school years have been made more successful?
2. What rights did Jake have to get special adaptations from his teachers?
3. How successful do you think Jake will be in college?

Attention deficit/hyperactivity disorder (ADHD) is a complex condition that has been a major concern in public education for several years. It is a complicated but intriguing condition and a real challenge for classroom teachers. This condition remains controversial because professional perspectives and personal opinions vary regarding the nature of ADHD and effective intervention techniques. In the past few years, awareness of this disability has significantly increased, along with successful intervention plans for students who struggle with it. The National Institutes of Health (NIH) released a consensus statement that despite the controversy, there is enough scientific evidence to conclude that ADHD is a valid disorder (National Institutes of Health, 2000). It is a lifelong condition, and it has negative impact on an individual's social, educational, and occupational life (Weyandt, 2001).

The legal basis for services and protection against discrimination for ADHD comes from IDEA and Section 504 of the Rehabilitation Act of 1973 (PL 93–112). When IDEA was reauthorized in 1990, a major debate took place as to whether to add ADHD as a separate handicapping condition. Some people were very disappointed when that change was not made. However, in 1991 the U.S. Department of Education did issue a policy memorandum indicating that students with attention deficit disorder (the department's term) who need special education or related services can qualify for those services under existing categories.

The category of "other health impaired" (OHI) was recommended as the appropriate classification for students whose primary disability is ADHD. This category includes "any chronic and acute condition that results in limited alertness and adversely affects educational performance" (U.S. Department of Education, 1991).

The final regulations for implementation of the 1999 amendments to IDEA actually amended the definition of OHI to add attention deficit disorder (ADD) and ADHD to the list of conditions that could render a child eligible under OHI. The definition provides the explanation that a child with ADD or ADHD has a heightened awareness or sensitivity to environmental stimuli, and this results in a limited alertness to the educational environment (U.S. Department of Education, 1999). In other words, the child is so busy paying attention to everything going on around him or her that attention is directed away from the important educational stimuli, and school performance is negatively affected. The category of "other health impaired" is currently considered the fastest growing category (Latham & Latham, 1999).

Before the 1999 U.S. Department of Education regulations were published, many professionals assumed that students with ADHD were being served under the category of learning disability, behavior disorders, or mental retardation (Reid, Maag, Vasa, & Wright, 1994). These categories may be used; however, the student with ADHD must also have the coexisting learning or emotional impairment. The number of students with ADHD requesting services under IDEA has grown dramatically, but a sizable number of students with ADHD are floundering in school and not qualifying for special services that would encourage academic success. In an effort to find a basis for services for this population, the U.S. Department of Education determined that Section 504 applies to these individuals and serves as a legal mandate to provide assessment and services. Section 504 has been and may continue to be the primary legal basis for services to this population.

Section 504 is not a special education law but a civil rights law. It mandates special education opportunities and related aids and services to meet individual educational needs for persons with disabilities as adequately as the needs of those who are not disabled. Section 504 provides protection for a larger group of individuals with disabilities and differs in some respects from IDEA. It protects any individual with a disability, defined as "any physical or mental impairment that substantially limits one or more major life activities." Since learning is one of the stated life activities, it was determined that this law does apply to schools, specifically those receiving federal funding. If a school has reason to believe that any student has a disability as defined under Section 504, the school must evaluate the student. If the student is determined to be disabled under the law, the

CONSIDER THIS

Do the results of the study by Reid and his colleagues surprise you? Although you have not yet studied behavior disorders or mental retardation, can you predict how they differ from learning disabilities? How would ADHD overlap with these other disabilities?

CROSS-REFERENCE

Section 504 of the Rehabilitation Act of 1973 and IDEA are introduced in Chapter 1. Compare the provisions of these important legislative acts.

school must develop and implement a plan for the delivery of services that are needed (Council of Administrators of Special Education, 1992).

If a student with ADHD does not qualify for services under IDEA, services might be made available under Section 504. Although its required services and procedures are not as specific as those found in IDEA, Section 504 does provide an avenue for accommodating the needs of students with ADHD in the schools. The intent of this law is to level the playing field for individuals with disabilities, creating an equal opportunity for success (Smith, 2002) Figure 5.1 is a flowchart demonstrating how both IDEA and Section 504 work together to provide appropriate services to students with ADHD.

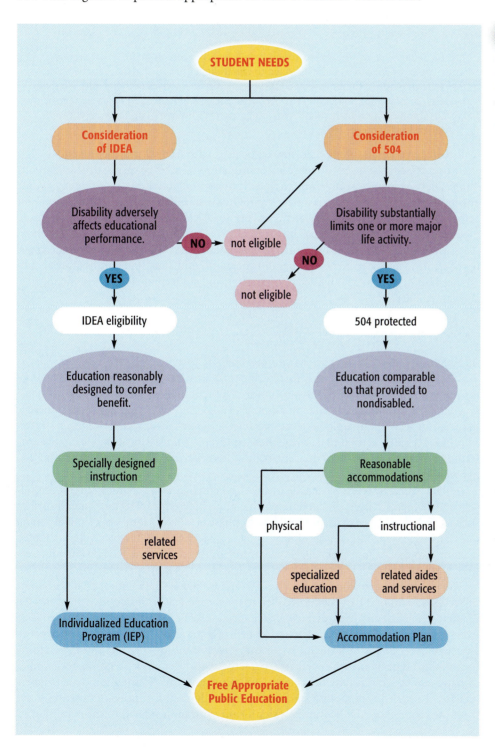

FIGURE 5.1

IDEA/504 Flowchart

From *Student Access: A Resource Guide for Educators: Section 504 of the Rehabilitation Act of 1973* (p. 25) by the Council for Administrators of Special Education, 1992, Reston, VA: Author. Used by permission.

Teachers must understand ADHD in order to recognize its characteristics and, most important, to implement effective intervention strategies and accommodations to facilitate success for affected children in their classrooms.

Basic Concepts About Attention Deficit/ Hyperactivity Disorder

Attention deficit/hyperactivity disorder is an invisible, hidden disability in that no unique physical characteristics and no definitive psychological or physiological tests differentiate these children from others. However, ADHD is not hard to spot in the classroom.

> Just look and listen as you walk through the places where children are—particularly those places where children are expected to behave in a quiet, orderly, productive fashion. In such places, children with ADHD will identify themselves quite readily. They will be doing or not doing something that frequently results in their receiving a barrage of comments and criticisms such as, "Why don't you ever listen?" "Think before you act." "Pay attention." (Fowler, 1992, p. 3)

Unfortunately, the disabling behaviors associated with ADHD may be misunderstood and misinterpreted as a sign of being lazy, unorganized, and even disrespectful. The condition can be recognized only through specific behavioral manifestations that may occur during the learning process. As a **developmental disability,** ADHD becomes apparent before the age of 7; however, in as many as 70% to 80% of the cases, it continues to cause problems in adulthood (Heiligenstein, Conyers, Beirns, & Smith, 1998). During the school years ADHD may have an impact on success in both academic and nonacademic areas. It occurs in various countries throughout the world and across all cultural, racial, and socioeconomic groups. It can also affect children and adults with all levels of intelligence (Weyandt, 2001).

Attention Deficit/Hyperactivity Disorder Defined

Although a variety of terms such as *minimal brain dysfunction* and *attention deficit disorder* have been used over the years to describe this disorder, currently the term *attention deficit/hyperactivity disorder* is most common. The terminology stems from the *Diagnostic and Statistical Manual of Mental Disorders* (4th ed.; DSM-IV; American Psychiatric Association, 1994). On a global level, the *International Classification of Diseases* (10th ed.; ICD–10, 1992) is used to describe these children. This classification system uses the term *hyperkinetic disorders* to describe conditions related to problems in attention and hyperactivity.

ADHD primarily refers to deficits in attention and behaviors characterized by impulsivity and hyperactivity. A distinction must be made between ADHD and other disorders such as sleep disorders, conduct disorder (e.g., physical fighting), and oppositional defiant disorder (e.g., recurrent patterns of disobedience). The DSM-IV has been widely adopted as a guide to the diagnosis of ADHD. According to this document, ADHD encompasses four types of disabilities. The diagnostic criteria for ADHD are presented in Figure 5.2.

The identification of the specific type of ADHD depends on the number of symptoms in Sections 1 and/or 2 that can be ascribed to the individual. For example, a combination of attention deficit and hyperactivity is designated if six or more symptoms are identified from each section. A diagnosis of attention deficit/hyperactivity with predominant problems with attention is indicated if six or more symptoms are identified from Section 1 only. A third type of attention deficit/hyperactivity disorder has a predominant number of hyperactivity-impulsivity behaviors. Last, a category called "attention deficit/hyperactivity disorder not otherwise specified" is typically used for individuals who do not meet the criteria for ADHD but have significant symptoms related to the condition.

ADHD encompasses four types of disabilities: inattention, hyperactivity-impulsivity, hyperactivity, and impulsivity.

FIGURE 5.2

Criteria for Attention Deficit/Hyperactivity Disorder

From *Diagnostic and Statistical Manual of Mental Disorders* (4th ed., pp. 83–85) by the American Psychiatric Association, 1993, Washington, DC: Author. Used by permission.

A. Either (1) or (2):
   (1) **Inattention:** At least six of the following symptoms of inattention have persisted for at least six months to a degree that is maladaptive and inconsistent with developmental level:
      (a) Often fails to give close attention to details or makes careless mistakes in school-work, work, or other activities
      (b) Often has difficulty sustaining attention in tasks or play activities
      (c) Often does not seem to listen to what is being said to him or her
      (d) Often does not follow through on instructions and fails to finish schoolwork, chores, or duties in the workplace (not due to oppositional behavior or failure to understand instructions)
      (e) Often has difficulties organizing tasks and activities
      (f) Often avoids and strongly dislikes tasks that require sustained mental effort (such as schoolwork and homework)
      (g) Often loses things necessary for tasks and activities (e.g., school assignments, pencils, books, tools, or toys)
      (h) Often is easily distracted by extraneous stimuli
      (i) Often is forgetful in daily activities
   (2) **Hyperactivity–Impulsivity:** At least six of the following symptoms of hyperactivity-impulsivity have persisted for at least six months to a degree that is maladaptive and inconsistent with developmental level:
      Hyperactivity:
      (a) Often fidgets with hands or feet or squirms in seat
      (b) Often leaves seat in classroom or in other situations in which remaining in seat is expected
      (c) Often runs about or climbs excessively in situations where it is inappropriate (in adolescents and adults, may be limited to subjective feelings of restlessness)
      (d) Often has difficulty playing or engaging in leisure activities quietly
      (e) Always is "on the go" or acts as if "driven by a motor"
      (f) Often talks excessively
      Impulsivity:
      (g) Often bursts out answers to questions before the questions have been completed
      (h) Often has difficulty waiting in lines or awaiting turn in games or group situations
      (i) Often interrupts or intrudes on others (e.g., butts into others' conversations or games)

B. Some symptoms that caused impairment were present before age 7.

C. Some symptoms that cause impairment are present in two or more settings (e.g., at school, work, and at home).

D. There must be clear evidence of clinically significant impairment in social, academic, or occupational functioning.

E. Does not occur exclusively during the course of a pervasive developmental disorder, schizophrenia or other psychotic disorder, and is not better accounted for by mood disorder, anxiety disorder, dissociative disorder, or a personality disorder.

Identification of the characteristics associated with ADHD is critical in the diagnosis. The teacher often brings the ADHD-like behaviors to the attention of the parents. When parents initiate contact with the school to find help, as Jake's parents did, they will be served best by teachers who are already well informed about this condition and the special education assessment process.

CONSIDER THIS

Review the characteristics and criteria in Figure 5.2. Can you think of examples of situations in which these characteristics might be observed in a school setting? at home? at work?

Prevalence and Causes of Attention Deficit/Hyperactivity Disorder

ADHD is more common than any other child psychiatric disorder (Nolan, Volpe, Gadow, & Sprafkin, 1999). Estimates of the prevalence of attention deficit/hyperactivity disorder in school-age children range from a conservative figure of less than 2% to a more liberal figure of 30%; however, 3%–5% is most probable (American Psychiatric Association, 1994). The extreme differences found in prevalence figures reflect the lack of agreement on a definition and the difficulty and variance in identification procedures. Regardless of the exact prevalence figure, a substantial number of students with this condition attend general education classrooms. Hyperactivity and impulsivity are most likely to be observed in preschool and elementary children; inattention is more common in adolescents. While boys are overrepresented in each subtype (Nolan et al., 1999), there is some concern that girls and children from minority families are at risk for not being identified to receive services (Bussing, Zima, Perwien, Belin, & Widawski, 1998). Several individuals have noted that the prevalence of ADHD is increasing; however, it is generally felt that this perception is due to the increased media attention that alerts parents and teachers and to better training of clinicians and physicians (Weyandt, 2001).

Although the exact cause of ADHD is unknown, several theories have been proposed, and rigorous research is ongoing. Most professionals agree that ADHD is a neurobiologically based condition. Following is a summary of the research on possible causes as summarized by Weyandt (2001):

▶ Neuroanatomical—related to brain structure. Unexplained differences such as smaller right frontal regions, smaller brain size in boys with ADHD, and a smaller cerebellum have been found. It is not known whether these differences are due to genetics or the environment, or if they are even related to or responsible for the symptoms of ADHD.

▶ Neurochemical—related to a chemical imbalance in the brain or a deficiency in chemicals that regulate behavior. This research usually focuses on neurotransmitters, chemicals in the brain responsible for communication between brain cells and necessary for behavior and thought to occur. Stimulant medication is proposed to stimulate or regulate production of the neurotransmitters and increase brain activity. As a result of conflicting findings, this research is currently inconclusive.

▶ Neurophysiological—related to brain function. Various medical tests such as the EEG and brain scans have suggested that individuals with ADHD have reduced brain activity (were found to be in a low state of arousal) and reduced blood flow in the right frontal region, an area that produces important neurotransmitters and helps regulate impulse control, attention, and planning. To be considered conclusive, these tests need to be validated on many more individuals at various ages and on both females and males.

▶ Neuropsychological—dysfunction of the frontal lobes resulting in deficits in attention, self-regulation, impulsivity, and planning, collectively called executive function. Renowned researcher Dr. Russell Barkley (1997) proposed a unifying theory that individuals with ADHD have deficits in behavioral inhibition that is caused by physiological differences in the brain. These differences result in the executive function deficits listed previously in addition to impairments in working memory, problem solving, motor control, and using internal speech (i.e., self-talk) to guide behavior. Other studies support this model, but again, more research is needed.

Some data suggest that genetics plays a significant role in ADHD, evidenced by a higher prevalence rate in some families. Studies have shown that biological parents, and siblings, and other family members of individuals with this disorder have higher rates of ADHD than expected in the general population. For example, one study found that if one biological parent has ADHD, there is a 57% chance that a child will have the condition (Biederman et al., 1995).

Barkley (1999–2000) also noted that pre- and postnatal events may cause ADHD. Premature birth is associated with ADHD; other events include complications during pregnancy, fetal exposure to tobacco or alcohol, head trauma, lead poisoning in preschool years, and strep infection. While many factors are still being seriously considered as a potential cause of ADHD, others have little or no evidence to support them. These include aspects of the physical environment such as fluorescent lighting, soaps, disinfectants, yeast, preservatives, food coloring, aspartame, certain fruits and vegetables, sugar, social factors, and poor parental management (Barkley, 1998; Weyandt, 2001). For most students, the precise cause of the problem may never be understood. Although many parents want to understand why their children have a developmental disability such as ADHD, its cause is really not relevant to educational strategies or medical treatment. These can succeed without pinpointing the root of the problem.

Characteristics of Students with Attention Deficit/Hyperactivity Disorder

The characteristics of ADHD manifest themselves in many different ways in the class-room. Recognizing them and identifying adaptations or strategies to lessen the impact in the classroom constitute a significant challenge for teachers. The characteristics listed in the DSM-IV criteria highlight the observable behaviors. Barkley (1998) groups these char-acteristics into the following three most common areas of difficulty:

1. *Limited sustained attention or persistence of attention to tasks:* Particularly during te-dious, long-term tasks, the students become rapidly bored and frequently shift from one uncompleted activity to another. They may lose concentration during long work periods and fail to complete routine work unless closely supervised. The problem is not due to inability to comprehend the instructions, memory impairment, or defiance. The instructions simply do not regulate behavior or stimulate the desired response.
2. *Reduced impulse control or limited delay of gratification:* Individuals often find it hard to wait their turn while talking to others or playing. Students may not stop and think before acting or speaking. They may have difficulty resisting distractions while con-centrating and working toward long-term goals and long-term rewards, preferring to work on shorter tasks that promise immediate reinforcement.
3. *Excessive task-irrelevant activity or activity poorly regulated to match situational demands:* Individuals with ADHD are often extremely fidgety and restless. Their movement seems excessive and often not directly related to the task—for example, tapping pen-cils, rocking, or shifting positions frequently. They also have trouble sitting still and inhibiting their movements when the situation demands it.

Other areas of difficulty in psychological functioning include working memory or remembering to do things, sensing time or using time as efficiently as their peers, and using their internal language to talk to themselves in order to think about events and purposefully direct their own behavior. They have problems inhibiting their reaction to events, often appearing more emotional or hotheaded and less emotionally mature. They are easily frustrated and seem to lack willpower or self-discipline. They may have difficulty following instructions or rules, even following their own "to-do" lists. They demonstrate considerable variation in the quantity, quality, and speed with which they perform their assigned tasks. Their relatively high performance on some occasions, coupled with low levels of accuracy on other occasions, can be baffling. Low levels of performance often occur with repetitive or tedious tasks.

The symptoms are likely to change from one situation to another. More ADHD symp-toms may be shown in group settings, during boring work, when students are without supervision, and when work has to be done later in the day. Individuals behave better when there is immediate payoff for doing the right thing, when they enjoy what they are doing or find it interesting, when they are in one-on-one situations, and when they can work earlier during the day (Barkley, 1998).

The characteristics of ADHD may also be present in adulthood; only an estimated 20% to 35% of children with the disorder will not be impaired as adults. For some individuals the condition continues to cause problems and limitations in the world of work, as well as in other life activities. Figure 5.3 provides a summary of common characteristics for varying age groups including adults. Barkley (1999–2000) reports that adults with ADHD are more likely to be fired, typically change jobs three times more often than adults with-out the disorder in a ten-year period, are more likely to divorce, and typically have more

CONSIDER THIS

Refer to the opening vignette in this chapter. Identify Jake's characteristics that would lead a teacher or parent to suspect ADHD.

TEACHING TIP

As another technique for recording a student's behavior, observe a child for 3–5 minutes every hour during a school day, and document whether the child is on or off task. Record what the child is supposed to be doing, what he or she is actually doing, and the consequences of that behavior (e.g., praise, ignoring). Figure the per-centage of on- and off-task behavior.

> **FIGURE 5.3**
>
> **Common Characteristics of Individuals with ADHD**
>
> From *An ADHD Primer* (p. 17) by L. L. Weyandt, 2001, Boston: Allyn and Bacon.
>
> **Early Childhood**
> Excessive activity level
> Talking incessantly
> Difficulty paying attention
> Difficulty playing quietly
> Impulsive and easily distracted
> Academic underachievement
>
> **Middle Childhood**
> Excessive fidgeting
> Difficulty remaining seated
> Messy and careless work
> Failing to follow instructions
> Failing to follow through on tasks
> Academic underachievement
>
> **Adolescence**
> Feelings of restlessness
> Difficulty engaging in quiet sedentary activities
> Forgetful and inattentive
> Impatience
> Engaging in potentially dangerous activities
> Academic underachievement
>
> **Adulthood**
> Feelings of restlessness
> Difficulty engaging in quiet sedentary activities
> Frequent shifts from one uncompleted activity to another
> Frequent interrupting or intruding on others
> Avoidance of tasks that allow for little spontaneous movement
> Relationship difficulties
> Anger management difficulties
> Frequent changes in employment

traffic citations and accidents. On the positive side, the outcome is much brighter for individuals with ADHD who receive treatment such as medication, behavior management, and social skills training. Research is currently investigating the best jobs for individuals with ADHD; highly intense jobs and those requiring brainstorming have been suggested. Up to 35% may be self-employed by the age of thirty. In any case, ADHD and the treatment of ADHD can have significant effects on adult outcomes. Teachers who can identify and plan meaningful interventions for students with ADHD can have a powerful impact on their success during the school years as well as their quality of life as adults.

Identification, Assessment, and Eligibility

For years the assessment and diagnosis of attention deficit/hyperactivity disorder were considered the responsibility of psychologists, psychiatrists, and physicians, and typically these individuals are still involved in the identification process. However, the mandates of Section 504 of PL 93–112 as interpreted by the assistant secretary for civil rights (Cantu, 1993) charged public education personnel with responsibility for this assessment as needed. If a school district suspects that a child has a disability that substantially limits a major life activity such as learning, the district is required to provide an assessment. If the disability is confirmed, the school district must then develop a plan and provide services. Since ADHD is often covered under Section 504, a child suspected of having it may be eligible both for assessment and services.

Because teachers are often the first to suspect the presence of ADHD, they should be familiar with its specific behaviors and the commonly used assessment techniques. Although specially trained school personnel must perform the formal assessment for ADHD, teachers participate on the interdisciplinary team that reviews the assessment data to determine whether the attention problems limit learning and to plan the individualized program, if appropriate. Teachers may also be called on to complete informal assessment instruments that, with other data, will help in determining the presence of ADHD.

Weyandt (2001) supports the participation of teachers as an important source of information in ADHD assessment. She notes that teachers spend a significant amount of time with students in a variety of academic and social situations and have a better sense of normal behaviors for the comparison group. Burnley (1993) proposes a four-part plan that could be implemented to structure the interdisciplinary assessment process for schools. This plan is similar to that used by school personnel as they determine eligibility for services under IDEA. A modified version of Burnley's process is described in the following sections. It is important to note that parents have rights guaranteed throughout this process (see Rights & Responsibilities).

Steps in the Assessment Process

Step 1: Preliminary Assessment and Initial Child Study Meeting   Initially, a teacher who has been trained in identifying the symptoms of attention deficit/hyperactivity disorder according to the school's criteria may begin to observe that a particular student manifests these behaviors in the classroom to a greater degree than his or her peers do. At this point, the teacher should begin to keep a log to document the child's ADHD-like behaviors,

Parent Rights Under Section 504

Section 504 of the Rehabilitation Act provides services for students identified as having a disability that substantially limits a major life activity. As parents, you have the following rights:

1. The right to be informed of your rights under Section 504 of the Rehabilitation Act.
2. The right for your child to have equal opportunities to participate in academic, nonacademic, and extracurricular activities in your school.
3. The right to be notified about referral, evaluation, and programs for your child.
4. The right for your child to be evaluated fairly.
5. The right, if eligible for services under 504, for your child to receive accommodations, modifications, and related services that will meet his/her needs as well as the needs of nondisabled students are met.

6. The right for your child to be educated with nondisabled peers as much as possible.
7. The right to an impartial hearing if you disagree with the school regarding your child's educational program.
8. The right to review and obtain copies of your child's school records.
9. The right to request attorney fees related to securing your rights under Section 504.
10. The right to request changes in the educational program of your child.

Signed: Parent(s): _____   Date: _____
School Representative: _____   Date: _____

For follow-up questions about parent rights under Section 504, go to Chapter 5 of the Companion Website (ablongman.com/sppd4e) and click Rights & Responsibilities.

From *Section 504 and Public Schools: A Practical Guide* (p. 73) by T. E. C. Smith and J. R. Patton, 1998, Austin, TX: Pro-Ed. Adapted by permission.

FIGURE 5.4

Sample Form for Documenting Classroom Manifestations of ADHD-like Behaviors

Teacher: _____   School: _____

Child: _____   Grade: _____   Age: _____

Class Activity	Child's Behavior	Date/Time

noting the times at which behaviors appear to be more intense, more frequent, or of a longer duration. Figure 5.4 provides a simple format for this observational log. For example, a teacher might document "bad behavior" such as constantly interrupting, excessive talking, not following directions, leaving a designated area, not finishing assignments, or not turning in homework.

If the teacher's anecdotal records confirm the continuing presence of these behaviors, the referral process should be initiated and the observational log turned in as documentation. At that point a less biased observer should come into the classroom to provide comparative information (Schaughency & Rothlind, 1991). Schaughency and Rothlind (1991) caution that this form of data collection is costly in terms of professional time; however, if the observation period is not long enough, behavior that occurs infrequently may be missed. The assessment team should realize that direct observation is just one source of information to be considered in the identification process.

As soon as the school suspects that a child is experiencing attention problems, the parents should be notified and invited to meet with the child study team. Often the parents, the teacher, the principal, and the school counselor will come together for the initial meeting. During this meeting parents should be asked to respond to the observations of the school personnel and describe their own experiences with problems in attention, impulsivity, and overactivity outside of the school setting. If the team agrees that additional testing is needed, a trained individual should step in to direct the assessment process. This person must understand the impact of ADHD on the family; the bias that might occur during the assessment process because of cultural, socioeconomic, language, and ethnic factors; and other conditions that may mimic ADHD and prevent an accurate diagnosis.

Step 2: Formal Assessment Process: Follow-Up Meeting of the Child Study Team   Although schools are not required to use a specific set of criteria to identify attention deficit/hyperactivity disorder, the DSM-IV criteria described earlier are highly recommended (Weyandt, 2001). The following questions, recommended by Schaughency and Rothlind (1991), need to be addressed during the formal assessment process:

1. Is there an alternative educational diagnosis or medical condition that accounts for the attention difficulties?
2. Are the behaviors demonstrated by the individual developmentally appropriate? (For example, individuals with mental retardation may be diagnosed correctly as having ADHD, but only if their attention problems are significantly different from those of the individuals at comparable developmental levels.)

3. Does the individual meet the DSM-IV criteria?
4. Do the ADHD-like behaviors affect the individual's functioning in several settings, such as home, school, and other social situations?

A variety of methods and assessment procedures will be needed to answer these questions and provide a thorough evaluation for ADHD. The school system will most likely interview the child, parents, and teachers; obtain a developmental and medical history; review school records; review and/or evaluate intellectual and academic performance; administer rating scales to parents, teachers, and possibly peers; and document the impact of the behavior through direct observation.

After the necessary observations have been made, the interview process can begin. According to Weyandt (2001), an interview with parents might include the following topics:

▶ The student's medical, social-emotional, and developmental history
▶ Family history
▶ Parental concerns and perception of the problem
▶ The student's behavior at home
▶ Academic history and previous testing

Woodrich (1994) recommends that the following areas be addressed during the teacher interview:

▶ Class work habits and productivity
▶ Skill levels in academic subjects
▶ Length of time attention can be sustained for novel tasks and for monotonous tasks
▶ Degree of activity during class and on the playground
▶ Class structure and standards for self-control
▶ Degree of compliance with class rules
▶ Manifestation of more serious conduct problems
▶ Onset, frequency, and duration of inappropriate behavior in the antecedent events
▶ Peer acceptance and social skills
▶ Previous intervention techniques and special services now considered appropriate

An interview with the child is appropriate in many cases, to determine the child's perception of the reports by the teacher, attitude toward school and family, and perception of relationships with peers. Although the child's responses will be slanted by personal feelings, the interview still is an important source of information.

The assessment of achievement and intelligence is not required in the identification of ADHD. However, the results of achievement and intelligence tests might suggest that the child can qualify for services under IDEA (1997) in categories of learning disabilities or mental retardation. Also, knowing the levels of intelligence and achievement will help eventually in developing an intervention plan.

Rating scales that measure the presence of ADHD symptoms are widely used to quantify the severity of the behaviors. They offer a way to measure the extent of the problem objectively. Several informants who know the child in a variety of settings should complete rating scales. The results should be compared to responses from interviews and the results of observations. Some rating scales are limited to an assessment of the primary symptoms contained in the DSM-IV criteria; other assessment instruments are multidimensional and might address emotional-social status, communication, memory, reasoning and problem solving, and cognitive skills such as planning and self-evaluation. Figure 5.5 contains an excerpt from the "Strengths and Limitations Inventory: School Version" (Dowdy, Patton, Smith, & Polloway, 1998).

A medical examination is not required in the diagnosis of ADHD; however, because symptoms of certain medical conditions may mimic those of ADHD, a medical exam should be considered. Schools may hesitate to recommend it because, according to federal law, any medical examination required to assist the team in making a school-related decision is considered a "related service," and the school must provide it at no cost to the

FIGURE 5.5   **Sample Test Items from "Strength and Limitations Inventory: School Version"**

	Never Observed	Sometimes Observed	Often Observed	Very Often Observed
ATTENTION/IMPULSIVITY/HYPERACTIVITY				
Exhibits excessive nonpurposeful movement (can't sit still, stay in seat).				
Does not stay on task for appropriate periods of time.				
Verbally or physically interrupts conversations or activities.				
Does not pay attention to most important stimuli.				
REASONING/PROCESSING				
Makes poor decisions.				
Makes frequent errors.				
Has difficulty getting started.				
MEMORY				
Has difficulty repeating information recently heard.				
Has difficulty following multiple directions.				
Memory deficits impact daily activities.				
EXECUTIVE FUNCTION				
Has difficulty planning/organizing activities.				
Has difficulty attending to several stimuli at once.				
Has difficulty monitoring own performance throughout activity (self-monitoring).				
Has difficulty independently adjusting behavior (self-regulation).				
INTERPERSONAL SKILLS				
Has difficulty accepting constructive criticism.				
Exhibits signs of poor self-confidence.				
EMOTIONAL MATURITY				
Inappropriate emotion for situation.				
Displays temper outbursts.				
Does not follow classroom or workplace "rules."				

From *Attention Deficit/Hyperactivity Disorder in the Classroom: A Practical Guide for Teachers* (pp. 112–113), by C. A. Dowdy, J. R. Patton, T. E. C. Smith, and E. A. Polloway, 1998, Austin, TX: Pro-Ed. Reprinted by permission.

parents (Worthington, Patterson, Elliott, & Linkous, 1993). No specific laboratory tests have been developed to diagnose ADHD (American Psychiatric Association, 1994). However, a physician might identify sleep apnea, anemia, allergies, lead poisoning, side effects from medication, or other medical conditions as the primary cause of problem behaviors.

When the child study team reconvenes to review all of the data, the following DSM-IV (1994) criteria should be considered:

▶ Six or more of the 9 characteristics of inattention and/or 6 or more of the 9 symptoms of hyperactivity-impulsivity should be demonstrated as present for longer than six months.

▶ The behaviors observed should be considered maladaptive and developmentally inconsistent.

▶ The symptoms should have been observed prior to or by age 7.

▶ The limitations that stem from the characteristics should be observed in two or more settings (e.g., home, school, work).

▶ The characteristics are not considered solely the result of schizophrenia, pervasive developmental disorder, or other psychiatric disorder, and they are not better attributed to the presence of another mental disorder such as anxiety disorder or mood disorder.

The child study team should look for consistency across reports from the assessment instruments and the informants to validate the existence of ADHD. If it is confirmed, the team must determine whether it has caused an adverse effect on school performance and whether a special educational plan is needed. Montague, McKinney, and Hocutt (1994) cite the following questions developed by the Professional Group on Attention and Related Disorders (PGARD) to guide the team in determining educational needs:

1. Do the ADHD symptoms negatively affect learning to the extent that there is a discrepancy between the child's productivity with respect to listening, following directions, planning, organizing, or completing academic tasks requiring reading, math, writing, or spelling skills?

2. Are inattentive behaviors the result of cultural or language differences, socioeconomic disadvantage, or lack of exposure to education?

3. Are the inattentive behaviors evidence of stressful family functioning (e.g., death or divorce), frustration related to having unattainable educational goals, abuse, or physical or emotional disorders (e.g., epilepsy or depression)?

If question 1 is answered positively and questions 2 and 3 are answered negatively, the team can conclude that an educational need exists that requires special services. At that point, a planning meeting should address the educational program.

Step 3: Collaborative Meeting for Strategy Development   The collaborative meeting for strategy development might be very emotional and overwhelming for parents, or it might generate relief and hope that the services can truly assist the child. The team must be sensitive to the feelings of the parents and take adequate time to describe the results of the testing. If the parents are emotionally upset, it may help to wait a week before developing the intervention plan for school services.

Step 4: Follow-Up and Progress Review   After the educational plan has been developed, the parents and school personnel should monitor the child's progress closely to ensure success. Adjustments may be needed occasionally to maintain progress. For example, reinforcement for good behavior may eventually lose its novelty and need to be changed. The ultimate goal is to remove accommodations and support as the child becomes capable of self-regulating his or her behavior. As the setting and school personnel change each year, reevaluating the need for special services will yield benefits. As the student becomes more efficient in learning and demonstrates better social skills under one plan, a new, less restrictive plan must be designed to complement this growth.

CONSIDER THIS

If your school has a policy stipulating that teachers should not recommend services that the school system might have to pay for (e.g., a medical exam), how will you proceed when you feel a child is in need of such services? What are your options?

TEACHING TIP

Begin a parent conference by talking about the strengths of the student! Give parents time to respond to the limitations observed in the school setting by having them report examples of behavior from home and other environments.

Cultural and Linguistic Diversity

When ADHD coexists with cultural and linguistic diversity, it presents a special set of challenges to the educator. Failure to address the special needs of these children can be detrimental to their academic success. Issues related to assessment and cultural diversity have been discussed previously; the same concerns exist in the identification and treatment of students with ADHD. To address the needs of multicultural students with ADHD, teachers must become familiar with their unique values, views, customs, interests, and behaviors and their relation to instructional strategies (Wright, 1995). DSM-IV (American Psychiatric Association, 1994) simply states that service-eligible behaviors cannot be the result of cultural differences.

Barkley (1998) raises the issue that the chaotic home environment of many minority populations existing below the poverty level exacerbates the problems of children with ADHD. When teachers use carefully organized and structured instruction, these students benefit. Streeter and Grant (1993) encourage teachers to make educational experiences more meaningful to students by developing activities and homework that acknowledge cultural differences and build on the specific experiences of the student. Teachers can integrate personal and community experiences into teaching an academic concept to help make it relevant. Strategies and adaptations described in the following sections will be appropriate for all students with ADHD including the culturally diverse.

> **CONSIDER THIS**
>
> Complete an in-depth study of the characteristics or educational needs of a particular culture. Share your findings with other groups in the class.

Strategies for Curriculum and Instruction for Students with Attention Deficit/Hyperactivity Disorder

Treatment for students with ADHD is unique because professionals outside of education are often involved in the process of identification and intervention. Although no magic cure has been discovered for this disorder, many treatments are effective in its management. Barkley (1998) suggests that education of the school staff, the family, and the individuals with ADHD is one of the most important treatments. He also reports that parent training in child management is helpful, particularly when children are preadolescent, and that family therapy is often needed to improve communication, especially with teens. General and special education teachers need to work closely with parents, physicians, and support personnel to develop, monitor, and maintain successful interventions. For many students, adaptations in general education classes are enough to improve learning; however, other students may need special education support services and placement. Research has also concluded that medication is one of the most successful treatments to enhance learning for students with ADHD (Barkley, 1999–2000; Weyandt, 2001). The following sections will discuss these issues.

Continuum-of-Placement Options

Under Section 504 and IDEA, a local education agency must provide a free appropriate public education to each qualified child with a disability. The U.S. Department of Education suggests that the placement of choice for children with ADHD should be the general education classroom, with appropriate adaptations and interventions.

Although students with ADHD may be found in a variety of special education settings, the majority of students classified as special education students spend more than 80% of the school day in general education classes (U.S. Department of Education, 1999) . Since the general education teacher is responsible for the learning experience of students with ADHD most of the time, it is imperative that these teachers understand the condition and have strategies for dealing with it in their classrooms. Special educators must be knowledgeable in order to collaborate effectively with general educators to develop educational plans that might adapt curriculum, instruction, and environment. Both special education

The U.S. Department of Education notes that most children with ADHD are in general education classrooms.

and general education teachers also need to be effective in providing behavioral support and skillful in teaching students to regulate their own behavior.

Developing Educational Plans

If a local education agency decides that a child has a disability under Section 504, the school must determine the child's educational needs for regular and special education or related aids and services. Although this law does not mandate a written individualized education program, implementation of a written IEP is recommended (U.S. Department of Education, 1991). Most school systems have opted to develop written plans; they are generally referred to as student accommodation plans, individual accommodation plans, or 504 plans.

It is recommended that this plan be developed by a committee that includes parents, professionals, and, as often as possible, the student. The areas identified as causing significant limitations in learning should be the targets of the intervention plan. The committee should determine the least amount of adaptations needed to stimulate success in learning and social development. If medication therapy is being used, the plan should also indicate the school's role in administering the medication and special precautions or considerations regarding side effects (Katisyannis, Landrum, & Vinton, 1997). When a conservative intervention plan has been developed and implemented, additional goals and interventions can be added as needed.

Each local education agency must have an identified 504 coordinator or officer responsible for maintaining a fair and responsive evaluation process and plan for developing 504 plans. They monitor students' needs and communicate with parents and teachers as necessary. Although it is much simpler than an IEP, a 504 plan serves to document legally the services agreed upon by the team members. Jake's 504 plan is included later in the chapter.

The Role of Medication

Since many students with ADHD will be prescribed medication by their physicians, teachers need to understand the types of medications used, commonly prescribed dosages, intended effects, and potential side effects. Medication therapy can be defined as

> **TEACHING TIP**
>
> When you are employed in a new school district, meet the special education and 504 coordinators to obtain an overview of policies and procedures for assessment and delivery.

CONSIDER THIS

Adolescents often refuse to take medication prescribed for ADHD. What do you think happens during this developmental period that might account for this behavior?

treatment by chemical substances that prevent or reduce inappropriate behaviors, thus promoting academic and social gains for children with learning and behavior problems (Dowdy et al., 1998). Studies have shown that different outcomes occur for different children. In 70% to 80% of the cases, children with ADHD (ages six and older) respond in a positive manner to psychostimulant medication (Baren, 2000; Barkley, 1999–2000). The desired outcomes include increased concentration, completion of assigned tasks, increased work productivity, better handwriting and motor skills, improved social relations with peers and teachers, increased appropriate behaviors and emotional control, and reduction of inappropriate, disruptive behaviors such as talking out loud, getting out of seat, and breaking rules. These changes frequently lead to improved academic and social achievement as well as increased self-esteem.

For some children, the desired effects do not occur. In these situations the medication has no negative effect, but simply does not lead to the hoped-for results. However, parents and teachers often give up too soon, prematurely concluding that the medication did not help. It is important to contact the physician when no effect is noticed, because the dosage may need to be adjusted or a different type of medication may be needed. Barkley (1999–2000) reports that when individuals continue to try different stimulants when one fails, the success rate rises to 90%.

Another possible response to medication is side effects. Side effects are changes that are not desired. The most common side effect, loss of appetite, occurs more than 50% of the time; however, it has not been found to affect adult stature (Barkley, 1999–2000). Figure 5.6 shows the most common side effects of the medications used for ADHD. Parents and teachers may use this rating scale when communicating with each other and physicians. Teachers should constantly be on the lookout for signs of side effects and report any concerns to parents or the child's physician.

The most commonly prescribed medications for ADHD are *psychostimulants* such as Dexedrine (dextroamphetamine), Ritalin (methylphenidate), and Adderall (amphetamine salts). Studies have shown that Ritalin accounts for 90% of the market in stimulants prescribed (Weyandt, 2001). This medication is considered a mild central nervous system stimulant, available as tablets of 5, 10, and 20 mg for oral administration. It is effective for approximately 4 hours and is at its peak after 1.5–2.5 hours (*Physicians' Desk Reference*, 1994, p. 835). A typical dosage of Ritalin for an initial trial is 5 mg, two to three times daily. The dosage will be increased until the optimal response is obtained with the fewest side effects. The medication is thought to stimulate the underaroused central nervous system of individuals with ADHD, increasing the amount or efficiency of the neurotransmitters needed for attention, concentration, and planning (Weyandt, 2001). Students who are described as anxious or tense, have tics, or have a family history or diagnosis of *Tourette's syndrome* are generally not given Ritalin (*Physicians' Desk Reference*, 1999). Adderall is gaining in usage partly because it is effective for up to 15 hours and a second dose does not have to be taken at school. The specific dose of medicine must be determined individually for each child. Generally, greater side effects come from higher dosages, but some students may need a high dosage to experience the positive effects of the medication. No clear guidelines exist as to how long an individual should take medication. Both adolescents and adults have been found to respond positively to these stimulants.

Antidepressants are also used to manage ADHD. They are prescribed less frequently than psychostimulants and might include Tofranil (imipramine), Norpramin (desipramine), and Elavil (amytriptyline). These medications are generally used when negative side effects have occurred with stimulants, when the stimulants have not been effective, or when an individual is also depressed. The long-term use of antidepressants has not been well studied. Again, frequent monitoring is necessary for responsible management. Other medications that are used much less frequently include antipsychotics such as Mellaril (thioridazine), Thorazine (chlorpromazine), Catapres (clonidine), Eskalith (lithium), and Tegretol (carbamazepine). Whatever medication is prescribed by the child's physician, teachers should refer to the current *Physicians' Desk Reference* or ask the physi-

Side Effects Checklist: Stimulants

Child _____ Date Checked _____

Person Completing Form _____ Relationship to Child _____

I. SIDE EFFECTS

Directions: Please check any of the behaviors which this child exhibits while receiving his or her stimulant medication. If a child exhibits one or more of the behaviors below, please rate the extent to which you perceive the behavior to be a problem using the scale below (1 = Mild to 7 = Severe).

	Mild						Severe
1. Loss of appetite	1	2	3	4	5	6	7
2. Stomachaches	1	2	3	4	5	6	7
3. Headaches	1	2	3	4	5	6	7
4. Tics (vocal or motor)	1	2	3	4	5	6	7
5. Extreme mood changes	1	2	3	4	5	6	7
6. Cognitively sluggish/disoriented	1	2	3	4	5	6	7
7. Excessive irritability	1	2	3	4	5	6	7
8. Excessive nervousness	1	2	3	4	5	6	7
9. Decreased social interactions	1	2	3	4	5	6	7
10. Unusual or bizarre behavior	1	2	3	4	5	6	7
11. Excessive activity level	1	2	3	4	5	6	7
12. Light picking of fingertips	1	2	3	4	5	6	7
13. Lip licking	1	2	3	4	5	6	7

II. PSYCHOSOCIAL CONCERNS

Please address any concerns you have about this child's adjustment to medication (e.g., physical, social, emotional changes; attitudes toward the medication, etc.).

III. OTHER CONCERNS

If you have any other concerns about this child's medication (e.g., administration problems, dosage concerns), please comment below.

IV. PARENT CONCERNS (FOR PARENTS ONLY)

Using the same scale above, please check any behaviors which this child exhibits while at home.

	Mild						Severe
1. Insomnia; sleeplessness	1	2	3	4	5	6	7
2. Possible rebound effects (excessive hyperactivity, impulsivity, inattention)	1	2	3	4	5	6	7

FIGURE 5.6

Stimulant Side Effects Checklist

From *ADHD Project Facilitate: An In-Service Education Program for Educators and Parents* (p. 10) by R. Elliott, L. A. Worthington, and D. Patterson, Tuscaloosa: University of Alabama. Used by permission.

cian or pharmacist for a thorough description of the possible positive and negative outcomes for that medication. Table 5.1 contains a list of common myths associated with medication treatment for ADHD.

The following are considerations for teachers of students taking medication (Fowler, 1992; Howell, Evans, & Gardiner, 1997):

▶ Handle the dispensing of medication discreetly, but according to school policy. Don't make announcements in front of the class that it's time for a child to take his or her pill. Students, especially teens, are often very embarrassed by the necessity to "take a pill" during school. If it is not given in private, they may refuse the medication.

▶ Make sure the medication is given as prescribed. Although the child should not be pulled away from an important event, the dosage should be given as close as possible to the designated time.

❱ Avoid placing too much blame or credit for the child's behavior on the medication. All children will have good and bad days. When problems arise, teachers should avoid such comments as "Did you take your pill this morning?" Don't assume that improvement will be automatic; academics and social skills need to be taught directly.
❱ Monitor the behavior of the child, looking for any side effects.
❱ Communicate with the school nurse, the parents, and/or the physician.

Remember, not all children diagnosed with ADHD need medication. The decision to intervene medically should come only after a great deal of thought about the possibility of a variety of interventions. Children whose impairments are minimal are certainly less likely to need medication than those whose severe impairments result in major disruptions.

Although teachers and other school personnel are important members of a therapeutic team involved in exploring, implementing, and evaluating diverse treatment methods, the decision to try medication is primarily the responsibility of the parents and the physician. Teachers are generally cautioned by their school systems not to specifically recommend medication because the school may be held responsible for the charges incurred. Educators, therefore, find themselves in a dilemma when they feel strongly that medication is needed to address the symptoms of the ADHD. However, teachers must also realize that medication alone is insufficient. Students with ADHD need a multimodal approach, including the cognitive and behavioral strategies addressed in the following section.

Occasionally teachers and parents will hear of alternative treatment therapies that seem to offer a "quick fix." These are often advertised in newspapers and popular magazines or seen on television, but they seldom appear in professional literature. Alternative approaches described by Barkley (1999–2000), Silver (2000), and Weyandt (2001) include the use of megavitamins, diet restrictions (e.g., sugar or additives), caffeine, massage ther-

---

T ABLE 5.1   **Common Myths Associated with ADHD Medications**

❱ Myth	❱ Fact
Medication should be stopped when a child reaches teen years.	Research clearly shows there is continued benefit to medication for those teens who meet criteria for diagnosis of ADHD.
Children tend to build up tolerance for medication.	Although the dose of medication may need adjusting from time to time due to weight gain or increased attention demands there is no evidence that children build up a tolerance to medication.
Taking medicine for ADHD leads to greater likelihood of later drug dependency or addiction.	A study by the National Institutes of Health (2000) suggested that Children and adolescents with ADHD who had used medication were less likely to engage in deviant behavior or substance abuse.
Positive response to medication is confirmation of a diagnosis of ADHD.	The fact that a child shows improvement of attention span or a reduction of activity while taking ADHD medication does not substantiate the diagnosis of ADHD. Even some normal children will show a marked improvement in attentiveness when they take ADHD medication.
Medication stunts growth.	ADHD medications may cause an initial and mild slowing of growth, but over time the growth suppression effect is minimal if not nonexistent in most cases.
Ritalin dulls a child's personality and can cause depression.	If a child's personality seems depressed or less spontaneous, the dosage should probably be lowered.
ADHD children who take medication attribute their success only to medication.	When self-esteem is encouraged, children taking medication attribute their success not only to the medication but to themselves as well.

Adapted from "What Teachers and Parents Should Know About Ritalin" (pp. 20–26) by C. Pancheri and M. A. Prater, 1999, *Teaching Exceptional Children* (March/April).

Diversity Forum

Appreciating Religious Diversity in the Referral Process

Will, a European American 11-year-old, is transitioning to middle school. Will's parents are concerned because his first progress report reflects attention problems and low grades. While his parents associate his high activity level with his gender and maturity level, his teachers are concerned that he may have ADHD. They think medication might help him be more successful. Will's parents are Christian Scientists, who believe in addressing physical and mental health problems through prayer and are opposed to medical intervention. Will's parents and teachers meet to discuss the possibility that special education services may be helpful.

Will's family and the school have different beliefs about appropriate ways to respond to Will's behavior; in this case, religious differences, rather than race, ethnicity, or social class, require cultural sensitivity and cross-cultural collaboration. Documenting problem-atic behavior is just the first step in the special education referral process. Problem solving and modifying the environment are equally important (Winzer & Mazurek, 1998). Placement in special education should not be viewed as inevitable.

When teachers and parents have differing views regarding disability and its treatment, listening to parents share strategies that work at home can provide teachers with alternative approaches that may be successful in addressing classroom concerns. With ADHD, resources for strategies, interventions, and accommodations beyond medical treatment are widely available. Home- and school-based interventions can be implemented in conjunction with rewards and consequences, such as structuring assignments with the use of written directions and checklists, or the use of daily self-assessment journals and home/school communication note-books (Weyandt, 2001). In Will's case, his parents would share strategies they have used successfully, such as the use of an immediate reward/consequence system and written checklists of directions. Will's teachers, who are concerned about his ability to use strategies independently, might try a daily self-assessment journal for him to complete during homeroom. Until more time is allowed to determine Will's progress, the discussion of medical treatment and special education services would be tabled.

Companion Website

For follow-up questions about prereferral interventions and ADHD, go to Chapter 5 of the Companion Website (ablongman.com/sppd4e) and click Diversity Forum.

---

apy, chiropractic skull manipulations, biofeedback, play therapy, and herbs. These authors caution that if an approach were that amazing, everyone would use it. They encourage asking to see the research supporting the treatment before submitting children to the treatment and investing resources.

Classroom Adaptations for Students with Attention Deficit/Hyperactivity Disorder

Since no two children with ADHD are exactly alike, a wide variety of interventions and service options must be used to meet their needs. Success for these students depends on the qualifications of the teacher, effective strategies for instruction, and classroom adaptations. The plan that was developed for Jake, the boy described in the opening vignette, is shown in the Section 504 Plan on page 144. Following is a discussion of these and other strategies that might be used to make school a more positive experience for students with ADHD.

Making Classroom Adaptations

Since ADHD describes a set of characteristics that affect learning, most interventions take place in the school setting. Any approach to addressing the needs of students with ADHD must be comprehensive. Figure 5.7 depicts a model of educational intervention built on four intervention areas: environmental management, instructional accommodations, student-regulated strategies, and medical management (Dowdy et al., 1998). Medical management was described previously. Strategies for addressing the challenges of ADHD in the classroom are discussed in the following sections.

Section 504 Plan for Jake

From *Section 504 and Public Schools* (p. 51) by T. E. C. Smith & J. R. Patton, 1998, Austin, TX: Pro-Ed. Used with permission.

Name: _Jake Smith_

School/Class: _11th grade — Central High School_

Teacher: _Pratt — History, Jordan — Literature_   Date: _9/29/97_

General Strengths: _Jake is a bright student, he wants to learn and make good grades. He is very ambitious and wants to go to college and become an engineer._

General Weaknesses: _Jake has been diagnosed with ADHD. His attention span is very short and he is easily distracted. He frequently gets out of his seat and walks around the room._

Specific Accommodations:

Accommodation #1

Class: _History_   Accommodation(s): _Jake will be given extra time to complete his assignments. He will be given assignments divided into shorter objectives so that his progress can be checked sooner._

Person Responsible for Accommodation #1: _Mr. Pratt — teacher_

Accommodation #2

Class: _History_   Accommodation(s): _Jake will sit at the front of the class._

Person Responsible for Accommodation #2: _Mr. Pratt — teacher_

Accommodation #3

Class: _Literature_   Accommodation(s): _Jake will work with selected other students in cooperative learning arrangements._

Person Responsible for Accommodation #3: _Ms. Jordan — teacher_

Accommodation #4

Class: _Literature_   Accommodation(s): _An assignment notebook will be sent home each day with specific assignments noted. Parents will sign the assignment notebook daily and return it to school._

Person Responsible for Accommodation #4: _Ms. Jordan — teacher_

Accommodation #5

Class: _All classes_   Accommodation(s): _A behavior management plan will be developed and implemented for Jake for the entire day. The plan will include time for Jake to take Ritalin and will focus on positive reinforcement._

Person Responsible for Accommodation #5: _Ms. Baker — asst. prin._

General Comments:
Jake's plan will be reviewed at the end of the fall term to ensure that it is meeting his needs.

Individuals Participating in Development of Accommodation Plan:

William Pratt — teacher	_Fred Haynes — 504 Coor._
Bonita Jordan — teacher	_Hank Smith — father_
Mary Baker — asst. prin.	

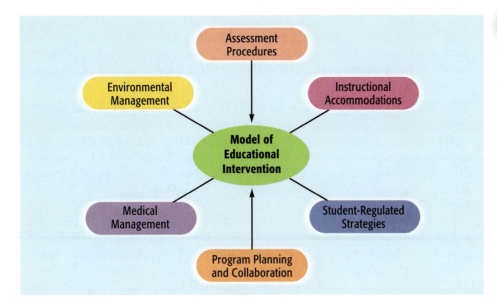

FIGURE 5.7

Model for ADHD Intervention

From *Attention-Deficit/Hyperactivity Disorder in the Classroom: A Practical Guide for Teachers* (p. 26) by by C. A. Dowdy, J. R. Patton, T. E. C. Smith, and E. A. Polloway, 1998, Austin, TX: Pro-Ed.

Managing the Classroom Environment

A classroom with even one or two students with ADHD can be difficult to control if the teacher is not skilled in classroom management. Rather than reacting spontaneously— and often inconsistently—to disruptive situations, teachers should have a management system to help avoid crises. Dowdy et al. (1998) define classroom management as a combination of techniques that results in an orderly classroom environment where social growth and learning can occur. Good classroom management is beneficial for all students, including those with ADHD. Techniques include group management, physical management, and behavior management.

Group Management Though they benefit all members of a class, group management techniques are critical in managing the behavior of individual students with ADHD. One of the most basic and effective techniques is to establish classroom rules and consequences for breaking those rules. Children with ADHD need to understand the classroom rules and school procedures in order to be successful. Jones and Jones (1995) suggest that students feel more committed to following rules when they have contributed to developing them. The rules should be displayed prominently in the room and reviewed periodically if students with ADHD are to retain and follow them. It is important for teachers to apply the rules consistently, even though students can sometimes frustrate teachers and make them want to "give in." Teachers may start the process of rule development by offering one or two rules of their own and then letting the children pick up with their own ideas. The following is a list of recommendations for developing rules (Dowdy et al., 1998):

CROSS-REFERENCE

Teachers should develop a list of procedures to make the classroom run smoothly. For example, how should students request help? How should they respond during a fire drill? For more tips in this area, refer to Chapter 14.

▶ State rules positively and clearly. A rule should tell students what to do instead of what not to do!
▶ Rules should be stated in simple terms so students can easily understand them. For young students, rules can be depicted with drawings and figures.
▶ The number of rules should be no more than five or six.
▶ Rules should be displayed conspicuously in the room.
▶ Rules should be practiced and discussed at the beginning of the year and periodically throughout the year.
▶ For students with ADHD, role-playing how to carry out the rules is an effective technique.
▶ Adopt rules and consequences that you are willing to enforce.

◗ Positively reinforce students who abide by the rules. It is more effective to reinforce the students who abide by the rules than to punish those who break them.

◗ To avoid misunderstandings, communicate rules and consequences to parents. It is helpful to have parents and students sign a contract documenting their understanding of the rules.

Time management is also important in effective classroom management. Students with ADHD thrive in an organized, structured classroom. Acting out and inappropriate behavior often occur during unscheduled, unstructured free time, when the number of choices of activities may become overwhelming. If free time is scheduled, limit the choices and provide positive reinforcement for appropriate behavior during free time. Encourage students to investigate topics that interest them and to complete projects that bring their strengths into play.

Polloway and Patton (2001) suggest that teachers begin each day with a similar routine. The particular activity is not as important as the consistency. For example, some teachers like to start the day with quiet reading, whereas others might begin with singing, recognizing birthdays, or talking about special events that are coming up. This routine sets the stage for a calm orderly day, and students will know what to expect from the teacher. Secondary teachers need to advise students of scheduling changes (e.g., assembly, pep rally) and provide a brief overview of the topics and activities to be expected during the class period.

Like the beginning of the day, closure on the day's or the class period's activities is important for secondary students. Reviewing the important events of the day and describing the next day's activities help students with ADHD. This is also an excellent time for teachers to provide rewards for students who have maintained appropriate behavior during the day. If parents are involved in a contract, this is the time to discuss the transmitted notes and to review homework that might have been assigned during the day.

To work successfully with students with ADHD, group students to create the most effective learning environment. They may be taught more effectively in small groups of four to seven students and complete work more successfully as a team. Perhaps two or three students may need to receive more individualized instruction. The teacher should plan the makeup of the groups to combine ADHD students with students who will be supportive, positive role models. The resulting peer pressure to abide by the rules is often more effective than teacher-directed behavior management. Also, students with ADHD may become friends with students without ADHD if they work together in cooperative learning groups (Landau, Milich, & Diener, 1998).

Teachers may want to offer incentives to individual students and groups to reward outstanding work. You might place a marble in a jar each time students are "caught being good." When the jar is filled the class receives an award such as a picnic or a skating party. Another technique involves adding a piece to a puzzle whenever the teacher recognizes that the class is working especially hard. When the puzzle is complete, the class is rewarded. These group incentives can be very effective; however, some students will need an individual contract or behavior management plan to help direct their behavior.

Physical Management   The physical environment of a classroom can also have an impact on the behavior of students with ADHD. The arrangement of the room is most important. The classroom needs to be large enough for students to have space between themselves and others, so they will be less likely to impose themselves on one another. Each student needs some personal space.

Desk arrangement is also important. Research has shown that distractions may be reduced by using standard rows or a semicircle; placing a child with ADHD with 5 or 6 students around a table can be very distracting (Flick, 1998). The student with ADHD may need to be near the teacher in order to focus attention on the information being presented in the classroom; however, students should never be placed near the teacher as a punitive measure. A seat near the front may help the student who is distracted by some-

CONSIDER THIS

What are some appropriate activities to begin and end the day or class period for elementary and secondary students?

one's new hairstyle or flashy jewelry. There should also be various places in the room where quiet activities can take place, where small groups can work together, where sustained attention for difficult tasks can be maintained, and where a relaxed and comfortable environment can be enjoyed for a change of pace. At one time, classrooms with lots of visual stimulation were considered inappropriate for students with ADHD, leading to the creation of sterile environments with colorless walls and no bulletin boards. This is no longer considered necessary; however, order is needed in the classroom; assignments should be posted in the same location daily, materials and completed assignments should be placed consistently in the same place, and bulletin boards should be well organized. Set aside places where students who seem to be overstimulated can work in a carrel or other private space with minimal visual and auditory stimuli, and have a place for a child who seems underaroused to be able to move around and get rejuvenated (Carbone, 2001).

Behavioral Support   Behavioral support techniques can enhance the education of students with ADHD, especially those that reward desired behavior. For example, when students with ADHD are attending to their tasks, following classroom rules, or participating appropriately in a cooperative learning activity, their behaviors should be positively reinforced. Unfortunately, teachers often ignore appropriate behavior and call attention only to what is inappropriate. When students receive attention for actions that are disruptive or inconsiderate, the negative behaviors can be reinforced and may thus increase in frequency. The Personal Spotlight presents a unique example of a student with ADHD who experienced behavior problems in school.

Positive reinforcement tends to increase appropriate behavior (Reid, 1999). Teachers should consider which rewards appeal most to the individuals who will receive them. Common ones include small toys, candy and other edibles, free time, time to listen to music, time in the gym, opportunities to do things for the teacher, having lunch with the teacher, praise, or hugs. Because a reward that acts as a reinforcer for one student may not work for another, teachers might generate a menu of rewards and allow students to select their own. Rewards do not have to be expensive; in fact, simply allowing students to take a break, time to get a drink of water, or time to sharpen a pencil, or giving a homework pass may be just as effective as expensive toys and games.

Another helpful idea in working with children with ADHD is called the Premack principle. Also known as "grandma's law," it is based on the traditional comment "If you eat your vegetables, then you can have your dessert" (Polloway & Patton, 2001, p. 74). The teacher announces that a reward or highly desired activity will be awarded to students after they complete a required or undesired activity. For example, students might be required to sit in their seats and complete work for 20 minutes; then a snack or free time will follow. This simple technique can be very effective for students with ADHD.

Often students need an individual contract that focuses on their particular needs. Together, student and teacher develop goals to improve behavior and then put these goals in writing. They also stipulate consequences for not following the contract and reinforcement for completing the contract. This instrument provides structure and forms an explicit way to communicate with children with ADHD and their parents. Downing (2002) offers the following guidelines for making and using such contracts:

▸ Determine the most critical area(s) of concern.
▸ Consider when the behavior usually occurs, the events that trigger it, and why you think the behavior is occurring.
▸ Specify the desired behavior in measurable terms, using clear, simple words.
▸ Specify the reinforcers that will be used and the consequences that will follow if the contract is not fulfilled.
▸ See that both teacher and student sign the contract (and the parents, when appropriate).
▸ Keep a record of the student's behavior.
▸ Provide the agreed-upon consequences or reinforcements in a timely fashion.

CONSIDER THIS

These ideas are effective with elementary age students. Generate some reinforcers that would be more effective in secondary settings.

CONSIDER THIS

Give examples of how the Premack principle can be applied for elementary, middle, and high school students.

◗ When the goal is reached, celebrate, and write a new contract! A sample contract is provided in Figure 5.8.

TEACHING TIP

One of the reasons children with ADHD don't take their medication or follow through with classroom adaptations is their embarrassment in front of peers. As a teacher, how can you provide adaptations for students with ADHD in a way that minimizes the stigma of special treatment?

Another behavior-management technique is cuing or signaling ADHD students when they are on the verge of inappropriate behavior. First, student and teacher sit down privately and discuss the inappropriate behavior that has been creating problems in the classroom. The teacher offers to provide a cue when the behavior begins to be noticed. Teachers and students can have fun working together on the signal, which might involve flipping the light switch, tapping the desk lightly, or simple eye contact. These cuing techniques help establish a collegial relationship between the teacher and the student that says, "We are working on this together; we have a problem, but we also have a plan" (Wood, 1984).

Making Instructional Adaptations

Barkley (1999–2000) says, "Knowing what to do is a strategy problem. Doing what you know is a motivational problem" (p. 134). His research suggests that ADHD may be

Personal Spotlight

Growing up with ADHD

Dave Birt has had ADHD as long as he can remember. Now age 29, he feels that he is still working to counteract the negative experiences of his school days. Upon entering kindergarten, he could already read, and throughout elementary school, he felt impatient when waiting for his peers to catch up. He qualified for the gifted program with an IQ well into the genius range, but even that program couldn't give him enough to do. He says, "The teachers would repeat things over and over. They only had to tell me once, and I learned it." As a result, Dave filled his time entertaining himself, and he soon became a behavior problem in the classroom. He was shuffled around suburban Pennsylvania school districts, but no one knew what to do for him. Soon, he simply became labeled a "troublemaker."

In the eighth grade, Dave was officially diagnosed with ADHD, but teachers still didn't know how to instruct him in the traditional classroom. The primary problem with the adaptations was the social stigma attached to them. For example, teachers had him keep assignment journals, but this special treatment made him feel like an outcast, so he didn't do it. The same applied to Ritalin—he didn't think it would help, and he wanted to avoid the stigma, so he didn't take it. Finally, a rural school district placed him in the program for students with behavior problems. Dave remembers, "They put me in the 'sped shed,' a program where the teacher had fewer students and could keep a closer eye on them. It worked to a point, but it was based on the idea that bad kids are dumb. My misbehavior was rebellion against being treated like an idiot or an attempt to keep myself entertained." Furthermore, the program was only set up for home-

Dave Birt

Boston, MA

room, study halls, and lunch, so it deprived students of important socializing opportunities with the rest of the school. Dave was reluctant to socialize with the other students in the program, some of whom are now in prison. He feels that the development of his social skills suffered as a result.

Eventually, Dave tired of this routine. He signed himself out of school in 11th grade and took the GED, scoring in the 97th percentile. He later joined the army, but the ADHD didn't allow him the patience necessary to wait for his peers to catch on to whatever they were doing.

Finally, Dave discovered something that held his interest—computers. He started his own small business building custom computers for clients, and he also took night classes and earned IT certifications. Currently he works for the wireless communications company Nextel, and he is considering attending college, perhaps to become a computer teacher. Because of his school experiences, though, he is hesitant about going back into the classroom as a full-time student. "What if I have professors who don't understand ADHD?" he worries. "I'm not going through that again." Still, he says, "I think I could be a good teacher because I understand how kids think. You have to keep them interested in order for them to learn."

For follow-up questions about this Personal Spotlight, go to Chapter 5 of the Companion Website (ablongman.com/sppd4e) and click Personal Spotlight.

I, Bobby, agree to:

▶ Follow the classroom rules and teacher's directions.

▶ Handle conflict situations appropriately, using the strategies I have learned rather than running away.

▶ Express my negative feelings in a calm, quiet voice without making threats and/or refusing to do what I am told.

For this effort, I will earn:

▶ Fifteen minutes of free time at the end of each successful day to play *The Magic School Bus Explores the Rainforest* computer game.

▶ A visit from Billy the Boa Constrictor at the end of every week if I am successful for at least 4 out of 5 days.

Date:

Student Signature:

Teacher Signature:

FIGURE 5.8

An Example of a Contingency Contract

From "Individualized Behavior Contracts" (p. 170) by J. A. Downing, 2002, *Intervention in School and Clinic, 37*(3).

caused by neurological differences in the motivational center of the brain; students with ADHD do not have a problem with skills, they have problems with performance. However, these students are often misunderstood and labeled lazy or unmotivated, as if they are choosing not to perform at their maximum potential. Teacher comments such as "I know you can do this work, because you did it yesterday" or "You can do better; you just aren't trying" probably suggest a lack of understanding of the inconsistent performance characteristic of this disability (Flick, 1998). Instead, teachers need to find ways to cope with the frustration and stress sometimes involved in working with these students, while modifying their teaching style, their curriculum, and possibly their expectations in order to engineer academic success for these students.

Modifying Teacher Behavior   Since students with ADHD are not easily stimulated, they need novelty and excitement in their learning environment. Although structure and consistency are extremely important, students need challenging, exciting activities to keep them focused and learning. The Web offers endless ideas for "jazzing up" lesson plans or developing new ones. See the nearby Technology Today feature to explore some options.

Weyandt (2001) reports that the incidence of inappropriate behavior increases during nonstimulating, repetitive activities. She suggests that teachers vary activities, allow and encourage movement that is purposeful and not disruptive, give frequent breaks, and even let students stand as they listen, take notes, or perform other academic tasks. "Legal movement" such as pencil sharpening or a hall pass for walking to the restroom or getting water might be preapproved for a student's restless times (Guyer, 2000). Here are some recommendations from Yehle and Wambold (1998) for enhancing large group instruction:

▶ Begin with an attention grabber (e.g., joke, question of the day).
▶ Distribute an outline of your lecture to assist with note taking; use the overhead projector and provide copies of overheads.

Web Tools for Lesson Plans

Use tools available on the Web like the following to enhance lesson plans and shorten preparation time:

▶ www.teach-nology.com/web_tools/ rubics/ Helps create assessment rubrics for any content area.
▶ www.classbuilder.com/
▶ www.edhelper.com/ Generates work sheets and puzzles for any content area.
▶ teachers.teach-nology.com/web_tools/ Generates planners, bingo cards, learning contracts, and more.

▶ www.educationalpress.org/ educationalpress/ Focuses on flash-cards and game boards for beginning reading skills.
▶ www.theeducatorsnetwork.com Provides comprehensive links to lessons.
▶ www.schoolexpress.com/ E-mails a free thematic unit each week.

▶ www.kimskorner4teachertalk.com Provides bulletin board ideas, ice-breakers, and more.

For more ideas visit www.TeachingK-8.com and click on "Classroom Activities."

For follow-up questions about lesson planning tools, go to Chapter 5 of the Companion Website (ablongman.com/sppd4e) and click Technology Today.

▶ Pace the lesson, giving more time for difficult concepts.
▶ Use visual aids such as a graphic organizer as often as possible.
▶ Clap, alter your tone of voice, or use different colored chalk to draw attention to important material.
▶ Repeat important information several times during the lecture; ask students to repeat in unison.
▶ Ask frequent questions of individual students by name throughout the presentation.
▶ Walk around the room monitoring and checking work frequently.
▶ Try to turn a lesson into a game format (e.g., the "Jeopardy!" game show) for a fun review.

Cuing or signaling students is one method that teachers can use to help get their attention.

▶ Stay close to students and use frequent eye contact.
▶ Close each lesson with a review, set the stage for the next lesson, and give reminders about homework.

Templeton (1995) suggests that teachers speak clearly and loudly enough for students to hear, but not too fast. She points out that enthusiasm and humor will help engage students and excite those who might become easily bored and distracted. She also recommends helping students see the value in what they learn and the importance of the material. During a long lecture period, teachers might list main ideas or important questions on the chalkboard or by using the overhead projector, to help students focus on the most important information. When a student's attention does wander, a small, unobtrusive signal such as a gentle pat on the student's shoulder can cue the student to return to the task. To perk up tiring students, teachers can try a quick game of Simon Says or assign purposeful physical activities such as taking a note to the office, feeding the animals in the classroom, or returning books to the library. Prater (1992) provides a self-assessment for teachers to determine if they are doing everything they can to increase each student's attention to task during instructional time. This strategy for improving instruction for all students is included in the nearby Inclusion Strategies feature.

Modifying the Curriculum   Although students with ADHD are typically taught in the general education classroom using the regular curriculum, they need a curriculum that focuses on "doing" and avoids long periods of sitting and listening. Such adaptations can benefit all students. For example, experience-based learning, in which students might develop their own projects, perform experiments, or take field trips, can help all students grow as active learners. Cronin (1993) suggests that teachers modify curriculum by using activities that closely resemble challenges and experiences in the real world. Resources can be found in story problems included in traditional textbooks, curriculum-based experiments and projects, or extended activities such as writing letters to environmental groups to obtain more information than is offered in a textbook.

Describing a related curriculum model, Stephien and Gallagher (1993) suggest that problem-based learning provides authentic experiences in the classroom. In this model, students are asked to solve an "ill-structured problem" before they receive any instruction. Teachers act as coaches and tutors, questioning the student's hypotheses and conclusions and sharing their own thoughts when needed during "time out" discussions. Students act as doctors, historians, or scientists, or assume other roles of individuals who have a real stake in solving the proposed problem. When students "take ownership" of the problem, motivation soars. Teachers can model problem-solving strategies by thinking out loud and questioning their own conclusions and recommendations. This model increases self-directed learning and improves motivation.

Teachers are also encouraged to vary their assessment techniques. Oral examinations, take-home or open-book exams, portfolio assessment, and informal measures are alternative assessment methods that provide a different perspective on what students know. Raza (1997) suggests that these techniques let students know that their teachers are not as concerned with how they perform on tests as they are with what the students have learned. Students with ADHD will generally be able to take the same tests as their peers; however, testing adaptations may be needed to specifically address the ADHD characteristics. These might include extra time to take the test (usually no more than time and a half), frequent breaks, taking the exam in a distraction-reduced environment, or using a computer to record responses. See the nearby feature Tips for Adapting a Lesson for Jake for examples of how to meet the needs of an individual student.

Developing Student-Regulated Strategies

The previous sections on classroom environment and instructional accommodations focused on activities that the teacher directs and implements to increase the success of

CONSIDER THIS

If you are currently teaching, complete the Time-on-Task Self-Assessment; if not, rewrite the questions and use them as an observation tool to evaluate a teacher who is willing to be observed. Analyze the results and identify changes that are indicated to improve learning in the classroom.

Time-on-Task Self-Assessment for Teachers

Read the following statements and rate yourself according to the following scale:

N	R	S	U	A
Never	Rarely	Sometimes	Usually	Always

During Group Instruction

1. Students are attending to me before I start the lesson. _____
2. Students use choral group responses to answer questions. _____
3. Individual students answer questions or orally read when called in a random order. _____
4. I ask a question, then call on a student to answer. _____
5. Students answer correctly most of the questions I ask. _____
6. I have all my materials and supplies ready before class begins. _____
7. If possible, I write all the necessary material on the board, an overhead, or poster before instructing. _____
8. I use some type of signal with group responses. _____
9. Students are involved in reading directions, practice items, or the answers. _____
10. Students are involved in housekeeping procedures such as passing out papers. _____

During Seatwork

11. I move around the classroom checking students' work. _____
12. I can make eye contact with all of my students. _____
13. I allow students to work together and to talk about their seatwork. _____
14. Immediately after instruction my students can work on their seatwork without any questions. _____
15. Students need not wait for my assistance if they have questions about their seatwork. _____
16. I spend little time answering questions about what the students are to do next. _____
17. Most of my students finish their work about the same time. _____

During Instruction or Seatwork

18. I spend little time reprimanding students for misbehavior. _____
19. My students are not restless. _____
20. My students follow a routine for transition times (i.e., getting materials ready, collecting papers, lining up for lunch). _____
21. My students respond quickly during transition times. _____
22. I have well-defined rules for appropriate behavior in my classroom. _____
23. I consistently provide appropriate consequences for students who are and remain on-task. _____
24. I teach my students self-management procedures (e.g., self-monitoring, self-instruction). _____

For follow-up questions about strategies for teachers to be time-on-task, go to Chapter 5 of the Companion Website (ablongman.com/sppd4e) and click Inclusion Strategies.

From "Increasing Time-on-Task in the Classroom" by M. A. Prater, 1992, *Intervention in School and Clinic, 28*(1), pp. 22–27.

children with ADHD. This section describes student-regulated strategies. Dowdy et al. (1998) define student-regulated strategies as interventions, initially taught by the teacher, that the student will eventually implement independently.

Fiore, Becker, and Nerro (1993) note that these cognitive approaches directly address core problems of children with ADHD, including impulse control, higher-order problem solving, and self-regulation. Because this is a new field, teachers are encouraged to validate their effectiveness in their classrooms (DuPaul & Eckert, 1998).

Tips for Adapting a Lesson for Jake

Since Jake's primary limitations include a short attention span, impulsive movement, and being easily distracted (as described in the chapter-opening vignette), the teacher's adaptations listed in his 504 plan and those recommended here should limit the impact of these challenges and help Jake make the good grades he needs to go to college.

Jake's teacher should

▶ allow Jake to sit by students who generally remain on task.

▶ provide a copy of notes and overheads.

▶ color-code or underline important concepts.

▶ give Jake permission to leave the room occasionally or walk in back of the room to provide authorized movement and not create a disturbance.

▶ take tests in a distraction-reduced environment and give extra time as needed.

▶ check often for understanding and review.

▶ vary activities.

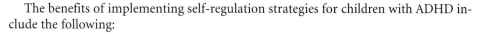

The benefits of implementing self-regulation strategies for children with ADHD include the following:

▶ Modifying impulsive responses
▶ Increasing selective attention and focus
▶ Providing verbal mediators to facilitate academic and social problem-solving challenges (e.g., self-talk to calm down during an argument)
▶ Teaching self-instructional statements to assist students in "talking through" problems and tasks
▶ Providing strategies that may develop prosocial behaviors and lead to improved peer relations (Rooney, 1993)

The following discussion addresses four types of student-regulated strategies: study and organizational tactics, self-management, learning strategies, and social skills.

Study and Organizational Tactics   Students with ADHD have difficulty organizing their work and developing effective study skills in general education classrooms. To help them with organization, teachers may designate space for students to keep materials, establish the routine of students writing down their assignments daily in an assignment notebook, and provide notebooks in different colors for each subject (Yehle & Wambold, 1998).

Hoover and Patton (1995) suggest teaching 11 study skills: increasing and/or adjusting reading rate according to the purpose for reading, listening, note taking, writing reports, giving oral presentations, using graphic aids, taking tests, using the library, using reference material, time management, and self-management. Students should practice planning as an organizational strategy. Before giving an assignment such as a term paper, deciding how to break the task into small parts and how to complete each part should be practiced. Students should also practice estimating how much time is needed for various activities so they can establish appropriate and realistic goals. Outlining skills can also help with organization and planning. Students may want to use a word processor to order their ideas and to help organize their work.

Self-Management   The primary goal of programs that teach self-management or self-control is to "make children more consciously aware of their own thinking processes and

TEACHING TIP

Practice what you teach! Identify an activity or task that you need to accomplish by a date in the future (e.g., develop a unit on ecology). Break down the steps to completion, including target dates. Model your planning skills by "thinking out loud" for your students. This will make the concept of planning and organizing more concrete for them.

task approach strategies, and to give them responsibility for their own reinforcement" (Reeve, 1990, p. 76). Here are some advantages of teaching self-control:

▶ It saves the teacher's time by decreasing the demand for direct instruction.
▶ It increases the effectiveness of an intervention.
▶ It increases the maintenance of skills over time.
▶ It increases a student's ability to use the skill in a variety of settings. (Lloyd, Landrum, & Hallahan, 1991, p. 201)

Polloway and Patton (2001) cite four types of self-regulation. In self-assessment, the individual determines the need for change and also monitors personal behavior. In self-monitoring, the student attends to specific aspects of his or her own behavior. While learning to self-monitor, a student can be given a periodic beep or other cue to signal that it is time for him or her to evaluate "on" or "off" task behavior. In self-instruction, the student cues himself or herself to inhibit inappropriate behaviors or to express appropriate ones. In self-reinforcement, the student administers self-selected reinforcement for an appropriate behavior that has been previously specified. Figure 5.9 contains a self-management strategy used to help students deal with anger. Figure 5.10 provides a self-monitoring sheet for the student to use to reflect on his or her use of the strategy. Eventually the student will begin to automatically self-monitor and will begin to use the appropriate response to situations that previously triggered an inappropriate display of anger. Other behaviors commonly targeted for self-regulation include completing assignments (productivity), appropriate classroom behavior (such as staying in one's seat), accuracy of work (such as percent correct), and staying on task (Johnson & Johnson, 1998).

Learning Strategies   Deshler and Lenz (1989) define a learning strategy as an individual approach to a task. It includes how an individual thinks and acts when planning, executing, or evaluating performance. The learning strategies approach combines what is going on in an individual's head (cognition) with what a person actually does (behavior) to guide the performance and evaluation of a specific task. All individuals use strategies; however, not all strategies are effective.

The learning strategies method of instruction will be described more fully in Chapter 6 as an effective method for improving academic performance for students with learning disabilities; however, this type of intervention is also particularly beneficial for students with ADHD (DuPaul & Eckert, 1998). Babkie and Provost (2002) encourage teachers and students to create their own strategies or cues to teach a difficult concept

---

FIGURE 5.9

A Self-Management Strategy for Dealing with Anger

From "Collaborating to Teach Prosocial Skills" (p. 145) by D. H. Allsopp, K. E. Santos, & R. Linn, 2000, *Intervention in School and Clinic, 35*(3).

1. **W**ATCH for the "trigger."
   ▶ Count to 10.
   ▶ Use relaxation techniques.

2. **A**NSWER, "Why am I angry?"

3. **I**DENTIFY my options.
   ▶ Ignore the other person.
   ▶ Move away.
   ▶ Resolve the problem.
   ▶ "I feel this way when you . . ."
   ▶ Listen to the other person.
   ▶ Talk to the teacher.

4. **T**RY an appropriate option for dealing with my anger.

What was the trigger?	Why was I angry?	Did I identify my options?	What option did I choose and was it successful?
1.			
2.			
3.			
4.			
5.			

FIGURE 5.10

A Self-Monitoring Sheet for Dealing with Anger

From "Collaborating to Teach Prosocial Skills" (p. 146) by D. H. Allsopp, K. E. Santos, & R. Linn, 2000, *Intervention in School and Clinic, 35*(3).

or behavior. A key word is identified that specifies the targeted area. A short phrase or sentence that tells the student what to do is written for each letter in the key word. Figure 5.11 shows a strategy developed to cue students to organize homework.

Social Skills Because students with attention deficit/hyperactivity disorder often do not exhibit good problem-solving skills and are not able to predict the consequences of their inappropriate behavior, specific and direct instruction in social skills may be necessary. Although it is better for students to be able to assess their own inappropriate behavior and adjust it to acceptable standards, many students may need social skills training first. Landau, Milich, and Diener (1998) recommended that training be done throughout the year in groups of 4–8, with classmates in groups of the same gender. The sessions should include practice, modeling, and reinforcement of appropriate behavior during real-life peer problem situations. Including appropriate, well-liked children in each group can promote desirable modeling and encourage important new friendships.

Promoting Inclusive Practices for Attention Deficit/Hyperactivity Disorder

The Professional Group for Attention and Related Disorders (PGARD) proposes that most children with ADHD can be served in the general education program by trained teachers providing appropriate instruction and modifications. In addition to activities

---

Organization: **HOMEWORK**

Have a place to work

Organize assignments according to difficulty

Make sure to follow directions

Examine the examples

Weave my way through the assignments

Observe work for errors and omissions

Return work to school

Keep up the effort!

FIGURE 5.11

A Learning Strategy for Homework

From "Select, Write, and Use Metacognitive Strategies in the Classroom" (p. 174) by A. M. Babkie and M. C. Provost, *Intervention in School and Clinic, 37*(3).

that teachers can use to promote a supportive classroom environment, Korinek, Walther-Thomas, McLaughlin, and Williams (1999) suggest that schoolwide support be promoted through disability-awareness activities, the use of positive discipline, and the use of adult volunteers. They add that the entire community can become involved through the establishment of business partnerships and the provision of organized activities like scouting and other forms of sports and recreation. Of course school administrators have to make a commitment to dedicate resources for training and to facilitate change.

The two critical features for successful inclusion of students with ADHD are the skills and behaviors of the teachers and the understanding and acceptance of the general education peers.

Community-Building Skills for Teachers

One of the most important aspects of promoting success for children with ADHD is the teacher. Fowler (1992) suggests that success for children with ADHD might vary from year to year, class to class, teacher to teacher. She reports that the most commonly cited reason for a positive or negative school experience is the teacher. She cites the following 17 characteristics of teachers as likely indicators of positive learning outcomes for students with ADHD:

1. Positive academic expectations
2. Frequent review of student work
3. Clarity of teaching (e.g., explicit directions, rules)
4. Flexibility
5. Fairness
6. Active interaction with the students
7. Responsiveness
8. Warmth
9. Patience
10. Humor
11. Structured and predictable approach
12. Consistency
13. Firmness
14. Positive attitude toward inclusion
15. Knowledge of and willingness to work with students with exceptional needs
16. Knowledge of different types of effective interventions
17. Willingness to work collaboratively with other teachers (e.g., sharing information, requesting assistance as needed, participating in conferences involving students) (p. 17)

Resources for Developing Awareness in Peers

Teachers with the traits listed in the preceding section will provide a positive role model for general education students in how to understand and accept children with ADHD. Teachers should confer with parents and the child with ADHD to obtain advice on explaining ADHD to other students in the classroom. The child with ADHD may wish to be present during the explanation or even to participate in informing his or her classmates. The following books and publications may help introduce this topic to students with ADHD and their peers.

Jumping Johnny Get Back to Work—A Child's Guide to ADHD/Hyperactivity
Michael Gordon, Ph.D., Author
Connecticut Association for Children with LD
18 Marshall Street
South Norwalk, CT 06854
(203) 838–5010

CONSIDER THIS

Use the characteristics of an effective teacher as a tool for self-assessment. Identify your strengths and determine goals for improving your teaching skills.

Shelley, the Hyperactive Turtle
Deborah Moss, Author
Woodbine House
5616 Fishers Lane
Rockville, MD 20852
(800) 843–7323

Sometimes I Drive My Mom Crazy, but I Know She's Crazy About Me!
Childworks
Center for Applied Psychology, Inc.
P.O. Box 61586
King of Prussia, PA 19406
(800) 962–1141

You Mean I'm Not Lazy, Stupid, or Crazy?
Peggy Ramundo and Kate Kelly, Authors
Tyrell & Jerem Press
P.O. Box 20089
Cincinnati, OH 45220
(800) 622–6611

Otto Learns About His Medicine
Michael Gaivin, M.D., Author
Childworks
Center for Applied Psychology, Inc.
P.O. Box 61586
King of Prussia, PA 19406
(800) 962–1141

Eagle Eyes: A Child's View of Attention Deficit Disorder
Jeanne Gehret, M.A., Author
Childworks
Center for Applied Psychology, Inc.
P.O. Box 61586
King of Prussia, PA 19406
(800) 962–1141

Feelings About Friends
Linda Schwartz, Author
The Learning Works
P.O. Box 6187
Santa Barbara, CA 93160
(800) 235–5767

Brakes: The Interactive Newsletter for Kids with ADHD
Magination Press
19 Union Square West
New York, NY 10003
(800) 825–3089

Collaborating with Parents of Students with Attention Deficit/Hyperactivity Disorder

Teachers can often promote success for students with ADHD by working closely with parents to practice and reinforce desirable academic and social behavior. Flick (1998) suggests the following parent-centered activities:

- Practice and reinforce school behaviors such as following directions, completing homework, getting along with siblings and friends, and obeying rules.
- Post and review home and school rules frequently.
- Use the same signal used by the teacher to cue the child when inappropriate behaviors are observed; examples include the commonly used finger placed over lips or a more personal or "secret cue" developed in collaboration among the child, parents, and the teacher.
- Develop a home-school reporting system that communicates positive behaviors and problem areas between parents and teachers

 **Summary**

Basic Concepts About Attention Deficit/Hyperactivity Disorder

- ADHD is a complex condition that offers a real challenge to classroom teachers.
- The legal basis for service delivery and protection for students with ADHD comes from IDEA and Section 504 of the Rehabilitation Act of 1973.

- Under IDEA, students with ADHD may be served through the category of "other health impaired"; children with ADHD as a secondary disability may be primarily diagnosed as behaviorally disordered, learning disabled, or mentally retarded.

▶ ADHD is a hidden disability with no unique physical characteristics to differentiate children who have it from others in the classroom.

▶ The diagnosis of ADHD is primarily based on the criteria in the *Diagnostic and Statistical Manual of Mental Disorders* (DSM-IV).

▶ Many theories exist to explain the cause of ADHD; however, ADHD is considered primarily a neurobiologically based condition.

▶ ADHD manifests itself across the life span; characteristics include limited sustained attention, reduced impulse control, excessive task-irrelevant activity, poor working memory, time-management problems, limited self-talk and behavior control, and greater than normal variability during task performance.

▶ The process for determining eligibility for services based on ADHD includes a preliminary assessment, an initial meeting of the child study team, a formal assessment and follow-up meeting of the child study team, a collaborative meeting to develop an intervention plan, and follow-up and progress reviews.

▶ Cultural and linguistic diversity complicates issues related to assessment and treatment for children with ADHD.

Strategies for Curriculum and Instruction for Students with Attention Deficit/Hyperactivity Disorder

▶ A continuum of placement options is available to students with ADHD, and the selected placement is based on their individual needs and abilities.

▶ The majority of students with ADHD spend all or most of the school day in general education classes.

▶ An individual accommodation plan is written collaboratively with parents, professionals, and when possible, the student, to identify interventions that will create success in the general education classroom.

▶ Medication is frequently used to enhance the educational experience of students with ADHD.

▶ The most commonly prescribed medication is a psychostimulant such as Dexedrine, Ritalin, or Adderall.

▶ Both positive outcomes and negative side effects should be monitored for individual children taking medication for ADHD.

Classroom Adaptations for Students with Attention Deficit/Hyperactivity Disorder

▶ Classroom adaptations include environmental management techniques, instructional adaptations, and student-regulated strategies.

▶ Techniques used to manage the classroom environment include strategies for group management, physical arrangement of the room, and individual behavior-management techniques.

▶ Through instructional adaptations, teachers modify their behavior to include novel and stimulating activity, to provide structure and consistency, to allow physical movement as frequently as possible, to include cooperative learning activities, and to give both spoken and written direction.

▶ The curriculum for students with ADHD should be stimulating and include experience-based learning as well as problem-solving activities.

▶ Student-regulated strategies include study and organizational tactics, self-management techniques, learning strategies, and social skills training.

▶ Effective teachers for students with ADHD provide positive classroom environments, frequently review student work, and are flexible, fair, responsive, warm, patient, consistent, firm, and humorous. They develop a knowledge of the strengths and needs of their students with ADHD and are knowledgeable about different intervention strategies. They are also willing to work collaboratively with other teachers, parents, and professionals.

Further Readings

Anastopoulos, A. D., Smith, J. M., & Wien, E. E. (1998). Counseling and training parents. In R. A. Barkley (Ed.), *Attention-deficit/hyperactivity disorder: A handbook for diagnosis and treatment* (2nd ed.). New York: Guilford Press.

Angold, A., Erkali, A., Egger, H. L., & Costell, J. E. (2000). Stimulant treatment for children: A community perspective. *Journal of the American Academy of Child and Adolescent Psychiatry, 39*(8), 975–987.

Anhalt, K., McNeil, C. B., & Bahl, A. B. (1998). The ADHD classroom kit: A whole-classroom approach for managing disruptive behavior. *Psychology in the Schools, 35*(1), 67–79.

Arnold, L. E. (1999). Treatment alternative for attention-deficit/hyperactivity disorder (ADHD). *Journal of Attention Disorders, 3*(1), 30–48.

Barkley, R. A. (1998). *Attention-deficit/hyperactivity disorder: A handbook for diagnosis and treatment* (2nd ed.). New York: Guilford Press.

DuPaul, G. J., & Eckert, T. L. (1998). Academic interventions for students with attention-deficit/hyperactivity disorder: A review of the literature. *Reading and Writing Quarterly, 14*, 59–82.

Filipek, P. A. (1999). Neuroimaging in the developmental disorders: The state of the science. *Journal of Child Psychology and Psychiatry, 40*, 113–128.

Hoagwood, K., Kelleher, K. J., Feil, M., & Comer, D. M. (2000). Treatment services for children with ADHD: A national perspective. *Journal of the American Academy of Child and Adolescent Psychiatry, 39*(2), 198–206.

Janover, C. (1997). *Zipper: The kid with ADHD.* Bethesda, MD: Woodbine House.

Jensen, P. S. (2000). Commentary: The NIH ADHD consensus statement: Win, lose, or draw? *Journal of the American Academy of Child and Adolescent Psychiatry, 39*(2), 194–197.

Jensen, P. S., Kettler, L., Roper, M., Sloan, M. T., Dulcan, M. K., Hoven, C., Bird, H. R., Bauermeister, J. J., & Payne, J. (1999). Are stimulants overprescribed? Treatment of ADHD in four US communities. *Journal of the American Academy of Child and Adolescent Psychiatry, 38*(7), 797–804.

Latham, P. S., & Latham, P. H. (1999). ADHD views from the courthouse. *The ADHD Report, 7*(4), 9–11, 14.

McKenzie, J. (1998). The WIRED classroom: Creating technology enhanced student-centered learning environments. *From Now On, 7*(6), 1–14. [Online]. Available at http://www.fromnowon.org/mar98/flotilla.html

Munden, A. C., & Archelus, J. (2001). *The ADHD handbook: A guide for parents and professionals.* New York: Jessica Kingsley.

National Institutes of Health. (2000). Consensus and development conference statement: Diagnosis and treatment of attention-deficit/hyperactivity disorder. *Journal of the American Academy of Child and Adolescent Psychiatry, 39*(2), 182–193.

Pentecost, D. (1999). Parenting the ADD child: Can't do? Won't do? Practical strategies for managing behavior problems in children with ADD and ADHD. New York: Jessica Kingsley.

Semrul-Clikerman, M., Steingard, R. J., Filipek, P., Biederman, J., Bekken, K., & Renshaw, P. F. (2000). Using MRI to examine brain-behavior relationships in males with attention-deficit hyperactivity disorder. *Journal of the American Academy of Child and Adolescent Psychiatry, 39*(4), 477–484.

Silver, L. B. (1999). *Attention deficit hyperactivity disorder: A clinical guide to diagnosis and treatment for health and mental health.* Washington, DC: American Psychiatric Press.

Smith, T. E. C., & Patton, J. R. (1998). *Section 504 and public schools.* Austin, TX: Pro-Ed.

Stormont-Spurgin, J. (1997). I lost my homework: Strategies for improving organization in students with ADHD. *Intervention in School and Clinic, 32*(5), 270–274.

 VideoWorkshop Extra!

If the VideoWorkshop package was included with your textbook, go to Chapter 5 of the Companion Website (www.ablongman.com/sppd4e) and click on the VideoWorkshop button. Follow the instructions for viewing video clip 5. Then consider this information along with what you've read in Chapter 5 while answering the following questions.

1. In this video clip, Dr. Goldsmith and the two teachers discussed the problems that Eric has with hyperactivity and aggression. They have determined that Eric needs to learn to work independently, express his needs verbally, and increase compliance. Using the information in the chapter regarding behavior contracts, write a contract for one of these goals.

2. Neither the doctor nor the teachers mentioned using medication with Eric. Based on what you saw in the video and read in the chapter, would you suggest medication to them? Explain your answer.

6 Teaching Students with Learning Disabilities

After reading this chapter, you should be able to

1. identify the characteristics of a learning disability (LD).
2. discuss the impact of cultural diversity on identification and intervention for LD.
3. describe the criteria for eligibility for LD services.
4. compare the traditional approaches to intervention for individuals with LD at the preschool, elementary, and secondary levels.
5. describe the challenges faced by adults with LD.
6. make modifications in teaching methods and classroom management to address academic, social, emotional, and cognitive differences.

E

mmanuel was six years old when he eagerly started first grade. Problems began to emerge as the reading program expanded from picture books with lots of repetition to books containing unknown words. Emmanuel had difficulty using context clues, and he had limited phonemic awareness in decoding a new word. His first report card showed "needs improvement" in reading, listening, and following directions. The bright spot in Emmanuel's first-grade achievement was his above-average functioning in math, his ability to pay attention, and good social skills. Emmanuel was promoted to second grade. Over the summer, his family moved to another state.

Emmanuel adjusted to the new school and everything was fine for the first nine weeks of review, and then he began to have trouble finishing his work. He became frustrated with written assignments and often complained of stomachaches, asking to stay home from school. His teachers felt that he was still adjusting to a new school.

By the middle of the year, his parents, teacher, and child study team agreed that adaptations were needed. The special education teacher put together material to develop phonemic awareness skills Emmanuel had not mastered. His parents agreed to work on this material at home. He also worked with a fifth-grade peer helper who read with him one-on-one three days a week. The classroom teacher agreed to restate oral instructions, to continue working on phonics, and to encourage Emmanuel to predict unknown words based on meaning and evaluate whether the word he guessed fit with the rest of the words in the sentence.

After six weeks the child study team still felt that Emmanuel was struggling too much, so they recommended a special education referral. His tests showed average intelligence and significant deficits in reading skills, writing, and listening. It was determined that Emmanuel had a learning disability, making him eligible for special education services.

Although signs of learning disabilities were present, the school proceeded slowly in identifying him as a child with a learning disability. (As discussed in Chapter 1, school personnel and parents often want to avoid labeling because it can be detrimental to children.) Emmanuel attended a resource class in third grade. Through these services, his reading of multisyllable words greatly improved as did his writing and listening skills. By fourth grade, he remained in the general education classroom full time, needing only periodic work with the learning disabilities teacher.

QUESTIONS TO CONSIDER

1. What alerted Emmanuel's teacher to a possible learning disability?
2. How might his move have been a factor in his school performance?
3. What would have happened to Emmanuel if he had not received special education services in third grade?

Just as it is difficult to distinguish children with LD from their peers by looks, you cannot distinguish adults with learning disabilities from other adults. You may be surprised to find that many important and famous people have made significant achievements in spite of experiencing a severe learning disability. Adults with learning disabilities can be found in all professions. They may be teachers, lawyers, doctors, blue-collar workers, or politicians! Read the examples that follow, and see whether you can identify the names of the individuals with learning disabilities.

During his childhood, this young man was an outstanding athlete, achieving great success and satisfaction from sports. Unfortunately, he struggled in the classroom. He tried very hard, but he always seemed to fail academically. His biggest fear was being asked to stand up and read in front of his classmates. He was frequently teased about his class performance, and he described his school days as sheer torture. His only feelings of success were experienced on the playing field.

When he graduated from high school, he didn't consider going to college because he "wasn't a terrific student, and never got into books all that much." Even though he was an outstanding high school pole vaulter, he did not get a single scholarship during his senior year. He had already gone to work with his father when he was offered a $500 football scholarship from Graceland College. He didn't accept that offer; instead he trained in track and field. Several years later, he won a gold medal in the Olympics in the grueling decathlon event! This story is about Bruce Jenner.

This individual was still illiterate at age 12, but he could memorize anything! Spelling was always impossible for him, and as he said, he "had trouble with the A, B, and that other letter." He also was a failure at math. He finally made it through high school, but he failed his first year at West Point. He did graduate, with the help of tutors, one year late. His special talent was in military strategy, and during World War II he became one of the United States' most famous generals. Of course, this story is about George Patton.

Other famous people with LD include Leonardo da Vinci, Tom Cruise, Cher, Nelson Rockefeller, Winston Churchill, Woodrow Wilson, F. W. Woolworth, Walt Disney, Ernest Hemingway, Albert Einstein, George Bernard Shaw, and Thomas Edison (Harwell, 1989; Silver, 1995). These and other individuals with learning disabilities are often misunderstood and teased early in life for their inadequacies in the classroom. To be successful, they had to be creative and persistent. Adults with learning disabilities succeed by sheer determination in overcoming their limitations and focusing on their talents.

Perhaps the most difficult aspect of understanding and teaching students with learning disabilities is the fact that the disability is hidden. When students with obviously normal intelligence fail to finish their work, interrupt inappropriately, never seem to follow directions, and turn in sloppy, poorly organized assignments, it is natural to blame poor motivation, lack of effort, and even an undesirable family life.

However, the lack of accomplishment and success in the classroom does have a cause; the students are not demonstrating these behaviors to upset or irritate their teachers. A **learning disability** is a cognitive disability; it is a disorder of thinking and reasoning. Because the dysfunction is presumed to be in the central nervous system, the presence of the disability is not visible.

The individuals with learning disabilities described earlier have experienced the frustration of living with a disability that is not easily identified. Children with learning disabilities look like the other students in their grade. They can perform like the other students in some areas, but not in others. Like Emmanuel in the chapter-opening vignette, a child may have good social skills and make good grades in math, but fail in reading. Another child may be able to read and write at grade level but fail in math and get in trouble for misconduct. Students with learning disabilities also may perform inconsistently. They may know spelling words on Thursday and fail the test on Friday.

In this chapter you will study the patterns of strengths and weakness of children, youth, and adults who experience unexplained underachievement. Professionals from many fields have joined the search for a definition and causes of these disabilities, as well as methods to identify affected children and to accommodate or remediate areas of the disability. Yet many questions remain.

In August 2001 a Learning Disability Summit was held in Washington, DC, to advance the "science" of dealing with LD and to provide leadership in this area for future reauthorizations of IDEA. Research presented at the summit is listed in Further Readings at the end of the chapter. You will see that the answers are still evolving, but much progress has been made in this exciting field (Polloway, 2002).

Basic Concepts About Learning Disabilities

Learning Disabilities Defined

Hallahan and Mercer (2001) discuss the history of LD, noting that the concept has long-standing recognition, dating back to a period they call the European Foundation Period (1800–1920). The early research focused on brain function. This era was followed by the Foundation Period (1920–1960), focusing on research on brain-injured adults with deficits in perception, attention, and the perceptual-motor area, and children with reading and language deficits. Since that time, more than 90 terms were introduced into the literature to describe these individuals. The most common terms include *minimal brain dysfunction (MBD), brain damage, central processing dysfunction,* and *language delay.* To add to the confusion, separate definitions were also offered to explain each term. The term *specific learning disabilities* was first adopted publicly in 1963 at a meeting of parents and professionals. Kirk (1962) developed the generic term *learning disabilities* in an effort to unite the field, which was torn between individuals promoting different theories regarding underachievement. The term was received favorably because it did not have the negative connotations of the other terms and did describe the primary characteristic of the children.

The Emergent Period (1960–1975) describes the development of professional and parent organizations to promote awareness of learning disabilities. During the Solidification Period (1975–1985), IDEA (then called PL 94–142) was passed, and it included learning disabilities as a disability category, citing a definition developed originally by a committee chaired by Kirk in 1968.

This definition, modified only slightly over the years, and retained in IDEA (1997), states:

> "Specific learning disability" means a disorder in one or more of the basic psychological processes involved in understanding or in using language, spoken or written, which may manifest itself in an imperfect ability to listen, think, speak, read, write, spell or to do mathematical calculations. The term includes such conditions as perceptual handicaps, brain injury, minimal brain dysfunction, dyslexia, and developmental aphasia. The term does not include children who have learning problems which are primarily the result of visual, hearing, or motor handicaps, of mental retardation, or emotional disturbance, or of environmental, cultural, or economic disadvantage. (USOE, 1977, p. 65083)

Hallahan and Mercer (2001) describe the period since this definition was published as the Turbulent Era. Dissension exists over the most effective methods to teach children with LD, as well as to identify and define them. A majority of states use the IDEA definition, but it has been criticized over the years for including concepts that are unclear or difficult to use to identify children with a learning disability (Swanson, 2000). The concept of deficits in "psychological processes" is the most nebulous and has been interpreted in several ways, including perceptual-motor deficits, deficits in the process of taking in information, difficulty in making sense of information and expressing knowledge effectively, and deficits in cognitive processes such as attention, memory, and metacognition (the way one thinks about and controls his or her cognitive processing, e.g., self-monitoring, predicting, and planning). As a result, the U.S. Office of Education did not include a measure of psychological processes when publishing the criteria for identifying students with learning disabilities. They focused instead on identifying a discrepancy between a child's ability and his or her achievement in reading, math, written language, speaking, or listening. These criteria will be described later in the chapter. A more straightforward definition is offered by Harwell (1989), who identifies an individual with a learning disability as one who

1. can see.
2. can hear.
3. has general intelligence in the near-average, average, or above-average range.
4. has educational difficulties that do not stem primarily from inadequate educational experience or cultural factors.
5. does not acquire and use information efficiently because of an impairment in perception, conceptualization, language, memory, attention, or motor control.

Prevalence and Causes of Learning Disabilities

In today's schools, there are by far more students with LD than with any other disability. Swanson (2000) proposes that the debate over the definition and eligibility criteria is to blame for the huge rise in the prevalence of LD. The number of students labeled as learning disabled has increased so significantly since it first was recognized as a disability that Swanson (2000) refers to the increase as epidemic. A report from the U.S. Department of Education (2000) shows that 51.2% of the students with disabilities between the ages of 6 and 21 were learning disabled (4.49 % of school children, with approximately four boys identified to every girl). It should be noted that this prevalence figure can vary widely between states and within a state, depending on the stringency of the method used to determine eligibility. For example, Kentucky reports the lowest prevalence figure (2.39%) and Massachusetts the highest (7.35%). A study completed in Michigan compared the learning disabilities eligibility criteria and procedures for identification across the 57 regional education service agencies in the state (RESA) (Haight, Patriarca, & Burns, 2001). The results showed that 21% of the RESAs had no written eligibility criteria or policies, the length of the written policies varied from one sentence to 112 pages, and the severe discrepancy formula score varied from 15 to 30 standard score points! It is possible for a student to move a few miles to the next school district and no longer be considered to have a learning disability. These results are also supported by a study in Georgia looking at the variability of minority representation across systems, with some systems identifying three to four times as many African Americans in learning disabilities classes as Caucasians, and other systems showing the opposite. National data suggest an equal distribution of Caucasian and African American students in learning disability classes (5.7%) (Colarusso, Keel, & Dangel, 2001).

Experts generally agree that learning is hindered in children with learning disabilities because of neurobiological abnormalities, or atypical brain development and/or function causing a problem in how the brain processes information (Fedorowicz, Benezra, MacDonald, McElgunn, Wilson, & Kaplan, 2001). This causes an unexpected discrepancy between intelligence and achievement. In a pamphlet for parents, the American Academy of Pediatrics (1988) describes the problem as

> similar to a distorted television picture caused by technical problems at the station. There is nothing wrong with the TV camera at the station or the TV set at home. Yet, the picture is not clear. Something in the internal workings of the TV station prevents it from presenting a good picture. There may be nothing wrong with the way the children take in information. Their senses of sight and sound are fine. The problem occurs after the eyes or ears have done their job. (p. 7)

Why this happens generally remains unknown. The literature suggests several causes, primarily hereditary factors and trauma experienced before birth, during birth, and after birth.

1. *Genetic factors:* Many studies have cited the large number of relatives with learning problems in children identified with learning disabilities. Chromosomal abnormalities and structural brain differences have been linked to learning disabilities. Raskind (2001) describes the progress that has been made identifying the gene location for a learning disability in reading. Research in this area continues to show promise.

2. *Causes occurring before birth:* Learning problems have been linked to injuries to the embryo or fetus caused by the birth mother's use of alcohol, cigarettes, or other drugs, such as cocaine and prescription and nonprescription drugs. Through the mother, the fetus is exposed to the toxins, causing malformations of the developing brain and central nervous system. Although significant amounts of overexposure to these drugs may cause serious problems, such as mental retardation, no safe levels have been identified.

3. *Causes occurring during birth process:* Traumas during birth may include prolonged labor, anoxia, prematurity, and injury from medical instruments such as forceps. Although not all children with a traumatic birth are found to have learning problems later, a significant number of children with learning problems do have a history of complications during this period.

4. *Causes occurring after birth:* High fever, encephalitis, meningitis, stroke, diabetes, and pediatric AIDS have been linked to LD. Malnutrition, poor postnatal health care, and lead ingestion can also lead to neurological dysfunction (Hallahan, Kauffman, & Lloyd, 1999; Fedorowicz et al., 2001).

> ### *T*EACHING TIP
>
> Often parents will ask teachers what causes a learning disability. To respond, you might discuss some of the possible causes and suggest that the specific cause is seldom identifiable for individual children. Reassure parents that pinpointing the cause is not important in planning and implementing effective intervention strategies.

Advances in neurological research and use of computerized neurological techniques such as computerized axial tomography (CAT) scan and positron emission tomography (PET) scan have made professionals more inclined to believe in a neurological explanation of learning disabilities. Widespread use of these tests to identify a learning disability has not been forthcoming for several reasons: such procedures are expensive and invasive, and the documented presence of a neurological dysfunction does not affect how the child is taught (Hallahan et al., 1999). However, this research is important to advance knowledge of this type of disability and in the future may help determine the effectiveness of various treatment techniques. Studies are currently under way to monitor the impact of various reading interventions on the results of neuroimaging (Pugh et al., 2001). A neurophysicist recently recommended using neuroimaging to identify young children with reading problems for treatment purposes, noting that learning to read can cause the brain to change and become like the brain of good readers (Richards, 2001). It is interesting to think about the possibility that one day brain imaging could be used to determine the best methods for teaching.

Characteristics of Students with Learning Disabilities

Learning disabilities are primarily described as deficits in academic achievement (reading, writing, and mathematics) and/or language (listening or speaking). However, children with learning disabilities may have significant problems in other areas, such as social interactions and emotional maturity, attention and hyperactivity, memory, cognition, metacognition, motor skills, and perceptual abilities. It is also important to understand that students with learning disabilities tend to be overly optimistic regarding some of their abilities, masking strategy and skill deficits. They may need more support in these areas than they report that they need (Klasson, 2002). Since learning disabilities are presumed to be a central nervous system dysfunction, characteristics may be manifested throughout the life span, preschool through adult (Bender, 2001).

The most common characteristics of students with LD are described briefly in the following sections, concentrating on the challenges they may create in a classroom. Students with learning disabilities are a heterogeneous group. A single student will not have deficits in all areas. Also, any area could be a strength for a student with learning disabilities, and the student might exceed the abilities of his or her peers in that area. An understanding of characteristics of children with learning problems is important in developing prereferral interventions, in making appropriate referrals, and in identifying effective adaptations and intervention strategies. Figure 6.1 displays the possible strengths and weaknesses of children with learning disabilities.

Academic Deficits   During the elementary years a discrepancy between ability and achievement begins to emerge in students with learning disabilities. Often puzzling to teachers, these students seem to have strengths similar to their peers in several areas, but their rate of learning in other areas is unexpectedly slower. The vignette that began this chapter profiles a typical child with learning disabilities: above-average ability in math; average ability in language, attention, and social skills; and severe deficits in reading, written expression, and listening. See the IEP Goals and Objectives for Emmanuel later in the chapter.

The academic problems that identify a learning disability fall into the areas of reading, math, and written expression. The most prevalent type of academic difficulty for students with learning disabilities is reading. Lyon et al. (2001) report that approximately 80% of the children identified as learning disabled have primary deficits in the area of reading and related language functions. Problems may be noted in *basic reading skills* and *reading comprehension.* Children with learning disabilities may struggle with oral reading tasks. They may read in a strained voice with poor phrasing, ignore punctuation, and grope for words like a much younger child. Oral reading problems cause tremendous embarrassment to these children. Polloway, Patton, and Serna (2001) confirm that a student's self-image and feelings of confidence are greatly affected by reading experience. Deficits in reading skills can also lead to acting-out behavior and poor motivation.

Some children with learning disabilities may be able to say the words correctly but not remember what they have read. Comprehension problems may include one or more of the following: (1) identifying the main idea, (2) recalling basic facts and events in a sequence, and (3) making inferences or evaluating what has been read. A child with a specific deficit in reading may be described as having **dyslexia.**

Another major academic problem area is mathematics. Students with learning disabilities may have problems in *math calculations* or *math reasoning* (USOE, 1977). These conceptual and skill areas include deficits in the four operations, the concept of zero, regrouping, place value, basic math concepts (e.g., one-to-one correspondence, sets), and solving math problems. Children may have *abilities* in calculation but have *disabilities* in

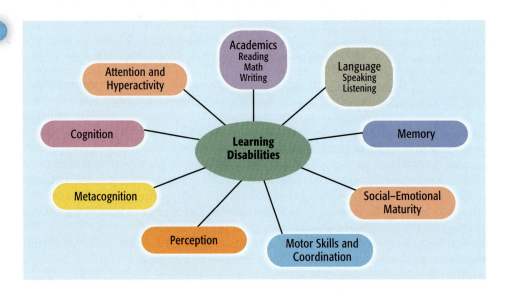

FIGURE 6.1

Areas of Possible Strengths and Deficits of Students with Learning Disabilities

During grades 2 through 6, academic problems begin to become very obvious.

math reasoning; they may make many errors in calculations but be able to perform calculations to solve a math word problem. Often the rate of response interferes with success in math; for example, a child may be able to perform the skill, but unable to complete the number of problems required during the time allowed. Robinson, Manchetti, and Torgeson (2002) proposed that for some children this math difficulty may be due to either deficits in the phonological processing of the features of spoken numbers or failure to grasp meaningful aspects of numbers. They note that 43% of the students with a math disability also have reading problems. It is hoped that math disabilities will soon be studied as intensely as reading disabilities. A disability in math is called **dyscalculia.**

Learning disabilities in the area of *written expression* are beginning to receive more recognition as a potentially serious problem. The three main areas of concern are handwriting, spelling, and written expression, including mechanics and creativity. The impact of written language problems increases with a student's age because so many school assignments require a written product. A learning disability in writing may be referred to as **dysgraphia.**

Language Deficits   Language deficits are found in the areas of *oral expression* and *listening comprehension.* Since these two areas control our ability to communicate with others, a deficit can have a major impact on quality of life—including life in a general education classroom. Studies have found that more than 60% of students with learning disabilities have some type of language disorder (Bryan, Bay, Lopez-Reyna, & Donahue, 1991). Common oral language problems include difficulty in retrieving words; children often use a less appropriate word because the right word will not come to them. The response rate of children with learning disabilities may be slower than that of their nondisabled peers, and they may speak more slowly. If ample time is not allowed for a response, the student's behavior may be misinterpreted as failure to understand or refusal to participate. Children with learning disabilities tend to use simpler, less mature language and confuse sequences in retelling a story. These deficits in expressive language suggest possible difficulties in receptive language or listening as well (Smith, 1994). Listening problems also can be easily misinterpreted. A child with a disability in listening demonstrates that disability in a negative way, for example, by failing to follow directions or by appearing oppositional or unmotivated. A teacher's careful observation and assessment of a student's language ability is important for ensuring the student's success.

A new area of concern and research for children with language-learning disabilities is the area of **pragmatics,** or use of language in social communication situations. Children with these disabilities are sometimes unsuccessful in fully participating in conversation. They may need extra time to process incoming information, or they may not understand the meaning of the words or word sequences. They may miss nonverbal language cues. They may not understand jokes; they may laugh inappropriately or at the wrong times. Group work is often difficult, as is giving or following directions. Language disabilities can contribute significantly to difficulties in other social situations as well.

Social-Emotional Problems   The literature suggests that to be socially accepted, students should be cooperative, share, offer pleasant greetings, have positive interactions with peers, ask for and give information, and make conversation (Gresham, 1982). Some children with learning disabilities have a real strength in the area of social skills. However, several characteristics of learning disabilities, like those noted concerning language, can create difficulties in social and emotional life. Social skills deficits of children with learning disabilities include resolving conflict, managing frustrations, initiating or joining a conversation or play activities, listening, demonstrating empathy, maintaining a friendship, and working in groups. About a third of the students with learning disabilities have nonverbal, or social, disabilities (Morris, 2002). These students and those with ADHD have also been shown to have lower self-concept in academics and social relations (Tabassam & Grainger, 2002).

A study by Kavale and Forness (1996) shows that a perception of low academic achievement was directly related to reduced acceptance, less interaction, greater rejection, and lower social status among peers. Often positive interactions and exchange of information do not occur between children with learning disabilities and their peers or teachers. Because of behavior and language differences, children with learning disabilities need more guidance and structure. Over time, this need can create feelings of overdependency, and eventually *learned helplessness* can occur. Social deficits have even been known to lead to school failure (Bryan, 1999).

Years of failure can create other concerns. Wright-Strawderman and Watson (1992) found that 36% of a sample of students with learning disabilities indicated depression. Other researchers have reported psychological problems including feelings of anxiety, inadequacy, frustration, and anger (Bender, 2002). Confusion and frustration can also result in aggressive behavior (Allsopp, Santos, & Linn, 2000). Research by Kavale and Forness (1996) demonstrated that 75% of students with learning disabilities were significantly different from their nondisabled peers on most measures of social competence.

By adolescence, a student's combined cognitive and language deficits can interfere significantly with deciding how to act in the new social situations brought about by increased independence. When interacting with normal adolescents who have advanced language skills, students with disabilities may experience greater failure in communication and may suffer more rejection (Morris, 2002). The negative self-image of teenagers with learning disabilities is evident in Geisthardt and Munsch's (1996) study, which found that adolescents with learning disabilities were more likely to report that they had failed a class and less likely to report that they had been selected for a school activity than their nondisabled peers. They were also less likely to call on peers for support when dealing with a personal or academic problem.

In summary, Gorman (1999) proposes that learning disabilities may result in or increase emotional distress. Emotional issues may mask or exacerbate a child's LD. However, she also notes that positive emotional health can enhance the performance of students with learning disabilities. By being sensitive to emotional issues, you can take care to include students with learning disabilities in supportive situations and provide reinforcement for specific successes. General praise statements such as "Good work!" or "You are really smart!" will not have much impact because they are not believable to the students. Commenting on or rewarding specific accomplishments will be more effec-

CROSS-REFERENCE

Often students with learning disabilities who have social-emotional difficulties will present challenges in behavior management in the classroom. Refer to Chapter 14 for more information in this area.

tive. Additional examples of appropriate interventions are discussed later in this chapter and in future chapters.

Attention Deficits and Hyperactivity   Attention is a critical skill in learning. Conte (1991) suggests that to be effective learners, children must be able to initiate attention, direct their attention appropriately, sustain their attention according to the task demands, and shift attention when appropriate. Deficits in these areas can have an impact on all aspects of success in school. When children are "not paying attention," they cannot respond appropriately to questions, follow directions, or take notes during a lecture. The excess movement of a hyperactive student can draw sharp criticism when it negatively affects the learning environment. Social problems occur when the student interrupts others and does not listen to his or her peers. Students with attention problems often have trouble finishing assignments or rush through their work with little regard for detail. Estimates of the number of students with learning disabilities that have attention problems range from 41% to 80% (DeLong, 1995).

Memory Deficits   Several studies have suggested that students with learning disabilities have more deficits in memory than students without learning disabilities except in the area of long-term memory (Swanson, 1994). Students with memory deficits have trouble retaining learned information. They may have difficulty in repeating information recently read or heard, following multiple directions, or performing tasks in the correct sequence. Teachers and parents may also report that the memory skills are inconsistent—for example, such a student may know the multiplication facts on Thursday and fail the test on Friday! O'Shaughenessy and Swanson (1998) suggest that the problem is mainly with an inability to code new information for memory storage and a decreased motivation for difficult mental effort. The good news is that when children with learning disabilities are taught a memory strategy, they perform memory tasks as well as non-learning-disabled students.

Cognition Deficits   Cognition refers to the ability to reason or think (Hallahan, Kauffman, & Lloyd, 1996). Students with problems in this area may make poor decisions or frequent errors. They may have trouble getting started on a task, have delayed verbal responses, require more supervision, or have trouble adjusting to change. Understanding social expectations may be difficult. They may require concrete demonstrations. They often have trouble using previously learned information in a new situation.

Metacognition Deficits   Hallahan et al. (1999) refer to **metacognition** as "thinking about thinking." Students with problems in this area might have difficulty focusing on listening, purposefully remembering important information, connecting that information to prior knowledge, making sense out of the new information, and using what they know to solve a problem. They often lack strategies for planning and organizing, setting priorities, and predicting and solving problems. An important component of metacognition is the ability to evaluate one's own behavior and behave differently when identifying inappropriate behavior or mistakes.

Perceptual Differences   Perceptual disorders affect the ability to recognize stimuli being received through sight, hearing, or touch and to discriminate between and interpret the sensations appropriately. A child with a learning disability might not have any problems in these areas, or he or she might have deficits in any or all of them. Research has shown that visual perception is more important at very young ages but is not a major requirement for higher level academics (Smith, 1994). Identification of deficits and training in the perceptual processes was emphasized in the early 1970s; however, it is no longer a prominent consideration in the education of children with learning disabilities.

CROSS-REFERENCE

Many students with learning disabilities have attention deficit/hyperactivity disorders. This topic is covered more extensively in Chapter 5.

Motor Skill and Coordination Problems   This area has also been deemphasized in the identification of an intervention for children with learning disabilities because it is not directly related to academics. However, it is common for children with learning disabilities to display problems in gross motor areas; they often cannot throw and catch a ball or may have a clumsy gait. Common fine motor deficits include difficulties with using scissors, buttoning clothing, and handwriting. Individuals with learning disabilities may also have a slow reaction time. Consideration of exceptionalities or disabilities in motor skills and coordination is especially important in the selection of postsecondary educational programs and ultimately in the identification of a career.

Identification, Assessment, and Eligibility

Because of the difficulty in measuring some of the nebulous constructs included in the definition of learning disabilities (e.g., psychological processes), the federal government has specified stronger criteria to assess and identify learning disabilities and to determine eligibility for special education services. Following a national debate that lasted for two years after PL 94–142 was passed in 1975, the federal regulations for definition and identification criteria for learning disabilities were published in the Federal Register (USOE, 1977). These are considered minimal standards, and states may require additional criteria. The criteria include the following:

▶ *Multidisciplinary team:* A group of individuals, including a classroom teacher, at least one individual qualified to perform diagnostic examinations of children, and a learning disabilities specialist, is required to determine eligibility.

▶ *Observation:* A student must be observed by at least one member of the team in the general education classroom. The purpose of the observation is to document the manifestation of the disability in the classroom.

▶ Criteria for determining a learning disability:
  1. The team must determine the existence of a severe discrepancy between achievement and intellectual ability in one or more of the following areas: (a) reading skills, (b) reading comprehension, (c) mathematical calculations, (d) mathematical reasoning, (e) written expression, (f) oral expression, and (g) listening comprehension. [An example is presented in Figure 6.2.]
  2. The team may not identify a student as having a specific learning disability if the severe discrepancy between ability and achievement is primarily the result of (a) a visual, hearing, or motor handicap, (b) mental retardation, (c) emotional disturbance, or (d) economic disadvantage.
  3. The team must document that appropriate learning opportunities have been provided.

▶ *Written report:* A written report is required to provide information to document that each of the above criteria was met. It must be noted on the report whether all team members agree with the findings. (USOE, 1977, p. 65083)

As mentioned earlier, the definition and criteria have been left unchanged since 1977 despite widespread criticism. Recently, however, government leaders in Washington, DC, have begun to emphasize the importance of developing a "genuine science" for dealing with learning disabilities (Elksnin et al., 2001). The reauthorization of IDEA debates will include serious discussion on whether significant changes are needed in the policies used to identify and serve students with learning disabilities. Following are a few of the issues. With the negative impact of the label (Higgins, Raskind, Goldberg, & Herman, 2002), some feel it is critical that we only apply the label to those who are truly learning disabled. Others have asked why students with specific learning disabilities are any more entitled to resources than those students who struggle for other reasons or are just slow (Finn, Rotherham, & Hokanson, 2002). MacMillian and Siperstein (2001) suggest that public schools are using low achievement alone without considering the discrepancy from aptitude, essentially making learning disabilities a "category of failure" or low achievement. Kavale (2001) suggests that without the discrepancy factor, the existence of learning disabilities as a category is endangered. However, he suggests that determining discrepancy

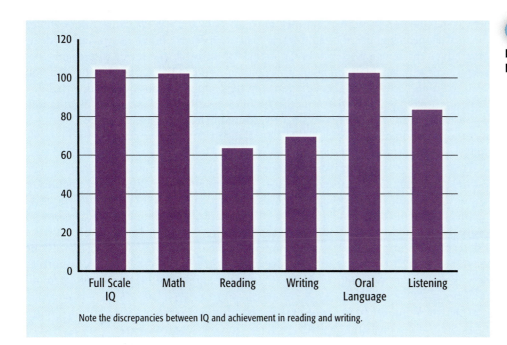

FIGURE 6.2

Profile of a Student with Learning Disabilities

Note the discrepancies between IQ and achievement in reading and writing.

should be only one component of the assessment process. Wise and Snyder (2001), primarily focusing on reading, recommend the use of clinical judgment to determine disability and to identify the most effective instructional interventions. Other researchers also studying reading found that the students with low achievement had scores that were higher than the students with learning disabilities, especially on timed measures requiring skills in comprehension. Their research suggests that students with learning disabilities may be the lowest of the low achievers. Still others suggest that it is the lack of response to intervention that separates learning disabilities from other low achieving groups, and they recommend that this be considered in identification (Fuchs et al., 2001). It will be interesting to see which recommendations are endorsed as the debate over identification is resolved for the reauthorization of IDEA.

Steps in the Assessment Process   When a student with deficits in areas of academic achievement is referred, the IEP team reviews the concerns stated on the referral and develops a comprehensive evaluation plan. One member of the evaluation team is assigned to observe the student in the general education classroom. This individual looks for any behaviors that might pose a limitation to success such as inattention, impulsivity, or difficulties following directions. The student's academic deficits are noted, as well as the teacher's instructional style, to determine whether modifications could be made to reduce deficits in learning.

The student is also evaluated for possible vision and hearing problems to determine whether these areas could be the cause of the learning problems. A professional with specialized training is assigned to administer an individualized intelligence test and evaluate the student in any academic areas in which there is a suspected deficit. Kavale (2001) recommends a combination of standardized, norm-referenced, and informal tests to measure achievement. In addition to measuring achievement, one or more teachers familiar with the student and often the student's parents complete a behavior rating scale. This behavioral assessment is completed in order to rule out the possibility that the primary cause of the deficit(s) in academic achievement is emotional or behavioral factors, suggesting that the child might be more appropriately served under the category seriously emotionally disturbed.

When all of the data have been collected, the team reviews the student's ability and determines whether or not there is a severe discrepancy between the student's ability and

CONSIDER THIS

Reflect on the characteristics of learning disabilities, such as deficits in attention, memory, cognition, and metacognition. What impact would these deficits have on success in the classroom?

achievement in one or more of the areas in which he or she was evaluated. Although this practice has been highly criticized (Meyer, 2000), this determination is typically made by obtaining a discrepancy score using a formula to quantify the severe discrepancy between achievement and potential (Kavale 2001). As noted earlier, there is wide variation in the formulas used. If there is a discrepancy, the team must consider whether that discrepancy could possibly be the result of a vision or hearing problem, mental retardation, emotional disturbance, or a disadvantaged economic status. It should be noted, however, that the exclusion of students with behavioral disturbance and social or cultural disadvantage has been highly questioned (Fletcher et al., 2001).

The team must also consider the student's history and document that appropriate learning opportunities have been provided. A child might not be determined eligible, for example, if a student's school attendance is reviewed and the team notes that the child has moved frequently during the school years, thus causing him or her to miss out on content as a result of the differences in each school's curriculum. If, after the review, the IEP team, including the parents, determines that the student is eligible for services, the team may decide to write the individualized educational plan immediately or return to develop the plan at a separate meeting. More information on educational plans is found in Chapter 4.

The criteria published in the Federal Register for identification of a learning disability (USOE, 1977) focus on the language, academic, and exclusion concepts and do not address the identification of deficits in areas like attention and memory. However, it is often these characteristics and others noted in the characteristics section that create the biggest barriers to success in the general education classroom and later in the workforce. Teachers should be very familiar with the characteristics of learning disabilities and the impact they might have on functioning in a general education classroom. They should also understand that these characteristics are not manifested intentionally but occur as a result of a presumed central nervous system dysfunction.

Difficulty of Identifying Preschool Students with Learning Disabilities   Because these criteria for determining a learning disability (USOE, 1977) mainly involve academic and language deficits that emerge in the elementary years, the identification of disabilities and delivery of special education services for preschool children are very controversial (Jenkins & O'Conner, 2001). The National Joint Committee on Learning Disabilities (NJCLD) issued a paper in 1988 describing this issue. They noted that the greatest complication in identifying preschool children with learning disabilities is the tremendous differences in growth and maturation that children manifest, which are normal and may not represent a learning disability. Hallahan et al. (1999) present two arguments against early identification of learning disabilities. The first concerns the difficulty in diagnosis that results from the inadequacy of assessment tools and procedures for this age group. Young children may have language and other skills that are lower than expected based on IQ, but it is difficult to determine whether these are the result of a learning disability, a maturational lag, or the effect of diverse educational experiences, language, and/or culture. The second argument takes into account the risk of diagnosing a learning disability where none exists, thus labeling and burdening the child unnecessarily. However, this argument does not address the fact that an equal risk is taken when a student who needs special educational services is not diagnosed and appropriately assisted; this student may be burdened by difficulties and failure that could have been avoided. Many authors of the Summit papers referenced at the end of the chapter in Further Readings stress the need for early intervention.

Critics call current practice for learning disabilities identification the "wait and fail" effect as the gap or discrepancy between ability and achievement becomes large enough to be labeled as a severe discrepancy that warrants services (MacMillian & Siperstein, 2001). Lyon et al. (2001) concluded that a child must be nine years old before discrepancy from IQ can be measured reliably. Thus, under the discrepancy model, potentially life-changing failure occurs for several years. They suggest that early intervention can be so critical for disabilities in the area of reading that children with a strong family history of attention difficulties or reading failure should be labeled at risk and placed in a preventive intervention program to strengthen their deficit areas. Currently each state determines the proper age for identifying a child with a learning disability or one who is at risk for early school failure. The American Academy of Pediatrics (1988) recommends the following benchmarks for ascertaining risk of learning disabilities:

1. *Language delay:* Children should be putting sentences together by age 2½.
2. *Difficulty with speech:* By the age of 3, a child's language should be understandable by adults more than 50% of the time.
3. *Coordination problems:* By the age of 5, children should be tying shoes, buttoning clothes, hopping, and cutting with scissors.
4. *Short attention span:* Although attention span increases with age, between ages 3 and 5, children should be sitting and attending while a short story is read to them. (p. 35)

Cultural and Linguistic Diversity

Since learning disabilities are found in approximately 5% of the school-age population and the number of school-age children with cultural and language diversity is growing steadily, inevitably many children will fall into both groups (Gerstan & Woodward, 1994). Although the issues related to educating all culturally diverse children apply to the population of children with learning disabilities as well, the existence of a learning disability does bring additional challenges in assessment for identification, program planning, instructional implementation, and personnel preparation.

Accurately identifying a learning disability in the presence of cultural diversity is no small challenge. School personnel must carefully determine that the differences related to diversity are not the primary cause of a student's learning difficulties. Teachers sometimes expect less from students from diverse cultural backgrounds and view special education as the most viable placement option for them (Gerstan, Brengelman, & Jimenez,

CONSIDER THIS

A child's having a language and vocabulary other than English has a significant impact on the assessment process. Inappropriate referrals, identification of a disability, and/or inappropriate programming might result.

Diversity Forum

From Learning to Read to Reading to Learn

Tyrone is struggling through his sixth grade year. In fourth grade he was diagnosed with a learning disability in the area of reading. His decoding skills are fair, but he struggles to understand what he has read. Now that he is in middle school, he receives 50 minutes of daily instruction in a reading and language arts resource setting with a teacher who provides explicit instruction in decoding or reading comprehension. Tyrone struggles to keep up with his content area work in science and social studies. His teachers want to know how to help.

Many students with learning disabilities in the area of reading struggle to keep up with the increased reading requirements of middle school (Bryant, Ugel, Thompson, & Hamff, 1999). By this time, they are expected to simultaneously decode and derive meaning from text. Often, teachers assume that middle school students have already mastered reading strategies, and they may spend little time building decoding and comprehension skills. They are also likely to underestimate the importance of students' culture and linguistic patterns in developing reading skills and motivating students to read. As a result, many African American learners with reading disabilities do not receive the support they need to read and appreciate complex texts.

To support middle school students' reading and comprehension, teachers can

▶ introduce new texts by discussing students' previous knowledge of the topic and allowing students to formulate reasons why mastery of new knowledge is relevant to their present and future circumstances.

▶ link previously learned concepts with new and complex vocabulary, and emphasize multiple ways of using this vocabulary in culture-specific situations.

▶ discuss new vocabulary and word use across contexts, a process that is critical because it assists students in accessing higher level, academic language that is needed for success in all areas of schooling.

▶ build students' word reading skills by incorporating brief yet explicit lessons in decoding.

For follow-up questions about middle school reading strategies and culture-specific contexts, go to Chapter 6 of the Companion Website (ablongman. com/sppd4e) and click Diversity Forum.

Companion Website

1994). As a result, a disproportionate number are referred for assessment and ultimately funneled into special education settings. Moecker (1992) found that too often a diagnosis of learning disability was based on intelligence and achievement tests administered in English without considering cultural and language difference. The referral itself may be made because a monolingual teacher has been ineffective in teaching a student who comes from another culture or who uses English as a second language. In this case, the child's failure to make progress may not be the result of a learning disability but the failure of the educational system to respect and adequately respond to cultural and language differences. However, it is certainly possible that a child with a low socioeconomic level or one who speaks English as a second language could have a central nervous system dysfunction that results in a learning disability. The IEP committee often has a big challenge in considering the diversity variable.

Strategies for Curriculum and Instruction for Students with Learning Disabilities

Over the years, treatment procedures for individuals with learning disabilities have been controversial. In the 1970s, advocates for perceptual training of auditory and visual processes debated those who advocated direct instruction in the deficit academic area(s) (Engelmann & Carnine, 1982). A convincing article by Hammill and Larsen (1974) analyzed research showing that perceptual training did little to improve basic academic skills. This triggered a move toward a skills approach, in which direct instruction was implemented in the areas of academic deficit. More recently, language, social-emotional, and cognitive-metacognitive areas have received positive attention. Many approaches have gained acceptance as research-based methods for improving the skills and developing the abilities of children and adults with learning disabilities. Other nontraditional approaches have been proposed, and some even have a large following, though they may not be supported by research. Teachers need to be well informed on all approaches so that they can provide objective information to parents who seek to understand and address their child's difficulties. The following section discusses the accepted traditional approaches for each age level and a brief overview of some of the nontraditional approaches.

Traditional Approaches

In a review of various treatment approaches, Elkins et al. (2001) conclude that no single approach to learning disabilities can be cited as the best. They suggest that each model has a "partial view of the truth" and "each individually is too narrow to be useful for all students" (p. 189). Lloyd (1988) suggests that the most effective ones are structured and goal-oriented, provide multiple opportunities for practice, include a strategy, foster independence, and are comprehensive and detailed. Many of the following approaches adhere to these time-tested principles. They all can be implemented in a general education classroom and may benefit many nondisabled students as well. The strategies are discussed according to age levels—preschool, elementary, secondary, and adult. The largest section concerns the elementary school student; however, many elementary-level techniques are equally effective at the secondary level. An understanding of these approaches is critical, as recent federal data indicate that in 1997–1998, 95.6% of students with learning disabilities received at least 60% of their instruction in the general education classroom.

Preschool Services   In addition to the controversy surrounding assessment and identification of learning disabilities in preschool children, much has been written for and against the educational effectiveness and cost-effectiveness of early intervention programs for these children. Bender (2001) summarizes research in this area by stating that

Most children with learning disabilities are identified during early elementary grades.

early intervention for some preschool children with learning disabilities—particularly those from low socioeconomic minority groups—is effective.

Mercer (1997) provides an overview of the curriculum models primarily used in preschool programs for children with learning disabilities. These include developmental, cognitive, and behavioral models. The **developmental model** stresses provision of an enriched environment. The child is provided numerous experiences and opportunities for learning. Development is stimulated through language and storytelling, field trips, and creative opportunities. These activities are particularly effective with diverse learners (Craig, Hull, Haggart, & Crowder, 2001).

The **cognitive model** (or constructionist model) is based on Piaget's work. Stimulating the child's cognitive or thinking abilities is the primary focus. Activities are designed to improve memory, discrimination, language, concept formation, self-evaluation, problem solving, and comprehension. This new area of research is experiencing great success.

Concepts learned by direct instruction and the theory of reinforcement form the basis for the **behavioral model.** Measurable goals are set for each student, behaviors are observed, and desirable behavior is reinforced. Direct instruction is provided to accomplish goals, and progress is charted to provide data that determine the next instructional task. For example, Abbott, Walton, and Greenwood (2002) used research on phonemic awareness to identify skills appropriate for K, 1, and 2. Students showing low performance during the regular shared book activities were given lessons several times a week depending on their level of deficit. Performance was closely monitored and intervention intensified as needed.

Mercer (1997) recommends a program that combines features from each approach. He suggests some structure, availability of free-choice activities, direct instruction in targeted areas, daily charting and feedback, developmental activities, and spontaneous learning experiences. McCardle, Cooper, Houle, Kart, and Paul-Brown (2001) speak to the importance of the birth-to-five period as the foundation for learning as children acquire knowledge and develop abilities—particularly in the area of reading. They like others speak against the "wait to fail" approach where children are not identified as struggling readers until the third or fourth grade. These researchers recommend a focus on book reading, writing, and fine-motor activities like coloring and drawing, as well as on developmental experiences that enhance vocabulary and increase language and communication skills.

These methods allow individual needs to be met in an inclusive setting without stigmatizing the children. Since children at this age are more likely to be falsely identified as learning disabled because of a maturational lag or lack of educational opportunities, it is particularly important to teach them in inclusive settings if at all possible. Lyons et al. (2001) agreed that the most efficient way to intervene early in reading is through general education. They and others recommend that resources be allocated for intervention instead of the expensive process of determining eligibility. Lyons et al. summarized several studies stating that when intervention is used with the bottom 18% of the student population and works on 70%, the number of at-risk children requiring services drops from 18 to 5.4%.

Elementary Services   The importance of intervention during the early elementary years is validated by Lyons et al. (2001) suggesting that over 70% of the children with a reading disability in the third grade remained disabled in the twelfth grade. Similarly, Cunningham and Stanovich (1997) found that reading ability in first grade was a strong predictor of reading ability in eleventh grade. As discussed in the section on characteristics, many of these deficits remain a problem throughout an individual's life. The intervention begun during elementary years may be equally important at the secondary level and for some adults. Intervention is important in academic and language deficits, social-emotional problems, and cognitive and metacognitive deficits.

Children with learning disabilities may have academic and language deficits in any or all of the following areas:

▶ Basic reading skills
▶ Reading comprehension
▶ Math calculation
▶ Math reasoning
▶ Written expression
▶ Oral expression
▶ Listening

Since these areas are usually the focus of an elementary curriculum, they can very often be addressed in the general education classroom. Both general and special education teachers have been trained to provide instruction in these areas, so collaborative teaching is possible. Because of the uneven skill development in children with learning disabilities, individualized assessment is generally required to identify areas that specifically need to be addressed. Informal methods, such as the curriculum-based assessment discussed in Chapter 4, are usually effective for planning instruction. This assessment should include an evaluation of the student's strengths, which may indicate the most effective method for instruction.

Because student strengths and weaknesses are so diverse, a single method of teaching may not meet the needs of all students with learning disabilities. For example, in the area of reading instruction, the majority of general education teachers use a reading approach based on reading literature for meaning; development in areas such as phonics is assumed to occur naturally as the reader becomes more efficient. In this method, often referred to as the **whole language method,** the teacher might note difficulty with a phonetic principle during oral reading and subsequently develop a mini-lesson using text to teach the skill. Resources are available on using this method to teach students with learning disabilities (Rhodes & Dudley-Marling, 1996). Unfortunately, many children with learning disabilities do not readily acquire the alphabet code because of limitations in processing the sounds of letters. Research has shown a dramatic reduction in reading failure when comprehensive, explicit instructions are provided in **phonemic awareness,** a **structured sequential phonics program** for decoding and fluent word recognition, processing text to construct meaning, vocabulary, spelling, and writing. A small number of children will need an intense small-group or one-on-one format (Foorman & Torgesen, 2001). A survey of teaching practices used by special education teachers nominated as effective literacy teachers showed that they used the best of whole language and direct instruction. See Table 6.1 to learn the practices and philosophies of these outstanding teachers.

One strength of the whole language method is its focus on the comprehension of authentic reading material; the teacher using the phonics method must purposely develop those important comprehension skills. Figure 6.3 describes an effective activity to engage students in writing and activities to help them remember what they read and use literature

TABLE 6.1 Philosophies, Learning Environments, and Instructional Processes and Practices Frequently Reported by Effective Special Education Teachers of Reading and Writing

General Philosophies and Learning Environments

Identify with a Whole Language Philosophy
Use of the language experience approach
Create a literate environment in the classroom, including in-class library, chart stories, signs and labels, and word lists
Use of themes to organize reading and writing instruction, with these themes extending into other curricular areas
Attempt to motivate literacy encouraging positive attitudes, providing positive feedback, reducing risks for attempting literacy activities, accepting where students are and working from that point, creating an exciting mood, encouraging personal interpretations, and conveying the importance of reading and writing in daily life
Encourage ownership and personal decision making

General Teaching Processes

Ability grouping for half of instruction, however, not in the form of traditional reading groups
Small group and individualized instruction is predominant
Direct instruction of attending behaviors
Direct instruction of listening skills
Assess learning styles and adjustment of instruction accordingly
Parent communication and involvement—specific reading and writing activities occurring with parents at home
Monitor progress several times a week by both formal and informal methods

Teaching of Reading

Types of Reading and Materials
Total class and individual silent reading
Individual oral reading, including round-robin reading
Different types of materials used—materials with controlled reading level, outstanding children's literature, materials that provide practice in specific phonetic elements and patterns (about half as often as the others)

What Is Taught
Concepts of print, including punctuation, sounds associated with print, concept of words and letters, parts of a book, directionality of print; taught both in context and isolation
Alphabetic principle and alphabet recognition; taught in context, isolation, with games and puzzles
Letter–sound associations, auditory discrimination, and visual discrimination; taught in context, isolation, with games and puzzles

Decoding skills taught several times a day in both context and isolation, most frequently teaching sounding out words and use of context cues
Explicit teaching of phonics based on individual student needs
Explicit teaching of sight words
Develop new vocabulary, using words from stories, other reading and writing, and student-selected words
Direct teaching of comprehension strategies, most frequently teaching prediction of upcoming events, finding the main idea, and activation of prior knowledge
Explicit attempts to develop background knowledge
Teach text elements, including character analysis, sequence of events, theme, details, and plot
Teach about various illustrators

Instructional Practice—Both Traditional and Whole Language
Use of worksheets and workbooks for specific instructional purposes
Use of frequent drill and repetition (for learning such things as sight words, phonic elements, spelling words, letter recognition), occurring both in the context of reading and writing and in more traditional practice methods
Tracing and copying of letters and words
Daily reading, both independent and in groups
Read stories to students with students "reading along"
Overt modeling of reading and writing
Comprehension questions asked for nearly all stories read
Weekly use of literature discussions
Use of story mapping or webbing to teach text elements
Publish students' work

Teaching Writing

Frequent writing (several times a week to several times a day)
Model the writing process
Students write stories, journals, and books
Guided writing
Write in response to reading
Teach planning, drafting, and revising as part of writing
Teach punctuation, both in context of real writing and in isolation
Teach spelling, including high-frequency words, words from spelling and reading curriculum, and words from students' writing
Acceptance and encouragement of invented spelling

From "Literacy in Special Education" (p. 221), by J. L. Rankin-Erickson and M. Pressley, 2000, *Learning Disabilities Research and Practice, 15*(4), 206–225.

IEP Goals and Objectives for Emmanuel

The chapter-opening vignette explains that Emmanuel is struggling primarily in the areas of reading, listening, and writing. The following sample from his IEP shows his top three goals and the objectives necessary to meet them.

Goal 1: Reading *Emmanuel will read orally and demonstrate comprehension of text on the third grade level.*

Objective 1: *Given a list of Dolch sight words, Emmanuel will read words through third grade level with 80% accuracy three times in a row.*

Objective 2: *Given a paragraph on his reading level, Emmanuel will use context clues to predict unknown words with 70% accuracy.*

Objective 3: *Given a list of 10 multisyllable words in isolation and a list of 10 multisyllable words in text, Emmanuel will correctly apply phonetic patterns in decoding the words with an 80% accuracy rate.*

Objective 4: *Given a paragraph at his reading level, Emmanuel will read the text and respond to comprehension questions orally or in writing with an 80% accuracy rate.*

Goal 2: Listening *Emmanuel will increase his listening skills.*

Objective 1: *Given a list of words orally, Emmanuel will display his increased phonemic awareness skills by repeating them in order with 80% accuracy.*

Objective 2: *After listening to a story read by the teacher, Emmanuel will retell it with age-appropriate detail, with 80% accuracy.*

Objective 3: *Given a multistep set of oral directions, Emmanuel will follow each step with 100% accuracy.*

Goal 3: Writing *Emmanuel will develop age-appropriate writing skills.*

Objective 1: *Given a list of Dolch words through third grade level, Emmanuel will spell the words correctly with 80% accuracy.*

Objective 2: *Given a list of Dolch words through third grade level, Emmanuel will apply phonetic patterns to spell multisyllable words with 80% accuracy.*

Objective 3: *Given the assignment to write in his daily journal, Emmanuel will write daily journal entries using age-appropriate vocabulary.*

Objective 4: *Given the assignment to write in his daily journal, Emmanuel will construct complete sentences, including correct capitalizations, punctuation, and grammar, with 80% accuracy.*

Objective 5: *Given a topic sentence, Emmanuel will generate a paragraph with at least five sentences, including a topic sentence, supporting details, and a concluding sentence, with 80% accuracy.*

to reinforce specific phonics skills. These two reading methods are discussed further in Chapter 15.

Another way to facilitate success for students with learning disabilities in inclusive settings is teaching a **strategy** to apply during the process of learning new information or skills. A strategy is defined by Deshler and Lenz (1989) as an individual's approach to a task. It includes how "a person thinks and acts when planning, executing, and evaluating performance on a task and its subsequent outcomes" (p. 203). Students with learning disabilities may not automatically develop strategies for learning, or the ones they develop may be inefficient. With the increased emphasis on state competency tests, it is more important than ever to remember academic content. Using mnemonic strategies can help students with learning disabilities having problems with memory. For example, to remember $4 \times 8 = 32$, the student might associate "door" for "4" and "gate" for "8" and

Main Idea Activity

Book Title	Chapter 1	Chapter 2	Chapter 3	Chapter 4
	Illustration Main Idea			
Chapter 5	Chapter 6	Chapter 7	Chapter 8	Student Name

Directions:

1. Fold a piece of paper into the appropriate number of squares.

2. After reading chapter one, write the main idea on your main idea poster.

3. Illustrate the main idea (see chart for a visual direction).

4. Go on to the next chapter.

Phonics Activity

Directions:

1. Fold a piece of paper to resemble a bookmark.

2. Draw a picture at the top of your bookmark. (Make sure it relates to your book.)

3. Locate words in your book that address the skill you are working on.

4. As you find words in your book, write them on the inside of the bookmark.

FIGURE 6.3

Reading Activities
From "Engaging Students in Meaningful Reading" (p. 17), by A. Rossow and C. Hess, 2001, *Teaching Exceptional Children, 33*(6), 15–20.

a "dirty shoe" for "32," so the association to visualize would be a door on a gate by a dirty shoe (Wood & Frank, 2000). The phases of one effective strategy to increase reading comprehension are highlighted in Inclusion Strategies. Additional strategies are discussed in Chapter 16.

Students with learning disabilities in the area of mathematics have been described by Gersten and Chard (1999) as lacking in "number sense." They propose that the traditional method of math instruction for students in special education that focuses on teaching algorithms and being drilled on number facts has led to a lack of general understanding. They described these students as being able to "do" math without "knowing" how to reason and communicate math meaning. Cawley and Foley (2001) describe methods of enhancing the quality of mathematics for students with learning disabilities by teaching the big ideas in math and using instructional techniques that promote students as problem solvers rather than routine followers. These methods in turn develop the "number sense" that encourages student to think about what they "know" and are "doing."

Written language is often difficult to master for children and adults with learning disabilities. Unfortunately, making too many adaptations in this area may result in underdeveloped skills. For example, if a student is always allowed to use another student's notes or allowed to take tests orally in place of written exams, the short-term benefits may be helpful, but instruction and experience in note taking and writing essay answers must be continued if growth is to occur in these areas. A study by Palinscar and Klenk (1992) suggests that special education teachers frequently limit students' writing tasks to copying words and filling out worksheets, so it is important in inclusive classrooms that students be exposed to a variety of writing opportunities. Students with learning disabilities must

TEACHING TIP

Many students with learning disabilities resist the challenge to write because of prior negative feedback. Try giving them multiple opportunities without grading, and then grade only one or two skills at a time. For example, one week you might grade punctuation, and the next, spelling. You can also give one grade for content and another for mechanics, and then average the two scores for the final grade.

Reading Comprehension Strategies for the General Education Classroom

Brainstorming:	Have students think about what they already know on the topic from prior lessons, reading, movies, and so forth.
Preview:	Have students work in small groups to preview assigned text. Give them 2 minutes to search for clues about key ideas, characters, settings, etc. Give students 6 minutes to discuss their predictions and develop their "preview."
Click:	After reading a designated portion of text, have students write down words they "click" on. These are words or information that they know about and that can extend information in text.
Clunk:	When students "clunk," they come to words or information they don't recognize or understand and need to know to learn new information. These words/ideas are written down to explore for them through a "declunking" strategy. Strategies for solving "clunks" are as follows:

Strategies for Solving Clunks

Clunk card #1:	Reread the sentence with the clunk and the sentences before or after the clunk, looking for clues.
Clunk card #2:	Reread the sentence without the word. Think about what would make sense.
Clunk card #3:	Look for a prefix or suffix in the word that might help.
Clunk card #4:	Break the word apart and look for smaller words.

For follow-up questions about reading comprehension strategies, go to Chapter 6 of the Companion Website (ablongman. com/sppd4e) and click Inclusion Strategies.

From "Teaching Reading Comprehension Skills to Students with Learning Disabilities in the General Education Classroom (Part II)" by S. Vaughn and J. Kingner, 1999, *Learning Disabilities, 9*(2), pp. 8–9. Used by permission.

be given specific instruction in the fundamental aspects of writing if they are to be competent in this area (Graham & Harris, 1997).

Improvement in oral language may be stimulated by promoting a better self-concept and enriching the language environment. These and other techniques are discussed by Candler and Hildreth (1990). They suggest that a poor self-concept can be addressed through encouraging more successful communication experiences and having the student self-evaluate the successes. The classroom can be designed with areas where students are encouraged to talk. Cooperative learning activities also promote increased verbal interactions. Providing opportunities for students to share their experiences and expertise is also a nonthreatening way to promote use of oral language. Listening and praise help reinforce talking.

Poor listening skills also limit individuals with learning disabilities, influencing success both in the classroom and in social interactions. In Heaton and O'Shea's (1995) effective strategy, which can be modified for use with all age groups, students follow these steps:

L	Look at the teacher.
I	Ignore the student next to you.
S	Stay in your place.
T	Try to visualize and understand the story.
E	Enjoy the story.
N	Nice job! You're a good listener.

Computers and other technology can assist in teaching individuals with learning disabilities in inclusive classrooms. Olsen and Platt (1996) describe the following advantages of technology:

- It is self-pacing and individualized.
- It provides immediate feedback.
- It has consistent correction procedures.
- It provides repetition without pressure.
- It confirms correct responses immediately.
- It maintains a high frequency of student response.
- It builds in repeated validation of academic success.
- It is an activity respected by peers.
- It is motivating.
- It encourages increased time on task.
- It minimizes the effects of the disability.

The computer can be used effectively for curriculum support in math, writing, language arts, social studies, science, and other areas. Various types of software provide instructional alternatives such as tutoring, drill and practice, simulation, and games. With so many choices available, teachers should carefully evaluate each program for ease of use and appropriateness for exceptional students.

Intervention related to social interactions and emotional maturity is critical for many students with learning disabilities. The inclusion movement provides opportunities for interactions; the question is how to best prepare both the children with disabilities and nondisabled children for positive interactions. Changing a student's self-image, social ability, and social standing is difficult. Until recently, the research and literature on learning disabilities focused primarily on the efficacy of treatments for the most obvious characteristic—academic deficits. The importance of social skills is just now being recognized and given the attention it deserves.

Intervention in the area of social standing and interaction can take two courses: changing the child or changing the environment. Optimally, both receive attention. Good teaching techniques can lead to academic achievement and eventually to higher self-esteem. Teachers can create a positive learning environment, incorporate praise and encouragement for specific accomplishments, such as making positive comments about themselves and others. Teachers should also set goals and be very explicit about expectations for academic work and behavior in the class; they should monitor progress closely and provide frequent feedback (Polloway et al., 2001).

Improvement in low academic self-concept has also been made by correcting maladaptive **attributional styles,** or teaching students to take credit for their successes. Students with higher academic self-concepts have been found to work harder to achieve (Tabassam & Grainger, 2002).

Modeling prosocial skills and positive self-talk is important, as well as providing natural opportunities for conversation and conflict resolution. A forum during group time can be used to pose potential problems and generate discussions to brainstorm possible solutions before the situations occur (Morris, 2002). Role-playing successful cooperation followed by experience in collaborative group projects can also provide positive social experiences if the teacher monitors closely. Table 6.2 provides a lesson plan in which the goal is to provide direct instruction to teach students to interact with other individuals.

The overall goal of social programs is to teach socially appropriate behavior and social skills that are self-generated and self-monitored. The cognitive problems of students with learning disabilities often make this type of decision making very difficult. FAST is an example of a strategy that can be effectively applied to the social-skills-training curriculum. It aids in interpersonal problem solving by developing skills in questioning and monitoring, brainstorming solutions, and developing and implementing a plan to solve the problem. The steps are displayed in Figure 6.4.

TEACHING TIP

The amount of software available for supporting instruction can be overwhelming, and costly mistakes can be made when ordering a program based on a catalog description alone. Organize a plan for the teachers in your school to share the names of effective software. Preview a copy before ordering whenever possible.

CONSIDER THIS

Describe some situations you have observed in which a child displayed inappropriate social skills or responses in the classroom. How could the FAST strategy have been used to prevent recurring problems?

TABLE 6.2   **Teaching Interaction**

Nonverbal Behavior
1. Face the student.
2. Maintain eye contact.
3. Maintain a neutral or pleasant facial expression.

Paraverbal Behavior
4. Maintain a neutral tone of voice.
5. Speak at a moderate volume.

Verbal Teaching Behavior
6. Begin with a compliment related to the student's efforts and achievements.
7. Introduce the social skill and define what the social skill means.
8. Give a rationale for learning the skill and for using the skill with others.
9. Share an experience when you used the social skill or could have used the social skill.
10. Specify each behavior (e.g., nonverbal and verbal behavior) to be considered when exhibiting the skill.
11. Demonstrate or model the use of the skill.
12. Have the student rehearse the social skill. (Observe the student's behavior.)
13. Provide positive corrective feedback.
    State what the student did correctly.
14. Practice the social skill with the student. (Make sure you do not prompt.)
15. Continue to provide corrective feedback to practice until the student masters (100%) the social skill in a novel situation.
16. Plan, with the student, when and where to use the social skill.

Remember: Make sure the student participates throughout the lesson. To do so, ask questions and let the student share ideas and thoughts. Always praise the student for participating and rehearsing the social skill.

From *Strategies for Teaching Learners with Special Needs* (p. 212), by E. A. Polloway, J. R. Patton, and L. Serna, 2001, Upper Saddle River, NJ: Merrill.

Intervention in cognitive and metacognitive skills has only recently received support from learning disabilities professionals. Powerful techniques are being studied to improve learning. Some of the ideas are relatively simple and require only common sense. First, and most important, is being sure a child is paying attention to the stimulus being presented.

FIGURE 6.4   **Strategies for Developing Interpersonal Problem Solving**

FAST Strategy

FREEZE AND THINK   What is the problem? Can I state the problem in behavioral terms?

ALTERNATIVES   What could I do to solve the problem? List possible alternatives.

SOLUTION   Which alternatives will solve the problem in the long run? Which are safe and fair? Select the best long-term alternative.

TRY IT   How can I implement the solution? Did it work? If this particular solution fails to solve the problem, return to the second step and pick another alternative that might solve the problem.

From "FAST Social Skills with a SLAM and a Rap" (p. 39), by R. McIntosh, S. Vaughn, and D. Bennerson (1995), *Teaching Exceptional Children, 28*(1), 37–41. Used by permission.

This purpose might be achieved by dimming the lights, calling for attention, or establishing eye contact. Without attention, learning will not take place.

Lerner (2000) suggests that teachers present new information in well-organized, meaningful chunks. As new information is presented to be memorized, it should be linked to previously learned, meaningful information. For example, to teach subtraction, the teacher would demonstrate the relationship to addition. Students should also be encouraged to rehearse new information and be given many opportunities for practice. These and other effective learning strategies are presented in Figure 6.5 and throughout the text.

Secondary Services   Academic and language deficits, social and emotional problems, and differences in cognitive and metacognitive functioning continue to plague many adolescents with learning disabilities. With the focus on content classes in middle and high

---

FIGURE 6.5   **Learning Strategies**

Self-Questioning

Students quietly ask themselves questions about the material. This process is also referred to as verbal mediation. The internal language, or covert speech, helps organize material and behavior. Camp and Bash (1981) suggest the following types of questions:

> What is the problem? (or) What am I supposed to do?
>
> What is my plan? (or) How can I do it?
>
> Am I using my plan?
>
> How did I do?

Verbal Rehearsal and Review

Students practice and review what they have learned. This self-rehearsal helps students remember. People forget when the brain trace, which is a physical record of memory, fades away. Recitation and review of material to be learned help the student remember.

> Students observe the instructor's modeling of verbalization of a problem.
>
> Students instruct themselves by verbalizing aloud or in a whisper.
>
> Students verbalize silently.

Organization

To aid in recall, students figure out the main idea of the lesson and the supporting facts. The organization of the material has a great deal to do with how fast we can learn it and how well we can remember it. Already-existing memory units are called chunks, and through chunking, new material is reorganized into already-existing memory units. The more students can relate to what they already know, the better they will remember the new material.

Using Prior Knowledge

New material is linked to already-existing memory units. The more students can relate what they are learning to what they already know, the better they will remember.

Memory Strategies

If new material is anchored to old knowledge, students are more likely to remember it. For example, one student remembered the word *look* because it had two eyes in the middle. Some pupils can alphabetize only if they sing the "ABC" song. Some adults can remember people's names by using a mnemonic device that associates the name with a particular attribute of that individual, for example "blond Bill" or "green-sweater Gertrude."

Predicting and Monitoring

Students guess about what they will learn in the lesson and then check on whether their guesses were correct.

Advance Organizers

This technique establishes a mindset for the learner, relating new material to previously learned material. Students are told in advance about what they are going to learn. This sets the stage for learning and improves comprehension and the ability to recall what has been learned.

Cognitive Behavior Modification

This behavioral approach teaches students self-instruction, self-monitoring, and self-evaluation techniques (Meichenbaum, 1977). There are several steps:

> The teacher models a behavior while giving an explanation.
>
> The student performs the task while the teacher describes it.
>
> The student talks the task through out loud.
>
> The student whispers it to himself or herself.
>
> The student performs the task with nonverbal self-cues.

Modeling

The teacher provides an example of appropriate cognitive behavior and problem-solving strategies. The teacher can talk through the cognitive processes being used.

Self-Monitoring

Students learn to monitor their own mistakes. They learn to check their own responses and become conscious of errors or answers that do not make sense. To reach this stage requires active involvement in the learning process to recognize incongruities.

From *Learning Disabilities: Theories, Diagnosis, and Teaching Strategies* (6th ed., pp. 207–208) by J. W. Lerner, 1993, Boston: Houghton Mifflin. Used by permission.

school, remediation of basic skills often is minimal. This situation can be problematic for students having difficulty passing the high school graduation exam required in many states for a regular diploma. Students who continue to benefit from remediation should be provided these opportunities.

However, the adaptations described in the next section and the learning strategies described in the previous section can also be used with secondary students to facilitate basic skill acquisition and to make learning and performance more effective and efficient (Deshler, Ellis, & Lenz, 1996). For example, instead of trying to bring basic skills to a level high enough to read a chapter in a content area textbook written on grade level, a teacher might assist students in comprehension by reading the heading and one or two sentences in each paragraph in a chapter. Figure 6.6 shows how the PASS method can be used as a reading comprehension strategy.

The teacher can also make an impact on student learning and performance by accounting for individual differences when developing and implementing lesson plans. Many students fail, not because of an inability to perform but because they do not understand directions, cannot remember all the information, or cannot process verbal information fast enough. Most adults and older children automatically lower the language they use when speaking to younger children or individuals with obvious disabilities. Unfortunately

FIGURE 6.6

PASS Reading Comprehension Strategy

From *Teaching Strategies and Methods* (2nd ed., p. 29) by D. Deshler, E. S. Ellis, and B. K. Lenz, 1996, Denver, CO: Love Publishing. Used by permission.

P **REVIEW, REVIEW, AND PREDICT**

Preview by reading the heading and one or two sentences.

Review what you know already about this topic.

Predict what you think the text will be about.

A **SK AND ANSWER QUESTIONS**

Content-Focused Questions

Who? What? When? Where? Why? How?

How does this relate to what I already know?

Monitoring Questions

Is my prediction correct?

How is this different from what I thought it was going to be about?

Does this make sense?

Problem-Solving Questions

Is it important that it make sense?

Do I need to reread part of it?

Can I visualize the information?

Do I need to read it more slowly?

Does it have too many unknown words?

Do I need to pay more attention?

Should I get help?

S **UMMARIZE**

Say what the short passage was about.

S **YNTHESIZE**

Say how the short passage fits in with the whole passage.

Say how what you learned fits with what you knew.

TEACHING TIP

When teaching the PASS strategy to students, model use of the strategy as you "think aloud" while applying the strategy to a chapter they have to read. This demonstration will make the process more concrete for students.

they do not typically do so when speaking to school-age children and adults with LD—even though the latter may have language-based learning disabilities. Johnson (1999) suggests the following strategies to meet the needs of students with language difficulties in an inclusive classroom setting:

▶ Be conscious of the level of language used, including rate of presentation, complexity of vocabulary, and sentence structure.
▶ Prepare a list of relevant terms prior to instruction; pretest students to determine their level of understanding.
▶ Adjust the level of language until students have basic concepts.
▶ Use demonstrations as needed.
▶ Repeat instructions individually to students if necessary.
▶ Select a method of testing knowledge to match the student's best method of communication. For example, a student may be able to select the correct answer from options given but not be able to answer open-ended questions. (p. 6)

As noted earlier in the chapter, a major problem for secondary students with learning disabilities is low self-concept and social and emotional problems that often stem from years of school failure. To help ameliorate unhappiness, school environments must be structured to create successful experiences. One method involves **self-determination,** or making students more active participants in designing their educational experiences and monitoring their own success; this can be done by teaching self-awareness and self-advocacy skills. Students should use these skills as active participants in their IEP meetings. Such participation is particularly important when a student is deciding whether to continue postsecondary education or to obtain employment after high school (Pocock et al., 2002).

While giving students more power and responsibility for determining their life outcome is very important at the secondary level, it is also important to maintain communication with parents and involve them in this process (Jayanthi, Bursuck, Epstein, & Polloway, 1999). Parents can promote responsibility in their children by setting clear expectations and consequences in regard to school achievement. Teachers can help by

▶ giving parents and students information on course assignments for the semester, available adaptations, and policies.
▶ providing progress reports, including descriptive comments on the quality of homework.

Adolescents should be active participants in meetings concerning them.

▶ putting assignment calendars on brightly colored paper to prevent misplacement.

▶ collaborating with other teachers to prevent homework overloads.

▶ communicating with parents regarding the amount of time students spend completing homework and adjusting workload correspondingly.

▶ understanding that homework may be a low priority in some families where other stressors such as family illness or school attendance may be a priority.

Motivation is also a key ingredient in successful high school programming. Fulk and Montgomery-Grymes (1994) suggest the following techniques for increasing motivation:

▶ Involve students in decision making.
  1. Provide a menu from which students can select assignments to demonstrate knowledge.
  2. Allow flexible due dates.
  3. Involve students in scoring and evaluating their own work.
  4. Vary the length of assignments for differing student abilities.
  5. Set goals with the students.
▶ Create and maintain interest.
  1. Challenge each student at the optimal level.
  2. Show enthusiasm as you introduce lessons.
  3. Give clear, simple directions.
  4. Set specific expectations.
  5. Explain the relevance of each lesson.
  6. Vary your teaching style.
▶ Address affective variables.
  1. Maintain a positive classroom environment.
  2. Give frequent feedback on performance.
  3. Acknowledge all levels of achievement. (p. 31)

High school students with learning disabilities especially need to acquire transition skills (e.g., abilities that will help students be successful after high school in employment and independent living). For students in inclusive settings, teachers can find ways to integrate transition topics into the regular curriculum. For example, when an English teacher assigns letter writing or term papers, students might focus their work on exploring different career opportunities. Math teachers can bring in income tax and budget forms to connect them to a variety of math skills. When planning any lesson, ask yourself, "Is there any way I can make this meaningful to their lives after high school?" See Table 6.3.

Adult Services   The instruction provided in high school classes can have a powerful impact on the outcome for adults with learning disabilities. The life skills applications of various school activities and lessons are described in Chapter 16. Relevant lessons in the general education curriculum can help adults be more successful in many aspects of independent living. Individuals with learning disabilities are often deficient in choosing and carrying out strategies, and they do not automatically generalize previously learned information to new challenges. Other cognitive difficulties include organizing thoughts and ideas, integrating and remembering information from a variety of sources, and solving problems (Ryan & Price, 1992). Intervention in these areas must often be implemented for adults if the high school curriculum is not based on future needs and challenges (Dowdy & Smith, 1991).

An important study by Raskind, Goldberg, Higgins, and Herman (2002) identified characteristics of highly successful adults with learning disabilities. Development of many of these factors can be encouraged by teachers and other individuals; however, some factors seem to be innate personality traits of the individuals themselves like emotional stability. One of the strongest predictors for success was the desire and willingness to persist and work extremely hard. Understanding one's strengths and limitations, identifying appropriate goals, and working proactively to meet them were also important. The successful adults developed a plan and then worked hard to accomplish their goals. They also

TABLE 6.3   Examples of Study Skill Functions In and Out of the Classroom

Study Skill	School Examples	Life Skills Applications
Reading Rate	Reviewing an assigned reading for a test Looking for an explanation of a concept discussed in class	Reviewing an automobile insurance policy Reading the newspaper
Listening	Understanding instructions about a field trip Attending to morning announcements	Understanding how a newly purchased appliance works Comprehending a radio traffic report
Note Taking/ Outlining	Capturing information given by a teacher on how to dissect a frog Framing the structure of a paper	Writing directions to a party Planning a summer vacation
Report Writing	Developing a book report Completing a science project on a specific marine organism	Completing the personal goals section on a job application Writing a complaint letter
Oral Presentations	Delivering a personal opinion on a current issue for a social studies class Describing the results of a lab experiment	Describing car problems to a mechanic Asking a supervisor/boss for time off work
Graphic Aids	Setting up the equipment of a chemistry experiment based on a diagram Locating the most densely populated regions of the world on a map	Utilizing the weather map in the newspaper Deciphering the store map in a mall
Test Taking	Developing tactics for retrieving information for a closed-book test Comparing notes with textbook content	Preparing for a driver's license renewal test Participating in television self-tests
Library Usage	Using picture files Searching a computerized catalog	Obtaining travel resources (books, videos) Viewing current periodicals
Reference Materials	Accessing CD-ROM encyclopedias Using a thesaurus to write a paper	Using the yellow pages to locate a repair service Ordering from a mail-order catalog
Time Management	Allocating a set time for homework Organizing a file system for writing a paper	Maintaining a daily "to do" list Keeping organized records for tax purposes
Self-Management	Ensuring that homework is signed by parents Rewarding oneself for controlling temper	Regulating a daily exercise program Evaluating the quality of a home repair

From *Teaching Students with Learning Problems to Use Study Skills: A Teacher's Guide* (p. 7) by J. J. Hoover and J. R. Patton, 1995, Austin, TX: Pro-Ed. Reprinted by permission.

developed and used support groups. These characteristics were more powerful predictors of success than academic achievement, IQ, life stressors, social-economic status, or race.

They also were able to reframe their feelings about having a learning disability, gradually identifying and accepting their own strengths and weaknesses. Once the weaknesses were identified, they took creative action to build strategies, techniques, and adaptations to offset the impact of the disability. The study also showed that it was important to find a "goodness of fit": choosing goals that would be possible to attain. Finally, successful adults were willing to seek help from supportive people, such as spouse or an individual at an agency. As one highly successful adult with learning disabilities said, "You must learn where your strengths are and how you can use them and where your weaknesses are and how to avoid them or compensate. I have learned to accept who I am, what I can do, what I cannot do, who I should not try to be, and who I should try to be" (Ginsberg, Gerber, & Reiff, 1994, p. 210).

The level of commitment and persistence shown by these successful adults is remarkable. One highly successful individual was told by his new boss that he was promoted to a higher level because he had a work ethic that had never been seen before. He never left until the job was done perfectly, and he was willing to do whatever was asked of him without complaining (Guyer, 2002).

Unfortunately, many adults leave high school without the skills and confidence necessary to find employment to help them realize their maximum potential and to live independently. According to Michaels (1994), problems in work settings can include the following:

▶ Following instructions
▶ Getting started on tasks
▶ Maintaining attention to task
▶ Organizing and budgeting time
▶ Completing tasks
▶ Checking for errors
▶ Requesting support when appropriate
▶ Using self-advocacy skills to obtain resources
▶ Having difficulty with interpersonal skills

TEACHING TIP

Ask students with disabilities to call the agencies listed in Figure 6.7 to identify services available in your local area. Have them research others and then create a resource directory. They might organize each entry by referral process, range of services, or cost.

These skills can be taught and should be addressed in a secondary curriculum. For adults with learning disabilities who still need support, a variety of agencies are available to address needs such as improving literacy skills, obtaining a high school equivalency certificate (called a GED), and meeting goals in areas such as financial aid for further education, employment, and independent living. Figure 6.7 lists examples of these important resources (excerpted from LDA *Newsbriefs*, 1996).

The primary adult agency that offers treatment and intervention to promote employment for adults with learning disabilities is the Rehabilitation Services Administration. An office of this vocational rehabilitation agency is located in every state. Vocational evaluators are trained to identify each individual's strengths and the characteristics that will limit employment. Counselors provide a variety of employment-related services to those who are eligible, often including financial support for postsecondary training (Dowdy, 1996). Other agencies are explored in a text on adult agencies by Cozzins, Dowdy, and Smith (1999).

Controversial Approaches

Some interventions, often presented to the public through television or newsstand magazines, are controversial and have not been validated as effective for students with learning disabilities. Educators may be asked for an opinion on these therapies by parents who

---

FIGURE 6.7 **Adult Agencies**

GED Hotline (1-800-626-9433)	General Education Development (GED) Hotline has a 24-hour operator service that provides information on local GED classes and testing services. They have an accommodations guide for people taking the GED who have a learning disability.
National Literacy Hotline (1-800-228-8813)	Literacy Hotline has a 24-hour bilingual (Spanish/English) operator service that provides information on literacy/education classes, GED testing services, volunteer opportunities, and a learning disabilities brochure.
HEATH Resource Center (1-800-544-3284)	National Clearinghouse on Postsecondary Education for Individuals with Disabilities (HEATH Resource Center) has information specialists available 9:00 A.M.–5 P.M. ET (Monday–Friday) who provide resource papers, directories, information on national organizations, and a resource directory for people with learning disabilities.
Learning Resources Network (1-800-678-5376)	Learning Resources Network (LERN) has an operator service 8:00 A.M.–5:00 P.M. ET (Monday–Friday) that provides information to practitioners of adult continuing education. They also give consulting information, take orders for publications, and provide phone numbers of associations and organizations that deal with learning disabilities.

From "Toll Free Access to Adult Services," *LDA Newsbriefs*, 1996, *31*, 22–24. Used by permission.

are attempting to find solutions to their children's frustrating problems. A brief overview of these nontraditional approaches follows. More extensive reviews are provided by Rooney (1991) and Silver (1995).

One controversial therapy involves the prescription of **tinted glasses** as a cure for dyslexia. In this approach, light sensitivity, said to interfere with learning, is treated by identifying a colored lens to reduce sensitivity. Rooney (1991) notes that the studies that support this treatment do not meet acceptable scientific standards and should be viewed with caution.

An older treatment theory is **orthomolecular therapy,** involving vitamins, minerals, and diet. Proponents of this treatment claim that large doses of vitamins and minerals straighten out the biochemistry of the brain to reduce hyperactivity and to increase learning. Hair analysis and blood studies are used to determine the doses needed.

Feingold's diet is another dietary treatment frequently cited. Feingold (1975) proposes that negative behaviors such as hyperactivity and limited learning are due to the body's reaction to unnatural substances such as food colorings, preservatives, and artificial dyes. His patients are asked to keep a comprehensive diary of their diet and to avoid harmful chemical substances. Other diets focus on avoiding sugar and caffeine.

Another proponent of orthomolecular therapy suggests that negative behaviors result from allergies to food and environmental substances (Silver, 1995). The research on the efficacy of these diet-related interventions usually consists of clinical studies without control groups. When control groups are used, the diets do not substantiate the claims made for them. Only a small percentage of children benefit from them.

Vision therapy or training is another controversial treatment for individuals with a learning disability. It is based on the theory that learning disabilities are the result of visual defects that occur when the eyes do not work together and that these deficits can be cured by visual training. This widespread practice has been supported primarily by groups of optometrists. The American Academy of Ophthalmology (1984) has issued a statement clearly stating that "no credible evidence exists to show that visual training, muscle exercises, perceptual, or hand/eye coordination exercises significantly affect a child's Specific Learning Disabilities" (p. 3).

Silver (1995) reviewed another controversial therapy involving the use of **vestibular dysfunction** medication to cure dyslexia. He notes that the relationship between dyslexia, the vestibular system, and the medication was not supported by research. Silver also warns that physicians often do not diagnose dyslexia consistently and are prescribing doses of medication for purposes other than those recommended by pharmaceutical companies.

CONSIDER THIS

Many parents are drawn to nontraditional approaches to treating learning disabilities because they promise a quick cure. How will you respond when a parent asks your opinion of the value of one of these approaches for his or her child?

Classroom Adaptations for Students with Learning Disabilities

One important consideration for individuals of all ages with disabilities, including learning disabilities, is the appropriate use of adaptations during testing. Use of these adaptations helps ensure that common characteristics of learning disabilities such as poor reading, distractibility, or slow work rate do not lower the results of an assessment of the child's learning. Care must be taken when implementing these adaptations because, while disallowing fair adaptations prevents a student from demonstrating his or her knowledge, overly permissive adaptations will inflate scores. Inflated scores may give students an overestimate of their abilities and may lead to unrealistic postsecondary goals. They also may reduce pressure on schools to maintain high expectations and offer students a challenging program with intense instruction (Fuchs & Fuchs, 2001). These researchers note, however, that when students can be penalized for low test scores, as is the case for "high stakes" assessment, which is the gateway to promotion or graduation, a more liberal allowance of adaptations should be made. Examples of reasonable adaptations are presented in Rights & Responsibilities.

Rights & Responsibilities

Examples of Accommodations for Assessments

Flexible Time	Flexible Setting	Alternative Presentation Format	Alternative Response Format
Extended time	Test alone in test carrel or separate room	Braille or large-print edition	Pointing to response
Alternating lengths of test sections (e.g., shorter and longer)	Test in small-group setting	Signing of directions	Using template for responding
More frequent breaks	Test at home (with accountability)	Interpretation of directions	Giving response in sign language
Extended testing sessions over several days	Test in special education classroom	Taped directions	Using a computer
	Test in room with special lighting	Highlighted keywords	Allow answers in test book

For follow-up questions about accommodations for assessments, go to Chapter 6 of the Companion Website (ablongman.com/sppd4e) and click Rights & Responsibilities.

From "The IDEA Amendments of 1997: Implications for Special and General Education Teachers, Administrators, and Teacher Trainers" by M. L. Yell and J. G. Shriner, 1997, *Focus on Exceptional Children, 30*(1), p. 8. Copyright 1997 by Love Publishing Co. Reprinted by permission.

When you are developing classroom adaptations, remember the wide range of behaviors identified earlier that might characterize individuals with learning disabilities. The heterogeneity in this population is sometimes baffling. No child with a learning disability is going to be exactly like any other, so teachers must provide a wide range of adaptations to meet individual needs. In the following sections, adaptations are discussed for each of the areas described earlier: academic and language deficits, social-emotional problems, and other differences such as attention, memory, cognition, metacognition, perception, and motor skills.

Academic and Language Deficits

Recall that students with learning disabilities may manifest deficits in the academic areas of reading skill, reading comprehension, math calculation, math applications, listening, speaking, and written language. Chapters 15 and 16 provide extensive adaptations and modifications for students with learning disabilities at the elementary and secondary levels. Some general guidelines proposed by Chalmers (1991) include these:

▶ Preteach vocabulary and assess the prior knowledge of students before you introduce new concepts.
▶ Establish a purpose for reading that gives students a specific goal for comprehension.
▶ Provide multiple opportunities to learn content: cooperative learning activities, study guides, choral responses, and hands-on participation.

▶ Reduce time pressure by adjusting requirements: give more time to complete a challenging project or shorten the assignment. Ask students to work every other problem or every third problem so they won't be overwhelmed.

▶ Provide frequent feedback, and gradually allow students to evaluate their own work.

▶ Have students use an assignment notebook to record important information and daily assignments.

▶ Provide options for students to demonstrate their knowledge or skill (e.g., videotape presentation, artwork, oral or written report).

▶ Use demonstrations and manipulatives frequently to make learning more concrete.

▶ Modify textbooks as shown in Figure 6.8.

▶ Avoid crowding too much material on a single page of a work sheet.

▶ Provide a listening guide or a partial outline to assist students in note taking.

▶ Use a buddy system for studying or for note taking. Allow a good note taker to work with the student with the learning disability, sharing notes duplicated on carbon paper or NCR paper.

▶ Allow students to tape-record lectures if necessary.

▶ Reduce the homework load, or allow the parent to write the student's dictated answers.

For students with learning difficulties in writing, a word processor can be invaluable. It allows students to see their work in a more legible format and simplifies proofreading and revising. The spell checker and grammar checker of many word processing programs can encourage success in writing, and a talking word processor may provide valuable assistance for students who also have difficulty in reading. The following list describes recommended programs (Pracek, 1996; MacArthur, 1998):

▶ *Write: Out Loud* has a speech-feedback component that highlights each word as it is "read" out loud to the student. (Wauconda, IL: Don Johnson, Inc.)

▶ *Dr. Peet's TalkWriter* is a talking program that includes letter recognition and simple word processing. Available from Hartley (1-800-247-1380), it uses the Echo Speech synthesizer and works on Apple computers.

▶ *Primary Editor Plus* is a talking word processing program that includes a spell checker and a feature that allows children to draw pictures using the mouse or keyboard. It is available from IBM Eduquest (1-800-426-4338).

▼EACHING TIP

Each word processing program has unique features. Try to have several programs available so students can experiment and find the one that works best for them. *Dyslexic* is a medical term to describe an individual with severe reading difficulties.

▼IGURE 6.8

Guidelines for Adapting Content Area Textbooks

Adapted from "Guidelines for Adapting Content Area Textbooks: Keeping Teachers and Students Content," by J. S. Schumm and K. Strickler, 1991, *Intervention in School and Clinic, 27*(2), pp. 79–84.

Determine "goodness of fit" by comparing the readability level of the text and the student's reading ability. If accommodations are needed, consider the following:

1. Substitute textbook reading by

▶ supplying an audiotape of the text.

▶ pairing students to learn text material together.

▶ substituting the text with direct experiences or videos.

▶ holding tutorial sessions to teach content to a small group.

2. Simplify text by

▶ developing abridged versions (volunteers may be helpful).

▶ developing chapter outlines or summaries.

▶ finding a text with similar content written at a lower level.

3. Highlight key concepts by

▶ establishing the purpose for reading.

▶ overviewing the assignment before reading.

▶ reviewing charts, graphs, vocabulary, and key concepts before reading.

▶ reducing amount of work by targeting the most important information or slowing down pace of assignments.

J.T.'s Writing Samples—Before and After

Each day during the study, J. T.'s class received a descriptive writing prompt, and then had 20 minutes to address this prompt in a journal entry. The entries shown here depict a prompt and J. T.'s corresponding journal response. On November 21, J. T. had not been introduced to the features of Co:Writer and was using word processing capabilities Write:OutLoud with the speech component disabled. By February, J. T. was using the intervention software when he composed his journal entries. This entry is a typical example of the longer entries he generated using Co:Writer and Write:OutLoud.

November 21
Prompt: Describe your idea of the "ideal" Thanksgiving dinner

MY FAVORITE FOOD IS A GRILL HOG IN A PUMPKIN IN A ROAST HAM IN A MAYBE A TURKEY my favorite DESSERT food strawberry pie THE END

February 27
Prompt: Describe your favorite clock

The clock that I have it is very old it was the first clock that my grandpa had it run off of current and it might go to the time it will go off in a little bird will comes at of the box. The box look like a house in it has a to pendulums on the bottom of the house inside of the house it has people in it. On the outside it has to door on it in it has to windows the color is color is brown on the top of the clock it is black.

For follow-up questions about technology that assists students with LD, go to Chapter 5 of the Companion Website (ablongman.com/sppd4e) and click Technology Today.

Adapted from "How Speech-Feedback and Work-Prediction Software Can Help Students Write" by S. Williams, 2002, *Teaching Exceptional Children, 34*(3), 72–78.

▶ *Co:Writer* is a word prediction program based on spelling, word frequency, and correct grammar. (Wauconda, IL: Don Johnson, Inc.)

▶ *FrEdWriter* is a public domain word processing program that may be copied freely. A Spanish version is also available. It works on an Apple computer.

▶ *Word Processing for Kids* is a public domain program that runs on MS-DOS. It was designed to teach word processing to students.

These and other types of technology can be critically important in facilitating success in inclusive settings for students with LD. Technology Today demonstrates the improvement made by a seventh-grade student, J. T., using the software *Write: Out Loud* and *Co:Writer*. When he began the program, J. T., who received all his instruction in an inclusive classroom, read on preprimer level and had many difficulties in the writing process. The assistive technology plan for J. T. was successful; however, some students are given assistive technology that is not a good match for their abilities or interests. The use of technology should be monitored closely to determine whether devices are being used successfully (Beigel, 2000).

Students and adults with LD in the area of reading are also eligible to apply for services from Reading for the Blind and Dyslexic. A catalog of services and application forms are available by calling (800) 221-4792. The forms require verification of the disability by a professional in disability services. This agency will provide a cassette tape of any book requested. The tapes are available at no cost; however, there may be a one-time charge for the special equipment needed to play the tapes. Taped trade books and textbooks would be an excellent adaptation for Emmanuel as his reading skills improve to allow him to be successful with printed material on his grade level. Other adaptations appropriate for Emmanuel are identified in Tips for Adapting a Lesson.

Social-Emotional Problems

As discussed earlier, the social and emotional problems of individuals with learning disabilities may be closely tied to academic failure. Many of the academic adaptations already described will encourage success in the classroom, which ultimately leads to a better

Tips for Adapting a Lesson for Emmanuel

Since Emmanuel's primary deficits include reading, listening, and writing (as described in the chapter-opening vignette), the teacher's adaptations recommended here should limit the impact of these challenges during the time he is receiving intense instruction to develop new skills.

Emmanuel's teacher should

▶ pair him with a peer helper or provide taped material to assist in reading difficult material.

▶ provide many opportunities to practice reading and writing for pleasure.

▶ develop cooperative learning groups and use group grades for projects in content subjects.

▶ allow extra time or require less work when reading or writing is involved.

▶ read tests or find alternative methods for assessment of knowledge other than reading questions and writing responses.

▶ have Emmanuel repeat oral directions to ensure understanding.

▶ provide lecture notes or copies of overheads.

▶ when grading Emmanuel's written work, limit points taken off to one skill at a time (e.g., punctuation, spelling, grammar).

▶ when grading spelling, give credit for all correct letters in a word.

▶ allow Emmanuel to be a peer tutor in a lower grade to reinforce reading skills and build self-concept.

self-concept, increased emotional stability, and greater confidence in approaching new academic tasks. A student who has deficits in social skills may need previously described training. However, some adaptations may still be needed even as the training begins to show results. Students may need to work in an isolated setting in the classroom during particularly challenging times. Distractions caused by peers may interfere with meeting academic challenges successfully. However, if teachers make the student with learning disabilities sit in a segregated portion of the room all the time, it sends a bad message to others. Including students with disabilities in group activities such as cooperative learning provides them with models of appropriate interactions and social skills. Identify the students in the classroom who seem to work best with individuals with a learning disability, and give them opportunities to interact. When conflicts arise, provide good modeling for the student by verbalizing the bad choices that were made and the good choices that could have been made.

Because these individuals may have difficulty responding appropriately to verbal and nonverbal cues, teachers should avoid sarcasm and use simple concrete language when giving directions and when teaching. If the student has difficulty accepting new tasks without complaint, consider providing a written assignment that the student can refer to for direction. When a student frequently upsets or irritates others in the classroom, you might agree on a contract to reduce the inappropriate behavior and reinforce positive peer interaction. Periodically review the rules for the classroom, and keep them posted as a quick reference. To assist students who have difficulty making and keeping friends, you can subtly point out the strengths of the individual with the learning disability to encourage the other students to want to be his or her friend. Allowing the student to demonstrate his or her expertise in an area or to share a hobby may stimulate conversations that can eventually lead to friendships.

Because many of these students cannot predict the consequences of negative behavior, teachers need to explain the consequences of rule breaking and other inappropriate behavior. Though you can implement many behavior management techniques to reinforce positive behavior, it is important to train the student in methods of self-monitoring and self-regulation. The ultimate goal is for the student to be able to identify socially inappropriate behavior and get back on track.

Cognitive Differences

Cognitive problems described earlier include deficits in attention, perception, motor abilities, problem solving, and metacognition. Adaptations for individuals exhibiting problems in attention were described more fully in Chapter 5. Adaptations can also help individuals with difficulties or preferences in the area of perception. For some students, presenting information visually through the overhead projector, reading material, videos, and graphics will be most effective. Other individuals will respond better by hearing the information. Teachers can accommodate these individual differences by identifying the preferred style of learning and either providing instruction and directions in the preferred style or teaching in a multisensory fashion that stimulates both auditory and visual perception. Combining seeing, saying, writing, and doing provides multiple opportunities for presenting new information. It also helps children remember important information.

Difficulties in the area of motor abilities might be manifested as poor handwriting skills or difficulty with other fine motor activities. Adaptations might include overlooking the difficulties in handwriting and providing a grade based not on the appearance of the handwriting but on the content of the material. You might allow these students to provide other evidence of their learning, such as oral reports or special projects. Let them select physical fitness activities that focus on their areas of strength rather than their deficits.

Students with difficulties in problem solving require careful direction and programming. Their deficits in reasoning skills make them especially prone to academic failures. The instructional strategies described earlier will help remedy problems in this area; also frequent practice and modeling of problem-solving strategies will strengthen developing skills.

Students with problems in the area of metacognition need to keep an assignment notebook or a monthly calendar to project the time needed to complete tasks or to prepare for tests. Students should be taught to organize their notebooks and their desks so that materials can be retrieved efficiently. If students have difficulty following or developing a plan, assist them in setting long-range goals and breaking down those goals into realistic steps. Prompt them with questions such as "What do you need to be able to do this?" Help students set clear time frames in which to accomplish each step. Assist them in prioritizing activities and assignments, and provide them with models that they can refer to often.

Encourage students to ask for help and to use self-checking methods to evaluate their work on an ongoing basis. Reinforce all signs of appropriate self-monitoring and self-regulation in the classroom. These behaviors will facilitate success after high school.

Adaptations for attention deficits and hyperactivity are addressed in Chapter 5. Other teaching tips for general educators are offered in Chapters 15 and 16, focusing on behavior support and classroom adaptations for either the elementary or secondary classrooms. The following list of recommended guidelines for teaching children and adolescents with learning disabilities has been compiled from work by Mercer (1997), Deiner (1993), and Bender (2001).

1. Be consistent in class rules and the daily schedule of activities.
2. State rules and expectations clearly. Tell children what to do—not what not to do. For example, instead of saying, "Don't run in the halls," say, "Walk in the halls."
3. Give advance organizers to prepare children for any changes in the day's events and to highlight the important points to be covered during instructional time.

4. Eliminate or reduce visual and auditory distractions when children need to concentrate. Help children focus on the important aspects of the task.

5. Give directions in clear, simple words. A long series of directions may need to be broken down and given one at time. Reinforcement may be needed as each step is completed. Have students rephrase directions to ensure understanding.

6. Begin with simple activities focused on a single concept and build to more abstract ideas as the child appears ready. If problems occur, check for the presence of the prerequisite skills or knowledge of the vocabulary being used.

7. Use concrete objects or demonstrations when teaching a new concept. Relate new information to previously known concepts.

8. Teach the children strategies for remembering.

9. Present information visually, auditorily, and through demonstration to address each child's preferred learning style.

10. Use a variety of activities and experiences to teach or reinforce the same concept. Repetition can be provided without inducing boredom.

11. Use activities that are short or that encourage movement. Some children may need to work standing up!

12. Incorporate problem-solving activities or other projects that involve the children. Use both higher level and lower level questions.

13. Always gain the student's attention before presenting important information.

14. Use cooperative instructional groupings and peer tutoring to vary modes of instruction.

15. Plan for success!

Promoting Inclusive Practices for Students with Learning Disabilities

After identifying an appropriate educational plan for individuals with learning disabilities and determining the adaptations that should lead to a successful educational program, the next challenge is to be sure the students in the general education classroom and the student with the learning disability understand the disability and the need for special education. Primarily, children should be made aware that all people are different. The Personal Spotlight shares the thoughts of a nationally recognized pediatrician who experiences the pain of learning disabilities personally and professionally. His story provides insight into the importance of promoting a sense of security and acceptance in inclusive classrooms.

Calloway (1999) provides the following techniques to promote friendship and establish a positive, accepting atmosphere in the general education classroom:

▶ Answer honestly and openly when students ask about disabilities.
▶ Let students talk about their own disabilities, if possible. Get their permission before asking specific questions.
▶ Keep the curriculum barrier free, ensuring that each child can participate in every activity.
▶ Brainstorm with other staff and students about adapting activities for students with disabilities.
▶ Include materials about children and adults with disabilities throughout the classroom so students become comfortable with the concept of disability.
▶ Create social opportunities by pairing children with disabilities with peers without disabilities to encourage positive social interactions.
▶ Use "friendship activities" like secret pal swaps.
▶ Allow nondisabled students to access adaptive equipment and assistive technology when it is not in use.

CONSIDER THIS

What are your personal strengths and challenges? How are you alike and different from your family members and your peers? We are all different. Can we learn to celebrate our differences?

Personal Spotlight

A Family History of Learning Disabilities

It was a Tuesday morning last December. I was getting ready to attend a staffing meeting at a nearby school to discuss a 10-year-old girl, who was in the fifth grade gifted and talented program. She breezed through grades one through four then was selected for the gifted program. She was a happy child with lots of friends who always loved school. In November of her fifth grade year, she began to cry each morning and not want to go to school. We discussed what was happening. She was very verbal and explained that her hand did not work right and that she could not keep up with the need to copy or to take notes or to do all the math or so many papers. Her teacher was angry with her for not completing her class work. With tears she said, *I never had a teacher mad at me before. I can't help it if writing is so hard for me.* She told me that she did her homework at different places around the house. The problem was that she often left it where she did it. She showed me her notebook and binders. It was a mess with everything shoved everyplace. She admitted that she lost and forgot things. *Sometimes when we clean out my backpack on the weekend, my mom finds work I should have turned in earlier in the week. Then, the teacher tells me I am just lazy and not trying hard enough.* She cried again. We discussed her other problems.

With her parent's agreement, I requested that the school professionals do a psycho-educational evaluation, because I suspected learning disabilities. Their response, *she is so bright. Anyone in a gifted program and succeeding does not qualify for testing.* Fortunately, these parents could afford a private evaluation. The results were clear. Very bright, yes; nonverbal learning disabilities, yes. (I think of the many parents who cannot afford private testing and have to wait until their child fails to get help.)

I arrived at the staffing. Most of the school professionals knew me and had worked with me over the years; so, the meeting was friendly. Her parents sat down. At my request, this young student was at the meeting. She sat between her mother and me. I presented the test results and we discussed my recommendation for services and accommodations. The meeting chairperson ended the discussion by saying, *she was not far enough behind to qualify for services.* How many times have I heard this? Some of the professionals sitting around the table looked down to avoid looking at me. I had planned a fall back proposal with her parents in advance. I said that this

family could not wait for their daughter to fail and to lose her self-confidence as a student. Thus, I mentioned that she also had ADHD and was on medication. Would the school do a 504 Plan to cover accommodations? Her parents would pay privately for the needed special education services. They could not say no. I could document the ADHD. I thought to myself, accommodations don't cost the school system money. I also thought of the many families who could not afford private services. The proposal was accepted. I did not tell them that the private special education services had already started.

I said good-bye to the team, kissed the mother who was my daughter, hugged the father, who is my son-in-law, and kissed my granddaughter. Then I quickly left the room. I quickly left because I did not want anyone to see the tears welling in my eyes.

I had been there as a student. Public school was a struggle. I did not really learn how to learn until mid-college. Life can be a struggle if I have a lot of reading to do or I have to write something by hand rather than by computer or I have to spell. How many times have people commented that I said the wrong word or name in a conversation? Another daughter, not this one, had been there. Fortunately, we gave her help through college. She is now a successful social worker. But, she will tell you how she feels when she makes mistakes in writing or misreads something. Now, my granddaughter. A third generation.

Yes, she will get all of the help possible.

Yes, she will have to face teachers who blame the victim by saying the student is lazy or unmotivated. I knew that each time this happened, her parents or I will be on the phone to that teacher. Yes, she will be successful. But, I can not take away her frustration and pain. Like her grandfather and aunt, she will have to deal with it. I walked out of the school with mixed feelings. Guilt for causing this. Relief that she will get all the help possible. Sadness that her path through education will not be as easy as others. And, more tears.

Larry Silver and Granddaughter   *Rockville, MD*

For follow-up questions about this Personal Spotlight, go to Chapter 6 of the Companion Website (ablongman.com/sppd4e) and click Personal Spotlight.

From "What Does It Mean to Have Learning Disabilities" by L. Silver, 2002, *LDA Newsbriefs,* January/February, p. 3.

- ◗ Model acceptance of children with disabilities; the other students will pick up the teacher's attitude.
- ◗ Use direct instruction to teach social skills and promote appropriate social interactions.
- ◗ Emphasize the unique skills and gifts of each child.
- ◗ Encourage students without disabilities to help their peers with disabilities, but encourage independence whenever possible.
- ◗ Intervene immediately if any child is rejected by another. Stress the expectation that all individuals must be treated with respect.
- ◗ Encourage small-group projects and other types of collaboration between students with and without disabilities.
- ◗ Provide simulations to allow students to experience specific disabilities. For example, blindfold children and have them identify people or objects by sound or touch.
- ◗ Invite people with disabilities to come to the class and discuss their lives as worthwhile members of the community.
- ◗ Explore similarities and differences between all people. Emphasize the positive side of uniqueness.
- ◗ Teach communication skills to the class, including nonverbal signs such as gestures, tone of voice, and facial expressions. (p. 177)

An important part of promoting acceptance is having the student with the disability, family members, and other teachers and professionals understand the disability, as well as how it can be manifested and successfully addressed in home and school environments.

Summary

Basic Concepts About Learning Disabilities

- ◗ LD is frequently misunderstood because it is hidden. It may be mistaken for purposely uncooperative behavior.
- ◗ The study of LD is a relatively young field, and basic definitions, etiology, and criteria for special education eligibility remain controversial.
- ◗ The most widely used criterion for identifying LD is a severe discrepancy between ability and achievement that cannot be explained by another disabling condition or lack of learning opportunity.
- ◗ School personnel must determine that the primary cause of a student's learning difficulties is not cultural or linguistic diversity.
- ◗ Cultural and linguistic differences need to be taken into account when any assessment of a student's skills occurs so that the student is not mistakenly referred to a special education setting.
- ◗ Characteristics of LD are manifested across the life span.
- ◗ LD is manifested in seven areas of academics and language: reading skills, reading comprehension, mathematical calculations, mathematical reasoning, written expression, oral expression, and listening comprehension.
- ◗ Other common characteristics of LD include social-emotional problems and difficulties with attention and hyperactivity, memory, cognition, metacognition, motor skills, and perceptual abilities.

Strategies for Curriculum and Instruction for Students with Learning Disabilities

- ◗ Teaching strategies for preschool children with LD include developmental, cognitive, and behavioral models.
- ◗ Interventions for elementary children with LD address academic and language deficits, social-emotional problems, and cognitive and metacognitive problems.
- ◗ Secondary students with LD continue to need remediation of basic skills, but they also benefit from strategies that will make them more efficient learners.
- ◗ A secondary curriculum that includes application of life skills can produce successful outcomes for adults with LD.
- ◗ Successful adults with LD are goal-directed, work hard to accomplish their goals, understand and accept their strengths and limitations, are advocates for themselves, and accept appropriate support.

Classroom Adaptations for Students with Learning Disabilities

- ◗ Adaptations in the general education classroom can address the academic, social-emotional, and cognitive, metacognition, and attentional differences of students with LD.
- ◗ The role of the classroom teacher includes using effective teaching strategies and adaptations to address the challenges of students with LD.

Promoting Inclusive Practices for Students with Learning Disabilities

▶ Classroom teachers need to help children with learning disabilities and other children in the general classroom understand and accept a learning disability.

▶ Students need to be aware that all people are different; this awareness will promote a positive, accepting atmosphere in the general education classroom.

Further Readings

Adams, M. J. (1990). *Beginning to read.* Cambridge, MA: MIT Press.

Blalock, G., & Patton, J. R. (1996). Transition and students with learning disabilities. *Journal of Learning Disability, 29,* 7–16

Dowdy, C. A. (1996). Vocational rehabilitation and special education. *Journal of Learning Disabilities, 2*(9), 137–147.

Finn, C. E., Rotherham, A. J., & Hokanson, C. R., Jr. (2001). *Rethinking special education for a new century.* Washington, DC: Thomas B. Fordham Foundation. Available on-line at http://www.edexcellence.net/library/special ed/index.html

Francis, D. J., Shaywitz, S. E., Stuebing, K. K., Shaywitz, B. A., & Fletcher, J. M. (1996). Developmental lag versus deficit models of reading disability: A longitudinal individual growth curve analysis. *Journal of Education Psychology, 88,* 3–17.

Fuchs, D., Fuchs, L. S., Mathes, P. G., Lipsey, M. W., & Roberts, P. H. (2001). *Is "learning disabilities" just a fancy term for low achievement: A meta-analysis of reading differences between low achievers with and without the label. LD Summit: Building a Foundation for the Future.* Available on-line from www.air.org/ldsummit

Gehret, J. (1993). *Before the well runs dry: Taking care of yourself as a parent of an LD/ADD child.* Springville, VA: EDRS. (For information on ordering, write to EDRS, 7420 Fullerton Road, Suite 110, Springville, VA, 22153-2852.)

Gehret, J. (1990). *The don't-give-up kid and learning disabilities.* Fairport, NY: Verbal Images.

Gersten, R. (1998). Recent advances in instructional research for students with learning disabilities: An overview. *Learning Disabilities Research & Practice, 13*(3), 162–170.

Gregg, N., Heggoy, S. J., Stapleton, M., Jackson, R. S., & Morris, R. (1996). Eligibility for college learning disability services. *Learning Disabilities: A Multidisciplinary Journal, 1,* 29–36.

Gresham, F. (2001). *Responsiveness to intervention: An alternative approach to the identification of learning disabilities. LD Summit: Building a Foundation for the Future.* Available on-line from www.air.org/ldsummit

Hadden, S., & Fowler, S. A. (1997). Preschool: A new beginning for children and parents. *The Council for Exceptional Children, 30*(1), 36–39.

Latham, P., & Latham, P. (1993). *Learning disabilities and the law.* Washington, DC: JKL Communication.

Justice, L. M., & Kaderavek, J. (2002). Using shared storybook reading to promote emergent literacy. *Teaching Exceptional Children, 34*(4), 8–13.

Kavale, K. A. (2001). *Discrepancy models in the identification of learning disability. LD Summit: Building a Foundation for the Future.* Available on-line from www.air.org/ldsummit

Kavale, K. A., & Forness, S. R. (2000). What definitions of learning disability say and don't say: A critical analysis. *Journal of Learning Disabilities, 33,* 239–245.

Meese, R. (1992). Adapting textbooks for children in mainstreamed classrooms. *Teaching Exceptional Children, 24,* 49–51.

National Reading Panel Report. (2000). *Report of the National Reading Panel: Teaching children to read.* Washington, DC: National Institutes of Health.

Smith, T. E. C., Dowdy, C., Polloway, E., & Blalock, G. (1997). *Children and adults with learning disabilities.* Boston: Allyn and Bacon.

Swanson, H. L. (1999). Instructional components that predict treatment outcomes for students with learning disabilities: Support for a combined strategy and direct instruction model. *Learning Disabilities Research and Practice, 14,* 129–140.

Swanson, H. L. (2000). Issues facing the field of learning disabilities. *Learning Disabilities Quarterly, 23*(1), 37–50.

Torgesen, J. J. (2001). *Empirical and theoretical support for direct diagnosis of learning disabilities by assessment of intrinsic processing weaknesses. LD Summit: Building a Foundation for the Future.* Available on-line from www.air.org/ldsummit

Wise, B. W., & Snyder, L. (2001). *Judgments in identifying and teaching children with language-based reading difficulties. LD Summit: Building a Foundation for the Future.* Available on-line from www.air.org/ldsummit

VideoWorkshop Extra!

If the VideoWorkshop package was included with your textbook, go to Chapter 6 of the Companion Website (www.ablongman.com/sppd4e) and click on the VideoWorkshop button. Follow the instructions for viewing video clips 1 and 6. Then consider this information along with what you've read in Chapter 6 while answering the following questions.

1. One issue that Bridget discusses at length in the video clip is social acceptance of students with dyslexia by other stu-dents. Based on suggestions in this chapter, what strategies do you believe could help promote social acceptance in Bridget's high school?

2. In Chapter 1 you read about the advantages and disadvantages of the Resource Room Model. Do you support Bridget's rejection of that model? Explain your answer.

3. In video clip 1, Doug is diagnosed as learning disabled. What are the academic and social-emotional issues that will need to be addressed in order to help Doug succeed? Review this chapter for suggestions.

7 Teaching Students with Emotional and Behavioral Disorders

After reading this chapter, you should be able to

1. define emotional and behavioral disorders.
2. describe the characteristics of children and youth with emotional and behavioral disorders (E/BD).
3. understand the nature of emotional and behavioral disorders.
4. discuss ways to identify and evaluate students with E/BD.
5. identify effective interventions for students with E/BD.
6. discuss the role of teachers in meeting the needs of students with E/BD in general education classrooms.

Frank is a seven-year-old first grader who often seems to be in trouble. On the first day of school, he stole some crayons from one of his new classmates. When confronted with the fact that the crayons in his desk belonged to another student, Frank adamantly denied stealing them. Frank's behavior became more difficult over the first six months of the school year. Ms. Walters, Frank's teacher, uses a classroom management system that rewards students with check marks for appropriate behaviors. Students can redeem their check marks at the end of the week for various toys. Frank has never earned enough check marks to get a toy. Now he openly states that he doesn't care if he ever receives any check marks.

Frank's primary behavioral difficulty is his inability to leave his classmates alone. He is constantly pinching, pulling hair, or taking things from other students. Ms. Walters has separated Frank's chair from those of the other students in an attempt to prevent him from bothering them. Still, he gets out of his chair and manages to create disturbances regularly. Ms. Walters has sent Frank to the principal's office on numerous occasions. Each time he returns, his behavior improves, but only for several hours. Then he returns to his previous behavioral patterns. Frank's schoolwork has suffered as a result of his behavior problems. While many of his classmates are reading and writing their names, Frank still has difficulties associating sounds with letters and can print his name only in a rudimentary fashion.

Ms. Walters has had four parent conferences about Frank. His mother indicates to Ms. Walters that she does not know what to do with Frank. There is no father figure in the home, and Frank has already progressed to the point where her discipline does not work. Ms. Walters and Frank's mother are both concerned that Frank's behavior will continue to get worse unless some solution is found. They are currently discussing whether to retain him in first grade for the next school year.

QUESTIONS TO CONSIDER
1. Why did the behavior management system used by Ms. Walters not work with Frank?
2. What positive behavior support strategies can Ms. Walters use that might result in an improvement in Frank's behavior?
3. Would retention be likely to benefit Frank? Why or why not?
4. How would it potentially help or hurt Frank if he were labeled as E/BD?

Although most children and youth are occasionally disruptive, the majority do not display negative behaviors sufficient to create serious problems in school. Most comply with classroom and school rules without needing extensive interventions. However, some students' behaviors and emotions result in significant problems for themselves, their peers, and their teachers, perhaps as a result of the way school personnel deal with various student behaviors. The behavior may continue even after several interventions have been tried. Students with significant school problems may require identification and intervention. At a minimum, classroom teachers should try different methods in an effort to enhance the student's school success and reduce the problem behavior.

Although emotional and behavioral problems may result in serious actions (e.g., aggression, attempted suicide), they far more often have been associated with acting out and disruptive behaviors in classrooms. The primary problem faced by most teachers when dealing with students with emotional and behavior problems is classroom discipline.

Behavior problems clearly are a major concern for professional educators. For example, in a survey of general education classroom teachers, the behavior of students was cited as a primary reason for their deciding to leave the teaching profession (Smith, 1990). Teachers noted that they spent too much time on student behavior problems and not enough on instruction. In a national study, Knitzer, Steinberg, and Fleisch (1990) reported that 80% of all students identified as having emotional and behavior problems are educated in regular schools. Nearly 50% of these students spend some or all of their school day in general education classrooms with general education classroom teachers, not special education teachers. The general public shares educators' concern about behavior problems. A Phi Delta Kappa/Gallup survey of attitudes toward public schools reveals that 15% of respondents ranked behavior problems and discipline as the number two problem in public schools, second only to drugs (Elam, Rose, & Gallup, 1996).

Basic Concepts About Emotional and Behavioral Disorders

CONSIDER THIS

What kinds of children do you think of when you hear the term emotionally disturbed? Can this term have an impact on teachers' expectations of children?

Students who experience emotional and behavioral disorders receive a variety of labels. The federal government historically has identified this group as **seriously emotionally disturbed (SED)** within the Individuals with Disabilities Education Act. Whereas SED is the category used in most states, others classify this group of children as having behavioral disorders. The most widely accepted term is **emotionally and behaviorally disordered (E/BD)** because this term better describes the students served in special education programs. *E/BD* is the term that will be used throughout this chapter.

This section provides basic information about emotional disturbance and behavioral disorders. Understanding children with these problems will aid teachers and other educators in developing appropriate intervention programs. Figure 7.1 illustrates a parent's perspective on intervention programs.

Emotional and Behavioral Disorders Defined

For students with emotional and behavioral disorders to be identified accurately and appropriately placed in educational programs, a critical prerequisite is the need for an acceptable definition. The challenges in developing an acceptable definition of emotional/behavioral disorders have been frequently stated. Kauffman (1995) indicated that the definitional problem has been made more difficult by the different conceptual models that have been used in the field (e.g., psychodynamic, biological, sociological, behavioral, ecological, educational), the different purposes for definition (e.g., educational, legal, mental

FIGURE 7.1   **A Parent's Perspective on E/BD: Patti Childress (Lynchburg, VA)**

From: pchildress [mailto: patti@inmind.com]

Sent: Tuesday, June 6, 2000 11:42 PM

TO: Polloway, Edward 'Ed'

Subject: Re: Concerns

Dr. Polloway:

Thanks for trying to help and please keep thinking about resources that can assist me as both a teacher and a parent.

It bothers me tremendously when I see children with E/BD often getting a "raw deal." People seem to think that it is fine for these children to have a disorder and maybe/maybe not receive special services, but heaven forbid if they can't control themselves or if they do something that appears to be a bit irrational. At times I feel like I am jumping in front of a firing squad to protect that [child whom some seem to see as that] "bad kid that shouldn't be in school anyway." I would like to work with a group that supports parents, provides understanding and advocacy regarding disorders, and seeks support and additional resources for help, etc. What is available in this field? Much is needed.

I have always had a huge heart for "the kid who is a little bit or a long way out there" even before I became a parent of a child with a mood disorder.

From an educational perspective, I know that these children can be very difficult in a group; however, they seem to function much better when they feel in control, are able to make choices, and are spoken to in a calm tone.

From a parent's perspective, I am an educated individual with a traditional home makeup: dad, mom, daughter, and son. . .and I know the difficulties of saying, "Yeah, we've got a very bright child with mood problems." We've been through every medication from ritalin to cylert and clonodone. The next stop would be lithium, weekly counseling, and psychiatric treatment to regulate the medications. I want teachers to understand that getting "meds" is not an easy task or a quick fix. It has taken us over a year of trying various medications until we have, hopefully, found the right combination for now. It requires the constant efforts of counselor, doctor, parents, and teachers working together and exchanging information.

Children without support have got to have advocates to help them get help. These children are very fragile and need to be treated as such. My heart goes out to such a child and the family that simply does not understand why their child is not like everybody else's. In the school environment, even when I listen to special education teachers, I do not find the same level of empathy and understanding for children with E/BD as for those with LD.

health), the difficulties in measuring both emotions and behavior, the range and variability of normal and deviant behavior, the complex relationships of emotional and behavioral disorders to other disabilities, and the transient nature of many emotional/behavioral problems. Although no single definition is accepted by all parties, the one currently used by the federal government for its category of seriously emotionally disturbed (SED) derives from the original work of Bower (1969) and is as follows:

(i) The term means a condition exhibiting one or more of the following characteristics over a long period of time and to a marked extent, which adversely affects educational performance:

(A) An inability to learn which cannot be explained by intellectual, sensory, or health factors;

(B) An inability to build or maintain satisfactory relationships with peers and teachers;

(C) Inappropriate types of behavior or feelings under normal circumstances;

(D) A general pervasive mood of unhappiness or depression; or

(E) A tendency to develop physical symptoms or fears associated with personal or school problems.

(i) The term includes children who are schizophrenic. The term does not include children who are socially maladjusted unless it is determined that they are seriously emotionally disturbed. (*Federal Register,* 1999, p. 12422; Algozzine, Serna, & Patton, 2001)

Although this definition has been used by most states and local educational agencies (e.g., Skiba, Grizzle, & Minke, 1994), it leaves much to be desired. The definition is vague and may leave the reader wondering just what a child with serious emotional disturbance is like. When this definition is interpreted broadly, many more children are served than when it is interpreted narrowly. As evidenced by the underserved nature of this disability category, most states and local school districts seem to interpret the definition narrowly and serve far fewer children in the category than prevalence estimates project as needing services.

Most agencies other than schools that provide services to children and adolescents with emotional problems use the definition and classification system found in the *Diagnostic and Statistical Manual of Mental Disorders* (DSM-IV). This manual, published by the American Psychiatric Association (1994), uses a definition and classification system different from the one used in public schools. This disagreement only adds to the confusion and results in fragmented services; some children are considered disabled according to one system but not according to the other.

More recently, K. Algozzine (2001) presented a definition to guide educational practices. While not adapted by any governmental agencies, it does illustrate a useful, alternative approach to defining this population:

Students with behavior problems are ones who, after receiving supportive educational services and counseling assistance available to all students, still exhibit persistent and consistent severe behavioral disabilities that consequently interfere with their productive learning processes as well as those of others. The inability of these students to achieve adequate academic progress and satisfactory interpersonal relationships cannot be attributed primarily to physical, sensory, or intellectual deficits. (p. 37)

Classification of Emotional and Behavioral Disorders

Children who experience emotional and behavioral disorders constitute a very heterogeneous population. Professionals typically have subcategorized the group into smaller, more homogeneous subgroups so that these students can be better understood and served (Wicks-Nelson & Israel, 1991). Several different classification systems are used to group individuals with emotional and behavioral disorders.

One classification system focuses on the clinical elements found in the field of emotional and behavior problems. This system is detailed in the DSM-IV (American Psychiatric Association, 1994), which is widely used by medical and psychological professionals, though far less frequently by educators. The manual categorizes emotional and behavioral

---

CONSIDER THIS

What impact can a definition that is vague, like the federal definition of SED, have on identification of and services to children?

CONSIDER THIS

Do some children reflect several of these different categories? If so, what is the purpose of placing them in the specific subcategory of E/BD?

TABLE 7.1   **Major Components of the DSM-IV Classification System**

Disorders usually first evident in infancy, childhood, or adolescence	Dissociative disorders
	Sexual disorders
Organic mental syndromes and disorders	Sleep disorders
Psychoactive substance use disorders	Factitious disorders
Schizophrenia	Impulse control disorders not elsewhere classified
Delusional disorders	Adjustment disorders
Psychotic disorders not elsewhere classified	Psychological factors affecting physical condition
Mood disorders	Personality disorders
Anxiety disorders	
Somatoform disorders	

From *Diagnostic and Statistical Manual of Mental Disorders* (4th ed.), by the American Psychiatric Association, 1994, Washington, DC: Author.

problems according to several clinical subtypes, such as developmental disorders, organic mental disorders, and schizophrenia. Educators need to be aware of the DSM-IV classification system because of the periodic need to interact with professionals from the field of mental health. Table 7.1 lists the major types of disorders according to this system.

A second classification system was developed by Quay and Peterson (1987). They described six major subgroups of children with emotional and behavior disorders as follows:

1. Individuals are classified as having a **conduct disorder** if they seek attention, are disruptive, and act out. This category includes behaving aggressively toward others.
2. Students who exhibit **socialized aggression** are likely to join a group of peers who are openly disrespectful to their peers, teachers, and parents. Delinquency and truancy are common among this group.
3. Individuals with **attention problems–immaturity** can be characterized as having attention deficits, being easily distractible, and having poor concentration. Many students in this group are impulsive and may act without thinking about the consequences.
4. Students classified in the **anxiety/withdrawal group** are self-conscious, reticent, and unsure of themselves. Their self-concepts are generally very low, causing them to retreat from immediate activities. They are also anxious and frequently depressed.
5. The subgroup of students who display **psychotic behavior** may hallucinate, deal in a fantasy world, and exhibit bizarre behavior.
6. Students with **motor excess** are hyperactive. They have difficulties sitting still, listening to other individuals, and keeping their attention focused.

At one time, children with *autism* were included in the federal definition of serious emotional disturbance. Since these children (and other children identified within the broader designation of autism spectrum disorders) frequently displayed behaviors that were considered extremely atypical, it was thought that they were experiencing emotional problems. However, professionals and advocates no longer classify autism as an emotional problem. It is best viewed as having a biological basis. The result has been the removal of autism from the SED (or E/BD) category.

Classification becomes less important when school personnel utilize a functional assessment and intervention model. This approach emphasizes determining which environmental stimuli result in inappropriate behaviors. Once these stimuli are identified and altered, the inappropriate behaviors may decrease or disappear (Foster-Johnson & Dunlap, 1993). In such instances, the process of classifying a student's problem becomes less relevant to the design of educational programs.

CROSS-REFERENCE

For more information on autism, see Chapter 10.

Prevalence and Causes of Emotional and Behavioral Disorders

Compared to children classified as having learning disabilities and mental retardation, the category of E/BD represents a much smaller number of children. In terms of prevalence, the *23rd Report to Congress on the Implementation of the Individuals with Disabilities Education Act* noted that 0.94% of the school population was served as EB/D during the 1999–2000 school year (U.S. Department of Education, 2001).

Because of the difficulty in defining and identifying emotional and behavioral disorders, the range of estimates of the prevalence of the disorder is great (Knitzer et al., 1990). The figure of 0.94% of students served under this category contrasts sharply with the 22% estimated by Cotler (1986) and the 14% to 20% estimated by Brandenburg, Friedman, and Silver (1990) as having moderate to severe behavioral disorders. The specific number depends on the definition used and the interpretation of the definition by individuals who classify students. However, the consensus clearly is that E/BD is a dramatically underserved category of disability with far more students in need of supports than the approximately 1% currently identified.

It is a safe assumption that students with emotional and behavioral disorders are typically the most underidentified in the school setting. Lambros, Ward, Bocian, MacMillan, and Gresham (1998) indicated that the reasons for this condition include the following: the ambiguity of definitions used by states; the limited training of school psychologists in conducting assessments for these students; the financial limitations of districts; and the general hesitation to apply labels such as behavioral disorder or seriously emotionally disturbed.

Among students classified as having emotional and behavioral disorders, the majority are males. Some studies have revealed that as many as 10 times more boys than girls are found in special classes for students with behavioral disorders (e.g., Rosenberg, Wilson, Maheady, & Sindelar, 1992).

Many factors can cause students to display emotional and behavioral disorders. These factors can be viewed through five different theoretical frameworks, including biological, psychoanalytical, behavioral, phenomenological, and sociological/ecological. Within each framework are numerous specific causal factors. Table 7.2 summarizes these variables by theoretical framework.

CONSIDER THIS

What factors will likely lead to larger or smaller numbers of children being identified as having emotional and behavioral disorders?

Depression is a characteristic of students with emotional and behavioral disorders.

TABLE 7.2	Causes of Serious Emotional and Behavioral Disorders
Theoretical Framework	**Etiologies/Causal Factors**
Biological	Genetic inheritance Biochemical abnormalities Neurological abnormalities Injury to the central nervous system
Psychoanalytical	Psychological processes Functioning of the mind: id, ego, and superego Inherited predispositions (instinctual process) Traumatic early-childhood experiences
Behavioral	Environmental events 1. Failure to learn adaptive behaviors 2. Learning of maladaptive behaviors 3. Developing maladaptive behaviors as a result of stressful environmental circumstances
Phenomenological	Faulty learning about oneself Misuse of defense mechanisms Feelings, thoughts, and events emanating from the self
Sociological/Ecological	Role assignment (labeling) Cultural transmission Social disorganization Distorted communication Differential association Negative interactions and transactions with others

From *Human Exceptionality* (p. 148) by M. L. Hardman, C. J. Drew, M. W. Egan, and B. Wolf, 1993, Boston: Allyn and Bacon. Used by permission.

It is critical to note that many students experience emotional and/or behavioral disorders because of the environmental factors that affect their lives. In American society, potential causative elements may include variables related to family, school, and community factors. In Figure 7.2, a model designed in reference to antisocial youth outlines this interaction of factors. Thus, it is essential that a broad view of the problems experienced by students be considered.

Characteristics of Students with Emotional and Behavioral Disorders

Students with emotional and behavioral problems exhibit a wide range of characteristics that differ in type as well as intensity. This wide range of behaviors and emotions reflects the broad variety of characteristics associated with individuals with emotional and behavior problems.

Problems typically associated with children with emotional and behavioral disorders include the following:

▶ Aggressive/acting-out behaviors (Grosenick, George, George, & Lewis, 1991; Kauffman, Lloyd, Baker, & Riedel, 1995)
▶ Social deficits (Smith & Luckasson, 1995)
▶ Inadequate peer relationships (Searcy & Meadows, 1994)
▶ Hyperactivity/distractibility
▶ Lying, cheating, and stealing (Rosenberg et al., 1992)
▶ Academic deficits (Bullock, 1992)
▶ Anxiety (Kauffman et al., 1995; Wicks-Nelson & Israel, 1991)

FIGURE **7.2**

The Development of Antisocial Behavior

From "Antisocial Behavior, Academic Failure, and School Climate: A Critical Review" (p. 133) by A. McEvoy & R. Welker, 2000, *Journal of Emotional and Behavioral Disorders, 8.*

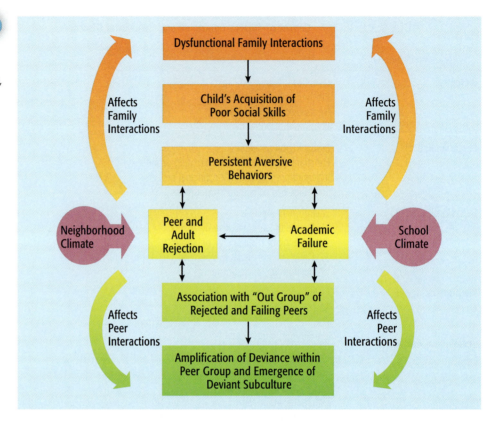

Children classified as having emotional and behavioral disorders do not exhibit all these characteristics. The ones exhibited by a particular child will depend on the nature of the emotional or behavioral problem.

A common, and helpful, way to conceptualize emotional and behavioral disorders is to categorize them as externalizing or internalizing behaviors. The list in Table 7.3 provides such an illustration.

TABLE **7.3**   **Categorizing Emotional and Behavioral Disorders**

Externalizing Behaviors

Aggressive toward people and objects	Temper tantrums
Defiant	Jealous
Disobedient	Distrustful, blames others
Noncompliant	Pattern of lying and stealing
Argumentative	Lack of self-control
Destructive	

Internalizing Behaviors

Withdrawn	Apathetic, restricted activity levels
Fixated on certain thoughts	Avoids social situations
Fearful, anxious	Inferiority
Sad, moody, depressed	Self-conscious, overly sensitive
Irritable	Inappropriate crying

From *Childhood Behavioral Disorders: Applied Research and Educational Practices* (2nd ed., p. 69) by R. Algozzine, L. Serna, & J. R. Patton, 2001, Austin, TX: Pro-Ed.

One problem often overlooked is depression. According to national estimates, approximately 2–4% of elementary school children and 4–8% of adolescents suffer from depression (CEC, 1999). Further, Forness (cited by CEC, 1999) has estimated that between 30 and 40% of students in E/BD classes suffer from depression. Depression may be a particularly significant issue for girls, which unfortunately may be underdiagnosed because it is a "silent" one, as opposed to acting-out problems. While depression may be more prevalent in young boys, Marcotte, Fortin, Potvin, and Papillon (2002) reported that this trend reverses during the teenage years. Negative body image and self-esteem as well as stressful life events were found to be related to this trend. Issues such as the stigma of being labeled, biological factors related to the causation of the disability, and failure experiences can all promote feelings of depression.

Teachers should be alert to signs of depression in order to assist students in the classroom where depression may be associated with an inability to concentrate or achieve. More dramatically, depression can be associated with suicide, estimated to be the third leading cause of death for adolescents and young adults.

While the focus of research on the characteristics of students with E/BD is often on social and behavioral concerns, nevertheless it should not be overlooked that academic problems are often a key concern as well. As Anderson, Kutash, and Duchnowski (2001, p. 6) note, students with E/BD and LD often are both frequently observed to exhibit "below-average achievement in content area courses, deficits in basic academics, a general lack of motivation toward school, and deficiencies in school-related skills such as note-taking and test-taking." Further, Anderson et al. (2001), in a five-year study of elementary school students, noted that students with E/BD made limited progress in academic achievement when compared to their peers identified as LD.

The relationship between academic achievement and behavioral disorders may be most pronounced in instances of more significant antisocial behavior. McEvoy and Welker (2000) summarized these issues as follows:

> Antisocial behavior and academic failure reinforce one another within the context of ineffective school practices and ineffective parenting strategies. . . . A pattern of academic failure provides few opportunities for the student to receive positive reinforcement. From the failing student's perspective, school then takes on aversive properties that increase the likelihood of escape, rebellion, uncooperativeness, and other negative behaviors. This cycle often results in school failure, dropping out, and involvement in delinquent groups. Conversely, ineffective school responses to antisocial conduct have negative implications and influence the academic performance of students in general. (p. 131)

Outcomes and Postschool Adjustment   A critical concern for students with emotional and behavioral disorders is the determination of postschool outcomes. In a comprehensive, longitudinal study of such students, Greenbaum and colleagues (1999) reported on students who were identified as SED and were served in either a publicly funded residential mental health facility or a community-based special education program. While the severity of the disorders that these students experienced is likely to be greater than those of students in general education classrooms, this information should alert educators to the potential challenges that these students face. The researchers found that approximately two-thirds (66.5%) of the individuals had at least one contact with police in which the person was believed to be the perpetrator of a crime, and 43.3% had been arrested at least once. The most commonly reported crimes were property related.

For this same sample of students, educational outcomes were generally poor. For those who were young adults (over 18 years of age) at the time of the follow-up, 75.4% were assessed to be below their appropriate reading levels, and 96.9% were below appropriate levels in math achievement. Only one in four had obtained a regular high school diploma; an additional 17.4% had completed a GED. Approximately 43% had dropped out of school programs.

These data are consistent with the challenging picture that emerges from the annual federal reports on IDEA, which indicate that students with E/BD are the most likely to drop out of school (50.6% of students exiting school in 1998–99). In addition to students with mental retardation and autism, these students are also among the least likely to receive a high school diploma or certificate (41.9%) (U.S. Department of Education, 2001).

One somewhat encouraging finding is that students with E/BD had greater success in adult education programs. Scanlon and Melland (2002) hypothesized that the context of adult programs may contribute to this success because such programs may be "less antagonizing and more accepting of any emotional or behavioral problems" (p. 253).

Students with emotional and behavioral disorders often have significant challenges in adjustment within the community. Maag and Katisyannis (1998) noted that successful adjustment is affected by the high dropout rate, which makes it difficult to establish and address transition goals within the student's IEP and individual transition plan. In addition, successful transition is affected by the high rates of unemployment, the increased likelihood of incarceration, and the persistence of mental health problems in adulthood.

A recent study reported by McConaughy and Wadsworth (2000) provided some guidance in predicting which individuals would fare better as adults. Based on life histories of these individuals, they concluded that young adults with good outcomes

> tended to have more stable and quality living situations, better family relationships, more positive relationships with friends, were more goal-oriented, and experienced more successes and fewer stresses than did young adults with poor outcomes. In addition, more young adults with good outcomes held full-time jobs in the community, and fewer associated with friends who used drugs or who were in trouble with the law or violent. (pp. 213–214)

Also, following up (after three years) on a group of adolescents who participated in a statewide system of care, Pandiani, Schacht, and Banks (2001) reported that these individuals, when compared to other young people, were eight times more likely to be hospitalized for behavioral health care and the young men in the sample were five times as likely to be incarcerated. For young women, the rate of maternity was generally similar to the general population.

In the area of employment, critical to successful transition, Rylance (1998) reported that the key variables that increase an individual's chances of employment included basic academic skills, higher functional competence levels in school-related areas, and high school graduation. Successful school programs for these students tended to be ones that included effective vocational education and counseling programs and that motivated students to persist in school and obtain a diploma. Chapter 16 provides more information about preparing students with disabilities for successful transitions to adult life.

In conclusion, Burns, Hoagwood, and Maultsby (1999) noted, "Consensus about the critical outcomes for children with serious emotional and behavioral disorders at home, in school, and out of trouble is not difficult to obtain. Achieving such outcomes and more is the challenge!" (p. 685).

Identification, Assessment, and Eligibility

Students with emotional and behavioral disorders are evaluated for several purposes, including identification, assessment to determine appropriate intervention strategies, and determination of eligibility for special education services. The first step is for students to be identified as potentially having emotional and behavioral problems. Teachers' awareness of the characteristics of students with these problems is critical in the identification process. Behavioral checklists can be used to identify students for possible referral.

Once students are identified as possibly having problems, they are referred for formal assessment to determine their eligibility for special education programs and to ascertain appropriate intervention strategies. Kaplan (1996) lists clinical interviews, observations, rating scales, personality tests, and neurological examinations as methods for obtaining relevant information. Table 7.4 summarizes these procedures.

⊤EACHING TIP

When you suspect a student of having an emotional or behavioral disorder, develop a systematic method of collecting information during observations of the student.

𝓣ABLE 7.4	Assessment Procedures Used for Students with Emotional and Behavioral Disorders
Clinical Interview	▶ The clinical interview is the most common tool for assessment. ▶ Questions are directed to the child and others regarding behaviors and any relevant relationships. ▶ Some questions are planned; some are developed as the interview progresses. ▶ The interview can be highly structured, using questions generated from the DSM-IV criteria.
Observation	▶ The observation can be structured with time limitations, or unstructured. ▶ Observations should occur in a variety of different settings and at different times.
Rating Scales	▶ A rating scale contains a listing of behaviors to note. ▶ It provides for much more structure than simple observation. ▶ It ensures that certain behaviors are observed or asked about.
Personality Tests	▶ The two kinds of personality tests include self-completed inventories and projective tests. ▶ Both kinds of personality tests can provide insightful information. ▶ Interpretation of personality tests is subjective and needs to be done by a trained professional.

From *Pathways for Exceptional Children: School, Home, and Culture,* by P. Kaplan, 1996, St. Paul, MN: West Publishing.

One encouraging new approach to the assessment of students with emotional and behavioral disorders is through the use of strength-based assessment. Unlike widely used deficit-oriented assessment models, strength-based assessment focuses on the student and his or her family "as individuals with unique talents, skills, and life events as well as with specific unmet needs. Strength-based assessment recognizes that even the most challenged children in stressed families have strengths, competencies, and resources that can be built on in developing a treatment approach" (Epstein, 1999, p. 258).

Epstein and Charma (1998) have developed a scale that complements assessment instruments that focus on difficulties experienced by the student in the school or home setting. As they noted (p. 3): "Strength-based assessment is defined as the measurement of those emotional/behavioral skills and characteristics that create a sense of personal accomplishment; contribute to satisfying relationships with family members, peers, and adults; enhance one's ability to deal with adversity and stress; and promote one's personal, social, and academic development."

Manifestation of the Disability   A key issue in the field of emotional and behavioral disorders is the relationship between the disability itself and the behaviors that are exhibited in school. Under IDEA guidelines, educators must determine whether the behavior in question functions as a **manifestation of the student's disability** (see Table 7.4). The key question is whether the student's disability impairs his or her ability to control the behavior and/or interferes with his or her awareness of the possible disciplinary action that may follow. The function of the guidelines is neither to exclude students with disabilities from normal disciplinary routines, nor to prevent educators from taking action to redirect troublesome behavior. Rather, the purpose is to prevent the misapplication of disciplinary actions that, owing to the student's particular disability, may fail to achieve the desired objective and create needless frustration for everyone involved (Buck, Polloway, Kirkpatrick, Patton, & Fad, 1999).

To complete a manifestation determination for students with emotional and behavioral disorders (as well as for other disabilities), school personnel should carefully consider the disability and the nature of the behavior to determine a possible relationship. Fad, Patton, and Polloway (2000) suggest that the following representative questions should be considered initially:

▶ Does the student know right from wrong?
▶ Does the disability limit the student's ability to handle stressful situations?
▶ Does the disability interfere with the student's ability to build or maintain appropriate peer and/or teacher relationships?
▶ Does the disability interfere with the student's ability to learn how to appropriately express his or her feelings?

After reviewing research on manifestation determination, Katsiyannis and Maag (2001, p. 93) developed a model for further conceptualizing key questions to consider. The four issues are summarized in Rights & Responsibilities.

Classroom teachers should be aware of the concept of manifestation of disability within the continuing debate about disciplinary procedures for students with disabilities, including those with emotional and behavioral disorders. The debate revolves around the issues of equity, discipline, school safety, and the legal rights of students with disabilities for a free and appropriate public education with accommodations designed to be consistent with students' individual needs.

Rights & Responsibilities   **Manifestation Determination**

Katsiyannis and Maag (2001, pp. 93–94) offered a reasoned critique of the application of the concept of manifestation determination. They proposed this model:

1. **Does the student possess the requisite skills to engage in an appropriate alternative behavior?** The team would break the behavior down into its subcomponents using task analysis, list the subcomponents on a checklist to note their presence or absence, and select a powerful reinforcer. The reinforcer is designed to motivate the student to use the targeted skills if they exist in his repertoire. If necessary, a relevant scenario would then be generated, and the student would be asked to role-play the skills for dealing with teasing appropriately in order to earn the reinforcer . . .

2. **Is the student able to analyze the problem, generate solutions, evaluate their effectiveness, and select one?** This question can be answered by interviewing the student. The evaluator would generate a scenario in which the aggressive behavior occurred. She would then determine how well the student could answer the following questions:
   • Can the student define the problem to be solved?
   • Can the student set realistic and concrete goals to solve the problem?
   • Can the student generate a wide range of possible alternative courses of action?
   • Can the student imagine and consider how others might respond if asked to deal with a similar problem?

• Can the student evaluate the pros and cons of each proposed solution and rank order the solutions from least to most practical and desirable?

3. **Does the student interpret the situation factually or distort it to fit some existing bias?** This question is aimed at discovering whether the student displays any cognitive distortions related to the situation. A cognitive distortion exists when a student does not factually interpret aspects of the situation. . . . In addition, an evaluator can interview a student to identify any discrepancies between the event and activated thoughts.

4. **Can the student monitor the behavior?** This deficit area is perhaps the most difficult to evaluate because the assessment and intervention techniques for this deficit area are identical. Namely, if we want to assess a student's skill at self-monitoring, we have him self-monitor. However, the process of self-monitoring results in reactivity—obtaining a positive change in the target behavior by virtue of the student observing and recording it.

 For follow-up questions about manifestation determination, go to Chapter 7 of the Companion Website (ablongman.com/sppd4e) and click Rights & Responsibilities.

Adapted from "Manifestation Determination as a Golden Fleece" (pp. 93–94) by A. Katsiyannis & J. W. Maag (2001), *Exceptional Children, 68.*

A survey reported by Butera, Klein, McMullen, and Wilson (1998) underscores the disciplinary issues in schools. They noted that

> the general and special educators interviewed did not differ in their opinions about the need for clearer school-wide discipline policies applied in an equitable fashion to all students. Special educators as well as general educators did not value IEP protection of students' rights. Especially noteworthy is our finding that schools did not often examine IEPs when making discipline decisions. Apparently educators do not see the necessity for individualized discipline procedures for students with disabilities nor do they readily acknowledge a relationship between disability and student misconduct. (p. 113)

Clearly, educators reflected a concern for discipline issues that did not precisely follow the issue of manifestation determination. Teachers are encouraged to closely follow the continuing discussions in the area of discipline. Concerns for school safety further exacerbate the resolution of this issue.

Functional Behavioral Assessment   One important approach to assessment warrants separate consideration because of its clear implications for intervention efforts. **Functional behavioral assessment (FBA)** provides a consideration of specific behaviors and behavioral patterns set within an environmental context. It has been defined as "an analysis of the contingencies responsible for behavioral problems" (Malott, Whaley, & Malott, 1997, p. 433). A sample FBA is presented in Figure 7.3.

When determining appropriate intervention strategies, functional behavioral assessment provides extensive information for teachers. A functional assessment helps teachers better understand disruptive behaviors; improved understanding can lead to an insightful intervention approach. Foster-Johnson and Dunlap (1993) identified the following variables that may influence behavior:

1. **Physiological factors**
   - Sickness or allergies
   - Side effects of medication
   - Fatigue
   - Frustration due to a fight, missing the bus, or a disrupted routine
2. **Classroom environment**
   - High noise level
   - Uncomfortable temperature
   - Over- or understimulation
   - Poor seating arrangement
   - Frequent disruptions
3. **Curriculum and instruction**
   - Few opportunities for making choices
   - Lack of predictability in the schedule
   - Inadequate level of assistance provided to the student
   - Unclear directions provided for activity completion
   - Few opportunities for the student to communicate
   - Activities that are too difficult
   - Activities that take a long time to complete
   - Activities for which the completion criterion is unclear
   - Activities that might not be perceived as relevant or useful

After reviewing these variables with a particular child in mind, teachers can devise interventions that target a specific variable to alter a particular behavior (Foster-Johnson & Dunlap, 1993). McConnell, Hilvitz, and Cox (1998) present a 10-step procedure for conducting a functional behavioral assessment. Their approach shows how writing a behavioral intervention plan (BIP) is a direct outgrowth of the assessment process. McConnell et al. (1998) stress that while an evaluation of the environmental context is necessary for developing hypotheses regarding the causes of a problem behavior, the only valid way to reach a conclu-

CONSIDER THIS

How can using functional behavioral assessment help teachers focus on specific issues related to inappropriate behaviors?

TEACHING TIP

Whenever possible, teach appropriate social skills in the context in which they will be used. If they must be taught in a different context, plan for their transfer to more typical settings.

The Functional Behavioral Assessment (FBA) addresses the relationship among precipitating conditions, the behavior, its consequences, and the function of the behavior. The FBA also reflects a consideration of all relevant data gathered, both as background information and by using specific assessment techniques. Refer to the Functional Behavioral Assessment Discussion Guide (found on page 16 of the manual) for assistance in completing this form.

Behavior # 3   Physical aggression/fighting

Precipitating Conditions
(Setting, time, or other situations typically occurring *before* the behavior)

- ☒ unstructured time in hallways/on the bus
- ☐ academic instruction in
- ☐ when given a directive to
- ☒ when close to smaller students
- ☐ when provoked by
- ☐ when unable to
- ☒ other when unsupervised
- ☐ none observed

Specific Behavior
(*Exactly* what the student does or does not do)

Casey pushes, hits, trips other students, often students who are smaller; Casey's aggression occurs more often when no adults are watching her (on bus; in halls).

Consequences
(Events that typically *follow* the behavior)

- ☒ teacher attention
- ☒ peer attention
- ☒ verbal warning/reprimand
- ☐ loss of privilege (what kind?)
- ☐ time out (where/how long?)
- ☒ detention (how long?) after school
- ☐ removal from class
- ☒ in-school suspension (how long?) 3 days
- ☐ other

Function of the Behavior
(*Hypothesized purpose[s]* the behavior serves)

- ☐ escape/avoidance
- ☐ gaining attention
- ☒ expression of anger
- ☐ frustration
- ☒ vengeance
- ☒ seeking of power/control
- ☒ intimidation
- ☐ sensory stimulation
- ☐ relief of fear/anxiety
- ☐ other

Specific Assessment Techniques Used to Analyze This Behavior

- ☒ Observation
- ☒ Behavior Checklist/Rating Scale
- ☐ Student Interview
- ☐ Video/Audio Taping
- ☒ Administrative Interview
- ☒ Teacher Interview
- ☒ Parent Interview
- ☐ Other

Relating Information/Considerations

Academic: Low grades—homework not turned in

Family: Casey's behavior has disrupted family life. Mother reports she is afraid of Casey.

Social/Peer: Few friends

Other:

FIGURE 7.3   **An Example of a Functional Behavioral Assessment (FBA)**

sion about behavioral influence is to change the environmental setting and/or the events associated with the behavior, and to observe whether or not a change in behavior results.

Strategies for Curriculum and Instruction for Students with Emotional and Behavioral Disorders

Students with emotional and behavioral disorders typically present significant problems for teachers in general education settings. Their behavior may affect not only their own learning but often the learning of others as well.

The challenges of appropriately serving students with emotional and behavioral disorders are emphasized by the realities of how schools respond to these students. See the Personal Spotlight for one educator's experience with these challenges.

Educational Placements

Students with emotional and behavioral disorders are commonly included in general education classrooms, albeit to a lesser extent than students with other types of disabilities. According to the 23rd annual report to Congress on the implementation of IDEA

Personal Spotlight

School Administrator

Mike Kelly took an interesting route to becoming a school administrator. After completing his undergraduate degree in special education, Mike taught for 11 years in both self-contained special education classrooms and resource rooms, primarily working with students with learning disabilities and those with emotional and behavioral problems. He then completed two master's degrees, one in school administration and the other in special education. He served for 12 years as an elementary school principal and now is a middle school principal.

Mike finds that inclusion is a powerful approach because it provides excellent learning opportunities for all students. At the same time, his experiences as a teacher and administrator reinforce the fact that successful inclusion stands or falls on access to necessary resources and supports. Reflecting back on his own teaching experience, Mike wishes there had been more opportunities for his own students to experience inclusion when he was teaching elementary and middle school children with disabilities.

As a principal, Mike has seen a number of successes that relate to inclusion. In particular, for students with emotional and behavioral disorders, the benefits of inclusion are most clearly seen when a student's behavior begins to change as a result of interaction with nondisabled peers and his or her social skills develop to a corresponding degree. While he would be reluctant to extol the virtues of inclusion for all students with severe behavior disorders, in many instances for students labeled E/BD, there were dramatic changes after inclusion in terms of appropriate behavior. "For example, one student identified as E/BD was placed in a general education

Mike Kelly
Bedford County, VA

classroom and initially continued the kinds of behaviors that had previously characterized his school performance. After a while, however, he seemed to realize that he was not getting the 'audience' that he had anticipated, and consequently, his inappropriate behaviors began to decrease and his prosocial interactions began to increase. He became a real success story." Mike continues, "While some indicate that inclusion may be difficult in schools with academically talented students, I believe that there are some special advantages in such a school. Because the students are quite committed to the learning process, they often consequently serve as very effective models for students who are experiencing both learning and behavioral difficulties."

Mike finds that the challenges for inclusion are more often in the academic domain. While some students have made remarkable progress in social adjustment, there is a significant need for supports in the classroom in order to make it work from an academic perspective. Paraprofessionals and the substantive involvement of special educators in support of classroom teachers can make the difference between successful and less successful inclusion experiences for individual learners as well as for their nondisabled peers.

Companion Website

For follow-up questions about this Personal Spotlight, go to Chapter 7 of the Companion Website (ablongman.com/sppd4e) and click Personal Spotlight.

(U.S. Department of Education, 2001), in the 1998–1999 school year 25.5% of all students identified as emotionally disturbed were taught in the regular class (i.e., general education) setting at least 79% of the time, while an additional 23% were served in these settings between 40% and 79% of the time. Combining these figures, we can conclude that approximately half of all students identified as E/BD will spend much of their time in general education–based programs. For those students who are placed in more restrictive settings, 33.1% were placed in separate classes, 13.3% in separate public or private day facilities, 3.5% in public or private residential facilities, and 1.3% in home or hospital environments.

The challenge of inclusion of students with E/BD has given rise to a number of perspectives on the relative advantages of inclusive versus restrictive settings, which can prove helpful to teachers as they plan inclusive programs. McConnell's (2001) perspectives are presented in Table 7.5.

Because many students with E/BD are included in general education classrooms, teachers and special education teachers need to collaborate in developing and implementing intervention programs. Without this collaboration, appropriate interventions will be difficult to provide. Consistency in behavior management and other strategies among teachers and family members is critical. If students receive feedback from the special education teacher that significantly differs from the feedback received from the classroom teacher, confusion often results.

As more students with disabilities are included in general education classrooms, many students with serious emotional disturbances and behavioral disorders are being reintegrated into general classrooms from more restrictive settings. The ability of students and teachers to deal effectively with behavior problems is critical for successful reintegration (Carpenter & McKee-Higgins, 1996). Rock, Rosenberg, and Carran (1995) studied the variables that affected this reintegration and reported that programs that were more likely to have success at reintegration included those with a more positive reintegration orien-

𝖳ABLE 7.5   **Advantages and Disadvantages of More Restrictive and Less Restrictive Placements for Students with Serious Emotional Disturbance**

▶ Placements	▶ Advantages	▶ Disadvantages
Less Restrictive Regular classrooms (with and without support) Resource rooms	Prevents the regular educator from giving up on the student and turning to "experts" Permits students to model appropriate behavior of their peers; increased interaction Possibly less expensive May be able to serve more students Students do not experience problems with reintegration Students follow general curriculum more easily	Expense and time required to train general educators to work with students and special educators to work collaboratively with general educators Problems with classroom management and discipline Lack of consistent expectations for the students Time and materials required for individualization Fear and frustration of general education
More Restrictive Separate classes Separate campuses Residential facilities Hospitals	Flexibility to provide different curricula and different goals Progress can be more closely monitored Accountability of program is more clearly defined Intervention can be more consistent Student follows only one set of guidelines and expectations One team for consistent discipline	Student's opportunities for peer interactions are limited, especially when student is not at neighborhood school with peers from neighborhood Travel time for students can be excessive No possible modeling of appropriate peers; no opportunities for socialization with nondisabled peers Difficulties with reintegration back into regular school or class

From "Placements" (p. 324) by K. McConnell, 2001, in R. Algozzine, L. Serna, & J. R. Patton (Eds.), *Childhood Behavior Disorders: Applied Research and Educational Practices* (2nd ed), Austin, TX: Pro-Ed.

IEP Goals and Objectives for Frank

The following IEP goals and objectives are consistent with the chapter-opening vignette of Frank (if Frank were subsequently identified as E/BD and found eligible for special education).

Goal 1   *Frank will interact appropriately with peers in the classroom.*
  Objective 1: *In classroom settings, Frank will ask permission to borrow or use items from classmates 90% of the time.*
  Objective 2: *In classroom settings, Frank will engage in disruptions of peers at a rate of three times or fewer per day, at least four days every week.*
  Objective 3: *In classroom settings, Frank will participate in group projects with peers without disruptions, independent of teacher monitoring of his behavior, 70% of the time.*

Goal 2   *Frank will complete the in-class and homework assignments successfully.*
  Objective 1: *Given an in-class assignment, Frank will work independently for a minimum of 15 minutes with one or no disruptions 80% of the time.*
  Objective 2: *Given homework assignments for one week, Frank will complete 75% of assignments on time.*
  Objective 3: *Given in-class assignments, Frank will complete 80% of them within the appropriate time frame.*

Goal 3   *Frank will demonstrate the ability to make sound-symbol correspondences for vowels and consonant sounds.*
  Objective 1: *Given a series of common consonants (i.e., b, d, f, l, m, n, p, r, s, t), Frank will correctly identify the associated sounds with 80% accuracy.*
  Objective 2: *Given a list of vowels, Frank will correctly identify all short vowel sounds with 90% accuracy.*
  Objective 3: *Given a set of vowels, Frank will correctly identify all long vowel sounds with 90% accuracy.*

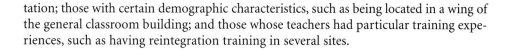

tation; those with certain demographic characteristics, such as being located in a wing of the general classroom building; and those whose teachers had particular training experiences, such as having reintegration training in several sites.

Effective Instruction

Teaching students with emotional and behavioral disorders is clearly challenging. Research, however, does offer promising directions for effective instructional practices. As adapted from Wehby, Symons, Canale, and Go (1998), these practices should include the following:

- providing appropriate structure and predictable routines
- establishing a structured and consistent classroom environment
- establishing a consistent schedule with set rules and consequences and clear expectations
- fostering positive teacher-student interaction with adequate praise and systematic responses to problem behaviors
- frequently implementing instructional sequences that promote high rates of academic engagement
- creating a classroom environment in which independent seat work is limited and sufficient time is allotted for establishing positive social interaction. (p. 52)

An important, emerging emphasis in effective instruction for students with E/BD is to use functional assessment procedures as a basis for making effective classroom adaptations. For example, Kerr, Delaney, Clarke, Dunlap, and Childs (2001) demonstrated that

Diversity Forum

African American Disproportionality: Is There a Problem?

Jamal is a 10-year-old African American fourth grader who repeatedly speaks out loudly without raising his hand. He is reprimanded for arguing with both the teacher, Ms. Wilson, and his peers. He appears to be in constant motion.

Ebony is another 10-year-old African American student in the same class. Ms. Wilson assigns books to be read silently the first 20 minutes of class, but Ebony refuses to finish reading her book and complains of boredom. She persists in talking throughout this time period. Ms. Wilson wonders if both Jamal and Ebony should be referred for special education because of their classroom behavior.

African American students are disproportionately referred and placed into classes for students with emotional and behavioral disorders. Students in high-poverty schools are also placed at higher risk than members of other socioeconomic groups to be identified as E/BD.

Ms. Wilson would benefit from knowing that behavior is defined differently within and across cultures. In Jamal's case, African American students are often perceived as talking loud, interrupting, and arguing when attempting to express or show interest in class activities. One suggestion is to provide flexible and interactive classrooms, which allow for greater movement, interaction, and opportunities for structured debate. This approach is consistent with African American social interaction styles and talent development.

In the case of Ebony, if Ms. Wilson allows her students to select their own books to read, they can engage in assignments that are reflective of their culture and personal interests. Promoting respect for diversity in the classroom and developing students' passions are tenets of culturally responsive pedagogy. Implementing these practices in education can help teachers recognize differences in behavior across cultures and also focus on developing a class-wide culture that is mutually respectful and conducive for critical inquiry (Denbo & Beaulieu, 2002).

For follow-up questions about cultural disproportionality and behavior, go to Chapter 7 of the Companion Website (ablongman.com/sppd4e) and click Diversity Forum.

---

adaptations based on assessment data, which identified activities associated with problem behavior and also activities not associated with such behavior, resulted in increased task employment, decreases in challenging behavior, and increased academic productivity—all without significant difficulties in implementation by the teacher. Further, Reid and Nelson (2002) reported that FBA provides a promising approach with research validation for planning positive behavioral interventions, which can have a significant effect on improving student behavior. They note that there remains a need for closer attention to the practicality of such interventions within the school setting to confirm that these methods will be acceptable to teachers. FBA-based approaches offer exciting opportunities to enhance instruction and influence successful inclusion practices. They will be discussed further later in the chapter.

Social Skills Instruction

Students with emotional and behavioral disorders frequently display deficits in social skills (Knitzer, 1990; Rosenberg et al., 1992). Elksnin and Elksnin (1998) stress the complexity of social skills, indicating that they include both overt, observable behaviors and covert actions that may relate more to problem solving. A list of typical social skills is presented in Table 7.6.

Social skills are best learned from observing others who display appropriate skills, but there are times when a more formal instructional effort must be made. When using a formal instructional process to teach social skills, the first step is to determine the student's level of social competence.

Assessing social skills requires eliciting informed judgments from persons who interact regularly with the student (Smith et al., 1993). Many different checklists are available to assist in assessing social competence. In addition, self-monitoring charts and sociometric measures may be used (Smith et al., 1993).

Following the assessment process, an instructional approach to teaching solutions to deficiencies in social skills must be developed. Numerous methods may be used to teach

TABLE 7.6   **Types of Social Skills**

Interpersonal Behaviors	"Friendship-making skills," such as introducing yourself, joining in, asking a favor, offering to help, giving and accepting compliments, and apologizing.
Peer-Related Social Skills	Skills valued by classmates and associated with peer acceptance. Examples include working cooperatively, asking for and receiving information, and correctly assessing another's emotional state.
Teacher-Pleasing Social Skills	School success behaviors, including following directions, doing your best work, and listening to the teacher.
Self-Related Behaviors	Skills that allow a child to assess a social situation, select an appropriate skill, and determine the skill's effectiveness. Other self-related behaviors include following through, dealing with stress, understanding feelings, and controlling anger.
Assertiveness Skills	Behaviors that allow children to express their needs without resorting to aggression.
Communication Skills	Listener responsiveness, turn taking, maintaining conversational attention, and giving the speaker feedback.

From "Teaching Social Skills to Students with Learning and Behavioral Problems" (p. 132) by L. K. Elksnin and N. Elksnin, 1998, *Intervention in School and Clinic, 33.*

social skills and promote good social relations, including modeling, direct instruction, prompting, and positive practice (Searcy & Meadows, 1994). Teachers must determine the method that will work best with a particular student.

Quinn, Kavale, Mathur, Rutherford, and Forness (1999) reported a comprehensive research analysis of the use of social skills training with students with E/BD. In general, they caution that only about half of students with E/BD have been demonstrated to benefit from social skills training, particularly when the focus was on the broader dimensions of the social domain. Greater success was obtained when the focus was on specific social skills (e.g., social problem solving, social interaction, cooperation). Forness (1999) and Kavale (2001) hypothesized that the reason more substantive positive effects have not been obtained from social skills training may be that the training programs within the research studies were too limited in duration and intensity.

One reason social skills instruction may be problematic is that its effectiveness is challenged by the difficulty of achieving generalization across settings. Scott and Nelson (1998) cautioned teachers to realize that educational practices for achieving generalization in academic instruction are often insufficient for achieving similar outcomes in social skills instruction. They stress that any such instruction in artificial contexts will create difficulty in generalization, and therefore schoolwide instruction, modeling, and the reinforcement of appropriate social behaviors taught within the context of the classroom are likely to be most effective. This instruction may be more effective when students who are not disabled are involved in the training. While they stress the complexity of teaching social skills, Scott and Nelson (1998) also similarly stress the critical nature of learning within this area. Teachers are advised to consider social skills programs cautiously, implement them experimentally, and confirm that positive outcomes are obtained.

Home-School Considerations

A collaborative effort between school and home is particularly important in educational programs for students with E/BD. The discussion in Chapter 3 about such programs is of significant merit as teachers and parents endeavor to address problems experienced in both venues.

Classroom Adaptations for Emotional and Behavioral Disorders

Effective classroom management is critical for teachers with students with emotional and behavioral disorders because of the interference of their behavior with their own learning and their impact on the learning of other students.

Standard Operating Procedures

CROSS-REFERENCE

For more information on management considerations, refer to Chapter 14.

Classroom rules and procedures are a critical management tool for students with E/BD. Rules should be developed with the input of students and should be posted in the room. Remember that "the process of determining rules is as important as the rules themselves" (Zabel & Zabel, 1996, p. 169). Walker and Shea (1995) give the following examples of classroom rules:

▶ Be polite and helpful.
▶ Keep your space and materials in order.
▶ Take care of classroom and school property.
▶ Raise your hand before speaking.
▶ Leave your seat only with permission.
▶ Only one person in the rest room at a time. (p. 252)

CONSIDER THIS

How can classroom rules and procedures result in improved behavior for children with emotional and behavioral disorders? Are they also effective with nondisabled students?

Teachers should establish classroom procedures to ensure an orderly environment. These include procedures for the beginning of a period or the school day, use of classroom equipment, social interaction, the completion of work, group and individual activities, and the conclusion of instructional periods and the school day (Walker & Shea, 1995).

Physical Accommodations

The physical arrangement of the classroom has an impact on the behaviors of students with emotional and behavioral disorders. Attention to the classroom arrangement can both facilitate learning and minimize disruptions (Zabel & Zabel, 1996). The following considerations can help maintain an orderly classroom:

▶ Arranging traffic patterns to lessen contact and disruptions
▶ Arranging student desks to facilitate monitoring of all students at all times
▶ Physically locating students with tendencies toward disruptive behaviors near the teacher's primary location
▶ Locating students away from stored materials that they may find tempting
▶ Creating spaces where students can do quiet work, such as a quiet reading area

Preventive Discipline

Probably the most effective means of working with students who display emotional and behavior problems is preventive in nature. If inappropriate behaviors can be prevented, then disruptions will be minimal, and the student can attend to the learning task at hand. **Preventive discipline** can be described as "the teacher's realization that discipline begins with a positive attitude that nurtures students' learning of personal, social, and academic skills" (Sabatino, 1987, p. 8). Rather than wait to respond to inappropriate behaviors, preventive measures remove the need for inappropriate behaviors.

Sabatino (1987) describes 10 components of a preventive discipline program:

1. Inform pupils of what is expected of them.
2. Establish a positive learning climate.
3. Provide a meaningful learning experience.
4. Avoid threats.
5. Demonstrate fairness.

The behaviors of teachers can have great impact on effective behavior management.

6. Build and exhibit self-confidence.
7. Recognize positive student attributes.
8. Recognize student attributes at optimal times.
9. Use positive modeling.
10. Structure the curriculum and classroom environment.

Teacher behavior can greatly facilitate preventive discipline. Teachers have to be consistent in discipline; they must not treat inappropriate behaviors from one student differently than they treat misbehavior from other students. Teachers must also apply consequences systematically. Disciplining a student for an inappropriate behavior one time and ignoring the same behavior another time will only cause the student to be confused over expectations. This discussion on preventative discipline is consistent with the trend toward positive behavioral supports discussed in the next section.

General Behavior Support Strategies

The development of **positive behavior supports** (**PBS**) has been a significant achievement in the education of students with special needs and has particular relevance for students with E/BD. Carr et al. (2002) describe PBS in this way:

> *Positive behavior* includes all those skills that increase the likelihood of success and personal satisfaction in . . . academic, work, social, recreational, community, and family settings. *Support* encompasses all those educational methods that can be used to teach, strengthen, and expand positive behavior and . . . increase opportunities for the display of positive behavior. The primary goal of PBS is to help an individual change his or her lifestyle in a direction that gives . . . teachers, employers, parents, friends, and the target person him- or herself the opportunity to perceive and to enjoy an improved quality of life. An important but secondary goal of PBS is to render problem behavior irrelevant, inefficient, and ineffective by helping an individual achieve his or her goals in a socially acceptable manner. (pp. 4–5)

Functional behavioral assessment is an important basis for the development of positive behavioral supports. PBS interventions provide an alternative to an emphasis on punitive disciplinary strategies and provide guidance to students with behavioral problems to make appropriate changes in their behavioral patterns. PBS emphasizes proactive, preventive strategies and early intervention with students deemed to be at risk.

As described by Lewis and Sugai (1999), an effective positive behavioral support program for a school should include the following components:

▶ specialized individual behavior support for students with chronic behavior problems
▶ specialized group behavior support for students with at-risk problem behavior
▶ universal group behavior support for most students. (p. 4)

The system that Lewis and Sugai have developed emphasizes schoolwide programs that put in place a preventive, proactive system and provide a foundation for the appropriate design of programs for individuals experiencing significant behavior problems.

Numerous positive behavioral support strategies have been developed for use with students experiencing emotional and behavioral problems. Along with additional strategies for classroom management, they will be discussed in detail in Chapter 14.

Particular behavioral strategies that have merit for use with students with E/BD include the good behavior game, contingency contracting, and individual behavior management plans (see Chapter 14). In addition, Webber and Scheuermann (1991) outlined several reinforcement programs that can be used to eliminate inappropriate behaviors. These examples utilize *differential reinforcement of zero rates of undesirable behaviors (DRO), differential reinforcement of incompatible behaviors (DRI), differential reinforcement of lower rates of behaviors (DRL), and differential rates of communicative behaviors (DRC).* Inclusion Strategies provides examples of these techniques.

TEACHING TIP

When students cannot reach a target behavior immediately, reinforce their efforts and their progress toward reaching the behavior.

Problem Classroom Behaviors and Differential Reinforcement Strategies

Problem Behavior	Differential Reinforcement Strategy
Talking back	Reinforce each 15- or 30-minute or 1-hour period with no talking back (DRO). Or reinforce each time that the student responds to the teacher without talking back (DRI).
Causing property damage	For each day that no property is damaged, reinforce the student and/or the class (DRO).
Cursing	Reinforce each 15- or 30-minute or 1-hour period with no cursing (DRO). Reinforce use of appropriate adjectives and exclamations (DRC).
Being off task	Reinforce each 5-, 10-, 15-, or 30-minute period of continuous in-seat behavior (DRI).
Failing to complete tasks	Reinforce each task that is completed, half completed, or started (DRI).
Tardiness	Reinforce each day or period that the student is on time (DRI).
Being out of seat	Reinforce 5-, 10-, 15-, or 30-minute periods of continuous in-seat behavior (DRI).
Fighting	Reinforce the student after each hour or 1/2 hour that the student does not fight (DRO). Reinforce talking about feelings (DRC).
Picking on others, name calling, teasing	Reinforce the student each time he or she interacts appropriately with another student (DRI). Or reinforce the student each hour that he or she does not tease, pinch, etc. (DRO).
Noncompliance	Reinforce the student for each direction that he or she follows within 5 seconds (DRI). The schedule can be thinned to every 3 directions followed, 8, 10, etc.
Talking out	Reinforce the student each time that he or she raises a hand and waits to be called on (DRI). Thin the schedule to 3, 5, 10 times, etc. Or reinforce progressively less talking out (DRI).

For follow-up questions about differential reinforcement strategies, go to Chapter 7 of the Companion Website (ablongman.com/sppd4e) and click Inclusion Strategies.

From "Accentuate the Positive . . . Eliminate the Negative!" by J. Webber and B. Scheuermann, 1991, *Teaching Exceptional Children, 24,* p. 16. Used by permission.

Cognitive approaches are of particular importance to students with E/BD. These interventions were discussed earlier in Chapters 5 and 6. For students with E/BD, a particular focus should be on the development of behavioral self-control in which students are taught to use self-management strategies throughout the day. A sample self-control plan is presented in Figure 7.4.

Another technique, the use of peer mediation, has also been used effectively with students with emotional and behavioral disorders. As Gable, Arllen, and Hendrickson (1994) noted, while most behavioral programs rely on adults to monitor and provide reinforcement for desirable behaviors, this technique instead relies on peers. After reviewing peer interaction studies, they concluded that peer behavior modifiers could be effective among students with emotional and behavioral problems: "The generally positive results surfacing from the modest number of investigations in which E/BD students have served as behavior modifiers underscore the relevance of this procedure for those facing the daunting task of better serving students with emotional/behavioral disorders" (p. 275). Peer mediation strategies are discussed further in Chapter 15.

Table 7.7 provides some sample hypothesis statements and possible interventions related to functional behavioral assessment-based interventions. Such an approach does not lock teachers into specific strategies, thus allowing them to tailor interventions to specific behaviors and causes (Kauffman et al., 1995).

Behavioral Intervention Planning

According to federal guidelines under the 1997 amendments to IDEA (and 1999 regulations), school district personnel are required to address the strategies to be employed for students with disabilities who exhibit significant behavioral problems. The required component is the development of a behavioral intervention plan (BIP). This plan is required in certain instances of serious misbehavior (e.g., using weapons or drugs) but also may be an effective response to other significant behavioral problems. The development of

TEACHING TIP

When using peers to assist with behavior changes, make sure that the students involved in the process are appropriately trained.

1. Rules needed to meet goal:
   a. Every day, after school, I will go to the library.
   b. I will study math for two hours at the library.
   c. I will monitor my time so only the time spent working on math will be attributed to the two-hour period.
   d. If I have trouble with my math assignment, I will ask the proctoring teacher for help.
   e. After the two-hour period, I can spend time with my friends, talk on the phone, or have leisure time alone.

2. Goal:
   I will improve my math grade by at least one letter grade in a six-week period.
   a. I will complete all my daily homework assignments.
   b. I will review each lecture on a daily basis.
   c. I will develop strategies that will help me remember problem-solving procedures for math problems.
   d. I will practice and review math problems.

3. Feedback:
   Prior to turning in my homework, I will ask my parent or teacher to check my work. I will correct any wrong answers.

4. Measurement—monitoring of rules and subgoals:
   a. *Rules:* Develop a monitoring system that indicates the time spent studying at the library and asking for help when needed.
   b. *Subgoals:* Develop a monitoring system that indicates whether the homework, review of lecture, strategies, or practice was completed during the two-hour period.
   c. *Products:* Improvement on math scores should indicate progress toward goal; if progress is not seen after a two-week period, reevaluate the plan.

FIGURE 7.4

Sample Behavioral Self-Control Plan for a Student Who Wants to Improve Math Scores

From "Cognitive-Behavioral Intervention" (p. 212), 2001, in R. Algozzine, L. Serna, & J. R. Patton (Eds.), *Childhood Behavior Disorders: Applied Research and Practices* (2nd ed.), Austin, TX: Pro-Ed.

TABLE 7.7 Sample Hypothesis Statements and Possible Interventions

Hypothesis Statements	Intervention	
	Modify Antecedents	Teach Alternative Behavior
Suzy pinches herself and others around 11:00 A.M. every day because she gets hungry.	Make sure Suzy gets breakfast. Provide a snack at about 9:30 A.M.	Teach Suzy to ask for something to eat.
Jack gets into arguments with the teacher every day during reading class when she asks him to correct his mistakes on the daily reading worksheet.	Get Jack to correct his own paper. Give Jack an easier assignment.	Teach Jack strategies to manage his frustration in a more appropriate manner. Teach Jack to ask for teacher assistance with the incorrect problems.
Tara starts pouting and refuses to work when she has to sort a box of washers because she doesn't want to do the activity.	Give Tara half of the box of washers to sort. Give Tara clear directions about how much she has to do or how long she must work.	
Frank kicks other children in morning circle time and usually gets to sit right by the teacher.	Give each child a clearly designated section of the floor that is his or hers.	Teach Frank how to ask the children to move over. Teach Frank how to ask the teacher to intervene with his classmates.
Harry is off task for most of math class when he is supposed to be adding two-digit numbers.	Ask Harry to add the prices of actual food items. Intersperse an easy activity with the more difficult math addition so Harry can experience some success.	Teach Harry how to ask for help. Teach Harry how to monitor his rate of problem completion, and provide reinforcement for a certain number of problems.

From "Using Functional Assessment to Develop Effective, Individualized Interventions for Challenging Behaviors" (p. 49) by L. Foster-Johnson and G. Dunlap, 1993, *Teaching Exceptional Children, 25.* Used by permission.

Tips for Adapting a Lesson for Frank

Based on the chapter-opening vignette describing Frank, the following sample classroom adaptations might be considered to enhance his learning and respond to his IEP goals and objectives.

Frank's teacher should

▶ establish a reinforcement system based on check marks earned for appropriate behavior with redemption for rewards or special activities twice daily on an initial basis.

▶ use peer-mediated interventions such as the "hero" technique in which Frank's appropriate social interactions with peers result in whole class reinforcement (e.g., special activity).

▶ use a peer tutor from an upper elementary grade to drill Frank on vowel and consonant sounds.

▶ set up a system of pictures to symbolize work assignments so Frank can monitor his own work completion as a basis for reinforcement.

▶ establish a home-school contract in which appropriate classroom behavior is linked with special opportunities provided by his mother.

▶ assign homework that can be completed in 10–15 minutes to reinforce effective work habits and task completion.

the BIP parallels the development of the IEP and includes input from professionals and parents. Detailed discussion on the development of BIPs is in Chapter 14.

Medication

Many students with emotional and behavioral problems experience difficulties in maintaining attention and controlling behavior. For students experiencing these problems, "medication is the most frequently used (and perhaps overused) intervention" (Ellenwood & Felt, 1989, p. 16). Many different kinds of medication have been found to be effective with students' behavior problems (Forness & Kavale, 1988) including stimulants, tranquilizers, anticonvulsants, antidepressants, and mood-altering drugs.

The use of medication to help manage students with emotional and behavior problems is controversial and has been investigated extensively. Findings include the following:

1. Medication can result in increased attention of students.
2. Medication can result in reduced aggressive behaviors.
3. Various side effects can result from medical interventions.
4. The use of medication for children experiencing emotional and behavioral problems should be carefully monitored. (Smith et al., 1993, p. 214)

Numerous side effects may accompany medications taken by children for emotional and behavioral problems. Ritalin is commonly prescribed to help students with attention and hyperactivity problems. Several potential side effects of Ritalin include nervousness, insomnia, anorexia, dizziness, blood pressure and pulse changes, abdominal pain, and weight loss. Teachers can monitor side effects by keeping a daily log of student behaviors that could be attributed to the medication (Dowdy, Patton, Smith, & Polloway, 1997).

Technology

Assistive technology offers a number of ways for teachers to adapt curriculum and instruction and respond to the needs of students with emotional and behavioral disorders. Technology Today on page 226 provides information on assistive technology products.

Promoting Inclusive Practices for Students with Emotional and Behavioral Disorders

Classroom teachers usually make the initial recommendation for prereferral review for child study or teacher accommodations for students with E/BD. Unless the problem exhibited by the student is severe, it may have gone unrecognized until the school years. In addition to referring students for initial review, classroom teachers must be directly involved in implementing the student's IEP because the majority of students in this category receive a portion of their educational program in general education classrooms. General education classroom teachers must deal with behavior problems much of the time, because there are large numbers of students who occasionally display inappropriate behaviors, although they have not been identified as having E/BD.

Promoting Community and Social Acceptance

Because students with emotional and behavioral disorders are generally placed in general education classrooms rather than in isolated special education settings, teachers must ensure their successful inclusion. Several tactics that teachers can use include

- using programs in which peers act as buddies or tutors.
- focusing on positive behaviors and providing appropriate reinforcements.
- using good-behavior games in which all students work together to earn rewards.

Teachers must make a special effort to keep themselves, as well as other students, from developing a negative attitude toward students with E/BD.

CONSIDER THIS

What role should mental health professionals play in serving students with E/BD? How can schools involve mental health professionals more?

Types of Assistive Technology

According to the Individuals with Disabilities Education Act Amendments (IDEA) of 1997, an assistive technology (AT) device refers to "any item, piece of equipment, or product system . . . that is used to increase, maintain or improve the functional capabilities of a child with a disability." The federal definition is quite broad and encompasses devices that are electronic (e.g., computer, scanner, tape recorder) and nonelectronic (e.g., pencil grip, manual typewriter). . . . In addition, the federal definition includes items such as computer-aided instructional software programs for reading and mathematics that can be used to remediate skill deficits. . . .

What Kinds of AT Are Available?

Writing Difficulties: word processors, spell checkers/talking spell checkers, proofreading programs (grammar checkers), speech synthesizers/screen readers (convert electronic text to synthetic speech), outlining programs, graphic organizers (create diagrams of ideas before writing), word prediction programs (predict and offer suggestions), alternative keyboards (customize key appearance and placement), and speech recognition systems (convert the spoken word to electronic text).

Reading Difficulties: tape recorders (e.g., books on tape), speech synthesis/screen reading systems, and optical character recognition/speech synthesis systems (scan hard copy text, convert to electronic text and synthetic speech).

Math Difficulties: talking calculators (use speech synthesis to speak numbers) and electronic computer-based worksheets (provide automatic alignment of numbers).

Listening Difficulties: personal FM listening devices (small transmitter and receiver that "brings" speaker's voice directly to the listener's ear) and variable speech-control tape recorders (slow down or speed up the recording).

Organization and Memory Difficulties: personal data managers (store and retrieve phone numbers, addresses, notes, etc.), free-form databases (note storage and retrieval software), and tape recorders.

Selecting the appropriate device . . . requires careful analysis of the interplay among (a) the individual's specific strengths, limitations, special abilities, prior experience/knowledge, and interests; (b) the specific tasks/functions to be performed (e.g., compensating for a reading, writing, or memory problem); (c) the specific contexts of interaction (across settings–school, home, work, and over time–over a semester or a lifetime); and (d) the specific device (e.g., reliability, operational ease, technical support, cost). . . .

There are limited resources to help offset the cost of AT. Under IDEA, public elementary and secondary schools are required to provide AT if an "educational professional" deems it necessary and technology is written into the student's Individualized Education Program (IEP).

For follow-up questions about types of assistive technology, go to Chapter 7 of the Companion Website (ablongman.com/sppd4e) and click Technology Today.

From "Assistive Technology" by M. Raskind, September 2002, information sheet, Council for Learning Disabilities.

Supports for General Education Teachers

CONSIDER THIS

Can general classroom teachers effectively deal with students with emotional and behavioral disorders? What factors will enhance the likelihood of success?

Since most students with emotional and behavioral disorders are educated in general classrooms, classroom teachers are the key to the success of these students. Too often, if these students do not achieve success, the entire classroom may be disrupted. Therefore, appropriate supports must be available to teachers. They include special education personnel, psychologists and counselors, and mental health service providers.

Special educators should be available to collaborate with teachers regarding the development of behavioral as well as instructional supports. A particularly helpful way to assist classroom teachers involves modeling methods of dealing with behavior problems. At times, it is best for students with emotional and behavioral problems to leave the general education setting and receive instruction from special educators.

School psychologists and counselors are other critical team members in providing a comprehensive program for students with E/BD. They can provide intensive counseling to students with emotional and behavioral disorders; they may also consult with teachers on how to implement specific programs, such as a student's individual behavior management plan. Finally, mental health personnel can provide helpful supports for teachers. Too often, mental health services are not available in schools; however, some schools are beginning to develop school-based mental health programs that are jointly staffed by school personnel and mental health staff and provide supports for teachers as well as direct interventions for students. If mental health services are not available, teachers should work with school administrators to involve mental health specialists with students who display emotional and behavioral problems.

ummary

Basic Concepts About Emotional and Behavioral Disorders

▶ Most children and youths are disruptive from time to time, but most do not require interventions. Some students' emotional or behavioral problems are severe enough to warrant interventions.

▶ Many problems complicate serving students with emotional and behavioral disorders, including inconsistent definitions of the disorder, the large number of agencies involved in defining and treating it, and limited ways to objectively measure the extent and precise parameters of the problem.

▶ Definitions for emotional disturbance and behavioral disorders are typically subject to alternative explanations.

▶ There is limited consistency in classifying persons with emotional and behavioral problems.

▶ Determining the eligibility of students with E/BD is difficult because of problems with identification and assessment.

▶ The estimated prevalence of students with emotional and behavioral problems ranges from a low of 1% to a high of 30%.

▶ Students with emotional and behavioral problems are significantly underserved in schools.

Strategies for Curriculum and Instruction for Students with Emotional and Behavioral Disorders

▶ Students with E/BD are commonly included in general education classes. General education teachers and special education teachers must collaborate so that there is consistency in the development and implementation of intervention methods.

▶ A variety of curricular, classroom, and behavioral management strategies are available to enhance the educational programs for students with E/BD.

▶ Social skills development is important for students with E/BD.

▶ Interventions based on functional behavioral assessment, preventive discipline, and positive behavioral supports are important methods for reducing the impact of problems or for keeping problems from occurring.

Promoting Inclusive Practices for Students with Emotional and Behavioral Disorders

▶ General education teachers must realize that the skills, attitudes, and beliefs needed to work effectively with students with E/BD may vary from those that are effective for nondisabled students.

▶ Positive reinforcement and peer tutoring are possible tactics for preventing students with E/BD from feeling isolated in the general education classroom.

▶ Special education teachers and mental health personnel need to be available to provide guidance for general education teachers who are implementing a student's behavior management plan.

Further Readings

Algozzine, R., Serna, L., & Patton, J. R. (2001). *Childhood behavior disorders: Applied research and educational practices* (2nd ed.). Austin, TX: Pro-Ed.

American Psychiatric Association. (1994). *Diagnostic and statistical manual of mental disorders* (DSM-IV). Washington, DC: Author.

Fad, K., Patton, J. R., & Polloway, E. A. (2000). *Behavioral intervention planning: Completing a functional behavioral assessment and developing a behavioral intervention plan* (2nd ed.). Austin, TX: Pro-Ed.

Katsiyannis, A., & Maag, J. W. (2001). Manifestation determination as a golden fleece. *Exceptional Children, 68,* 85–96.

Kauffman, J. M. (1993). *Characteristics of emotional and behavioral disorders of children and youth.* Columbus, OH: Merrill.

Zabel, R. H., & Zabel, M. K. (1996). *Classroom management in context.* Boston: Houghton Mifflin.

 # VideoWorkshop Extra!

If the VideoWorkshop package was included with your textbook, go to Chapter 7 of the Companion Website (www.ablongman.com/sppd4e) and click on the VideoWorkshop button. Follow the instructions for viewing video clip 10. Then consider this information along with what you've read in Chapter 7 while answering the following questions.

1. Nick's teacher, Ms. Naputi, noted that he has academic strengths and while he has behavior problems, he is manageable and responds to feedback and redirection. How might these management strategies be used to reintegrate Nick into a general education classroom? Explain your answer.

2. Nick has experienced success in controlling his behavior in self-contained and special programs for several years, and his academic achievement indicates an ability to learn in a general education setting. What social skills strategies would you use to help Nick reintegrate into the general education classroom? Explain your choices.

8 Teaching Students with Mental Retardation

After reading this chapter, you should be able to

1. discuss the concept of mental retardation.
2. provide personal perspectives on mental retardation.
3. summarize key definitions and classifications.
4. identify the instructional implications of common characteristics of students with mental retardation.
5. describe the transitional needs of students with mild mental retardation.
6. apply considerations of the needs of students with mental retardation to curriculum design.
7. enhance the successful inclusion of students with mental retardation.

Orlando is currently a junior at Shifflett High School in Virginia. He has been receiving special education supports throughout his school career. Prior to kindergarten, he had been identified as "at-risk" in part because of language delays and also in part because of the difficult home situation in which he was raised (his grandmother has been his guardian since his mother was incarcerated when Orlando was four years old; his father has not been part of his life since he was an infant).

When Orlando began elementary school, he was identified as developmentally delayed, a term in Virginia that allows the school division to provide special education services in primary school without a formal categorical label. However, when assessments were completed on Orlando at age 8, he was formally identified as mentally retarded. His language, academic, and social skills were deemed most consistent with the traditional label of mild retardation.

Orlando has progressed well in part because of his continued involvement in general education classrooms through middle school and into the first several years of high school. With in-class support and periodic remedial instruction, he has developed his reading skills to the equivalent of fourth grade level with comparable achievement in mathematics and other academic areas. Currently, the focus of his program is on building his academic skills in the inclusive environment and complementing these with a functional curriculum to prepare him for success in the community.

Orlando has become an active participant in the development of his individualized educational program and, more recently, his individual transition plan. His short-term objective is to obtain his driver's license, for which he is currently eligible based on chronological age. He is currently enrolled in both an instructional program to complete the written portion of the test and the behind-the-wheel component. A longer term focus of his program is to prepare him for competitive employment in the community. Through a series of community-based instructional programs, he has become aware of the options that are available to him, and an apprenticeship program in maintenance at the local Wal-Mart will be available next year. Orlando's success is a combination of his motivation to succeed, detailed planning by key individuals in his life, and ongoing support provided by teachers, his grandmother, his football coach, and several significant peers who are more academically able.

QUESTIONS TO CONSIDER

1. How can Orlando's curriculum include peers who are not disabled and use the functional curriculum designed by special educators?
2. How can the curriculum balance short-term objectives and preparation for competitive employment and independent living?
3. What strategies can enhance a positive influence from peers?
4. What available community resources will aid his transition to independent living?

Basic Concepts About Mental Retardation

Mental retardation is a powerful term used to describe a level of functioning significantly below what is considered to be "average." It conjures up a variety of images including a stereotypical photo of an adolescent with Down syndrome, a young child living in poverty and provided with limited experience and stimulation, and an adult striving to adjust to the demands of a complex society. Since it is a generic term representing a very diverse group of individuals, ironically all of the images of mental retardation and, at the same time, none of these images, can be assumed to be accurate ones.

In the public schools, the most recent national database (for 1999–2000) indicates that 1.15% of the estimated enrollment (ages 6–17) is identified as mentally retarded (U.S. Department of Education, 2001). However, a closer look at these data reveals a substantial variance in prevalence from 2.63% in Alabama to 1.12% in Virginia to 0.48% in California. Even a naive observer would at once conclude that the concept is not defined, or the condition is not conceptualized, in the same way across the states. Further, the prevalence of mental retardation in individuals of school age tends to be higher than in adults because of the challenges of formal education for school age individuals as well as the relative lack of identification in adulthood; thus, Larson et al. (2001) estimate the prevalence at 0.78% for the general population.

CONSIDER THIS

Why do you think the prevalence of mental retardation varies so much from state to state?

Terminology

Adding complexity to the discussion of concepts, the term *mental retardation* itself is often avoided in many areas. As Warren (2000) noted:

> The term has been in widespread use in the United States for roughly 50 years, having replaced earlier terms such as "feebleminded" and "moron." In recent years [however] . . . it has been attacked as promoting stigma and negative stereotyping in our society, many self-advocates hate it and consider it demeaning, and others point out that it lacks sufficient specificity for meaningful clinical, educational, and professional application. (p. 1)

As a consequence, *intellectually impaired* or *educationally disabled* or other terms are often seen as more palatable and may be the preferred description in a given state. Nevertheless, although the term *mental retardation* has been widely criticized and proposals for alternative terms have been made periodically (e.g., Terrill, 2001; Schalock, 2001), a recent survey found that educational departments in 26 states (51%) continue to use the term, while an additional 14 states (27.4%) use similar terms (e.g., mental disability, mental impairment) (Denning, Chamberlain, & Polloway, 2000). This finding is consistent with a broad survey by Sandieson (1998) that looked at worldwide trends. For this reason we continue to use the term *mental retardation* in this text, although we caution the reader that it is value-laden. Indeed, the underlying message is clear: Without question, being labeled mentally retarded can be stigmatizing and the label is often seen as offensive by persons to whom it refers (*MRDD Express,* 2001). Avoiding labels or using more positive labels, as well as providing opportunities to be with peers who are not disabled, must be pursued in order to ensure the prospect of a positive quality of life for those people who are identified as mentally retarded.

In the field of mental retardation, the late 20th century witnessed momentous changes, which have washed away the realities of restricted, and often abusive, settings that characterized many of the so-called services for persons with mental retardation through the 1970s. Shifts in public attitudes toward persons with mental retardation and the resulting development and provision of services and supports for them have been truly phenomenal. Consequently, this is an exciting time to be participating in the changing perspectives on mental retardation. Thus, while the discussion of definitional aspects of mental retardation unfortunately creates a focus on deficits, the more powerful and relevant message of the 21st century is that persons with mental retardation are capable of significant achievements as we develop their strengths and assets.

Mental retardation is a broad concept that has been used to refer to a wide range of functioning levels, from mild disabilities to more severe limitations. The discussion in this chapter initially addresses the global concept of mental retardation. Then the remainder of the chapter focuses primarily on the educational implications of mild mental retardation. More severe disabilities receive detailed attention in Chapter 10, which focuses on a variety of low-incidence disabilities.

Mental Retardation Defined

It has been difficult for professionals to formulate definitions of mental retardation that could then be used to govern practices such as assessment and placement. Nevertheless, a number of aspects of the definitional concepts have been consistently followed over the years. Mental retardation has been most often characterized by two dimensions: limited intellectual ability and difficulty in coping with the social demands of the environment. Greenspan (1996) described mental retardation primarily as a problem in "everyday intelligence"; thus, persons with retardation can be viewed as those who are challenged by adapting to the demands of daily life in the community.

All individuals with mental retardation must, by most definitions, demonstrate some degree of impaired mental abilities, most often reflected in an intelligence quotient (IQ) significantly below average. In addition, these individuals would necessarily demonstrate less mature adaptive skills, such as social behavior or functional academic skills, when compared to their same-age peers. For some individuals this discrepancy can be somewhat subtle and not be readily apparent in a casual interaction in a nonschool setting. These individuals may be challenged most dramatically by the school setting, and thus between the ages of 6 and 21 their inability to cope may be most evident, for example, in problems with peer relationships, with difficulty in compliance with adult-initiated directions, or in meeting academic challenges.

1983 Definition   The American Association on Mental Retardation (AAMR) has concerned itself for decades with developing and revising the definition of mental retardation. This organization's efforts are broadly recognized, and its definitions have often been incorporated, with modifications, into state and federal statutes. Although usage in the states in terms of educational regulations and practice has been uneven (Denning et al., 2000; Frankenberger & Harper, 1988), the organization's definitions frequently have been considered as the basis for diagnosis in the field.

The Grossman (1983) definition was as follows:

> Mental retardation refers to significantly subaverage general intellectual functioning resulting in or associated with concurrent impairments in adaptive behavior and manifested during the developmental period. (p. 11)

Three concepts are central to this definition: intellectual functioning, adaptive behavior, and the developmental period. **Intellectual functioning** is intended as a broad summation of cognitive abilities, such as the capacity to learn, solve problems, accumulate knowledge, adapt to new situations, and think abstractly. Operationally, however, it has often been reduced to performance on a test of intelligence. "Significantly below average" is defined in the 1983 AAMD definition as below a flexible upper IQ range of 70 to 75. Research indicates that this approximate IQ range remains a relatively common component of state identification practices if an IQ cut-off score is required at all (Denning et al., 2000).

It is worth considering how an IQ score relates to this first criterion for diagnosis. Since an IQ of 100 is the mean score on such tests, a person receiving a score of 100 is considered to have an average level of cognitive functioning. Based on statistical analysis, approximately 2.3% of IQs would be expected to lie below 70 and a like percentage above

CONSIDER THIS

What are some of the dangers in relating the concept of mental retardation to a numerical index, such as IQ?

130. Thus, to limit the diagnosis of mental retardation to persons with IQs of about 70 or below is to suggest that, hypothetically, about 2%–3% of the tested population may have significantly subaverage general intellectual functioning. However, as the definition clearly states, low IQ scores alone are not sufficient for diagnosis. Hence, we must next consider the adaptive dimension.

An individual's **adaptive behavior** represents the degree to which the individual meets "the standards of maturation, learning, personal independence, and/or social responsibility that are expected for his or her age level and cultural group" (Grossman, 1983, p. 11). Continuing with this concept, Grossman (1983) emphasized the idea of coping: "Adaptive behavior refers to the quality of everyday performance in coping with environmental demands. . . . Adaptive behavior refers to what people do to take care of themselves and to relate to others in daily living rather than the abstract potential implied by intelligence" (p. 11). Particularly important to the concept of adaptive behavior are the skills necessary to function independently in a range of situations and to maintain responsible social relationships. The importance of adaptive behavior is reflected in the fact that, in the most recent survey of the states, 98% required consideration of this dimension for eligibility (Denning et al., 2000). Table 8.1 lists key adaptive skill areas. These skills are each age-relevant and represent core areas of concern for both elementary and secondary educators.

The third component of the definition is the **developmental period.** It is typically defined as the period of time between conception and 18 years of age. Below-average intellectual functioning and disabilities in adaptive behavior must appear during this period in order for an individual to be considered to have mental retardation.

1992 Definition   In 1992, the AAMR revised its definition in order to reflect changes in current thinking about persons with mental retardation. According to Luckasson et al. (1992),

> Mental retardation refers to substantial limitations in present functioning. It is manifested by significantly subaverage intellectual functioning, existing concurrently with related limitations in two or more of the following applicable adaptive skill areas: communication, self-care, home living, social skills, community use, self-direction, health and safety, functional academics, leisure, and work. Mental retardation begins before age 18. (p. 8)

CONSIDER THIS

Without an operational definition derived from the 1983 AAMR definition, could you identify a person as having mental retardation?

TABLE 8.1   **Examples of Conceptual, Social, and Practical Adaptive Skills**

Conceptual	Practical
▶ Language (receptive and expressive)	▶ Activities of daily living
▶ Reading and writing	Eating
▶ Money concepts	Transfer/mobility
▶ Self-direction	Toileting
	Dressing
Social	▶ Instrumental activities of daily living
▶ Interpersonal	Meal preparation
▶ Responsibility	Housekeeping
▶ Self-esteem	Transportation
▶ Gullibility (likelihood of being tricked or manipulated)	Taking medication
▶ Naiveté	Money management
▶ Follows rules	Telephone use
▶ Obeys laws	▶ Occupational skills
▶ Avoids victimization	▶ Maintains safe environments

From *Mental Retardation: Definition, Classification, and Systems of Supports* (p. 42) by R. Luckasson et al., 2002, Washington, DC: American Association on Mental Retardation.

The Luckasson et al. (1992) definition retained the focus of earlier AAMR definitions on the two key dimensions of intelligence and adaptation as well as the modifier of age of onset. However, the conceptual basis varies from those earlier efforts. The 1992 definition reflected a more functional approach, thus shifting focus to the individual's functioning within the community rather than giving weight mainly to the psychometric and clinical aspects of the person (e.g., IQ scores, limited adaptive behavior evaluations).

Denning et al. (2000) reported on the definitional basis for state guidelines across the 50 states and the District of Columbia. They found that the Grossman (1983) definition continued to be used by 35 states (68.6%) in an adapted version and by 9 (17.6%) verbatim. The Luckasson et al. (1992) definition was reported to be used by 3 states in either the verbatim or adapted form. Table 8.2 provides a summary of the findings by state.

A number of responses were made to the Luckasson et al. (1992) definitional system (e.g., Schalock et al., 1994; MacMillan, Gresham, & Siperstein, 1993; Polloway, 1997; Luckasson, Schalock, Snell, & Spitalnik, 1996; and Smith, 1994). These responses and others provided the basis for further work, which led to the 2002 revision.

2002 Definition The most recent effort by the AAMR is currently under review by the organization's Terminology and Classification Committee. The proposed definition has been modified to read as follows (Luckasson et al., 2002):

> Mental retardation is a disability characterized by significant limitations both in intellectual functioning and in adaptive behavior as expressed in conceptual, social, and practical adaptive skills. This disability originates before age 18. The following five assumptions are essential to the application of the stated definition of mental retardation.
> 1. Limitations in present functioning must be considered within the context of community environments typical of the individual's age peers and culture.
> 2. Valid assessment considers cultural and linguistic diversity as well as differences in communication, sensory, motor, and behavioral factors.
> 3. Within an individual, limitations often coexist with strengths.
> 4. An important purpose of describing limitations is to develop a profile of needed supports.
> 5. With appropriate personalized supports over a sustained period, the life functioning of the person with mental retardation generally will improve. (p. 1)

Diversity Forum

Integrating Cultural Values with IEP Goals and Objectives

Susan, an 11- year-old Navajo student, is receiving services under the category of mild mental retardation. Her teacher, Mr. Garza, has developed a buddy system to help Susan learn new material and practice new skills. He is concerned that Susan prefers to work on her own instead of collaborating with her buddies. During a conference with Susan's family to discuss her goals, Mr. Garza is surprised to learn that the family wants Susan to be more independent. Her grandmother is reluctant to pressure Susan to work with a buddy because in their Navajo community, preadolescent children are expected to become more self-reliant and to make their own decisions.

When working with exceptional learners from diverse cultural backgrounds, teachers should keep in mind that the primary caregiver's goals for a student may reflect very different cultural values than those held by educators. For example, the age at which children are expected to master self-help and academic skills can vary widely depending on the family's cultural background. So, while an early-childhood teacher's first goal for a student with mild mental retardation may be toilet training, traditional Filipino families may not view this as a concern until after age four. In contrast, Korean families may begin toilet training a child at 3–4 months of age.

Culturally responsive special education services begin by integrating a student's and family's cultural values and beliefs with goals and objectives in the IEP (Deyhle & LeCompte, 1999; Lynch & Hanson, 1998). Factors to be considered may include

- parameters of acceptable behavior.
- views of child independence in the student's community.
- the amount and extent of interaction desired with the community.
- gender-specific roles.
- expectations for economic self-sufficiency.
- independent living for people with disabilities.

Companion Website

For follow-up questions about integrating cultural beliefs into a student's IEP, go to Chapter 8 of the Companion Website (ablongman.com/sppd4e) and click Diversity Forum.

TABLE 8.2   **State Guidelines for Mental Retardation: Definition and Classification**

State	Term[1]	Definition[2]	IQ Cut-off	Require Adaptive Behavior?	Age Ceiling	Classification System[3]
Alabama	MR	GV	70	YES	NO	No
Alaska	MR	GA	2 SD	YES	NO	No
Arizona	MR	GA	2 SD	YES	NO	M/M/S/P
Arkansas	MR	GA	No	YES	NO	No
California	MR	GA	No	YES	NO	M/M/S/P
Colorado	SLIC	GA	2 SD	YES	NO	No
Connecticut	MR	GA	2 SD	YES	NO	NO
Delaware	MD	GA	70	YES	NO	EMR/TMR/S
District of Columbia	MR	GA	70	YES	NO	M/M/S/P
Florida	MH	GV	2 SD	YES	NO	EMR/TMR/P
Georgia	ID	GV	70	YES	NO	M/M/S/P
Hawaii	MR	GA	2 SD	YES	NO	M/M/S
Idaho	MR	GA	70	YES	NO	NO
Illinois	MI	GA	NO	YES	NO	M/M/S/P
Indiana	MH	GA	2 SD	YES	18	M/M/S
Iowa	MD	GV	75	YES	21	NO
Kansas	MR	LV	2 SD	YES	NO	MR/SMD
Kentucky	MD	O	2 SD	YES	21	M/FMD
Louisiana	MD	GA	70	YES	NO	M/M/S/P
Maine	MR	GA	NO	YES	NO	NO
Maryland	MR	GV	NO	YES	NO	NO
Massachusetts	II	O	NO	NO	NO	NO
Michigan	MI	O	2 SD	YES	NO	EMR/TMR/S/P
Minnesota	MI	GA	70	YES	NO	M/M/S/P
Mississippi	ED	GA	2 SD	YES	NO	EMR/TMR/S
Missouri	MR	GA	2 SD	YES	18	M/M/S/P
Montana	CD	GA	NO	YES	18	NO
Nebraska	MH	GA	2 SD	YES	NO	M/M/S/P
Nevada	MR	GA	NO	YES	21	M/M/S/P
New Hampshire	MR	GA	NO	YES	NO	NO
New Jersey	CI	LA	2 SD	YES	NO	M/S CI
New Mexico	ID	GA	NO	YES	NO	NO
New York	MR	GA	1.5 SD	YES	NO	NO
North Carolina	MD	GA	70	YES	NO	EMR/TMR
North Dakota	MR	GV	70	YES	NO	EMR/TMR
Ohio	DH	GV	80	YES	NO	DH
Oklahoma	MR	GA	2 SD	YES	18	NO
Oregon	MR	GA	2 SD	YES	NO	NO
Pennsylvania	MR	GA	80	YES	NO	NO
Rhode Island	MR	GA	70	YES	YES	M/M/S/P
South Carolina	MD	GV	70	YES	18	EMR/TMR
South Dakota	MR	GA	70	YES	18	NO
Tennessee	MR	LA	74	YES	NO	NO
Texas	MR	GA	2 SD	YES	NO	NO
Utah	ID	GA	NO	YES	NO	NO
Vermont	LI	GA	70	YES	NO	NO
Virginia	MR	GA	NO	YES	NO	EMR/TMR
Washington	MR	GA	2 SD	YES	NO	NO
West Virginia	MI	LA	70–75	YES	18	M/M/S/P
Wisconsin	CD	GV	70–75	YES	NO	M/M/S/P
Wyoming	MD	GA	NO	YES	NO	NO

Table 8.2 continued

1. CD=cognitively delayed/cognitive disability, CI=cognitive impairment, DH=developmentally handicapped, ED=educational disability, ID=intellectual disability, II=intellectual impairment, LI=learning impairments, MD=mental disability, MH=mentally handicapped, MI=mental impairment, MR=mental retardation, SLIC=significantly limited intellectual capacity.

2. GA=Grossman adapted, GV=Grossman verbatim, LA=Luckasson adapted, LV=Luckasson verbatim, O=other.

3. EMR=educable mentally retarded, M/FMD=mild and functional mental disability, M/M=mild/moderate, M/SCD=mild and severe cognitive disability, P=profound, S=severe, SMD=severe multiple disabilities, TMR=trainable mentally retarded.

From "An Evaluation of State Guidelines for Mental Retardation: Focus on Definition and Classification Practices" (p. 117), by C. Denning, J. Chamberlain, and E. A. Polloway, 2000, *Education and Training in Mental Retardation and Developmental Disabilities, 35,* 111–119.

This definition reflects some similarities to the Luckasson et al. (1992) definition (e.g., set of assumptions used to clarify intent) and some modifications in presentation (e.g., description of adaptive skills). It represents a next logical step in the continued efforts by professionals to define the concept of mental retardation.

Classification

Historically, classification in this field has been done by both etiology (i.e., causes) or level of severity. While the former has limited application to nonmedical practice, the latter has been used by a range of disciplines, including education and psychology. The classification system cited most often in the professional literature continues to be the one recommended by Grossman (1983). This system uses the terms **mild, moderate, severe,** and **profound mental retardation,** which are summative judgments reflecting more significant degrees of disability as based on both intelligence and adaptive behavior assessment. Often, however, the emphasis has been on the former only, so IQ scores have frequently and unfortunately been equated with level of functioning.

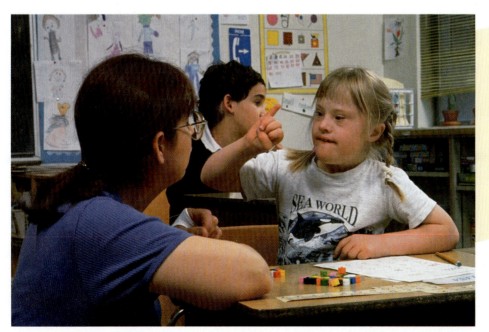

Terms such as educable *and* trainable *have often been used to categorize students with mental retardation.*

Terms such as **educable** and **trainable** reflect an alternative system that has been used in school environments. These archaic terms remain in use today in many places; it is not uncommon to hear students referred to as EMR (educable mentally retarded) and TMR (trainable mentally retarded). The terms roughly correspond somewhat to the 1983 AAMR terms mild and moderate/severe retardation, respectively. However, by nature, these terms are inherently stereotypical and prejudicial, and consequently (and appropriately) have been criticized, thus leading to decreased use, although some derivatives of this system continue to be reflected in state guidelines (see Table 8.2).

One alternative is to classify mental retardation according to only two levels of functioning (i.e., mild and severe) and to avoid sole reliance on IQ scores in considerations of level of severity. With such a less formal approach, the consideration of levels of adaptive skills serves as the yardstick for determining level of retardation, resulting in a more meaningful and broad-based, though less precise, system of classification. This approach is commonly used in the field and is generally reflected in the distinctions made between mild and severe retardation in this text.

An alternative to this deficit approach is the classification system of Luckasson et al. (1992), which has particular merit for use in inclusive settings. According to this system, classification is not derived from levels of disability, or deficit, but rather from needed **levels of support.** As defined by Luckasson et al. (2002, p. 151), "supports are resources and strategies that aim to promote the development, education, interests, and personal well-being of a person and that enhance individual functioning." Thus, this system would classify the *needs* rather than the *deficits* of the individual. Individuals would be designated as needing intermittent, limited, extensive, or pervasive levels of support as related to each of the adaptive skills areas (see Table 8.1). Of course, in a given area, an individual may also not need any support to function successfully. These levels of support are defined as follows:

> *Intermittent:* Supports on an "as needed basis," characterized by their episodic (person not always needing the supports) or short-term nature (supports needed during life-span transitions, e.g., job loss or acute medical crisis). Intermittent supports may be high or low intensity when provided.
>
> *Limited:* An intensity of supports characterized by consistency over time, time-limited but not of an intermittent nature, may require fewer staff members and less cost than more intense levels of support (e.g., time-limited employment training or transitional supports during the school-to-adult period).
>
> *Extensive:* Supports characterized by regular involvement (e.g., daily) in at least some environments (e.g., school, work, or home) and not time-limited nature (e.g., long-term support and long-term home living support).
>
> *Pervasive:* Supports characterized by their constancy, high intensity, provision across environments, potentially life-sustaining nature. Pervasive supports typically involve more staff members and intrusiveness than do extensive or time-limited supports. (adapted from Luckasson et al., 2002, p. 152)

The supports classification system of the AAMR manual (Luckasson et al., 1992) was further explained in a publication by Luckasson et al. (1996). Table 8.3 presents a grid showing different levels of intensity of supports to illustrate the way that this classification system can be put into practice. In Table 8.4, a portrait of the concept of supports is provided by describing support functions and selected representative activities.

The Luckasson et al. (1992) classification received general support in the field, particularly in the area of programs for adults with mental retardation, although it did not have a significant impact on research and school practices after its development. Polloway, Smith, Chamberlain, Denning, and Smith (1999) found that 99% of research papers that were published in three mental retardation journals (1993–1997) and that relied on a system to describe research participants continued to use the levels-of-deficit model from the Grossman (1983) manual rather than relying on the levels-of-support system.

CONSIDER THIS

What are some advantages to using a classification system based on levels of support rather than levels of deficit?

	Intermittent	Limited	Extensive	Pervasive
Time Duration	As needed	Time limited, occasionally ongoing	Usually ongoing	Possibly lifelong
Time Frequency	Infrequent, low occurrence	Regular, anticipated, could be high frequency		High rate, continuous, constant
Settings Living, Work, Recreation, Leisure, Health, Community, etc.	Few settings, typically one or two settings	Across several settings, typically not all settings		All or nearly all settings
Resources Professional/ Technological Assistance	Occasional consultation or discussion, ordinary appointment schedule, occasional monitoring	Occasional contact or time limited but frequent regular contact	Regular, ongoing contact or monitoring by professionals typically at least weekly	Constant contact and monitoring by professionals
Intrusiveness	Predominantly all natural supports, high degree of choice and autonomy	Mixture of natural and service-based supports, lesser degree of choice and autonomy		Predominantly service-based supports, controlled by others

TABLE 8.3   Levels of Supports × Intensity Grid

From "The 1992 AAMR Definition and Preschool Children: Response from the Committee on Terminology and Classification" (p. 250) by R. Luckasson, R. Schalock, M. Snell, and D. Spitalnik, 1996, *Mental Retardation, 34.*

In their review of state educational guidelines, Denning et al. (2000) reported that no states were using the levels-of-support model as their classification system. Most commonly used were a variety of deficit models based on either the AAMR system of mild/moderate/severe/profound or the traditional school-based system of educable/trainable (see Table 8.3).

Prevalence, Causes, and Characteristics

As discussed previously, *prevalence* data based on the 23rd annual report from the U.S. Department of Education for IDEA indicated that 1.15% of the estimated enrollment (ages 6–17) was identified as having mental retardation in school year 1999–2000 (U.S. Department of Education, 2001). This represents a significant change from the time when the national school prevalence for mental retardation was approximately 3%, and thus mental retardation was one of the two largest categories of disabilities, and mild retardation, in particular, was the most significant high-incidence disability related to learning problems in the schools. Currently, it is likely that, of the approximately 1% of the school population that is identified with mental retardation, approximately 60% might be viewed as mildly retarded, with the remainder having more severe disabilities.

A key reason for the decrease in the reported incidence of mild mental retardation which became most apparent first in the 1980s (e.g., MacMillan, 1989; Reschly, 1988) was the concern about the overrepresentation of minority children under this label. However, while effort has been made to prevent potential bias in the system (see MacMillan & Forness, 1998), African American students are estimated to be 2.4 times more likely to be identified as having mild mental retardation than their non–African American peers (Oswald, Coutinho, Best, & Singh, 1999). Nevertheless, to appreciate the ethnic breakdown within educational programs, it is important to note that the U.S. Department of

| TABLE 8.4 | Support Functions and Representative Activities |

Support Function*	Representative Activities		
Teaching	Supervising Giving feedback Organizing the learning environment	Training Evaluating Supporting inclusive classrooms	Instructing Collecting data Individualizing instruction
Befriending	Advocating Car pooling Supervising Instructing	Evaluating Communicating Training Giving feedback	Reciprocating Associating and disassociating Socializing
Financial Planning	Working with SSI–Medicaid Advocating for benefits	Assisting with money management Protection and legal assistance	Budgeting Income assistance and planning/ considerations
Employee Assistance	Counseling Procuring/using assistive technology devices	Supervisory training Job performance enhancement	Crisis intervention/assistance Job/task accommodation and redesigning job/work duties
Behavioral Support	Functional analysis Multicomponent instruction Emphasis on antecedent manipulation	Manipulation of ecological and setting events Teaching adaptive behavior	Building environment with effective consequences
In-home Living Assistance	Personal maintenance/care Transfer and mobility Dressing and clothing care Architectural modifications	Communication devices Behavioral support Eating and food management Housekeeping	Respite care Attendant care Home-health aides Homemaker services
Community Access and Use	Carpooling/rides program Transportation training Personal protection skills	Recreation/leisure involvement Community awareness opportunities Vehicle modification	Community use opportunities and interacting with generic agencies Personal protection skills
Health Assistance	Medical appointments Medical interventions Supervision Med Alert devices	Emergency procedures Mobility (assistive devices) Counseling appointments Medication taking	Hazard awareness Safety training Physical therapy and related activities Counseling interventions

*The support functions and activities may need to be modified slightly to accommodate individuals of different ages.

Adapted from *Mental Retardation: Definition, Classification, and Systems of Supports* (pp. 153–154) by R. Luckasson et al., 2002, Washington, DC: American Association on Mental Retardation.

CROSS-REFERENCE

Review the causes of other disabilities (see Chapters 5–11) to determine the possible overlap of etiological factors.

Education (2001) reports that 53.8% of students with mental retardation are white compared with 34.2% who are black and 9.1% Hispanic.

There are hundreds of known causes of retardation, and at the same time, numerous cases for which the cause is unknown. Table 8.5 outlines some representative causes to show the complexity of this area of concern. While this information is limited to selected causes and brief, related information, the reader is referred to Polloway and Smith (2002) for a fuller discussion of biological causes and prevention and Kim and Ittenbach (2002) for an analysis of psychosocial aspects.

Given the diversity of persons who may be identified as mentally retarded, or even mildly retarded, the drawing of a portrait of characteristics must be done with caution. Nevertheless, some generalizations are reasonable.

In their review of characteristics, Beirne-Smith, Ittenbach, and Patton (2002) discussed demographic aspects. In addition to the ethnic issues discussed previously, other key considerations include gender (with a significantly larger number of boys identified than girls

TABLE 8.5	Selected Causes of Mental Retardation	
Cause	**Nature of Problem**	**Considerations**
Down Syndrome	Trisomy 21 (3 chromosomes on this pair) IQ range from severe retardation to nonretarded	Wide variance in learning characteristics Classic physical signs Most common chromosomal anomaly
Environmental Disadvantage	Elements of poverty environment (e.g., family constellation, resources, educational role models)	Can be related to mild retardation Commonly associated with school failure
Fetal Alcohol Syndrome	Caused by drinking during pregnancy Related to toxic effects of alcohol	Associated with varying degrees of disability May be accompanied by facial and other malformations and behavioral disturbances Among the three most common biologically based causes of retardation
Fragile X Syndrome	Genetic disorder related to the gene or X chromosome	Most often transmitted from mother to son Frequently associated with retardation in males and learning disabilities in females (in some instances) May be accompanied by variant patterns of behavior (e.g., self-stimulation), social skills difficulties, language impairment
Hydrocephalus	Multiple causes (e.g., genetic, environmental) Disruption in appropriate flow of cerebrospinal fluid on the brain	Previously associated with enlarged head and brain damage Controlled by the implantation of a shunt
Phenylketonuria	Autosomal recessive genetic disorder	Associated with metabolic problems in processing high-protein foods Can be controlled via restrictive diets implemented at birth
Prader-Willi Syndrome	Chromosomal error of the autosomal type	Associated with biological compulsion to excessive eating Obesity as a common secondary trait to retardation
Tay-Sachs Disease	Autosomal recessive genetic disorder	Highest risk for Ashkenazic Jewish persons Associated with severe disabilities and early mortality No known cure Prevention by means of genetic screening

in the schools) and socioeconomic and family patterns (with a disproportionate number of children with mental retardation coming from single-parent families and low-income homes).

Mental retardation is associated with a number of characteristics that are in turn related to specific challenges to learning. Table 8.6 identifies the most significant learning domains, lists representative problem areas, and notes certain instructional implications. In addition, the table summarizes information on motivation as well as cognitive, language, academic, and sociobehavioral development.

While a discussion of learning characteristics inevitably concerns deficiencies related to students with mental retardation (Kavale & Forness, 1999), nevertheless teachers should keep in mind the importance of retaining high expectations for their students. As Wehmeyer, Lattin, and Agran (2001) noted, the fact that these students are often held to low expectations can have a deleterious effects on outcomes. A commitment to challenging these learners to succeed and build on their assets is clearly called for.

Recent research on learning in students with mental retardation has been relatively limited. For example, Kavale and Forness (1999) reported that the majority of the studies in this area useful for ascertaining learning characteristics were more than 25 years old.

T ABLE 8.6   **Characteristics and Implications of Mental Retardation**

Domain	Representative Problem Areas	Instructional Implications
Attention	Attention span (length of time on task) Focus (inhibition of distracting stimuli) Selective attention (discrimination of important stimulus characteristics)	Train students to be aware of the importance of attention. Teach students how to actively monitor their attention (i.e., self-monitoring). Highlight salient cues.
Use of Mediational Strategies	Production of strategies to assist learning Organizing new information	Teach specific strategies (rehearsal, labeling, chunking). Involve student in active learning process (practice, apply, review). Stress meaningful content.
Memory	Short-term memory (i.e., over seconds, minutes)—common deficit area Long-term memory—usually more similar to that of persons who are nondisabled (once information has been learned)	Because strategy production is difficult, students need to be shown how to use strategies in order to proceed in an organized, well-planned manner. Stress meaningful content.
Generalization Learning	Applying knowledge or skills to new tasks, problems, or situations Using previous experience to formulate rules that will help solve problems of a similar nature	Teach in multiple contexts. Reinforce generalization. Teach skills in relevant contexts. Remind students to apply what they have learned.
Motivational Considerations	External locus of control (attributing events to others' influence) Outerdirectedness (in learning style) Lack of encouragement to achieve and low expectations by others Failure set (personal expectancy of failure)	Create environment focused on success opportunities. Emphasize self-reliance. Promote self-management strategies. Teach learning strategies for academic tasks. Focus on learning to learn. Encourage problem-solving strategies (versus only correct responses).
Cognitive Development	Ability to engage in abstract thinking Symbolic thought, as exemplified by introspection and developing hypotheses	Provide concrete examples in instruction. Provide contextual learning experiences. Encourage interaction between students and the environment, being responsive to their needs so that they may learn about themselves as they relate to the people and objects around them.
Language Development	Delayed acquisition of vocabulary and language rules Possible interaction with cultural variance and language dialects Speech disorders (more common than in general population)	Create environment that facilitates development and encourages verbal communication. Provide appropriate language models. Provide opportunities for students to use language for a variety of purposes and with different audiences. Differentiate cultural variance and language delay or difficulties. Encourage student speech and active participation.
Academic Development	Delayed acquisition of reading, writing, and mathematical skills, decoding, and comprehension of text Problem-solving difficulties in mathematics	Use learning strategies to promote effective studying. Promote literacy acquisition. Teach sight words with emphases on functional applications (see Polloway, Smith, & Miller, 2003). Teach strategies for decoding unknown words and place skills in context of literacy development (Katims, 2001). Provide strategies to promote reading comprehension and math problem solving. Adapt curriculum to promote success.
Sociobehavioral Considerations	Social adjustment Social perception and awareness Self-esteem Peer acceptance Suggestability Classroom behavioral difficulties (e.g., disruptions, lack of involvement)	Promote social competence through direct instruction in social skills. Reinforce appropriate behaviors. Seek an understanding of reasons for inappropriate behavior. Involve peers as classroom role models. Program for social acceptance. Use peers in reinforcing interventions.

Thus, while the population has changed over time, there has been rather limited attention to the study of these changes.

An important area of the study with direct implications for instruction is strategy training. Clearly it remains critical for teachers of students with mental retardation to focus not only on the content to be learned but also on the learning process itself so that students can lessen their learning deficits through systematic strategy training. Kavale and Forness (1999) underscore the importance of focusing on strategy training so that students learn effective ways to acquire, retain, and master relevant skills within the curriculum.

While the obvious focus in the field of mental retardation is on the cognitive characteristics of students with mental retardation, practitioners should not overlook the fact that socioemotional factors are also critical to successful functioning. For example, Masi, Mucci, and Favilla (1999) studied a group of adolescents with mild mental retardation and found depressed moods, psychomotor agitation, and loss of energy and interest as the more common problems experienced by these students.

Identification, Assessment, Eligibility, and Placement

Procedures for the identification of mental retardation proceed directly from the specific AAMR scheme that is followed. The proposed revision to the AAMR manual (Ad Hoc Committee, 2001) provides a framework for the consideration of diagnosis, classification, and the planning of supports as outlined in Figure 8.1.

FIGURE 8.1   **Proposed Framework for Diagnosis, Classification, and Planning of Supports**

Function	Purposes	Assessment	
		Matching Measures to Purposes	**Guidelines and Considerations That May Be Important[†]**
Diagnosis	Service eligibility Research Legal	IQ test* Adaptive behavior* Age*	Appropriateness for person (age group, cultural group, primary language, means of communication, gender)
Classification	Service reimbursement/funding Grouping for research Grouping for services Communication about selected characteristics	Supports intensities (e.g., support needs scale) IQ ranges or levels (e.g., IQ tests) Special education categories Environment (e.g., PASS, UN Rules) Etiology (e.g., ICD-10) Severity (e.g., adaptive behavior levels) Mental health (e.g., DSM-IV)	Psychometric characteristics of measures selected Stated or selected purpose for measurement Physical or mental health Opportunities/experiences Physical/emotional behavior in assessment situation Clinical/social history
Planning supports	Facilitate person-referenced outcomes ▶ Independence/interdependence ▶ Productivity/meaningful activities ▶ Community participation ▶ Personal well-being	Personal appraisal and functional assessment measures	Personal goals Team input Relevant context/environments Social roles Participation, interactions

*All required for diagnosis of mental retardation
†Always adhere to published best practices from relevant discipline

From "Request for Comments on the Proposed New Edition of *Mental Retardation: Definition, Classification, and Systems of Supports*" (p. 11) by Ad Hoc Committee, 2001, *AAMR News and Notes, 14*(5).

Personal Spotlight

Sibling

Max Lewis is a clinical psychologist. He has a 51-year-old sister, Judy, with mental retardation. Because Judy is older than Max, he only remembers her as having mental retardation; she was diagnosed in her first few years. Many professionals told Max's parents that Judy should be institutionalized. Despite these recommendations, Judy's parents kept her at home and struggled to obtain an appropriate education for her in public schools, but most public schools did not have programs for Judy. It was not until she was in the eighth grade that she actually went to a public school. Prior to this time, Judy attended segregated programs that focused on children with developmental disabilities.

Max Lewis

Bellingham, WA

During the few years that Judy attended public schools, she was still very segregated from nondisabled children. "The students with disabilities were segregated to the point," notes Max, "that they were allowed to leave their classrooms only when the other students were not around." The students with disabilities were treated nearly like "untouchables." Max says that as an adolescent, his sister was somewhat of an embarrassment to him. He rarely told his friends that he had a sister with mental retardation for fear of their rejecting him.

Judy is now living with her parents, which is a concern for all the family. Max and his brother are both aware that when their parents die, Judy will be without a home. Although the family will provide whatever supports are necessary for Judy, they are concerned that she will have a very difficult time adjusting to any new living situation. Max believes that had there been other alternatives for Judy while she was growing up, this would not be a problem now. Had she been more involved with nondisabled students, she very likely would be more independent now.

Max believes that current practices in public schools for children with disabilities are significantly superior to the situation that existed when Judy was growing up. He states that "Schools are so much better now simply because they are trying to deal with the problems of these children." Unfortunately for Judy, and for thousands of children who grew up before special education services were expanded, many opportunities for individual growth and development were simply not available.

For follow-up questions about this Personal Spotlight, go to Chapter 8 of the Companion Website (ablongman.com/sppd4e) and click Personal Spotlight.

The challenges of accurate identification, assessment, and eligibility criterion procedures have been faced by the field for many years. The Personal Spotlight feature provides a perspective on this process by offering a biographical sketch of an individual who was misdiagnosed as having severe mental retardation.

Students with mental retardation are the individuals with disabilities that traditionally have been least likely to be included within general education classrooms. According to the U.S. Department of Education (2001), during the 1998–1999 school year, 13.7% of the students were served in regular classes (for at least 79% of the school day), 29.2% of the students were served outside of regular classes between 21% and 60% of the school day (e.g., resource room), and 51% were placed in special education programs for at least 61% of the day. An additional 5.9% of students were served in alternative settings (e.g., separate day and residential facilities, homebound). When these numbers are compared with other areas of exceptionality (i.e., the average across disabilities is 47% of students served in regular classes more than 79% of the school day) (U.S. Department of Education, 2001), it is apparent that students with other kinds of disabilities are more commonly served in general education classrooms than are students with mental retardation. However, the trend since 1992 has been toward an increase in general education and resource placement and a decrease in separate class placement (Katsiyannis, Zhang, & Archwamety, 2002).

When evaluating placement considerations for students with mental retardation (as well as with other disabilities), educators should realize that setting alone does not represent effective "treatment" for the students. Too often the debate in education has concerned placement to the exclusion of a careful analysis of what constitutes effective instructional practices. In fact, it is quite likely that "features of instruction are probably the major influence on outcomes, but these are not unique to setting. Setting is thus a macro variable; the real question becomes one of examining what happens in that setting" (Kavale & Forness, 1999, p. 70).

Transition Considerations

Occupational success and community living skills are among the critical life adjustment variables that ensure successful transition into adulthood. Numerous studies and case histories confirm the successes that individuals achieve, often thanks to the supports of teachers, family, and friends. Two general and equally critical considerations are these: (1) Through which means do students exit special education? and (2) What opportunities and supports are available to them during adulthood?

The U.S. Department of Education (2001) tracks exit data on all students who leave special education. For students with mental retardation, the data (from the 1998–99 academic year) on special education exits illustrate some interesting points. Not including those students who move from a school division but are continuing in special education in another location, the reasons for exit include the following: graduated with diploma (41.7%), graduated through certificate of completion (22.2%), "aged out" of education (4.7%), returned to regular education (5.8%), died (0.78%), moved and were not known to continue their education (12.5%), and dropped out (24.9%). The key conclusion that can be drawn is that about half of students with mental retardation completed the designated academic curriculum with either a diploma or a certificate while a large number of students instead either leave because of age or formally or less formally (i.e., moved, not known to continue) drop out of school. The same federal report indicates an estimated 26.7% of students (ages 14–21) with mental retardation who left school in 1997–1998 had dropped out. In terms of students with mental retardation earning a diploma or a certificate, Katsiyannis et al. (2002, p. 143) note a "disturbing trend" of a decreased annual percentage having completed secondary school with this recognition. However, they urged caution in an interpretation of these findings because of the complexity of variables influencing these data.

In terms of postschool adjustment, Polloway, Patton, Smith, and Roderique (1992) posed the question "What happens when students who are mildly retarded get older?" They considered in particular the data that Edgar (1987, 1988, 1990) and Affleck, Edgar, Levine, and Kortering (1990) reported, indicating that of the students who went through special education programs, less than one half were either working or involved in training programs while only 21% were living independently 30 months after secondary school. The transition period was seen as a time of "floundering" (Edgar, 1988), particularly for students with mild retardation who were not afforded effective transition programming. More recent outcomes have been more optimistic when effective transition programs are in place. Examples of the challenges of adulthood in terms of life demands are summarized in Table 8.7.

In general, the clear majority of adults with mental retardation can make successful transitions and obtain and maintain gainful employment. A number of critical factors influence their success. First, postschool adjustment hinges on their ability to demonstrate personal and social behaviors appropriate to the workplace. Second, the quality of the transition programming provided will predict subsequent success. Such programs recognize that programming must reflect a top-down perspective (i.e., from community considerations to school curriculum) that bases curriculum on the demands of the next environment in which the individual will live, work, socialize, and recreate.

Third, the workplace of the future poses special challenges. The more complex demands of the workplace will become increasingly problematic for this group. Many of the

CONSIDER THIS

Why do you think the prevalence of students identified as having mental retardation has declined over the past 30 years?

TEACHING TIP

Students with mental retardation should be taught functional (i.e., life) skills that will prepare them for success as adults.

TABLE 8.7 **Major Life Demands**

Domain	Subdomain	Sample Life Demands
Employment/Education	General job skills	Seeking and securing a job Learning job skills Maintaining one's job
	General education/training considerations	Gaining entry to postsecondary education/training settings (higher education, adult education, community education, trade/technical schools, military service) Finding financial support Utilizing academic and system survival skills (e.g., study skills, organizational skills, and time management)
	Employment setting	Recognizing job duties and responsibilities Exhibiting appropriate work habits/behavior Getting along with employer and coworkers
Home and Family	Home management	Setting up household operations (e.g., initiating utilities) Cleaning dwelling Laundering and maintaining clothes and household items
	Financial management	Creating a general financial plan (e.g., savings, investments, retirement) Paying bills Obtaining government assistance when needed (e.g., Medicare, food stamps, student loans)
	Family life	Preparing for marriage, family Maintaining physical/emotional health of family members Planning and preparing meals (menu, buying food, ordering take-out food, dining out)
Leisure Pursuits	Indoor activities	Performing individual physical activities (e.g., weight training, aerobics, dance, swimming, martial arts) Participating in group physical activities (e.g., racquetball, basketball)
	Outdoor activities	Engaging in general recreating activities (e.g., camping, sightseeing, picnicking)

jobs that traditionally have been available to individuals with mental retardation (e.g., in the service industry) may be in shorter supply. Finally, individuals with mental retardation are likely to have increased leisure time. Thus an important component of transition planning should be preparing students to use their leisure time in rewarding and useful ways (Patton, Polloway, & Smith, 2000).

While general education teachers would be quite unlikely to have full responsibility for meeting the transitional needs of students with mental retardation, nevertheless this focus is one of the most critical curricular and instructional aspects of their needs. Patton and Dunn (1998) summarized the essential features of transition, highlighting the following:

▶ Transition efforts must start early and planning must be comprehensive.
▶ Decisions must balance what is ideal with what is possible.
▶ Active and meaningful student participation and family involvement are essential.
▶ Supports are beneficial and used by everyone.
▶ Community-based instructional experiences have a major impact on learning.
▶ The transition planning process should be viewed as a capacity-building activity.
▶ Transition planning is needed by all students.

Transition planning is critical to success for students with mental retardation, and therefore school districts can profit significantly from analyzing the life outcomes of their graduates. Sitlington and Frank (1998) developed a practitioner's handbook for conducting follow-up studies that provides an appropriate approach to collecting such data.

Strategies for Curriculum and Instruction for Students with Mental Retardation

The education of students with mental retardation in inclusive settings presents a unique opportunity for students with mental retardation, their peers, and their teachers. Without question educators must deliver quality programs, or else the prognosis for young adults with mental retardation, as noted earlier, will not reflect the positive quality of life to which they, like all persons, aspire.

Challenges for General Education

The data on postschool outcomes point to areas that teachers who work with students with mild retardation in inclusive settings must address. These concerns should be kept in mind as curricula and instructional plans are developed and implemented in conjunction with special education teachers. Patton et al. (1996) identified four primary goals for individuals with retardation: productive employment, independence and self-sufficiency, life skills competence, and opportunity to participate successfully within the schools and the community. These goals should guide the long-term goals for educational programs for these students.

The four overarching goals identified by Patton et al. (1996) are discussed further in the following paragraphs. The key challenge for teachers is to find ways to structure educational programs so that these important emphases can be related to curricular and instructional strategies.

In terms of *employment,* teachers should build students' career awareness and help them see how academic content relates to applied situations; at the secondary level, this effort should include training in specific job skills. This concern should be the primary focus of vocational educators who work with these students.

In terms of *independence and economic self-sufficiency,* young adults need to become as responsible as possible for themselves. As Miller (1995) states, the educational goal "is to develop self-directed learners who can address their own wants and concerns and can advocate for their goals and aspirations" (p. 12). Thus, the successful inclusion of students with mental retardation depends on the ability of teachers, peers, and the curriculum to create a climate of empowerment. Empowerment involves self-efficacy, a sense of personal control, self-esteem, and a sense of belonging to a group. Empowerment is not an automatic by-product of inclusive classrooms. However, when students are members of the group and retain the right to make decisions for themselves, they are being prepared for the challenges and rewards of life.

One essential element of empowerment is self-determination (Wehmeyer, 1993, 1994). As Wehmeyer (1993, p. 16) noted:

> Self-determination refers to the attitudes and abilities necessary to act as the primary causal agent in one's life, and to make choices and decisions regarding one's quality of life free from undue external influence or interference.

A series of specific behaviors constitute self-determination. For example, Zhang (2001) included the following: "making choices, making decisions, solving problems, setting and attaining goals, being independent, evaluating our performance, self-studying, speaking up for self, having internal motivations, believing in one's own abilities, being aware of personal strengths and weaknesses, and applying strengths to overcome weaknesses" (p. 339).

A third key consideration is the inclusion of *life skills* in the curriculum, focusing on the importance of competence in everyday activities. This area includes, but is not limited to, use of community resources, home and family activities, social and interpersonal skills, health and safety skills, use of leisure time, and participation in the community as

TEACHING TIP

Instructional activities for students with mental retardation should focus on the development of self-determination skills.

IEP Goals and Objectives for Orlando

The importance of a focus on educational programs is reflected in this set of IEP goals and objectives for Orlando (from the chapter-opening vignette). These are as follows:

Goal 1: *To obtain a valid Virginia driver's license.*

Objective 1: *Given a teacher-developed test orally, which parallels the requirements for a driver's license, Orlando will score an 80% accuracy.*

Objective 2: *Given a written form of a teacher-made driver's test, Orlando will score an 80% accuracy (with graduated, less intrusive prompts).*

Objective 3: *Given the state-required written test, Orlando will successfully pass the test.*

Objective 4: *Given the opportunity to enroll in the school's behind-the-wheel educational program, Orlando will complete the program.*

Objective 5: *Given the opportunity to enroll in the required behind-the-wheel driver's test, Orlando will complete the program at an acceptable competency level.*

Goal 2: *To successfully complete the apprenticeship program at Wal-Mart.*

Objective 1: *Given a job application for Wal-Mart, Orlando will accurately complete the application for an apprentice position with 100% accuracy.*

Objective 2: *Given the opportunity to use public transportation, Orlando will effectively use the transportation to arrive on time for work on a daily basis with 100% accuracy.*

Objective 3: *Given the workplace setting, Orlando will demonstrate the correct application of the safety rules with 100% accuracy.*

Objective 4: *Given the necessary tools and equipment to clean the floor at work, Orlando will demonstrate the specific skills required for cleaning the floor and emptying trash receptacles with 100% accuracy.*

Goal 3: *To demonstrate the ability to handle personal finances in the areas of housing, food, leisure, and transportation.*

Objective 1: *Given a set income level, Orlando will establish a realistic weekly budget to cover daily living expenses.*

Objective 2: *Given the opportunity to eat whatever he wants, Orlando will identify elements of a nutritious diet with 80% accuracy.*

Objective 3: *Given the opportunity to live alone, Orlando will be able to identify appropriate supports and be able to access assistance as needed for personal budget management 100% of the time.*

Objective 4: *Given the opportunity to live alone, Orlando will be able to determine areas of preferred leisure activities and identify community opportunities when asked 80% of the time.*

a citizen (e.g., compliance with legal and cultural standards). With the increased commitment to inclusion, a particularly challenging consideration for both general and special educators will be ways to include a life skills and transitional focus within the general education curriculum beginning at the elementary school level and reflected throughout formal schooling.

A critical concern relative to school and community inclusion and to life adjustment is the acquisition of social skills. A useful model has been developed by Sargent (1991). It embraces three processes: development of social affect (appearance to others), social skills (specific behaviors that are central to interactions), and social cognition (understanding and being able to respond appropriately to various social situations).

A fourth consideration, *successful community involvement,* requires that students experience inclusive environments. Students with mental retardation can learn to participate in school and community by being included in general education classrooms. Although school inclusion may be viewed by some as an end in itself, it is better viewed as a condition that can provide instruction and training for success in subsequent inclusive community activities. As a necessary step toward this goal, individuals with mental retardation should be included to the maximum extent possible while there is assurance that such placement facilitates their learning and ultimately their preparation for adulthood.

Finally, consideration must be given to the perspectives of the individuals themselves about educational programs and their outcomes. To provide a picture of the views of the outcomes of interventions with persons with mental retardation, Fox and Emerson (2001) solicited input from persons with mental retardation, parents, clinical psychologists, nurses, program managers, and direct support workers. The focus was on two groups of individuals with mental retardation who also had challenging behaviors: children and young adults living at home and young adults in group homes. The most salient outcomes for these two groups identified by stakeholders present an interesting contrast. While program managers, nurses, and psychiatrists, for example, stressed reductions in the severity of challenging behaviors for both groups of individuals, persons with mental retardation from both groups identified increased friendships and relationships as their priority outcome goals.

General Considerations for Inclusion

The key to including students with mental retardation in the general education classroom is providing necessary and appropriate supports. These include personal supports, natural supports (e.g., parents, friends), support services, and technical supports. This model, **supported education,** assumes that individuals should be maintained in inclusive classroom settings to the maximum degree possible and supported in those locations in order to ensure successful learning.

Strains have occurred during the movement to the supports model because a too frequent tendency has been simply to physically place the student in the classroom, rather

A key to successful inclusion for students with mental retardation is provision of appropriate supports.

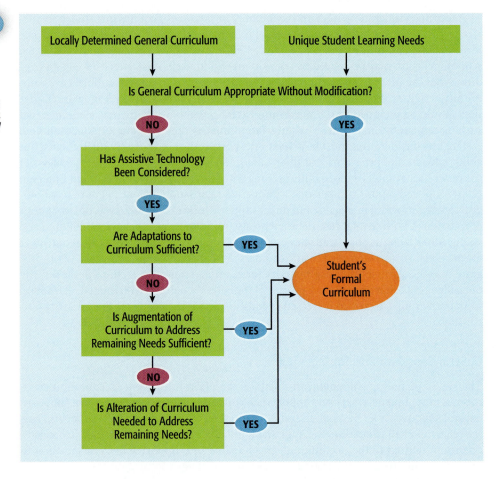

FIGURE 8.2

A Model to Gain Access to the General Curriculum

From "Achieving Access to the General Curriculum for Students with Mental Retardation: A Curriculum Decision-Making Model" (pp. 327–342) by M. L. Wehmeyer, D. Latton, & M. Agran, 2001, *Education and Training in Mental Retardation and Developmental Disabilities, 36.*

CROSS-REFERENCE

See Chapters 1 and 2 to review the purposes of including students with disabilities in general education settings.

than achieve the more appropriate goal of supported education. Inclusion should involve supported education and focus on welcoming and involving persons with retardation in the general education classroom. Merely placing students in general education without social integration and active classroom participation is not the intent of inclusion and will be far less likely to result in positive gains for students. Likewise, adults with mental retardation who live in the community but do not participate in community activities do not fulfill the true spirit of inclusion.

Wehmeyer, Latton, and Agran (2001) developed a model related to access to the general curriculum for individuals with mental retardation. Presented in Figure 8.2, the model reflects the fact that a series of key decisions need to be made in curriculum development in order for students to succeed in the general education classroom. Particular emphases include the use of assistive technology, the development of curricular adaptations (see the next section), the augmentation of the curriculum (to include emphases on strategy training, self-determination), and the availability of curricular alternatives (which stress a more functional emphasis often not present in the general curriculum).

Classroom Adaptations for Students with Mental Retardation

As inclusion becomes a more common alternative for students with disabilities in general, and individuals with mental retardation in particular, the regular curriculum has become the "program of choice" for more students with mental retardation. Review of data on the preferences of general education teachers concerning modifications and adaptations for such students indicates that preferred adaptations typically revolve more around changes in instructional delivery systems and response modes (e.g., testing adaptations such as extended time) than in changes in the actual curriculum or the standards associated with the curricular content (e.g., Polloway, Epstein, & Bursuck, 2002; Polloway, Bursuck, Jayanthi, Epstein, & Nelson, 1996; see also Chapter 15). Therefore, to the extent that these observations are verified, it is likely that a specialized curriculum may less commonly be available for students with mild mental retardation (Patton et al., 2000). Nevertheless, given the preceding discussion, teachers need to be aware of the importance of a functional focus within the curriculum in order to enhance learning and adult outcomes for students with mental retardation.

Table 8.6 presents an outline of the common characteristics associated with retardation, along with their implications for instruction. When they are considered collectively, certain instructional themes emerge. Teachers should focus on teaching and learning adaptations that

▶ ensure attention to relevant task demands.
▶ teach ways to learn content while teaching content itself.
▶ focus on content that is meaningful to the students, to promote learning as well as to facilitate application.
▶ provide training that crosses multiple learning and environmental contexts.
▶ offer opportunities for active involvement in the learning process.

One promising approach that has merit for all students and can particularly benefit students with retardation is the use of cognitively oriented instructional methods (e.g., strategy training, as discussed earlier in the chapter). Based on the premise that learning problems experienced by low-achieving students are due more to a lack of knowledge regarding the processes involved in independent learning than to underlying deficits, these approaches incorporate learning strategies, metacognition, and cognitive behavior modification (e.g., self-monitoring) as alternatives to traditional instructional practices. Their potential for students with mild mental retardation is clear (see Polloway, Patton, Smith, & Buck, 1997).

Curricular adaptations are likewise important to consider. In general, the key focus should be on relevant and meaningful curricular content that students can master and apply to their current and future lives. Teachers should focus on the subsequent environments for which students will prepare (in terms of learning, working, residing) as a basis for curriculum design. The subsequent-environments rationale has applicability across the school levels as individuals prepare for successful transitions and life challenges. Most important is the assurance that the secondary school curriculum prepares students with mental retardation (as well as all students) for adulthood, whether that means further education, job placement, or independent living.

To make the curriculum appropriate for students with mental retardation, specific adaptations can enhance learning and increase relevance. One format, developed by Wehman (1997), offers useful ideas for curricular initiatives (Table 8.8).

Assistive technology can further enhance classroom adaptations. Although students with mental retardation can benefit from a variety of technological applications, the key concern is that technology be used in a way that effectively enhances learning such as through the acquisition of new skills, the development of fluency and proficiency, and the maintenance of skills over time and can promote generalization to new situations (Hasselbring & Goin, 1993). Conscious attention to the use of technology for each of these four respective stages of learning will greatly enhance the effectiveness of technological approaches in supporting classroom adaptations. The nearby Technology Today feature describes how assistive technology devices can affect the learning environment.

TABLE 8.8 Typical and Modified Curriculum Outcomes for Students with Mental Retardation

Grade Level	Typical Outcomes	Modified Outcomes
Grade 2: Language Arts	Learn 10 spelling words per week and be able to use them correctly in sentences.	Identify 15 safety words (e.g., *stop, poison*) and functional words (e.g., *men, women*).
Grade 4: Language Arts	Read a book and write a two-page report, using correct grammar, punctuation, and spelling.	Listen to taped book, tape a personal reaction to the story, and illustrate the story.
Grade 6: Social Studies	Locate all 50 states on a map, and name their capitals.	Locate own state and those immediately adjacent to it, and name the capitals.
Grade 8: Social Studies	Name and explain the functions of each branch of the government.	Describe the jobs of the president, the vice president, a member of Congress, and a judge, and tell where each works.
Grade 10: Science	Describe the body systems of three different mammals, and identify the major components and functions for each system.	Label diagrams of the human body, identifying each body system and its purpose and naming major body organs.

Adapted from *Exceptional Individuals in School, Community, and Work* (p. 131) by P. Wehman, 1997, Austin, TX: Pro-Ed. Used by permission.

Tips for Adapting a Lesson for Orlando

The following selected adaptations reflect the learning and life needs as well as the classroom challenges for Orlando (as described in the chapter-opening vignette). They provide an illustration of adaptations which may be effective with students with special needs.

Orlando's teacher should

▶ use video-based training to learn the key elements in the driving manual.

▶ use a computer-simulated behind-the-wheel driving program.

▶ use community-based instruction to illustrate application of academic concepts (e.g., consumer math) in shopping.

▶ read test questions to Orlando in social studies.

▶ use weighted grades to emphasize laboratory assessment (versus test grades) in assigning report card grades in science.

▶ develop cooperative learning groups and use group grades for literature projects in English.

Assistive Technology

Assistive technology can be low- or high-tech devices designed to remove barriers or provide practical solutions to common everyday problems. . . . [Such] devices can be applied in the classroom to assist a student with learning curriculum content or in a community setting to promote skill development and participation.

Assistive technology can include such complex devices as (1) an environmental control unit to allow an individual with little or no mobility to control his or her environment (e.g., turn on the lights), (2) a voice-activated computer to allow an individual with mobility or sensory impairments to input data on a computer and receive output information, (3) augmentative communication systems to allow an individual with poor speech to be able to communicate with others (e.g., electronic communication aids), and (4) microswitches to allow an individual to perform a more complex task by reducing the number of steps to complete it to one press on the switch or to allow someone with poor motor skills to

access something by touching a very large switch pad as opposed to a small button or lever. In addition, switches can be activated by a number of means, such as sound, air, light, or movement, and are very versatile as to the functions they can perform.

Assistive technology can also include low-tech devices or modifications that can be very inexpensive and easy to apply, such as (1) a reach device to assist an individual with picking things off the floor or taking something off a high shelf, (2) a pre-coded push button phone to allow an individual with poor memory to complete a call to an important or frequently used number by lightly touching a large color-coded button, (3) audiotape instruction to allow an individual with cognitive or sensory impairments to have access to the instructions, directions, or classroom materials in a for-

mat that can be repeated as often as necessary to either learn or perform a task, and (4) a holder made out of wood with suction cups on the bottom that will keep a bowl or pan in place to allow an individual to mix ingredients using only one hand.

The range of high- and low-tech devices to assist with completing an activity or just to make the task easier is virtually endless. Many of these devices are commercially available while others can oftentimes be developed by any interested persons. The major ingredients for developing useful assistive technology devices are creativity, open-mindedness, and resourcefulness.

 For follow-up questions about assistive technology, go to Chapter 8 of the Companion Website (ablongman.com/sppd4e) and click Technology Today.

Adapted from "Severe Mental Retardation" by P. Wehman and W. Parent (pp. 170–171), in *Exceptional Individuals in School, Community, and Work,* edited by P. Wehman, 1997, Austin, TX: Pro-Ed. Used by permission.

Teachers need to promote an environment where social relationships can be developed.

Circles of Friends in Schools

Marsha Forest came away from her Joshua Committee experiences as if she had put on a better pair of glasses. Her position as a professor of special education suddenly seemed less important to her. She spent long hours on the road helping school boards, principals, and teachers to see how everybody can experience richness when someone with a disability is placed in a regular classroom and the so-called regular students are encouraged to form a circle of friends around that person.

Forest always believed in getting teaching down to meticulous detail when it came to educating persons with disabilities. Now, however, she saw that some of the most valuable educational steps can come *naturally* from regular classmates, if the right conditions exist in the classroom.

She also knew that parents and teachers fear peer group pressure. After all, when kids get together these days, they can give themselves quite an education—one that often shapes lives more powerfully than adults can shape them. But peer group education doesn't always lead to belligerence and destruction and drugs. It can lead to caring and nurturing and helping others do healthy things they had never done before.

This twist, however, generated fears in some teachers when it dawned on them that a circle of friends might foster better growth and development in a student than they were capable of teaching.

And so Marsha moved into regular schools and worked hard at

1. helping boards and principals understand the circles-of-friends process.
2. finding a teacher and class willing to include a person with a disability.
3. helping the regular teacher handle any initial fears about the venture.
4. letting the teacher and class call the shots as much as possible.
5. providing strong support persons who would assist only when they really were needed.
6. then finding a handful of kids willing to work at being friends with their classmate with the disability.

"The first placement in a school is the toughest," she said. "After that, it's usually easy to include others."

Forest sees building a circle of friends as a person-by-person process, not an all-encompassing program. So she focuses on students with disabilities one at a time, and sets up a framework that enables a circle to surround that person.

Because no two settings are alike, she watches as the circle, the regular teacher, and the rest of the students develop and coordinate their own routines for helping. Then, never predicting an outcome, she waits. And when new learning takes place in the person with the disability, Forest moves in and makes all the students, the teacher, the principal—even the board members—feel simply great.

According to her, the average school can handle up to twelve of these arrangements. After that, the efficiency of the process may diminish.

She doubts that circles of friends will work in every school. "If a school is all screwed up," she said, "and if it has lost its zest and commitment for really helping kids learn—forget it. On the other hand, I'm sure that circles of friends can help make a good school—and especially the kids—better. Then coming to school takes on fresh values and meaning. Some enjoy coming to school as they never did before."

For follow-up questions about circles of friends, go to Chapter 8 of the Companion Website (ablongman.com/sppd4e) and click Inclusion Strategies.

Adapted from *Circles of Friends: People with Disabilities and Their Friends Enrich the Lives of One Another* (pp. 39–40) by R. Perske, 1988, Nashville, TN: Abingdon Press.

Promoting Inclusive Practices for Students with Mental Retardation

Beyond the curricular and instructional considerations summarized previously, several other considerations are central to the successful inclusion of students with mental retardation. The first concern is the creation of a sense of community in the school in general and the classroom in particular. As noted earlier, successful inclusion represents supported education—an environment where students succeed because they are welcomed, encouraged, and involved (i.e., supported) in their learning.

The challenge for teachers seeking to successfully include students with mental retardation thus reaches beyond the students' acquisition of, for example, specific academic skills. Rather, it requires finding ways to provide a "belonging place" for them in the general education classroom. Such a place can be created through friendships, a key priority outcome as expressed by persons with mental retardation (Fox & Emerson, 2001).

Despite the broad support for inclusion, it does bring with it the potential loss of friendships present in traditional, self-contained classes. For example, Stainback, Stainback, East, and Sapon-Shevin (1994) note the concern of adolescents (and their parents) over finding dating partners in general education classes. Teachers should be sensitive to this consideration and promote an environment in which the benefits of friendships can be realized.

A helpful strategy for promoting social acceptance for students (and young adults) with mental retardation involves "circles of support," or "circles of friends." The Inclusion Strategies feature discusses an example of such a program. As teachers consider developing such systems, they should not overlook the benefits to students who are not disabled, which may include enhanced attitudes, personal growth, and a sense of civic responsibility in addition to the benefits of friendship (Hughes et al., 2001).

Final Thoughts

As special and general education teachers jointly develop and implement educational programs for students with mental retardation, they should keep in mind that these students require a comprehensive, broad-based curriculum to meet their needs. The most effective programs will provide appropriate academic instruction, adapted to facilitate learning. However, the curriculum cannot solely be academic in orientation; rather, it should focus also on developing social and life skills and transition skills to facilitate not only the students' success in general education classrooms but also their subsequent inclusion into the community.

In making curricular choices, teachers will have to evaluate the responsiveness of the general education classroom and curriculum to the needs of students with mental retardation. The ultimate goal is not simply school inclusion but rather community or "life" inclusion; the curriculum that achieves that purpose most effectively is the most appropriate one. As Cassidy and Stanton (1959) suggested over four decades ago, the key question in evaluating the effectiveness of programs for students with mental retardation is *effective for what?* What is it the schools are to impart to the students? The challenge of inclusion for students with mental retardation is to ensure that the curriculum they pursue prepares them for their future.

TEACHING TIP

Curricular decisions for students with mental retardation should always be made with the students' future needs in mind.

Summary

Basic Concepts About Mental Retardation

▸ The concept of mental retardation has varying meanings to professionals and the public.

▸ The three central dimensions of the definition are lower intellectual functioning, deficits or limitations in adaptive skills, and an onset prior to age 18.

▸ The 1992 AAMR definition retains the three dimensions, but also stresses the importance of four assumptions: cultural and linguistic diversity, an environmental context for adaptive skills, the strengths of individuals as well as their limitations, and the promise of improvement over time. A draft definition (2001) has been proposed to further update work in this area.

▸ Common practice in the field has been to speak of two general levels of mental retardation, mild and severe, but emerging efforts in classification stress levels of needed supports rather than levels of disability.

▸ The prevalence of mental retardation in schools decreased dramatically throughout the 1980s and early 1990s but has now stabilized at approximately 1%.

▸ Social competence is a critical component of instructional programs for students with mental retardation. Teaching social skills can have a positive effect on successful inclusion both in school and in the community.

▸ Educational programs must be outcomes-oriented and attend to transitional concerns so that students receive the appropriate training to prepare them for subsequent environments. The curriculum should thus have a top-down orientation.

Strategies for Curriculum and Instruction for Students with Mental Retardation

▸ Teachers should teach not only content but also mediation strategies that facilitate learning. Examples include rehearsal, classification, and visual imagery.

▸ Attention difficulties can be addressed by modifying instruction to highlight relevant stimuli and by training students to monitor their own attention.

▸ Cognitive development for students with mental retardation can be enhanced by emphasizing active interaction with the environment and the provision of concrete learning experiences.

Classroom Adaptations for Students with Mental Retardation

▸ Many students with a history of failure have an external locus of control, which can be enhanced by an emphasis on success experiences and by reinforcement for independent work.

▸ To enhance language development, teachers should provide a facilitative environment, structure opportunities for communication, and encourage verbal language.

Promoting Inclusive Practices for Students with Mental Retardation

▸ Opportunities for inclusion are essential and should focus on social benefits such as friendship while not neglecting critical, functional curricular needs.

Further Readings

Beirne-Smith, M., Ittenbach, R., & Patton, J. R. (2002). *Mental retardation* (6th ed.). Columbus, OH: Merrill.

Luckasson, R., Coulter, D., Polloway, E. A., Reiss, S., Schalock, R., Snell, M., Spitalnik, D., & Stark, J. (1992). *Mental retardation: Definition, classification and systems of supports.* Washington, DC: American Association on Mental Retardation.

Luckasson, R., et al. (2002). *Mental retardation: Definition, classification and systems of supports.* Washington, DC: American Association on Mental Retardation.

Patton, J. R., Polloway, E. A., Smith, T. E. C., Edgar, E., Clark, G. M., & Lee, S. (1996). Individuals with mild mental retardation: Post-secondary outcomes and implications for educational policy. *Education and Training in Mental Retardation and Development Disabilities, 31,* 77–85.

Polloway, E. A., Smith, T. E. C., Patton, J. R., & Smith, J. D. (1996). Historical perspectives in mental retardation. *Education and Training in Mental Retardation and Developmental Disabilities, 31,* 3–12.

Wehmeyer, M., & Patton, J. R. (2001). *Mental retardation in the 21st century.* Austin, TX: Pro-Ed.

VideoWorkshop Extra!

If the VideoWorkshop package was included with your textbook, go to Chapter 8 of the Companion Website (www.ablongman.com/sppd4e) and click on the VideoWorkshop button. Follow the instructions for viewing video clip 7. Then consider this information along with what you've read in Chapter 8 while answering the following questions.

1. Teacher comments made in the video clip indicate that Carlyn has had a successful first year in preschool. Describe the teacher behaviors that contributed to Carlyn's success.
2. In order to prepare Carlyn for transition to an integrated kindergarten, what skills would you target so that Carlyn's inclusion will continue to be successful?

9 Teaching Students with Sensory Impairments

After reading this chapter, you should be able to

1. explain the nature of low-incidence disabilities.
2. define hearing impairment and visual impairment.
3. describe educationally relevant characteristics of students with hearing impairments and visual impairments.
4. describe accommodations and modifications for students with hearing impairments and visual impairments.

Monique is 15 years old. She was diagnosed with a hearing loss when she was 14 months old. She has a bilateral loss that is considered to be severe to profound. Although she uses a hearing aid, her primary mode of communication is through sign language. Monique attended the state residential school for the deaf as a day student from kindergarten through 3rd grade. Beginning in the 4th grade, she enrolled in her regular elementary school and was assigned a sign language interpreter. Each year she has split her classroom time between the general education classroom and resource room. In the resource room, Monique has received individual assistance with some of her content courses; she has also received speech therapy services weekly. Monique is beginning to think about life after high school. Her goal is to go to college and major in deaf education. While she has the support of her family and teachers, Monique's main barrier is her ability to self-advocate. She is rather shy and does not become involved in academic or social activities without facilitation. Her family and teachers know that Monique needs to become a better self-advocate in order to be successful after she exits high school and before she enters college. (Adapted from Luckner, 2002)

QUESTIONS TO CONSIDER

1. How have Monique's school placements (residential school and general education classroom) been an asset to her academic and social development?
2. What can Monique's teachers do to help her become a better self-advocate?
3. What skills are critical for Monique to have in order to be successful in a post-secondary educational setting?

s with all students with special needs, there remains some debate regarding the best setting in which to provide services to students with **sensory impairments,** which include visual and hearing impairments. Whereas many students with sensory impairments were historically served in residential settings, today many students with these conditions are placed in general education settings. Most are capable of handling the academic and social demands of these settings. However, for these students to receive an appropriate education, a variety of accommodations may be needed, ranging from minor seating adjustments to the use of sophisticated equipment for communicating, listening, or navigating. Students with these impairments may also need the support of additional personnel (e.g., an *interpreter* or *Braille instructor*).

To provide appropriate accommodations, teachers must have accurate information about how to modify their classrooms and adapt instruction to meet student needs. In addition, they need to understand the psychosocial aspects of these types of disabilities. For some students with severe sensory problems, special consultants may also be needed to assist general education teachers. Ultimately, teachers must feel comfortable and confident that they can address the range of needs these students present.

Sensory impairments are considered *low-incidence disabilities,* since there are not large numbers of these students in the school population. The number of students (ages 6 to 21) with hearing or visual impairments who were officially identified and provided with special education or related services nationally for the school year 1999–2000 is reported in Figure 9.1. These are small numbers, considering the total number of students in this age range. Furthermore, these groups represent a very small percentage of all students who are disabled.

However, having only one of these students in a classroom may seem overwhelming, as this student may require a variety of modifications in classroom management and in certain instructional practices. Students who have both vision and hearing losses present significant challenges for educators; *deaf-blindness* is covered in Chapter 10.

CONSIDER THIS

Should students whose only disability is hearing or visual impairment be segregated in state residential schools, often many miles away from their families?

Basic Concepts About Hearing Impairment

Hearing impairment is a hidden disability—an observer typically cannot tell from looking at physical features alone that a person's hearing is impaired. However, in any context where communicative skills are needed, hearing limitations become evident.

FIGURE 9.1

Students of Ages 6 Through 21 Served Under IDEA and Chapter 1 in 1999–2000

Note: For comparative purposes, 2,756,000 students with learning disabilities and 603,400 students with mental retardation were served during the same period.

From *21st Annual Report to Congress on the Implementation of IDEA* (p. 11), by U.S. Department of Education, 2001, Washington, DC: Author.

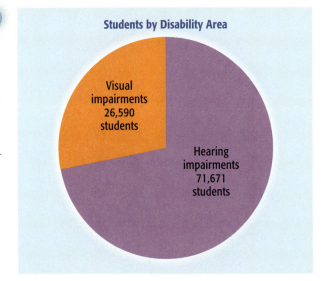

Students by Disability Area

Visual impairments 26,590 students

Hearing impairments 71,671 students

Students with a hearing disability pose a variety of challenges to the general classroom teacher. Although their numbers are increasing, relatively few students with profound hearing loss (deafness) are educated in general education settings (Brackett, 1997). When these students are placed in general education classes, they need major accommodations (e.g., an interpreter).

The number of students who have some degree of hearing loss (i.e., mild to severe) is more noteworthy, because these students can function in general education settings more easily when certain accommodations are provided. To achieve this purpose, it is critical for teachers to understand the nature of hearing impairments and to know how to address the needs associated with these conditions. In addition to these students, other students have minimal hearing loss. These students have hearing losses that are not severe enough to be eligible for special education services; however, they are at a distinct disadvantage in the general education classroom if the teacher does not recognize their problem (Kaderavek & Pakulski, 2002).

The importance of language acquisition and usage to the development of cognitive abilities and achievement in academic subject areas is unassailable (Polloway, Miller, & Smith, 2003). While the greatest effect of a hearing impairment is on a students' ability to hear someone speak, "its impact on communication development dramatically alters social and academic skill acquisition" (Brackett, 1997, p. 355). Language is a dominant consideration when discussing appropriate education for students with hearing losses (Mayer, Akamatsu, & Stewart, 2002).

The following sections provide basic information on hearing impairments. Teachers who build a solid working knowledge in this area can teach more effectively and communicate more clearly with other professionals and with families.

Hearing Impairment Defined

The fact that a number of different terms are associated with hearing loss often causes confusion. Three terms frequently encountered in print and in professional conversation are *hearing impairment, deafness,* and *hard of hearing.*

1. *Hearing impairment* is the generic term that has frequently been used to cover the entire range of hearing loss.
2. *Deafness* describes hearing loss that is so severe that speech cannot be understood through the ear alone, with or without aids.
3. *Hard of hearing* describes individuals who have a hearing loss that makes it difficult, but not impossible, to understand speech through the ear alone, with or without a hearing aid. (Moores, 2001)

Some school systems use other terminology, such as *auditorily impaired,* to describe persons with hearing loss.

Hearing loss is often measured in decibel (dB) loss. Individuals with losses from 25 to 90 dB are considered hard of hearing, whereas those with losses greater than 90 dB are classified as deaf.

Most schools use the definitions of hearing impairment found in IDEA. The federal definitions of deafness and hearing impairment are as follows:

> Deafness means a hearing impairment that is so severe that the child is impaired in processing linguistic information through hearing, with or without amplification, that adversely affects a child's educational performance. (300.7(c)(3), Final Regulations, IDEA, 1997)
>
> Hearing impairment means an impairment in hearing, whether permanent or fluctuating, that adversely affects a child's educational performance but that is not included under the definition of deafness in this section. (300.7(c)(7), Final Regulations, IDEA, 1997)

Minimal hearing loss, which is not included in the federal definition of hearing impairment but which can cause problems for students, is defined as a loss of between 16 and 25 decibels (Kaderavek & Pakulski, 2002).

CONSIDER THIS

Do some of the terms used in this chapter—for example, hearing impairment—convey a clear understanding of a particular hearing disability? Which terms in the text are the most descriptive and useful to teachers?

Classification of Hearing Impairment

CONSIDER THIS

Is it important for teachers to know the type of hearing loss experienced by a student? Why or why not?

Hearing loss can be categorized in several different ways. Diefendorf (1996) organized hearing loss into four different groups: conductive hearing loss (mild loss in both ears), unilateral hearing loss (loss only in one ear), mild bilateral sensorineural hearing loss (caused by sound not being transmitted to the brain), and moderate-to-severe bilateral sensorineural hearing loss (more severe loss in both ears). Table 9.1 summarizes the audiological, communicational, and educational implications for each type of loss. Each specific type and degree of loss poses challenges in learning and communicating.

TABLE 9.1 **Symptoms Associated with Conductive Hearing Loss; Unilateral Hearing Loss; Mild, Bilateral Sensorineural Hearing Loss; and Moderate-to-Severe Bilateral Sensorineural Hearing Loss**

	Audiological	Communicative	Educational
Conductive Hearing Loss	▶ Hearing loss 30 dB (range 10–50 dB) ▶ Poor auditory reception ▶ Degraded and inconsistent speech signal ▶ Difficulty understanding under adverse listening conditions ▶ Impaired speech discrimination ▶ Hearing loss overlays developmental requirement for greater stimulus intensity before infants can respond to and discriminate between speech ▶ Inability to organize auditory information consistently	▶ Difficulty forming linguistic categories (plurals, tense) ▶ Difficulty in differentiating word boundaries, phoneme boundaries ▶ Receptive language delay ▶ Expressive language delay ▶ Cognitive delay	▶ Lower achievement test scores ▶ Lower verbal IQ ▶ Poorer reading and spelling performance ▶ Higher frequency of enrollment in special support classes in school ▶ Lower measures of social maturity
Unilateral Hearing Loss	▶ Hearing loss moderate to profound ▶ Impaired auditory localization ▶ Difficulty understanding speech in presence of competing noise ▶ Loss of binaural advantage: binaural summation, binaural release from masking	▶ Tasks involving language concepts may be depressed	▶ Lags in academic achievement: reading, spelling, arithmetic ▶ Verbally based learning difficulties ▶ High rate of grade repetition ▶ Self-described: embarrassment, annoyance, confusion, helplessness ▶ Less independence in the classroom
Mild Bilateral Sensorineural Hearing Loss	▶ Hearing loss 15–20 dB ▶ Speech recognition depressed ▶ Auditory discrimination depressed ▶ Amplification considered: FM systems, classroom amplification	▶ Potential problems in articulation ▶ Problems in auditory attention ▶ Problems in auditory memory ▶ Problems in auditory comprehension ▶ Possible delays in expressive oral language ▶ Impact on syntax and semantics	▶ Impact on vocabulary development ▶ Lowered academic achievement: arithmetic problem solving, math concepts, vocabulary, reading comprehension ▶ Educational delays progress systematically with age
Moderate-to-Severe Bilateral Sensorineural Hearing Loss	▶ Hearing loss 41 dB–90 dB ▶ Noise and reverberation significantly affect listening and understanding ▶ Audiologic management: essentials, amplification recommendations, monitor hearing for: –otitis media –sudden changes in hearing –progressive hearing loss	▶ Deficits in speech perception ▶ Deficits in speech production (mild-to-moderate articulation problems) ▶ Language deficits from slight to significant: syntax, morphology, semantics, pragmatics ▶ Vocabulary deficits	▶ Slight to significant deficits in literacy (reading and writing) ▶ Deficits in academic achievement ▶ High rate of academic failure ▶ Immaturity ▶ Feelings of isolation and exclusion ▶ Special education supports needed

From "Hearing Loss and Its Effect" (p. 5), by A. O. Diefendorf, in *Hearing Care for Children,* edited by F. N. Martin and J. G. Clark, 1996, Boston: Allyn and Bacon. Used by permission.

Prevalence and Causes of Hearing Impairment

As noted in Figure 9.1, more than 71,000 students are served in special education programs for students with hearing impairments. This figure represents only about 0.11% of the total school population (U.S. Department of Education, 2001). While the number of children with hearing impairments significant enough to be eligible for special education is small, the Centers for Disease Control and Prevention (CDC) have estimated that as many as 15% of all children experience some degree of hearing loss (Crawford, 1998). This estimate includes those children with minimal hearing loss which does not result in eligibility for special services (Kaderavek & Pakulski, 2002).

Many different factors can lead to hearing impairments. These include genetic causes (Moores, 2001); developmental anomalies (Clark & Jaindl, 1996); toxic reaction to drugs, infections, prematurity, and Rh incompatibility (Moores, 2001); birth trauma (Chase, Hall, & Werkhaven, 1996); and allergies (Lang, 1998). Knowing the specific cause of a hearing impairment is usually not important for school personnel, since the cause rarely affects interventions needed by students.

Characteristics of Students with Hearing Impairment

The characteristics of students with hearing impairment vary greatly. Four categories of characteristics are especially meaningful to the classroom setting: (1) psychological, (2) communicational, (3) academic, and (4) social-emotional. Specific characteristics that fall into each of these general categories are listed in Table 9.2. (Table 9.1 listed characteristics associated with types and degrees of hearing losses.)

Identification, Assessment, and Eligibility

The ease of identifying students with hearing impairment is related to the degree of hearing loss. Students with severe losses are more easily recognized, while those with mild losses may go unrecognized for many years or even their entire school career (Kaderavek & Pakulski, 2002). In fact, the prevalence of hearing loss among children is higher than

T ABLE 9.2   **Possible Characteristics of Students with Hearing Impairments**

Area of Functioning	Possible Effects
Psychological	▶ Intellectual ability range similar to hearing peers ▶ Problems with certain conceptualizations
Communicational	▶ Poor speech production (e.g., unintelligibility) ▶ Tested vocabulary limited ▶ Problems with language usage and comprehension, particularly abstract topics ▶ Voice quality problems
Social–Emotional	▶ Less socially mature ▶ Difficulty making friends ▶ Withdrawn behavior—feelings of being an outsider ▶ Possible maladjustment problems ▶ May resent having to wear a hearing aid or use other amplification devices ▶ May be dependent on teacher assistance
Academic	▶ Achievement levels significantly below those of their hearing peers ▶ Reading ability most significantly affected ▶ Spelling problems ▶ Limited written language production ▶ Discrepancy between capabilities and performance in many academic areas

cited in previous reports because of delayed identification, which often results in serious consequences for children. As noted previously, data indicate that as many as 15% of children in the United States have low- or high-frequency hearing loss that is often too mild to allow easy identification (Herer & Reilly, 1999). Teachers should be aware of certain indicators of possible hearing loss and refer students who show these signs for a comprehensive assessment (Stewart & Kluwin, 2001). Teachers should consider referring a student for an evaluation if some of the following behaviors are present (Kaderavek & Pakulski, 2002; Moores, 2001; Stewart & Kluwin, 2001):

▶ Turns head to position an ear in the direction of the speaker
▶ Asks for information to be repeated frequently
▶ Uses a loud voice when speaking
▶ Pulls or presses on ear
▶ Does not respond when spoken to
▶ Gives incorrect answers to questions
▶ Has frequent colds, earaches, or infections
▶ Appears inattentive and daydreams
▶ Has difficulty following directions
▶ Is distracted easily by visual or auditory stimuli
▶ Misarticulates certain speech sounds or omits certain consonant sounds
▶ Withdraws from classroom activities that involve listening
▶ Has a confused expression on face
▶ Has a restricted vocabulary
▶ Figdets or moves about in seat

A teacher's careful observations and referral can spare a student months or years of struggle and frustration. While all students referred will not be found to have a significant hearing loss, they should be referred so that an assessment can be made to determine which students need additional supports.

Formal Assessment   The assessment of hearing ability requires the use of various audiological techniques. The most common method of evaluating hearing is the use of **pure-tone audiometry,** in which sounds of different frequencies are presented at increasing levels of intensity. Bone conduction hearing (related to the outer and middle ear) can also be assessed to determine if there are problems in the sensorineural portion of the hearing mechanism (occurring in the inner ear). The role of pediatric audiology has grown significantly in the past years. With new technology, audiologists are going to be more involved in assessment (Herer & Reilly, 1999).

Informal Assessment   In addition to the formal assessment conducted by audiologists, teachers and other school personnel should engage in informal assessment of students, especially those suspected of having a hearing impairment. Informal assessment focuses on observing students for signs that might indicate a hearing loss. Tables 9.1 and 9.2 list indicators that, if recorded over a period of time, show that a student may need formal assessment.

Eligibility   The eligibility of students for special education and related services is determined by individual state departments of education. Most states follow the federal guidelines for eligibility and add certain levels of decibel loss as criteria. The federal criteria are included in the definitions cited previously. In order to be eligible under the category of hearing impairment, the students must meet the definitions and must need special education.

Teachers should not be concerned about specific eligibility criteria, but should refer students who display characteristics suggesting the presence of a hearing loss. The evaluation/eligibility committee will be responsible for making the decisions.

*T*EACHING TIP

Teachers should keep records of students who display these types of behaviors to determine whether there is a pattern that might call for a referral.

Strategies for Curriculum and Instruction for Students with Hearing Impairments

Students with hearing impairment may present a significant challenge for general education teachers. Language is such an important component of instruction that students who have problems processing language because of hearing losses make it difficult for teachers to use standard instructional methods effectively. Teachers have to rely on the supports provided by special education staff and specialists in hearing impairments to assist them in meeting the needs of these students.

Realities of the General Education Classroom

Students with hearing impairments vary greatly in their need for supports in the general education classroom. Students with mild losses, generally classified as hard of hearing, need minimal supports. In fact, these students resemble their nondisabled peers in most ways. If amplification assistance can enable these students to hear clearly, they will need little specialized instruction (Dagenais, Critz-Crosby, Fletcher, & McCutcheon, 1994).

Students with severe hearing impairments, those classified as deaf, present unique challenges to teachers. Specialized instructional techniques usually involve alternative communication methods; the use of interpreters is typically a necessity for these students. General education teachers must know how to utilize the services of an interpreter to facilitate the success of students with significant hearing losses.

Continuum of Placement Options   Students with hearing impairments are educated in the complete continuum of placement options, depending on their individual needs. These options range from general education classrooms to residential schools for the deaf. The topic of educational placement for students with hearing impairments has been the most controversial aspect of educating this group of students (Edwards, 1996). As with all students with disabilities, there is no single educational setting that is best for all students with hearing impairments. The placement decision for students with hearing impairments should be based on the unique needs of the student and the IEP process (Edwards, 1996).

Still, the trend continues toward educating more students with hearing impairments in the general education classroom. During the 1998–1999 school year, almost 60% of all students with hearing impairments were educated in general education classrooms for at least 40% of the school day (U.S. Department of Education, 2001). This figure compares with approximately 44% served in the same types of settings during the 1986–1987 school year (U.S. Department of Education, 1989). During the 1998–1999 school year, fewer than 10% of these students were educated in residential settings, the most likely placement prior to the passage of Public Law 94–142 (U.S. Department of Education, 2001). The trend, therefore, favors inclusion, which in turn signals a need for supports and services to help students succeed. Figure 9.2 on page 264 describes the types of supports that students with hearing impairments will need in inclusive settings. They resemble those needed by students with other disabilities, except for a few services specific to students with hearing problems.

Classroom Adaptations for Students with Hearing Impairments

As mentioned before, the general education setting is appropriate for most students who are hard of hearing and for many students who are deaf. However, this statement is true only if the specific needs of these students are taken into consideration.

CONSIDER THIS

How do educational needs differ for these two students: one with a mild hearing loss who can effectively use a hearing aid and one who is not disabled?

CONSIDER THIS

What are some obvious advantages and disadvantages of various placement options for students with hearing impairments?

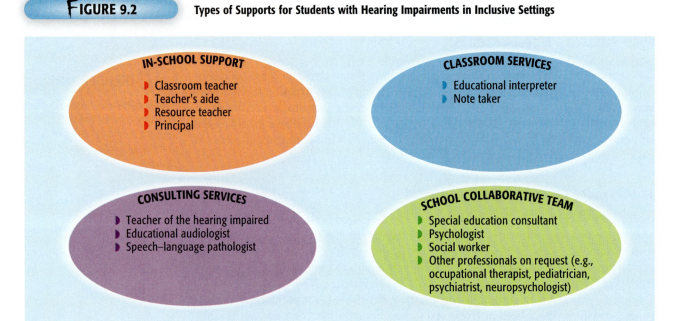

FIGURE 9.2   **Types of Supports for Students with Hearing Impairments in Inclusive Settings**

From "Educational Management of Children with Hearing Loss" (p. 306) by C. Edwards, in *Hearing Care for Children,* edited by
F. N. Martin and J. G. Clark, 1996, Boston: Allyn and Bacon. Used by permission.

The following sections provide recommendations for accommodating these students in general education classrooms. Specific suggestions are also given. Both general recommendations and specific suggestions are clustered under four major areas: management considerations, curricular and instructional accommodations, social-emotional interventions, and technology.

Management Considerations

The effective management of a classroom is critical to maximizing the potential for learning. This important topic is covered in detail in Chapter 14. Attention to classroom management can help include students with various degrees of hearing impairment in general education settings.

CROSS-REFERENCE

Preview the section in Chapter 14 on rules and procedures appropriate for all students with disabilities and for students without disabilities.

Standard Operating Procedures   The dimension of standard operating procedures refers to the rules, regulations, and procedures that operate in a classroom. Students who have hearing impairments must be subject to the same requirements as other students. Some procedures may have to be modified to accommodate special needs. For instance, students may be allowed to leave their seats to get the attention of a student who cannot hear a spoken communication.

Teachers should always confirm that students understand the rules and procedures developed for the classroom. Teachers may also want to establish a buddy system (i.e., a peer support system). With such a system, a student with normal hearing is assigned to assist the student with a hearing impairment in, for example, following procedures for a fire drill or helping the student take notes during a class lecture.

Physical Considerations   Seating is the major consideration related to the physical setup of the classroom. Teachers need to ensure that students are seated to maximize the use of their residual hearing or to have an unobstructed view of an interpreter. Since information presented visually is extremely helpful to these students, they need to be positioned to take advantage of all visual cues (Berry, 1995). Following are some specific suggestions Luckner & Denzin, 1998):

▶ Seat student in the best place to facilitate attending and participating.
▶ Seat students in a semicircular arrangement to increase sight lines for students and teacher.
▶ Position teacher so that student can read lips.
▶ Position teacher so that he or she faces students when talking.

In addition, make sure that you seat students who use interpreters so that they can easily see the interpreter, the teacher, and any visuals that are used. Unfortunately, seating a student with a hearing loss near the front of the class is rarely the only modification that needs to be made. In contrast to teaching methods of the past, today very little may happen at the front of the room (Crawford, 1998).

Creating a Favorable Environment for Students   As noted in the preceding section, more than preferential seating is necessary for students with a hearing loss. Attention must be given to creating a supportive acoustical environment throughout the classroom. Modifications that can be made to provide an accommodating acoustical environment include the following (Scott, 1997):

▶ Acoustical ceiling tiles
▶ Carpeting
▶ Thick curtains
▶ Rubber tips on chair and table legs
▶ Proper maintenance of ventilation systems, lighting, doors, and windows

Preinstructional Considerations   Teachers must also carefully plan ahead to deliver instruction in a way that will benefit students with hearing impairments. The following list gives many practical suggestions:

▶ Allow students to move about the classroom to position themselves for participation in ongoing events.
▶ Let students use swivel chairs.
▶ Reduce distracting and competing noise by modifying the classroom environment (e.g., carpeting on floor, corkboard on walls).
▶ Ensure that adequate lighting is available.
▶ Provide visual reminders indicating the amount of time left for an activity or until the end of class.
▶ Use cooperative learning arrangements to facilitate student involvement with hearing peers.
▶ Include a section of the lesson plan for special provisions for students with hearing impairments.
▶ Acquire or develop visually oriented materials to augment orally presented topics— use overhead projection systems when appropriate.
▶ Use homework assignment books and make sure that students understand their assignments.

Specific suggestions related to grouping, lesson planning, materials acquisition and adaptation, and homework systems can be found in Chapter 14.

Curricular and Instructional Considerations

All basic elements of effective instructional practice will benefit students with hearing impairment. However, certain specific ideas will enhance their learning experiences.

Communication   Perhaps the most challenging aspect of teaching students whose hearing is impaired is making sure that (1) they participate in communicational activities (i.e., teacher to student, student to teacher, student to student) in the classroom and (2) they are

CONSIDER THIS

How can teachers use seating as an effective accommodation even when there is a great deal going on in different parts of the room?

able to handle the reading and writing demands of the class. Language and communication tend to dominate the teaching of these students (Mayer et al., 2002). Students who have profound hearing loss must rely on alternative methods of communication such as sign language or speech reading. Because these students typically do not become facile with standard forms of English, they can have significant problems in the areas of reading and writing. Sign language does not follow the grammatical conventions of English.

When students using some form of manual communication, usually **American Sign Language (ASL),** are in general education classrooms, teachers are not required to learn this language. However, teachers should make an effort to know some of the more common signs and to be able to finger-spell the letters of the alphabet as well as the numbers one to ten. If students can communicate only by using sign language, an interpreter will most likely need to be present. Teachers should know basic information about the role and functions of an interpreter.

Still another form of communication that may be effective is **cued speech** (Stewart & Kluwin, 2001). Cued speech is a system of hand cues that enhances lipreading. Eight different hand shapes represent consonant sounds and four hand positions represent vowel sounds. Using the hand signs near the lips provides students with cues that help with their lipreading (Blasi & Priestley, 1998).

Teachers should be conscious of how well they are communicating with their students. The teacher's speech, location, and movement in the classroom can affect the facility with which a student with a hearing impairment can follow a discussion or lecture. The proper use of assistive equipment (e.g., amplification devices) can also make a difference. This topic is covered in a subsequent section.

Delivery of Instruction   Teachers need to utilize a host of practices that allow students to learn more effectively and efficiently. One suggestion already mentioned, the use of visually oriented material, is especially valuable for students with hearing problems. The following are additional suggestions:

▶ Make sure students are attending.
▶ Provide short, clear instructions.
▶ Speak clearly and normally—do not exaggerate the pronunciation of words.
▶ Keep your face visible to students.
▶ Avoid frequent movement around the classroom, turning your back on students while talking, and standing in front of a bright light source.
▶ Use gestures and facial expressions.
▶ If the student reads speech, make sure that your mustache and beard are trimmed to maximize visibility.
▶ Maintain eye contact with the student, not the interpreter.
▶ Check with students to confirm that they understand what is being discussed or presented.
▶ Encourage students to request clarification and to ask questions.
▶ Identify other speakers by name so that students can more easily follow a discussion among more than one speaker.
▶ Repeat the comments of other students who speak.
▶ Paraphrase or summarize discussions at the end of a class session.
▶ Write information when necessary.
▶ Have students take responsibility for making themselves understood.
▶ Provide students with advance organizers such as outlines of lectures and copies of overhead transparencies.
▶ Preview new vocabulary and concepts prior to their presentation during a lecture.
▶ Use the demonstration-guided practice-independent practice paradigm as often as possible (see Polloway & Patton, 1993, for more information).
▶ Utilize a variety of instructional formats, including demonstrations, experiments, and other visually oriented activities.

▶ Emphasize the main points covered in a lecture both verbally and visually.

▶ Use lots of visual aids (e.g., overhead transparencies, slides, diagrams, charts, multi-media) to explain material.

▶ Provide summaries, outlines, or scripts of videotapes, videodiscs, or films.

▶ Let students use microcomputers for word processing and for checking their spelling and grammar.

Teaching secondary-level content classes to students with hearing impairments is uniquely challenging. The nearby Inclusion Strategies feature provides suggestions for teaching science to students who are deaf. Also, see the nearby Tips for Adapting a Lesson for Monique.

Co-teaching has been shown to be one effective method for teaching students with hearing losses in general education classes. This model encourages general classroom teachers and teachers of students with hearing losses to combine their skills in an inclusive setting. "Coteaching allows teachers to respond to the diverse needs of all students, provides another set of hands and eyes, lowers the teacher-student ratio, and expands the amount of professional expertise that can be directed to student needs" (Luckner, 1999, p. 150).

Social-Emotional Considerations

Classrooms constitute complex social systems. In addition to development of scholastic abilities and academic support skills, personal development is also occurring. Students need to learn how to get along with their peers and authority figures while they learn how to deal with their beliefs and emotions. While the available research suggests that students with hearing impairments develop similarly, socially and emotionally, to their hearing peers (Moores, 2001), teachers still need to be able to help students develop a realistic sense of their abilities, become more responsible and independent, interact appropriately

Teaching Science to Deaf Students

The following are several suggestions on how to give better individual attention in teaching science to deaf students:

1. Individualize assignments so that students progress at their own rate and, at the end of the period, hand in what they have accomplished. This may be a laboratory or written assignment.

2. Extend special recognition to a student who goes beyond minimum acceptance level for doing and formulating laboratory investigation.

3. Use multiple resources, including texts, in class. If a slow student has difficulty reading one text, endeavor to find another or attempt to help him or her learn the material in ways other than through books.

4. Offer special activities for the academically talented. Let them assist you in preparing solutions and materials for laboratory work. They should be involved in experiences that are educationally desirable and not just prepared for a future working at a menial job.

5. Encourage students to do research. They should consult with a scientist or engineer in the community on their research problem. Local industries, museums, zoos, botanical gardens, and hospitals have resource people who will often help.

6. Have students from the upper grades go to some of the lower grades and demonstrate a scientific principle or explain a science project. This approach has the advantage of giving recogni-

tion to the younger students and motivating them to greater achievement.

7. Encourage parents to obtain books and to take trips advantageous to science students. Parents often welcome a suggestion from the teacher about books and type of trips to help enrich their children's science education.

For follow-up questions about teaching science to deaf students, go to Chapter 9 of the Companion Website (ablongman.com/sppd4e) and click Inclusion Strategies.

Tips for Adapting a Lesson for Monique

The following are some ways to infuse concepts related to deaf studies and self-advocacy throughout the social studies curriculum for Monique.

Monique's teacher should

▶ examine laws that have impacted the lives of deaf and hard of hearing people (e.g., Americans with Disabilities Act, Vocational Rehabilitation Act of 1973).

▶ examine the concept of "access" as it applies to deaf and hard of hearing people as well as to people with other disabilities.

▶ debate society's obligation to ensure that all citizens have access to basic services and information.

▶ compare the principles associated with access to those associated with the civil rights movements of African Americans.

▶ discuss the dynamics of social change as it pertains to deaf and hard of hearing people and the responsibilities that students have to ensure progress in improving the lives of deaf and hard of hearing people.

Adapted from Teaching deaf and hard of hearing students: Content, strategies, and curriculum (p. 67) by D. A. Steward & T. N. Kluwin, 2001, Needham Heights, MA: Allyn & Bacon. Used with permission.

with their peers, and enhance their self-concept and sense of belonging (Luckner, 1994). The following are some specific suggestions:

▶ Create a positive, supportive, and nurturing classroom environment.

▶ Encourage class involvement through active participation in classroom activities and interaction in small groups.

▶ Let students know that you are available if they are experiencing problems and need to talk.

▶ Help the students with normal hearing understand the nature of hearing impairment and what they can do to assist.

▶ Practice appropriate interactive skills.

▶ Encourage and assist students to get involved in extracurricular activities.

▶ Help them develop problem-solving abilities.

▶ Help students develop realistic expectations.

▶ Prepare students for dealing with the demands of life and adulthood.

Technology

Technology has been a boon for individuals with hearing impairments (Stewart & Kluwin, 2001). Students with hearing impairments placed in general education classrooms often use devices to help them to maximize their communicational abilities (Easterbrooks, 1999), and they need a supportive environment in which to use these devices (McAnally, Rose, & Quigley, 1999). Teachers need a working knowledge of these devices so that they can ensure that the student benefits from the equipment.

Assistive Listening Devices   *Assistive listening devices (ALDs)* include hearing aids and other devices that amplify voices and sounds, communicate messages visually, or alert users to environmental sounds (Marschark, Lang, & Albertini, 2002).

Children with even small losses, those in the 16 to 25 dB range, may have problems hearing faint or distant speech without some amplification (Iskowitz, 1998). Hearing aids are the predominant ALDs found in schools. These devices pick up sound with a microphone, amplify and filter it, and then convey that sound into the ear canal through a loud-

TEACHING TIP

When students in your classroom use assistive listening devices, learn as much about the devices as possible so that you will be able to maximize their use.

TABLE 9.3   **Media, Materials, and Technology for Students with Hearing Losses**

Visual Technology, Media, and Materials	▶ Microcomputers and computer systems such as ENFI ▶ Captioning systems ▶ Computer-assisted notetaking ▶ Videotapes and interactive video discs ▶ Instructional CDs and software ▶ Telecommunication technology ▶ Printed materials, programs, and packages
Auditory Technology, Media, and Materials	▶ Induction loops ▶ FM systems ▶ Programmable hearing aids ▶ Soundfield amplification systems ▶ Cochlear implants ▶ Instructional CDs, interactive listening developmental program, and software ▶ Audiocassette programs ▶ Computer-based speech training systems

From Bruce, Peyton, & Batson (1993); Kaplan, Mahshie, Moseley, Singer, & Winston (1993).

speaker, also called a receiver (Marschark et al., 2002). They work very well with students who experience mild-to-severe hearing losses (Iskowitz, 1997).

To assist students in maximizing the use of their ALDs, teachers should

▶ know what type of ALD a student uses.
▶ understand how the device works: on/off switch, battery function (e.g., selection, life span, insertion), volume controls.
▶ be able to determine whether a hearing aid is working properly.
▶ help students keep their hearing aids functioning properly (e.g., daily cleaning, appropriate storage).
▶ make sure students avoid getting their hearing aids wet, dropping or jarring them, spraying hairspray on them, and exposing them to extreme heat (Shimon, 1992).
▶ keep spare batteries on hand.
▶ ensure that the system is functioning properly.
▶ be sure that students turn the transmitter off when not engaged in instructional activities to prevent battery loss.
▶ perform daily troubleshooting of all components of the system (Brackett, 1990).
▶ make sure background noises are minimized.

Table 9.3 includes a list of media, materials, and technology available for students with hearing losses. This information should provide teachers with a beginning understanding of how to meet the needs of students with hearing loss. We strongly recommend that teachers consult with a hearing specialist to determine the best possible accommodations to provide an appropriate educational environment for students with hearing problems.

Promoting Inclusive Practices for Students with Hearing Impairments

Being an integral part of the inclusive school community is important for students with hearing impairments who receive their educational programs in public schools, especially for those placed in general education classrooms. Simply physically situating students in

Diversity Forum

Creating a Community of Sharing: Monica's Story

My name is Monica; I am a Mexican-American, deaf high school student. My goal is to go to college and major in deaf education, but my parents are worried about letting me move so far away from home. On the other hand, my teachers say that I need to become independent and take care of myself so that I can live on my own and go to college. I'm really excited about learning more about deaf culture and going to college, but I know I will miss my family, and I don't want them to feel left out of my life. It seems like I'm always juggling the different expectations of the important people in my life—my parents, my teachers, my deaf culture, and the hearing world.

Many hearing people I know think of my deafness as a hearing loss, and they don't even realize that deaf people share a culture of their own. American Sign Language, or ASL, is the primary method of communication for many deaf people, but it's also important to realize that there are many other sign systems available. Being Mexican-American, deaf, and a student in public school, I have learned Spanish, ASL, English, and other sign systems. For me, the use of an interpreter has been especially helpful in bridging cultures because Mary, my interpreter, signs ASL *and* speaks Spanish. Mary meets with my teachers before a lesson to get an outline, handouts, and key vocabu-

lary and concepts that will be taught so that she can figure out how best to interpret for me. For example, Mary explains new terminology/concepts to me in Spanish and ASL. Seating is arranged so that Mary is next to me and I have a clear view of all the speakers in the classroom. We also get short breaks at least every hour to give us both a rest (Christensen & Delgado, 1993; National Association for the Deaf, 2002).

For follow-up questions about deafness and culture, go to Chapter 9 of the Companion Website (ablongman.com/sppd4e) and click Diversity Forum.

CONSIDER THIS

Do you think that students with hearing impairments can be accepted in the classroom by their peers in spite of their differing language skills? Should students with hearing impairments be isolated in institutions with other students who have hearing losses? Why or why not?

classrooms does not automatically make them included members of the class. This statement especially holds true for children with hearing impairments who have a very difficult time associating with the "hearing" culture (Andrews & Jordan, 1998). Therefore, teachers must ensure that these students become part of the community of the school and class and are socially accepted by their peers.

Teachers may have to orchestrate opportunities for interaction between students with hearing impairments and their nondisabled peers. These could include grouping, pairing students for specific tasks, assigning buddies, and establishing a circle of friends. Kluwin (1996) suggests using dialogue journals to facilitate this interaction. Students are paired (one hearing and one nonhearing) to make journal entries and then exchange them. Rather than assign deadlines, allow students to exchange journal entries whenever they want to. You may need to give them ideas appropriate for sharing to get them started. Reward students for making and exchanging journal entries. This approach encourages interactions between students with hearing impairments and their nondisabled peers without using a rigidly structured activity or assignment.

Supports for the General Education Teacher

Students with hearing impairments often create major challenges for general classroom teachers, primarily because of the language barrier that hearing loss often creates. Therefore, teachers must rely on support personnel such as educational consultants who specialize in the area of hearing impairment, as well as interpreters, audiologists, and medical personnel, to assist them in their efforts to provide appropriate educational programs.

Basic Concepts About Visual Impairments

Students with visual impairments also pose unique challenges to teachers in general education classrooms. Although the number of students whose vision creates learning-related problems is not large (see Figure 9.1), having one such student in a classroom may require a host of accommodations.

Vision plays a critical role in the development of concepts, the understanding of spatial relations, and the use of printed material. Thus children with visual problems have unique educational needs. "Learning the necessary compensatory skills and adaptive techniques—such as using Braille or *optical devices* for written communication—requires specialized instruction from teachers and parents who have expertise in addressing disability-specific needs" (Corn, Hatlen, Huebner, Ryan, & Siller, 1995, p. 1). See Technology Today for examples of optical devices and technology available for students with visual impairments. Teachers may be able to use their usual instructional techniques with some modifications with students who have some functional vision. But for students who have very little or no vision, teachers will need to implement alternative techniques to provide effective educational programs.

General education classes are appropriate settings for many students with visual impairments. However, teachers working with these students need to understand the nature of a particular student's vision problem to be able to choose appropriate accommodative tactics. They need basic information related to four categories: (1) fundamental concepts of vision and visual impairment, (2) signs of possible visual problems, (3) typical characteristics of students with visual problems, and (4) specific accommodative techniques for meeting student needs.

Visual Impairments Defined

Because a number of different terms are associated with the concept of visual impairment, confusion regarding the exact meaning of visual terminology is often a problem. These are the most frequently used terms and their definitions:

▶ *Visual impairment* is a generic term that includes a wide range of visual problems.
▶ *Blindness* has different meanings depending upon context, resulting in some confusion. *Legal blindness* refers to a person's visual acuity and field of vision. It is defined as a visual acuity of 20/200 or less in the person's better eye after correction, or a field of vision of 20 degrees or less. An educational definition of *blindness* implies that a student must use Braille (a system of raised dots that the student reads tactilely) or aural methods in order to receive instruction (Heward, 2000).
▶ *Low vision* indicates that some functional vision exists to be used for gaining information through written means with or without the assistance of optical, nonoptical, or electronic devices (Kirk, Gallagher, & Anastasiow, 2000).

Students with low vision are capable of handling the demands of most classroom settings. However, they will need some modifications to perform successfully. Students who are blind (i.e., have very little or no vision) will need major accommodations to be successful in general education settings.

Classification of Visual Impairments

Visual problems can be categorized in a number of ways. One typical method organizes visual problems as refractive errors (e.g., farsightedness, nearsightedness, and astigmatism); retinal disorders; disorders of the cornea, iris, and lens; and optic nerve problems. In addition to common refractive problems, which usually can be improved with corrective lenses, other visual problems include the following:

▶ *Strabismus*—improper alignment of the eyes
▶ *Nystagmus*—rapid involuntary movements of the eye
▶ *Glaucoma*—fluid pressure buildup in the eye
▶ *Cataract*—cloudy film over the lens of the eye
▶ *Diabetic retinopathy*—changes in the blood vessels of the eye caused by diabetes

TEACHING TIP

Try using an idea from a children's game to work with children with visual impairments. Just as you would ask a blindfolded child what information he or she needs to make progress in the game, ask the children with visual impairments what assistance or information they need in order to benefit from your teaching.

CONSIDER THIS

Some students who are classified as blind are actually able to read print and do not need to use Braille. Are there descriptors other than "blind" and "low vision" that would better describe students with visual impairments for educational purposes?

Assistive Technology for Visual Impairments

The following equipment is available at the MSU Resource Center for Persons with Disabilities (RCPD) Assistive Technology Center.

AI Squared, ZoomText Xtra Level 2

This software-based screen magnifier enlarges all text and graphics on the Windows display. It also features contrast and color enhancements that make it easy for the visually impaired user to locate key items such as pointers and highlight bars. Although this is primarily a screen magnifier, the product can also deliver some spoken output, reducing eye fatigue during prolonged reading.

Alva Access Group, OutSpoken for Macintosh

This screen reader for the Macintosh represents the only commercially available solution for blindness access to the Macintosh. It uses the built-in speech system of the Macintosh to read important elements of the screen as the user navigates around the display.

Alva Access Group, InLarge for Macintosh

This software-based screen magnifier enlarges all text and graphics on the Macintosh screen. It also features contrast and color enhancements that make it easy

for the visually impaired user to locate key items such as pointers and highlight bars.

Arkenstone, An Open Book

This customized Optical Character Recognition system enables students with visual impairments or learning disabilities to read typewritten materials without human intervention. The system uses a computer and scanner to take a digital picture of a printed page. The software then converts the digital picture into the equivalent of typewritten text. The text is then either displayed on the computer screen in enhanced print, displayed in Braille on a refreshable Braille display, or read aloud via a speech synthesizer.

Artic Technologies, TransType

This portable electronic note-taking device is designed specifically for blind individuals requiring a mobile method for taking, storing, and retrieving notes. The device is no larger than a notebook-computer-style keyboard. Since it has no display, the device is light, rugged, and quite portable. The built-in speech synthesizer allows the user to easily review the contents of many different files stored in the unit's memory. The note taker includes several applications including alarms, stopwatch, terminal

program, and a talking five-function calculator. When connected to a computer via a serial connection, the device can serve as a speech synthesizer on nearly any computer. The TransType also connects easily to a printer for hard copy production.

Blazie Engineering, Braille n' Speak/Type n' Speak

This family of portable electronic note takers allow blind students to independently take written notes in class or on the go. As the note takers use a built-in speech synthesizer to review created files, no display is required or included. In addition to being highly portable note takers, these units also contain a number of built-in options including a talking scientific calculator. The Braille n' Speak (BNS) requires the user to enter all information via its seven-key Braille keyboard, while the Type n' Speak (TNS) has a QWERTY style keyboard. Both units can be connected to either a Braille embosser or ink printer for hard-copy printouts.

Duxbury Systems, Duxbury Braille Translator

This Braille translation software allows the user to transform a common word processor file from ASCII characters to Grade II Braille. Once translated, the file can be sent to one of several Braille embossers on campus.

Enabling Technologies, Juliet Braille Embosser

This device is the Braille equivalent to an ink printer. It allows the computer to

▶ *Macular degeneration*—damage to the central portion of the retina, causing central vision loss

▶ *Retinitis pigmentosa*—genetic eye disease leading to total blindness (Smith & Luckasson, 1998)

Tunnel vision denotes a condition caused by deterioration of parts of the retina, which leaves the person with central vision only. Individuals who have tunnel vision can see as if they are looking through a long tube; they have little or no peripheral vision.

Regardless of the cause of the visual problem, educators primarily have to deal with its functional result. Whether or not the student has usable residual vision is an important issue, as is the time at which the vision problem developed. Students who are born with significant visual loss have a much more difficult time understanding some concepts and developing basic skills than students who lose their vision after they have established certain concepts (Warren, 1994).

produce the Braille system of characters on heavy card-stock paper. Unlike many Braille embossers, the Juliet is capable of embossing on both sides of a page, thus dramatically reducing paper use and the bulk of documents printed on a single-sided embosser. This device must be used in conjunction with a Braille translator such as the Duxbury Braille Translator to produce properly formatted Grade II Braille.

Franklin Electronic Publishing, Language Master

These handheld devices allow students to quickly search for definitions and spellings of difficult or troublesome words. The systems also allow the user to locate synonyms and antonyms for particular words. Finally, the units include a speech synthesizer allowing them to read definitions and spellings aloud.

Henter-Joyce, JAWS for Windows (JFW)

This powerful screen-reading package affords speech output and Braille access to the newest operating systems (Windows 95, Windows 98, Windows NT, and Windows 2000). Its high configurability makes it a good choice for the most demanding screen reading tasks. With JFW, blind or visually impaired computer users can independently use most Windows-based software including e-mail, web browsers, word processing, spreadsheets, and databases. The software uses a standard sound card to produce a clear synthesized voice in any of several languages. For users who prefer Braille output over speech, JFW supports full access to the computer via a

refreshable Braille display such as the Braille Window.

HumanWare, Braille Window

This 45-cell refreshable Braille display allows blind and deaf-blind users to access a variety of Windows-based software through tactile Braille output. The display is used in conjunction with a PC and either a screen-reading software package like JAWS for Windows or other Braille ready software such as An Open Book. The display supports both the common six-dot Braille or eight-dot computer Braille.

HumanWare, Keynote Companion

This palm-top-sized note taker is equipped with both speech synthesis and a small LCD display. The intuitive word processor software allows the user to create a variety of documents that can be easily modified, stored, and reviewed with speech. The device easily connects to a printer for a hard-copy printout of important information. The device also features a talking scientific calculator and a telecommunications program.

Kurzweil Educational Systems, Kurzweil 1000

This powerful Optical Character Recognition software allows the computer to scan printed materials and render them in a spoken and large-print output. The system features voice recognition allowing control over scanning and reading operations by voice in addition to traditional keyboard control. Finally, the built-in definitions dictionary provides full definitions and synonyms for hundreds of thousands of words.

Optalec, SVGA Closed-Circuit Television (CCTV)

This device assists students with visual impairments or learning disabilities by allowing them to enlarge and embolden the contents of printed materials. As with a traditional CCTV, the user places the printed material on an X-Y table. The image is then captured by a video camera, allowing the user to adjust magnification level, focus, brightness, contrast, and coloration. This unit differs from a traditional CCTV in that it shares a single display/monitor with an existing PC. The user can thus (with the press of a button or foot pedal) select a full-screen view of the computer, CCTV, or a split screen containing both. This system allows the user to easily read printed materials while working simultaneously with a computer.

Telesensory, Versapoint Braille Embosser

This Braille embosser allows a PC running a Braille translation software package to emboss Braille on heavy tractor-fed paper. A Braille embosser is the Braille equivalent of an ink printer.

 For follow-up questions about assistive technology for students with visual impairments, go to Chapter 9 of the Companion Website (ablongman.com/sppd4e) and click Technology Today.

Adapted from Assistive Technology Center, MSU Resource Center for Persons with Disabilities (RCPD), East Lansing, MI 48824-1033. Used with permission

Prevalence and Causes of Visual Impairments

Vision problems are common in American society. Fortunately, corrective lenses allow most individuals to see very efficiently. However, many individuals have vision problems that cannot be corrected in this way. As with hearing impairments, the number of individuals who have visual impairments increases with age. In the school-age population, approximately 0.04% of students are classified as visually impaired. During the 1999–2000 school year, 26,590 students, ages 6–21, were classified as having visual impairments in the United States (U.S. Department of Education, 2001).

Etiological factors associated with visual impairments include genetic causes, physical trauma, infections, premature birth, anoxia, and retinal degeneration. *Retrolental fibroplasia (RLF)* was a common cause of blindness in the early 1950s, resulting when premature infants were exposed to too much oxygen in incubators. Once the cause of this problem was understood, it became nearly nonexistent. However, this cause of blindness

CONSIDER THIS

How does the low incidence of visual impairments affect a school's ability to provide appropriate services? How can small systems meet the needs of these children when there may be only one child with a visual impairment in a district?

is reasserting itself as medical science faces the challenge of providing care to infants born more and more prematurely. Blindness sometimes accompanies very premature birth.

Characteristics of Students with Visual Impairments

The most educationally relevant characteristic of students who have visual impairments is the extent of their visual efficiency. More specific characteristics can be categorized as psychological, communicational, academic, and social-emotional. These characteristics are listed in Table 9.4.

Identification, Assessment, and Eligibility

Students with visual impairments can be easily identified if their visual loss is severe. However, many students have milder losses that are much more difficult to identify and may go several years without being recognized. Teachers must be aware of behaviors that could indicate a vision problem. Table 9.5 summarizes possible symptoms of vision problems.

Formal Assessment   Students are screened for vision problems in schools, and when problems are suspected, a more in-depth evaluation is conducted. The typical eye examination assesses two dimensions: visual acuity and field of vision. Visual acuity is most often evaluated by the use of a **Snellen chart.** As Smith (2001) notes, two versions of this chart are available: the traditional version using alphabetic letters of different sizes, and the other version using the letter *E* presented in different spatial arrangements and sizes. Regardless of the assessment used, the person conducting it should have expertise in the area of visual impairment (Corn et al., 1995).

Once students are identified as having possible vision problems, they should be referred for more extensive evaluations. Ophthalmologists, medical doctors, and optometrists (who specialize in evaluating vision and prescribing glasses) are typically involved in this more extensive evaluation. These specialists determine the specific nature and extent of any vision problem.

TEACHING TIP

For students who are not doing well academically and who display symptoms of visual impairment, conduct a functional visual screening to determine whether the child should be referred for more formal screening.

TABLE 9.4   **Possible Characteristics of Students with Visual Impairments**

Area of Functioning	Possible Effects
Psychological	▶ Intellectual abilities similar to those of sighted peers ▶ Concept development can depend on tactile experiences (i.e., synthetic and analytic touch) ▶ Unable to use sight to assist in the development of integrated concepts ▶ Unable to use visual imagery
Communicational	▶ Relatively unimpaired in language abilities
Social/Emotional/ Behavioral	▶ May display repetitive, stereotyped movements (e.g., rocking or rubbing eyes) ▶ Socially immature ▶ Withdrawn ▶ Dependent ▶ Unable to use nonverbal cues
Mobility	▶ Distinct disadvantage in using spatial information ▶ Visual imagery and memory problems with functional implications
Academic	▶ Generally behind sighted peers

T ABLE 9.5   **Symptoms of Possible Vision Problems**

Behavior	▶ Rubs eyes excessively
	▶ Shuts or covers one eye, tilts head, or thrusts head forward
	▶ Has difficulty in reading or in other work requiring close use of the eyes
	▶ Blinks more than usual or is irritable when doing close work
	▶ Holds books close to eyes
	▶ Is unable to see distant things clearly
	▶ Squints eyelids together or frowns
Appearance	▶ Crossed eyes
	▶ Red-rimmed, encrusted, or swollen eyelids
	▶ Inflamed or watery eyes
	▶ Recurring styes
Complaints	▶ Eyes that itch, burn, or feel scratchy
	▶ Cannot see well
	▶ Dizziness, headaches, or nausea following close eye work
	▶ Blurred or double vision

From *Exceptional Learners: Introduction to Special Education* (7th ed., p. 358) by D. P. Hallahan and J. M. Kauffman, 1997, Boston: Allyn & Bacon. Used by permission.

Informal Assessment   A great deal of informal assessment should be completed by school personnel. Like that of students with hearing impairments, the informal assessment of students with visual impairments focuses on observation. Teachers and other school personnel note behaviors that might indicate a vision loss or change in the vision of the child. Once students are identified as having a problem, school personnel must be alert to any changes in the student's visual abilities.

Eligibility   Most states adhere to the eligibility guidelines established in IDEA for students with visual impairments. These guidelines focus on the visual acuity of students. Students with a 20/200 acuity or worse, in the better eye with best correction, are eligible as blind students, whereas those with a visual acuity of 20/70 to 20/200 are eligible as low-vision students. Like all other students with disabilities served under IDEA, these students must evidence need of special education services in order to be eligible for them.

Strategies for Curriculum and Instruction for Students with Visual Impairments

Students with visual impairments need specific curricular and instructional modifications. For students with low vision, these modifications may simply mean enlarging printed materials to sufficient size so that the student can see them. For students with little or no vision, modifications must be more extensive.

Realities of the General Education Classroom

Students with visual impairments present a range of needs. Those who are capable of reading print, with modifications, often require minimal curricular changes; those who must read using Braille require significant changes. Teachers should remember that even

IEP Goals and Objectives for Monique

Goals and objectives for Monique, whom you met in the introductory vignette, might include the following (Luckner, 2002):

Goal 1:   *To take and successfully pass college preparatory courses.*
  Objective 1:   *Given a college preparatory textbook, Monique will identify the textbook features and text structures with 90% accuracy.*
  Objective 2:   *Given a chapter to read, Monique will use summarization strategies when asked, 100% of the time.*
  Objective 3:   *Given an assignment to study for tests and quizzes, Monique will identify and use appropriate study strategies 90% of the time.*
  Objective 4:   *Given tests, Monique will be successful (minimum 70% accuracy) 80% of the time.*

Goal 2:   *To increase her ability to advocate for herself.*
  Objective 1:   *Given the opportunity to explain her need for accommodations, Monique will be able to explain her specific needs with 100% accuracy, 100% of the time.*
  Objective 2:   *Given difficult situations in a classroom, Monique will be able to ask appropriate questions to seek assistance 90% of the time.*
  Objective 3:   *Given her presence at her IEP meeting, Monique will be able to successfully facilitate the meeting 100% of the time.*

students who are capable of reading print may need modifications in many day-to-day activities. These may be as simple as ensuring appropriate contrast in printed materials and having students sit in a place that will optimize their vision.

Continuum of Placement Options

CONSIDER THIS

What are some typical reasons teachers might give for not wanting children with visual impairments in their general classrooms? Can these reasons be overcome or not?

Like students with hearing impairments, students with visual problems may be placed anywhere on the full continuum of placement options, ranging from general education classrooms to residential schools for students with visual impairments. *The National Agenda for the Education of Children and Youth with Visual Impairments, Including Those with Multiple Disabilities* calls for all schools to offer programs that will give all students a full array of placement options (Corn et al., 1995). Students must be evaluated individually to determine the appropriate educational placement. Although some totally blind students function very well in general education settings, many are placed in residential schools where they receive more extensive services.

The trend for placement of students with visual impairment is in the direction of inclusive settings. During the 1998–1999 school year, more than 85% of all students with visual impairments were served in general education classrooms at least 40% of each school day. Almost 50% were in general classrooms more than 80% of the school day. During this same year, fewer than 10% were educated in residential schools (U.S. Department of Education, 2001).

Classroom Adaptations for Students with Visual Impairments

Certain classroom accommodations will enhance the quality of programs for students with visual problems. This section recommends ways to address the needs of these students, organized according to five categories: general considerations, management considerations, curricular and instructional accommodations, social-emotional interventions, and technology.

General Considerations

When educating students with visual impairments, the unique needs of each student must be considered (Desrochers, 1999). However, some general practices apply for most, if not all, students with these problems. These practices include the following:

▶ Ask the student if assistance is needed.
▶ Do not assume that certain tasks and activities cannot be accomplished without accommodations or modifications.
▶ Include students with visual impairments in all activities that occur in the class.
▶ Use seating arrangements to take advantage of any vision the child can use.
▶ Encourage the use of residual vision.

Remember that many characteristics of students with visual impairment (e.g., intelligence, health) may not be negatively affected by the vision problem.

Management Considerations

A variety of classroom management tactics can be helpful to students who have vision problems. Classroom management is discussed in detail in Chapter 14. When students with vision problems are present, attention needs to be given to standard operating procedures, physical considerations, and preinstructional considerations.

Standard Operating Procedures   The same standards of expected behavior should be applied to all students, including those who have visual problems. However, students with visual limitations may need special freedom to move around the classroom, to find the place where they can best see demonstrations or participate in activities.

Physical Considerations   Students with visual problems need to know the physical layout of the classroom so that they can navigate through it without harming themselves. Teachers have to orient these students to the classroom by taking them around the classroom and noting certain features, such as the location of desks, tables, and materials. A clock orientation approach is useful—for example, the front of the class is 12 o'clock, at

Classmates can assist students with visual problems in areas such as mobility.

3 o'clock is the teacher's desk, at 6 o'clock is the reading table, and at 9 o'clock is the area for students' coats and backpacks. Appropriate seating is extremely important for students who are able to use their existing vision. Placement of the student's desk, lighting, glare, and distractions should be considered when situating such students in the classroom.

Preinstructional Considerations   Teachers should plan ahead to adapt instruction to the needs of students with visual impairments. Class schedules must allow extra time for students who use large-print or Braille materials, as it takes longer to use these materials.

Test-taking procedures may need to be modified. Modifications might involve preparing an enlarged version of the test, allowing extra time, or arranging for someone to read the test to the student.

Some students may need special instruction in study skills such as note taking, organizational skills, time management, and keyboarding. These become increasingly important as students move to middle school and high school. The following are some specific accommodation suggestions:

TEACHING TIP

Have vision specialists, such as an orientation and mobility specialist, visit your class to demonstrate sighted guide techniques that provide support for students with visual impairments.

▶ Assign a classmate to assist students who may need help with mobility in emergency situations.
▶ Teach all students in the class the proper techniques of being a sighted guide.
▶ In advance, inform staff members at field-trip sites that a student with a visual problem will be part of the visiting group.
▶ Tell students with visual problems that you are entering or leaving a room so that they are aware of your presence or absence.
▶ Have all students practice movement patterns that you expect of them, to maintain an orderly classroom.
▶ Orient students to the physical layout and other distinguishing features of the classroom.
▶ Maintain consistency in the placement of furniture, equipment, and instructional materials—remove all dangerous obstacles.
▶ Keep doors to cabinets, carts, and closets closed.
▶ Assist students in getting into unfamiliar desks, chairs, or other furniture.
▶ Eliminate auditory distractions.
▶ Seat students to maximize their usable vision and listening skills—often a position in the front and center part of the room is advantageous.
▶ Seat students so that they are not looking into a source of light or bothered by glare from reflected surfaces.
▶ Ensure that proper lighting is available.
▶ Create extra space for students who must use and store a piece of equipment (e.g., Brailler, notebook computer).
▶ As a special section of the lesson plan, include notes for accommodating students with visual problems.

Curricular and Instructional Considerations

Teacher-Related Activities   As the principal agents in delivering instruction, teachers should use techniques that will ensure success for students who have visual problems. A special challenge involves conveying primarily visual material to those who cannot see well. For example, it will require some creativity on the part of the teacher to make a graphic depiction of the circulatory system in a life science book (a two-dimensional illustration) accessible to a student who can see little or not at all. Three-dimensional models or illustrations with raised features might address this need. Teachers have to decide what should be emphasized in the curriculum when students with visual impairments are in their classes. As a result of the wide array of curricular options for these student, teachers must "(a) address the multifaceted educational requisites of their students, (b) ensure that instruction occurs in all areas of greatest need and (c) ensure that sufficient instructional time is allocated for identified educational priorities" (Lueck, 1999, p. 54).

Materials and Equipment   Special materials and equipment can enhance the education of students who have visual impairments. Some materials (e.g., large-print materials) are not appropriate for all and must be considered in light of individual needs. Vision specialists can help teachers select appropriate materials and equipment.

Many materials found in general education classrooms may pose difficulties for students with vision problems. For instance, the *size* and *contrast* of print materials have a real effect on students with visual problems. Print size can generally be taken care of with magnification devices; however, little can be done to enhance the poor contrast often found on photocopies. Consider these points when using photocopies:

▶ Avoid using both sides of the paper (ink often bleeds through, making it difficult to see either side).
▶ Avoid old or light work sheet masters.
▶ Avoid work sheet masters with missing parts or creases.
▶ Give the darkest copies of handouts to students with visual problems.
▶ Do not give a student with a visual impairment a poor copy and say, "Do the best you can with this."
▶ Copy over lines that are light with a dark marker.
▶ Make new originals when photocopies become difficult to read.
▶ Avoid the use of colored inks that may produce limited contrast.
▶ Do not use colored paper—it limits contrast.

Although large-print materials seem like a good idea, they may be used inappropriately. Barraga and Erin (1992) recommend that these materials be used only as a last resort, since they may not be readily available. They believe that large-print materials should be utilized only after other techniques (e.g., optical devices or reduction of the reading distance) have been tried.

Teachers also may want to use concrete materials (i.e., realistic representations of actual items). However, concrete representations of large real-life objects may not be helpful for young students, who may not understand the abstract notion of one thing representing another. Teachers must carefully ensure that all instructional materials for students with visual impairments are presented in the appropriate medium for the particular student (Corn et al., 1995).

Various optical, nonoptical, and electronic devices are also available for classroom use. These devices help students by enlarging existing printed images. If these devices are recommended for certain students, teachers will need to learn about them to ensure that they are used properly and to recognize when there is a problem. Teachers should practice the use of optical and electronic devices with students after consultation with a vision specialist.

Some students with more severe visual limitations may use Braille as the primary means of working with written material. They may use instructional materials that are printed in Braille and may also take notes using it. Through the use of computers, a student can write in Braille and have the text converted to standard print. The reverse process is available as well. If a student uses this system of communication, the teacher should consult with a vision specialist to understand how it works.

Following are some specific accommodation suggestions:

▶ Call students by name, and speak directly to them.
▶ Take breaks at regular intervals to minimize fatigue in listening or using a Brailler or optical device.

TEACHING TIP

Make sure that students with visual impairments have ample storage areas near their desks for materials such as large-print or Braille books and other equipment.

TEACHING TIP

Have a student who uses a Braille writer demonstrate the Braille code and methods of writing Braille to members of the class so they can understand the learning medium used by their classmate.

◗ Ensure that students are seated properly so that they can see you (if they have vision) and hear you clearly.

◗ Vary the type of instruction used, and include lessons that incorporate hands-on activities, cooperative learning, or the use of real-life materials.

◗ Use high-contrast materials, whether on paper or on the chalkboard—dry-erase boards may be preferable.

◗ Avoid using materials with glossy surfaces and, if possible, dittoed material.

◗ Use large-print materials only after other methods have been attempted and proved unsuccessful.

◗ Use environmental connectors (e.g., ropes or railing) and other adaptations for students with visual problems for physical education or recreational activities (Barraga & Erin, 1992).

◗ Avoid using written materials with pages that are too crowded.

Social-Emotional Considerations

Although the literature is mixed on whether students with visual impairments are less well adjusted than their sighted peers (Hallahan & Kauffman, 2000), there is evidence that some students with this disability experience social isolation (Huurre, Komulainen, & Aro, 1999). As a result, many students with visual problems will benefit from attention to their social and emotional development. Social skill instruction may be particularly useful (Sacks, Wolffe, & Tierney, 1998). However, because social skills are typically learned through observing others and imitating their behaviors, it is difficult to teach these skills to students who are not able to see.

Concern about emotional development is warranted for all students, including those with visual problems. Teachers should make sure that students know that they are available to talk about a student's concerns. A system can be developed whereby a student who has a visual impairment can signal the need to chat with the teacher. Being accessible and letting students know that someone is concerned about their social and emotional needs are extremely important.

The following are some specific accommodation suggestions:

◗ Encourage students with visual problems to become independent learners and to manage their own behaviors.

◗ Create opportunities for students to manipulate their own environment (Mangold & Roessing, 1982).

◗ Reinforce students for their efforts.

◗ Help students develop a healthy self-concept.

◗ Provide special instruction to help students acquire social skills needed to perform appropriately in classroom and social situations.

◗ Teach students how to communicate nonverbally (e.g., use of hands, etc.).

◗ Work with students to eliminate inappropriate mannerisms that some students with visual impairments display.

Technology

Like students with hearing impairments, those with visual problems often use technological devices to assist them in their academic work and daily living skills. Low-vision aids include magnifiers, closed-circuit televisions, and *monoculars.* These devices enlarge print and other materials for individuals with visual impairments.

Many other technological devices are used by students with visual impairments. Refer back to Technology Today for samples of some of these technological devices.

While access to the Internet is relatively easy for students without visual problems, many students with visual impairments may have difficulty. Certain technological devices can make access to the Internet available. Braille printers and speech input/output devices can help achieve access. Access and computer training can give students with visual impairments a vast resource that can have a profound positive impact on their education (Heinrich, 1999).

Promoting Inclusive Practices for Students with Visual Impairments

Students with visual impairments, like those with hearing impairments, need to be part of the school community. Many can be included without special supports. However, for others, teachers may need to consider the following (Amerson, 1999; Desrochers, 1999; Torres & Corn, 1990):

1. Remember that the student with a visual impairment is but one of many students in the classroom with individual needs and characteristics.
2. Use words such as *see, look,* and *watch* naturally.
3. Introduce students with visual impairments the same way you would introduce any other student.
4. Include students with visual impairments in all classroom activities, including physical education, home economics, and so on.
5. Encourage students with visual problems to seek leadership and high-visibility roles in the classroom.
6. Use the same disciplinary procedures for all students.
7. Encourage students with visual problems to move about the room just like other students.
8. Use verbal cues as often as necessary to cue the student with a visual impairment about something that is happening.
9. Provide additional space for students with visual impairments to store materials.
10. Allow students with visual impairments to learn about and discuss with other classmates special topics related to visual loss.
11. Model acceptance of visually impaired students as an example to other students.
12. Encourage students with visual impairments to use their specialized equipment, such as a Braille writer.
13. Discuss special needs of the child with a visual impairment with specialists, as necessary.
14. Always tell a person with a visual impairment who you are as you approach.
15. Help students avoid inappropriate mannerisms associated with visual impairments.
16. Expect the same level of work from students with visual impairments as you do from other students.
17. Encourage students with visual impairments to be as independent as possible.
18. Treat children with visual impairments as you treat other students in the classroom.
19. Provide physical supports for students with concomitant motor problems.
20. Include students with visual impairments in outdoor activities and team sports.

In your efforts to promote a sense of community, consider that some students with visual impairments may have different cultural backgrounds than the majority of students in the school. School personnel must be sensitive to different cultural patterns. Bau (1999) noted seven different cultural values that could have an impact on the provision of services to students with visual impairments. These include communication, health beliefs, family structure, attitude toward authority, etiquette, expectations of helping, and time

Teachers should be sensitive to the cultural values of families of students with visual impairments.

orientation. To communicate clearly with a family that speaks a different language, you may need to use a language interpreter. Being sensitive to the culture and family background of students with visual impairments facilitates the delivery of appropriate services.

Supports for the General Education Teacher

CONSIDER THIS

Students with visual impairments may not be able to monitor visual cues from peers regarding social behaviors. How can you teach students with visual impairments to understand these visual cues?

As noted earlier, general education teachers can effectively instruct most students with visual impairments, with appropriate supports. A vision specialist may need to work with students on specific skills, such as Braille; an orientation and mobility instructor can teach students how to travel independently; an adaptive physical education instructor can help modify physical activities for the student with visual impairment (see nearby Personal Spotlight).

Counselors, school health personnel, and vocational specialists may also provide support services for general education teachers. School personnel should never forget to include parents in helping develop and implement educational supports for students with visual impairments. In a recent study, McConnell (1999) found that a model program that included family involvement and support greatly assisted adolescents with visual impairments to develop career choices and values. Other ways to enhance the education of students with visual impairments are the following:

▶ Get help from others. Teach other students to assist in social as well as academic settings. Call parents and ask questions when you don't understand terminology, equipment, or reasons for prescribed practices.
▶ Learn how to adapt and modify materials and instruction.
▶ Learn as much as you can, and encourage the professionals you work with to do the same. Find out about training that may be available and ask to go.
▶ Suggest that others become informed, especially students. Use your local library and bookstores to find print material that you can read and share. (Viadero, 1989)

Personal Spotlight

Itinerant Service Specialist

Bonnie Lawrence is currently an orientation and mobility specialist working with children with visual impairments who live in their communities and receive educational services in local public schools. She is classified as an itinerant service provider. Her current caseload of 35 students includes children who are classified as totally blind as well as other students who have varying degrees of vision loss. Bonnie's primary responsibility is to train students in developing independent travel skills by using a long cane and in using technological aids, such as a monocular. She works with children in all grades, kindergarten through high school. Although most of her time is spent with children in school settings, she also works with them in the community to help them develop independent travel skills outside the school setting. Bonnie says that she likes many different things about her job, but the thing she likes best is that the students she works with live with their families and go to school with their nondisabled peers rather than receiving educational services in a residential school program. She likes the independence associated with her job and the fact that she can make a real difference with

Bonnie Lawrence
Orientation and Mobility Specialist

Arkansas Education Services for the Visually Impaired

the students she serves. "It is so gratifying to be able to see students with visual problems be able to go from one point to another without having to depend on someone else to help them. They truly become more independent in all aspects of their life as a result of being able to travel independently."

Bonnie doesn't dislike anything about her job. The only negative aspect is the amount of time she has to spend traveling from one student to another. She works with children who live in a large geographical area and often has to drive several hours to work with only one student. But despite this inconvenience, she knows that itinerant services are the only effective method of serving students with visual impairments in rural areas in their home and school settings. In Bonnie's words, "I can't imagine doing anything else; I love what I do."

For follow-up questions about this Personal Spotlight, go to Chapter 9 of the Companion Website (ablongman.com/sppd4e) and click Personal Spotlight.

Summary

Basic Concepts About Hearing Impairment
- Many students with sensory deficits are educated in general education classrooms.
- For students with sensory impairments to receive an appropriate education, various accommodations must be made.
- Students with hearing and visual problems represent a very heterogeneous group.
- Most students with hearing problems have some residual hearing ability.
- The term hearing impairment includes individuals with deafness and those who are hard of hearing.

Strategies for Curriculum and Instruction for Students with Hearing Impairments
- The effect of a hearing loss on a student's ability to understand speech is a primary concern of teachers.
- An audiometric evaluation helps to determine the extent of a hearing disorder.

- Several factors should alert teachers to a possible hearing loss in a particular student.

Classroom Adaptations for Students with Hearing Impairments
- Teachers in general education classrooms must implement a variety of accommodations for students with hearing impairments.
- The seating location of a student with hearing loss is critical for effective instruction.
- Specialized equipment, such as hearing aids, may be necessary to ensure the success of students with hearing losses.

Promoting Inclusive Practices for Students with Hearing Impairments
- The most challenging aspect of teaching students with hearing problems is making sure that they participate in the communicational activities that occur in the classroom.

▶ Teachers need to encourage interaction between students with hearing impairments and their nondisabled classmates (e.g., grouping, assigning buddies).

Basic Concepts About Visual Impairment

▶ Vision plays a critical role in the development of concepts such as understanding the spatial relations of the environment.

▶ Teachers must use a variety of accommodations for students with visual disabilities.

▶ Most students with visual disabilities have residual or low vision.

▶ Refractive errors are the most common form of visual disability.

▶ Visual problems may be congenital or occur later in life.

Strategies for Curriculum and Instruction for Students with Visual Impairments

▶ The most educationally relevant characteristic of students who have visual impairments is the extent of their visual efficiency.

▶ Special materials may be needed when working with students with visual problems.

▶ Using large-print and nonglare materials may be sufficient accommodation for many students with visual disabilities.

▶ Provide ample storage space for students' materials.

▶ Allow students additional time, as Braille and large-print reading are slower than regular-print reading.

Classroom Adaptations for Students with Visual Impairments

▶ A very small number of students require instruction in Braille.

▶ Specialists to teach Braille and develop Braille materials may be needed in order to successfully place students with visual disabilities in general education classrooms.

▶ Academic tests may need to be adapted when evaluating students with visual disabilities.

▶ Allow students to hold materials as close as necessary.

▶ Facilitate all technology needed by students.

Promoting Inclusive Practices for Students with Visual Impairments

▶ It is critical that students with visual impairments be socially accepted in their general education classrooms.

▶ Orchestrate social opportunities for students.

▶ Encourage students with visual impairments to demonstrate any specialized equipment they may use.

Further Readings

American Foundation for the Blind. (1998). *AFB directory of services for blind and visually impaired persons in the United States and Canada* (27th ed.). New York: Author.

Beukelman, D. R., & Mirenda, P. (1998). *Augmentative and alternative communication* (2nd ed.). Baltimore: Brookes.

Caton, H. (Ed.). (1997). *Tools for selecting appropriate learning media.* Louisville, KY: American Printing House for the Blind.

Corn, A. L., & Koening, A. J. (Eds.). *Foundations of low vision: Clinical and functional perspectives.* New York: American Foundation for the Blind.

Jahoda, G. (1993). *How can I do this if I can't see what I'm doing?* Washington, DC: National Library Service for the Blind and Physically Handicapped.

Kluwin, T. N., Moores, D. F., & Gaustad, M. G. (Eds.). (1998). *Toward effective public school programs for deaf students: Context, process, and outcomes.* New York: Teachers College Press.

Koenig, A. J., & Holbrook, M. C. (1995). *Learning media assessment of students with visual impairments: A resource guide for teachers* (2nd ed.). Austin, TX: Pro-Ed.

Lucas, C. (Ed.). (1990). *Sign language research.* Washington, DC: Gallaudet University Press.

Martin, D. S. (1991). *Advances in cognition, education, and deafness.* Washington, DC: Gallaudet University Press.

Moores, D. (2001). *Educating the deaf: Psychology, principles, and practices* (5th ed.). Columbus, OH: Merrill.

Paul, P. V. (1998). *Literacy and deafness: The development of reading, writing, and literate thought.* Boston: Allyn and Bacon.

Sacks, S. Z., & Silberman, R. K. (1998). *Educating students who have visual impairments with other disabilities.* Baltimore: Brookes.

Smith, A., & Cote, K. S. (1983). *Look at me: A resource manual for the development of residual vision in multiple impaired children.* Philadelphia: College of Optometry Press.

Articles in *American Annals of the Deaf*

Articles in *Journal of Visual Impairment and Blindness*

Articles in *RE:view*

VideoWorkshop Extra!

If the VideoWorkshop package was included with your text-book, go to Chapter 9 of the Companion Website (www.ablongman.com/sppd4e) and click on the VideoWorkshop button. Follow the instructions for viewing video clips 8 and 9. Then consider this information along with what you've read in Chapter 9 while answering the following questions.

1. Students with visual impairments may miss the visual cues that are essential in social and classroom situations, such as when Kyle was facing the wrong way on stage. How will you provide the support required to ensure that students like Kyle are active members of your class?

2. The aide in the video mentioned that teachers were good about providing visuals to help the student. How will you do this in your classroom? What other adaptations are important for students with hearing impairments, especially if they do not have an interpreter?

10 Teaching Students with Autism, Traumatic Brain Injury, and Other Low-Incidence Disabilities

After reading this chapter, you should be able to

1. define and describe students with autism and Asperger syndrome.
2. define and describe students with traumatic brain injury.
3. define and describe students with health problems and physical disabilities.
4. describe various intervention strategies for students with autism, traumatic brain injury, health problems, and physical disabilities.

Charlie's parents noted something different about their child when he was about 2 years old. Up until that time he had developed perfectly. He walked at 13 months, started babbling at about 15 months, and loved to play with adults and other children. Then things began to change. His babbling stopped, he developed sort of a blank stare, his early success at toilet training seemed to be reversed, and he stopped paying any attention to other children and adults. When he was about 3 years old, his parents took him to the state children's hospital, and the diagnosis was autism. What a shock! Charlie was placed in a preschool program and has been in special education services ever since. Now at the age of 7 he is enjoying being in a regular second grade classroom. In his kindergarten and first grade he was placed in a self-contained special education classroom. During these two years Charlie seemed to regress. He actually started picking up some of the other children's stereotypical, self-stimulating behaviors. His parents convinced the school to give Charlie a try in the regular second grade, with some special education support. Now, in December, Charlie seems to be doing very well. While he has very little oral language, he seems to enjoy being with his nondisabled peers and is able to do most of the academic work with the assistance of a paraprofessional.

QUESTIONS TO CONSIDER

1. Is there a preferred placement for children with autism?
2. What kinds of supports should be available for Charlie to facilitate his success in the regular classroom?
3. Is a child ever *ready* for inclusion, or does the school have to make the placement decision and provide the necessary supports to make it work?

The previous chapter focused on students with sensory impairments, typically considered low-incidence disabilities because they do not occur in many children. In addition to these two categories of disabilities, many other conditions that occur relatively rarely in children can result in significant challenges for these students, their families, school personnel, and other professionals. These conditions include autism, traumatic brain injury (TBI), and a host of physical and health problems that may be present in school-age children, such as cerebral palsy, spina bifida, AIDS, cystic fibrosis, epilepsy, and diabetes.

CONSIDER THIS

What are some problems that may be encountered by general classroom teachers with which specialists could provide assistance?

Many general education classroom teachers will teach their entire careers without encountering children with these problems. However, as a result of IDEA and the inclusion of students with a wide range of disabilities in general education classrooms at least part of the school day, teachers need to generally understand the conditions and how to support these students in the classroom.

This chapter will provide substantial information on autism and traumatic brain injury, two disability categories recognized in the Individuals with Disabilities Education Act (IDEA). Other conditions, primarily subsumed under the *other health impaired* and *orthopedically impaired* categories in IDEA, will be presented more briefly. IDEA defines other health impaired as "having limited strength, vitality or alertness, due to chronic or acute health problems such as a heart condition, tuberculosis, rheumatic fever, nephritis, asthma, sickle cell anemia, hemophilia, epilepsy, lead poisoning, leukemia, or diabetes that adversely affects a child's educational performance" [300.7(b)(8)].

Orthopedic impairment is defined in IDEA as "a severe orthopedic impairment that adversely affects a child's educational performance. The term includes impairments caused by congenital anomaly (e.g., clubfoot, absence of some member, etc.), impairments caused by disease (e.g., poliomyelitis, bone tuberculosis, etc.), and impairments from other causes (e.g., cerebral palsy, amputations, and fractures or burns, that cause contractures)" [300.7(b)(7)].

Often, schools and state education agencies provide support personnel for teachers and students with these types of problems. Therefore, teachers should not have to "go it alone" when working with students with these disabilities. Behavioral specialists, psychologists, physical therapists, occupational therapists, nurses, and other health personnel are often available to provide services to students and supports to their teachers (Wadsworth & Knight, 1999). The fact that many different professionals are involved in providing services for some of these children may have repercussions for students of certain cultural backgrounds. Individuals from some cultures, for example, prefer to interact with only one person at a time, rather than a team of individuals.

Describing every aspect of autism, TBI, and other low-incidence disabilities is not possible here. However, this chapter discusses the more common, and in some cases, unique, aspects of these conditions. Figure 10.1 shows the number of children in each group served in special education programs.

Basic Concepts About Autism

Autism is a pervasive developmental disorder that primarily affects social interactions, language, and behavior. Although autism has been glamorized by several movies, such as *Rain Man* (1988), many students with this condition do not have the incredible abilities reflected in the movie. Also, even for students with extraordinary skills, the presence of autism still has a significant impact on individuals and their families. The characteristics displayed by individuals with autism vary significantly; some individuals are able to assimilate into community settings and activities, whereas others have major difficulties achieving such normality (Scheuermann & Webber, 2002). Needless to say, "children

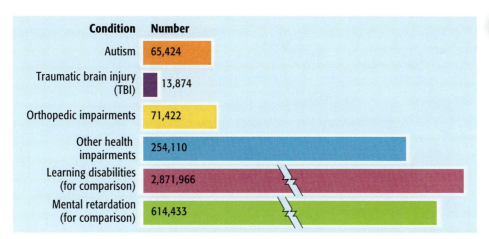

FIGURE 10.1

Number of Students, Ages 6–21, with Autism, TBI, and Health and Physical Disabilities Served in Public Schools During the 1999–2000 School Year

From 23rd *Annual Report to Congress on the Implementation of the Individuals with Disabilities Education Act* (p. 11), U.S. Department of Education, 2002, Washington, DC: Author.

and youth with autism spectrum disorders are a particularly unique group, even when compared with other children with disabilities" (Simpson, 2001, p. 68).

The study of autism has had a confusing and controversial history since the condition was first described less than 50 years ago by Dr. Leo Kanner (Scheuermann & Webber, 2002). Some of the early controversy centered on attempts to relate the cause of autism to poor mother-child bonding. Eventually this hypothesis was disproved, but it caused a great deal of guilt, confusion, and misunderstanding. Many professionals once thought that children with autism made a conscious decision to withdraw from their environment because of its hostile nature. During the 1980s, autism was found to be an organic disorder, eliminating much of this speculation (Eaves, 1992).

Autism was not a separate category under IDEA until 1990 (Kaplan, 1996). Prior to this change in the original law, children with autism were eligible for special education services only as *other health impaired.* Parents and other advocates for children with autism convinced Congress that children with this disability deserved their own category.

Defining Autism

Although many definitions of autism have been developed, no single definition has been universally accepted. However, it is important to be familiar with two definitions: the one in IDEA, primarily used by educators, and the one found in the *Diagnostic and Statistical Manual of Mental Disorders,* fourth edition (DSM-IV), used by psychologists and medical professionals. IDEA defines autism as "a developmental disability that primarily results in significant deficits in verbal and non-verbal communication and social interactions, generally evidenced before the age of 3 years and adversely affects the child's educational performance" [34 CFR §300.7(b)(1)]. Figure 10.2 provides the DSM-IV definition and diagnostic criteria.

The IDEA and DSM-IV definitions are the most widely used; however, there are other definitions popular among some groups. The Autism Society of America, the primary parent advocacy group associated with autism, defines autism using the following definition (Autism Society of America, 2000):

Autism is a complex developmental disability that typically appears during the first three years of life. The result of a neurological disorder that affects the functioning of the brain, autism and its associated behaviors have been estimated to occur in as many as 1 in 500 individuals. Autism is four times more prevalent in boys than girls and knows no racial, ethnic, or social boundaries. Family income, life-style, and educational levels do not affect the chance of autism's occurrence.

Autism interferes with the normal development of the brain in the areas of social interaction and communication skills. Children and adults with autism typically have difficulties in verbal and non-verbal communication, social interactions, and leisure or

CONSIDER THIS

How can movies that depict persons with disabilities help, as well as hurt, the cause of providing appropriate educational opportunities to students with disabilities?

FIGURE 10.2

Definition of Autism Using DSM-IV

From *Diagnostic and Statistical Manual of Mental Disorders* (4th ed., p. 32), American Psychiatric Association, 1994, Washington, DC: Author. Used by permission.

A. A total of six (or more) items from (1), (2), and (3), with at least two from (1), and one each from (2) and (3):
   (1) qualitative impairment in social interaction, as manifested by at least two of the following:
      (a) marked impairment in the use of multiple nonverbal behaviors such as eye-to-eye gaze, facial expression, body postures, and gestures to regulate social interaction
      (b) failure to develop peer relationships appropriate to developmental level
      (c) a lack of spontaneous seeking to share enjoyment, interests, or achievements with other people (e.g., by a lack of showing, bringing, or pointing out objects of interest)
      (d) lack of social or emotional reciprocity
   (2) qualitative impairments in communication as manifested by at least one of the following:
      (a) delay in, or total lack of, the development of spoken language (not accompanied by an attempt to compensate through alternative modes of communication such as gesture or mime)
      (b) in individuals with adequate speech, marked impairment in the ability to initiate or sustain a conversation with others
      (c) stereotyped and repetitive use of language or idiosyncratic language
      (d) lack of varied, spontaneous make-believe play or social imitative play appropriate to developmental level
   (3) restricted repetitive and stereotyped patterns of behavior, interests, and activities, as manifested by at least one of the following:
      (a) encompassing preoccupation with one or more stereotyped and restricted patterns of interest that is abnormal either in intensity or focus
      (b) apparently inflexible adherence to specific, nonfunctional routines or rituals
      (c) stereotyped and repetitive motor mannerisms (e.g., hand or finger flapping or twisting, or complex whole-body movements)
      (d) persistent preoccupation with parts of objects

B. Delays or abnormal functioning in at least one of the following areas, with onset prior to age 3 years: (1) social interaction, (2) language as used in social communication, or (3) symbolic or imaginative play.

C. The disturbance is not better accounted for by Rett's Disorder or Childhood Disintegrative Disorder (two pervasive developmental disorders characterized by impairment in the development of reciprocal social interaction).

play activities. The disorder makes it hard for them to communicate with others and relate to the outside world. They may exhibit repeated body movements (hand flapping, rocking), unusual responses to people or attachments to objects, and they may resist changes in routines. (p. 3)

Identification of Children with Autism

Just as autism is hard to define, children with autism are difficult to identify. Problems related to the identification of these children include the following:

▶ Children with autism display many characteristics exhibited by individuals with other disabilities, such as speech and language disorders.
▶ Many children with autism, because they exhibit disorders across multiple domains, are mistakenly classified as having multiple disabilities.
▶ No stable classification system is used among educators and other professionals who encounter children with autism. (Eaves, 1992)

Still another problem in identifying children with autism is the large, diverse group of professionals involved in the evaluation and diagnosis. In diagnosing some disabilities, educators function as the lead professionals; in the area of autism, pediatricians, speech-language pathologists, psychologists, audiologists, and social workers are typically involved as well (Powers, 1989). Working with such a large group of individuals can cause difficult logistical problems. Diverse definitions and eligibility criteria, different funding agencies, and varying services complicate the process of identifying and serving these children and adults. The nearby Rights & Responsibilities feature summarizes some of the legal decisions concerning the rights of students with autism.

Prevalence and Causes of Autism

There is no single specific cause of autism, but a variety of factors can result in this disability. Organic factors such as brain damage, genetic links, and complications during pregnancy may cause this condition, though in most cases no cause can be confirmed (Kaplan, 1996). Some children have a higher risk for autism than others. For example, children who are born with rubella and those classified as having fragile X syndrome are more likely to develop autism than other children (Blackman, 1990). In general, however, autism strikes randomly in all segments of society.

Autism is a relatively rare condition, although the number of children identified over the past few years has increased dramatically (Zirkel, 2002). The incidence of autism varies directly with the definition used. More restricted definitions result in approximately 0.7 to 2.3 individuals per 10,000 being identified, while less restrictive definitions may result in the identification of as many as 7 to 14 per 10,000 (Koegel et al., 1995; Locke, Banken, & Mahone, 1994). The Autism Society of America estimates as many as one in 500 may have autism (2002).

Regardless of the definition used, however, autism represents a very low-incidence disability. During the 1999–2000 school year, 65,424 children were classified as having autism

Rights & Responsibilities

Court Decisions Related to Interventions and Treatment Programs for Students with Autism

Delaware County IU#25 v. Martin K. (1993)   When programs are new or considered pilot programs, programs with documented benefits (e.g., the program developed by Lovaas) will be considered more effective.

Mark Hartmann v. Loudoun County Board of Education (1997)   A student's IEP should reflect individual needs; an IEP that strictly focuses on a singular emphasis, such as social skills training, will likely be considered inappropriate.

Cordrey v. Euckert (1990)   Benefit alone is insufficient to justify extended school year services. Parents may be required to show that regression will occur without extended services.

Johnson v. Independent School District No. 4 of Bixby (1990)   In addition to regression/recoupment, other factors that must be included when determining the need for an extended school year for students with autism are the degree of impairment, the ability of the child to interact with others, the child's rate of progress, and professional opinion predicting the student's progress toward goals.

Byron Union School District 35, IDELR 49 (SEA CA 2001)   A district hearing officer ruled that an 11-year-old student with autism did not require placement in a special day class to receive a free appropriate public education. Evidence and testimony supported the fact that the student was able to benefit from academic instruction in the general education classroom and therefore did not need to be placed in the special school.

Sanford School Committee v. Mr. And Mrs. L., No. CIV.00–CV113 PH (D. Me.2001)   A student with autism was found to be denied his free appropriate public education when an IEP was developed that did not take into consideration his needs. In developing the IEP, it was determined that the district never considered whether the proposed placement would meet the needs of the student (Special Education Law Update, 2001).

How might these court decisions affect the classroom teacher who has a student with autism?

 For follow-up questions about court decisions related to autism, go to Chapter 10 of the Companion Website (ablongman.com/sppd4e) and click Rights & Responsibilities.

From "Interventions for Children and Youth with Autism: Prudent Choices in a World of Exaggerated Claims and Empty Promises," Heflin and Simpson, 1998, *Focus on Autism and Other Developmental Disabilities, 13*, pp. 212–220.

for IDEA reporting purposes. This group accounted for only 0.10% of children in public schools, making it one of the smallest disability categories recognized in schools (U.S. Department of Education, 2001).

Characteristics of Individuals with Autism

A wide variety of characteristics are associated with autism. Some of the more pervasive include verbal and nonverbal communication impairments (Dyches, 1998), auditory-based sensory impairments (Orr, Myles, & Carlson, 1998), and problems relating to other individuals (Autism Society of America, 2000). Scheuermann and Webber (2002) describe the characteristics of autism using two major groups: behavioral deficits and behavioral excesses.

1. Behavioral deficits
   - Inability to relate to others
   - Lack of functional language
   - Sensory processing deficits
   - Cognitive deficits
2. Behavioral excesses
   - Self-stimulation
   - Resistance to change
   - Bizarre and challenging behaviors
   - Self-injurious behaviors

Although most of these characteristics are negative, some children with autism present some positive, as well as unexpected, characteristics. For example, Tirosh and Canby (1993) describe children with autism who also have hyperlexia, which is defined as "an advance of at least one standard deviation (SD) in the reading over the verbal IQ level" (p. 86). For these children, spelling and contextual reading also appeared to be advanced.

In some cases, children with autism display unique **splinter skills,** or islands of precocity where they display areas of giftedness. "Common splinter skills include (1) calendar abilities, such as being able to give the day of the week for any date you might provide (e.g., May 12, 1896); (2) the ability to count visual things quickly, such as telling how many toothpicks are on the floor when a box is dropped; (3) artistic ability, such as the ability to design machinery; and (4) musical ability, such as playing a piano" (Scheuermann & Webber, 2002, p. 9).

Classroom Adaptations for Students with Autism

Formerly, the prognosis for individuals with autism was pessimistic; most children with autism would grow into adulthood with severe impairments. However, intensive intervention programs have been somewhat effective with this group. No single method is effective with all children with autism, partly because these children display widely variable characteristics (Heflin & Simpson, 1998). However, several different techniques have shown positive results (Kaplan, 1996). Table 10.1 summarizes some of these techniques.

Growing evidence shows that placing children with autism with their nondisabled peers in general education settings, with appropriate supports, can make a significant difference in their behaviors. The nearby Personal Spotlight features one professional's perspective on including this group of students.

Appropriate role models appear to be very important. Recent research also indicates that behavioral treatment of children with autism, especially young children, may result in significant long-term gains in intellectual and adaptive behavior areas (McEachlin et al., 1993). Also, social skills training has been shown to be effective for this group of children (Kamps et al., 1992). (See Chapter 6 for more information on behavior management and social skills instruction.)

CROSS-REFERENCE

Review Chapter 7 on children with serious emotional disturbance (SED). Compare the characteristics of children with autism and those with SED. How are these children similar and different?

CONSIDER THIS

How do splinter skills often confuse family members concerning the abilities and capabilities of a child with autism?

TEACHING TIP

Peer buddies can be very useful when a student with autism is included in a general classroom. Peers can serve as excellent role models and provide support for these students.

TABLE 10.1   **Classroom Tips for Teaching Children with Autism**

Tip	Reason
1. Teaching a child with autism should be seen as a team approach with many professionals helping the classroom teacher.	The child with autism being educated in a regular class has probably been treated by many professionals who have extensive experience with the child. Their experiences and suggestions are of great help to the teacher. Regular consultations should be scheduled.
2. Learn everything possible about the child's development, behavior, and what services the child has received.	Understanding the nature of the child's difficulties and what has been accomplished previously can serve as a beginning for designing a program that will enable the child to learn.
3. Try to foster an atmosphere of shared decision making with other professionals responsible for the child's progress.	Successful models for integration of children with autism into regular classes show that shared decision making among all professionals leads to superior results.
4. Do not assume that children with autism have mental retardation.	The serious behavioral and linguistic difficulties of these children may lead to the assumption that they have mental retardation. The meaning of intelligence tests for children with autism is subject to question.
5. Beware of even suggesting that parents have caused their children's difficulties.	Blaming parents is counterproductive since parental help is so often required. However, in the case of autism, old discredited theories did suggest such a connection. Even though these ideas have been proven false, parental guilt may be present.
6. Prepare the class for the child with autism.	Discussing the nature of autism and some behaviors, such as rocking, may help allay the concerns of other children in the class.

From *Pathways for Exceptional Children* (p. 595) by P. S. Kaplan, 1996, St. Paul, MN: West Publishing. Used by permission.

Regardless of the specific intervention used, professionals developing programs for children with autism should ask these questions (Heflin & Simpson, 1998):

1. What are the anticipated outcomes of the programming option?
2. What are the potential risks?
3. How will the option be evaluated?
4. What proof is available that the option is effective?
5. What other options would be excluded if this option is chosen?

Since there is no single, best method for teaching students with autism, school personnel must have available a variety of intervention strategies. Ruble and Dalrymple (2002) suggest a variety of environmental supports that can facilitate the success of students with autism. These are listed in Table 10.2.

In addition, Egel (1989) has emphasized two important principles that should inform educational programs for children with autism: the use of functional activities and an effort to make programs appropriate for the student's developmental level and chronological age. Children with autism grow up to be adults with autism; the condition cannot be cured. As a result, educational programs should help them deal with the daily needs that will extend throughout their lives. To help educators focus more on the functionality of curriculum choices, they should ask themselves the following questions:

1. Does the program teach skills that are immediately useful?
2. Will the materials used be available in the student's daily environment?
3. Will learning certain skills make it less likely that someone will have to do the task for the student in the future?

If the answer to any of these questions is no, then the instructional program should be changed.

TEACHING TIP

Always remember that students with autism present a wide range of characteristics, strengths, and weaknesses. Treat each child as a unique individual, and do not expect them all to need the same kinds of services.

CONSIDER THIS

How should the curriculum for students with autism be balanced between academic skills and functional life skills? Should skills from both areas be taught to all students with autism?

CROSS-REFERENCE

Review program recommendations for students with mental retardation found in Chapter 8. How are programs for these two groups of students similar and different?

Personal Spotlight

A Professional's Opinion on Inclusion

Kim **Carper** is the coordinator of educational and training programs at the University of Central Florida's Center for Autism and Related Disabilities (CARD). In addition to her job, Kim is currently pursuing her PhD in special education at UCF. Her research and training interests include alternative communication systems, curriculum development, personnel preparation, family advocacy, and inclusion. As coordinator, Kim deals regularly with the question of the appropriate placement for students with autism.

On the topic of inclusion, Kim makes the following statement: "I feel very strongly about the inclusion of people with autism and other related disorders. I am acutely aware that inclusion means different things to different people; my definition consists of each individual getting what he or she needs out of an educational environment with typical peers. It is a process that must be conducted by a team and determined carefully based upon each individual's needs. Special education has its place in this process, specifically, as a specialized setting in which to prepare children to best work within regular classrooms. When I was teaching, I always viewed my classroom as a MASH unit or a 'triage center.' By this, I mean that I felt it was my responsibility to stabilize my students in preparation for them to go out into regular classroom settings. For my students with autism, an intense focus on social skills instruction

Kim Carper
Coordinator of Educational & Training Programs

Center for Autism & Related Disabilities, University of Central Florida

was required to assist them in successful inclusive situations, as well as in the development of friendships. Additionally, my students often required some form of communicative and behavioral support to successfully navigate the school and/or regular classrooms. Along with the skills I taught my students, I often found myself educating other teachers and administrators about the capabilities, gifts, and talents of my students with autism. I often iterated the great need for opportunities in settings that valued differences and created opportunities for all students to work together as a 'community.' I have long held the belief that our society would function at a much greater capacity if it were more tolerant of the individual differences among all people."

Kim definitely supports the philosophy of inclusion for students with autism and other related disorders. Her experience with children and adolescents with these disorders gives her significant credibility in her opinions about where these students should be placed.

For follow-up questions about this Personal Spotlight, go to Chapter 10 of the Companion Website (ablongman.com/sppd4e) and click Personal Spotlight.

Self-management is a promising intervention strategy for children with autism.

TABLE 10.2	**Environmental Supports for Children with Autism**

Communicating to the Person (Receptive Language Supports)
Slow down the pace
State positively what to do (e.g., "Let's walk" instead of "Stop running")
Provide more information in visual format

Encouraging Communication from the Person (Expressive Language Supports)
Pause, listen, and wait
Encourage input and choice when possible
Provide alternative means, such as written words or pictures, to aid communication
Encourage and respond to words and appropriate attempts, rather than to behavior

Social Supports
Build in time to watch, encourage watching and proximity
Practice on specific skills through natural activities with one peer
Structure activities with set interaction patterns and roles
Provide cooperative learning activities with facilitation
Facilitate recruitment of sociable peers to be buddies and advocates
Provide opportunity for shared experiences using interests and strengths

Expanding Repertoires of Interests and Activities
Capitalize on strengths and individual learning styles
Over time, minimize specific fears and frustrations
Use rehearsal with visuals

From "COMPASS: A Parent-Teacher Collaborative Model for Students with Autism" (p. 76) by L. A. Ruble & N. J. Dalrymple, 2002, *Focus on Autism and Other Developmental Disabilities, 17.* Used with permission.

Programs for students with autism should also be age appropriate and **developmentally appropriate.** The individual's chronological age and developmental status must be considered together. Sometimes a real incongruence exists between these two realms, making program planning a challenge (McDonnell, Hardman, McDonnell, & Kiefer-O'Donnell, 1995). In this case, developmentally appropriate materials must be modified to make them as age appropriate as possible. The nearby IEP Goals and Objectives for Charlie are developmentally appropriate for him. Remember to keep chronological and developmental status in mind when developing and implementing individualized education programs. These developmental levels should also be taken into consideration when implementing classroom adaptations. See Tips for Adapting a Lesson for Charlie for examples of the adaptations that might be appropriate for him.

A promising intervention strategy for children and adults with autism is **self-management**—implementing a variety of techniques that assist in self-control (see nearby Inclusion Strategies). Although total self-management is not possible for many students with autism, most can be taught to improve their skills in this area (Alberto & Troutman, 1995). Koegel et al. (1992) studied four children with autism who displayed a variety of inappropriate behaviors, including **self-injurious** behaviors (or self-abusive behaviors), running away from school personnel, delayed echolalic speech (repeating what is said to them), hitting objects, and stereotypical twirling of hair. After several sessions in which the children were taught how to use self-management strategies, such as **self-recording** (documenting their own behavior) and **self-reinforcement** (giving themselves reinforcers), marked improvement occurred. The results indicate that "the lack of social responsivity that is so characteristic in autism can be successfully treated with self-management procedures, requiring minimal presence of a treatment provider in the children's natural environments" (p. 350). This particular study focused on self-management related to social skills, yet hints at the possibility that such interventions could be successful in other areas.

IEP Goals and Objectives for Charlie

For Charlie, the second grader introduced in the opening vignette, appropriate goals and objectives might include the following:

Goal 1:   *To reproduce written materials*
Objective 1: *Given a set of letter and word templates, Charlie will be able to trace the letters and words with 80% accuracy.*
Objective 2: *Given a set of letters and words on a piece of paper, Charlie will be able to write the letters and words with 80% accuracy.*
Objective 3: *Given the assignment to write his name and a four-sentence story, Charlie will write his name with 100% accuracy and the story with 70% accuracy.*

Goal 2:   *To participate in group activities*
Objective 1: *During a recess game, Charlie will be able to remain with a selected group without disruptions or leaving the group 80% of the time.*
Objective 2: *Given the opportunity to participate in a cooperative learning activity, Charlie will do so for at least 10 minutes without any inappropriate behaviors, 80% of the time.*

Goal 3:   *To increase expressive vocabulary*
Objective 1: *Given an opportunity to express himself verbally, Charlie will increase his expressive vocabulary by 10 words over a two-week period.*
Objective 2: *Given the need to go to the bathroom, Charlie will verbally communicate the need to go to the bathroom appropriately 100% of the time.*

Tips for Adapting a Lesson for Charlie

Based on the opening vignette, the following adaptations for Charlie seem appropriate.

Charlie's teacher should

▶ make sure that Charlie is attending before starting instruction.
▶ make the instruction clear and brief.
▶ make sure the instruction is appropriate and relevant.
▶ be consistent with instructions.
▶ use effective but not unintended prompts.
▶ fade prompts as appropriate.
▶ make consequences contingent, immediate, consistent, and clear.
▶ positively reinforce appropriate responses.
▶ change consequences if they are ineffective.

Adapted from Scheuermann & Webber (2002).

Teaching Self-Management Skills

Teaching students with autism to increase their self-management skills is an area that is appropriate for many of these students. The following provides examples of self-management goals and supports that could help students achieve these goals:

Goal 1: To independently transition from one activity to another using a picture/word schedule

Supports
- Imitate peers
- Learn by observing
- Provide visual supports including schedule for the day, steps in each activity, completion of activity, and time to move
- Train peers in how to use schedule
- Peer models

Goal 2: To stay in bounds at recess

Supports
- Imitate skills
- Learn by observing
- Teach and practice skills
- Use flags to show playground boundaries
- Use peers to model staying within boundaries
- Reinforce appropriate behaviors

Goal 3: To work quietly during individual work time

Supports
- Imitation skills
- Academic ability
- Motivation to do what other students are doing
- Peer models

- Visual reminders about being quiet
- Social story for quiet work
- Positive reinforcement for appropriate behaviors

For follow-up questions about self-management skills for students with autism, go to Chapter 10 of the Companion Website (ablongman.com/sppd4e) and click Inclusion Strategies.

Adapted from "COMPASS: A Parent-Teacher Collaboration Model for Students with Autism" (pp. 76–83) by L. A. Ruble and M. J. Dalrymple, 2002, *Focus on Autism and Other Developmental Disabilities, 17.*

Over the past several years, a major controversy has erupted in the education of children with autism over the use of **facilitated communication,** a process in which a facilitator helps the person with autism (or some other disability related to expressive language) to type or use a keyboard for communication purposes. The process is described by Biklen et al. (1992) as follows:

> Facilitated communication involves a series of steps. The communicator types with one index finger, first with hand over hand or hand-at-the-wrist support and then later independently or with just a touch to the elbow or shoulder. Over time, the communicator progresses from structured work such as fill-in-the-blanks/cloze exercises and multiple-choice activities to open-ended, typed, conversational text. (p. 5)

Although this method was once touted as the key to establishing communication with children with autism, recent studies have cast doubt on its authenticity. The heart of the controversy concerns how to validate the technique. Advocates of the method offer numerous qualitative research studies as proof of success, yet recent quantitative research raises significant questions about the program. After reviewing much of the empirical research related to facilitated communication, Kaplan (1996) reported that evidence often shows that the facilitator influences the person with autism, though the facilitator may be unaware of it. Yet despite the growing evidence questioning the efficacy of facilitated communication, Kaplan says that "it would be incorrect to suggest that because excesses sometimes creep into the way the method is used, it should completely be abandoned" (p. 585). In other words, although little empirical evidence supports facilitated communication, it could still be an effective means of communication for some individuals and should not be abandoned totally until more study is done. It is unlikely, however, that facilitated communication is the miracle many people had hoped it would be.

CONSIDER THIS

How can the use of procedures that have not yet been validated harm students? Why do some of these ideas become so popular with some educators and family members before they are proven effective?

Asperger Syndrome

During the past few years a condition associated with autism has received a great deal of attention. This condition, called **Asperger syndrome,** was first described in 1944 by Hans Asperger (Griswold et al., 2002) but largely ignored until it was first included in DSM-IV (Safran, 2002a). In general, students classified as having Asperger syndrome share many of the same characteristics of children with autism, but also display some unique features. "Clinical features of Asperger syndrome include social interaction impairments, speech and communication characteristics, cognitive and academic characteristics, sensory characteristics, and physical and motor-skill anomalies" (Myles & Simpson, 1998, p. 3). These characteristics, for the most part, are the same as those found in children with autism (McLaughlin-Cheng, 1998). Children with Asperger syndrome differ from those with autism in having higher cognitive development and more typical communication skills. Table 10.3 shows the similarities and differences of the behavioral characteristics of children with Asperger syndrome and children with autism.

TABLE 10.3   Behavioral Comparison of Asperger Syndrome and Autism

	Asperger Syndrome	Autistic Syndrome
1. Intelligence measures		
Standardized scores	Average to high average range	Borderline through average range
2. Language		
Development	Normal development	Delayed onset, deficits
Pragmatic language		
a. Verbal	Deficits can be observed	Delayed and disordered
b. Nonverbal	Deficits (e.g., odd eye gaze)	Deficits can be severe
3. Communication		
Expressive	Within normal limits	Deficits can be observed
Receptive	Within normal limits	Deficits can be observed
4. Social responsiveness		
Attachment		
a. Parents	Observed responsiveness	Lack responsiveness
b. Caregivers	Observed responsiveness	Lack responsiveness
c. Peers	Observed responsiveness	Lack responsiveness
Interactions		
a. Initiations to peers	Frequent, poor quality	Minimal frequency
b. Positive responses to peers	Frequent, awkward, and pertains to self-interests	Minimal frequency
c. Symbolic play	No impaired symbolic play	Absence of symbolic play
d. Reciprocal play	Observed but awkward	Minimal frequency
e. Coping	Deficits observed in quality	
f. Friendships	Minimal frequency	Minimal frequency
g. Requests for assistance	Observed but awkward	Minimal frequency
Emotional self-regulation		
a. Emotional empathy	Observed but awkward	Deficits can be observed
b. Emotional responsiveness	Observed but could be extreme	Aloof, indifferent
5. Physical/motor		
a. Gross motor	Observed deficits—controversial	No observed deficits
b. Repetitive behavior	Observed	Observed

From "Asperger Syndrome and Autism: A Literature Review and Meta-analysis" (p. 237) by E. McLaughlin-Cheng, 1998, *Focus on Autism and Other Developmental Disabilities, 13.* Used by permission.

Just as there is no single method to teach children with autism, there is also not a preferred educational intervention for children with Asperger syndrome. Teachers must address several issues when dealing with these children and develop effective strategies for each child on an individual basis. Areas that should be considered include using visual strategies, which takes advantage of their more intact learning modality; using structural strategies, such as preparing students for changes in schedules and routines; and providing an instructional sequence that follows a logical progression for learning (Myles & Simpson, 1998).

Safran (2002b) provides the following tips for teachers working with students with Asperger syndrome:

- Carefully structure seating arrangements and group work.
- Provide a safe haven.
- Save the student from himself or herself.
- Prepare for changes in routine.
- Use available resources/make needed accommodations.
- Connect with each other, parents, Internet support groups, and other groups.
- Promote positive peer interactions.
- Capitalize on special interests.
- Don't take it personally.
- Help your classroom become a caring community. (p. 64)

Basic Concepts About Traumatic Brain Injury

Traumatic brain injury (TBI) was added to the special education categories under IDEA in 1990. The condition is defined in the law as an acquired injury to the brain caused by an external physical force, resulting in total or partial functional disability or psychosocial impairment, or both, that adversely affects a child's educational performance. The term applies to open or closed head injuries resulting in impairments in one or more areas, such as cognition, language, memory, attention, reasoning, abstract thinking, judgment, problem solving, sensory, perceptual, and motor abilities, psychosocial behavior, physical functions, information processing, and speech. The term does not apply to brain injuries that are congenital, degenerative, or induced by birth trauma (IDEA, 1997).

Traumatic brain injury is the most common cause of death and disability among children in the United States. Every year, more than one million children suffer from TBI, and between 9% and 38% of these students are referred for special education services (Keyser-Marcus et al., 2002). During the 1999–2000 school year, nearly 14,000 students were served in special education programs because of TBI (U.S. Department of Education, 2001). This fact means that many children who suffer from TBI are not in special education, making it even more important that general classroom teachers understand this disability. TBI can result from a wide variety of causes, including falls, vehicle accidents, and even abuse. It can also be caused by lack of oxygen to the brain, infections, tumors, and strokes (Garcia, Krankowski, & Jones, 1998).

The social-emotional and cognitive deficits caused by the injury may persist long after physical capabilities recover. Students with TBI can experience a host of confusing and frustrating symptoms. "There is an inability to concentrate; short-term memory is affected; one's self-confidence is undermined; self-esteem is diminished; the personality changes; . . . the family and friends are affected" (Infusini, 1994, pp. 4–5). Teachers must guard against minimizing an injury because it presents no visible evidence and many children exhibit typical behaviors.

The prognosis for recovery depends on many variables. Initially, it is "influenced by the type of injury and the rapidity and quality of medical and surgical care" (Bigge, 1991, p. 197). Later, it will be influenced by the nature of rehabilitative and educational intervention. Some students with TBI will become successful students, while others will have long-term lingering effects of their injury (Table 10.4).

TABLE 10.4   **Persisting Features of Traumatic Brain Injury**

Area of Functioning	Possible Effects
Physical/Medical	◗ Fatigue and reduced stamina ◗ Seizures (5%) ◗ Headaches ◗ Problems with regulation of various functions (e.g., growth, eating, body temperature)
Sensory	◗ Hearing problems (e.g., conductive and/or sensorineural loss) ◗ Vision problems (e.g., blurred vision, visual field defects)
Cognitive	◗ Memory problems (e.g., storage and retrieval) ◗ Attentional difficulties ◗ Intellectual deficits ◗ Reasoning and problem-solving difficulties
Language-Related	◗ Word retrieval difficulties ◗ Motor-speech problems (e.g., dysarthria) ◗ Language comprehension deficits (e.g., difficulty listening) ◗ Difficulty acquiring new vocabulary and learning new concepts ◗ Socially inappropriate verbal behavior
Behavioral/Emotional	◗ Problems in planning, organizing, and problem solving ◗ Disinhibition ◗ Overactivity ◗ Impulsivity ◗ Lack of self-direction ◗ Helplessness or apathy ◗ Inability to recognize one's injury

From *Traumatic Brain Injury in Children and Adolescents: A Sourcebook for Teachers and Other School Personnel* (pp. 71–72) by M. P. Mira, B. F. Tucker, and J. S. Tyler, 1992, Austin, TX: Pro-Ed. Used by permission.

Classroom Adaptations for Students with Traumatic Brain Injury

CONSIDER THIS

What can school personnel do to facilitate the transition of children with TBI from hospital and residential settings to public school? What kind of relationship should school personnel and hospital personnel maintain after the transition is completed?

The transition of students with TBI from rehabilitation facilities to school settings needs to be coordinated among a number of people. Intervention involves the efforts of professionals from many different disciplines, including teachers (Bergland & Hoffbauer, 1996). In addition to the injury itself and its implications on functioning and potential learning, students probably will have missed a significant amount of schooling. All these factors can have a significant impact on educational performance. An effective educational program creates a positive attitude about the student's prognosis. Such a program reaches beyond just speaking positively. Teachers communicate a positive attitude by the type of programming they present and by the level of expectations they establish. Remember to "keep expectations for students' performance high. Often, this means providing students with mild TBI with multiple opportunities for practice that do not carry penalties for inaccuracy" (Hux & Hackley, 1996). This will show the students that programs and instruction are designed to support them and not just to give them a grade. They will respond better when programs do not seem punitive.

Under the Individuals with Disabilities Education Act of 1997, TBI is a distinct category of disability, although some students may be provided services under Section 504. If they are identified under IDEA, they will have a written IEP; if served under Section 504, they will have an appropriate accommodation plan. Whatever plan is used, teachers

TABLE 10.5	Recommended Instructional Strategies for Children with TBI

Use a multimodal approach (overheads, videos, hands-on activities) when presenting material and instructions for assignments.

Teach compensatory strategies to students and structure choices.

Begin class with review and overview of topics to be covered.

Provide the student with an outline of the material to be presented, to assist in comprehension.

Emphasize main points and key ideas frequently.

Incorporate repetition into instruction.

Provide specific, frequent feedback on student performance and behavior.

Encourage questions.

Break down large assignments into smaller components.

Use task analyses to determine skill acquisition and maintenance.

Ask the student how he or she could improve learning.

Use a variety of open-ended and multiple-choice questions to encourage independent thinking.

Present difficult material in a simplified fashion, using illustrations or diagrams if possible.

Provide the student with cues when appropriate.

From "Enhancing the Schooling of Students with Traumatic Brain Injury" (p. 65) by L. Keyser-Marcus, L. Briel, P. Sherron-Targett, S. Yasuda, S. Johnson, & P. Wehman, 2002, *Teaching Exceptional Children, 34.* Used with permission.

will need to address the specific areas that have been identified as problematic. Table 10.5 gives ideas for helping students with problems that may result from TBI.

A well-planned program of instruction should focus on "retaining impaired cognitive processes, developing new skills or procedures to compensate for residual deficits, creating an environment that permits effective performance, identifying effective instructional procedures, and improving metacognitive awareness" (Ylvisaker et al., 1994, p. 17). The impact of the injury may require that the student learn compensatory strategies to make up for deficits. Such strategies can address problems with attending, language comprehension, memory, sequencing, and thought organization.

TEACHING TIP

Develop and implement intervention programs based on the student's specific needs. TBI causes a wide variety of deficits, resulting in a great diversity of intervention needs.

Basic Concepts About Low-Incidence Health Problems and Physical Disabilities

As noted in the beginning of this chapter, many health and physical disabilities may be present in children that result in a need for special education and related services. The remainder of this chapter will provide a quick guide to some of these disabilities and some considerations for educators. Teachers who work with children with one of these conditions should refer to a more thorough reference work to learn more about it. The Further Readings list at the end of this chapter suggests such sources of information.

Asthma

Asthma is the most common chronic illness in children, affecting approximately 3 million children and youth under the age of 15 (American Academy of Allergy and Immunology, 1991; Bauer et al., 1999).

It is characterized by repetitive episodes of coughing, shortness of breath, and wheezing, resulting from the narrowing of small air passages, caused by irritation of the bronchial tubes by allergic reactions to various substances, such as animal dander, air pollutants, and pollens (McEwen et al., 1998). Asthma attacks can be very dangerous and should be taken seriously by school personnel. Specific suggestions for teachers include the following:

▶ Know the signs and symptoms of respiratory distress (Getch & Neuharth-Pritchett, 1999).
▶ Ensure that students have proper medications and that they are taken at the appropriate times.
▶ Allow students to rest when needed, as they often tire easily.
▶ Eliminate any known allergens found in the classroom.
▶ Determine what types of physical limitations might have to be set (e.g., restriction of a certain physical activity that can induce attacks), but otherwise encourage students to play games and participate in activities.
▶ Recognize the side effects of prescribed medication.
▶ Remain calm if an attack occurs.
▶ Allow the student to participate in nonstressful activity until an episode subsides.
▶ Introduce a vaporizer or dehumidifier to the classroom when recommended by the student's physician.
▶ Work on building up the student's self-image.
▶ Sensitize other students in the class to the nature of allergic reactions.
▶ Develop an effective system for helping the student keep up with schoolwork, as frequent absences may occur.

Educators can ask the following questions to determine whether a school is prepared to deal with students with asthma (National Heart, Lung, and Blood Institute, 1998):

1. Is the school free of tobacco smoke all of the time, including during school-sponsored events?
2. Does the school maintain good indoor air quality?
3. Is a school nurse in the school all day, every day?
4. Can children take medicines at school as recommended by their doctor and parents?
5. Does the school have an emergency plan for taking care of a child with a severe asthma attack?
6. Does someone teach school staff about asthma, asthma management plans, and asthma medicines?
7. Do students with asthma have good options for fully and safely participating in physical education class and recess? (p. 168)

Childhood Cancer

Childhood cancer occurs in approximately 1 in 330 children prior to the age of 19 years (National Cancer Foundation, 1997). Childhood cancer can take several different forms, including leukemia, lymphoma, tumors of the central nervous system, bone tumors, tumors affecting the eyes, and tumors affecting various organs (Heller, Alberto, Forney, & Schwartzman, 1996). Treatment of cancer includes chemotherapy, radiation, surgery, and bone marrow transplantation. Suggestions for teachers and administrators who have students with cancer include the following:

▶ Express your concern about a student's condition to the parents and family.
▶ Learn about a student's illness from hospital personnel and parents.
▶ Inquire about the type of treatment and anticipated side effects.
▶ Refer the student for any needed special education services.
▶ Prepare for a student's terminal illness and possible death.
▶ Encourage discussion and consideration of future events.
▶ Allow for exceptions to classroom rules and procedures when indicated (e.g., wearing a baseball cap to disguise hair loss from chemotherapy).

CONSIDER THIS

What are some ways that teachers can maintain contact with students with cancer during their extended absences from the classroom? How can the teacher facilitate contact between classmates and the student with cancer?

Teachers who have students with cancer should learn about the child's illness from medical personnel.

▶ Be available to talk with a student when the need arises.

▶ Share information about the student's condition and ongoing status with teachers of the student's siblings.

▶ Be prepared to deal with issues concerning death and dying with students. Provide information to school staff and parents, as needed (Hoida & McDougal, 1998).

▶ Facilitate the student's reentry into school after an extended absence.

Cerebral Palsy

Cerebral palsy (CP) is a disorder of movement or posture that is caused by brain damage. It affects the voluntary muscles and often leads to major problems in communication and mobility. Cerebral palsy is neither progressive nor communicable (Gersh, 1991; Schleichkorn, 1993). It is also not "curable" in the usual sense of the word, although education, therapy, and applied technology can help persons with cerebral palsy lead productive lives.

Between 6 and 10 individuals for every 10,000 in the population have cerebral palsy (Eaves, 1992). There are three primary methods for classifying individuals with cerebral palsy: by type (physiological), by distribution (topological) (Inge, 1992), and by degree of severity (Bigge, 1991). Table 10.6 describes the different types of cerebral palsy according to two classification systems.

The primary intervention approach for children with cerebral palsy focuses on their physical needs. Physical therapy, occupational therapy, and even surgery often play a part. Specific suggestions for teachers include the following:

▶ Create a supportive classroom environment that encourages participation in every facet of the school day.

▶ Allow extra time for students to move from one location to another.

▶ Ask students to repeat verbalizations that may be hard to understand because of their speech patterns.

▶ Provide many real-life activities.

▶ Learn the correct way for the student to sit upright in a chair or wheelchair and how to use adaptive equipment (e.g., prone standers).

▶ Understand the functions and components of a wheelchair and any special adaptive pieces that may accompany it.

TEACHING TIP

Develop some simulation activities for nondisabled students that will help them understand mobility problems. The use of wheelchairs and restricting the use of students' arms or hands will help them understand the problems experienced by some students with CP.

TABLE 10.6　　　**Classification of Cerebral Palsy**

Topographical Classification System	Classification System by Motor Symptoms (Physiological)
A. *Monoplegia:* one limb	A. Spastic
B. *Paraplegia:* legs only	B. Athetoid 　1. Tension 　2. Nontension 　3. Dystonic 　4. Tremor
C. *Hemiplegia:* one-half of body	
D. *Triplegia:* three limbs (usually two legs and one arm)	
E. *Quadriplegia:* all four limbs	C. Rigidity
F. *Diplegia:* more affected in the legs than the arms	D. Ataxia
	E. Tremor
G. *Double hemiplegia:* arms more involved than the legs	F. Atonic (rare)
	G. Mixed
	H. Unclassified

From *Understanding Physical, Sensory, and Health Impairments* (p. 95) by K. W. Heller, P. A. Alberto, P. E. Forney, and M. N. Schwartzman, 1996, Pacific Grove, CA: Brooks/Cole. Used by permission.

▶ Consider the use of various augmentative communication techniques with students who have severe cerebral palsy (Musselwhite, 1987).
▶ Encourage students to use computers that are equipped with expanded keyboards if necessary or other portable writing aids for taking notes or generating written products.
▶ Consult physical and occupational therapists to understand correct positioning, posture, and other motor function areas.

Assistive technology (AT) can also play a significant role in the education of students with cerebral palsy. The nearby Technology Today provides a means of determining the use of assistive technology in a particular school. After determining its use, school personnel can develop a plan of action to implement appropriate assistive technology supports.

Cystic Fibrosis

Cystic fibrosis is an inherited, fatal disease that results in an abnormal amount of mucus throughout the body, most often affecting the lungs and digestive tract. It occurs in approximately 1 in 2,000 live births (Hill et al., 1993). On the average, children with the disease will live to their midteens. Teachers must make sure that children with cystic fibrosis take special medication before they eat. As the disease progresses, it greatly affects stamina and the student's physical condition. Here are some specific suggestions for dealing with students with this disease:

▶ Prepare students in class for the realities of this disease (e.g., coughing, noncontagious sputum, gas).
▶ Learn how to clear a student's lungs and air passages, as such assistance may be needed after certain activities.
▶ Know the medications a student must take and be able to administer them (e.g., enzymes, vitamins).
▶ Consider restricting certain physical activities.
▶ Inquire about the therapies being used with the student.
▶ Support the implementation of special diets if needed.
▶ Provide opportunities for students to talk about their concerns, fears, and feelings.
▶ Ensure that the student is included in all class activities to whatever extent is possible.
▶ Prepare students for the eventual outcome of the disease by discussing death and dying.

Schoolwide Assistive Technology Database Sample

AT Needs	Have	Class/Instructor	Hours of Usage	Hours Available
Books on Tape			Period	Period
1. Our World Today	Yes	1. 7th SS/Brown	1 2 3 4 5 6	1 2 3 4 5 6
2. World History	No	2. 8th Hist/White	1 2 3 4 5 6	1 2 3 4 5 6
3.		3.	1 2 3 4 5 6	1 2 3 4 5 6
4.		4.	1 2 3 4 5 6	1 2 3 4 5 6
Franklin Spellers			Period	Period
1. Set of 35	Yes	1. 6th Eng/Green	1 2 3 4 5 6	1 2 3 4 5 6
2. 20 additional	Yes	2. Individual Checkout	1 2 3 4 5 6	1 2 3 4 5 6
3.		3.	1 2 3 4 5 6	1 2 3 4 5 6
4.		4.	1 2 3 4 5 6	1 2 3 4 5 6
Calculators			Period	Period
1. Set of 35	Yes	1. 6th Math/Black	1 2 3 4 5 6	1 2 3 4 5 6
2. 30 additional	Yes	2. Individual Checkout	1 2 3 4 5 6	1 2 3 4 5 6
3.		3.	1 2 3 4 5 6	1 2 3 4 5 6
4.		4.	1 2 3 4 5 6	1 2 3 4 5 6
Computers			Period	Period
1. IBM	No	1. 6th Eng/Green	1 2 3 4 5 6	1 2 3 4 5 6
2. IBM Lab	Yes	2. Lab/Tann	1 2 3 4 5 6	1 2 3 4 5 6
3.		3.	1 2 3 4 5 6	1 2 3 4 5 6
4.		4.	1 2 3 4 5 6	1 2 3 4 5 6
Software (Title)			Period	Period
1. MS Word	Yes	1. 6th Eng/Green	1 2 3 4 5 6	1 2 3 4 5 6
2. Type to Learn	No	2. Keyboard/Tann	1 2 3 4 5 6	1 2 3 4 5 6
3.		3.	1 2 3 4 5 6	1 2 3 4 5 6
4.		4.	1 2 3 4 5 6	1 2 3 4 5 6
NCR paper/Peer Helper			Period	Period
1. 2 students	Yes	1. 6th Eng/Green	1 2 3 4 5 6	1 2 3 4 5 6
2. 3 students	Yes	2. 7th SS/Brown	1 2 3 4 5 6	1 2 3 4 5 6
3. 1 student	Yes	3. 6th Math/Black	1 2 3 4 5 6	1 2 3 4 5 6
4.		4.	1 2 3 4 5 6	1 2 3 4 5 6
Other			Period	Period
1.		1.	1 2 3 4 5 6	1 2 3 4 5 6
2.		2.	1 2 3 4 5 6	1 2 3 4 5 6
3.		3.	1 2 3 4 5 6	1 2 3 4 5 6
4.		4.	1 2 3 4 5 6	1 2 3 4 5 6

For follow-up questions about schoolwide assistive technology databases, go to Chapter 10 of the Companion Website (ablongman.com/sppd4e) and click Technology Today.

From "Planning and Organizing Assistive Technology Resources in Your School" (p. 53) by B. J. Webb, *Teaching Exceptional Children, 32.* Used with permission.

Deaf-Blind

Students who have visual impairments or auditory impairments create unique problems for educators. When students present deficits in both sensory areas, resulting in their being **deaf-blind,** their needs become extremely complex. Although the term *deaf-blind* continues to be found in federal legislation and regulations, including IDEA, the terms *dual sensory impairment* or *multiple sensory impairments* are considered more appropriate (Marchant, 1992). For purposes of being eligible for special education services under IDEA, *deaf-blind* is still the label for such students.

Students who are classified as being deaf-blind may be blind or deaf, or they may have degrees of visual and auditory impairments that do not classify as blindness or deafness. "The Helen Keller National Center estimates that about 94% of such individuals have residual hearing or residual sight that can facilitate their educational programs" (Marchant, 1992, p. 114). During the 1999–2000 school year, only 1,845 students nationwide were identified as being deaf-blind and served in special education programs (U.S. Department of Education, 2001).

Obviously, individuals classified as being deaf-blind present a variety of characteristics. While these characteristics represent those exhibited by students who only have visual or hearing impairments, the overlap of these two disabilities results in significant educational needs. Wolfe (1997) suggests the following educational techniques for teachers to use when working with students classified as deaf-blind:

▶ Use an ecological approach to assessment and skill selection to emphasize functional needs of students.
▶ Use a variety of prompts, cues, and reinforcement strategies in a systematic instructional pattern.
▶ Use time delay prompting, where time between prompts is increased.
▶ Use groups and cooperative learning strategies.
▶ Implement environmental adaptations, such as enlarging materials, using contrasting materials, altering seating arrangements, and reducing extraneous noises to maximize residual hearing and vision of the student.

Diabetes (Juvenile Diabetes)

Affecting nearly 8 million people in the United States, diabetes is a metabolic disorder in which the pancreas cannot produce sufficient insulin to process food (Holcomb et al., 1998). Teachers should be alert to possible symptoms of diabetes, including increased thirst, appetite, and urination; weight loss; fatigue; and irritability. Children with type I (**insulin-dependent**) diabetes must take daily injections of insulin. School personnel must have knowledge of the special dietary needs of these children and understand their need for a daily activity regimen. Some specific suggestions on dealing with diabetic students follow:

▶ Communicate regularly with the family to determine any special needs the student may have.
▶ Schedule snacks and lunch at the same time every day.
▶ Be prepared for hypoglycemia—a situation in which the student needs to have sugar.
▶ Help the student deal with the disease.
▶ Understand the distinction between having too much insulin in the body and not having enough. Table 10.7 describes both these conditions and actions to address them.

Epilepsy

Epilepsy is a series of recurrent convulsions, or seizures, that are caused by abnormal electrical discharges in the brain (Smith, 1998). There are several different types of epilepsy, determined by the impact of abnormal brain activity. Table 10.8 describes four types.

TEACHING TIP

Be prepared to deal with students with diabetes in your classroom before an emergency develops. Keep a list of symptoms and things to do if a student has too much insulin or if a student has too little insulin readily available.

TABLE 10.7   **Hyperglycemia and Hypoglycemia**

Category	Possible Symptoms	Cause	Treatment
Ketoacidosis; hyperglycemia (too much sugar)	Symptoms occur gradually (over hours or days): polyuria; polyphagia; polydipsia; fatigue; abdominal pain; nausea; vomiting; fruity odor on breath; rapid, deep breathing; unconsciousness	Did not take insulin; did not comply with diet	Give insulin; follow plan of action
Insulin reaction; hypoglycemia (too little sugar)	Symptoms occur quickly (in minutes): headache; dullness; irritability; shaking; sweating; lightheadedness; behavior change; paleness; weakness; moist skin; slurred speech; confusion; shallow breathing; unconsciousness	Delayed eating; participated in strenuous exercise; took too much insulin	Give sugar; follow plan of action

From *Understanding Physical, Sensory, and Health Impairments* (p.78) by K. W. Heller, P. A. Alberto, P. E. Forney, and M. N. Schwartzman, 1996, Pacific Grove, CA: Brooks/Cole. Used by permission.

Approximately 1% of the population of the United States has epilepsy (Jan, Ziegler, & Erba, 1991). No common characteristics are shared by individuals with epilepsy. The Epilepsy Foundation of America (1992) notes the following significant signs of the disorder: (1) staring spells, (2) tic-like movements, (3) rhythmic movements of the head, (4) purposeless sounds and body movements, (5) head drooping, (6) lack of response, (7) eyes

TABLE 10.8   **Four Types of Seizures**

Generalized (grand mal)	• Sudden cry, fall, rigidity, followed by muscle jerks • Shallow breathing, or temporarily suspended breathing, bluish skin • Possible loss of bladder or bowel control • Usually lasts 2–3 minutes
Absence (petit mal)	• Blank stare, beginning and ending abruptly • Lasting only a few seconds • Most common in children • May be accompanied by blinking, chewing movement • Individual is unaware of the seizure
Simple Partial	• Jerking may begin in one area of body, arm, leg, or face • Cannot be stopped but individual is aware • Jerking may proceed from one area to another area
Complex Partial	• Starts with blank stares, followed by chewing and random activity • Individual may seem unaware or dazed • Unresponsiveness • Clumsy actions • May run, pick up objects, take clothes off, or other activity • Lasts a few minutes • No memory of what occurred

From *Understanding Physical, Sensory, and Health Impairments* (p. 78) by K. W. Heller, P. A. Alberto, P. E. Forney, and M. N. Schwartzman, 1996, Pacific Grove, CA: Brooks/Cole. Used by permission.

rolling upward, and (8) chewing and swallowing movements. Medical intervention is the primary recourse for individuals with epilepsy. Most people with epilepsy are able to control their seizures with the proper regimen of medical therapy (Agnew, Nystul, & Conner, 1998).

Even persons who respond very well to medication have occasional seizures. Therefore teachers and other school personnel must know what actions to take should a person experience a generalized seizure. Figure 10.3 summarizes the steps that should be taken when a child has a seizure. Teachers, parents, or others need to record behaviors that occur before, during, and after the seizure because they may be important to treatment of the disorder.

HIV and AIDS

Human immunodeficiency virus (HIV) infection occurs when the virus attacks the body's immune system, leaving an individual vulnerable to infections or cancers. In its later stages, HIV infection becomes **acquired immunodeficiency syndrome (AIDS).** Two of the fastest-growing groups contracting HIV are infants and teenagers (Johnson, Johnson, & Jefferson-Aker, 2001). HIV/AIDS is transmitted only through the exchange of blood or semen. As of September 1996, 7,472 cases of AIDS in children under 13 years of age were reported to the Centers for Disease Control (Centers for Disease Control, 1997). Students with HIV/AIDS may display a variety of academic, behavioral, and social-emotional problems. Teachers need to take precautions when dealing with children with

---

FIGURE 10.3

Steps to Take When Dealing with a Seizure

From *Seizure Recognition and Observation: A Guide for Allied Health Professionals* (p. 2), Epilepsy Foundation of America, 1992, Landover, MD: Author. Used by permission.

In a generalized tonic–clonic seizure, the person suddenly falls to the ground and has a convulsive seizure. It is essential to protect him or her from injury. Cradle the head or place something soft under it—a towel or your hand, for example. Remove all dangerous objects. A bystander can do nothing to prevent or terminate an attack. At the end of the episode, make sure the mouth is cleared of food and saliva by turning the person on his or her side to provide the best airway and allow secretions to drain. The person may be incontinent during a seizure. If the assisting person remains calm, the person will be reassured when he or she regains consciousness.

Breathing almost always resumes spontaneously after a convulsive seizure. Failure to resume breathing signals a complication of the seizure such as an aspiration of food, heart attack, or severe head or neck injury. In these unusual circumstances, cardiopulmonary resuscitation must start immediately. If repeated seizures occur, or if a single seizure lasts longer than five minutes, the person should be taken to a medical facility immediately. Prolonged or repeated seizures may suggest *status epilepticus* (nonstop seizures), which requires emergency medical treatment. In summary, *first aid for generalized tonic–clonic seizures is similar to that for other convulsive seizures.*

▶ Prevent further injury. Place something soft under the head, loosen tight clothing, and clear the area of sharp or hard objects.

▶ Force no objects into the person's mouth.

▶ Do not restrain the person's movements unless they place him or her in danger.

▶ At the end of the episode, turn the person on his or her side to open the airway and allow secretions to drain.

▶ Stay with the person until the seizure ends.

▶ Do not pour any liquids into the person's mouth or offer any food, drink, or medication until he or she is fully awake.

▶ Start cardiopulmonary resuscitation if the person does not resume breathing after the seizure.

▶ Let the person rest until he or she is fully awake.

▶ Be reassuring and supportive when consciousness returns.

▶ A convulsive seizure is not a medical emergency unless it lasts longer than five minutes or a second seizure occurs soon after the first. In this situation, the person should be taken to an emergency medical facility.

FIGURE 10.4

Universal Precautions for Prevention of HIV, Hepatitis B, and Other Blood-Borne Pathogens

From *AIDS Surveillance Report* (p. 7), Centers for Disease Control, 1988, Atlanta, GA: Author. Used by permission.

The Centers for Disease Control and the Food and Drug Administration (1988) published guidelines designed to protect health care workers and to ensure the confidentiality of patients with HIV infection. These guidelines include the following information that is useful for classroom teachers.

▶ Blood should always be handled with latex or nonpermeable disposable gloves. The use of gloves is not necessary for feces, nasal secretions, sputum, sweat, saliva, tears, urine, and vomitus unless they are visibly tinged with blood. Handwashing is sufficient after handling material not containing blood.

▶ In all settings in which blood or bloody material is handled, gloves and a suitable receptacle that closes tightly and is child-proof should be available. Although HIV does not survive well outside the body, all spillage of secretions should be cleaned up immediately with disinfectants. This is particularly important for cleaning up after a bloody nose or a large cut. Household bleach at a dilution of 1:10 should be used. Only objects that have come into contact with blood need to be cleaned with bleach.

▶ When intact skin is exposed to contaminated fluids, particularly blood, it should be washed with soap and water. Handwashing is sufficient for such activities as diaper change; toilet training; and clean-up of nasal secretions, stool, saliva, tears, or vomitus. If an open lesion or a mucous membrane appears to have been contaminated, AZT therapy should be considered.

HIV/AIDS, hepatitis B, or any other blood-borne pathogen. See Figure 10.4 for specific precautions. Some specific suggestions for teachers include the following:

▶ Follow the guidelines (universal precautions) developed by the Centers for Disease Control and the Food and Drug Administration for working with HIV-infected individuals (see Figure 10.4).
▶ Ask the student's parents or physician whether there are any special procedures that must be followed.
▶ Discuss HIV/AIDS with the entire class, providing accurate information, dispelling myths, and answering questions.
▶ Discuss with students in the class the fact that a student's skills and abilities will change over time if he or she is infected with HIV/AIDS.
▶ Prepare for the fact that the student may die, especially if AIDS is present.
▶ Ensure that the student with HIV/AIDS is included in all aspects of classroom activities.
▶ Be sensitive to the stress that the student's family is undergoing.

CONSIDER THIS

Students with HIV and AIDS should not be allowed to attend school because of their potential ability to infect other students. Do you agree or disagree with this statement? Why or why not?

Muscular Dystrophy

Muscular dystrophy is an umbrella term used to describe several different inherited disorders that result in progressive muscular weakness (Tver & Tver, 1991). The most common and most serious form of muscular dystrophy is **Duchenne dystrophy.** In this type of muscular dystrophy, fat cells and connective tissue replace muscle tissue. Individuals with Duchenne dystrophy ultimately lose their ability to walk, typically by age 12. Functional use of arms and hands will also be affected. Muscle weakness will also result in respiratory complications. Teachers must adapt their classrooms to accommodate the physical needs of these students. Most individuals with this form of muscular dystrophy die during young adulthood. Specific suggestions for teachers include the following:

▶ Be prepared to help the student deal with the loss of various functions.
▶ Involve the student in as many classroom activities as possible.
▶ Using assistive techniques that do not hurt the individual, help the student as needed in climbing stairs or in getting up from the floor.
▶ Understand the functions and components of wheelchairs.
▶ Monitor the administration of required medications.
▶ Monitor the amount of time the student is allowed to stand during the day.

CONSIDER THIS

Should students who require extensive physical accommodations be placed in the same school, so that all schools and classrooms do not have to be accessible? Defend your response.

Diversity Forum

AIDS/HIV Epidemics in African American and Hispanic American Communities

Estrellita, a 13-year-old Hispanic American girl with HIV, wants to try out for the basketball team, but her parents are worried about the effects on her health. Coach Robinson feels it would promote social acceptance and decides to have a conference with her parents, who are monolingual Spanish speakers.

Eight-year-old Tanisha is new to Mr. Peterson's classroom. Her parents have provided consent for her AIDS condition to be disclosed but are concerned about her acceptance by peers and her social development in the classroom. Tanisha is one of three African American students at her school.

The percentage of children with HIV/AIDS among Hispanic and African American communities has risen to epidemic proportions. Between 1999 and 2000, while African American children

made up 65% of all AIDS pediatric cases. Children with HIV/AIDS and their families face many cultural, social, and economic barriers that discourage them from seeking out much-needed health and social services (National Minority AIDS Education and Training Center, 1999).

In school settings, these barriers are likely to surface in a variety of ways. For instance, fear and negative reactions to HIV/AIDS may further isolate children who are already marginalized because of their racial, linguistic, and cultural differences. Interventions are more likely to succeed if they are culturally responsive to the values, beliefs, and goals of the student and family (see Diversity Forum for Chapter 3). For example, student participation in sports can be an effective way to promote growth

and provide opportunities for the development of social skills.

Coach Robinson's conference with Estrellita's parents will be more successful if the school arranges for an interpreter to be present and if the parents can participate in determining which activities are appropriate for her. Similarly, Mr. Peterson's efforts to promote acceptance and social development for Tanisha would have to address any rejection she may be experiencing from her peers on the basis of race, in addition to educating students about AIDS.

Companion Website

For follow-up questions about students with HIV/AIDS, go to Chapter 10 of the Companion Website (ablongman.com/sppd4e) and click Diversity Forum.

TEACHING TIP

Get in a wheelchair and try to move about your classroom to see whether it is fully accessible; often, areas that look accessible are not.

▶ Be familiar with different types of braces (e.g., short leg, molded ankle-foot) students might use.
▶ Prepare other students in class for the realities of the disease.

Spina Bifida

Spina bifida is a "congenital condition characterized by a malformation of the vertebrae and spinal cord" (Gearheart, Weishahn, & Gearheart, 1996). It affects about 1 in 2,000

Children in wheelchairs need opportunities for social interactions.

births (Bigge, 1991). There are three different types of spina bifida: spina bifida occulta, meningocele, and myelomeningocele (Gearheart et al., 1996; Robertson et al., 1992).

The least serious form of spina bifida is spina bifida occulta. In this type, the vertebral column fails to close properly, leaving a hole in the bony vertebrae that protect the delicate spinal column. With this form of spina bifida, surgically closing the opening to protect the spinal column is generally all that is required and does not result in any problems. **Meningocele** is similar to spina bifida occulta in that the vertebral column fails to close properly, leaving a hole in the bony vertebrae. Skin pouches out in the area where the vertebral column is not closed. In meningocele, the outpouching does not contain any nerve tissue. Surgically removing the outpouching and closing the opening usually result in a positive prognosis without any problems. **Myelomeningocele** is the most common and most severe form of spina bifida. Similar to meningocele, it has one major difference: nerve tissue is present in the outpouching. Because nerve tissue is involved, this form of spina bifida generally results in permanent paralysis and loss of sensation. Incontinence is also a possible result of this condition (Bigge, 1991; Robertson et al., 1992). School personnel must ensure appropriate use of wheelchairs and make accommodations for limited use of arms and hands. Teachers should do the following when working with a child with spina bifida:

▶ Inquire about any acute medical needs the student may have.
▶ Learn about the various adaptive equipment a student may be using (see Baker & Rogosky-Grassi, 1993).
▶ Maintain an environment that assists the student who is using crutches by keeping floors from getting wet and removing loose floor coverings.
▶ Understand the use of a wheelchair as well as its major parts.
▶ Learn how to position these students to develop strength and to keep sores from developing in parts of their bodies that bear their weight or that receive pressure from orthotic devices they are using. Because they do not have sensation, they may not notice the sores themselves. Healing is complicated by poor circulation.
▶ Understand the process of **clean intermittent bladder catheterization (CIC),** as some students will be performing this process to become continent and avoid urinary tract infections—the process involves insertion of a clean catheter through the urethra and into the bladder, must be done four times a day, and can be done independently by most children by age 6.
▶ Be ready to deal with the occasional incontinence of students. Assure the student with spina bifida that this is not a problem and discuss this situation with other class members.
▶ Learn how to deal with the special circumstances associated with students who use wheelchairs and have seizures.
▶ Ensure the full participation of the student in all classroom activities.
▶ Help the student with spina bifida develop a healthy, positive self-concept.
▶ Notify parents if there are unusual changes in the student's behavior or personality or if the student has various physical complaints such as headaches or double vision— these may indicate a problem with increased pressure on the brain (Deiner, 1993).

Tourette Syndrome

Tourette syndrome is a neuropsychiatric disorder that occurs in males three times as often as in females, resulting in a prevalence rate for males as high as 1 in 1,000 individuals (Hansen, 1992). The syndrome is "characterized by multiple motor and one or more vocal tics, which occur many times a day, nearly every day or intermittently, throughout a period of more than one year" (Crews et al., 1993, p. 25). Characteristics include various motor tics; inappropriate laughing; rapid eye movements; winks and grimaces; aggressive behaviors; in infrequent cases, mental retardation; mild to moderate incoordination; and peculiar verbalizations (Woodrich, 1998). Most important, school personnel

CONSIDER THIS

How should students with Tourette syndrome be dealt with when they shout obscenities and display other inappropriate disruptive behaviors?

should be understanding with children who have Tourette syndrome. Monitoring medication and participating as a member of the interdisciplinary team are important roles for teachers and other school personnel.

Summary

▶ Children with physical and health needs are entitled to an appropriate educational program as a result of IDEA.
▶ Physical and health impairments constitute low-incidence disabilities.
▶ The severity, visibility, and age of acquisition affect the needs of children with physical and health impairments.
▶ Students with physical and health problems display a wide array of characteristics and needs.
▶ Students with physical problems qualify for special education under the *orthopedically impaired* category of IDEA.
▶ Students with health problems qualify for special education under the *other health impaired* category of IDEA.

Basic Concepts About Autism
▶ Autism is a pervasive developmental disability that primarily affects social interactions, language, and behavior.
▶ Although originally thought to be caused by environmental factors, autism is now considered to be caused by organic factors, including brain damage and complications during pregnancy.

Classroom Adaptations for Students with Autism
▶ Growing evidence suggests that placing students with autism in general education classrooms with their nondisabled peers results in positive gains for them.

Asperger Syndrome
▶ A condition associated with autism, Asperger syndrome was first included in the fourth edition of the *Diagnostic and Statistical Manual of Mental Disorders*.
▶ Although many of the behavioral characteristics displayed by children with Asperger syndrome are similar to those displayed by children with autism, the former generally have higher cognitive development and more typical communication skills.

Basic Concepts About Traumatic Brain Injury
▶ Traumatic brain injury (TBI) is one of the newest categories recognized by IDEA as a disability category eligible for special education services.
▶ Children with TBI exhibit a wide variety of characteristics, including emotional, learning, and behavior problems.

Classroom Adaptations for Students with Traumatic Brain Injury
▶ Teachers need to maintain as high a level of expectation as possible for students with TBI.

▶ Teachers must familiarize themselves with any specific equipment or medications that students with TBI might need and modify the classroom accordingly.

Low-Incidence Health Problems and Physical Disabilities
▶ Asthma affects many children; teachers primarily need to be aware of medications to control asthma, side effects of medication, and the limitations of students with asthma.
▶ The survival rates for children with cancer have increased dramatically over the past 30 years.
▶ Teachers need to be prepared to deal with the emotional issues surrounding childhood cancer, including death issues.
▶ Children with cancer may miss a good deal of school; the school should make appropriate arrangements in these situations.
▶ Cerebral palsy is a condition that affects muscles and posture; it can be described by the way it affects movement or which limb is involved.
▶ Physical therapy is a critical component of treatment for children with cerebral palsy. Accessibility, communication, and social-emotional concerns are the primary areas that general educators must attend to.
▶ Cystic fibrosis is a terminal condition that affects the mucous membranes of the lungs.
▶ Juvenile diabetes results in children having to take insulin injections daily. Diet and exercise can help children manage their diabetes.
▶ Epilepsy is caused by abnormal activity in the brain that is the result of some brain damage or insult.
▶ Teachers must know specific steps to take in case children have a generalized tonic-clonic seizure in their classrooms.
▶ Infants and teenagers are two of the fastest-growing groups to contract HIV.
▶ Teachers need to keep up to date with developments in HIV/AIDS prevention and treatment approaches.
▶ Muscular dystrophy is a term used to describe several different inherited disorders that result in progressive muscular weakness and may cause death.
▶ Spina bifida is caused by a failure of the spinal column to close properly; this condition may result in paralysis of the lower extremities.
▶ Tourette syndrome is a neuropsychiatric disorder that is characterized by multiple motor tics, inappropriate laughter, rapid eye movements, winks and grimaces, and aggressive behavior.

Further Readings

Batshaw, M. L., & Parret, Y. M. (1986). *Children with handicaps: A medical primer.* Baltimore: Brookes.

Blackman, J. A. (Ed.). (1984). *Medical aspects of developmental disabilities in children birth to three.* Rockville, MD: Aspen.

Gillberg, C. (Ed.). (1989). *Diagnosis and treatment of autism.* New York: Plenum Press.

Koegel, R. L., & Koegel, L. K. (1995). *Teaching children with autism.* Baltimore: Brookes.

National Head Injury Foundation. (1988). *An educator's manual: What educators need to know about students with traumatic brain injury.* Southborough, MA: Author.

Pless, I. B. (Ed.). *The epidemiology of childhood disorders.* (1994). New York: Oxford University Press.

Savage, R. C., & Wolcott, G. F. (Eds.). (1995). *Educational dimensions of acquired brain injury.* Austin, TX: Pro-Ed.

Schopler, E., & Mesibov, G. B. (Eds.). (1995). *Learning and cognition in autism.* New York: Plenum Press.

Smith, M. D., Belcher, R. G., & Juhrs, P. D. (1995). *A guide to successful employment for individuals with autism.* Baltimore: Brookes.

Wetherby, A. M., & Prizant, B. M. (Eds.). (2000). *Autism spectrum disorders: A transactional developmental perspective.* Baltimore: Brookes.

VideoWorkshop Extra!

If the VideoWorkshop package was included with your textbook, go to Chapter 10 of the Companion Website (www.ablongman.com/sppd4e) and click on the VideoWorkshop button. Follow the instructions for viewing video clips 11 and 12. Then consider this information along with what you've read in Chapter 10 while answering the following questions.

1. Educational programs for students like Matt, who experience TBI, should focus on retraining impaired cognitive processes while developing new compensatory skills and providing a supportive environment. If Matt's age permitted him to be in your classroom, how would you support his reentry?

2. Students like Oscar who have paraplegia have many special needs and typically have assigned support staff to aid them. Reflect on and list the issues that will concern you about situations like Oscar's. How will you address these concerns in your classroom?

11 Teaching Students with Communication Disorders

Peggy Kipping and Kathleen McConnell Fad

After reading this chapter, you should be able to

1. define the concept of communication and describe its major components, language, and speech.
2. describe typical speech and language development in children.
3. discuss communication disorders, including the different types of disorders and some of their characteristics.
4. describe various classroom accommodations appropriate for students with speech and language disorders.
5. discuss language differences that are due to culture and ways that teachers can deal with these differences.
6. discuss augmentative and alternative communication techniques.
7. describe trends that are shaping provision of speech therapy services in the schools.

avid is an eight-year-old who recently began stuttering in the classroom. At first David's second grade teacher, Mr. Parker, wasn't concerned because David's dysfluencies were infrequent and short both in duration and in intensity. But lately, it seems to be becoming more of a problem. Mr. Parker has noticed that David has stopped participating in class and that he doesn't seem to be playing with his friends on the playground as he used to.

Mr. Parker called David's parents to schedule a parent-teacher conference. At the conference, David's parents said that they had also noticed David's stuttering, but that it didn't seem as severe at home as at school. They were very concerned about how David's stuttering might affect his educational, emotional, and behavioral development. They indicated that there was a history of disfluency in their family, and they knew how important it was that David begin receiving therapy as soon as possible.

Mr. Parker and David's parents requested an in-depth evaluation by the school's speech–language pathologist, Mrs. Woods. Mrs. Woods began by chatting with David about his stuttering. David said that he was aware of his stuttering and that he was really embarrassed and ashamed of it. He said that his stuttering was worse when he talked to his friends and when he talked on the phone or with adults with whom he was less familiar. David was clearly upset about his stuttering and even began crying during one part of the interview.

After completing the interview with David as well as the formal assessment, Mrs. Woods scheduled the IEP meeting. At the meeting, she recommended that David begin receiving speech therapy services three times weekly for thirty minutes each session. David would join a small group of two other boys from his school who were also stuttering. Mrs. Woods gave David's parents and Mr. Parker some brochures and pamphlets that provided information about stuttering, speech therapy, and how to help David communicate better in school and at home. The IEP team agreed on David's goals and objectives for the coming school year, and discussed how to modify lessons to help David participate to the fullest extent possible.

QUESTIONS TO CONSIDER

1. What should Mr. Parker tell the students in his classroom about stuttering?
2. What could Mr. Parker and Mrs. Woods do to help David better interact with his peers in settings other than the classroom?
3. Should Mr. Parker expect David to give oral reports in front of class? Why or why not?
4. Why would asking David to "slow down" or "relax" not help him to speak more fluently?

For most of us, the ability to communicate is a skill we take for granted. Our communication is effortless and frequent. In one day, we might share a story with family members, discuss problems with our coworkers, ask directions from a stranger on the street, and telephone an old friend. When we are able to communicate easily and effectively, it is natural to participate in both the commonplace activities of daily living and the more enjoyable experiences that enrich our lives.

However, when communication is impaired, absent, or qualitatively different, the simplest interactions may become difficult or even impossible. Moreover, because the communication skills that most of us use fluently and easily almost always involve personal interactions with others, disorders in speech or language may also result in social problems. For children, these social problems are most likely to occur in school. School is a place not only for academic learning, but also for building positive relationships with teachers and enduring friendships with peers. When a student's communication disorder, however mild, limits these experiences, makes him or her feel different and inadequate, or undermines confidence and self-esteem, the overall impact can be devastating.

Communication problems are often complex. There are many types of communication disorders, involving both speech and language. This chapter describes strategies that teachers can use with students who have such disorders. Suggestions will address specific communication disorders as well as associated problems in socialization and adjustment.

Basic Concepts About Communication Disorders

Communication and Communication Disorders Defined

Speech and **language** are interrelated skills, tools that we use to communicate and learn. Heward (1995) defines the related terms this way:

> *Communication* is the exchange of information and ideas. Communication involves encoding, transmitting, and decoding messages. It is an interactive process requiring at least two parties to play the roles of both sender and receiver. . . . *Language* is a system used by a group of people for giving meaning to sounds, words, gestures, and other symbols to enable communication with one another. . . . *Speech* is the actual behavior of producing a language code by making appropriate vocal sound patterns. Although it is not the only possible vehicle for expressing language (gestures, manual signing, pictures, and written symbols can also be used to convey ideas and intentions), speech is a most effective and efficient method. Speech is also one of the most complex and difficult human endeavors. (pp. 234–236)

Various cultures develop and use language differently, and the study of language is a complex topic. The **American Speech-Language-Hearing Association (ASHA)** (1982) includes the following important considerations in its discussion of language: (1) language evolves within specific historical, social, and cultural contexts; (2) language is rule-governed behavior; (3) language learning and use are determined by the interaction of biological, cognitive, psychosocial, and environmental factors; and (4) effective use of language for communication requires a broad understanding of human interactions, including associated factors such as nonverbal cues, motivation, and sociocultural roles (p. 949).

Because language development and use are such complicated topics, determining what is *normal* and what is *disordered* communication is also difficult. According to Emerick and Haynes (1986), a communication difference is considered a disability when

▶ the transmission or perception of messages is faulty.
▶ the person is placed at an economic disadvantage.
▶ the person is placed at a learning disadvantage.
▶ the person is placed at a social disadvantage.

▶ there is a negative impact upon the person's emotional growth.
▶ the problem causes physical damage or endangers the health of the person. (pp. 6–7)

In order to better understand communication disorders, it is helpful to be familiar with the dimensions of communication and the terms used to describe related disorders.

Types of Communication Disorders   In its definition of communicative disorders, ASHA (1982) describes both speech disorders and language disorders. **Speech disorders** include impairments of *voice, articulation,* and *fluency.* **Language disorders** are impairments of *comprehension or use of language,* regardless of the symbol system used. A language disorder may involve the *form* of language, the content of language, or the *function* (use) of language. Specific disorders of language form include **phonologic, syntactic,** and **morphologic impairments. Semantics** refers to the content or meaning of language, and **pragmatics** is the system controlling language function. Figure 11.1 contains the definitions of communication disorders as described by ASHA. The terms in this figure are discussed in more detail later in the chapter. The category of communication disorders is broad in scope and includes a wide variety of problems, some of which may overlap.

CONSIDER THIS

Can you think of instances in which communication between two or more people was so poor that problems resulted?

COMMUNICATION DISORDERS

A. A *speech disorder* is an impairment of voice, articulation of speech sounds, and/or fluency. These impairments are observed in the transmission and use of the oral symbol system.
1. A *voice disorder* is defined as the absence or abnormal production of voice quality, pitch, loudness, resonance, and/or duration.
2. An *articulation disorder* is defined as the abnormal production of speech sounds.
3. A *fluency disorder* is defined as the abnormal flow of verbal expression, characterized by impaired rate and rhythm, which may be accompanied by struggle behavior.

B. A *language disorder* is the impairment or deviant development of comprehension and/or use of a spoken, written, and/or other symbol system. The disorder may involve (1) the form of language (phonologic, morphologic, and syntactic systems), (2) the content of language (semantic system), and/or (3) the function of language in communication (pragmatic system) in any combination.
1. Form of language
   a. *Phonology* is the sound system of a language and the linguistic rules that govern the sound combinations.
   b. *Morphology* is the linguistic rule system that governs the structure of words and the construction of word forms from the basic elements of meaning.
   c. *Syntax* is the linguistic rule governing the order and combination of words to form sentences, and the relationships among the elements within a sentence.
2. Content of language
   Semantics is the psycholinguistic system that patterns the content of an utterance, intent, and meanings of words and sentences.
3. Function of language
   Pragmatics is the sociolinguistic system that patterns the use of language in communication, which may be expressed motorically, vocally, or verbally.

COMMUNICATION VARIATIONS

A. *Communicative difference/dialect* is a variation of a symbol system used by a group of individuals that reflects and is determined by shared regional, social, or cultural/ethnic factors. Variations or alterations in use of a symbol system may be indicative of primary language interferences. A regional, social, or cultural/ethnic variation of a symbol system should not be considered a disorder of speech or language.

B. *Augmentative communication* is a system used to supplement the communicative skills of individuals for whom speech is temporarily or permanently inadequate to meet communicative needs. Both prosthetic devices and/or nonprosthetic techniques may be designed for individual use as an augmentative communication system.

FIGURE 11.1

Definitions of Communication Disorders from ASHA

From "Definitions: Communicative Disorders and Variations," by the American Speech-Language-Hearing Association, 1982, *ASHA, 24,* pp. 949–950. Reprinted by permission of the American Speech-Language-Hearing Association.

It is not surprising that this group of disorders includes a large proportion of all students with disabilities.

Prevalence and Causes of Communication Disorders

Approximately 1,089,964 children and youth, about 2% of the school-age population, were classified as having speech or language impairments during the 1999–2000 school year (U.S. Department of Education, 2002). These students have impairments in their ability to send or receive a message, to articulate clearly or fluently, or to comprehend the pragmatics of social interactions. Because many other students have other conditions as their primary disability but still receive speech–language services, the total number of students served by **speech–language pathologists** is about 5% of all school-age children, two-thirds of whom are boys. Students with communication disorders constitute about 20% of all students with disabilities. The number of students in this classification increased during the 1999–2000 school year (U.S. Department of Education, 2002). Of the more than 1 million students identified as speech- or language-impaired, about 90% (over 900,000) are 6 to 11 years of age (U.S. Department of Education, 2002). Thirty-four percent of students aged 6–11 who have been identified as requiring special education services are classified as having a speech or language impairment (SLI). For this reason, most of the suggestions in this chapter focus on that age group, although many of the language development activities would also be useful for older students.

Identification, Assessment, and Eligibility

CONSIDER THIS

What are the advantages of serving most of the students with communication disorders in general education classrooms?

Placement patterns for students with disabilities vary by disability, according to students' individual needs. Usually, the milder the disability, the less restrictive the placement. Students with speech or language impairments are the most highly integrated of all students with disabilities. Since 1985, most students with SLI have been served in either general education classes or resource rooms. During the 1998–1999 school year, 88.5% of students with communication disorders were served in general education classroom placements and 6.5% were served in resource rooms (U.S. Department of Education, 2002). The small proportion served in separate classes most likely represents students with severe language delays and disabilities. For classroom teachers, having students with communication disorders in their classes is more the rule than the exception. The Rights & Responsibilities feature highlights students with speech impairments rights to related services when they are in the general education classroom.

Rights & Responsibilities

The Right to "Related Services" for Students with Speech Impairments

Students with speech impairments are generally served in general education classes. They are usually in need of related services. Related services are "to benefit the student" so that he or she may

▶ Advance appropriately toward attaining annual goals;
▶ Be involved and progress in the general curriculum and participate in extracurricular activities and other nonacademic activities; and
▶ Be educated and participate with other children with disabilities and nondisabled children in those extracurricular and nonacademic activities. (Turnbull & Turnbull, 2000, p. 193)

Related services include speech pathology and speech–language pathology. IDEA defines these as "identification, diagnosis, and appraisal of specific speech or language impairments; referral to or provision of speech and language, medical, or other services; and counseling and guidance of parents, children, and teachers regarding speech and language impairments" [34 C.F.R., 300.24(b)(14)].

For follow-up questions about rights for students with speech impairments, go to Chapter 11 of the Companion Website (ablongman.com/sppd4e) and click Rights & Responsibilities.

Because so many students with communication disorders are included in general education classrooms, it is important that teachers be able to identify those students who may have speech or language problems, be familiar with common causes of communication disorders, know when problems are serious enough to require referral to other resources, and have some effective strategies for working with students in the general education environment.

Speech Disorders

This section of the chapter discusses speech disorders that include problems in *phonology, voice,* and *fluency.* The discussion includes (1) a description and definition, (2) a brief explanation of causes, and (3) information related to identifying problems serious enough to require a referral for possible assessment or remediation.

Articulatory and Phonological Disorders

Articulatory and **phonological disorders** are the most common speech disorders, affecting about 10% of preschool and school-age children (ASHA, 2002). The ability to articulate clearly and use the phonological code correctly is a function of many variables, including a student's age, developmental history, oral-motor skills, and culture. Although some articulatory and phonological errors are normal and acceptable at young ages, when students are older these same errors may be viewed as developmentally inappropriate and problematic. However, by the time students begin kindergarten, they should be easily understood by their teacher and their peers. McReynolds (1990) has described the most common types of articulation errors: **distortions, substitutions, omissions,** and **additions** (Table 11.1).

Causes of Problems in the Phonological System   Articulatory and phonological impairments can be either organic (i.e., having an identifiable physical cause) or functional (i.e., having no identifiable cause). Children with functional disorders account for 99% of the articulation caseloads of speech–language pathologists in the schools (ASHA, 1999). Some functional disorders may be related to the student's opportunities to learn appropriate and inappropriate speech patterns, including opportunities to practice appropriate speech, transient hearing loss during early development, and the absence or presence of good speech models. Some functional phonological problems have causes that may be

> **CROSS-REFERENCE**
>
> Review Chapter 9 on sensory impairments to see the impact of a hearing loss on articulation skills.

TABLE 11.1   **The Four Kinds of Articulation Errors**

Error Type	Definition	Example
Distortion	A sound is produced in an unfamiliar manner.	Standard: Give the pencil to Sally. Distortion: Give the pencil to Sally. (the /p/ is nasalized)
Substitution	Replace one sound with another sound.	Standard: The ball is red. Substitution: The ball is wed.
Omission	A sound is omitted in a word.	Standard: Play the piano. Omission: P_ay the piano.
Addition	An extra sound is inserted within a word.	Standard: I have a black horse. Addition: I have a balack horse.

From *Human Communication Disorders* (3rd ed., p. 219) by G. H. Shames and E. H. Wiig, 1990, New York: Macmillan. Copyright © 1990 by Macmillan Publishing Company. Reprinted by permission.

related to complex neurological or neuromuscular deficits and might never be specifically identified. Differences in speech can also be related to cultural and linguistic variables. These differences often do not constitute a speech disorder and will be discussed later in the chapter.

Organic articulatory and phonological disorders are related to the neurological and physical abilities required in the process of producing speech sounds, which is a highly complex activity involving intricate, precise, and rapid coordination of neuromuscular, sensory, and cognitive systems. According to the American Psychiatric Association (2000), organic causes of speech impairments may include hearing loss, cleft palate, dental malformations, or tumors. Brain damage and related neurological problems may also result in disorders of speech production such as verbal apraxia and dysarthria. The severity of articulatory and phonological disorders can vary widely, depending in part on the causes of the disorders.

When Articulatory and Phonological Errors Are a Serious Problem   Because we know the developmental patterns for normal sound production, we can recognize those children who are significantly different from the norm. According to Sander (1972), the normal pattern of consonant sound production falls within relatively well-defined age limits. For example, children usually master the consonant /p/ sound by age 3, but may not produce a correct /s/ sound consistently until age 8. Although young children between ages 2 and 6 often make phonological errors as their speech develops, similar errors in older students would indicate a problem. At age 3 it might be normal for a child to say *wabbit* instead of *rabbit*. If a 5-year-old consistently made the same error, it would be considered a problem, and the teacher should refer the student to a speech–language pathologist for evaluation. Figure 11.2 presents this pattern of normal development for production of consonants among speakers of Standard American English.

For a general education teacher, evaluating a student's phonological errors involves looking at the big picture, that is, how well the student is doing in class and whether the disorder is interfering with either overall academic performance or social adjustment. A

Articulation problems can result in problems in socialization or adjustment.

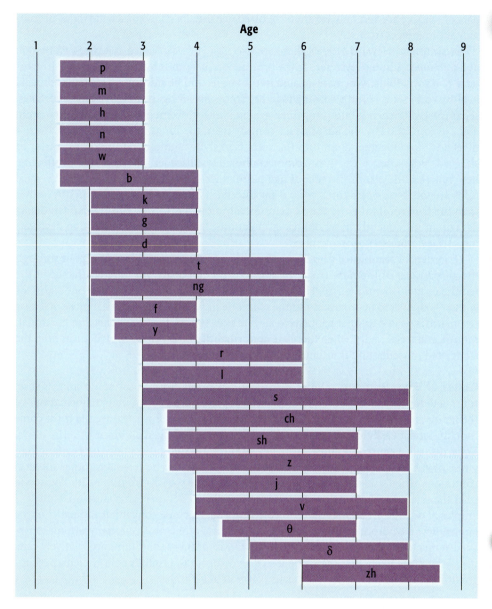

Age

FIGURE 11.2

Ages at Which 90% of All Children Typically Produce a Specific Sound Correctly

Note: Average estimates and upper age limits of customary consonant production. The solid bar corresponding to each sound starts at the median age of customary articulation; it stops at an age level at which 90% of all children are customarily producing the sound. The ø symbol stands for the breathed "th" sound, as in *bathroom,* and the ∂ symbol stands for the voiced "th" sound, as in *feather* (Smith and Luckasson, 1992, p. 168).

From "When Are Speech Sounds Learned?" by E. K. Sander, 1972, *Journal of Speech and Hearing Disorders, 37,* p. 62. Reprinted by permission of the American Speech-Language-Hearing Association.

CONSIDER THIS

How could cultural differences influence a child's development of the specific sounds listed in Figure 11.2?

few common-sense considerations may give some insight into whether the student has a serious problem and what, if anything, should be done about it:

▶ Take note of how understandable or intelligible the student's speech is.
▶ Consider how many different errors the student makes.
▶ Evaluate whether the speech errors may have an impact on the student's ability to read and write.
▶ Observe whether the articulation errors cause the student problems in socialization or adjustment.
▶ Consider whether the errors could be due to physical problems.

Voice Disorders

Voice disorders are abnormalities of speech related to volume, quality, or pitch. Voice problems are not very common in children, and it is sometimes difficult to distinguish an unpleasant voice from one that would be considered disordered. People generally tolerate a wide range of voices. Because our voices are related to our identities and are an integral

TEACHING TIP

General classroom teachers should screen all students in their classes, especially during the early elementary grades, to determine which students have articulation problems that might require intervention.

part of who we are and how we are recognized, we usually allow for a wide range of individual differences in voice.

According to Heward (1995), there are two basic types of voice disorders, *phonation* and *resonance*. **Phonation** refers to the production of sounds by the vocal folds. Humans have two vocal folds, which are located in the larynx and lie side by side. When we speak, healthy vocal folds vibrate, coming together smoothly along the length of their surfaces, separating, and then coming together again. These movements are usually very rapid and are controlled by the air pressure coming from the lungs. If the vocal folds do not meet and close together smoothly, the voice is likely to sound breathy, hoarse, husky, or strained. Hoarseness is the most common phonatory disorder among children, affecting between 18 and 23% of the school-age population (ASHA, 2002). If a student's vocal folds are too tense or lax, or if voice is produced by vibrating laryngeal structures other than the true vocal folds, he might demonstrate a pitch disorder. Although pitch disorders occur infrequently in school-age populations, they can sometimes lead to devastating social-emotional consequences.

Disorders of **resonance** usually involve either too many sounds coming out through the air passages of the nose (hypernasality) or the opposite, too little resonance of the nasal passages (hyponasality). Hypernasality sounds like talking through one's nose or with a "twang," and hyponasality sounds like one has a cold or a congested nose. Because resonance is related to what happens to air that travels from the vocal folds into the throat, mouth, and nasal cavity, when there are abnormalities in any of these structures or in the associated musculature, resonance problems can result.

Causes of Voice Disorders Voice disorders can result from vocal abuse and misuse, trauma to the larynx from accidents or medical procedures, congenital malformations of the larynx, nodules, or tumors. Disorders caused by abuse or misuse are the most common and most easily prevented voice disorders in school-aged children (ASHA, 1999). Voice disorders caused by abuse or misuse of the vocal folds affect boys more often than girls (ASHA, 2002). Because some voice disorders can also be related to other medical conditions, when students evidence a voice disorder, the speech–language pathologist will refer them to an otolaryngologist (ear, nose, and throat doctor) for evaluation. Some examples of organic problems related to voice disorders include congenital anomalies of the larynx, Reye's syndrome, juvenile arthritis, psychiatric problems, Tourette syndrome, physical trauma to the larynx, and cancer. Because most of these conditions are relatively rare, it may be more likely that the student's voice disorder is a functional problem, perhaps resulting from learned speech patterns (Oyer et al., 1987).

When Voice Disorders Are a Serious Problem Classroom teachers can help prevent voice disorders among their students by modeling and promoting healthy voice habits in the classroom, on the playground, and at home. A student who is suspected of having a voice disorder should be observed over the course of several weeks, since many symptoms of voice disorders are similar to other temporary conditions such as colds, seasonal allergies, or minor respiratory infections (Oyer et al., 1987). One way to get a meaningful measure of the student's speech during this time is to tape-record him or her several times during the observation period. The tape recordings will be helpful to the speech-language pathologist and will provide a basis for comparison. Again, our voices are part of our identity, and, quite often, differences in voice quality, volume, or pitch may be considered to be part of who we are, rather than a problem that requires correction. Teachers might ask themselves the following questions before referring a student for evaluation of a voice disorder:

▶ Is the student's voice having such an unpleasant effect on others that the student is teased or excluded from activities?
▶ Does the student habitually abuse or misuse his voice?
▶ Is there a possibility that the voice disorder is related to another medical condition?
▶ Does the student's voice problem make him difficult for others to understand?

CONSIDER THIS

How can a student's voice quality affect classroom and peer acceptance? What are some things that teachers can do to influence this impact?

◗ Has there been a recent, noticeable change in the student's vocal quality?
◗ Might the voice quality be related to a hearing loss?

Fluency Disorders

Fluency refers to the pattern of the rate and flow of a person's speech. Normal speech has a rhythm and timing that is regular and steady; however, normal speech patterns also include some interruptions in speech flow. We all sometimes stumble over sounds, repeat syllables or words, mix up speech sounds in words, speak too fast, or fill in pauses with "uh" or "you know." Often normal dysfluencies of speech are related to stressful or demanding situations. When the interruptions in speech flow are so frequent or pervasive that a speaker cannot be understood, when efforts at speech are so intense that they are uncomfortable, or when they draw undue attention, then the dysfluencies are considered a problem (Hallahan & Kauffman, 1995).

Many young children, especially those between ages 2 and 5, demonstrate dysfluencies in the course of normal speech development. Parents and teachers may become concerned about young children's fluency, but most of these dysfluencies of early childhood begin to disappear by age 5. The most frequent type of fluency disorder is **stuttering,** which affects about 2% of school-age children, more often boys than girls (Smith & Luckasson, 1992). Cluttering, another type of fluency disorder, occurs infrequently in school-age children. Disturbances of prosody and intonation are also rare in children, and are often associated with other, more serious communication problems.

Fluency problems usually consist of blocking, repeating, prolonging, or avoiding sounds, syllables, words, or phrases. In *stuttering,* these interruptions are frequently obvious to both the speaker and the listener. Often, they are very disruptive to the act of speaking, much more so than disorders of articulation or voice. When the speech dysfluencies occur, listeners may become uncomfortable and look away or try to finish the speaker's words, phrases, or sentences. This discomfort is exacerbated when dysfluent speech is accompanied by unusual gestures, facial contortions, or other movements. Because stuttering can lead to such a pronounced interruption of normal speech and also has a profound impact on listeners, the disorder receives a lot of attention, even though it is not as prevalent as other communication disorders (Hardman, Drew, Egan, & Wolf, 1993).

Causes of Stuttering   Although many causes of stuttering have been suggested over the years, the current thinking among professionals in the field of communication disorders is that there may be many different causes of the disorder. According to Van Riper and Emerick (1984), these theories include (1) the view that stuttering is related to emotional

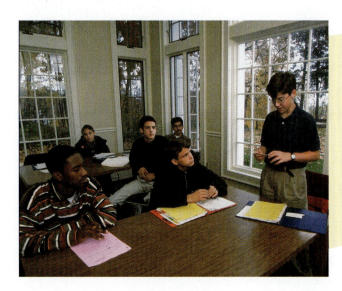

Stuttering is the most frequent type of fluency disorder, affecting about 2% of school-age children, more often boys than girls.

problems, (2) the idea that stuttering is the result of a person's biological makeup or of some neurological difference, and (3) the view that stuttering is a learned behavior. Recent studies have focused on the growing evidence supporting a genetic and physiologic basis of stuttering (Agrawal, 2001; Budgar, 2001).

There seems to be no doubt that the children who stutter are very vulnerable to the attitudes, responses, and comments of their teachers and peers. When considerable attention is focused on normal dysfluencies or when students begin to have negative feelings about themselves because of their stuttering, they may become even more anxious and their stuttering may get worse. Most students who stutter will require therapy by a speech–language pathologist if they hope to avoid a lifelong problem that will affect their ability to communicate, learn, work, and develop positive interpersonal relationships.

When Fluency Disorders Are a Serious Problem   Although we know that many children will naturally outgrow their speech dysfluencies, we are unable to predict those children who will not. Therefore, classroom teachers should be sure to refer any children who show signs of dysfluency so they can be evaluated by the speech–language pathologist and, if necessary, receive speech therapy. Teachers should consider the following questions when deciding whether speech dysfluencies are serious:

▶ Are the dysfluencies beginning to occur more often in the student's speech or beginning to sound more effortful or strained?
▶ Is there a pattern to situations in which the student stutters?
▶ Is the student experiencing social problems?
▶ Is the student concerned about his dysfluencies?

Classroom Adaptations for Students with Speech Disorders

Build a Positive Classroom Climate

Regardless of the type of speech disorder that students in general education classes demonstrate, it is crucial that teachers make every effort to create a positive, accepting, and supportive climate. The following points are helpful to remember when dealing with children who have speech disorders:

▶ Talk with the student privately about his or her speech problems. Acknowledge your awareness of the problem, and stress your belief that speech will improve with practice.
▶ Encourage the student's family to actively support the student's educational and communication goals.
▶ Don't think of or refer to students with speech disorders in terms of their behaviors ("students," not "stutterers").
▶ Work closely with the speech–language pathologist, following suggestions and trying to reinforce specific skills.
▶ Encourage the student.
▶ Be positive.
▶ Accept the child just as you would any other student in the class.
▶ Provide lots of opportunities for students to participate in oral group activities.
▶ Give students lots of chances to model and practice appropriate speech.
▶ Maintain eye contact when the student speaks.
▶ Be a good listener.
▶ Don't interrupt or finish the student's sentence for him or her.
▶ When appropriate, educate other students in the class about speech disorders and about acceptance and understanding.
▶ Reward the child just as you would reward any student.

See Tips for Adapting a Lesson for David for specific recommendations for the student profiled in the chapter-opening vignette.

TEACHING TIP

Teachers who have students who stutter should attempt to reduce the stress on these students and create an accepting atmosphere.

TEACHING TIP

Teachers should keep a log to record instances of stuttering and the activities occurring with the student and the rest of the class when stuttering occurs and when it does not occur.

Tips for Adapting a Lesson for David

Based on the chapter-opening vignette, several adaptations are appropriate for David.

David's teacher should do the following:

▶ Do not complete sentences for David; be patient and allow him time to get the words out.

▶ Do not ask David to "slow down" or "relax"; these instructions are not helpful to him.

▶ During group instruction, call on David fairly early in the discussion and ask David questions that can be answered with relatively few words.

▶ Speak slowly during group instruction to help slow the pace of all interactions in class.

▶ Have the same academic expectations for David as for any other student in the class.

▶ Talk about stuttering with the class and with David just as you would any other matter. It is nothing to be ashamed of.

Help Students Learn to Monitor Their Own Speech

By using simple contract formats, teachers can help students focus on using the skills they learn in speech therapy. When students are aware of how to make sounds correctly, they can then practice, monitor their own performance, and earn reinforcement from the teacher or parents whenever specific criteria are met.

Pair Students for Practice

If students are to master speech skills, they will need to practice the skills taught by the speech–language pathologist frequently in many different settings. One way for students to practice specific sounds is to use practice exercises like those in Loehr's *Read the Picture Stories for Articulation* (Loehr, 2002; Figure 11.3). With a partner, students can use short periods of downtime such as those between or before classes to work on their articulation. First, the student is trained in the speech therapy setting on a specific phoneme in a particular position of words, for example, the initial /s/ sound in seal. After the student has reached 90% mastery of the /s/ sound in the beginning of words, she or he then reads a story that is saturated with words beginning with the /s/ sound to a classmate. Each practice session should take no more than five minutes and will provide students with practice that is simple and fun. Both partners should be reinforced for their participation. This practice format can also be used at home with parents.

Teach Students Affirmations and Positive Self-Talk

For students with speech disorders, especially stuttering, having self-confidence and a positive attitude are as important as learning specific speech skills. Research has supported the premise that we all talk to ourselves all of the time, and the more we talk to ourselves in certain ways, the more we think about ourselves in those same ways. Although negative **self-talk** is common among individuals who have speech disorders, it is possible to change negative patterns to more positive ones.

Affirmations like those suggested by Daly (1991) can enable students to build their confidence. The goal of positive self-talk is to replace negative patterns, which might include the statements "I could never do that" or "I can never talk on the phone without stuttering" with positive statements such as "I am positive and confident. I know that I can handle any speaking situation by being in control of my speech" and "I enjoy saying my name clearly and smoothly when answering the telephone." Whenever a student slips

TEACHING TIP

Self-monitoring strategies, such as record keeping, can facilitate a student's attempts to monitor his or her own speech.

FIGURE 11.3 **Sample Form for Articulation Practice**

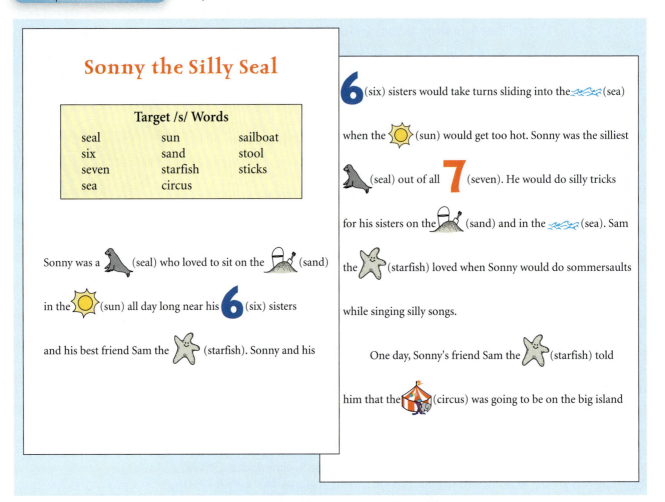

From *Read the Picture Stories for Articulation* (2nd ed., pp. 19–20) by J. Loehr, 2002, Austin, TX: Pro-Ed. Used by permission.

back into a negative frame of mind, encourage him or her to mentally erase the negative ideas and immediately think of something positive. Students should also write their affirmations in their own words, so that they will remember them easily and will more likely use them.

Modify Instruction and Materials

The *Pre-Referral Intervention Manual (PRIM)* (McCarney & Wunderlich, 1988) presents numerous ways of intervening with students who demonstrate speech errors. Some of the suggestions include the following:

▶ Set up a system of motivators to encourage students' efforts.
▶ Highlight material to identify key syllables and words in a passage.
▶ Give students practice listening so that they can learn to discriminate among sounds, fluent speech patterns, and good vocal habits.
▶ Tape-record the students' reading so that they can evaluate themselves related to their communication goals.
▶ Reduce the emphasis on competition. Competitive activities may increase students' stress and result in even more speech errors.

Encourage Parents to Work with Their Children

There are many ways to structure practice activities so that students can work at home with their parents. One program is described in the book *Oral-Motor Activities for School-Aged Children* (Mackie, 1996; Figure 11.4). This series of homework activities is designed to help build the skills that are prerequisite to producing sounds in words. They are designed to be an enjoyable approach to improving the coordination, sensory awareness, and muscle strength needed to produce the sounds of speech. By completing the activities, students assume responsibility for practicing skills learned in the therapy room in other environments. It is suggested that students complete one activity per day and have their parents discuss it with them and provide feedback and guidance.

Teach Students Their Own Strategies

Many of the speech problems that students demonstrate while young can be corrected and modified with therapy. While the therapy is going on, the teacher should focus on giving students strategies for successful learning. The strategies are little "tricks of the trade" that students can use to maximize their academic and social strengths. Some of these strategies also require accommodations on the part of the teacher in structuring situations and requirements.

▶ Teach them to relax with breathing exercises or mental imagery.
▶ Encourage them to participate in groups in which responses do not have to be individually generated.

FIGURE 11.4

Speech Activities That Parents Can Use

From *Oral-Motor Activities for School-Aged Children* by E. Mackie, 1996, Austin: Pro-Ed.

1. What sound are you working on? Write it down. List 10 words with your sound.
   My sound _____

   _____   _____
   _____   _____
   _____   _____
   _____   _____
   _____   _____

2. List the parts of your mouth used to produce your sound.

   _____
   _____
   _____

3. Identify the stability and mobility points needed to produce your sound.

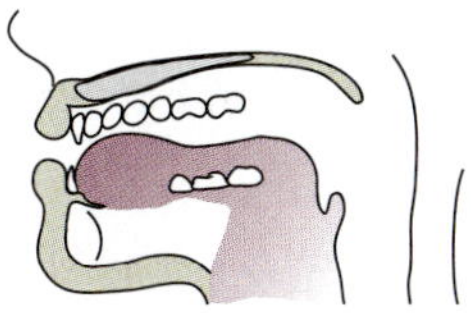

4. Mark the parts of the tongue you need to work on to produce your sound correctly.

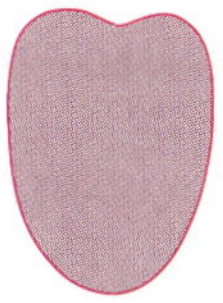

5. Describe what is happening to your mouth when you say your sound incorrectly.

6. Be ready to define the words *stability, mobility,* and *separation (differentiation)* at your next speech session.

Helper _____   Date _____

IEP Goals and Objectives for David

Goal 1:   *David will read in variety of settings with normal fluency.*
  Objective 1:   *Given a short passage to read in the therapy setting, David will read the passage with normal fluency in 75% of trials.*
  Objective 2:   *Given a short passage at home, David will read the passage with normal fluency in 75% of trials.*
  Objective 3:   *Given a short passage in the classroom, David will read the passage with normal fluency in 75% of trials.*

Goal 2:   *David will learn techniques that facilitate fluent speech.*
  Objective 1:   *Given the opportunity to describe and demonstrate breathing techniques in the therapy setting and at home, David will do so appropriately in 70% of the trials.*
  Objective 2:   *Given the opportunity to demonstrate mastery of relaxation techniques in the therapy setting and at home, David will do so successfully in 70% of trials.*
  Objective 3:   *Given the opportunity to demonstrate the use of slow, easy speech in the therapy setting and at home, David will do so successfully in 70% of trials.*
  Objective 4:   *Given the opportunity to demonstrate the use of fluency-facilitating techniques in small groups in the classroom, David will do so successfully in 70% of opportunities.*

▶ Teach them to reinforce themselves by recognizing when they are doing well and by appreciating themselves.
▶ Let them practice skills with a friend in real situations so that they are not afraid or nervous when it's the "real thing."
▶ Let them tape-record their own speech and listen carefully for errors so that they can discriminate between correct and incorrect sounds.
▶ Help them come up with strategies for dealing with specific people or situations that make them nervous (walking away, counting to 10 before they speak, deep breathing, etc.).

The IEP Goals and Objectives for David feature includes examples of the strategies recommended for David to try on his own.

Language Disorders

Language is the system we use to communicate our thoughts and ideas to others. According to Lahey (1988), language is a code "whereby ideas about the world are expressed through a conventional system of arbitrary signals for communication" (p. 2). The interrelationships of what we hear, speak, read, and write become our format for sharing information.

For most of us, spoken language is the tool we use to communicate our ideas, but even the most articulate, fluent, pleasant speech would be useless without a language system that enables us to understand and be understood. Language is an integral component of students' abilities in reading, writing, speaking, and listening. Disorders of language often have a serious impact on academic performance. In recent years, the emphasis in the field of communication disorders has shifted to encompass an increased focus on language disorders. Estimates today are that 50% to 80% of the children seen by speech–language pathologists have language disorders (Wiig, 1986).

More important for classroom teachers, however, is the fact that remediation of language disorders will often be as much their responsibility as it is the speech–language pathologist's. Although remediation of speech problems is provided primarily in a therapeutic setting and then supported and reinforced by the classroom teacher, classroom teachers will often direct and manage the overall language development of their students in collaboration with the speech–language pathologist and other special education staff.

We know that humans can communicate in several ways. Heward (1995) describes a child's process for learning language this way: "A child may learn to identify a familiar object, for example, by hearing the spoken word *tree,* by seeing the printed word *tree,* by viewing the sign language gesture for *tree,* or by encountering a combination of these signals" (p. 235). We generally describe modes of communication as either **receptive language,** which involves receiving and decoding or interpreting language, or **expressive language,** which is the encoding or production of a message. Reading and listening are examples of receptive language; writing and speaking are forms of expressive language.

As with speech disorders, knowing the normal sequence of language development is important in working with students with language disorders. Some children may be delayed in their development of language but still acquire skills in the same general sequence as other children. Other children may acquire some age-appropriate language skills but have deficits in other specific areas. Table 11.2 shows the normal patterns of language development for children with language disorders and children without language disorders. Although they may refer to these general patterns of language development to judge students' overall progress, teachers should not expect every child to follow this precise sequence on these exact timelines.

Dimensions of Language

Earlier in the chapter, some terminology related to language disorders was introduced. In addition, we refer to the dimensions of language and their related impairments in terms of form, content, and function (or use). Students can demonstrate impairments in any or all of these areas.

Form Form describes the rule systems used in oral language. Three different rule systems are included when we discuss form: *phonology, morphology,* and *syntax.*

Phonology is the rule system that governs the individual and combined sounds of a language. Phonological rules vary from one language to another. For example, some of the guttural sounds heard in German are not used in English, and some of the vowel combinations of English are not found in Spanish. The ability to process and manipulate the phonological components of language has been shown to be a critical component in the development of early reading skills.

Morphology refers to the rule system controlling the structure of words. Because the structures of words govern their meanings, comparative suffixes such as *-er* or *-est* and plural forms such as the *-s* that changes *book* to *books* are important. Oyer et al. (1987) provide an example of how morphemes (units of meaning) can change a basic word into similar words with many different meanings:

> The word "friend" is composed of one free morpheme that has meaning. One or more bound morphemes may be added, making "friendly," "unfriendly," "friendless," "friendliness," "friendship," and "friendlier." There are rules for combining morphemes into words that must be followed (e.g., "disfriend" is not an allowable word and thus has no meaning). (p. 61)

Syntax is the ordering of words in such a way that they can be understood. Syntax rules determine where words are placed in a phrase or sentence. Just like phonology, syntax rules vary from one language to another. Rules governing negatives, questions, tenses,

TABLE 11.2   **Language Development for Children with Language Disorders and Without Language Disorders**

Language-Disordered Child			Normally Developing Child		
Age	Attainment	Example	Age	Attainment	Example
27 months	First words	*this, mama, bye bye, doggie*	13 months	First words	*here, mama, bye bye, kitty*
38 months	50-word vocabulary		17 months	50-word vocabulary	
40 months	First two-word combinations	*this doggie more apple this mama more play*	18 months	First two-word combinations	*more juice here ball more TV here kitty*
48 months	Later two-word combinations	*Mimi purse Daddy coat block chair dolly table*	22 months	Later two-word combinations	*Andy shoe Mommy ring cup floor keys chair*
52 months	Mean sentence length of 2.00 words		24 months	Mean sentence length of 2.00 words	
55 months	First appearance of -ing	*Mommy eating*	24 months	First appearance of -ing	*Andy sleeping*
63 months	Mean sentence length of 3.10 words		30 months	Mean sentence length of 3.10 words	
66 months	First appearance of is	*The doggie's mad*	30 months	First appearance of is	*My car's gone!*
73 months	Mean sentence length of 4.10 words		37 months	Mean sentence length of 4.10 words	
79 months	Mean sentence length of 4.50 words		37 months	First appearance of indirect requests	*Can I have some cookies?*
79 months	First appearance of indirect requests	*Can I get the ball?*	40 months	Mean sentence length of 4.50 words	

From "Language Disorders in Preschool Children" by L. Leonard, in *Human Communications Disorders: An Introduction* (4th ed., p. 179), edited by G. H. Shames, E. H. Wiig, and W. A. Second, 1994, New York: Macmillan. Copyright © 1994. Reprinted with permission of Merrill, an imprint of Macmillan Publishing Company.

and compound or simple sentences determine the meanings of word combinations. For example, the same words used in different combinations can mean very different things: *The boy hit the ball* is not the same as *The ball hit the boy.*

All these rule systems affect how we use and understand language. Children's abilities to understand and correctly use all these rules related to form develop sequentially as their language skill develops. Language form is important not only in spoken language, but also in written and sign language systems, as well as in augmentative and alternative communication (AAC), discussed later in this chapter.

Content   Content refers to the intent and meaning of language and its rule system; *semantics* deals with the meaning of words and word combinations. Without specific words to label and describe objects or ideas, our language would have no meaning. When students fail to comprehend concrete and abstract meanings of words, inferences, or figurative expressions, it is difficult for them to understand more subtle uses of language such as jokes, puns, similes, proverbs, or sarcasm. As children mature, they are better able to differentiate meanings of similar words, classify them according to similarities and differences, understand abstract meanings of words, and comprehend figurative language.

Use   When we use language in various social contexts, we follow another set of rules, *pragmatics*. The purpose and setting of our communication as well as the people with whom we are communicating determine the type of language we use. If children are to build and maintain successful relationships with others, it is important that they understand and effectively use skills appropriate to the context. For example, when children speak to adults, it is helpful if they use polite, respectful language; when they speak to their friends, they will most likely use less formal spoken language, demonstrate more relaxed body language, and take turns while talking (Owens, 1984).

The unique language environment of traditional American classrooms places special demands on language use and comprehension that can be particularly challenging to students from diverse cultural and linguistic backgrounds. For example, maintaining eye contact during communication exchanges, naming common objects, and answering "wh" questions are skills at which middle- and upper-class English-speaking children are usually adept, because these skills are valued and supported by their linguistic community. However, because these behaviors may not be at all desirable or encouraged in children from communities with a different cultural heritage or linguistic tradition, these children begin their educational career at a distinct disadvantage.

Types and Causes of Language Disorders

Hallahan and Kauffman (1991) have described four basic categories of language disorders: absence of verbal language, qualitatively different language, delayed language development, and interrupted language development. Table 11.3 from Naremore (1980) summarizes these four categories and includes some suspected causes of each. For children who are not deaf, a complete absence of language would likely indicate severe emotional disturbance or a severe developmental disorder. Qualitatively different language is also associated with developmental disorders and emotional disturbance. A good example of this type of problem is the echolalic speech of children with autism, who may repeat speech they hear in a singsong voice and fail to use their spoken language in a meaningful way. Delayed language occurs when a child develops language in the same approximate sequence as other children, but at a slower rate. Causes of delayed language include mental retardation, hearing loss, or lack of stimulation or appropriate experiences. Sometimes language development is interrupted by illness or physical trauma. This type of language problem is increasingly common among children as a result of traumatic brain injury (TBI). In general education classrooms, teachers may encounter any or all of these types of language disorders ranging from very mild to severe.

Indicators of Language Impairments

Some teachers may have an overall sense that a student is demonstrating language problems; others may not notice anything amiss. Wiig and Semel (1984) have identified some indicators of language problems by grade levels.

▶ *Primary Grades*
- Problems in following verbal directions
- Difficulty with preacademic skills
- Phonics problems
- Poor word-attack skills
- Difficulties with structural analysis
- Problems learning new material

TABLE 11.3   Types of Language Disorders and Their Causes

Type	Commonly Suspected Causative Factors or Related Conditions
No Verbal Language Child does not show indications of understanding or spontaneously using language by age 3.	▶ Congenital or early acquired deafness ▶ Gross brain damage or severe mental retardation/developmental disabilities ▶ Severe emotional disturbance
Quantitatively Different Language Child's language is different from that of nondisabled children at any stage of development—meaning and usefulness for communication are greatly lessened or lost.	▶ Inability to understand auditory stimuli ▶ Severe emotional disturbance ▶ Learning disability ▶ Mental retardation/developmental disabilities ▶ Hearing loss
Delayed Language Development Language follows normal course of development, but lags seriously behind that of most children who are the same chronological age.	▶ Mental retardation ▶ Experiential deprivation ▶ Lack of language stimulation ▶ Hearing loss
Interrupted Language Development Normal language development begins but is interrupted by illness, accident, or other trauma; language disorder is acquired.	▶ Acquired hearing loss ▶ Brain injury due to oxygen deprivation, physical trauma, or infection

Adapted from "Language Disorders in Children" by R. C. Naremore. In *Introduction to Communication Disorders* (p. 224), edited by T. J. Hixon, L. D. Shriberg, and J. H. Saxman, 1980, Englewood Cliffs, NJ: Prentice-Hall. Used by permission.

▶ *Intermediate Grades*
- Word substitutions
- Inadequate language processing and production that affects reading comprehension and academic achievement

▶ *Middle and High School*
- Inability to understand abstract concepts
- Difficulties connecting previously learned information to new material that must be learned independently
- Widening gap in achievement when compared to peers

In addition, teachers can check for linguistic, social, emotional, and academic problems that are related to language disorders (Ratner & Harris, 1994). These problems are shown in Table 11.4.

Children who have language disorders sometimes develop patterns of interaction with peers, teachers, and family members that may result in behavior problems. The behavior problems might seem to have nothing to do with language problems but may in fact have developed in response to inabilities to read, spell, talk, or write effectively.

Classroom Adaptations for Students with Language Disorders

Numerous strategies can be used in general education classrooms to improve students' language skills and remedy language deficits. Consult with the speech–language pathologist as well as with other special education personnel to develop individualized classroom modifications for students with language disorders. The following sections present some ways of structuring learning situations and presenting information to enhance communication.

TABLE 11.4   Linguistic, Social, Emotional, and Academic Problems Related to Language Disorders

Linguistic Problems	Language structure	Omissions and distortions of speech sounds Omissions of parts of words or word endings Sounds or syllables of words out of sequence Immature sentence structure
	Language meaning	Difficulty understanding directions and questions Confusion of basic concepts and ideas Limited vocabulary Literal interpretation of figurative language and jokes Poor word classification and association skills
	Language use	Difficulty beginning, maintaining, and ending conversations Difficulty taking turns in conversations and other classroom activities Difficulty understanding the listener's point of view Overuse of pauses, fillers, and repetitions in conversation
	Metalinguistics	Difficulty expressing ideas about language Poor phonemic awareness skills (rhyming, syllabification, phonics)
Social Problems	Conversational deficits	Poor eye contact Inappropriate comments and responses to questions Providing insufficient information when describing, relaying information, or giving directions Poor social language use (please, thank you)
	Social interaction issues	Poor sense of fair play Unable to set limits or boundaries Difficulty with new situations Difficulty expressing wants, needs, and ideas
Emotional Problems	Personal issues	Poor self-concept Low frustration level Perseverative and repetitious
	Emotional-interaction issues	Inability to accept responsibility Gullible Sensitive to criticism Poor coping strategies
Academic Problems	Classroom issues	Poor retention of learning Problems with organizing and planning Difficulty problem solving Left/right confusion Symbol reversals Difficulty expressing known information Poor generalization of knowledge to new situations Difficulty with higher-level thinking skills (deduction, inference) Poor judgment and understanding of cause and effect Inability to monitor and self-correct Poor memory
	Metacognition	Inability to talk about academic tasks Inability to self-regulate behaviors

Teach Some Prerequisite Imitation Skills

Nowacek and McShane (1993) recommend the following activities:

▶ Show a picture (of a girl running) and say, "The girl is running."
▶ Ask the student to repeat a target phrase.
▶ Positively reinforce correct responses.
▶ Present a variety of subject/verb combinations until the student correctly and consistently imitates them.

Improve Comprehension in the Classroom

CROSS-REFERENCE

When reading Chapters 15 and 16, consider specific activities that could be used to teach listening skills to elementary and secondary students.

Clary and Edwards (1992) suggest some specific activities to improve students' receptive language skills:

▶ *Give students practice in following directions.* Begin with one simple direction, and then increase the length of the list of directions.
▶ *Have students pair up and practice descriptions.* Place two students at a table separated by a screen. Place groups of identical objects in front of both students. Have one describe one of the objects; the other must determine which object is being described. Reverse roles with new sets of objects.
▶ *Let students work on categorizing.* Orally present a list of three words. Two should be related in some way. Ask a student to tell which two are related and why (e.g., horse, tree, dog).

The nearby Inclusion Strategies feature provides some additional suggestions for teaching listening skills.

Give Students Opportunities for Facilitative Play

Facilitative play provides modeling for the students so that they can imitate and expand their own use of language. The following is an abbreviated sequence for this type of interaction:

▶ The teacher models self-talk in a play activity. ("I'm making the cars go.")
▶ The teacher elicits comments from the student and then expands on them. ("Yes, the cars are going fast.")
▶ The teacher uses "buildups" and "breakdowns" by expanding on a student's ideas, breaking them down, and then repeating them. ("Red car go? Yes, look at the red car. It's going fast on the road. It's going to win the race.") (Nowacek & McShane, 1993)

Encourage Students to Talk with Their Teachers and Peers

Sometimes students who are reluctant to speak require encouragement. In addition to encouraging them with positive social interactions, teachers might also have to structure situations in which students must use language to meet some of their needs in the classroom. The strategies that follow should prompt students to use language when they otherwise might not.

▶ Place items out of reach so that the child has to ask for them.
▶ When a child asks for an item, present the wrong item (e.g., the child asks for a spoon and you present a fork).
▶ Give a child an item that is hard to open so that he or she has to request assistance.
▶ When performing a task, do one step incorrectly (forget to put the milk in the blender with the pudding mix).
▶ Make items difficult to find.
▶ Give students an item that requires some assistance to work with (e.g., an orange that needs peeling).

Teaching Strategies to Help Problem Listeners in the Classroom

▶ Allow for clarification and repetition of questions during oral tests.

▶ Avoid use of figurative language and complex or passive sentences.

▶ Be an interesting speaker—use gestures, facial expressions, movement, and variety in your voice.

▶ Encourage students to ask questions.

▶ Identify problem and at-risk listeners and pair them with "study buddies."

▶ Keep sentence structures simple and direct.

▶ Limit concentrated listening time to short intervals.

▶ Make simple adaptations in your classroom to improve the acoustics.

▶ Reduce noise levels in the classroom during listening tasks.

▶ Refer problem listeners for hearing screenings.

▶ Repeat and rephrase.

▶ Seat problem listeners strategically.

▶ Speak slowly and pause between thoughts.

▶ Use advanced organizers and preview questions to help focus listening.

▶ Use the blackboard and other visual aids.

For follow-up questions about teaching strategies for problem listeners, go to Chapter 11 of the Companion Website (ablongman.com/sppd4e) and click Inclusion Strategies.

Adapted from *It's Time to Listen: Metacognitive Activities for Improving Auditory Processing in the Classroom* (2nd ed., pp. 9–15) by P. A. Hamaguchi, 2002, Austin, TX: Pro-Ed.

Use Naturalistic Techniques and Simulated Real-Life Activities to Increase Language Use

Often, the most effective techniques to instill language acquisition and use are those that will be easy for teachers to use and easy for students to generalize to everyday situations. Teachers can encourage generalization by using naturalistic and situational strategies and real-life activities.

▶ *Naturalistic Techniques*
  • Try cloze activities. ("What do you need? Oh, you need paint and a _____. That's right, you need paint and a brush.")
  • Emphasize problem solving. ("You can't find your backpack? What should you do? Let's look on the hook. Is your coat there? What did we do to find your coat? That's right, we looked on the hook.")
  • Use questioning techniques. ("Where are you going? That's right, you are going to lunch.")

▶ *Simulated Real-Life Activities*
  • Let students role-play a newscast or commercial.
  • Have students write and follow their own written directions to locations in and around the school.
  • Play "social charades" by having students act out social situations and decide on appropriate responses.
  • Have one student teach an everyday skill to another (e.g., how to shoot a basket).
  • Using real telephones, give students opportunities to call each other, and to give, receive, and record messages.

CONSIDER THIS

When using some of these strategies to facilitate the development of students' speech and language skills, what can you do to make it more likely that the student will continue to speak without these strategies?

Encourage Students' Conversational Skills Through Story Reading

McNeill and Fowler (1996) give some excellent suggestions for helping students with delayed language development. Since students with language development problems often do not get the results they want through their ordinary conversations, they need more practice. What better way to practice effective language skills than through story reading! Students of all ages enjoy being read to, whether individually or in small groups while students are young, or in larger classes when they are in intermediate or secondary grades.

These authors suggest four specific strategies for teachers to use when reading stories aloud: (1) praise the students' talk, (2) expand on their words, (3) ask open-ended questions, and (4) pause long enough to allow students to initiate speaking. In addition, they emphasize taking turns, so that students have an opportunity to clarify their messages, hear appropriate language models, and practice the unspoken rules of communication.

McNeill and Fowler (1996) also recommend coaching parents in how to give their children opportunities to talk and how to respond when their children do talk. When parents pause, expand on answers, and ask open-ended questions that require more than just "yes" or "no" responses, they can become their children's best teachers.

Use Music and Play Games to Improve Language

Teachers should always try to have some fun with students. Using music and playing games are two ways language can be incorporated into enjoyable activities.

▶ *Music*
  • Use songs that require students to request items (e.g., rhythm sticks or tambourines passed around a circle).
  • Have picture symbols for common songs so that students can request the ones they like.
  • Use props to raise interest and allow students to act out the story (e.g., during "Humpty Dumpty" the student falls off a large ball).
  • Use common chants such as "When You're Happy and You Know It," and let students choose the action (e.g., clap your hands).
▶ *Games That Require Language Comprehension and Expression Skills*
  • Play "Simon Says."
  • Play "Musical Chairs" with words rather than music. (Pass a ball around a circle. When the teacher says a magic word, the student with the ball is out.)
  • Use key words to identify and organize students. ("All the boys with red hair stand up. Everyone who has a sister sit down.")
  • Play "Twenty Questions." ("I'm thinking of a person." Students ask yes-or-no questions.)

Arrange Your Classroom for Effective Interactions

For students who have either speech or language problems, the physical arrangement of the classroom can contribute to success. The following guidelines may improve students' language development:

▶ Give instructions and important information when distractions are at their lowest.
▶ Use consistent attention-getting devices, either verbal, visual, or physical cues.
▶ Be specific when giving directions.
▶ Write directions on the chalkboard, flip chart, or overhead so that students can refer to them.
▶ Use students' names frequently when talking to them.
▶ Emphasize what you're saying by using gestures and facial expressions.
▶ Pair students up with buddies for modeling and support.
▶ Allow for conversation time in the classroom so that students can share information and ideas.
▶ Encourage students to use calendars to organize themselves and manage their time. (Breeding, Stone, & Riley, n.d.)

Use Challenging Games with Older Students

Older students may require continued intervention to improve language skills. However, the activities chosen must be appropriate and not seem like "baby" games. Thomas and Carmack (1993) have collected ideas to involve older students in enjoyable, interactive tasks:

- Read fables or stories with morals. Discuss outcomes and focus on the endings.
- Do "Explain That." Discuss common idiomatic phrases, and help students discover the connection between the literal and figurative meanings (e.g., She was on pins and needles).
- "Riddlemania" presents riddles to students and has them explain what makes them humorous.
- Have "Sense-Able Lessons." Bring objects to see, taste, hear, and smell, and compile a list of students' verbal comments. (p. 155)

Modify Strategies to Develop Students' Learning Tools

When facilitating language development for older students, help them develop their own strategies to use in challenging situations (Thomas & Carmack, 1993). Requiring them to use higher-order thinking skills will both require and stimulate higher-level language.

- Pair students to find word meanings. Use partners when working on categories such as synonyms or antonyms. Let students work together to master using a thesaurus.
- Teach students to categorize. Begin with concrete objects that they relate to easily, such as types of cars or names of foods, and then move to more abstract concepts such as feelings or ideas.
- Play reverse quiz games like "Jeopardy!" in which students have to work backward to think of questions for answers. (pp. 155–163)

Work Collaboratively with the Speech–Language Pathologist

LINC (Language IN the Classroom) is a program adapted for use in many school districts (Breeding et al., n.d.). The program philosophy holds that language learning should occur in the child's most natural environment and in conjunction with other content being learned. The development of students' language should relate to their world and should be a learning experience, not a teaching experience.

The purpose of the program is to strengthen the language system of those students in general education classrooms who need to develop coping and compensatory skills to survive academically. Another goal is to transfer language learned from the therapy setting to the classroom, thereby allowing children to learn to communicate, rather than merely *talk*. The teacher and the speech–language pathologist must both be present for the approach to be successful. The two professionals work together to plan unit lessons that develop language skills in students.

Hiller (1990) presents an example of how LINC works. His elementary school implemented classroom-based language instruction. At the beginning of the program, the speech–language pathologist visited each classroom for a specified amount of time each week (90 minutes) during the language arts period. The first 45 minutes were used for an oral language activity, often a cooking activity from the *Blooming Recipes* workbook (Tavzel, 1987). During the second 45 minutes, students wrote paragraphs. For example, after preparing peanut butter and raisins on celery ("Bumps on a Log"), students responded to the following questions:

1. What was the name of the recipe we made?
2. Where did we do our preparing?
3. Who brought the peanut butter, celery, and raisins?
4. How did we make "Bumps on a Log"?

5. When did we eat "Bumps on a Log"?
6. Why do you think this recipe is called "Bumps on a Log"?

Responses were written on the board or on an overhead transparency. Students copied the responses in paragraph format.

Teachers and speech–language pathologists later extended the activities to teaching language lessons on current topics, team-teaching critical thinking activities during science experiments, and team planning and teaching social studies units. Reports from Hiller's and other schools using LINC programs described better collaboration among professionals, more accurate language referrals, and increased interest in speech–language activities among the entire staff. The nearby Personal Spotlight describes how a speech–language pathologist views collaboration.

Use Storytelling and Process Writing

When children listen to and retell a story, they incorporate it into their oral language repertoire. McKamey (1991) has described a structure for allowing students to retell stories they had heard, to tell stories from their own experience, and to write down and illustrate their oral presentations. In process writing, students are instructed based on what they can already do. This and other balanced literacy approaches often allow students who have had negative language experiences to begin to succeed, to link written and spoken language, and to grow as communicators.

Personal Spotlight

Speech–Language Pathologist

Martha Drennan has been a speech–language pathologist for eight years. She has been employed in both a large, urban district and a small, rural district. Currently she works for the Rison School District in Rison, Arkansas. One of the most significant changes Martha has observed in her field is that many children now receive speech–language services in a general education setting rather than being pulled out for services in a segregated, speech classroom. Martha likes this change. She notes that there are several advantages to providing services to these children in general classrooms rather than pulling them out. Among these advantages are that

Martha Drennan

Rison School District, Rison, AR

▶ more students can be served because the speech–language pathologist can work with several students at the same time. Often an entire class is the target of a lesson conducted by the speech–language pathologist so that all students benefit.

▶ some students, especially older ones, do not feel the stigma of receiving services as part of their general education classroom whereas they did when they had to leave the room for speech.

Martha notes that many older students really resent having to go to the speech room. She especially sees serving students in the general education setting as beneficial for this group of students.

Despite benefits, there are also some negative factors associated with this newer service delivery model. Martha said that "some teachers would simply rather teach all the lessons in their classroom themselves because they feel like they do not have the luxury to give another teacher time." Another negative to providing services in the general education classroom is that students with speech–language needs do not get the individual attention in general education classes that they would if they were to receive their services in the speech room.

Overall, Martha is very pleased with serving students with speech and language needs in general education classes. She noted that "virtually all general education teachers are very happy when you go into their classroom and provide a language lesson for all kids." She also stated that the collaboration needed to ensure an effective, smooth lesson requires time for general education teachers and speech–language pathologists to plan, something that seems to always be a problem.

For follow-up questions about this Personal Spotlight, go to Chapter 11 of the Companion Website (ablongman.com/sppd4e) and click Personal Spotlight.

Language Differences

Children's patterns of speech and use of language reflect their culture, socioeconomic status, and gender and may be different from that of some of their peers. It is important not to mistake a language *difference* for a language *disorder,* but also a disorder must not be overlooked in a student with language differences. Variations in family structure, child-rearing practices, family perceptions and attitudes, regional dialects, and language and communication styles can all influence students' communication (Wayman, Lynch, & Hanson, 1990).

CONSIDER THIS

What are some of the ways that culture can have an impact on a child's language, which in turn will affect the child's functioning in school?

Acquiring English as a Second Language

Students who are learning English as a second language often exhibit error patterns that can look like language disorders, when they are, in fact, part of the normal process of second-language acquisition (Roseberry-McKibbin & Brice, 2002). It is crucial that teachers of students who are English-language learners recognize these patterns as language differences rather than communication disorders in order to avoid unnecessary referrals:

▶ *Interference or transfer:* Students may make errors in English form because of the influence of structures or patterns in their native language.
▶ *Silent period:* Children who are learning a new language focus on listening to and attempting to understand the new language before trying out what they have learned. This silent period may last as long as a year in very young children and as briefly as a few weeks or months in older children.
▶ *Codeswitching:* Languages are blended in phrases or sentences such that students alternate between the two.
▶ *Subtractive bilingualism:* As students learn English, they can begin to loose skill and proficiency in their native language if it is not also supported and valued.

Relationship Between Communication Style and Culture

Culture has a strong influence on the style of communication. Many areas of communication style can be affected by factors including gender, status, dialect, and age roles; rules governing interruptions and turn taking; use of humor; and how to greet or leave someone (Erickson, 1992). Teachers must be aware of the many manifestations of culture in nonverbal communication, as well. Differences in rules governing eye contact, the physical space between speakers, use of gestures and facial expression, and use of silence can cause dissonance between teachers and students of differing cultures. Walker (1993) has described how differences such as directness of a conversation, volume of voices, and reliance on verbal (low-context) versus nonverbal (high-context) parts of communication affect attitudes toward the speaker. Teachers can respond to cultural differences in several ways. These suggestions are adapted from Walker (1993, p. 2) and should be helpful for teachers who want to enhance both overall achievement and communication skills with students who are culturally or linguistically different:

▶ Try to involve community resources, including churches and neighborhood organizations, in school activities.
▶ Make home visits.
▶ Allow flexible hours for conferences.
▶ Question your own assumptions about human behavior, values, biases, personal limitations, and so on.
▶ Try to understand the world from the student's perspective.
▶ Ask yourself questions about an individual student's behavior in light of cultural values, motivation, and world views, and how these relate to his or her learning experiences.

The cultural background of a child will influence many aspects of the style of communication that is used.

▶ Remind yourself and your students to celebrate and value the cultural and linguistic differences among individuals in their school and community.

▶ Consult with the speech–language pathologist to understand how to differentiate between students who have language differences and those who have disorders.

Multicultural Considerations in Assessment

TEACHING TIP

Remember the basic tenets of nondiscriminatory assessment when evaluating students with diverse cultural backgrounds or when reviewing assessment data that have already been collected.

Assessment in the area of communication disorders is often complicated, just as it is for students with other disabilities. Because of the increasing numbers of students who are culturally and linguistically different and who require services in ESL (English as a Second Language) or who are Limited English Proficient (LEP), teachers should consult with personnel in special education, ESL, speech and language services, and bilingual education to obtain appropriate evaluation and programming services. Observation is an important form of assessment, particularly when assessing students who are linguistically different.

Because of the increasing number of students in public schools from cultural or linguistic minority groups, teachers are recognizing the need for information related to learning and communication styles as well as modifications to curriculum and instruction. Although many of these children will never be identified as having a communication disorder, teachers in general education must be aware that differences in language and culture may often impact a student's apparent proficiency in both oral and written communication.

Augmentative and Alternative Communication (AAC)

The term **augmentative communication** denotes techniques that supplement or enhance communication by complementing whatever vocal skills the individual already has (Harris & Vanderheiden, 1980). Research has demonstrated that the use of communication devices does not inhibit the development of natural speech. Other individuals (e.g., those who are severely neurologically impaired and cannot speak) must employ techniques that serve in place of speech—in other words, **alternative communication.** According to Shane and Sauer (1986), the term *alternative communication* applies when "the production of speech for communication purposes has been ruled out" (p. 2).

Diversity Forum

Language Disorder or Language Difference: Sol's Story

Sol's parents report that their five-year-old daughter is having difficulty expressing her needs in Spanish, their home language. The family speaks Spanish to Sol but note that she very seldom initiates conversations. To interact with others, Sol usually pulls on people's clothes or points to things. She has few friends and prefers to play by herself.

According to Mrs. Foster, Sol's kindergarten teacher, Sol is a quiet, somewhat withdrawn child who sometimes attempts Spanish communication with classmates. However, other children have difficulty understanding Sol because she "speaks funny." Though Sol knows some basic English words, she does not use them at school. In addition to having access to Spanish speakers at home, Sol works with a tutor who engages her in activities encouraging language growth. Still, she does not talk much. Sol produces two- to three-word utterances, and her pronunciation is still developing. She repeats things said to her but does not seem to understand the words' meaning. Following simple directions is also difficult.

Mrs. Foster and Sol's parents share concerns about Sol's language development. They consult with other school personnel and develop a plan to help Sol develop expressive language skills. A timeline for implementing the plan's strategies will be agreed upon before discussing further evaluation. During this time period, Sol will be encouraged to assume leadership roles in academic and social interactions. The teacher will focus on language development in Spanish and in English. Simple vocabulary and grammatical forms will be modeled for Sol in Spanish and in English. Consistent efforts will be made to praise and reinforce Sol's social interactions in classroom and social settings (Brice, 2002).

For follow-up questions about language differences versus language disorders, go to Chapter 11 of the Companion Website (ablongman.com/sppd4e) and click Diversity Forum.

AAC is a multimodal system consisting of four components (symbols, aids, techniques, and strategies) that can be utilized in various combinations to enhance communication. Communication techniques used in AAC are usually divided into either *aided* or *unaided* forms. Unaided techniques include nonverbal methods used in normal communication and do not require any physical object or entity in order to express information (e.g., speech, signing, gestures, and facial expressions). Aided communication techniques require a physical object, device, or external support to enable the individual to communicate (e.g., communication boards, charts, and mechanical or electrical devices). Because substantial numbers of individuals lack functional speech secondary to mental retardation, traumatic brain injury, deafness, neurological disorders, or other causes, there has been increased demand for augmentative and alternative communication in recent years. A student's communication skills and needs will change over time, as will the types of technology and methods available to support communication. Thus, the educational team should continually monitor and periodically reevaluate the usefulness of each AAC approach used by their students.

Students who cannot use spoken language may use a basic nonautomated communication device with no electronic parts. Examples include communication boards, charts, frames, and books that can be based upon symbols, words, or letters. Typically, this kind of device will contain representations of common objects, words, phrases, or numbers and can be arranged in either an alphabetic or nonalphabetic format (Figure 11.5). Because they are easy to construct and can be modified to fit the student's vocabulary and communication context, nonautomated communication devices are very useful in communicating with teachers, family members, and peers. There are several commercially available sets of symbols, including the *Picture Communication Symbols* (Mayer-Johnson, 1986) and *The Oakland Picture Dictionary* (Kirsten, 1981). Computer software programs that contain picture communication symbols can also be used to generate communication boards, picture schedules, instruction sheets, and other communication tools.

Electronic communication aids encompass a wide variety of capabilities, from simple to complex. Aids that produce voice are known as voice output communication aids or VOCAs. There are a large number of different voice output communication aids available that vary greatly in their level of sophistication and complexity. They range from aids that

FIGURE 11.5

Communication Board

From *Functional Language Instruction* (p. 87) by C. Cottier, M. Doyle, & K. Gilworth, 1997, Austin, TX: Pro-Ed.

speak just one message to aids that provide access to keyboards for virtually unlimited messaging capacity. The voice output may be amplified, digitized, or synthetic speech. Often, a voice synthesizer is used to produce speech output, and written output is produced on printers or displays. Software, which is becoming increasingly sophisticated, can accommodate the many different needs of individuals who cannot produce spoken and/or written language. Some examples of electronic communication aids and their key features are shown in Table 11.5.

Because recent evidence has shown that *everyone* can communicate, the focus of contemporary AAC assessment and intervention is on developing and fine-tuning individualized methods that promote functional communication abilities in school, home, and community settings (Sevcik & Romski, 2000). The Technology Today feature on page 344 lists some of the approaches and facilitating strategies for developing an effective team approach to serve students using AAC in the classroom.

Facilitated Communication

Facilitated communication is a process that has been used with individuals who have developmental disabilities, including autism. First introduced by Rosemary Crossley in Australia, facilitated communication usually involves having someone (a facilitator) support the arm or wrist of the person with autism, who then points to pictures, objects, printed letters, and words, or types letters on a keyboard. The keyboard is often connected to a computer so that the individual's words can be displayed or printed (Kirk, Gallagher, & Anastasiow, 1993). Supposedly the support of the facilitator enables the individual to type out words and phrases.

TABLE 11.5   **Electronic Communication Aids and Their Key Features**

BigMack

A large, colorful, single message digitizer.
Record and re-record a message, song, sound, story line, or choice of up to 20 seconds.
A picture or label can easily be stuck to the large button.
Can be accessed by pressing anywhere on the large button or by a separate switch.
Can be used as a switch to control other devices, toys, or appliances.

Lightwriter SL35

A compact, portable keyboard will speak what is typed into it.
Text messages are displayed on the two-way screen, and synthesized speech is used.
Can be customized for people with more complex needs.
Add-ons such as key guards can be purchased, and a range of models are available.
Reduces keystrokes by using memory and word prediction.

ChatPC

Based on a palmtop Windows CE computer.
Housed in a durable case to give additional protection and additional amplification.
Has a color touch screen, and over a hundred pages of messages can be programmed.
An onscreen keyboard is available, and this speaks out what is typed into it.
3000+ symbols are supplied and can be supplemented with scanned or digital images.
Speech output can be digital or synthetic.
Changes can be made on the device or on a computer and then downloaded.

Dynavox 3100

Touchscreen device offers word layouts, symbol layouts, or a combination of both.
Many preprogrammed page sets, suitable for users with a wide range of ability levels.
Flexible layout can be thoroughly customized.
Symbol-supported word prediction encourages literacy.
DecTalk speech synthesis offers nine different voices.
Can be accessed via touchscreen, mouse, joystick, or switches.
Auditory and visual scanning modes are possible.
Built-in infrared for environmental controls and computer access.

Biklen (1990) has conducted much of the work done in facilitated communication and has reported anecdotal success with the procedure. However, results of objective research on the effectiveness of facilitated communication have found no conclusive evidence supporting the method (see Chapter 10). The American Speech-Language-Hearing Association (ASHA) has issued a position paper on facilitated communication which cautions that the validity and reliability of this method have yet to be proven (ASHA, 1995).

Promoting Inclusive Practices for Students with Communication Disorders

Until very recently, the traditional service delivery model for speech therapy included a twice-weekly, 30-minutes-per-session, pull-out model in which speech–language pathologists worked with students in a small room away from the regular education classroom. Even though this model may still be appropriate with some students some of the time, there are other effective approaches for provision of speech–language therapy services in public school settings. Just as academic services to students with disabilities have become more and more integrated into general education programs, speech–language services are now following more inclusive models. This collaboration between regular and special

CONSIDER THIS

What are some of the advantages and disadvantages, to both the student and general classroom teacher, of pull-out speech therapy services?

Developing an Effective Team Approach to Serve Students Using AAC in the Classroom

Approach	Facilitating Strategies
Collaborative teaming	Regularly scheduled team meetings
	Roles and responsibilities of team members are clearly defined
	Mutual respect among team members
	Team members communicate effectively and take a proactive approach
	Flexible interpretation of traditional roles of team members
Providing access to the curriculum	All team members have a working knowledge of the curriculum
	Assessment of the student's learning style by each member of the team
	Vocabulary and support are provided for use of the device across all classroom activities and school events
Cultivating social supports	Facilitate social interactions between the student and his peers
	Identifying and using natural supports in the classroom
	Training peers as communication partners
	Foster the independence and autonomy of the student
AAC system maintenance and operation	Team members are familiar with the basic maintenance, operation, and elements of the AAC device
	Team members know how to access help and additional resources as necessary
	Peers are familiarized with the device and regarding how to provide communication support
Building a supportive classroom community	Use of cooperative learning strategies
	Team teaching between general and special education personnel
	Working together to support all students in the classroom
	Promoting appreciation of differences within the classroom

For follow-up questions about a team approach using AAC, go to Chapter 11 of the Companion Website (ablongman.com/sppd4e) and click Technology Today.

Adapted from "Professional Skills for Serving Students Who Use AAC in General Education Classrooms: A Team Perspective" (pp. 51–56) by G. Soto, E. Muller, P. Hunt, and L. Goetz, 2001, *Language, Speech, and Hearing Services in the Schools, 32.*

education staff might involve speech–language pathologists visiting the classroom to work with individual students or with small groups, the teacher and speech–language pathologist teaching alternate lessons or sections of a particular lesson, or professionals co-teaching the same lesson at the same time. The following delivery options have been recommended for the provision of speech and language services in the schools: direct instruction (pull-out), classroom-based, community-based, and consultation (ASHA, 1996). These service-delivery options can be implemented independently or in any combination in order to best meet the individual needs of the student.

▶ The traditional pull-out model is indicated for students who are in particular stages of the intervention process or for those who have very specific communication goals. Pull-out services are often provided within the classroom or in the therapy room and with individual students or in small groups.

▶ Classroom-based service delivery options usually involve a collaborative effort between teachers and speech–language pathologists. This model is particularly appropriate at the preschool and kindergarten grades and in classrooms with large numbers of students who have been identified as having communication disorders or as being at risk. This collaboration can involve the speech–language pathologist providing individual or small group instruction in the classroom or participating in team teaching or co-teaching lessons with the classroom teacher.

▶ The community-based service delivery model indicates that therapy services are being provided in more natural communication environments such as at home, on the playground, or in other age-appropriate community settings. Providing speech and language therapy in a community-based setting is ideal for students who have pragmatic language disorders, for those who need to generalize new skills to a variety of settings, and for students who are enrolled in vocational programs.

▶ Consultation is a model of service delivery in which the speech–language pathologist does not provide direct instruction to the student. Instead, the family, teacher, or other school staff are provided with assistance in the form of information, training, or resources to help the student reach specific communication goals. The provision of consultation services is indicated for those students who are working on generalization of communication skills or for those students who are receiving communication programming from other instructional staff.

As schools try to maximize the positive impact of professional collaboration, it is important to recognize and overcome the barriers inherent in the process.

According to Kerrin (1996), the barriers to greater collaboration among speech–language professionals and teachers can include the following:

▶ Territorial obstacles ("This is my job; that is your job.")
▶ Time concerns ("When are general education teachers supposed to find the time to meet, plan, and modify?")
▶ Terror ("I'm afraid this new way won't work.")

Fortunately, Kerrin has also offered some good ideas for overcoming these obstacles. She suggests that team members try the following tips:

▶ Try to be flexible and creative when scheduling conferences.
▶ Encourage everyone involved to ask questions.
▶ Invite speech–language professionals into the classroom.
▶ Ask for assistance in planning.
▶ Maintain open, regular communication.
▶ Keep an open mind, a cooperative spirit, and a sense of humor.

Future Trends

Several forces are changing the field of communication disorders as practiced in the public schools. First, general education teachers are likely to see more students with moderate to severe disabilities in their classrooms. The movement toward more inclusive environments for students will require classroom teachers to provide more instruction for these students. Moreover, recent legislation and research suggest a shift away from the use of standardized assessment instruments toward the employment of dynamic, authentic, and curriculum-based assessment methods. The observations and input of the classroom teacher play a crucial role in each of these models of assessment.

As a result of expanding knowledge and skills among professionals trained in speech–language pathology, the scope of practice of the profession has been increasing and will continue to do so in the future. In addition to providing services in the more traditional area of oral communication skills, speech–language pathologists now working in the schools are often called upon to have expertise in swallowing disorders, Medicaid billing, selecting AAC systems, providing intervention and recommending classroom modifications for children with TBI and other complex neurological disorders, and promoting and enhancing literacy skills (Montgomery & Herer, 1999).

The caseloads of speech–language pathologists are continuing to grow, and there is an ever-increasing demand for services, especially in the area of language disorders. At the same time, there is expected to be an increasing shortage of speech–language pathologists employed to meet these increasing demands. Although "pull-out" speech–language remediation will still be offered to some students, many of the services will be delivered in an increasingly collaborative and consultative framework, with teachers and speech–language pathologists cooperating and sharing resources. In areas where shortages are particularly acute, schools will need to consider alternate methods of providing services to students with communication disorders. Some methods that might be employed in order to compensate for shortages in specialty personnel include employment of speech–language pathology assistants, flexible scheduling, cross-disciplinary service provision, peer tutoring, and increased use of natural supports.

The social trends that are shaping American society in general will have an increasing effect on the provision of speech therapy services in the schools. These trends include an increasingly multicultural and multilinguistic society, an increase in the numbers of children living in poverty without access to adequate health care and early intervention services, and the changing role of the school in the community.

Another area of change is the expected continuation of technological advances. Some of the improved technology has already been described here; however, it is virtually impossible to keep up with the rapid improvements in this area. With continued improvements in technology, students with more severe communication disorders will have opportunities to interact with family members, teachers, and peers, perhaps participating in activities that would have seemed impossible ten years ago. Distance learning and telehealth services will become more commonplace, particularly in traditionally underserved areas such as inner-city, geographically remote, and rural schools (Montgomery & Herer, 1994).

Authors' note: The authors would like to express their appreciation to Janice Maxwell, MS, CCC-SLP, for her assistance in providing much of the practical information that was presented in this chapter. Janice is an exemplary speech pathologist and a wonderful friend to teachers in general education.

 **Summary**

Basic Concepts About Communication Disorders

▶ Although most people take the ability to communicate for granted, communication problems can result in difficulties in even the most simple of interactions and lead to problems in socialization and emotional adjustment. Speech and language are the interrelated, rule-governed skills that we use to communicate.

▶ About 2% of the school-age population has been identified as having speech or language impairments.

▶ Because most students with speech and language impairments are served in a regular classroom or resource room placement, having students with speech and language disorders in the classroom is more the rule than the exception.

Speech Disorders

▶ Speech disorders include impairments of phonology, voice, and fluency, with phonological disorders being the most common.

▶ Speech disorders can either be functional or organic in origin.

Classroom Adaptations for Students with Speech Disorders

▶ Teachers can make numerous accommodations and modifications for students with speech disorders. For example, building a positive classroom environment is an important accommodation that can make inclusion easier for these students.

Language Disorders

▶ Language disorders can be expressive or receptive in nature and can affect the form, content, or use of language.

▶ Disorders of language can be classified into four basic categories: absence of verbal language, qualitatively different language, delayed language development, and interrupted language development.

▶ Significant language disorders directly impact a student's ability to interact with family, peers, and teachers.

Classroom Adaptations for Students with Language Disorders

▶ Specific, individualized intervention and instructional modifications (e.g., storytelling, facilitative play, classroom arrangement) are required.

Language Differences

▶ Individual social and cultural experiences often affect the way in which we use speech and language as tools for communication and learning.

▶ Teachers should be aware of the influence that culture has on the style and nonverbal aspects of communication.

▶ Special consideration should be given during assessment of students having diverse cultural and linguistic heritage. Some speech and language differences can be attributed to cultural diversity or environmental factors and are not considered disorders.

Augmentative and Alternative Communication

▶ All students can communicate.

▶ Augmentative and alternative communication options can facilitate the communicative abilities of persons with severe speech and language disorders.

▶ The level and type of technology needed to support augmentative and alternative communication methods varies widely.

▶ Objective research on the facilitated communication method has not shown it to be reliable or valid.

Promoting Inclusive Practices for Students with Communication Disorders

▶ Speech–language pathologists employ a variety of service delivery models that can be used independently or in combination to meet the individual needs of each student. Most of these models involve some level of professional collaboration and consultation with the classroom teacher.

▶ The speech–language pathologist can work with the classroom teacher to make necessary modifications to the classroom environment, methodology, and curriculum in order to accommodate the needs of students with communication disorders in inclusive settings.

▶ Teachers and therapists need to work as a team to overcome common barriers to greater collaboration.

Future Trends

▶ The movement toward more inclusive environments for students will require classroom teachers to serve greater numbers of students with moderate and severe communication disorders.

▶ Increasing caseloads, an expanding scope of practice, and personnel shortages will lead speech–language pathologists to provide many services using collaborative, consultative, and alternative models of service delivery rather than the more traditional "pull-out" approach.

▶ Technological advances will offer increased options for provision of services to students with severe communication disorders and increased opportunities for students to interact with others and participate in a wider range of activities.

Further Readings

American Speech-Language-Hearing Association. (1996, Spring). Inclusive practices for children and youth with communication disorders: Position statement and technical report. *ASHA, 38*(16), 35–44.

American Speech-Language-Hearing Association. (2001). *Roles and responsibilities of speech–language pathologists with respect to reading and writing* (position statement and guidelines). Rockville, MD: Author.

Fahey, K. B., & Reid, D. K. (2000). *Language development, differences, and disorders.* Austin, TX: Pro-Ed.

Kerrin, R. G. (1996). Collaboration: Working with the speech–language pathologist. *Intervention in School and Clinic, 21,* 56–59.

McNeill, J. H., & Fowler, S. A. (1996). Using story reading to encourage children's conversations. *Teaching Exceptional Children, 28,* 43–47.

Miller, R. (1996). *The developmentally appropriate inclusive classroom in early education.* Albany, NY: Delmar.

Parette, P., Hourcade, M., & Van-Biervliet, R. (1993, Spring). "Selection of appropriate technology for children with disabilities." *Teaching Exceptional Children, 26,* 40–44.

Shames, G. H., Wiig, E. H., & Secord, W. A. (1994). *Human communication disorders: An introduction* (4th ed.). New York: Merrill.

VideoWorkshop Extra!

If the VideoWorkshop package was included with your textbook, go to Chapter 11 of the Companion Website (www.ablongman.com/sppd4e) and click on the VideoWorkshop button. Follow the instructions for viewing video clip 1. Then consider this information along with what you've read in Chapter 11 while answering the following questions.

1. The team agrees that Doug has an articulation disorder that makes him eligible for related services as part of his IEP. Based on the videoclip and this chapter, what issues should be considered when making such a diagnosis?

2. If you are a general educator, how can you support the speech/language therapist and Doug's personal efforts?

12 Teaching Students Who Are Gifted

After reading this chapter, you should be able to

1. define giftedness.
2. describe the characteristics of gifted students.
3. describe ways to identify and evaluate gifted students.
4. discuss the curricular needs of gifted students.
5. describe appropriate instructional methods for gifted students.
6. identify ways to enhance curriculum and instruction within the general education setting.

Carmen is truly an amazing young woman. She was a student in classes for gifted/talented/creative students for six years, from the first to the sixth grade. Her story provides a glimpse of what giftedness might look like in a student. However, not all students who are gifted display the breadth of exceptionality that Carmen does.

Learning came very easily for Carmen, and she excelled in all subjects. However, mathematics was her personal favorite. When she was in the fifth grade, she successfully completed pre-algebra, and, when she was a sixth grader, Carmen attended a seventh- and eighth-grade gifted mathematics class, where she received the highest grades in algebra. Carmen's writing skills were also well developed. Several of her essays and poems have already been published. When Carmen was a fourth grader, she presented testimony to a NASA board defending and encouraging the continuation of the junior astronaut program. After completing her first year of junior high school, Carmen was awarded two out of five academic awards given to seventh-grade students at her school for outstanding achievement in science and mathematics. As a tenth grader, she took the PSAT, and received a perfect score!

Carmen is also musically talented. When she was in second grade, a music specialist who came to school on a weekly basis informed her teacher that Carmen should be encouraged to continue with piano lessons because she demonstrated concert pianist abilities. When Carmen entered junior high school, she took up playing the clarinet in the band. At the end-of-the-year banquet, she received the top honor after being in the band for only one year.

Additionally, Carmen is psychomotorically talented. She is an accomplished gymnast, dances both the hula and ballet, has been a competitive ice skater (an unusual sport for someone from Hawaii), played soccer for two years on champion soccer teams, and was a walk-on for her junior high's cross-country track team.

Carmen also has artistic strengths, demonstrates leadership abilities, has good social skills, and, wouldn't you know it, is simply beautiful.

Carmen's career goals have remained consistent for a long time. She wants to be either a dentist or an astronaut; she can probably be either one.

QUESTIONS TO CONSIDER

1. What kinds of challenges can students like Carmen create for teachers and for themselves?
2. How do individuals like Carmen who are highly gifted differ from other students who are gifted?
3. Should children like Carmen be included in general education classrooms all the time, separated from time to time, or provided with a completely different curriculum?

hildren and youth such as Carmen, who perform or have the potential to perform at levels significantly above those of other students, have special needs as great as those of students whose disabilities demonstrably limit their performance. These needs are notable because most of these students are likely to spend much of their school day in general education settings, if they are attending public schools. As a result, teaching students who are gifted provides challenges to general education teachers that are equal to, if not greater than, those associated with meeting the needs of students with other special needs (McGrail, 1998). To feel confident to work with students who are gifted, classroom teachers should have basic information about giftedness and be able to implement some useful techniques for maximizing the educational experiences of these students.

Although there is no general agreement concerning the best way to educate students who are gifted, many professionals argue that such students benefit from a curricular focus different from that provided in general education. Yet, as noted, the vast majority of students who are gifted spend a considerable amount of time in the general education classroom, offering teachers the challenges of working with them, along with some amazing rewards.

Although a set of exact competencies that general education teachers should have in working with students who are gifted remains elusive, certain ones are emerging as necessary. Nelson and Prindle (1992) surveyed teachers and principals and identified six competencies on which these groups tended to agree:

1. Promotion of thinking skills
2. Development of creative problem solving
3. Selection of appropriate methods and materials
4. Knowledge of affective needs
5. Facilitation of independent research
6. Awareness of the nature of gifted students

The purpose of the chapter is twofold: (1) to provide basic information about giftedness in children and youth and (2) to suggest practices for working with these students in inclusive settings. This chapter is a primer only; confidence and competence in teaching students who are gifted come with study and experience. More in-depth information about teaching students who are gifted can be found elsewhere (Clark, 2002; Colangelo & Davis, 2003; Coleman & Cross, 2001; Davis & Rimm, 1998).

Basic Concepts About Students Who Are Gifted

tudents with exceptional abilities continue to be an underidentified, underserved, and too often inappropriately served group. Unlike the situation for students with disabilities, no federal legislation mandates appropriate education for these students. Moreover, states and local school districts vary greatly in the type and quality of services provided—if indeed they are provided at all.

Students who could benefit from special programming are often not identified because of several factors. Teachers in general education may not be aware of the characteristics that suggest giftedness, particularly those associated with students who differ from the general student populations because of culture, gender, or disability. Historically, ineffective assessment practices have not identified gifted students coming from diverse backgrounds.

For students who are identified as gifted, a common problem is a mismatch between their academic, social, and emotional needs and the programming they receive. In many schools, a limited amount of instructional time is devoted to special activities. The point is reflected in the current focus on equity in education associated with the recent educational reform movement. As Gallagher (1997) notes, "It is this value that leads one to

CROSS-REFERENCE

Carmen is an example of a highly gifted student that will be discussed later in the chapter.

CROSS-REFERENCE

The issue of teacher preparation is very important and will be addressed later in the chapter.

CONSIDER THIS

Should there be federal mandates to provide appropriate educational programs for students who are gifted and talented?

heterogeneous grouping, whereby no one gets any special programming or privileges, and thus all are 'equal'" (p. 17). Furthermore, some gifted programming that exists today favors students who are gifted in the linguistic and mathematical areas only. In too many instances, gifted students do not receive the type of education in the general education classroom that addresses their needs.

Services to gifted students remain controversial, partly because the general public and many school personnel hold misconceptions about these students. Hallahan and Kauffman (2002) highlight some of these misguided beliefs:

▶ People with special intellectual gifts are physically weak, socially inept, narrow in interests, and prone to emotional instability or early decline. *Fact:* There are wide individual variations, and most gifted individuals are healthy, well adjusted, socially attractive, and morally responsible.

▶ Children with special gifts or talents are usually bored with school and antagonistic toward those who are responsible for their education. *Fact:* Most gifted children like school and adjust well to their peers and teachers, although some do not like school and have social or emotional problems.

▶ Students who have a true gift or talent will excel without special education. They need only the incentives and instruction that are appropriate for all students. *Fact:* Some gifted children will perform at a remarkably high level without special education of any kind, and some will make outstanding contributions even in the face of great obstacles to their achievement. But most will not come close to achieving at a level commensurate with their potential unless their talents are deliberately fostered by instruction that is appropriate for their advanced abilities. (p. 455)

The portrayal of individuals who are gifted in movies is noteworthy. As Coleman and Cross (2001) note, too often the portrayal has negative connotations. They described the features of key characters in a number of recent movies, as highlighted in Table 12.1. The problem with negative portrayals of individuals who are gifted is that it leads to inaccurate perceptions and attitudes, ultimately resulting in unfair, and often discriminatory, practices.

Many professionals in the field of gifted education find current services unacceptable and are frustrated by the lack of specialized programming for these students (Feldhusen, 1997). Undoubtedly, the programming provided in inclusive settings to students who are gifted should be improved. VanTassel-Baska (1997), highlighting key beliefs regarding curriculum theory, remarks that gifted students should be provided with curriculum opportunities that allow them to attain optimum levels of learning. In addition, these curriculum experiences need to be carefully planned, implemented, and evaluated.

> **CONSIDER THIS**
>
> Why do you think misconceptions about children and adults who are gifted and talented have developed and continue to exist?

TABLE 12.1   Portrayal of Gifted Characters in Movies

Movie	Year	Portrayal
Little Man Tate	1991	Dysfunctional
Searching for Bobby Fischer	1993	Dysfunctional
Powder	1995	Frail
Shine	1996	Bespectacled
The Nutty Professor	1996	Idealistic Misguided
Good Will Hunting	1997	Violent
A Beautiful Mind	2001	Psychiatric problems

From *Being Gifted in School: An Introduction to Development, Guidance, and Teaching* (p. 3) by L. J. Coleman and T. L. Cross, 2001, Waco, TX: Prufrock Press. Copyright 2002 by Prufrock Press. Reprinted by permission.

"Gifted" Defined

Our understanding of giftedness has changed over time, and the terminology used to describe it has also varied. The term **gifted** is often used to refer to the heterogeneous spectrum of students with exceptional abilities, although some professionals restrict the use of this term only to certain individuals who display high levels of intelligence. Other terms such as *talented* and *creative* are used to differentiate subgroups of gifted people.

CROSS-REFERENCE

The individuals who were in Terman's original study are still being studied today.

Historical Context A number of attempts to define giftedness have been made. One of the earliest efforts, and one that has received a fair amount of attention, is the work of Terman that began in the early 1920s. Collectively the Terman work is entitled the *Genetic Studies of Genius,* and this research was still being conducted in recent times. Terman and colleagues identified 1,500 individuals with high IQs (i.e., over 140), collected data on their mental and physical traits, and also studied their lives longitudinally (Sears, 1979; Terman, 1926; Terman & Oden, 1959; Tomlinson-Keasey & Little, 1990). The research was important because it represented a major attempt to look closely at individuals who were exceptional and dispelled some early misconceptions relating high intelligence and neurotic behavior. This work also provided some beginning conceptualizations of giftedness.

However, as Turnbull and Turnbull (2001) point out, Terman's work also led to some misconceptions. First, he equated genius with IQ, thus excluding other areas such as artistic ability. Second, Terman stressed the strong association of genius and genetics, thus precluding the fact that some variability in intelligence can occur due to psychosocial factors and other life-related opportunities.

Throughout the years, other definitional perspectives emerged. Most of these were associated with federal legislation that recognized students who were gifted (e.g., the Elementary and Secondary Education Act) or were developed by the U.S. Commissioner of Education (Marland, 1972). Attention was directed to this topic as a function of the creation of various professional organizations as well—for example, the American Association for the Study of the Gifted in 1946; the National Association for Gifted Children in 1954; and the Association for the Gifted, part of the Council for Exceptional Children, in 1958.

Federal Definition The current definition of giftedness promoted by the U.S. Department of Education comes from the Jacob K. Javits Gifted and Talented Education Act of 1988 (reauthorized in 1994). It contains many of the key concepts included in previous definitions.

CROSS-REFERENCE

Review the definitions of other categories of disabilities discussed in previous chapters to compare components of definitions.

> Children and youth with outstanding talent perform or show the potential for performing at remarkably high levels of accomplishment when compared with others of their age, experience, or environment. These children and youth exhibit high performance capability in intellectual, creative, and/or artistic areas, possess an unusual leadership capacity, or excel in specific academic fields. They require services or activities not ordinarily provided by schools. Outstanding talents are present in children and youth from all cultural groups, across all economic strata, and in all areas of human endeavor. (U.S. Department of Education, 1993, p. 3)

A number of interesting observations can be made regarding this definition. First, attention is given to potential—students who have not yet produced significant accomplishments may be considered gifted. Second, there is no mention of giftedness in athletics because this area is already addressed in existing school programs. Third, the need for special services or activities for these students is clearly stated, along with the observation that such intervention is not ordinarily provided. Finally, the fact that students who are gifted come from a range of diverse backgrounds is affirmed.

A Developmental Perspective Attentive to the fact that changes occur with age, Coleman and Cross (2001) propose a definition that is considerate of developmental factors.

The definition . . . differs from others by proposing a change in the criteria that describe giftedness, accounting for changes in abilities with advancing age in school. The criteria become narrower with increased age. This means that in early grades, giftedness would appear more in the areas of general ability or specific skills; but, as the child moves through the grades, evidence of ability and achievement would manifest within specific areas of study. . . . In this model, preadolescent gifted children have potential or demonstrated high ability in two areas: general cognitive ability and creative ability. Adolescent gifted children have demonstrated ability in abstract thinking, have produced creative works in some worthwhile area, and have demonstrated consistent involvement in activities of either type. (pp. 19–20)

This definitional perspective contains elements of the various conceptualizations of giftedness, as discussed in the next section.

Other Conceptualizations of Giftedness

Many different ways to understand giftedness have been presented in the professional literature. Three of the more popular and better-received conceptualizations are highlighted in this section. They include Renzulli's "three-ring" conception of giftedness, Sternberg's "triarchic theory" of intelligence, and Gardner's theory of "multiple intelligences."

Renzulli   One way to conceptualize giftedness is to consider the interaction of three interlocking clusters of traits (Renzulli, 1979; Renzulli & Reis, 1991) as essential elements associated with outstanding accomplishments. The three clusters are as follows, their interacting nature is depicted in Figure 12.1.

▶ High ability—including high intelligence
▶ High creativity—the ability to formulate new ideas and apply them to the solution of problems
▶ High task commitment—a high level of motivation and the ability to see a project through to its completion

These criteria are found in the two types of people who are truly gifted and noted in the U.S. Office of Education definition: those who produce and those who perform (Tannebaum, 1997).

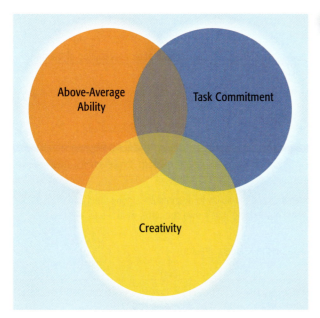

FIGURE 12.1

Renzulli's Three-Ring Conception of Giftedness

From *What Makes Giftedness?* (Brief #6, p. 10), by J. Renzulli, 1979, Los Angeles: National/State Leadership Training Institute. Reprinted by permission.

Sternberg   A popular theory of intellectual giftedness has been developed by Sternberg (1991). His theory includes three types of abilities: analytic giftedness (i.e., ability to dissect a problem and understand its parts); synthetic giftedness (i.e., insight, intuitive creativity, or skill at coping with relatively novel situations); and practical giftedness (i.e., ability to apply aspects of analytical and synthetic strengths to everyday situations). All individuals demonstrate some blend of these three abilities. However, gifted individuals show high ability in one or more of these areas.

Gardner   Another perspective, constituting a broad theory of intelligence, has important applications for conceptualizing giftedness and for programming. Gardner and his colleagues (Gardner, 1983; Gardner & Hatch, 1989) have developed a very popular model that proposes the idea of **multiple intelligences.** This model currently comprises nine areas of ability. Originally the model included only seven areas, but an eighth area (naturalistic) and ninth area (existential) have been added in recent years. Table 12.2 describes the features of each type of intelligence and provides a possible role that might be characteristic of a person with a high degree of a given intelligence.

If Gardner's ideas were followed closely, students would be assessed in all areas of intelligence. If found to have strengths in an area, students would be given opportunities to expand their interests, skills, and abilities accordingly. This conceptualization is attractive because (1) it acknowledges some ability areas that are frequently overlooked and (2) it recognizes the importance of different types of intelligences and gives them all equal footing.

Concept of Creativity

Creativity is included as an element of the federal definition of giftedness, and it is a major part of Renzulli's three-ring model. The concept is difficult to pinpoint, yet its importance

TABLE 12.2   **Multiple Intelligences**

Intelligence	End States	Core Components
Logical–Mathematical	Scientist Mathematician	Sensitivity to, and capacity to discern, logical or numerical patterns; ability to handle long chains of reasoning
Linguistic	Poet Journalist	Sensitivity to the sounds, rhythms, and meanings of words; sensitivity to the different functions of language
Musical	Composer Violinist	Abilities to produce and appreciate rhythm, pitch, and timbre; appreciation of the forms of musical expressiveness
Spatial	Navigator Sculptor	Capacities to perceive the visual–spatial world accurately and to transform one's initial perceptions
Bodily–Kinesthetic	Dancer Athlete	Abilities to control one's body movements and to handle objects skillfully
Interpersonal	Therapist Salesperson	Capacities to discern and respond appropriately to the moods, temperaments, motivations, and desires of other people
Intrapersonal	Person with detailed, accurate self-knowledge	Access to one's own feelings and the ability to discriminate among them and draw upon them to guide behavior; knowledge of one's own strengths, weaknesses, desires, and intelligences
Naturalistic	Naturalist Park Ranger	Affinity and appreciation for the wonders of nature

Adapted from "Multiple Intelligences Go to School: Educational Implications of the Theory of Multiple Intelligences" (p. 6) by H. Gardner and T. Hatch, 1989, *Educational Researcher, 18*(8). Copyright © 1989 by the American Educational Research Association. Reprinted by permission.

as it relates to individuals who are gifted makes it a current topic for debate and discussion. As Coleman and Cross (2001) note, this topic has been part of the ongoing discussion of gifted individuals ever since the publication in 1959 of Guilford's seminal work on this topic.

As indicated previously, the concept is somewhat elusive, and no one definition explaining it has become popular. The concept can be characterized by the phrase "You know it when you see it." Coleman and Cross (2001) aptly describe the state of affairs:

> A single accepted definition of creativity does not exist. In fact, neither is there universal agreement about what relevant attributes are needed to define an act as creative. The difficulty of selecting relevant attributes illustrates the problem of defining creativity. The terms originality and novelty pervade the literature on creativity. They express a quantitative and a qualitative standard, but they fail to say to what criterion a person is being compared. (p. 240)

The concept of creativity continues to receive wide attention, and efforts to better understand it and be able to apply it in meaningful ways within the context of education are warranted. Clark (2002) has created a listing of conditions that facilitate and inhibit the development of creativity. This list is useful for developing instructional activities to allow for creative expression.

Prevalence and Origins of Giftedness

The number of students who display exceptional abilities is uncertain. It is, of course, influenced by how giftedness is defined and how it is measured. Figures of 3% to 5% are typically cited to reflect the extent of giftedness in the school population (National Center for Education Statistics, 1989).

The critical reader should also note the distinction between the number of students served and the number of students who might be gifted. Only certain types of gifted students may be served because of the methods used for identification. Another cautionary note is that such figures generally underestimate the number of gifted students who are ethnically or culturally different, disabled, or female. These subgroups are underrepresented in programs for students with exceptional abilities.

Much professional discussion has focused on what contributes to giftedness in a person. Terman's early work made a strong case for genetics. Without question, research has shown that behavior is greatly affected by genetics. Although this notion is sometimes overemphasized, genetic factors do play a role in giftedness. Most researchers suggest that giftedness results from the interaction between biology and environment. In addition to genetic code, other biological factors, such as nutrition, also have an impact on an individual's development.

The environment in which a child is raised also affects later performance and intellectual abilities. Homes in which significant amounts of stimulation and opportunity to explore and interact with the environment exist, accompanied by high expectations, tend to produce children more likely to be successful scholastically and socially.

CONSIDER THIS

How can the way in which "gifted" is defined influence the prevalence of children classified?

Characteristics of Students Who Are Gifted

Students who are gifted demonstrate a wide range of specific aptitudes, abilities, and skills. Though they should not be overgeneralized or considered stereotypical, certain characteristics distinguish students who are gifted or talented. A comprehensive list, depicting the characteristics of gifted students, has been developed by Clark (2002); a summary is presented in Table 12.3.

An interesting phenomenon is the paradoxical negative effect of seemingly desirable behaviors displayed by gifted students. For instance, sincere, excited curiosity about a topic being covered in class can sometimes be interpreted as annoying or disruptive by a teacher or fellow students. Their quick answers or certainty that they are right may be misconstrued

*T*ABLE 12.3	Differentiating Characteristics of the Gifted
Domain	**Characteristic**
The Cognitive Function	▶ Extraordinary quantity of information; unusual retentiveness ▶ Advanced comprehension ▶ Unusual varied interests and curiosity ▶ High level of language development ▶ High level of verbal ability ▶ Unusual capacity for processing information ▶ Accelerated pace of thought processes ▶ Flexible thought processes ▶ Comprehensive synthesis ▶ Early ability to delay closure ▶ Heightened capacity for seeing unusual and diverse relationships, integration of ideas, and disciplines ▶ Ability to generate original ideas and solutions ▶ Early differential patterns for thought processing (e.g., thinking in alternatives; abstract terms; sensing consequences; making generalizations; visual thinking; use of metaphors and analogies) ▶ Early ability to use and form conceptual frameworks ▶ An evaluative approach toward oneself and others ▶ Unusual intensity; persistent goal-directed behavior
The Affective Function	▶ Large accumulation of information about emotions that have not been brought to awareness ▶ Unusual sensitivity to the expectations and feelings of others ▶ Keen sense of humor—may be gentle or hostile ▶ Heightened self-awareness, accompanied by feelings of being different ▶ Idealism and a sense of justice, which appear at an early age ▶ Earlier development of an inner locus of control and satisfaction ▶ Unusual emotional depth and intensity ▶ High expectations of self and others, often leading to high levels of frustration with self, others, and situations; perfectionism ▶ Strong need for consistency between abstract values and personal actions ▶ Advanced levels of moral judgment ▶ Strongly motivated by self-actualization needs ▶ Advanced cognitive and affective capacity for conceptualizing and solving societal problems ▶ Leadership ability ▶ Solutions to social and environmental problems ▶ Involvement with the metaneeds of society (e.g., injustice, beauty, truth)
The Physical/Sensing Function	▶ Unusual quantity of input from the environment through a heightened sensory awareness ▶ Unusual discrepancy between physical and intellectual development ▶ Low tolerance for the lag between their standards and their athletic skills ▶ Cartesian split—can include neglect of physical well-being and avoidance of physical activity
The Intuitive Function	▶ Early involvement and concern for intuitive knowing and metaphysical ideas and phenomena ▶ Open to experiences in this area; will experiment with psychic and metaphysical phenomena ▶ Creative approach in all areas of endeavor ▶ Ability to predict; interest in future

From *Growing Up Gifted* (6th Ed.) by Barbara Clark. Copyright 2002 by Merrill/Prentice Hall. Reprinted by permission.

as brash arrogance. Such desirable behavior can be misperceived as problem behavior for students who are gifted.

Some characteristics can outright be problematic for students who are gifted. For instance, characteristics such as uneven precocity, interpersonal difficulties (possibly due to cognitive differences), underachievement, nonconformity, perfectionism, and frustration and anger may indeed be negative features (Davis & Rimm, 1998).

Clark (2002) also points out that different levels of ability and performance exist within the ranks of those who are gifted. She distinguishes among students who would be considered typical or moderately gifted, those who are highly gifted, and those who are exceptionally gifted. Carmen, who was introduced at the beginning of the chapter, represents an individual who could be considered highly gifted. According to Clark, highly gifted students "tend to evidence more energy than gifted individuals; they think faster and are more intent and focused on their interests and they exhibit a higher degree of ability in most of the traits . . . identified with giftedness" (p. 63). Clark describes exceptionally gifted as those who "seem to have different value structures . . . tend to be more isolated by choice and more invested in concerns of a meta-nature (e.g., universal problems) . . . seldom seek popularity or social acclaim" (p. 63). Both highly gifted and exceptionally gifted students pose significant challenges to educators in meeting their needs within the general education classroom. Most of the discussion in this chapter is directed toward the typical gifted student.

A notable characteristic that has important classroom implications is the gifted student's expenditure of minimum effort while still earning high grades (Reis & Schack, 1993). Many gifted students are able to handle the general education curriculum with ease. But the long-term effect of being able to excel without working hard may be a lack of the work habits needed for challenging programs at a later point in time (i.e., advanced placement classes in high school or the curriculum of an upper-tier college).

Identification, Assessment, and Eligibility

General education teachers need to know about the assessment process used to confirm the existence of exceptional abilities. General education teachers play a crucial role in the initial stages of the process, for they are likely to be the first to recognize that a student might be gifted. For this reason, teachers should provide opportunities across the range of ability areas (e.g., multiple intelligences) for students to explore their interests and abilities, particularly at the preschool and elementary levels. Ramos-Ford and Gardner (1997) suggest that such opportunities may help students discover certain abilities that might otherwise go unnoticed.

The assessment process includes a sequence of steps, beginning with an initial referral (i.e., nomination) and culminating with the validation of the decision. Schools typically send out announcements to all parents, notifying them that testing to screen for students who are gifted will occur and asking them if they would like for their son or daughter to be considered for this assessment. As mentioned, general education teachers also play a role in identifying gifted students. Although some children displaying exceptional abilities may be spotted very early (i.e., preschool years), many are not recognized until they are in school. For this reason, teachers need to be aware of classroom behaviors that gifted students typically display. A listing of such behaviors is provided in Table 12.4.

Teachers who recognize behaviors highlighted in Table 12.4 should determine whether a student should be evaluated more comprehensively. Teachers should share their observations with the student's parents. Eventually, teachers may want to nominate the student for gifted services. Teachers can be involved in the next step in the assessment process as well.

After a student has been nominated or referred, teachers can assemble information to help determine whether the student should receive special services. The following sources of information can contribute to understanding a student's demonstrated or potential ability: formal test results; informal assessments; interviews with teachers, parents, and peers; and actual student products. For example, a public elementary school may use various screening instruments to identify gifted students, including a standardized ability test, standardized creativity test, teacher observation form, student portfolio, and parent observation form. This phase should be followed by a set of nondiscriminatory evaluation procedures, as suggested in Table 12.5.

A helpful technique used in many school systems to determine the performance capabilities of students is **portfolio assessment.** Portfolios contain a collection of student-generated products, reflecting the quality of a student's work. They may also contain

TEACHING TIP

Classroom teachers need to be alert to students who may be gifted and talented and refer students to appropriate professionals for testing and services.

TABLE 12.4 **Classroom Behaviors of Gifted Students**

Does the child

▶ Ask a lot of questions?
▶ Show a lot of interest in progress?
▶ Have lots of information on many things?
▶ Want to know why or how something is so?
▶ Become unusually upset at injustices?
▶ Seem interested and concerned about social or political problems?
▶ Often have a better reason than you do for not doing what you want done?
▶ Refuse to drill on spelling, math, facts, flash cards, or handwriting?
▶ Criticize others for dumb ideas?
▶ Become impatient if work is not "perfect"?
▶ Seem to be a loner?
▶ Seem bored and often have nothing to do?
▶ Complete only part of an assignment or project and then take off in a new direction?
▶ Stick to a subject long after the class has gone on to other things?
▶ Seem restless, out of seat often?
▶ Daydream?
▶ Seem to understand easily?
▶ Like solving puzzles and problems?
▶ Have his or her own idea about how something should be done? And stay with it?
▶ Talk a lot?
▶ Love metaphors and abstract ideas?
▶ Love debating issues?

This child may be showing giftedness cognitively.

Does the child

▶ Show unusual ability in some area? Maybe reading or math?
▶ Show fascination with one field of interest? And manage to include this interest in all discussion topics?
▶ Enjoy meeting or talking with experts in this field?

▶ Get math answers correct, but find it difficult to tell you how?
▶ Enjoy graphing everything? Seem obsessed with probabilities?
▶ Invent new obscure systems and codes?

This child may be showing giftedness academically.

Does the child

▶ Try to do things in different, unusual, imaginative ways?
▶ Have a really zany sense of humor?
▶ Enjoy new routines or spontaneous activities?
▶ Love variety and novelty?
▶ Create problems with no apparent solutions? And enjoy asking you to solve them?
▶ Love controversial and unusual questions?
▶ Have a vivid imagination?
▶ Seem never to proceed sequentially?

This child may be showing giftedness creatively.

Does the child

▶ Organize and lead group activities? Sometimes take over?
▶ Enjoy taking risks?
▶ Seem cocky, self-assured?
▶ Enjoy decision-making? Stay with that decision?
▶ Synthesize ideas and information from a lot of different sources?

This child may be showing giftedness through leadership ability.

Does the child

▶ Seem to pick up skills in the arts—music, dance, drama, painting, etc.—without instruction?
▶ Invent new techniques? Experiment?
▶ See minute detail in products or performances?
▶ Have high sensory sensitivity?

This child may be showing giftedness through visual or performing arts ability.

From *Growing Up Gifted* (3rd ed., p. 332) by B. Clark, 2002, Upper Saddle River, NJ: Merrill/Prentice Hall. Copyright 2002 by Pearson Education. Reprinted by permission.

permanent products such as artwork, poetry, or videotapes of student performance (e.g., theatrical production, dance or music recital).

As VanTassel-Baska, Patton, and Prillaman (1989) point out, students who are culturally different and those who come from socially and economically disadvantaged backgrounds are typically overlooked in the process of identifying students for gifted programs. For the most part, this problem results from entry requirements that stress performance on standardized tests. When students obtain low test scores on standardized instruments that may be biased against them, exclusion results. VanTassel-Baska et al. provide these recommendations for improving the identification and assessment process:

▶ Use nontraditional measures for identification purposes.
▶ Recognize cultural attributes and factors in deciding on identification procedures.
▶ Focus on strengths in nonacademic areas, particularly in creativity and psychomotor domains. (p. 3)

It has also been difficult to identify and serve students who are twice exceptional—gifted and having a disability. For instance, the problems that characterize a learning disability (e.g., problems in language-related areas) often mask high levels of accomplish-

T ABLE 12.5   **Nondiscriminatory Evaluation Procedures and Evaluations**

Assessment Measures	Findings That Suggest Giftedness
Individualized intelligence test	Student scores in the upper 2 to 3 percent of the population (most states have cutoff scores of 130 or 132 depending on test). Because of cultural biases of standardized IQ tests, students from minority backgrounds are considered if their IQs do not meet the cutoff but other indicators suggest giftedness.
Individualized achievement test	The student scores in the upper 2 to 3 percent in one or more areas of achievement.
Creativity assessment	The student demonstrates unusual creativity in work products as judged by experts or performs exceptionally well on tests designed to assess creativity. The student does not have to be academically gifted to qualify.
Checklists of gifted characteristics	These checklists are often completed by teachers, parents, peers, or others who know the student well. The student scores in the range that suggests giftedness as established by checklist developers.
Anecdotal records	The student's records suggest high ability in one or more areas.
Curriculum-based assessment	The student is performing at a level beyond peers in one or more areas of the curriculum used by the local school district.
Direct observation	The student may be a model student or could have behavior problems as a result of being bored with classwork. If the student is perfectionistic, anxiety might be observed. Observations should occur in other settings besides the school.
Visual and performing arts assessment	The student's performance in visual or performing arts is judged by individuals with expertise in the specific area. The student does not have to be academically gifted to qualify.
Leadership assessment	Peer nomination, parent nomination, and teacher nomination are generally used. However, self-nomination can also be a good predictor of leadership. Leadership in extracurricular activities is often an effective indicator. The student does not have to be academically gifted to qualify.
Case-study approach	Determination of student's giftedness is based on looking at all areas of assessment described above without adding special weight to one factor.

From *Exceptional Lives: Special Education in Today's Schools* (p. 239) by R. Turnbull, A. Turnbull, M. Shank, S. Smith, and D. Leal, 2002. Upper Saddle River, NJ: Merrill/Prentice Hall. Copyright 2002 by Pearson Education. Reprinted by permission.

ment in other areas such as drama, art, or music. Special assessment considerations of this unique population are warranted.

After the student has been identified as gifted and begins to participate in special programs or services, ongoing assessment should become part of the student's educational program. Practical and personal needs should be monitored regularly (Del Prete, 1996). Practical concerns, such as progress in academic areas and realization of potential, can be evaluated. Nevertheless, the personal needs of students who are gifted (e.g., feeling accepted and developing confidence), which should be addressed as well, may require additional time and effort.

Gifted students are not entitled to receive special services under IDEA, unless, of course, they also have a disability that has a significant impact on their education. As a result, "special education" for gifted students is not guaranteed, and various due process safeguards, as provided by IDEA, are not applicable to these students and their families. The nearby Rights & Responsibilities feature summarizes some court cases dealing with this group of students.

Multicultural Issues

As pointed out earlier, cultural diversity remains an area of concern in the education of gifted students. Too few students who are culturally different from the majority of their peers are identified and served through programs for gifted students. "Culturally diverse children have much talent, creativity, and intelligence. Manifestations of these characteristics may be different and thus require not only different tools for measuring these

Rights & Responsibilities

State Programs for Gifted Children

The Individuals with Disabilities Education Act (IDEA) does not include rights for gifted children. Some states, however, do provide programs for this group of students. Examples of state cases involving gifted students include:

1. In a court case in Pennsylvania, *Ellis v. Chester Upland School Dist.,* 651 A.2d 616 (Pa.Cmwlth. 1994), the court ruled that the school did not have to pay out-of-state tuition to a private school for a child who was classified as gifted because the state law did not entitle a gifted student to such services.
2. In the case *Broadley v. Bd. of Educ. of the City of Meriden,* 229 Conn. 1, 639 App.2d 502 (1994), the court ruled that the state of Connecticut did not have to provide special education to gifted children because, even though they were within the broad definition of exceptional children, the law only required special education for children with disabilities.
3. In *Centennial School Dist. v. Commonwealth Dept. of Educ.,* 539 A.2d 785 (Pa.1988), the court ruled that the school district had to provide an IEP and special pro-

grams for gifted students because they were classified as exceptional. The court ruled, however, that this requirement did not entitle the student to specialized instruction beyond enrichment.

4. In *Student Roe v. Commonwealth,* 638 F.Supp. 929 (E.D.Pa. 1986), the court ruled that while Pennsylvania law provides for children with an IQ of 130 and above to be admitted to its gifted programs, IDEA did not apply to children unless they had a disability as defined in the act. Therefore, while state law did require some programs for gifted children, this did not result in gifted students being eligible for IDEA protections.

 For follow-up questions about rights for gifted students, go to Chapter 12 of the Companion Website (ablongman.com/sppd4e) and click Rights & Responsibilities.

From *Students with Disabilities and Special Education* (14th ed., p. 249), 1997, Burnsville, MN: Oakstone Publishing.

Too few students from minority cultural groups are identified as gifted and talented.

*T*ABLE 12.6	Observational Checklist for Identifying Strengths of Culturally Diverse Students

Ability to express feeling and emotions

Ability to improvise with commonplace materials and objects

Articulateness in role-playing, sociodrama, and storytelling

Enjoyment of and ability in visual arts, such as drawing, painting, and sculpture

Enjoyment of and ability in creative movement, dance, drama, etc.

Enjoyment of and ability in music and rhythm

Use of expressive speech

Fluency and flexibility in figural media

Enjoyment of and skills in group or team activities

Responsiveness to the concrete

Responsiveness to the kinesthetic

Expressiveness of gestures, body language, etc., and ability to interpret body language

Humor

Richness of imagery in informal language

Originality of ideas in problem solving

Problem-centeredness or persistence in problem solving

Emotional responsiveness

Quickness of warmup

From "Identifying and Capitalizing on the Strengths of Culturally Different Children" (p. 469) by E. P. Torrance, in *The Handbook of School Psychology,* edited by C. R. Reynolds and J. B. Gulkin, 1982, pp. 451–500. New York: Wiley. Copyright 1982 by John Wiley & Sons. Reprinted by permission.

strengths, but also different eyes from which to see them" (Plummer, 1995, p. 290). Teachers should look for certain behaviors associated with giftedness in children who are culturally different. An example of an observational checklist for accomplishing this task is presented in Table 12.6.

Even when culturally diverse students have been identified as gifted, programming often has not been sensitive to their needs. As Plummer (1995) notes, few programs have the resources (i.e., personnel, materials) available to tap the interests and strengths of these students. Often the general education teacher needs such supports to address these students' educational needs in inclusive settings. The twofold challenge for teachers is (1) to respect ethnic and cultural differences of students from diverse backgrounds and (2) to integrate diverse cultural topics into the curriculum (Plummer, 1995).

Strategies for Curriculum and Instruction for Students Who Are Gifted

The literature on providing effective services for students with exceptional abilities consistently stresses the need for **differentiated programming.** Very simply, this means that learning opportunities provided to these students must differ according to a student's needs and abilities. Differentiation includes the content of what students learn, the processes used in learning situations, and the final products that students develop. Furthermore, as Lopez and MacKenzie (1993) note, "Difference lies in the depth, scope, pace, and self-directedness of the expectations" (p. 288).

CONSIDER THIS

How can teachers take into consideration multicultural issues when designing instruction for students who are gifted?

Diversity Forum

To Be Young, Gifted, and . . . Different

Someday
By Sonny B.

I was identified as gifted in the third grade. . . . I feel that I have had some unique learning experiences, but there has been one drawback—I have been the only Indian in all of the programs that I have participated in. . . . I look forward to participating in an all-Indian program and sharing my experiences with other Indian students like myself. (Callahan & McIntire, 1994, p. 3)

Students like Sonny—young, talented, and from a cultural heritage different from many of their peers—are often overlooked when schools conduct screenings to identify students who are gifted. Educators often have difficulty recognizing characteristics associated with highly talented children in students whose languages, cultures, and life experiences are vastly different from their own (Belcher & Fletcher-Carter, 1999). For instance:

▶ Students who are learning English as a second language may not be able to express their creativity and intellectual potential to monolingual English teachers.

▶ What is valued and viewed as a gift in the student's culture may be different from what is valued in U.S. public schools and reflected in identification measures and procedures.

▶ Economic barriers may prevent some children from participating in activities that develop their potential.

▶ Students' reactions to a culturally unfamiliar school or classroom climate may make them appear unmotivated.

Identification procedures that are more successful in identifying gifted students from these underrepresented groups tend to "recognize alternative, culturally relevant indicators of outstanding talent and can translate them into effective assessment strategies and programming models for children not from the dominant culture" (Callahan & McIntire, 1994, p. 7). Examples of these effective procedures include the following:

▶ School personnel are sensitive to the cultural and social orientation of the student and family.

▶ School personnel collaborate with community members in determining how talent will be defined and identified in the school setting.

▶ Assessment tools and activities are multidimensional and include input from community members, parents, teachers, and students themselves.

▶ Eligibility criteria place greater emphasis on information provided by the family and community rather than school-based criteria.

For follow-up questions about cultural heritage and giftedness, go to Chapter 12 of the Companion Website (ablongman.com/sppd4e) and click Diversity Forum.

CROSS-REFERENCE

Review Chapters 5–11 and compare curriculum and instruction modifications suggested for students with other special needs.

VanTassel-Baska (1989) notes some of the mistaken beliefs that some educators have about educating students with exceptional abilities:

▶ A "differentiated" curriculum for the gifted means "anything that is different from what is provided for all learners." *Fact:* A "differentiated" curriculum implies a coherently planned scope and sequence of instruction that matches the needs of students and that typically does differ from the regular education curriculum.

▶ All experiences provided for gifted learners must be creative and focused on process. *Fact:* Core content areas are important areas of instructional focus.

▶ One curriculum package will provide what is needed for the entire gifted population. *Fact:* Students need a variety of materials, resources, and courses.

▶ Acceleration, moving through the curriculum at a more rapid pace, can be harmful because it pushes children socially and leaves gaps in their knowledge. *Fact:* This approach to meeting the needs of students with exceptional abilities is the intervention technique best supported by research. (pp. 13–14)

CONSIDER THIS

Is the argument for separate programming for gifted students out of phase with the inclusion movement?

Many professionals in the field of gifted education argue that the preferred setting for these students, particularly for highly and exceptionally gifted students, is not general education; they recommend differentiated programs delivered in separate classes for the greater part, if not all, of the school day. However, in reality gifted students are more likely to spend a significant part of their instructional week in general education settings, possibly receiving some differentiated opportunities in a pull-out program. The nearby Inclusion Strategies feature lists curricular goals for gifted children.

Goals for Curricula of Gifted Children

▶ Include more elaborate, complex, and in-depth study of major ideas, problems, and themes—those that integrate knowledge with and across systems of thought.

▶ Allow for the development and application of productive thinking skills that enable students to reconceptualize existing knowledge or generate new knowledge.

▶ Enable students to explore constantly changing knowledge and information, and to develop the attitude that knowledge is worth pursuing in an open world.

▶ Encourage exposure to, selection of, and use of appropriate and specialized resources.

▶ Promote self-initiated and self-directed learning and growth.

▶ Provide for the development of self-understanding and the understanding of one's relationship to persons, societal institutions, nature, and culture.

▶ Evaluate students with stress placed on their ability to perform at a level of excellence that demonstrates creativity and higher-level thinking skills.

For follow-up questions about curricula for gifted students, go to Chapter 12 of the Companion Website (ablongman.com/sppd4e) and click Inclusion Strategies.

From *Diverse Populations of Gifted Children* (pp. 15–16) by S. Cline and D. Schwartz, 1999, Columbus, OH: Merrill.

Continuum of Placement Options

A variety of ways exist for providing educational programs to students who are gifted and talented. Figure 12.2 illustrates various options, as developed by Clark (2002), that might be considered for use with different types of gifted learners. Certain options, used more commonly in the public schools settings, include specialized grouping within the general education setting, independent study, various adjunct programs (e.g., mentorships, internships), special classes outside of general education, special schools, and special summer programs. Another option that some families have chosen is to place their son or daughter in a private school that specializes in providing differentiated programming for gifted students. The value of a particular option reflects the extent to which it meets an individual's needs. As Clark (2002) points out, all the options have some merit; none address the needs of all students with exceptional abilities; however, the general education classroom as traditionally organized in terms of curriculum and instruction is inadequate for true gifted education. For this reason, school systems should provide a range of programmatic alternatives.

Gifted students who are in general education classrooms for the entire instructional day can have some of their needs met through a variety of special provisions such as enrichment, certain acceleration options, or special grouping. The challenge for teachers is to coordinate these provisions with those required for other students in the classroom. It should be noted that some parents make a conscious decision not to have their gifted children participate in the gifted programming offered by a school. This decision might be made for a number of reasons; sometimes it is made because the quality of the gifted programming is poor.

In many schools, students who have been identified as gifted are pulled out for a specified period of time each day to attend a special class for gifted students. When they are in the general education setting, it may be possible for them to participate in an individualized program of study, apart from the regular curriculum.

Gifted students may also participate in various adjunct programs such as mentorships, internships, special tutorials, independent study, and resource rooms—many of which occur outside the regular classroom. For students at the secondary level, spending time in special programming for part of the day, attending heterogeneous classes, or attending a magnet school are other possibilities.

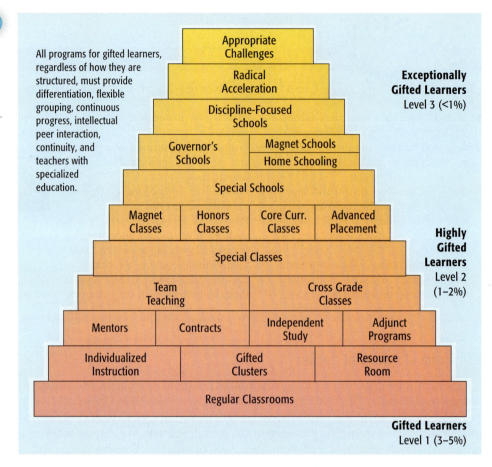

FIGURE 12.2

Placement Options for Gifted Students

From *Growing Up Gifted* (3rd ed., p. 256) by B. Clark, 2002, Upper Saddle River, NJ: Merrill/Prentice Hall. Copyright 2002 by Pearson Education. Reprinted by permission.

These programmatic options affect the role and responsibilities of the general education teacher. In some situations, the general education teacher will be the primary source of instruction for these students. In others, the general education teacher may serve as a manager, coordinating the services provided by others. However, it is probable that most teachers will be responsible for providing some level of instruction to gifted students.

Realities of the General Education Classroom

More attention is being directed to the reality that most gifted students in public school settings will spend a significant amount of time in general education settings. Many innovative and useful techniques exist for addressing the needs of students in these inclusive settings. The section of the chapter on classroom accommodations will highlight many of the techniques. However, cautions remain in regard to meeting the needs of gifted students in general education settings.

In general education settings, students who are gifted or talented are sometimes subject to conditions that diminish the possibility of having their individual needs met. The U.S. Department of Education (1993) has noted the following concerns related to educating gifted students in general education settings:

▶ *Elementary level*
  • The general education curriculum does not challenge gifted students.
  • Most academically talented students have already mastered up to one half of the required curriculum offered to them in elementary school.
  • Classroom teachers do little to accommodate the different learning needs of gifted children.

CONSIDER THIS

How should general classroom teachers be prepared to teach students who are gifted?

- Most specialized programs are available for only a few hours a week.
- Students talented in the arts are offered few challenging opportunities.

▶ *Secondary level*
- Appropriate opportunities in middle schools are scattered and uncoordinated.
- High school schedules do not meet the needs of talented students (i.e., pacing or content of coverage).
- The college preparatory curriculum in the United States generally does not require hard work from able students.
- Small-town and rural schools often have limited resources and are unable to offer advanced classes and special learning opportunities.
- Specialized schools, magnet schools, and intensive summer programs serve only a fraction of the secondary students who might benefit from them.
- Dual enrollment in secondary school and college is uncommon.

Other more specific practices that can be problematic for gifted students include the following:

▶ When involved in group activities (i.e., cooperative learning), gifted students may end up doing all the work (Clinkenbeard, 1991).
▶ They are often subjected to more stringent grading criteria (Clinkenbeard, 1991).
▶ When they finish assignments early, they are given more of the same type of work or assigned more of the same types of tasks at the outset (Shaner, 1991).
▶ They are overused as co-teachers to help students who need more assistance.
▶ Vocabulary use in the average classroom is inappropriate for advanced learners (Clark, 1996).
▶ Advanced levels of critical thinking are not typically incorporated into lessons (Clark, 1996).
▶ Instructional materials in general education classrooms are frequently limited in range and complexity (Clark, 1996).
▶ Problem-solving strategies are not used in classrooms (Gallagher, 1997).

Unfortunately, most general education teachers are not provided with the necessary understanding, skills, and resources to deal appropriately with this population—an issue that will be addressed in more detail later in the chapter. This situation is exacerbated by the fact that teachers have to deal with a wide range of abilities and needs in their classrooms. The composition of the general education classroom in many of today's public schools requires a staggering array of competence in providing appropriate accommodations.

In addition, some teachers feel uncomfortable working with students who have exceptional abilities. Figure 12.3 highlights this situation by way of a personal experience. Shaner (1991) remarks that a teacher who is working with a gifted student can be "intimidated by him or her, paralyzed with a fear of not being able to keep up, or threatened by the student's challenges to authority" (pp. 14–15). Teachers are also concerned about being asked questions they are unprepared to answer or challenged on points they may not know well. These are reasonable fears; however, they can be minimized by using these opportunities as a way of increasing everyone's knowledge—a teacher's as well—and by understanding how to address gifted students' needs within the general classroom setting.

Differentiated programming for students with exceptional abilities, wherever it occurs, must address individual needs and interests in the context of preparing the students for a world characterized by change and complexity. Reis (1989) suggests that we reassess how we look at gifted education and move away from the content-based nature of most current curriculums to an orientation based on a realistic view of future education.

Approaches to Programming

A number of general approaches exist for designing programs for students who have exceptional abilities. While a variety of options might exist in any given school system,

FIGURE 12.3

A Personal Experience

From *Exceptional Children in Focus* (p. 216), by J. R. Patton, J. Blackbourn, and K. Fad, 1996, Columbus, OH: Merrill. Used by permission.

Not long ago, I was invited to go on a "reef walk" with a class of gifted third- and fourth-graders. It was a very educational experience.

While we were wading in shallow water, we came upon a familiar marine organism commonly called a feather duster (tube worm). Forgetting that these students had vocabularies well advanced of their nongifted age peers, I was ready to say something like, "Look how that thing hangs on the rock."

Before I could get my highly descriptive statement out, Eddie, who always amazes us with his comments, offered the following: "Notice how securely anchored the organism is to the stationary coral?"

All I could reply was "Yes. I did."

certain options are most commonly used. Many elementary schools rely on a pull-out program to provide enrichment-type experiences for students. The approaches most likely to be used in general education settings involve acceleration, enrichment, and special grouping.

Acceleration refers to practices that introduce content, concepts, and educational experiences to gifted students sooner than for other students. According to Coleman and Cross (2001) accelerations can be thought of as a way "in which the learner completes a course of study in less time than ordinarily expected" (p. 298). This approach presents gifted students with more advanced materials appropriate to their ability and interests. There are many types of accelerative practices, as reflected in the array of options provided by Southern and Jones (1991) in Table 12.7.

All the acceleration options described by Southern and Jones (1991) have relevance for gifted students in general education classrooms. The techniques that have the most direct application in the general education classroom are continuous progress, self-paced instruction, subject-matter acceleration, combined classes, curriculum compacting, and curriculum telescoping. All of these practices require teachers to plan and implement instructional activities accordingly.

Other accelerative practices have a more indirect impact on ongoing activities in the general education classroom. Nevertheless, teachers should be aware of them. They include early entrance to school, grade skipping, mentorships, extracurricular programs, concurrent enrollment, advanced placement, and credit by examination.

According to Gallagher and Gallagher (1994), the most common acceleration practices are (1) primary level—early admittance to school, ungraded primary; (2) upper elementary—ungraded classes, grade skipping; (3) middle school—three years in two, senior high classes for credit; and (4) high school—extra load (early graduation), advanced placement (AP). Interestingly, some professionals (Davis, 1996) advocate separate advanced placement classes for gifted students because their needs differ from those of nongifted students enrolled in AP classes.

Enrichment refers to techniques that provide topics, skill development, materials, or experiences that extend the depth of coverage beyond the typical curriculum. Coleman and Cross (2001) explain enrichment in the following way: "In its broadest interpretation, enrichment encompasses a number of modifications in standard educational practices. In its narrowest interpretation, enrichment means providing interesting and stimulating tributaries to the mainstream of school" (p. 298).

This practice is commonly used in general education classes to address the needs of students who move through content quickly. Many teachers' manuals and guides provide

CROSS-REFERENCE

These techniques along with other useful strategies are described in Table 12.7.

TABLE 12.7	**Range and Types of Accelerative Options**
1. Early entrance to kindergarten or first grade	The student is admitted to school prior to the age specified by the district for normal entry to kindergarten or first grade.
2. Grade skipping	The student is moved ahead of normal grade placement. This may be done during an academic year (placing a third-grader directly into fourth grade), or at year end (promoting a third-grader to fifth grade).
3. Continuous progress	The student is given material deemed appropriate for current achievement as the student becomes ready.
4. Self-paced instruction	The student is presented with materials that allow him or her to proceed at a self-selected pace. Responsibility for selection of pacing is the student's.
5. Subject matter acceleration	The student is placed for a part of a day with students at more advanced grade levels for one or more subjects without being assigned to a higher grade (e.g., a fifth-grader going to sixth grade for science instruction).
6. Combined classes	The student is placed in classes where two or more grade levels are combined (e.g., third- and fourth-grade split rooms). The arrangement can be used to allow younger children to interact with older ones academically and socially.
7. Curriculum compacting	The student is given reduced amounts of introductory activities, drill review, and so on. The time saved may be used to move faster through the curriculum.
8. Telescoping curriculum	The student spends less time than normal in a course of study (e.g., completing a one-year course in one semester, or finishing junior high school in two years rather than three).
9. Mentorships	The student is exposed to a mentor who provides advanced training and experiences in a content area.
10. Extracurricular programs	The student is enrolled in course work or summer programs that confer advanced instruction and/or credit for study (e.g., fast-paced language or math courses offered by universities).
11. Concurrent enrollment	The student is taking a course at one level and receiving credit for successful completion of a parallel course at a higher level (e.g., taking algebra at the junior high level and receiving credit for high school algebra as well as junior high math credits upon successful completion).
12. Advanced placement	The student takes a course in high school that prepares him or her for taking an examination that can confer college credit for satisfactory performances.
13. Credit by examination	The student receives credit (at high school or college level) upon successful completion of an examination.
14. Correspondence courses	The student takes high school or college courses by mail (or, more recently, through video and audio presentations).
15. Early entrance into junior high, high school, or college	The student is admitted with full standing to an advanced level of instruction (at least one year early).

From *Academic Acceleration of Gifted Children* (Figure 1.1) by W. T. Southern and E. D. Jones, 1991, New York: Teachers College Press. Copyright © 1991 by Teachers College, Columbia University. All rights reserved. Used by permission.

ideas on how to deliver enriching activities to students who finish their work quickly. Comprehensive lesson plans should include a section on "early finishers," which will often include gifted students, so that enriching activities are available for those who complete assignments before the rest of the class.

As Southern and Jones (1991) note, some enrichment activities ultimately involve acceleration. For instance, whenever topics of an advanced nature are introduced, a form of acceleration is actually being employed. There is, however, a distinction between materials or activities that are accelerated and involve a dimension of difficulty or conceptual complexity and materials or activities that provide variety but do not require advanced skills or understanding.

Special grouping refers to the practice whereby gifted students of similar ability levels or interests are grouped together for at least part of the instructional day. One commonly cited technique is the use of cluster grouping within the general education classroom. This practice allows for interaction with peers who share a similar enthusiasm, bring different perspectives to topics, and stimulate the cognitive and creative thinking of others in the group.

Classroom Adaptations for Students Who Are Gifted

This section highlights techniques for addressing the needs of students with exceptional abilities who are in general education classes. Teachers who will be working closely with these students are encouraged to consult resources that thoroughly discuss teaching gifted students in general education settings—see Maker (1993), Parke (1989), Smutny, Walker, and Meckstroth (1997), or Winebrenner (1992).

First and foremost, teachers should strive to create classroom settings that foster conditions in which gifted students feel comfortable and are able to realize their potential. They need a comprehensive long-term plan of education and must enjoy learning experiences that reflect this plan (Kitano, 1993).

Although special opportunities for enrichment, acceleration, and the use of higher-level skills are particularly beneficial to gifted students, these opportunities can also be extended to other students when appropriate (Roberts, Ingram, & Harris, 1992). Many students in general education settings will find practices such as integrated programming (combining different subject matter) to be exciting, motivating, and meaningful.

Management Considerations

It is essential to organize and systematically manage the classroom environment. Teachers must create a psychosocial climate that is open to a "variety of ideas, materials, problems, people, viewpoints, and resources" (Schiever, 1993, p. 209). The learning environment should be safe, accepting, and supportive. It is also useful to design instructional activities that allow for extensive social interactions among all students in the class.

Grouping gifted students for instructional purposes is useful and can be done in a variety of ways. These might include cooperative cluster grouping on the basis of similar abilities or interests, dyads, or seminar-type formats. Gifted students should be afforded an opportunity to spend time with other gifted students, just as competitive tennis players must play opponents with similar or more advanced ability in order to maintain their skills.

Even though the merits of cooperative learning in classroom settings have been established, heterogeneous cooperative learning arrangements involving gifted students must be managed carefully, as there are some potential pitfalls. Teachers must guarantee that most of the work does not always fall on gifted students in such arrangements. Cooperative learning arrangements can be used effectively but need to be continually monitored to ensure productiveness and fairness.

Teachers should develop effective record-keeping systems that monitor the progress of all students, including gifted students who may be involved in a mix of enrichment and accelerated activities. A differentiated report card may be useful for conveying to parents more information about a gifted student's performance. An example of such a report is shown in Figure 12.4. Qualitative information about student performance that parents will find extremely helpful in understanding the progress of their gifted son or daughter can be communicated through this document.

The following are some specific management-related suggestions on dealing with gifted students:

▶ Get to know gifted students early in the school year through interviews, portfolios of previous work, child-created portfolios, and dynamic assessment (test-teach-retest) (Smutny et al., 1997).
▶ Enlist parents as colleagues early in the school year by soliciting information and materials (Smutny et al., 1997).

CONSIDER THIS

How can special opportunities for gifted and talented children benefit other students, including those with other special needs?

TEACHING TIP

Pairing gifted students with students who are not gifted can make an excellent cooperative learning situation for all students.

Differentiated–Integrated Curriculum Report

Student: _____
Teacher: _____
Semester/Year: _____

DISCIPLINES

CONTENT

Area of Study	Broad-Based Theme	Language Arts Enrichment/Acceleration				Math/Science Enrichment		Social Science	Arts	Individual Extension Activities
		Reading	Written Expression	Oral Expression	Spelling	Math	Science	Social Studies/Social Issues	Music/Visual Arts/Performance Arts	

PROCESSES

Basic Skills

Research Skills
- Reading for general information
- Creating hypothesis
- Taking notes
- Making an outline
- Reading for supportive evidence
- Writing the thesis
- Using various sources
- Writing bibliography
- Making appendices

Productive Thinking/Critical Thinking Skills

Brainstorm	Compare	Elaborate
Observe	Categorize	Hypothesize
Classify	Synthesize	Exhibit awareness
Interpret	Exhibit fluency	Appreciate
Analyze	Display flexibility	Create
Evaluate	Demonstrate originality	Redesign
Judge	Problem solve	Prove

PRODUCTS

a variety of ways to communicate and express selves ▲ the opportunity to share information with an audience

☐ Proposed } in-depth study of student's choice.
☐ Completed }

FIGURE 12.4

Differentiated–Integrated Curriculum Report

Adapted from S. N. Kaplan by J. Kataoka, revised 1990. Copyright © ASSETS 1986.

▶ Require gifted students to follow classroom rules and procedures while allowing them to explore and pursue their curiosity when appropriate (Feldhusen, 1993a, 1993b).

▶ Include gifted students in the development of class procedures that emerge during the course of a school year (e.g., introduction of animals in the room).

▶ Explain the logic and rationale for certain rules and procedures.

▶ Use cluster seating arrangements rather than strict rows (Feldhusen, 1993a).

▶ Identify a portion of the room where special events and activities take place and where stimulating materials are kept.

▶ Include instructional ideas for gifted students within all lesson plans.

▶ Let students who are working in independent arrangements plan their own learning activities (Feldhusen, 1993a).

▶ Use contracts with students who are involved in elaborate independent study projects to maximize communication between teacher and students (Rosselli, 1993).

▶ Involve students in their own record keeping, thus assisting the teacher and developing responsibility.

▶ Use periodic progress reports, daily logs, and teacher conferences to monitor and evaluate students who are in independent study arrangements (Conroy, 1993).

Curricular and Instructional Considerations

General education teachers should develop instructional lessons that consider a range of abilities and interests. For gifted students, instructional activities may be qualitatively, and even quantitatively, different from those assigned to the class in general—or completely different if certain accelerative options are being used.

Guiding Questions　When designing instructional activities for the entire class, teachers can use the following series of questions offered by Kitano (1993) to guide planning for gifted students:

▶ Do the activities include provisions for several ability levels?

▶ Do the activities include ways to accommodate a variety of interest areas?

▶ Does the design of activities encourage development of sophisticated products?

▶ Do the activities provide for the integration of thinking processes with concept development?

▶ Are the concepts consistent with the comprehensive curriculum plan? (p. 280)

Select Programming Ideas　An accelerative technique that can be used effectively with gifted students in general education classes is **curriculum compacting,** which allows students to cover assigned material in ways that are faster or different. As Renzulli, Reis, and Smith (1981) point out, this process involves three phases: the assessment of what students know and the skills they possess, identification of various ways of covering the curricular material, and suggestions for enrichment and accelerative options. Renzulli et al. have developed a form to assist teachers in compacting curriculum. This form is presented in Figure 12.5.

Another recommended way to address the needs of gifted students within the context of the general education classroom is to use enrichment techniques. Figure 12.6 provides an example of enrichment by showing how the play *Romeo and Juliet* can be taught, keeping in mind the needs of both nongifted and gifted students who are participating in this same lesson. This example developed by Shanley (1993) shows how the content of the play and the activities used by the teacher can be adapted for gifted students.

The following are more specific suggestions related to instructional strategies and product differentiation:

▶ Balance coverage of basic disciplines and the arts (Feldhusen, 1993a).

▶ Consult teacher/instructor guides of textbook series for ideas for enrichment activities.

CONSIDER THIS

How can differential programming be used effectively with students with a variety of different learning needs?

TEACHING TIP

Nearly all teacher's guides that accompany textbook series used in schools today include suggestions for providing "extension" activities.

Individual Educational Programming Guide
The Compactor

Name _____   Age _____   Teacher(s) _____   Individual conference dates and persons participating in planning of IEP

School _____   Grade _____   Parent(s) _____

Curriculum areas to be considered for compacting. Provide a brief description of basic material to be covered during this marking period and the assessment information or evidence that suggests the need for compacting.	Procedures for compacting basic material. Describe activities that will be used to guarantee proficiency in basic curricular areas.	Acceleration and/or enrichment activities. Describe activities that will be used to provide advanced-level learning experiences in each of the regular curricula.

FIGURE 12.5

Curriculum Compacting Form

From *The Revolving Door Identification Model* (p. 79) by J. Renzulli, S. Reis, and L. Smith, 1981, Mansfield Center, CT: Creative Learning Press. Reprinted with permission from Creative Learning Press, copyright © 1981.

▶ Incorporate Internet-based activities into lessons.

▶ Acquire an array of different learning-related materials for use with gifted students—these can include textbooks, magazines, artifacts, software, CD-ROMs, Internet sources, and digital media, as well as other types of media.

▶ Include time for independent study—use independent study contracts (Pugh, 1999).

▶ Teach research skills (data-gathering and investigative techniques) to gifted students to develop their independent study abilities (Reis & Schack, 1993).

▶ Use integrated themes for interrelating ideas within and across domains of inquiry (VanTassel-Baska, 1997). This type of curricular orientation can be used for all students in the general education setting, with special activities designed for gifted students.

▶ Include higher-order thinking skills in lessons (Johnson, 2001; Winocur & Mauer, 1997)—for example, include questions that are open-ended and of varying conceptual levels in class discussions—see Table 12.8.

▶ Allocate time for students to have contact with adults who can provide special experiences and information to gifted students (e.g., mentors).

▶ Avoid assigning regular class work missed when gifted students spend time in special programs.

▶ Manage classroom discussions so that all students have an equal opportunity to contribute, feel comfortable doing so, and understand the nature of the discussion.

▶ Use standard textbooks and materials carefully, as gifted students will typically be able to move through them rapidly and may find them boring.

IGURE 12.6 **Adapting Curricular Content for Teaching *Romeo and Juliet***

APPROPRIATE CONTENT FOR REGULAR STUDENTS

1. Discuss qualities of drama that make drama a unique genre of literature.
2. Discuss terms used in discussion of drama, such as *aside, soliloquy, prologue, epilogue, dramatic irony,* and *foreshadowing.*
3. Discuss overview of Elizabethan time period, political system, and the role of arts in the society.
4. Distinguish between Shakespeare's time period and setting of the play, giving brief explanation of Verona's social and political characteristics.
5. Discuss structure of Shakespeare's plays, using terms such as *act, scene,* and *line count.*
6. Discuss Shakespeare's language and such terms as *puns* and *asides.*
7. Discuss main plot, characterization, conflict, and ending of the play.

POSSIBLE ASSIGNMENTS:
a. Write an "updated" scene from Romeo and Juliet, stressing the same relationships, but making the scene's setting, names, language more contemporary.
b. Act out the original or rewritten scenes with emphasis on staging considerations.

ROMEO AND JULIET

APPROPRIATE CONTENT FOR GIFTED STUDENTS

1. Arrange students in small group to read play at rate appropriate to level of understanding.
2. Provide reference material dealing with Elizabethan time period, political and social characteristics, English theater, and time period information about Verona and play's setting.
3. Provide reference material on critical analysis of *Romeo and Juliet.*
4. Encourage awareness of concepts found in play, such as decision making, personal identity, interpretation of the law.
5. Complete a Taba Teaching Strategy (Application of Generalization or Resolution of Conflict), stressing concepts as areas for individual research.
6. Facilitate student research and projects on conceptual subject matter from play.

POSSIBLE ACTIVITIES:
a. Visit and interview local agency for counseling youth or counseling for suicide prevention.
b. Become involved in local drama group.
c. Write an original play dealing with similar or related concepts found in *Romeo and Juliet.*

From "Becoming Content with Content" (p. 74) by R. Shanley, in *Critical Issues in Gifted Education: Vol. 1. Defensible Programs for the Gifted* (pp. 43–89), edited by C. J. Maker, 1993, Austin, TX: Pro-Ed. Used by permission.

TABLE 12.8 **Question Analysis Chart for a Class Discussion on George Washington Carver**

	Question Type	Explanation	Example
1.	Data-recall questions	Requires remembering	What was the name given to George Washington Carver's laboratory?
2.	Naming questions	Lacks insight	Name 10 peanut products developed by George Washington Carver.
3.	Observation questions	Requires minimal understanding	What obstacles did George Washington Carver overcome as a black scientist?
4.	Control questions	Modifies behavior	How will you remember George Washington Carver's scientific contribution to the farming community?
5.	Pseudo-questions	Conveys expected answer	Were George Washington Carver's accomplishments inspirational to black people?
6.	Hypothesis-generating questions	Involves speculation	Would George Washington Carver have been famous if he were white?
7.	Reasoning questions	Requires rationale	Why did George Washington Carver want to preserve the small family farm?
8.	Personal response questions	Invites personal opinions	What, in your opinion, was George Washington Carver's greatest accomplishment?
9.	Discriminatory questions	Requires weighing of pros and cons	Which of George Washington Carver's discoveries was the most significant, those evolving from the sweet potato or the peanut?
10.	Problem-solving questions	Demands finding ways to answer questions	If you were to design a memorial for George Washington Carver, what sources would you study for inspiration?

From "Process Differentiation for Gifted Learners in the Regular Classroom: Teaching to Everyone's Needs" (p. 151) by H. Rosselli, in *Critical Issues in Gifted Education: Vol. 3. Programs for the Gifted in Regular Classrooms* (pp. 139–155), edited by C. J. Maker, 1993, Austin, TX: Pro-Ed. Used by permission.

Websites That Offer Curriculum, Strategies, and Interventions

▶ www.kn.pacbell.com/wired/bluewebn
(lesson plans and teaching resources)

▶ www.education-world.com
(curriculum ideas)

▶ www.yahooligans.com
(child-safe search engine, links, discussion groups)

▶ rtec.org
(links to 6 regional technology consortia to support improved teaching)

▶ www.nyu.edu/projects/mstep/menu.html
(lesson plans, activities, and information for math and science teachers)

▶ www.planemath.com/
(InfoUse with NASA provides student activities in math and aeronautics)

▶ mathforum.org
(database of math lesson plans by topic and grade level)

▶ www.enc.org
(variety of math and science lessons for grades 4–12)

For follow-up questions about website resources, go to Chapter 12 of the Companion Website (ablongman.com/sppd4e) and click Technology Today.

From *Quick Guide to the Internet for Special Education* (2000 edition) by M. Male and D. Gotthoffer, 2000, Boston: Allyn and Bacon.

▶ Ensure that gifted students have access to technology—especially various types of software applications (e.g., word processing, spreadsheets, databases, presentation, photo editing) and various interactive/telecommunications options (e-mail, mailing lists, discussion groups, bulletin boards). See the nearby Technology Today for some websites that contain curriculum-appropriate suggestions for students and teachers.

▶ Provide a range of options for demonstrating student mastery of curricular/instructional objectives—for instance, consider a range of options for final product development—see Figure 12.7 for a list of examples.

Career Development   Gifted and talented students need to learn about possible career choices that await them. They may need to do so at an earlier time than other students because they may participate in accelerated programs that necessitate early decisions about career direction. Students should learn about various career options, the dynamics of different disciplines, and the training required to work in a given discipline.

Teachers can select different ways to address the career needs of students. One way is to ensure that gifted students have access to mentor programs, spending time with adults who are engaged in professional activities that interest them. Another method is to integrate the study of careers into the existing curriculum by discussing various careers when appropriate and by requiring students to engage in some activities associated with different careers. Students can become acquainted with a number of different careers while covering traditional subject areas and through the use of resources like the *Occupational Outlook Handbook,* which is available on-line (http://www.bls.gov/oco/home.htm).

Career counseling and guidance are also recommended. As Hardman, Drew, Egan, and Wolf (1993) point out, because of their multiple exceptional abilities and wide range of interests, some gifted students have a difficult time making career choices or narrowing down mentorship possibilities. These students should spend some time with counselors or teachers who can help them make these choices and other important postsecondary decisions.

> **TEACHING TIP**
>
> Arrange a career day for students, and have community members discuss various careers with students.

Social-Emotional Considerations

Gifted students have the same physiological and psychological needs as their peers. Yet, as Cross (1999) points out, "The lives of gifted students are both the same as and different from other students' lives" (p. 33). They may also be dealing with perplexing concepts that are well ahead of the concerns of their peers. For instance, a gifted fourth-grade girl asked her teacher questions related to abortion—a topic with which she was already dealing conceptually. In addition, gifted students may be dealing with some issues that are different

FIGURE 12.7   **Outlet Vehicles for Differentiated Student Products**

LITERARY

- Literary magazine (prose or poetry)
- Newspaper for school or class
- Class reporter for school newspaper
- Collections of local folklore (*Foxfire*)
- Book reviews of childrens' books for children, by children
- Storytelling
- Puppeteers
- Student editorials on a series of topics
- Kids' page in a city newspaper
- Series of books or stories
- Classbook or yearbook
- Calendar book
- Greeting cards (including original poetry)
- Original play and production
- Poetry readings
- Study of foreign languages
- Organizer of story hour in local or school library
- Comic book or comic book series
- Organization of debate society
- Monologue, sound track, or script

MATHEMATICAL

- Contributor of math puzzles, quizzes, games for children's sections in newspapers, magazines
- Editor/founder of computer magazine or newsletter
- Math consultant for school
- Editor of math magazine, newsletter
- Organizer of metrics conversion movement
- Original computer programming
- Programming book
- Graphics (original use of) films

MEDIA

- Children's television show
- Children's radio show
- Children's reviews (books, movie) on local news shows
- Photo exhibit (talking)
- Pictorial tour
- Photo essay
- Designing advertisement (literary magazine)
- Slide/tape show on self-selected topic

ARTISTIC

- Displays, exhibits
- Greeting cards
- Sculpture
- Illustrated books
- Animation
- Cartooning

MUSICAL, DANCE

- Books on life of famous composer
- Original music, lyrics
- Electronic music (original)
- Musical instrument construction
- Historical investigation of folk songs
- Movement—history of dance, costumes

HISTORICAL AND SOCIAL SCIENCES

- Roving historian series in newspaper
- "Remember when" column in newspaper
- Establishment of historical society
- Establishment of an oral history tape library
- Published collection of local folklore and historical highlight stories
- Published history (written, taped, pictorial)
- Historical walking tour of a city
- Film on historical topic
- Historical monologue
- Historical play based on theme
- Historical board game
- Presentation of historical research topic (World War II, etc.)
- Slide/tape presentation of historical research
- Starting your own business
- Investigation of local elections
- Electronic light board explaining historical battle, etc.
- Talking time line of a decade (specific time period)
- Tour of local historical homes
- Investigate a vacant lot
- Create a "hall" of local historical figures
- Archaeological dig
- Anthropological study (comparison of/within groups)

SCIENTIFIC

- Science journal
- Daily meteorologist posting weather conditions
- Science column in newspaper
- Science "slot" in kids television show
- Organizer at a natural museum
- Science consultant for school
- "Science Wizard" (experimenters)
- Science fair
- Establishment of a nature walk
- Animal behavior study
- Any prolonged experimentation involving manipulation of variables
- Microscopic study involving slides
- Classification guide to natural habitats
- Acid rain study
- Future study of natural conditions
- Book on pond life
- Aquarium study/study of different ecosystems
- Science article submitted to national magazines
- Plan a trip to national parks (travelogue)
- Working model of a heart
- Working model of a solar home
- Working model of a windmill

From "Differentiating Products for the Gifted and Talented: The Encouragement of Independent Learning" (p. 169) by S. M. Reis and G. D. Schack, in *Critical Issues in Gifted Education: Vol. 3. Programs for the Gifted in Regular Classrooms* (pp. 161–186), edited by C. J. Maker, 1993, Austin, TX: Pro-Ed. Used by permission.

Personal Spotlight

Special Education Teacher

Joy Kataoka has taught students with special needs for ten years. While teaching students with many different types of disabilities, she believes that the most challenging teaching year she had was with students with learning disabilities, some of whom were also gifted. To meet the unique needs of these students, Joy had to develop an approach that met individual student needs while challenging their intellectual advancement. In order to do this, she selected a differentiated-integrated curriculum, which is a common approach for students classified as gifted. "I selected a broad-based theme that was implemented throughout the entire school year."

Using this model, learning activities and experiences were developed that related to the theme as well as to the basic skill needs of some of the students. For example, one year the theme "change" was chosen. Activities associated with this theme included the study of weather, seasons, the theory of continental drift, the theory of evolution, the Civil Rights movement, and people who made significant contributions to the Civil Rights movement. Conflict resolution in literature and factors that influence change in people were topics that were also included. In addition, students were also engaged in taking a scientific phenomenon such as lightning, thunder, or rain, and researching how it was represented in mythology, examining the scientific explanation, and also looking at how different poets describe the scientific occurrence in poetry.

The implementation of the curriculum required some individualization. Basic concepts were presented to the entire class, and all students participated in class discussions. However, each student was evaluated based on what he or she could successfully accomplish. Gifted students were required to complete projects in much more detail and at a higher level of sophistication than students who were not gifted. However, all students had to meet certain basic or minimum requirements.

Joy noted that "although such a diverse group of learners in one classroom initially presented a challenge, this curricular approach turned out to be the most successful and productive teaching experience in my career." Inclusion often results in having to teach students with diverse needs and abilities. Teachers must analyze the situation and develop an approach that can meet the needs of all students.

Joy Kataoka　　　　*Austin, TX*

For follow-up questions about this Personal Spotlight, go to Chapter 12 of the Companion Website (ablongman.com/sppd4e) and click Personal Spotlight.

---

from their nongifted peers, such as stress, hypersensitivity, control, perfectionism, underachievement/lack of motivation, coping mechanisms, introversion, peer relationships, need for empathy, self-understanding, and self-acceptance (Smutny et al., 1997).

Perhaps the most important recommendation is for teachers to develop relationships with students that make them feel comfortable discussing their concerns and questions. Teachers can become important resources to gifted students, not only for advice, but also for information. Regularly scheduled individual time with a teacher can have important paybacks for both the student and the teacher.

Teachers may also find it beneficial to schedule weekly room meetings (Feldhusen, 1993b) or class councils (Kataoka, 1987) to identify and address social, procedural, or learning-related problems that arise in the classroom. The group discussion includes articulation of a problem, brainstorming and discussion of possible solutions, selection of a plan of action, and implementation, evaluation, and reintroduction of the problem if the plan of action is not effective.

The Personal Spotlight highlights one teacher's suggestions for adjusting the curriculum to meet the individual needs of all the students in the classroom. Following are some specific suggestions for dealing with the social-emotional needs of gifted students:

▶ Know when to refer students to professionals trained to deal with certain types of emotional problems.

▶ Create a classroom atmosphere that encourages students to take academic risks and allows them to make mistakes without fear of ridicule or harsh negative critique.

▶ Provide time on a weekly basis, if at all possible, for individual sessions with students so that they can share their interests, ongoing events in their lives, or concerns.

▶ Maintain regular, ongoing communication with the families of gifted students, notifying them of the goals, activities, products, and expectations you have for their children.

▶ Require, and teach if necessary, appropriate social skills (e.g., appropriate interactions) to students who display problems in these areas.

▶ Work with parents on the personal development of students.

▶ Use different types of activities (e.g., social issues) to develop self-understanding and decision-making and problem-solving skills. Rosselli (1993) recommends the use of bibliotherapy (literature that focuses on children with disabilities).

▶ Teach gifted students how to deal with their "uniqueness."

▶ Recognize that gifted students may experience higher levels of social pressure and anxiety—for example, peer pressure not to achieve at a high level or lofty expectations originating internally or from others (Del Prete, 1996).

Promoting Inclusive Practices for Students Who Are Gifted

Addressing the needs of students with exceptional abilities in the context of the general education classroom is a monumental challenge. Current realities and probable trends in programming for gifted students suggest that general education will continue to be the typical setting in which they receive instruction. Thus, it is important that we do all that we can to enrich the educational experiences of this population in these settings. To do so requires some thoughtful planning and revision to the modus operandi. First, we need to create classrooms where gifted students feel wanted and supported, in addition to having their instructional needs met by appropriate programming. Second, we must identify and provide appropriate programming to gifted students who are currently underidentified. Third, it is essential that the necessary supports be provided to general education teachers to achieve desired outcomes for this group of students. Fourth, supports must be offered to parents and families. Last, the way general education teachers are prepared must be examined to ensure that attention is given to the topic of giftedness.

Classroom Climate

The climate of any classroom is determined by the interaction between the teacher, the students in the class, and other regular participants in classroom dynamics; in particular, the teacher plays a leading role in establishing the parameters by which a classroom operates and the foundation for classroom dynamics. The degree to which a classroom becomes a community in which students care for one another and strive to improve the daily experience for everyone will depend on each class's unique dynamics. When a healthy and nurturing classroom context is established, students who are gifted can be important members of the classroom community. In such an environment, their abilities are recognized as assets to the class rather than something to be jealous of, envied, or despised.

To promote acceptance of gifted students, teachers should strive to dispel prevailing stereotypes, as perpetuated by myths and misconceptions. Teachers should discuss the uniqueness of these students in terms of the diversity of the classroom, implying that everyone is different. The notion that we all have strengths and weaknesses is also useful.

Instructionally, many of the strategies suggested for gifted students can also be used successfully with nongifted students (Del Prete, 1996). By taking this approach, teachers can accommodate the needs of gifted students without drawing undue attention to the special programming they are receiving.

CROSS-REFERENCE

Review Chapters 5–11 to determine whether methods of enhancing an inclusive classroom for students with other special needs will be effective with students who are gifted and talented.

TEACHING TIP

Assigning students who are gifted and talented to be peer tutors can both enhance their acceptance and give them opportunities for leadership.

Teachers must create a psychological classroom climate that is conducive to a variety of ideas and viewpoints.

Addressing the Needs of Special Populations

It is particularly important to address the needs of students who are typically underidentified as being gifted, such as females, students with disabilities, those who are economically disadvantaged, those who underachieve in school, and those who come from different ethnic or cultural backgrounds. Critical issues related to serving these groups focus on nurturing abilities of students in general education, recognizing their potential and discovering exceptional abilities in academic and nonacademic areas, and providing appropriate intervention.

Some general suggestions for improving the nature of services are the following:

▶ *Nurturing student development*
- Create a supportive, caring, nurturing classroom environment, as noted earlier.
- Establish high expectations for all students in the general education classroom.
- Encourage all students to do their best.
- Emphasize that everyone has strengths and areas needing improvement.
- Identify areas of student interest—this effort often leads to recognition of areas where a student finds some degree of success.

▶ *Recognizing hidden giftedness*
- Regularly examine the qualitative aspects of students' performance on academic tasks.
- Make sure that certain factors such as a specific learning-related problem (e.g., memory problems) or English not being the student's first language do not mask strength in a variety of areas.
- Use a variety of assessment techniques for screening and eligibility determination purposes.
- Seek parent input on students who are very shy and passive in class activities—these students are often overlooked.

▶ *Providing appropriate services*
- Consider a student's personal style and cultural background in the selection of various programming options—for instance, heavy reliance on special ability group work may not be the best first choice for some students.
- Be aware that some enrichment-related activities, while perhaps engaging, may be in conflict with a student's family and personal beliefs.

Methods that are effective with gifted students are also useful for nongifted students.

The needs of gifted females have received more attention over the years. Various lists of suggestions (Silverman, 1986) have been generated to assist teachers, parents, and others to better attend to the needs of this group of students. A recent article by Reis (2001) looked at some of the extant barriers that gifted girls and woman still face. She provided a list of general recommendations to help gifted girls understand and do something about the external barriers that inhibit their talent development—a selection of some of the recommendations is provided in Table 12.9.

Supports for the General Education Teacher

The responsibility to deliver a quality education to gifted students in general education settings rests on the shoulders of the instructional staff, especially general education teachers. Given the realities of the general education classroom, teachers face a mighty challenge in meeting the needs of gifted students. To maximize the chances of successfully addressing the needs of gifted students who are in these settings, Coleman (1998) recommends that schools

▶ group students in teachable clusters—groups of 6–10 students whose instructional needs are similar.
▶ reduce class size.
▶ provide additional instructional resources.
▶ modify schedules so that there are greater amounts of time available to work with gifted students.
▶ provide additional support personnel.
▶ require and/or provide training in working with gifted students.

School-based supports such as teacher assistance teams (Chalfant & Van Dusen Pysh, 1993) can also assist with addressing the needs of gifted students. When staffed properly, these teams become a rich resource of experience and ideas for dealing with a myriad of student needs. Parents also play an important, and often indirect, role in the school-based programs of their children. As Riley (1999) suggests, it is worthwhile to develop parents into good "dance partners" (i.e., to create and maintain positive relationships) in this process.

CONSIDER THIS

What other kinds of supports might contribute to the effectiveness of general classroom teachers in meeting the needs of gifted students in their classes?

TABLE 12.9   Recommendations for Girls and Women

Gifted and Talented Girls Should	Teachers Should	Parents, Teachers, and Counselors Should
Have exposure or personal contact with female role models and mentors who have successfully balanced career and family;	Provide equitable treatment in a nonstereotyped environment and in particular, provide encouragement;	Form task forces to advocate for programming and equal opportunities and to investigate opportunities for talented, creative girls;
Participate in discussion groups and attend panel discussions in which gifted and talented girls and women discuss the external barriers they have encountered;	Reduce sexism in classrooms and create an avenue for girls to report and discuss examples of stereotyping in schools;	Spotlight achievements of talented females in a variety of different areas, encourage girls and young women to become involved in as many different types of activities, travel opportunities, and clubs as possible;
Pursue involvement in leadership roles and extracurricular activities;	Help creative, talented females appreciate and understand healthy competition;	Encourage girls to take advanced courses in all areas as well as courses in the arts and reinforce successes in these and all areas of endeavor; ensure equal representation of girls in advanced classes;
Participate in either sports, athletics, and multiple extracurricular activities in areas in which they have an interest;	Group gifted females homogeneously in math/science or within cluster groups of high ability students in heterogeneous groups;	Encourage relationships with other creative girls who want to achieve;
Discuss issues related to gender and success such as family issues in supportive settings with other talented girls; and	Encourage creativity in girls;	Maintain options for talented, creative girls in specific groups such as self-contained classes, groups of girls within heterogeneous classes and in separate classes for gifted girls, science and math clubs, or support groups; and
Participate in career counseling at an early age and be exposed to a wide variety of career options and talented women who pursue challenging careers in all areas.	Use problem solving in assignments and reduce the use of timed tests and timed assignments within class periods; rather, provide options for untimed work within a reasonable time frame;	Consistently point out options for careers and encourage future choices but help girls focus on specific interests and planning for future academic choices, interests, and careers.
	Expose girls to other creative, gifted females through direct and curricular experiences—field trips, guest speakers, seminars, role models, books, videotapes, articles, movies;	
	Provide educational interventions compatible with cognitive development and styles of learning (i.e., independent study projects, small group learning opportunities, and so forth) and use a variety of authentic assessment tools such as projects and learning centers instead of just using tests;	
	Establish equity in classroom interactions; and	
	Provide multiple opportunities for creative expression in multiple modalities.	

Support for Parents and Families

In addition to the usual suggestion about the importance of establishing a good home-school collaborative arrangement, some parents of gifted students may need additional information and support. Cases exist where parents of highly gifted students did not recognize that their son or daughter might be gifted. These parents are likely to need information about their child as well as information about the different programming that might be available to address their child's needs.

TEACHING TIP

Teachers are well advised to set up an efficient and effective system for informing and involving parents in the education of their gifted son or daughter.

Parents are faced with the same challenges arising from the gifted characteristics that teachers encounter in the classroom. Often these desirable characteristics can become points of contention. Parents can benefit from the advice of teachers in dealing with these student capabilities and in challenging their child at home during the time when the student is not in school.

Parents can also benefit from obtaining information about careers and further education. Most families are very familiar with the college selection process; however, some families are not, particularly those where the parents may not have gone to postsecondary education.

Teacher Preparation

To be a successful general education teacher of gifted students, a wide range of competencies are needed. A set of national standards for teacher preparation is not presently available (Cline & Schwartz, 1999). As a result, training programs, where they do exist, may vary widely in terms of the required coursework and the content of courses offered.

Maker (1993) highlighted the following personal features as important in teaching gifted students: commitment, belief that people learn differently, high expectations, organization, enthusiasm, willingness to talk less–listen more, facilitative abilities, creativity, and the ability to juggle. Others (see Davis & Rimm, 1998) have discussed the personal characteristics desirable in teachers of gifted students.

It is important to acknowledge the point made by Cline and Schwartz (1999) that "no one teacher can be expected to have complete expertise in meeting the needs of every type of learner" (p. 172). However, general education teachers should be exposed to some basic set of knowledge and skills to better address the needs of gifted students who will be in their classrooms. Research has validated the fact that teachers who have had specialized training in addressing the needs of gifted students are more effective (Hansen & Feldhusen, 1994). A basic list of knowledge/understanding and skills/competencies suggested for general education teachers is provided in Table 12.10.

TABLE 12.10   **What General Education Teachers Need to Know**

Knowledge and Understanding	*Skills and Competencies*
Cognitive and affective differentiating characteristics of gifted learners	Instructional modification techniques
Educational needs of gifted, creative, and talented (GCT) learners	Instructional design strategies
Future studies	Teaching strategy selection
Creativity, creative thinking strategies	Higher order questioning
Specific instructional materials and curriculum already designed for basic content areas	Creative problem-solving
Nature of giftedness, intelligence	Futuring
	Group process
	Parent conferencing

From "Training Teachers of the Gifted: What Do They Need to Know?" (p. 146) by K. B. Rogers, 1989, *Roeper Review, 11*(3). Copyright 1989 by Roeper Review. Reprinted by permission.

> ## TABLE 12.11   A Declaration of the Educational Rights of the Gifted Child
>
> It is the right of a gifted child to engage in appropriate educational experiences even when other children of that grade level or age are unable to profit from the experience.
>
> It is the right of a gifted child to be grouped and to interact with other gifted children for some part of their learning experience so that the child may be understood, engaged, and challenged.
>
> It is the right of a gifted child to be taught rather than to be used as a tutor or teaching assistant for a significant part of the school day.
>
> It is the right of a gifted child to be presented with new, advanced, and challenging ideas and concepts regardless of the materials and resources that have been designated for the age group or grade level in which the child was placed.
>
> It is the right of a gifted child to be taught concepts that the child does not yet know instead of relearning old concepts that the child has already shown evidence of mastering.
>
> It is the right of a gifted child to learn faster than age peers and to have that pace of learning respected and provided for.
>
> It is the right of a gifted child to think in alternative ways, produce diverse products, and to bring intuition and innovation to the learning experience.
>
> It is the right of a gifted child to be idealistic and sensitive to fairness, justice, accuracy, and the global problems facing humankind and to have a forum for expressing these concerns.
>
> It is the right of a gifted child to question generalizations, offer alternative solutions, and value complex and profound levels of thought.
>
> It is the right of a gifted child to be intense, persistent, and goal-directed in the pursuit of knowledge.
>
> It is the right of a gifted child to express a sense of humor that is unusual, playful, and often complex.
>
> It is the right of a gifted child to hold high expectations for self and others and to be sensitive to inconsistency between ideals and behavior, with the need to have help in seeing the value in human differences.
>
> It is the right of a gifted child to be a high achiever in some areas of the curriculum and not in others, making thoughtful, knowledgeable academic placement a necessity.
>
> It is the right of a gifted child to have a low tolerance for the lag between vision and actualization, between personal standards and developed skill, and between physical maturity and athletic ability.
>
> It is the right of a gifted child to pursue interests that are beyond the ability of age peers, are outside the grade level curriculum, or involve areas as yet unexplored or unknown.
>
> From *Growing Up Gifted* (3rd ed., pp. 19–20) by B. Clark, 2002, Upper Saddle River, NJ: Merrill/Prentice Hall. Copyright 2002 by Pearson Education. Reprinted by permission.

Final Thought

If the topics and issues presented in this chapter are addressed correctly, we will do a great service to students with exceptional abilities. Furthermore, gifted students should be entitled to a set of educational rights, as Clark (2002) has suggested, on which efforts to provide appropriate education to this population should be based. Her 15 educational rights are listed in Table 12.11. It is only when these conditions are met that teachers will be able to "stimulate the imagination, awaken the desire to learn, and imbue the students with a sense of curiosity and an urge to reach beyond themselves" (Mirman, 1991, p. 59).

Summary

Basic Concepts About Students Who Are Gifted

- Gifted students continue to be an underidentified, underserved, and often inappropriately served segment of the school population. A host of misconceptions exist in the minds of the general public about these individuals.
- Definitional perspectives of giftedness and intellectual abilities vary and contribute to some of the problems related to identification, eligibility, and service delivery. A key component of most definitions is the student's remarkable potential to achieve at levels above the level of peers, as well as high ability, high task commitment, and high creativity.
- The notion of multiple intelligences suggests that there are different areas where one can show high ability.
- The identification of gifted students is a complex and multifaceted process. Multiple sources of information are needed to determine whether a student is gifted.
- Gifted students with diverse cultural backgrounds are underrepresented in gifted programs, often because of biased assessment practices. Special effort must be given to serving all students who show promise.

Strategies for Curriculum and Instruction for Students Who Are Gifted

- Most educators of gifted students prefer programs that are typically apart and different from those of nongifted students. The reality, however, is that most gifted students are in general education classes for most of their education.

- The major ways of addressing the needs of gifted students in general education are through the use of acceleration, enrichment, or special grouping.

Classroom Adaptations for Students Who Are Gifted

- The special methods used with gifted students are often effective with other students as well.
- The career development needs of gifted students must also be addressed.

Promoting Inclusive Practices for Students Who Are Gifted

- Teachers can do a great deal to promote a sense of community and social acceptance of gifted students in their classrooms. It is difficult to address the needs of gifted students in the context of a large class with a great range of diverse needs.
- Supports to teachers, as well as to parents and families, are needed to effectively address the needs of students who are gifted.
- The probability of successfully helping gifted students reach their potential is contingent upon a number of key factors.
- Understanding the needs of special populations of gifted students (females, disabled, economically disadvantaged, underachievers, and those from ethnically and culturally different backgrounds) is essential.

Further Readings

Baum, S. M., Owen, S. V., & Dixon, J. (1991). *The gifted and learning disabled.* Mansfield Center, CT: Creative Learning Press.

Castellano, J. A., & Díaz, E. I. (2002). *Reaching new horizons: Gifted and talented education for culturally and linguistically diverse students.* Boston: Allyn and Bacon.

Clark, B. (2002). *Growing up gifted* (6th ed.). Upper Saddle River, NJ: Merrill/Prentice Hall.

Cline, S., & Schwartz, D. (1999). *Diverse populations of gifted children.* Boston: Allyn and Bacon.

Colangelo, N., & Davis, G. A. (Eds.). (In press). *Handbook of gifted education* (3rd ed.). Boston: Allyn and Bacon.

Coleman, L. J., & Cross, T. L. (2001). *Being gifted in school: An introduction to development, guidance, and teaching.* Waco, TX: Prufrock Press.

Csikszentmihalyi, M., Rathunde, K., & Whalen, S. (1997). *Talented teenagers: The roots of success and failure.* Cambridge, UK: Cambridge University Press.

Davis, G. A., & Rimm, S. B., (1998). *Education of the gifted and talented* (4th ed.). Boston: Allyn and Bacon.

Delisle, J. R. (2000). *Once upon a mind: The stories and scholars of gifted child education.* Fort Worth, TX: Harcourt Brace.

Gardner, H. (1993). *Multiple intelligences: The theory in practice.* New York: Basic Books.

Heller, K., Monks, F., & Passow, A. H. (Eds.). (1993). *International handbook of research and development of giftedness and talent.* Oxford, UK: Pergamon Press.

Maker, C. J. (Ed.). (1993). *Critical issues in gifted education: Vol. 3. Programs for the gifted in regular classrooms.* Austin, TX: Pro-Ed.

Rogers, K. B. (2002). *Re-forming gifted education: Matching the program to the child.* Scottsdale, AZ: Great Potential Press.

Smutny, J. F., Walker, S. Y., & Meckstroth, E. A. (1997). *Teaching young gifted children in the regular classroom: Identifying, nurturing, and challenging ages 4–9.* Minneapolis: Free Spirit.

Subotnik, R. F., & Arnold, K. D. (Eds.). (1994). *Beyond Terman: Contemporary longitudinal studies of giftedness and talent.* Norwood, NJ: Ablex.

VanTassel-Baska, J. (1998). *Gifted and talented learners.* Denver: Love.

Winebrenner, S. (1992). *Teaching gifted kids in the regular classroom: Strategies and techniques every teacher can use to meet the academic needs of the gifted and talented.* Minneapolis: Free Spirit.

VideoWorkshop Extra!

If the VideoWorkshop package was included with your text-book, go to Chapter 12 of the Companion Website (www. ablongman.com/sppd4e) and click on the VideoWorkshop button. Follow the instructions for viewing video clip 8. Then consider this information along with what you've read in Chapter 12 while answering the following questions.

1. Kyle has musical and theatrical talents. How has his school accommodated both his exceptionalities? Is there more that might be done for Kyle?
2. What are the implications for classroom instruction in Kyle's case? How can classroom teachers use his special abilities to enhance his educational experience?

13 Teaching Students Who Are at Risk

After reading this chapter, you should be able to

1. define students who are considered to be at risk.
2. describe the different types of children who are considered at risk for developing learning and behavior problems.
3. discuss general considerations for teaching at risk students.
4. describe specific methods that are effective for teaching at risk students.

Lisa is a 9-year-old girl with blond hair and blue eyes. She is currently in third grade; she was kept back once in kindergarten. Mr. Sykes, her teacher, does not know how to help her. He referred Lisa for special education, but the assessment revealed that she was not eligible. Although her intelligence is in the low-average range, she does not have mental retardation or any other qualifying disability. Lisa is shy and very insecure.

Lisa has significant problems in reading and math. Although she seems sharp at times, she is achieving below even her own expected level. Her eyes fill with tears of frustration as she sits at her desk and struggles with her work.

She frequently cries if Mr. Sykes leaves the classroom; she is very dependent on her teacher. She should have a cluster of good friends, but she is a social outcast. Even though on rare occasions a few of the other girls in the classroom will include her, she is typically teased, ridiculed, and harassed by her peers. She has been unable to establish and maintain meaningful relationships with her classmates and adults. Lisa's attempts to win friends are usually couched in a variety of undesirable behaviors, yet she craves attention and friendship. She just does not demonstrate the appropriate social skills requisite of her age.

Lisa lives with her mother and one younger brother in a small apartment. Her mother has been divorced twice and works as a waitress at a local restaurant. Her mother's income barely covers rent, utilities, groceries, and other daily expenses. Occasionally, when Lisa's mother gets the chance to work extra hours at the restaurant, she will do so, leaving Lisa in charge of her brother. Although Lisa's mother appears interested in Lisa's schoolwork, she has been unable to get to a teacher's meeting with Mr. Sykes, even though several have been scheduled. Lisa's mother's interest in helping her daughter with her homework is limited by the fact that Lisa's mother did not complete school and does not have a great command of the content that Lisa is studying.

Mr. Sykes knows that Lisa is not likely to qualify for special education services under IDEA; however, he also recognizes that Lisa could benefit from some assistance, particularly in reading and in social/affective areas.

One thing that can be done for Lisa is prereferral intervention. This option is available in many schools to help general education teachers address the needs of students in their classes who are experiencing problems. These services are called prereferral because they are meant to deal with issues prior to a formal referral to special education. If prereferral interventions are successful, further consideration for special education may not be necessary.

QUESTIONS TO CONSIDER

1. What types of interventions does Lisa need? What services would you recommend?
2. Should Lisa be considered for special education?
3. What can teachers do with Lisa and students like her to help prevent failure?

Basic Concepts About Students Who Are at Risk

The movement to include students with special needs in general education has made substantial progress over the past several years. One beneficial result has been the recognition that many students who are not officially eligible for special education services may need, and can benefit from, special supports. Although certain students like Lisa do not manifest problems severe enough to result in a disability classification, these students are at risk for developing achievement and behavior problems that could limit their success in school and later as young adults.

Lisa, the student in chapter-opening vignette, is a good example of a child who is already experiencing some problems that are limiting her ability to succeed, and she is very much at risk for developing major academic and behavior problems. In the current system, children like Lisa cannot be provided with special education and related services from federal programs. The result, too often, is that Lisa and children like her find school to be frustrating and basically an undesirable place to be. Ultimately, these students are likely to drop out of school and experience major problems as adults.

"At Risk" Defined

The term *at risk* can be defined in many different ways. It is often used to describe children who have personal characteristics, or who live in families that display characteristics, that are associated with problems in school (Bowman, 1994). Using education as our frame of reference, we are defining **at risk** children and youth as those who are in situations that can lead to academic, personal, and behavioral problems that could limit their success in school and later in life.

Students identified as being at risk generally have difficulty learning basic academic skills, exhibit unacceptable social behaviors, and cannot keep up with their peers (Pierce, 1994). They represent a very heterogeneous group (Davis, 1995). Unlike students with disabilities, who have historically been segregated full-time or part-time from their age peers, students who are considered at risk are typically fully included in educational programs. Unfortunately, rather than receiving appropriate interventions, they have been neglected in the classroom and consigned to failure. Although not eligible for special education and related services, students who are at risk need special interventions. Without them, many will be retained year after year, become behavior problems, develop drug and alcohol abuse problems, drop out of school, fail as adults, and possibly even commit suicide (Huff, 1999). School personnel need to recognize students who are at risk for failure and develop appropriate programs to facilitate their success in school and in society. Not doing so will result in losing many of these children, and "to lose today's at risk students implies [that] society is more than a little out of control itself" (Greer, 1991, p. 390).

Although certain factors can increase the vulnerability of students becoming at risk as we have defined the term, it is important to recognize that this phenomenon is not only associated with students who are poor or educationally disadvantaged in some other way. Barr and Parrett (2001) underscored this point:

> . . . any young person may become at risk . . . the risks now facing our youths have become a matter of life and death. It is now clear that students who are at risk are not limited to any single group. They cut across all social classes and occur in every ethnic group. (p. 2)

Prevalence and Factors Related to Being at Risk

Many factors place students at risk for developing school problems. These include poverty, homelessness, single-parent homes, abusive situations, substance abuse, and unrec-

---

CONSIDER THIS

Should students at risk for failure be identified as disabled and served in special education programs? Why or why not?

TABLE 13.1   **Factors That Place Students at Risk**

▶ Attempted suicide during the past year	▶ Other family members used drugs during past year
▶ Used drugs or engaged in substance abuse	▶ Attended three or more schools during past five years
▶ Has been a drug "pusher" during the past year	▶ After grades were below C last school year
▶ Sense of self-esteem is negative	▶ Was arrested for driving while intoxicated
▶ Was involved in a pregnancy during the past year	▶ Has an IQ score below 90
▶ Was expelled from school during the past year	▶ Parents divorced or separated last year
▶ Consumes alcohol regularly	▶ Father is unskilled laborer who is unemployed
▶ Was arrested for illegal activity	▶ Mother is unskilled laborer who is unemployed
▶ Parents have negative attitudes toward education	▶ Father or mother died during the past year
▶ Has several brothers or sisters who dropped out	▶ Diagnosed as needing special education
▶ Was sexually or physically abused last year	▶ English is not first language
▶ Failed two courses last school year	▶ Lives in an inner city, urban area
▶ Was suspended from school twice last year	▶ The mother is only parent living in the home
▶ Student was absent more than 20 days last year	▶ Is year older than other students in same grade
▶ Parent drinks excessively and is an alcoholic	▶ Mother did not graduate from high school
▶ Was retained in grade (i.e., "held back")	▶ Father lost his job during the past year
▶ One parent attempted suicide last year	▶ Was dropped from athletic team during past year
▶ Scored below 20th percentile on standardized test	▶ Experienced a serious illness or accident

From Frymier, Barber, Denton, Johnson-Lewis, & Robertson (1992)

ognized disabilities. Frymier and Gansneder (1989) studied factors associated with at risk students and identified and ranked 45 key indicators. The results of their work are presented in Table 13.1. Although the presence of these factors often makes failure more likely for students, it is important not to label every child who is poor or who lives with a single parent as an at risk student. Many students are very resilient even when faced with some difficult life situations. Although overly simplistic conclusions should not be drawn concerning students at risk, research identifies certain factors as having a clear correlation with school problems.

According to Barr and Parrett (1995), it is possible to predict, with a high degree of accuracy, which students at the third grade are likely to drop out of school at a later point in time. For example, in a government report, McPartland and Slavin (1990) reported that third graders who read one year below grade level, have been retained in one grade, come from low socioeconomic backgrounds, and attend school with many other poor children have almost no chance of graduating from high school. Figure 13.1 on page 388 depicts the relationship between these four factors that are such strong predictors of school failure.

Even when children are strongly indicated as being at risk, school personnel must be cautious about predicting their actual abilities and potential for achievement. Such care is particularly important when considering students from ethnically and culturally different backgrounds who appear to be experiencing school-related difficulties. Some cautions to be taken when initially considering special education referral for students from such backgrounds are provided in Table 13.2 on page 388. Addressing these issues will decrease the likelihood of referring students for special education programs when in-class interventions might be effective.

Select at Risk Groups

This section explores the challenges that nine at risk groups present to school-based personnel.

FIGURE 13.1

Research on Third-Grade Students

From *Policy Perspectives Increasing Achievement of at-Risk Students at Each Grade Level,* by J. M. McPartland and R. E. Slavin, 1990, Washington, D.C.: U.S. Department of Education. Cited in *Hope at Last for at-Risk Youth* (p. 10), by R. D. Barr and W. H. Parrett, 1995, Boston: Allyn and Bacon. Used by permission.

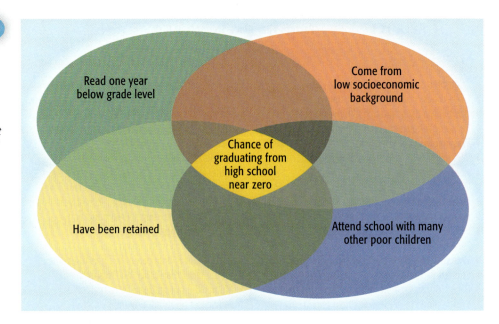

CROSS-REFERENCE

For the impact of poverty on mental retardation and learning disabilities, review Chapters 6 and 8.

Students Who Grow Up in Poverty

Poverty is a social condition associated with many different kinds of problems. Poverty has been related to crime, physical abuse, learning problems, behavior problems, and emotional problems. Professionals in the field of learning disabilities have even begun to

TABLE 13.2   **Issues to Consider Before Referring Students from Culturally Diverse Backgrounds for Special Education Programs**

Stage of language development: At what stage of language proficiency, oral and written, is the student in L1 (student's first language) and L2 (student's second language)? What impact have past educational experiences had on language development? Will the environment facilitate further development?

Language skills: What are the particular strengths and weaknesses of the student in oral and written L1 and L2 skills? What curriculum materials and instructional expertise are available to meet the student's needs? What skills are the parents able to work on at home?

Disability/at risk status: What impact does the student's specific disability or at risk circumstances have on the acquisition of language skills in L1 and L2 and on other academic skills? Does the teacher have an adequate knowledge base to provide effective services? Does the school have access to community supports?

Age: What impact does the student's age have on the ability to acquire L1 and L2 and to achieve in content areas? Is there a discrepancy between a child's age and emotional maturity? Is the curriculum developmentally appropriate?

Needs of the student: What are the short-term and long-term needs of the student in academic, vocational, and community life? What are the needs of the student in relation to other students in the environment?

Amount of integration: How much time will be spent in L1 and L2 environments? Will the student be able to interact with students who have various levels of ability?

Personal qualities: How might the student's personality, learning style, and interests influence the acquisition of L1 and L2, achievement in content areas, and social–emotional growth? How might personal qualities of the student's peers and teacher influence learning?

From *Assessment and Instruction of Culturally and Linguistically Diverse Students with or at Risk of Learning Problems* (pp. 221–222), by V. Gonzalez, R. Brusca-Vega, and T. Yawkey, 1997, Boston: Allyn and Bacon. Used by permission.

Diversity Forum

Leave No School or Teacher Behind

It is the end of the school year; results of the state-mandated achievement test have just come in for Johnston Elementary School. The number of African American and Latino students passing all subtests is about 10–15% lower than the number of white students. At a faculty meeting to review these results, some teachers voice their reactions:

"We've tried everything we can, but these kids aren't motivated—school's just not important to them!" "How can we expect school to be important when their parents have to work three jobs to pay the bills?" "That's beyond our control!"

Is the students' success really beyond their control? While traditional definitions of educational risk have emphasized student and family background, many students from diverse cultural and linguistic communities have experienced academic difficulties because of school-related factors. For these students and their teachers, *risk* can be the result of a disconnect between students' learning styles and needs, and the school and classroom environments (García, Wilkinson, and Ortiz, 1995; Wang & Gordon, 1994). In fact, many educators find themselves inadequately prepared to meet the educational needs of a growing diverse student community.

Prevention and intervention models of curriculum and instruction are more effective when

1. school-based support systems are in place for students, families, and teachers, which provide access to needed resources and foster teachers' ability to design appropriate interventions.
2. teachers have consistently high expectations, develop supportive personal relationships with students, and provide academically challenging instruction.
3. teachers know how to gather information about students' sociocultural and linguistic backgrounds and can use this information to make instruction relevant and meaningful.
4. the values, beliefs, languages, and cultures of students, families, and communities are integrated with the culture and activities of the school.
5. teachers and other school personnel use a variety of approaches to reduce student vulnerability and stress, and to build resilience and academic success.
6. there is a culture of shared responsibility for all students, regardless of the special services they may receive through bilingual education, ESL, or special education.

Companion Website

For follow-up questions about prevention and intervention models for students at risk, go to Chapter 13 of the Companion Website (ablongman.com/sppd4e) and click Diversity Forum.

realize that poverty can be a significant factor in the etiology of that particular disability (Young & Gerber, 1998). Davis (1993) notes that poverty is the number one factor that places children at risk for academic failure.

Unfortunately, poverty is a fact of life for many children. In 1997, 19.9% of children 18 years old and younger lived in poverty in the United States. While this number was down from 22% in 1992, it still represented more than 14 million children. The rate of poverty among children varies significantly from state to state and race to race. For example, while only 16.1% of white children lived in poverty in 1997, 36.8% of Hispanic children and 37.2% of African American children lived in such circumstances. And, during the same year, 59.1% of children in a household with a single female parent lived in poverty (*Poverty in the United States: 1998*). Figure 13.2 shows the greater incidence of poverty among Hispanic and African American children as compared to white children. Although the overall numbers have not gotten worse, the disheartening fact is that they have not improved significantly in recent years.

Poverty is associated with different kinds of disabilities (Smith & Luckasson, 1992), including mental retardation (Beirne-Smith, Ittenbach, & Patton, 2002), learning disabilities (Smith, Dowdy, Polloway, & Blalock, 1997; Young & Gerber, 1998), and various health problems. Poverty is also associated with poor prenatal care, poor parenting, hunger, limited health care, single-parent households, poor housing conditions, and even homelessness (Yamaguchi, Strawser, & Higgins, 1997). Elders (2002) remarked that most children who are poor will be members of only one club in their lives—the "Five-H Club." Members carry the following credentials—they are hungry, healthless, homeless, hugless, and hopeless. Using hyperbole, Elders was trying to accentuate some of the key issues confronting many children living in poverty. Most importantly, all these issues are addressable. Her reference to "hugless" was meant to stress the need to have an array of people in their lives who sincerely care and show it—it was not meant to imply that all children who live in poverty

Percentages of Children Less Than 18 Years Old Who Live in Families with Incomes Below the Poverty Level: Selected Years, 1960–1997

From *Poverty in the United States,* 1998, Washington, D.C.: U.S. Census Bureau.

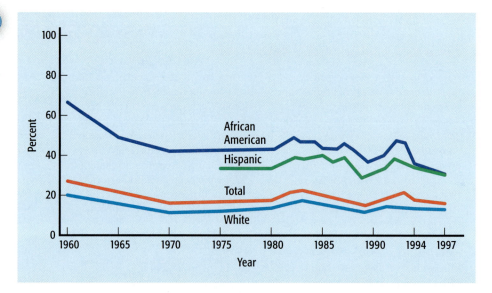

What kinds of actions can American society take that could have an impact on the level of poverty? What are some barriers to doing these things?

are devoid of love at home. Her point regarding "hope" merely points to the need to provide children and youth with promise and motivation to make changes.

Hunger   Although many people have a difficult time believing it, thousands of children go to bed hungry every night. "It is estimated that at least 5.5 million children (1 in 8 children today in the United States) are regularly hungry, while another 6 million other children younger than age 12 are in families living on the edge of poverty and face chronic food shortages" (Davis, 1993, p. 11). Hunger leads to malnutrition, which in turn can result in damage to a developing neurological system. Children who are hungry have a difficult time concentrating on schoolwork and frequently display behavior problems in the classroom. Although free school lunch and breakfast programs have been expanded over the past years, hunger among schoolchildren still remains a significant problem in the United States.

Health Care   Children who grow up in poverty are unlikely to receive adequate health care. Although significant progress with childhood diseases such as polio and whooping cough has been made over the past 40 years, the health status of many children today is below that of children in other countries. Twenty-one developed countries have a lower rate of infant mortality than that of the United States (Davis, 1993). In 1993, 20.1% of poor children had no health insurance (U.S. Department of Commerce, 1995). Poverty appears to be directly associated with many of the health problems experienced by children today (*Healthy People 2000,* 1992). Just as children who are hungry have difficulties concentrating, children who are unhealthy may miss school and fall behind academically.

Implications for School Personnel   Unfortunately, teachers and other school personnel cannot do much to alleviate directly the base cause of poverty experienced by students. However, teachers can reduce the impact of poverty on achievement and behavior by:

▶ Recognizing the impact that poverty can have on students.
▶ Making all students in the classroom feel important.
▶ Avoiding placing students in situations in which limited family finances become obvious to other students.
▶ Initiating and coordinate with school social workers or other school personnel who can work with family members to secure social services.
▶ Realizing and preparing for the reality that students may not have supplies and other equipment required for certain class activities. Seeking contingency funds or other means that could be used to help pay for these items.

A teacher should have a pool of supplies that all students can use when they do not have the necessary materials.

See the nearby Personal Spotlight feature, which further highlights this issue.

Personal Spotlight

School Counselor

Sara Gillison has been a school counselor for seven years. During that time, she has generally worked in inner-city schools where poverty is a fact of life for many children. In the two schools where she serves as the elementary counselor, approximately 35% of students qualify for a free or reduced-price lunch. Many of the problems that she deals with as the school counselor are related to poverty.

"One of the most difficult things for me to do is identify with these families. Unlike most of my friends growing up, many of the students I see on a daily basis do not have many of the basic things they need. They may not have decent clothes, or even enough to eat at night. I have to try to remember every day that my life experiences are just different and try not to project onto my students and their families the same experiences I have had."

Sara notes that the poverty many of her students experience has a wide-ranging impact on their performances in school. She stated, "Many of the children who come from obvious poverty are less likely to be prepared for school every day. They often appear to be tired and uninterested. I wonder, sometimes, how much rest they get at home." She notes that while some poor children do well in school, for most it seems to be a struggle that closely relates to their struggle with everyday life.

Sara has had to attempt to understand the impact of poverty on the families she counsels. She notes, "The first time I tried to

Sara Gillison

Lakewood Elementary School, North Little Rock, AR

have a parent conference with a student who was not doing well, I could not understand why the mother or father would not come to a meeting. Finally I realized that not only did they feel uncomfortable because of their personal history of school problems, but also that they did not have transportation. Not having access to personal transportation is not something I used to think of. However, after working with students who come from impoverished backgrounds, one of the first things I try to find out is whether or not the family has a car or access to transportation, and whether or not they have a telephone."

Sara does believe school personnel can deal effectively with children who come from poverty, although it is very difficult. The best advice she can give to teachers and other school people is to try to make these students feel good about themselves and experience success. "Success goes so far with all students," notes Sara, "but for students who are poor, school success can mean the difference between being a failure in life or making it."

For follow-up questions about this Personal Spotlight, go to Chapter 13 of the Companion Website (ablongman.com/sppd4e) and click Personal Spotlight.

Students Who Are Homeless

A tragedy of the new century is the growing number of homeless people in the United States. The number of individuals who do not have homes has risen to epidemic proportions. While historically the homeless population has been thought to be made up of aging adults, often with mental illness or alcohol problems, today as many as 25% of all homeless persons are children (U.S. Conference of Mayors, 1998). "On any given night, it is estimated that between 50,000 and 200,000 children are homeless in the United States" (Davis, 1993, p. 16). The National Coalition for the Homeless (1999) underscored the impact that homelessness has on families:

> Homelessness is a devastating experience for families. It disrupts virtually every aspect of family life, damaging the physical and emotional health of family members, interfering with children's education and development, and frequently resulting in the separation of family members. (p. 1)

Federal Backdrop   Federal legislation now exists to guide policy and practice throughout the United States. The McKinney-Vento Act (2001), which was part of the No Child Left Behind Act of 2001, is a reauthorization of previously enacted legislation (McKinney Homeless Assistance Act of 1987) regarding this population. Following is the definition of "homeless children and youth" under the current law.

(A) individuals who lack a fixed, regular, and adequate nighttime residence . . . , and
(B) includes—
  (i) children and youths who are sharing the housing of other persons due to loss of housing, economic hardship, or a similar reason; are living in motels, hotels, trailer parks, or camping grounds due to the lack of alternative accommodations; are living in emergency or transitional shelters; are abandoned in hospitals; or are awaiting foster care placement;
  (ii) children and youths who have a primary nighttime residence that is a public or private place not designed for or ordinarily used as a regular sleeping accommodation for human beings . . .
  (iii) children and youths who are living in cars, parks, public spaces, abandoned buildings, substandard housing, bus or train stations, or similar settings; and
  (iv) migratory children who qualify as homeless for the purposes of this subtitle because the children are living in circumstances described in clauses (i) and (iii). (Sec. 725)

This act requires that each state have on record a plan for the education of homeless students. Every local school system must designate someone as liaison for homeless students and must provide access to appropriate education for these students.

Presenting Issues   Poverty and the lack of affordable housing are directly associated with homelessness. As Elders (2002) noted, the key issues and problems of poverty also affect this group of children. The added impact of not having a home greatly compounds problems of poverty. Children and youth who are homeless experience health problems, hunger, poor nutrition, academic achievement deficits, depression, and behavioral problems (Yamaguchi et al., 1997). In addition, children who are homeless are usually very embarrassed by the fact that they do not have a place to live. The dissolution of families is great as well.

Implications for School Personnel   Although some homeless students are lucky enough to stay in a shelter, many live on the streets, in cars, or in other public settings with their parents. Of course, school personnel can do little to find homes for these children. Probably the best advice is to avoid putting students in situations in which their homelessness will result in embarrassment. For example, going around the room after the students' birthday and having everyone tell, in graphic detail, about every gift they received may be very uncomfortable for students who do not even have a home to go to after school.

It is also important to realize that parents of homeless children are very likely to do everything they can to hide the fact that their family is homeless. As a result, they are very unlikely to inform school personnel of significant situations related to a student's life that would be beneficial to know. They are fearful of having their children taken away from them if they are discovered.

A few other recommendations are the following:

▶ Realize that a large percentage of homeless students will not attend school on a regular basis.
▶ Be vigilant and sensitive to students who may be homeless—the students may need services, but their families may fear that to get needed services discovery is required and forced breakup of the family may follow.
▶ Monitor behavior and progress in the classroom—paying particular attention to physical, health, emotional, and social manifestations.
▶ Do not expect homework of the same quality as that of children who have homes.
▶ Become a safe resource for students and their parents.

In order to work with parents who are homeless, teachers and other school personnel should consider the following:

1. Arrange to meet parents at their place of work or at school.
2. Offer to assist family members in securing services from available social service agencies.

TEACHING TIP

For students who are homeless, reduce the amount of homework and do not lower the student's grade because the work may be less neat than that of other students.

3. Do not require excessive school supplies that many families cannot afford.

Schools can use any of several program models when working with students who are homeless. A description of some of these programs can be found in Table 13.3.

TABLE 13.3   **Program Models for the Education of Students Who Are Homeless**

Outreach Programs

District-based programs that employ a coordinator whose duties may include

▶ maintaining communication among schools, shelters, and social service agencies;
▶ visiting shelters on a daily basis to identify children who may need assistance with school enrollment;
▶ assisting families with referrals to appropriate agencies for accessing necessary services;
▶ providing students with clothing and school supplies;
▶ assisting with school transportation arrangements; and
▶ conducting in-service training programs at school sites or to parent groups.

District Schools

Schools located in the area of homeless shelters that provide special programs for students who are homeless. Programs include

▶ assisting with the school registration process;
▶ assisting with applications for appropriate services, such as free school breakfast and lunch and before/after school programs;
▶ providing a free clothing and school supplies closet located at the school;
▶ assessing the student's present academic levels for appropriate classroom placement; and
▶ tutoring and social skills programs for the student.

Transition Room in Neighborhood Schools

A classroom located in the student's school that provides a temporary setting for children. Characteristics of the transition room include

▶ providing a safe environment where children become acquainted with the school and teachers before moving into their permanent classrooms;
▶ emphasizing the emotional needs of the child;
▶ emphasizing the assessment of academic skills;
▶ establishing good rapport with the family of the child;
▶ providing assistance for the family as necessary; and
▶ providing clothing and school supplies as needed.

Transition and Shelter Schools

Schools whose specific purpose is to serve students who are homeless. These may be located within a shelter or close to a shelter. When students are functioning well in this setting, they are moved into larger schools in the district. In this setting the goals include

▶ providing intense and temporary assistance;
▶ working on basic skills;
▶ providing emotional support to help the children cope with the various levels of stress in their lives; and
▶ assisting with the basic needs of clothing, school supplies, food, and health services.

After-School Programs

Programs that include all or some of the following:

▶ one-on-one tutoring;
▶ help with homework;
▶ opportunities to build friendships;
▶ counseling and emotional support; and
▶ recreation, field trips, and other leisure activities.

From "Children Who Are Homeless: Implications for Educators" (p. 94) by B. J. Yamaguchi, S. Strawser, and K. Higgins, 1997, *Intervention in School and Clinic, 33.* Used by permission.

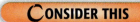

What factors found in single-parent homes have an impact on the level of parent involvement with schools?

Students in Single-Parent Homes

The nature of the American family has changed dramatically over the past 25 years. "During the 1980s, only 6% of all U.S. families fit the mold of the 1950s 'Ozzie and Harriet family': a working father, a housewife mother, and two children of public school age" (Davis, 1993, p. 14). The following facts describe the families of the late 1990s:

▶ The percentage of children living in a home with only one parent went from 12.8% in 1970 to 27% in 1998.

▶ About 55% of African American children live in a home with only one parent.

▶ Approximately 31% of Hispanic children live in a home with only one parent.

▶ Nearly 70% of all children have working mothers (U.S. Census Bureau, 1999).

Figure 13.3 shows the composition of family groups with children, by race, from 1970 to 1998.

Many factors result in children being reared in single-parent homes, including divorce, death of a parent, significant illness of a parent, or a parent being incarcerated.

FIGURE 13.3

Composition of Family Groups with Children, by Race: 1970 to 1998

From *Population Profile of the United States, 1999* (p. ix), by U.S. Department of Commerce, Washington, DC: Bureau of the Census

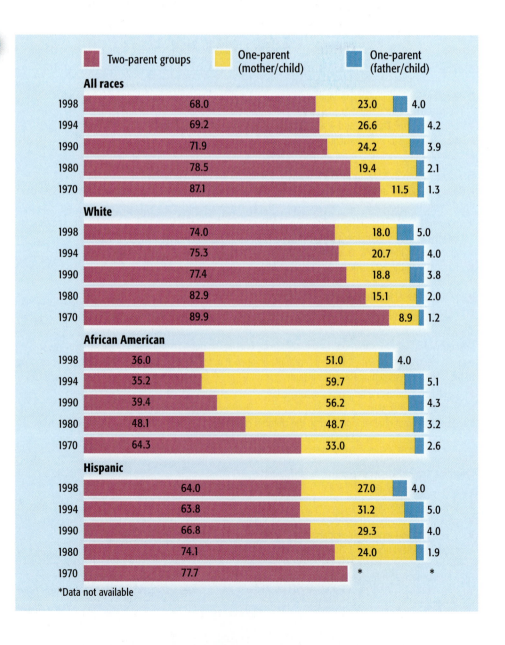

Children of Divorced Parents   Divorce in the United States is on an upward trend that shows no signs of decreasing. It is estimated that half of all new marriages will end in divorce. Although the birth rate is declining, the number of divorces in which children are involved is increasing (Chiriboga & Catron, 1991). Forty-four percent of all children live in a nontraditional family unit, most often headed by a single, working mother (Austin, 1992). Divorce is a disorganizing and reorganizing process, particularly when children are involved, and the process often extends over several years (Morgan, 1985). Divorce offers the potential for growth and new relationships, but too often it creates only problems for children and youth, and although some children cope very well with the trauma surrounding divorce, many react with major problems (Munger & Morse, 1992). The central dilemma in many divorces is the conflict of interest between the child's need for continuity of the family unit and the parents' decision to break up the family that has provided the child's main supports. Children react in many different ways to divorce, including the following: feeling guilt, developing anxiety, exhibiting social problems, experiencing grief, being angry, and displaying hostility.

Children in Homes Headed by Single Mothers   Most single-parent homes are headed by mothers (see Figure 13.3). The absence of a father figure may have a significant impact on the psychological development of children (Saintonge, Achille, & Lachance, 1993). The academic achievement of both boys and girls has been shown to be affected by the absence of the father, with lower achievement correlating with limited presence of the father.

Children in Homes Headed by Single Fathers   Although not nearly as prevalent as single-parent homes headed by mothers, the number of single-parent homes headed by fathers has increased significantly over the past decade. The effects of growing up in a single-parent home headed by a father vary a great deal from child to child. Some of the findings of studies indicate that fathers are more likely to use other adults in their support networks than are single-parent mothers, and children seem to fare better with a large adult support network than a limited one (Santrock & Warshak, 1979).

Implications for School Personnel   Children who find themselves in single-parent families as a result of divorce, death, illness, or incarceration require a great deal of support. For many of these children, the school may be their most stable environment. School

> **TEACHING TIP**
>
> Involve school counselors and other support personnel when dealing with the emotional impact of divorce on children.

> **TEACHING TIP**
>
> Have male staff in the school take the lead in working with single fathers.

More than one-quarter of all children live with a single parent, usually a mother.

CONSIDER THIS

What things could school personnel do to make children from single-parent homes feel more secure?

personnel must develop supports to prevent negative outcomes, such as school failure, manifestation of emotional problems, or the development of behavior problems. An interview conducted with children residing in single-parent homes resulted in the following conclusions concerning the positive role schools can play:

1. Schools are a place of security and safety for students from single-parent homes.
2. Students who lose parents due to death are often treated differently by school personnel than when the loss is from divorce. Unfortunately, the child's needs are similar in both situations.
3. Teachers are the most important people in the school for children who are in single-parent homes because of their tremendous influence on self-esteem.
4. Students want to be treated just as they were before they became part of a single-parent home.
5. Trust with peers and teachers is the most important factor for students from single-parent homes.
6. School personnel need to be more sensitive to the new financial situation of families with only one parent.
7. Keeping a log or diary is considered an excellent method for children to explore feelings and create opportunities for meaningful discussions. (Lewis, 1992)

CROSS-REFERENCE

Review Chapter 4 for due-process requirements of schools, and consider the impact single-parent homes have on these requirements.

There are many things schools should and should not do when dealing with students who are from single-parent homes (Wanat, 1992; Figure 13.4). For children whose parents are divorced, schools must consider the involvement of the noncustodial parent. Unfortunately, many schools do not even include spaces for information on forms for students' noncustodial parents (Austin, 1992). In order to ensure that noncustodial parents are afforded their rights regarding their children, and to actively solicit the involvement of the noncustodial parent, school personnel should

1. establish policies that encourage the involvement of noncustodial parents.
2. maintain records of information about the noncustodial parent.
3. distribute information about school activities to noncustodial parents.
4. insist that noncustodial parents be involved in teacher conferences.

FIGURE 13.4

Some DOs and DON'Ts When Working with Children with Single Parents

From "Meeting the Needs of Single-Parent Children: School and Parent Views Differ" (p. 47) by C. L. Wanat, 1992, NAASP Bulletin, 76, pp. 43–48. Used by permission.

Some DOs
- Collect information about students' families.
- Analyze information about students' families to determine specific needs.
- Create programs and practices that address areas of need unique to particular schools.
- Include curricular areas that help students achieve success, such as study skills.
- Provide nonacademic programs such as child care and family counseling.
- Involve parents in determining appropriate roles for school and family.
- Take the initiative early in the year to establish a communication link with parents.
- Enlist the support of both parents, when possible.
- Provide a stable, consistent environment for children during the school day.

Some DON'Ts
- Don't treat single parents differently than other parents.
- Don't call attention to the fact that a child lives with only one parent.
- Limit activities such as "father/son" night or other events that highlight the differences in a single-parent home.
- Don't have "room mothers," have "room parents."
- Don't overlook the limitations of single-parent homes in areas such as helping with projects, helping with homework, and so forth.

5. structure parent conferences to facilitate the development of a shared relationship between the custodial and noncustodial parent.
6. conduct surveys to determine the level of involvement desired by noncustodial parents. (Austin, 1992)

Students Who Experience Significant Losses

Although the continued absence of one or both parents through separation or divorce is considered a loss, the loss created by the death of a parent can result in significantly more problems for children. Unlike children living in earlier centuries, when extended families often lived together and children actually observed death close at hand, often in the home environment with grandparents, children of today are generally insulated from death. Therefore, when death does occur, especially that of a significant person in a child's life, the result can be devastating, often resulting in major problems in school.

Death of a Parent   When a child's parent dies, external events impinge on the child's personality in three main ways (Felner, Ginter, Boike, & Cowan, 1981; Moriarty, 1967; Tennant, Bebbington, & Hurry, 1980):

1. The child must deal with the reality of the death itself.
2. The child must adapt to the resulting changes in the family.
3. The child must contend with the perpetual absence of the lost parent.

Children respond in many different ways to a parent's death. Some responses are guilt, regression, denial, bodily distress, hostile reactions to the deceased, eating disorders, enuresis (incontinence), sleep disturbances, withdrawal, anxiety, panic, learning difficulties, and aggression (Anthony, 1972; Elizer & Kauffman, 1983; Van Eerdewegh, Bieri, Parrilla, & Clayton, 1982). It is also not unusual for sibling rivalry to become very intense and disruptive. Often, extreme family turmoil results from the death of a parent, especially when the parent who dies was the controlling person in the family (Van Eerdewegh et al., 1982).

Death of a Sibling   A sibling plays an important and significant part in family dynamics, so the death of a sibling can initiate a psychological crisis for a child. Sometimes the grief of the parents renders them unable to maintain a healthy parental relationship with the remaining child or children, significantly changing a child's life situation.

When experiencing the death of a sibling, children frequently fear that they will die. When an older sibling dies, the younger child may revert to childish behaviors in hopes of not getting older, thereby averting dying. Older children often react with extreme fear and anxiety if they are ignored by parents during the grieving period. Often these children become preoccupied with the horrifying question about their own future "Will it happen to me tomorrow, or next week, or next year?" (McKeever, 1983). Children can also develop severe depression when a sibling dies (McKeever, 1983).

Implications for School Personnel   For the most part, the best advice for teachers is to be aware of how the student who experiences loss is doing when in school. Equally important is knowing when to contact the school counselor, if he or she is not already involved in some ongoing work with the student. Some of the issues that may arise require intervention that is outside the training and expertise of most teachers. So, knowing about other school-based and outside school resources is valuable.

Students Who Are Abused and Neglected

Growing up in an abusive or neglectful family places children at significant risk. Child abuse and neglect occur in families from every socioeconomic level, race, religion, and ethnic background. Family members, acquaintances, or strangers may be the source of

> **TEACHING TIP**
>
> Involve the school counselor, mental health professionals, and other support personnel when providing information on death and dying; invite these persons into the class when a student is confronted with this issue.

the abuse. Although there is no single cause, there are many factors that add to the likelihood of abuse and neglect. These include poverty, large family size, low maternal involvement with children, low maternal self-esteem, low father involvement, and a stepfather in the household (Brown, Cohen, Johnson, & Salzinger, 1998).

There are two major types of abuse (1) emotional abuse and (2) physical abuse, which includes sexual abuse. **Emotional abuse,** which accompanies all other forms of child abuse, involves unreasonable demands placed on children by parents, siblings, peers, or teachers, and the failure of parents to provide the emotional support necessary for children to grow and develop (Thompson & Kaplan, 1999). Research has revealed that verbal abuse, by itself, can result in lowered self-esteem and school achievement (Solomon & Serres, 1999). Although difficult to identify, several characteristics may be exhibited by children who are being emotionally abused. These include the following:

CONSIDER THIS

Think how being abused would affect you at this point in your life; then transfer those feelings into a young child's perspective. How would they affect the child's school activities?

- Absence of a positive self-image
- Behavioral extremes
- Depression
- Psychosomatic complaints
- Attempted suicide
- Impulsive, defiant, and antisocial behavior
- Age-inappropriate behaviors
- Inappropriate habits and tics
- Enuresis
- Inhibited intellectual or emotional development
- Difficulty in establishing and maintaining peer relationships
- Extreme fear, vigilance
- Sleep and eating disorders
- Self-destructive tendencies
- Rigidly compulsive behaviors (Gargiulo, 1990, p. 22)

Physical abuse is more easily identified than emotional abuse and includes beating, strangulation, burns to the body, and other forms of physical brutalization. It is defined as "any physical injury that has been caused by other than accidental means, including any injury which appears to be at variance with the explanation of the injury" (*At Risk Youth in Crisis,* 1991, p. 9). The rate of child abuse in the United States is staggering. Prevent Child Abuse America (1998) reported that over 3 million children were referred for child protective service agencies in the United States in 1997. More than one million children were confirmed as victims of abuse. The number of child abuse cases increased 41% between 1988 and 1997. Statistics indicate that the prevalence of child abuse is 1 out of every 1,000 U.S. children (Prevent Child Abuse America, 1998).

Children who are physically abused are two to three times more likely than nonabused children to experience failing grades and to become discipline problems. They have difficulty with peer relationships, show physically aggressive behaviors, and frequently are substance abusers (Emery, 1989). Studies also show that children who suffer from physical abuse are likely to exhibit social skill deficits, including shyness, inhibited social interactions, and limited problem-solving skills. Deficits in cognitive functioning are also found in greater numbers in students who are abused than in their nonabused peers (Weston, Ludolph, Misle, Ruffins, & Block, 1990).

CROSS-REFERENCE

Review Chapter 7 on emotional and behavioral disorders and consider the impact of child abuse on emotional and behavioral functioning.

Sexual abuse is another form of physical abuse that puts children at risk for school failure. The rate for sexual abuse of female children in the United States ranges from 15% to 32%, depending on the method of calculation used. Sexual abuse is more likely to occur in girls younger than the age of 15 (Vogeltanz et al., 1999). Children may be sexually abused by their own families as well as by strangers. Sexual abuse can include actual physical activities, such as touching a child's genital areas, attempted and completed sexual intercourse, and the use of children in pornography. Exposing children to sexual acts by adults with the intention of shocking or arousing them is another form of sexual abuse (Jones, 1982; Williamson, Borduin, & Howe, 1991). Children who are sexually abused not only are at risk for developing problems during their school years, but also will typically manifest problems throughout their adulthood (Silverman, Reinherz, & Giaconia, 1996).

School personnel should be aware of typical physical and behavioral symptoms of sexual abuse:

▶ Physical injuries to the genital area
▶ Sexually transmitted diseases
▶ Difficulty in urinating
▶ Discharges from the penis or vagina
▶ Pregnancy
▶ Aggressive behavior toward adults, especially a child's own parents
▶ Sexual self-consciousness
▶ Sexual promiscuity and acting out
▶ Inability to establish appropriate relationships with peers
▶ Running away, stealing, and abusing substances
▶ Using the school as a sanctuary, coming early, and not wanting to go home

Neglect refers to situations where a child is exposed to a substantial risk of harm. Neglect is much more difficult to recognize, as no visible physical signs of neglect are evident—unless, of course, physical harm does occur. Signs of neglect are reflected through behaviors. Examples of neglect could include placing a child in an unsupervised situation that could result in bodily injury, failing to seek and obtain proper medical care for a child, or failing to provide adequate food, clothing, or shelter. As mentioned earlier, it is this last element that casts fear into the minds of parents who are homeless.

Implications for School Personnel   The first thing that school personnel should be prepared to do when dealing with children who might be abused or neglected is to report any incident to the appropriate agencies. School personnel have a moral and legal obligation to report suspected child abuse. For instance, Texas statutes (Texas Family Code) include the following mandate:

> Any person having cause to believe that a child's physical or mental health or welfare has been or may be adversely affected by abuse or neglect must report the case to any local or state law enforcement agency and to the Texas Department of Protective and Regulatory Services. (Chapter 34)

Failure to report a case is a punishable offense. The Suspected Child Abuse Network (**SCAN**) provides a reporting network for referral purposes. School personnel need to understand their responsibility in reporting suspected abuse and know the specific procedures to follow when making such a report. In addition to reporting suspected cases of abuse, schools in general can do the following:

▶ Work with local government officials to establish awareness of child abuse and neglect as a priority in the community.
▶ Organize a telephone "hotline" service where parents or other caregivers can call for support when they believe a crisis is impending in their families.
▶ Offer parent education programs that focus on parenting skills, behavior management techniques, child care suggestions, and communication strategies.
▶ Establish a local chapter of **Parents Anonymous,** a volunteer group for individuals who have a history of abusing their children.
▶ Develop workshops on child abuse for concerned individuals and disseminate literature on the topic.
▶ Arrange visits by public health nurses to help families at risk for abuse after the birth of their first child.
▶ Provide short-term respite day care through a Mother's Day Out program.
▶ Encourage individuals to serve as foster parents in the community.

▶ Institute a parent aide program in which parent volunteers assist single-parent homes by providing support.

▶ Make structured group therapy available to abuse victims (Kruczek & Vitanza, 1999).

School-based personnel should consider the following suggestions:

▶ Provide a safe classroom where students can flourish.

▶ Be vigilant for the signs of abuse and neglect in students.

▶ Make yourself recognizable as a person in whom a student can confide very personal information—every student needs someone like this.

▶ Try not to show any extreme emotion when a student discloses information to you. Remain calm, interested, and reassuring.

▶ Report any suspected situations knowing that you are immune from civil or criminal liability as long as the report was made in good faith and without malice.

▶ Understand that a student who confides in you (i.e., shares very personal information about being abused) in all likelihood will ask you not to tell anyone—and yet you will have to do so. As a result, avoid promising to abide by any preconditions a student may ask of you.

▶ Understand that initially a student who confided information to you on which you had to take action will feel that you betrayed him or her. For a period of time your relationship with this person will be rough. Ultimately, the student is likely to come around and appreciate what you did.

Students Who Abuse Substances

Substance abuse among children and adolescents results in major problems and places students significantly at risk for school failure (Vaughn & Long, 1999). Students who are abusing substances have a much more difficult time succeeding in school than their peers. While most people consider substance abuse to relate to the improper use of alcohol and drugs, it can also refer to the use of tobacco, as many health issues are related to tobacco.

Although there were indicators that substance abuse among children declined during the late 1980s and early 1990s, data indicate that substance abuse is on the rise again (*Teen drug use is on the rise again,* 1996; *The condition of education,* 1998). In 1997, according to the National Center for Education Statistics, 74.8% of high school seniors reported using alcohol during the previous school year. Elders (2002) reported that a third of high school students said that they engaged in binge drinking. Table 13.4 shows the percentage of seniors using drugs, by type of drug, between 1975 and 1997. While there was a definite decline in the use of some substances during this period, there appears to be an increase in other areas. The disturbing fact is that after years of drug abuse education, the use of alcohol and drugs has not been significantly influenced (*The condition of education,* 1998).

A disturbing fact about substance abuse is that while the level of use by high school seniors has remained virtually constant, the level of use by younger students has increased significantly. For example, in 1991 only 3.2% of eighth graders indicated that they had used marijuana or hashish during the previous 30 days. This number had increased to 10.2% in 1997 (*The condition of education,* 1998). Nagel et al. (1996) report that boys have a tendency to use illegal drugs slightly more than girls, but that girls actually use more over-the-counter drugs inappropriately than boys do.

While no factors are always associated with drug use in children, some appear to increase the likelihood of such use. Parental factors, such as (1) drug use by parents, (2) parents' attitudes about drug use, (3) family management styles, and (4) parent-child communication patterns, have an impact on children's drug use (Young, Kersten, & Werch, 1996). Additional cross-pressures such as the perception of friends' approval or disapproval of drug use, peer pressure to use drugs, and the assessment of individual risk also play a role (Robin & Johnson, 1996).

Although a great deal of attention has been paid to the impact of marijuana, cocaine, and alcohol abuse on children and youth, only recently has attention been focused on

CONSIDER THIS

Why do violence, drug abuse, and other problems seem to be affecting younger children than they did ten years ago?

TABLE 13.4   Percentage of High School Seniors Who Reported Using Alcohol or Drugs Any Time During the Previous Year, by Type of Drug

Type of Drug	1975	1976	1977	1978	1979	1980	1981	1982	1983	1984	1985	1986
Alcohol	84.8	85.7	87.0	87.7	88.1	87.9	87.0	86.8	87.3	86.0	85.6	84.5
Marijuana	40.0	44.5	47.6	50.2	50.8	48.8	46.1	44.3	42.3	40.0	40.6	38.8
Any illicit drug other than marijuana	26.2	25.4	26.0	27.1	28.2	30.4	34.0	30.1	28.4	28.0	27.4	25.9
Stimulants	16.2	15.8	16.3	17.1	18.3	20.8	26.0	20.3	17.9	17.7	15.8	13.4
LSD	7.2	6.4	5.5	6.3	6.6	6.5	6.5	6.1	5.4	4.7	4.4	4.5
Cocaine	5.6	6.0	7.2	9.0	12.0	12.3	12.4	11.5	11.4	11.6	13.1	12.7
Sedatives	11.7	10.7	10.8	9.9	9.9	10.3	10.5	9.1	7.9	6.6	5.8	5.2
Tranquilizers	10.6	10.3	10.8	9.9	9.6	8.7	8.0	7.0	6.9	6.1	6.1	5.8
Inhalants	–	3.0	3.7	4.1	5.4	4.6	4.1	4.5	4.3	5.1	5.7	6.1

Type of Drug	1987	1988	1989	1990	1991	1992	1993	1994	1995	1996	1997
Alcohol	85.7	85.3	82.7	80.6	77.7	76.8	*72.7	*73.0	*73.7	*72.5	*74.8
Marijuana	36.3	33.1	29.6	27.0	23.9	21.9	26.0	30.7	34.7	35.8	38.5
Any illicit drug other than marijuana	24.1	21.1	20.0	17.9	16.2	14.9	17.1	18.0	19.4	19.8	20.7
Stimulants	12.2	10.9	10.8	9.1	8.2	7.1	8.4	9.4	9.3	9.5	10.2
LSD	5.2	4.8	4.9	5.4	5.2	5.6	6.8	6.9	8.4	8.8	8.4
Cocaine	10.3	7.9	6.5	5.3	3.5	3.1	3.3	3.6	4.0	4.9	5.5
Sedatives	4.1	3.7	3.7	3.6	3.6	2.9	3.4	4.2	4.9	5.3	5.4
Tranquilizers	5.5	4.8	3.8	3.5	3.6	2.8	3.5	3.7	4.4	4.6	4.7
Inhalants	6.9	6.5	5.9	6.9	6.6	6.2	7.0	7.7	8.0	7.6	6.7

—Not available

*In 1993, the questions regarding alcohol consumption changed; therefore, data for alcohol use from 1993 through 1997 may not be comparable to earlier years. For example, in 1993, the original wording produced an estimate of 76 percent for alcohol use. The new wording produced an estimate of 73 percent.

Note: Only drug use not under a doctor's orders is included.

From *The Condition of Education* (p. 277) by Office of Educational Research and Improvement, 1998, Washington, DC: U.S. Department of Education.

inhalants. Inhalant use increased for every grade level from 1991 to 1995 (*The condition of education*, 1998). One of the problems with inhalants is the wide number that can be used by students, many of which are readily available. Examples include cleaning solvents, gasoline, room deodorizers, glue, perfume, wax, and spray paint.

Implications for School Personnel   School personnel must be alert to the signs of substance abuse, whether the substance is alcohol, marijuana, inhalants, or something else. The following characteristics, though they may not imply abuse in and of themselves, can be associated with substance abuse:

- Inability to concentrate
- Chronic absenteeism
- Poor grades or neglect of homework
- Poor scores on standardized tests not related to IQ or learning disabilities
- Uncooperative and quarrelsome behavior
- Sudden behavior changes
- Shy and withdrawn behavior
- Compulsive behaviors
- Chronic health problems
- Low self-esteem
- Anger, anxiety, and depression
- Poor coping skills

▶ Unreasonable fears
▶ Difficulty adjusting to changes

Once a student is identified as having a substance abuse problem, a supportive classroom environment must be provided (Lisnov, Harding, Safer, & Kavenagh, 1998). This includes a structured program to build self-esteem and create opportunities for students to be successful. Research has shown that substance-abusing adolescents do not respond positively to lecturing. Rather, successes appear to be related to the development of self-esteem and interventions that are supportive. School personnel involved with students who are substance abusers should consider establishing connections with Alcoholics Anonymous and Narcotics Anonymous to help provide support (Vaughn & Long, 1999).

Students Who Become Pregnant

Teenage pregnancy in the United States continues at an extremely high rate, even though it has decreased in recent years (Elders, 2002). In fact, teenage pregnancy rates in the United States are the highest of any Western nation. While there are many unfortunate outcomes from teenage pregnancy, including an increased risk that the resulting child will have problems, one of the most prevalent is that the teenage mother will drop out of school (Trad, 1999). In an era of extensive sex education and fear of HIV/AIDS, the continued high levels of teenage pregnancy are surprising. Despite all the information available for adolescents about sex and sexually transmitted diseases (STDs), it appears that many adolescents continue to engage in unprotected sexual activity (Weinbender & Rossignol, 1996).

School personnel should get involved in teenage pregnancy issues before pregnancy occurs. Sex education, information about HIV, and the consequences of unprotected sex should be a curricular focus. Unfortunately, sex education and practices such as distributing free condoms are very controversial, and many schools refuse to get involved in such emotion-laden issues.

Implications for School Personnel   In addition to having a pregnancy prevention program, school personnel can do the following to intervene in teenage pregnancy situations:

▶ Provide counseling and parent skills training for girls who become pregnant.
▶ Develop programs that encourage girls who are pregnant to remain in school—these programs need to include the availability of a school-based child care program.
▶ Do not discriminate against students who become pregnant, have children, or are married.
▶ Work with families of girls who are pregnant to ensure that family support is present.
▶ Provide counseling support and parent skills training for boys who are fathers.

Students Who Are Gay, Lesbian, Bisexual, or Transgendered

One of the most vulnerable and overlooked groups who might be at risk comprises those students whose sexually identity differs from those around them. Currently referred to in general as GLBT youth, this group includes students who are gay, lesbian, bisexual, or transgendered. Statistics point to the fact that theses students have experienced some uncomfortable situations when at school. A study conducted by the Gay, Lesbian, and Straight Education Network (GLSEN) (1999) found that GLBT youth had experienced the following:

▶ 61% were verbally harassed.
▶ 47% were sexually harassed.
▶ 28% were physically harassed (shoved, hit).
▶ 18% were physically assaulted (beaten, punched, kicked).

The home environment for this population may also be an unsafe environment. This is especially true in cases where parents have a difficult time accepting a child who "comes

TEACHING TIP

Work with school health personnel or state department of education personnel to obtain useful and appropriate teaching materials and suggestions for HIV/AIDS education.

out" or tells family members about this difference. Many GLBT youth experience physical violence at home.

Presenting Issues Youth who are GLBT come to school feeling that very few, if any, school-based staff understand their situation. To a great extent, they are correct. Most school personnel do lack understanding of their needs and the daily dynamics of their lives at school. Most of the time, this lack of understanding is unintentional; sometimes it is not. This group of students in general is prone to being absent more frequently than their classmates and to dropping out of school more often as a result of their discomfort and lack of safety at school.

On a personal level, GLBT youth are at greater risk for depression and attempting suicide. They often feel alienated and isolated. Substance abuse is greater with this group. Furthermore, these students find themselves homeless more often than their straight peers, as they are sometimes thrown out of their homes by parents. It should be noted that some GLBT students report very positive and productive school experiences.

Implications for School Personnel A number of actions can be taken to improve the climate of acceptance for GLBT youth. Some district and school level suggestions include the following:

▶ Include sexual orientation in all anti-harassment and anti-discrimination policies.
▶ Educate all school-based personnel regarding GLBT issues.
▶ Commit resources to this issue.
▶ Have diversity days that include GLBT youth.
▶ Establish a clear anti-slur policy.
▶ Develop and disseminate positive images and resources. (American Civil Liberties Union Freedom Network, n.d.)

Teachers, as mentioned earlier, play a key role. The following suggestions can be helpful to teachers and students who are GLBT:

▶ Recognize your own attitudes about this topic.
▶ Refer GLBT youth who are experiencing personal problems to personnel who are more comfortable with this issue, if you are not.
▶ Recognize your obligations to act on the behalf of GLBT youth when their rights are violated or policies are disregarded (e.g., harassment).
▶ Create and maintain a safe classroom environment.
▶ Let students know if you are a "safe" person with whom they can consult if they need to do so.
▶ Create and maintain a classroom environment where diversity is respected and different points of view are welcomed.
▶ Use language in the classroom that is sexual orientation neutral.
▶ Include GLBT topics in the curriculum if at all possible.

Students Who Are Delinquents

Students who get into trouble with legal authorities are frequently labeled as *socially maladjusted* or *juvenile delinquents*. Morrison (1997) defines delinquency as "behavior that violates the rules and regulations of the society" (p. 189). *Juvenile delinquency* often results in school failure; students who are involved in illegal activities often do not focus on school activities. Juvenile delinquency must be considered in conjunction with other factors related to at risk students, although the relationship of these factors may be difficult to discern. Juvenile delinquency is highly correlated with substance abuse and may be found in higher rates among poor children than among children who are raised in adequate income environments. It is also more prevalent in single-parent homes (Morgan, 1994).

Juvenile delinquency is frequently related to gang activity. Gangs currently represent a major problem for adolescents, especially in large urban areas. In 1997, there were approximately 30,500 gangs in the United States with 816,000 gang members (National Youth Gang Center, 1999). Morgan (1994) cites numerous studies showing that adolescents raised in single-parent homes or homes that sustain a great deal of conflict often join gangs and exhibit other delinquent behaviors. Again, although no single factor leads children to delinquent behaviors, certain factors can indicate high risk. Delinquent behaviors often disrupt school success. School personnel need to work with legal and social service agencies to reduce delinquency and academic failure. In addition, the educational needs of children with disabilities who are in the juvenile justice system must be met the same as for other children with disabilities (Robinson & Rapport, 1999).

Strategies for Curriculum and Instruction for Students Who Are at Risk

There are four primary approaches to dealing with students who are at risk for failure in schools: prevention programs, compensatory education, intervention programs, and transition programs. Figure 13.5 depicts these four orientations.

Prevention programs focus on developing appropriate skills and behaviors that lead to success and, if used, are incompatible with other undesirable behaviors. Prevention programs also attempt to keep certain negative factors from having an impact on students. Drug prevention programs, antismoking educational efforts, and sex education programs are examples of efforts designed to establish responsible behaviors and keep students from developing problem behaviors.

Compensatory education programs "are designed to compensate or make up for existing or past risk factors and their effects in students' lives" (Morrison, 1997, p. 192). Head Start and Chapter I reading programs are examples of efforts to reduce the impact of poverty on children (Morrison, 1997). Reading Recovery, a program that is gaining popularity, has been shown to effectively improve the reading skills of at risk students (Dorn & Allen, 1995; Ross, Smith, Casey, & Slavin, 1995).

Intervention programs focus on eliminating risk factors. They include teaching teenagers how to be good parents and early intervention programs that target at risk preschool children (Sexton et al., 1996).

Finally, transition programs are designed to help students see the relationship between what they learn in school and how it will be used in the real world. School-to-Career programs, which help students move from school to work, are effective transition programs (Morrison, 1997).

CONSIDER THIS

How can programs like Head Start have an impact on students who are at risk? Should these programs be continuously emphasized? Why or why not?

FIGURE 13.5

Four Approaches to Education for Students at Risk

From *Teaching in America* (p. 193) by G. S. Morrison, 1997, Boston: Allyn and Bacon. Used by permission.

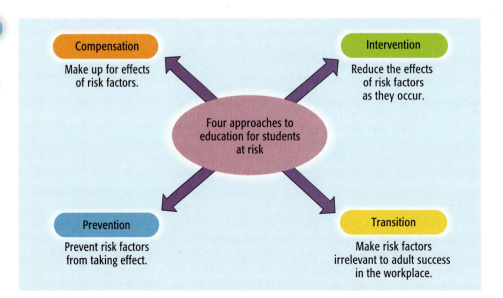

- **Compensation** — Make up for effects of risk factors.
- **Intervention** — Reduce the effects of risk factors as they occur.
- Four approaches to education for students at risk
- **Prevention** — Prevent risk factors from taking effect.
- **Transition** — Make risk factors irrelevant to adult success in the workplace.

After-school programs, along with involvement with various school-sponsored extra-curricular activities, provide schools with an opportunity to implement many strategies that are effective with at risk students. Many students who are at risk for problems face extreme challenges in the afternoon hours following school.

> School-age children and teens who are unsupervised during the hours after school are far more likely to use alcohol, drugs, and tobacco, engage in criminal and other high-risk behaviors, receive poor grades, and drop out of school than those children who have the opportunity to benefit from constructive activities supervised by responsible adults. (*Safe and smart*, 1998, p. 5)

After-school programs combine prevention, intervention, and compensatory programs.

Schools must use a variety of programs to prevent problems from developing and to address problems that do develop. The use of technology often proves beneficial. The nearby Technology Today feature provides information about how computers can be used with multicultural and bilingual groups, two at risk populations.

Schools must ensure that they do not discriminate against at risk students because of their race or socioeconomic status. The use of nondiscriminatory assessment is mandated by IDEA. The nearby Rights & Responsibilities feature focuses on this issue.

Characteristics of Effective Programs

Several factors are associated with schools that provide effective programs for students who are at risk. The U.S. Department of Education has noted that some research-based school reform models have been very successful in improving the achievement scores of students who are at risk for school failure. While differing in many respects, successful programs appear to share several characteristics (*Tools for schools*, 1998):

> ▶ They provide a clear blueprint with specific instructions for the changes that are to be made by the school in order to improve its educational performance;
> ▶ They offer a system of guidance and technical assistance for schools, often by the developer, and, in order to have the widest application, offer instructions on how the model may be scaled up at a large number of sites;
> ▶ The changes that the models propose for implementation are comprehensive, involving school organization, social relations (parental involvement, relationships between school staff and student), curriculum and instruction, and educational standards and goals;
> ▶ The models are flexible, which allows them to be implemented on variable time scales and with adaptations to meet local circumstances; and
> ▶ The model designs are based on up-to-date research on curriculum and the learning environment (p. 2).

Effective programs are those that see through the myths that have evolved in relation to at risk students and have become barriers to successful efforts. Barr and Parrett (2001) identified seven myths that must be overcome.

1. At risk youth need slow learning. *They need to be academically challenged like all students.*
2. At risk youth should be retained during the early grades until they are ready to move forward. *Research has shown that this can have disastrous effects.*
3. At risk youth can be educated with the same expenditures as other students. *Additional programming that might be needed will require additional funds.*
4. Classroom teachers can adequately address the needs of at risk youth. *Classroom teachers can contribute, but addressing the needs of at risk students requires a team effort.*
5. Some students can't learn. *Reaffirmation of this overriding education theme is often needed.*
6. The most effective way to improve instruction for at risk youth is to reduce classroom size. *This is a desirable but not necessary element.*
7. Students who are having learning difficulties need special education. *A tendency to refer to special education must be balanced with the idea of addressing the needs of at risks students within the general education classroom with necessary assistance and supports.*

CONSIDER THIS

Why have research-based reform models been successful in improving the achievement scores of students who are at risk for failure?

Using Technology with Multicultural and Bilingual Students Who May Be at Risk

Microcomputers

As computerized language translators begin to develop, there may be a significant impact for special education students with a primary language other than English. Imagine if the student could use a computer to write an assignment in his or her primary language, check the spelling and punctuation, then press a button to translate the work into English and transmit it to the teacher. Or perhaps the student wrote the assignment in a dialect, and then the computer was able to translate it into the standard form of that language. Such technology is possible.

One successful use of the microcomputer has been for the students to write their journals and for the teacher to respond via computer (Goldman and Rueda, 1988). Multicultural bilingual special education students were successful in developing their writing skills and their interaction skills with their teacher.

George Earl (1984) created a Spanish-to-English as well as an English-to-Spanish computerized version of the word game "hangman." Hangman is one of the many instructional games used by special education teachers to help improve language skills. Although the program had some difficulty (Zemke, 1985) with dialects (it translates standard Spanish), it demonstrates how technology can be applied to the learning needs of children who are multicultural and bilingual.

Computers have contributed to improved education for migrant children. A nationwide computerized transcript service, the Migrant Student Record Transfer System (MSRTS) in Little Rock, Arkansas, serves as a centralized location for transcripts and health records. A special education component contains information on the existence of a disability, assessment results, related services provided, and IEPs.

 For follow-up questions about technology for students at risk, go to Chapter 13 of the Companion Website (ablongman.com/sppd4e) and click Technology Today.

From *Introduction to Special Education* (3rd ed.) (p. 71) by D. D. Smith and R. Luckasson, 1998, Boston: Allyn and Bacon. Used by permission.

Technology applications can reduce the chance of failure for some at risk students.

Rights & Responsibilities   At Risk Children's Right to Nondiscriminatory Assessment

Schools are required, under IDEA, to use nondiscriminatory practices when evaluating students, since many at risk children experience poverty and come from single-parent homes and homes where English is not the primary language. The case law supporting this requirement came out of the *Larry P. v. Riles* case that was first filed in 1972. The court in this case

> held that schools no longer may use standardized IQ tests for the purpose of identifying and placing African American children into segregated special education classes for students classified as educable mentally retarded. . . .
>
> The district court found that the Stanford-Binet, Wechsler, and Leiter IQ tests discriminate against African Americans on several grounds.
>
> 1. They measure achievement, not ability.
> 2. They rest on the "plausible but unproven assumption that intelligence is distributed in the population in accordance with a normal statistical curve" and thus are "artificial tools to rank individuals accord-

> ing to certain skills, not to diagnose a medical condition (the presence of retardation)."
> 3. They "necessarily" lead to placement of more African Americans than Whites into classes for students with mild or moderate mental retardation."

On appeal, the Ninth Circuit Court of Appeals affirmed the lower court decision and rejected the state's argument that tests are good predictors of academic performance, even if they have a discriminatory impact; found that the state did not use any means of diagnosing disability other than IQ tests; and agreed that inappropriate placement of children can result in a profound negative impact on their education (Turnbull & Turnbull, 2000, pp. 153–154).

For follow-up questions about assessment for students at risk, go to Chapter 13 of the Companion Website (ablongman.com/sppd4e) and click Rights & Responsibilities.

Table 13.5 provides a list of factors, culled from research over the last 25 years, that have been found to be essential to school programs where at risk students are learning effectively.

The movement to include students with disabilities in general education classrooms provides an opportunity to meet the needs of at risk students as well. In an inclusive classroom, students should be educated based on their needs rather than on their clinical labels. In fact, inclusion, rather than separate programming, is supported by the lack of evidence that different teaching techniques are required by students from different disability groups.

The elements that are needed to create and maintain an inclusive classroom (as discussed in Chapter 2), which include specific techniques targeted for a specific population, often benefit everyone. When schools remove labels from students and provide programs based on individual needs, students who are at risk can benefit from the strategies and activities supplied for students with various disabilities (Wang, Reynolds, & Walberg, 1994/1995).

Specific Strategies for Students at Risk

In addition to the general principles cited earlier, specific programs can prove effective with these students. These include an emphasis on teaching every child to read, accelerated schools, alternative schools, one-on-one tutoring, extended day programs, cooperative learning activities, magnet schools, teen parent programs, vocational-technical programs, mentoring, and school-to-work programs (Barr & Parrett, 2001).

One program that has been used effectively in many schools is *mentoring* (Slicker & Palmer, 1993). Elementary, middle, and high schools design such programs to provide students with a positive personal relationship with an adult—something that many children and youth lack (Barr & Parrett, 2001). A **mentor** can be any person of any background who is committed to serving as a support person for a child or youth.

TABLE 13.5   **Essential Components of Effective Programs**

Positive School Climate
    Choice, commitment, and voluntary participation
    Small, safe, supportive learning environment
    Shared vision, cooperative governance, and local autonomy
    Flexible organization
    Community partnerships and coordination of services

Customized Curriculum and Instructional Program
    Caring, demanding, and well-prepared teachers
    Comprehensive and continuing programs
    Challenging and relevant curricula
    High academic standards and continuing assessment of student progress
    Individualized instruction: personal, diverse, accelerated, and flexible
    Successful transitions

Personal, Social, and Emotional Growth
    Promoting personal growth and responsibility
    Developing personal resiliency
    Developing emotional maturity through service
    Promoting emotional growth
    Promoting social growth

From *Hope Fulfilled for at-Risk and Violent Youth: K–12 Programs That Work* (p. 73) by R. D. Barr and W. H. Parrett, 2001, Boston: Allyn and Bacon. Copyright 2001 by Allyn and Bacon. Reprinted by permission.

Mentor programs provide opportunities for at risk students to meet with adults in the community and develop positive personal relationships.

Components of Effective Mentoring Programs for at Risk Students

▶ *Program compatibility:* The program should be compatible with the policies and goals of the organization. In a program for students in a community group, for example, program organizers should work closely with school personnel to ensure that the mentoring they provide complements the student's education.

▶ *Administrative commitment:* The program must be supported from the top as well as on a grass-roots level. In a school-based program, all school and district administrators, teachers, and staff must provide input and assistance. For a sponsoring business, the president or chief executive officer must view the program as important and worthy of the time and attention of the employees.

▶ *Proactive:* Ideally the programs should be proactive; that is, not a quick-fix reaction to a crisis. Successful mentoring programs for youth work because they are well thought out, they have specific goals and objectives, and they exist within a larger realm of programs and policies that function together.

▶ *Participant oriented:* The program should be based on the goals and needs of the participants. These goals will de-

termine the program's focus, recruitment, and training. For example, if the primary aim of a mentoring program is career awareness, students should be matched with successful businesspeople in the youth's area of interest. Activities and workshops should be job related.

▶ *Pilot program:* The first step should be a pilot program of 6 to 12 months, with 10 to 40 participants, in order to work out any problems before expanding to a larger audience. Trying to start out with a large-scale plan that includes more than this number can prove unwieldy and disastrous. In the words of Oregon's guide to mentorship programs, "Think big but start small."

▶ *Orientation:* An orientation should be provided for prospective participants. It will help determine interest and enthusiasm, as well as give prospective mentors and students an idea of what to expect. In addition, it will provide them with opportunities to help design the program.

▶ *Selection and matching:* Mentors and their protégés should be carefully selected and matched. Questionnaires are helpful in determining needs, areas of interest, and strengths.

▶ *Training:* Training must be provided for all participants, including support people, throughout the program. Assuming that because a person is knowledgeable, caring, and enthusiastic he or she will make a good mentor is a mistake. Training must be geared to the specific problems experienced by at risk youth as well as different styles of communication.

▶ *Monitoring progress:* The program should be periodically monitored for progress and results to resolve emerging conflicts and problems.

▶ *Evaluation and revision:* The program should be evaluated with respect to how well goals and objectives are achieved. This can be done using questionnaires, interviews, etc.

For follow-up questions about mentoring programs for students at risk, go to Chapter 13 of the Companion Website (ablongman.com/sppd4e) and click Inclusion Strategies.

From *Mentoring Programs for at-Risk Youth* (pp. 5–6) by National Dropout Prevention Center, 1990, Clemson, SC: Clemson University.

Mentor programs range in scope from national programs such as Big Brothers/Big Sisters to programs developed by and for specific schools, such as a program wherein adults employed in the community have lunch with students (Friedman & Scaduto, 1995). Programs large and small have proved effective for many children. It is important to ensure that a positive match is made between the mentor and the child. Other features of successful mentor programs are listed in the nearby Inclusion Strategies feature.

CROSS-REFERENCE

Review some of the strategies included in Chapters 5–9 and determine whether any of these methods would be effective with children at risk for school problems.

Final Thought

The population of at risk children and youth is incredibly diverse. Many different professionals need to get involved in developing and implementing programs for this group of students. Nevertheless, general classroom teachers will continue to play a major role in the lives of students who are at risk. Because teachers and students will spend a considerable amount of time together during the week, the importance of the teacher-student relationship is critical.

Elders' (2002) thoughts about the key elements that should guide school-based efforts with at risk students serve as a wonderful final thought for this chapter.

They come to us like a sponge and we must ensure that they leave with four things. We want them to leave with that voice in the ear that can hear all of those less fortunate so that they can have compassion. We want them to leave with a vision in their eye that extends much farther than the eye can see. We want them to have a scroll in their hand, which is a good education, and a song in their heart to carry them through when things get tough, as we know they will. (p. 1)

Summary

Basic Concepts About Students Who Are at Risk

▶ Students who are at risk may not be eligible for special education programs.
▶ At risk students include those who are in danger of developing significant learning and behavior problems.

Select at Risk Groups

▶ Poverty is a leading cause of academic failure.
▶ Poverty among children is increasing in the United States.
▶ Poverty is associated with homelessness, poor health care, hunger, and single-parent households.
▶ Hunger is a major problem in the United States.
▶ As many as 25% of all homeless people are children.
▶ Students in single-parent homes face major problems in school.
▶ About 25% of all children live in single-parent homes.
▶ Divorce is the leading reason for which children live in single-parent homes.

▶ Children react in many different ways to divorce.
▶ Schools must take into consideration the rights of the non-custodial parent.
▶ The death of a parent, sibling, or friend can have a major impact on a child and school success.
▶ Child abuse is a major problem in the United States and causes children to experience major emotional trauma.
▶ School personnel are required by law to report suspected child abuse.
▶ Drug use among students is on the increase after several years of decline.
▶ Teenage pregnancy continues to be a problem, despite the fear of AIDS and the presence of sex education programs.

Strategies for Curriculum and Instruction for Students Who Are at Risk

▶ Numerous programs and interventions have proved effective in working with at risk students.

Further Readings

Annie E. Casey Foundation. (1998). *1998 kids count data book: Overview.* Baltimore, MD: Author.

Barnes, K. E. (1982). *Preschool screening: The measurement and prediction of children at risk.* Springfield, IL: Thomas.

Barr, J. R., & Parrett, S. (1995). *Hope at last for at-risk youth.* Boston: Allyn and Bacon.

Carnegie Council on Adolescent Development. (1989). *Turning point: Preparing American youth for the 21st century.* New York: Author.

National Education Goals Panel. (1998). *Ready schools.* Washington, DC: Author.

National Law Center on Homelessness and Poverty. (1990). *Shut out: Denial of education to homeless children.* Washington, DC: Author.

Office of Education Research and Improvement. (1988). *Youth indicators, 1988: Trends in the well-being of American youth.* Washington, DC: U.S. Department of Education.

Office of Juvenile Justice and Delinquency Prevention. (1995). *Juvenile offenders and victims: A national report.* Pittsburgh, PA: National Center for Juvenile Justice.

Siccone, F. (1995). *Celebrating diversity: Building self-esteem in today's multi-cultural classrooms.* Boston: Allyn and Bacon.

U.S. Department of Education. (1998). *Tools for schools: From at-risk to excellence.* Washington, DC: Author.

U.S. Department of Education. (1998). *Safe and smart: Making the after-school hours work for kids.* Washington, DC: Author.

U.S. Department of Education. (1999). *The condition of education, 1998.* Washington, DC: Author.

Ysseldyke, J. E., Algozzine, B., & Thurlow, M. L. (2000). *Critical issues in special education* (3rd ed.). Boston: Houghton Mifflin.

VideoWorkshop Extra!

If the VideoWorkshop package was included with your textbook, go to Chapter 13 of the Companion Website (www. ablongman.com/sppd4e) and click on the VideoWorkshop button. Follow the instructions for viewing video clip 4. Then consider this information along with what you've read in Chapter 13 while answering the following questions.

1. When classroom teachers notice that students who are not native English speakers fail to achieve at an age-appropriate rate, they may consider referring such students for special education. What are the issues to consider before referral is made? Suggest two or three intervention strategies you might use in your classroom.

2. Technology can provide very useful learning tools for students who are not native English speakers. Recall the assistive and educational technology suggestions from this and previous chapters. What technology might you use in your classroom to support student learning?

14 Classroom Organization and Management

After reading this chapter, you should be able to

1. identify the key components of classroom management.
2. describe the roles of students, teachers, peers, and family members in promoting a positive classroom climate.
3. describe ways to increase desirable behaviors, decrease undesirable classroom behaviors, and maintain behaviors over time.
4. identify self-regulatory approaches and procedures.
5. identify possible strategies to enhance classroom and personal organization.

This year has been particularly challenging for Jeannie Chung. Jeannie has been teaching fifth grade for ten years, but she cannot recall any year in which her students' needs were more diverse and the tasks of managing the classroom and motivating her students were more challenging.

While many of her students present unique needs, 11-year-old Sam clearly stands out as the most difficult student in the class. Sam is too frequently out of his seat and often yells out to other students across the room. He has great difficulty staying on task during instructional periods and at times spreads a contagion of misbehavior in the classroom.

During large-group language arts lessons, Sam is inattentive and frequently uncooperative. Jeannie is beginning to believe that his high level of inattentive behavior may make it virtually impossible for him to progress and achieve in the general education classroom, although, at the same time, Jeannie does not see him as a candidate for a special class or other pull-out program. Further, his inattentive behavior is gradually resulting in his falling far behind academically. Although it is only November, Jeannie seriously wonders whether this will be a productive year for Sam.

Sam currently receives no special education supports or services. However, Jeannie has referred Sam to the child study team, and they are pondering suggestions that may be effective within Jeannie's classroom as well as considering a request for a more comprehensive assessment that may elucidate instructional and/or curricular alternatives.

QUESTIONS TO CONSIDER

1. What recommendations would you give Jeannie for focusing on Sam's behavior and its consequences?
2. Which procedures can Jeannie use to significantly increase Sam's attention to task behaviors?
3. How can Sam's peers be involved in a comprehensive behavior management program?
4. How can cooperative teaching facilitate successful intervention in the inclusive classroom?

A teacher's ability to manage his or her classroom effectively and efficiently can greatly enhance the quality of the educational experience for all students. Well-organized and well-managed classrooms allow more time for productive instruction for all students, including those with special needs.

The overriding theme of the chapter relates back the notion of creating a classroom community, as discussed in Chapter 2. As noted by Kohn (1996), we should strive to "make the classroom a community where students feel valued and respected, where care and trust have taken the place of restrictions and threats" (p. ix). The absence of heavy-handed adult-directed management systems is characteristic of classrooms where students are valued and solid relationships between teachers and students are established (Bender, 2003). When attention is given to preventive action rather than reactive intervention, classrooms run smoothly and without notice.

This chapter presents a model for thinking about the major dimensions of *classroom management,* a discussion of these dimensions, and specific suggested pedagogical practices for creating an effective learning environment. Sound organizational and management tactics promote learning for all students and are particularly relevant to the successful inclusion of students with special learning needs. When management/organization tactics are devised by general and special educators working collaboratively, the likelihood of establishing an effective learning setting is further enhanced.

Basic Concepts About Classroom Management and Organization

The importance of good classroom management and organization techniques has been affirmed numerous times by professionals in the field of education. Although much attention is given to curricular and instructional aspects of students' educational programs, organizational and management dimensions are typically underemphasized, despite their importance as prerequisites to instruction. This area is consistently identified as most problematic by first-year teachers. Further, the smooth functioning of the general education classroom often represents a challenge for teachers as classrooms become more diverse. Evertson, Emmer, and Worsham (2003) accurately articulate the relationship between the diversity found in today's schools and the need for well-run classrooms.

> Students entering the nation's schools come with such widely diverse backgrounds, capabilities, interests, and skills that meeting their needs and finding appropriate learning activities requires a great deal of care and skill. Because one of the first and most basic tasks for the teacher is to develop a smoothly running classroom community where students are highly involved in worthwhile activities that support learning, establishing an effective management system is a first priority. (p. ix)

We feel that this particular topic is too important to be overlooked, as attention to the elements described within this chapter can benefit a wide range of students with special needs in the general education classroom. Although reading about classroom management cannot take the place of practice and experience, this chapter offers a variety of management strategies to assist both new and experienced educators.

Most definitions describe **classroom management** as a systematic designing of the classroom environment to create conditions in which effective teaching and learning can occur. This chapter broadly defines the concept as all activities that support the efficient operations of the classroom and that help establish optimal conditions for learning (i.e., creating an effective learning environment). Noting Kohn's objections to the use of the term "management," because of its origins from business and overtones of directing and controlling, we will still use the term. However, our conceptualization of management and organization is not incompatible with Kohn's overall desire to empower students.

CONSIDER THIS

Does the inclusion of students with special needs result in greater need for good classroom management? If so, why?

Model of Classroom Management

Every classroom environment involves a number of elements that have a profound impact on the effectiveness of instruction and learning (Doyle, 1986). Six of these are described briefly here:

1. *Multidimensionality* refers to the wide variety of activities that occur in a classroom within the course of an instructional day.
2. *Simultaneity* refers to the fact that many different events occur at the same time.
3. *Immediacy* refers to the rapid pace at which events occur in classrooms.
4. *Unpredictability* refers to the reality that some events occur unexpectedly and cannot consistently be anticipated, but require attention nonetheless.
5. *Publicness* refers to the fact that classroom events are witnessed by a significant number of students who are very likely to take note of how teachers deal with these ongoing events.
6. *History* refers to the reality that, over the course of the school year, various events (experiences, routines, rules) will shape the evolving dynamics of classroom behavior.

Considering these elements reaffirms the complexity of teaching large numbers of students who have diverse learning needs in our schools today. To address these classroom dynamics, teachers need to identify ways to organize and manage their classrooms to maximize the potential opportunities for learning. Figure 14.1 depicts a model of classroom organization and management that highlights the multifaceted dimensions of this topic. This particular model of organization and management evolved from one designed by Polloway, Patton, and Serna (2001), reflecting an adaptation of what they identify as "precursors to teaching."

The effective and efficient management of a classroom is based on numerous considerations. To create a positive, supportive, and nurturing environment conducive to learn-

FIGURE 14.1   Dimensions of Classroom Organization and Management

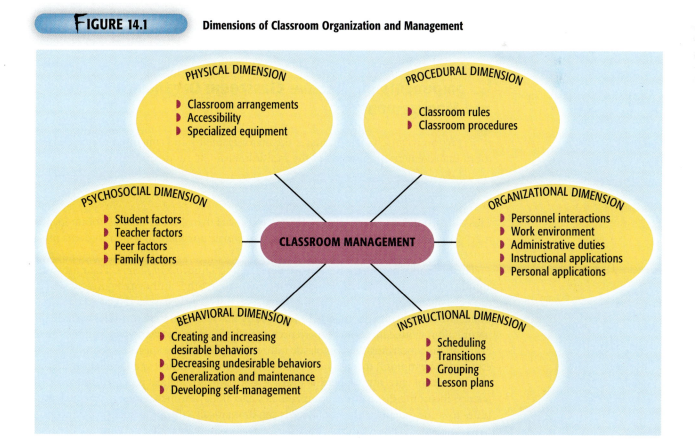

ing, teachers must pay attention to psychosocial, procedural, physical, behavioral, instructional, and organizational variables that have a critical impact on learning and behavior. Teachers need to consider much of the content of the dimensional model (see Figure 14.1), discussed in this chapter, *before* the beginning of the school year to prevent classroom-related issues from developing. Prevention is frequently more effective than behavioral interventions that might be needed after issues have become significant problems.

Guiding Principles

TEACHING TIP

Teachers need to have a comprehensive behavior management plan that includes not only consequences for actions by students (reactive elements) but also rules, procedures, and overall classroom organization (proactive elements).

Ten overarching principles guide the development and implementation of appropriate classroom organization and management procedures:

1. All students must be valued.
2. Meaningful relationships between teachers and students need to be developed and cultivated (Bender, 2003).
3. Successful management derives from a positive classroom climate.
4. Good classroom organization and management must be planned ahead of time.
5. Affording students choices contributes to effective classroom dynamics.
6. Teachers and students in effective classrooms are considerate of individual differences, including cultural and familial differences.
7. Proactive management is preferable to reactive approaches.
8. Consistency is the key to establishing an effective management program.
9. Two characteristics identified in classic classroom research enhance a teacher's ability to manage classrooms effectively (Kounin, 1970):
   • *With-it-ness:* Overall awareness of what is happening in the classroom.
   • *Overlap:* The ability to deal with more than one event simultaneously.
10. Although sound classroom management practices are useful in working with all students, the recommendations provided in this chapter are particularly helpful for students who have special needs and require individualized consideration. Without question, these students struggle to learn in environments that are not well organized and effectively managed.

Components of Effective Classroom Organization and Management

This section of the chapter discusses the major elements and subcomponents of classroom management highlighted in the multidimensional model in Figure 14.1.

Psychosocial Dimension

This dimension refers to the psychological and social dynamics of the classroom. Its primary focus is on **classroom climate,** the classroom atmosphere in which students must function.

The dynamics of classrooms are influenced by certain *student factors.* Their attitudes about school and their relationships with teachers and other authority figures, as well as their classmates, can have a remarkable impact on how they behave and react to organizational and management demands. Other factors that shape student attitudes include the nature of previous educational experiences, how they feel about themselves, and their own expectations concerning their scholastic futures (i.e., potential for success or failure). Teachers need to be mindful that all these factors are subject to cultural and familial variations.

The psychological atmosphere of any classroom depends in great part on certain *teacher factors,* including disposition, competencies and skills, and behaviors. A teacher's attitudes toward students with special needs can dramatically affect the quality of education that a student will receive during the time he or she is in that teacher's classroom. Personal

The dynamics of a classroom are determined by many different student factors.

philosophies about education, management and discipline, and curriculum weigh heavily as well. The type of expectations a teacher holds for students can significantly influence learning outcomes.

One particular set of skills that has bearing on the psychological aspects of the classroom is teacher communication skills. Evertson and colleagues (2003) note that the ability to communicate clearly and effectively with students influences the nature of ongoing dynamics in the classroom. They stress that to become an effective communicator, teachers need to display three related skills: constructive assertiveness (e.g., describing concerns clearly); empathic responding (e.g., listening to the student's perspective); and problem solving (e.g., ability to reach mutually satisfactory resolutions to problems).

Peers are also key players in forming the psychological and social atmosphere of a classroom, especially among middle and high school students. Teachers must understand peer values, pressures, and needs and use this knowledge to benefit students with special needs. Valuable cooperative learning opportunities can evolve based on successful peer involvement strategies. As Kohn (1996) remarked, "Communities are built upon a foundation of cooperating throughout the day, with students continually being invited to work, play, and reflect with someone else" (p. 113).

The final component involves a variety of *family-related factors.* Three major issues, all of which have cultural implications, include family attitudes toward education, level of family support and involvement in the student's education, and amount of pressure placed on a child by the family. Extremes can be problematic—for example, a family that burdens a student (e.g., a gifted child) with overwhelming pressure to succeed can cause as many difficulties as one that takes limited interest in a child's education.

Efforts should be undertaken to establish relationships with parents and guardians. At very least, a letter (with correct grammar, punctuation, and spelling) should be sent to each family, describing the nature of the classroom management system. This is particularly important if no other means exists for conveying this information, such as some type of orientation. A benefit of developing a relationship with parents is that the teacher can determine a family's status on the dimensions mentioned in the previous paragraph.

The following recommendations should help create a positive, nurturing environment that contributes to positive outcomes for all students:

▶ Let students know that you are sensitive to their needs and concerns.
▶ Convey enthusiasm about learning and the school experience.

▶ Create a supportive, safe environment in which students who are different can learn without fear of being ridiculed or threatened.

▶ Treat all students with fairness.

▶ Acknowledge all students in some personal way each day to affirm that they are valued within the room.

▶ Create a learning environment that is built on success and minimizes failure experiences common to the learning histories of students with disabilities.

▶ Understand the family and cultural contexts from which students come.

▶ Establish that each student in the classroom has rights (e.g., not to be interrupted when working or responding to a teacher inquiry) and that you expect everyone to respect those rights.

▶ Instill in students the understanding that they are responsible for their own behavior.

▶ Convey to students that every student's thoughts and ideas are important.

▶ Encourage risk taking and nurture all students (i.e., gifted, average, and disabled) to take on scholastic challenges.

Procedural Dimension

As noted in Figure 14.1, the procedural dimension refers to the rules and procedures that are part of the operating program of a classroom. The guidelines discussed here provide direction to school staff and students as to what is expected of all. The teacher must identify all rules, procedures, and regulations before the school year begins and should plan to *teach* them to students during the first days of the school year.

Equally important is preparation for dealing with violations of rules. Immediate and consistent consequences are needed. Various disciplinary techniques can be implemented to ensure that inappropriate behavior is handled effectively. (These will be covered in a subsequent section of the chapter.)

Students with exceptional needs will benefit from being taught systematically the administrative and social rules operative in a classroom. The suggestions provided in this section focus on classroom rules and in-class procedures.

Most individuals respond best when they know what is expected of them. *Classroom rules* provide a general sense of what is expected of students. The rules that are chosen should be essential to classroom functioning and help create a positive learning environment (Christenson, Ysseldyke, & Thurlow, 1989; Smith & Rivera, 1995). Reasonable

T ABLE 14.1   **Recommendations for Classroom Rules**

Develop no more than seven rules for the classroom.
Involve students in rule setting.
Keep the rules brief, and state them clearly.
Explain the rules thoroughly, and discuss the specific consequences if they are violated.
State the rules in a positive way—avoid statements that are worded in a negative way, such as "not allowed."
Post the rules in a location that all students can see.
Discuss exceptions in advance so that students understand them.
Teach the rules through modeling and practice and verify that all have been learned.
Review the rules on a regular basis and when new students join the class.
Use reminders of rules as a preventive measure for times when possible disruptions are anticipated.

classroom rules, presented appropriately, will be particularly beneficial to students with special needs who are in general education settings because this process assists in clarifying expectations. Some specific suggestions related to classroom rules are presented in Table 14.1.

An area of classroom management that may be overlooked is the development of logical *classroom procedures.* Classroom procedures refer to the specific way in which various classroom activities will be performed or the way certain situations will be handled. For example, depending on age, procedures may need to be established for using the pencil sharpener, using the rest room, and entering and leaving the classroom. Evertson and colleagues have identified five general areas in which specific procedures should be developed:

▶ Room use: teacher's desk, student desks, storage, drinking fountains, sink, pencil sharpener, centers, computer stations, board.
▶ Individual work and teacher-led activities: attention during presentations, participation, talk among students, obtaining help, when work has been completed.
▶ Transitions into and out of the room: beginning of the day, leaving the room, returning to the room, ending the day.
▶ Procedures during teacher-led, small-group instruction: getting the class ready, student movement, expected behavior in the group, expected behavior of the students out of group, materials and supplies.
▶ General procedures: distributing materials, classroom helpers, interruptions or delays, rest rooms, library usage, office visits, cafeteria, playground, fire and disaster drills. (pp. 38–39)

Again, clearly defined procedures are of particular importance especially for some students with special needs who may have difficulty attending to details or following instructions. This is one area where adequate consideration of these classroom/school activities can prevent many behavioral-related problems from developing.

Failing to address procedural issues in the classroom can cause distress for teachers if not attended to at the beginning of the school year. Teachers are often surprised by the complexity and detail associated with many seemingly trivial areas. The procedures for these areas combine to form the mosaic of one's management system. Here are some suggestions:

▶ Identify all situations for which a procedure will be needed.
▶ Develop the procedures collaboratively with the students.
▶ Explain (describe and demonstrate) each procedure thoroughly.
▶ *Teach* each procedure through modeling, guided practice, independent practice and feedback, allowing every student to have an opportunity to practice the procedure and demonstrate learning on an appropriate level.
▶ Introduce classroom procedures during the first week of school, scheduling priority procedures for the first day and covering others on subsequent days.
▶ Avoid introducing too many procedures at once.
▶ Incorporate any school regulation of importance and relevance into classroom procedures instruction (e.g., hall passes).

Physical Dimension

The physical dimension includes the aspects of the physical environment that teachers can manipulate to enhance the conditions for learning. For students with certain disabilities, some features of the physical setting may need to be especially arranged to ensure that individual needs are met.

Classroom arrangements refer to physical facets of the classroom, including classroom layout (i.e., geography of the room), arrangement of desks, storage, wall space, and signage. Teachers are encouraged to consider carefully where to seat students who have problems with controlling their behaviors, those who experience attention deficit, and

CONSIDER THIS

Why are classroom rules such an important component of classroom management? Describe the likely climate of classrooms with effective rules and those without effective rules.

T ABLE 14.2   Seating Arrangements

Seat students with behavior problems first so that they are in close proximity to the teacher for as much of the time as possible.

After more self-control is demonstrated, more distant seating arrangements are possible and desirable.

Locate students for whom visual distractions can interfere with attention to tasks (e.g., learning and attentional problems, hearing impairments, behavior problems) so that these distractions are minimized.

Establish clear lines of vision (a) for students so that they can attend to instruction and (b) for the teacher so that students can be monitored throughout the class period (Rosenberg et al., 1991).

Ensure that students with sensory impairments are seated so that they can maximize their residual vision and hearing.

Consider alternative arrangements of desks (e.g., table clusters) as options to traditional rows.

students with sensory impairments. Table 14.2 provides recommendations on seating arrangement. The judicious use of seating arrangements can minimize problems as well as create better learning opportunities for students. Carbone (2001) provides a host of suggestions for arranging the physical dimensions of a general education classroom for addressing the needs of students with ADHD.

Other suggestions for classroom arrangement are listed here:

▶ Consider establishing areas of the classroom for certain types of activities (e.g., discovery or inquiry learning, independent reading).
▶ Clearly establish which areas of the classroom, such as the teacher's desk, are off limits—this recommendation is also a procedural one.
▶ Begin the year with a more structured environment, moving to more flexibility after rules and procedures have been established.
▶ Notify students with visual impairments of changes made to the physical environment.
▶ Arrange furniture so that the teachers and students can move easily around the classroom.
▶ Direct students' attention to the information to be learned from bulletin boards, if they are used for instructional purposes.
▶ Establish patterns that students can use in moving around the class which minimize disruption.
▶ Secure materials and equipment that are potentially harmful, if used without proper supervision, such as certain art supplies, chemicals, and science equipment.
▶ Avoid creating open spaces that have no clear purpose, as they often can become staging areas for problem behaviors (Rosenberg et al., 1991).
▶ Provide labels and signs for areas of the room to assist younger or more delayed students in better understanding what and where things are.

The accessibility of the classroom warrants special attention because of legal mandates (e.g., Section 504 of the Rehabilitation Act of 1973). The concept of **accessibility**, of course, extends beyond physical accessibility, touching on overall program accessibility for students with special needs. Students who are identified as disabled under IDEA as well as students qualifying as having substantial limitations in a major life function such as walking or learning are able to benefit from needed accommodations.

Students with disabilities must be able to utilize the classroom like other students and the room must be free of potential hazards. Most of the time, making a classroom physically accessible is neither difficult nor costly. Specific suggestions for creating an accessible classroom include the following:

▶ Ensuring that the classroom is accessible to students who use wheelchairs, braces, crutches, or other forms of mobility assistance—this involves doorways, space to move within the classroom, floor coverings, learning centers, microcomputers, chalkboards or dry-erase boards, bookshelves, sinks, tables, desks, and any other areas or physical objects that students use.

▶ Guaranteeing that the classroom is free of hazards (e.g., low-hanging mobiles or plants) that could injure students who have a visual impairment.

▶ Labeling storage areas and other parts of the classroom for students with visual impairments by using raised lettering or braille.

▶ Paying special attention to signs identifying hazards by providing nonverbal cautions for nonreaders.

Some students with disabilities require the use of *specialized equipment,* such as wheelchairs, hearing aids and other types of amplification systems, communication devices, adaptive desks and trays, prone standers (i.e., stand-up desks), and medical equipment. This equipment allows programmatic accessibility and, in many instances, access to the general education curriculum. These types of assistive devices were introduced earlier in the book so that teachers may understand how the equipment works, how it should be used, and what adaptations will need to be made to the classroom environment to accommodate the student using it. The other students in the classroom should be introduced to the special equipment as well. Instructional lessons on specific pieces of equipment will not only be helpful in creating an inclusive environment, but may also provide a basis for curricular tie-ins in areas including health and science. Suggestions include the following:

▶ Identify the special equipment that will be used in the classroom prior to the arrival of the student who needs it.

▶ Learn how special equipment and devices work and how to identify problems or malfunctions.

▶ Find out how long students need to use time-specified equipment or devices.

▶ Structure learning activities in which the student with a disability (perhaps paired with a peer) demonstrates appropriate usage of the specialized equipment.

Behavioral Dimension

The ability to manage inappropriate behaviors that may disrupt the learning environment is an important component of classroom management. Yet, this ability is only a part of a comprehensive behavior management program. Such a plan should also include techniques for developing new behaviors or increasing desirable behaviors within the students' repertoire. Moreover, a sound program must ensure that behaviors learned or changed will be maintained over time and generalized (e.g., demonstrated in different contexts). It must also teach self-control and self-regulatory mechanisms. Table 14.3 describes the basic components of a behavior management plan based on functional assessment procedures.

Recently more attention is being given to behavior that goes beyond the typical emphasis on external behavioral tactics. Bender (2003) promotes the concept of "relational discipline."

> Relational discipline focuses squarely on the relationship between the teacher and the student, and various tactics and strategies are implemented within that broader context. For it is this relationship, rather than the specific disciplinary tactics that are used, that forms the basis for appropriate classroom behavior and that eventually develops into self-discipline. (p. 3)

Related to the notion that relationship is important, Bender points out that "behavioral interventions practices" (i.e., disciplinary tactics) must be understood from a developmental perspective. Differential techniques must be considered in terms of age-related

CROSS-REFERENCE

Review Chapter 10 on students with low-incidence disabilities and Chapter 9 on those with sensory impairments, and consider the implications of equipment needed by these groups of students.

CONSIDER THIS

IDEA requires that attention be given to positive behavioral interventions.

> ### TABLE 14.3   Components of a Behavior Management Plan
>
> *Conduct a Functional Assessment*
> 1. Collect information.
>   - Identify and define the target behavior.
>   - Identify events/circumstances associated with the problem behavior.
>   - Determine potential function(s) of the problem behavior.
> 2. Develop hypothesis statements about the behavior.
>   - Events/circumstances associated with the problem behavior.
>   - Function/purpose of the behavior.
>
> *Develop an Intervention (Based on Hypothesis Statements)*
> 1. Teach alternative behavior.
> 2. Modify events/circumstances associated with the problem behavior.
>
> From "Using Functional Assessment to Develop Effective, Individualized Interventions for Challenging Behaviors" (p. 46) by L. F. Johnson and G. Dunlap, 1993, *Teaching Exceptional Children, 25.* Used by permission.

needs and predominant influences operative at a given age. Figure 14.2 illustrates these points. Bender notes that few disciplinary systems have, to any reasonable extent, built upon the influence of peer groups with older students.

Given the importance of the behavioral dimension, most general educators will probably work regularly with special educators to develop effective programs for students with disabilities and for other students with behavioral problems. To provide a flavor of the areas for possible emphasis, Etscheidt and Bartlett (1999) identified the following sample factors:

▶ *Skill Training:* Could the student be involved in social skill instruction? Does the student need counseling?

▶ *Behavior Management Plan:* Does the student need a behavior management plan that describes a reinforcement system, supportive signals, and corrective options?

▶ *Self-Management:* Could the student use self-monitoring of target behaviors?

▶ *Peer Support:* Could peers help monitor and/or redirect behavior? Could peers take notes, help prepare for exams, etc.?

▶ *Class-Wide Systems:* Could the teacher implement an interdependent group contingency for the class? Could a "Circle of Friends" be initiated? (p. 171)

Because research confirms the effectiveness of behavioral techniques for promoting learning in students with special needs (see Lloyd, Forness, & Kavale, 1998), such interventions should clearly be key components of a teacher's repertoire. Today, professionals in the area of behavior have been stressing the need to implement positive behavioral interventions and supports. This emphasis has been accompanied by a deemphasis on the use of more negative and punitive tactics.

TEACHING TIP

Students should be involved in selecting positive reinforcers to make sure that they are indeed attractive to the student.

FIGURE 14.2

Relational Discipline

From *Relational Discipline: Strategies for In-Your-Face Kids* (p. 35) by W. N. Bender, 2003, Boston: Allyn and Bacon. Copyright 2003 by Pearson Education. Reprinted by permission.

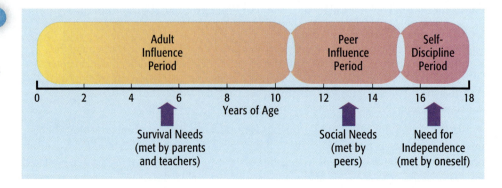

Not all facets of behavior management can be covered in sufficient detail in this chapter. However, the following sections provide recommendations that should guide practice in increasing desirable behaviors, decreasing undesirable behaviors, promoting generalization and maintenance, and enhancing self-management. The final section revisits the mandated requirement in IDEA for behavioral intervention plans (BIPs).

Creating and Increasing Desirable Behaviors   The acquisition of desired new behaviors, whether academic, personal, behavioral, social, or vocational, is a classroom goal. A new desired behavior can be affirmed with a **reinforcer,** any event that rewards, and thus strengthens, the behavior it follows. **Positive reinforcement** presents a desirable consequence for performance of an appropriate behavior. Positive reinforcers can take different forms; however, what serves as reinforcement for one individual may not hold true for another. Reinforcers can consist of praise, physical contact, tangible items, activities, or privileges. The use of reinforcement is the most socially acceptable and instructionally sound tactic for increasing desired behaviors. The goal of most behavioral regimens is to internalize the nature of reinforcement (i.e., self-reinforcement).

Three basic principles must be followed for positive reinforcement to be most effective. It must be meaningful to the student, contingent upon the proper performance of a desired behavior, and presented immediately. In other words, for positive reinforcement to work, students must find the reinforcement desirable in some fashion, understand that it is being given as a result of the behavior demonstrated, and receive it soon after they do what was asked. Principles for the use of positive reinforcement are presented in Table 14.4. Generally, attention to the systematic nature of the reinforcement program should parallel the severity of a student's intellectual, learning, or behavioral problem. All too often, teachers do not pay close enough attention to the principles that we have noted, and, as a result, do not implement techniques with any power. Another potential problem is that some powerful positive behavioral interventions cannot be implemented because of such factors as cost or complexity (Bender, 2003).

The first illustrative application of the principle of positive reinforcement is **contingency contracting,** a concept introduced by Homme (1969). With this method, the teacher develops contracts with students that state (1) what behaviors (e.g., academic work, social

> **CONSIDER THIS**
>
> Some people say that contracts, as well as other forms of positive reinforcement, amount to little more than bribery. Do you agree or disagree, and why?

TABLE 14.4   **Implementing Positive Reinforcement Techniques**

Determine what reinforcements will work for particular students:

1. Ask the child by using direct formal or informal questioning or by administering an interest inventory or reinforcement survey.
2. Ask those knowledgeable about the student (e.g., parents, friends, or past teachers).
3. Observe the student in the natural environment as well as in a structured observation (e.g., arranging reinforcement alternatives from which the student may select).

Select meaningful reinforcers that are easy and practical to deliver in classroom settings (Idol, 1993).

"Catch" students behaving appropriately, and provide them with the subsequent appropriate reinforcement (referred to as the differential reinforcement of behavior incompatible with problem behavior). Begin this technique early so that students experience the effects of positive reinforcement.

Use the Premack (1959) principle ("Grandma's law": "eat your vegetables and then you can have dessert") regularly.

Use reinforcement techniques as the student makes gradual progress in developing a desired behavior that requires the mastery of numerous substeps (reinforce each successive approximation). This concept is called shaping.

Demonstrate to a student that certain behaviors will result in positive outcomes by reinforcing nearby peers.

behaviors) students are to complete or perform and (2) what consequences (e.g., reinforcement) the instructor will provide. These contracts are presented as binding agreements between student and teacher. To be most effective, contracts should (1) initially reward imperfect approximations of the behavior, (2) provide frequent reinforcement, (3) reward accomplishment rather than obedience, and (4) be fair, clear, and positive. Figure 14.3 shows an example of a contract for a secondary school student.

Group contingencies, which are set up for groups of students rather than individuals, provide excellent alternatives for managing behavior and actively including students with special needs in the general education classroom. There are three types:

1. *Dependent contingencies:* All group members share in the reinforcement if one individual achieves a goal (i.e., the "hero" strategy).
2. *Interdependent contingencies:* All group members are reinforced if all collectively (or all individually) achieve the stated goal.
3. *Independent contingencies:* Individuals within the group are reinforced for individual achievement toward a goal.

Whereas independent contingencies are commonly used, the other two forms are less widely seen in the classroom. The dependent strategy is sometimes referred to as a "hero approach" because it singles out one student's performance for attention. Although it can be abused, such an approach may be particularly attractive for a student who responds well to peer attention. A student with special needs may feel more meaningfully included in class when his or her talents are recognized in this way.

Others may feel reinforced and accepted as part of a group when interdependent contingencies are employed. The most common use of an interdependent strategy is the "good behavior game." Because it is most often used as a behavioral reduction intervention, it is discussed later in the chapter.

The benefits of group-oriented contingencies (or peer-mediated strategies, as they are often called) include the involvement of peers, the ability of teachers to enhance motivation, and increased efficiency for the teacher. In some instances, students will raise ques-

FIGURE 14.3

Sample Contract Between Student and Teacher

From *Behavior Management: Applications for Teachers and Parents* (p. 189) by T. Zirpoli and G. Melloy, 1993, Columbus, OH: Merrill. Used by permission.

Contract

_____ will demonstrate the following appropriate behaviors
(Student's name)

in the classroom:

1. Come to school on time.
2. Come to school with homework completed.
3. Complete all assigned work in school without prompting.
4. Ask for help when necessary by raising hand and getting teacher's attention.

_____ will provide the following reinforcement:
(Teacher's name)

1. Ten tokens for the completion of each of the above four objectives. Tokens for the first two objectives will be provided at the beginning of class after all homework assignments have been checked. Tokens for objectives 3 and 4 will be provided at the end of the school day.
2. Tokens may be exchanged for activities on the Classroom Reinforcement Menu at noon on Fridays.

_____   _____
Student's signature   Teacher's signature

                                                   _____
                                                   Date

tions of fairness concerning group contingency programs. Those who typically behave appropriately may feel that they are being penalized for the actions of others if reinforcement occurs only when the whole group evidences a desired behavior. You can assure them that, ultimately, they and everyone else will benefit from group success with particular guidelines or goals. Two resources—one for young students [*Practical Ideas That Really Work with Students Who Are Disruptive, Defiant, and Difficult: Preschool Through Grade 4* (McConnell, Ryser, & Patton, 2002a)] and the other for older students [*Practical Ideas That Really Work with Students Who Are Disruptive, Defiant, and Difficult: Grades 5–12* (McConnell, Ryser, & Patton, 2002b)]—include many practical ideas for using individual and group contingencies.

Decreasing Undesirable Behaviors   Every teacher will face situations involving undesirable behaviors that require behavior reduction techniques. Teachers can select from a range of techniques; however, it is usually best to begin with the least intrusive interventions (Smith & Rivera, 1995) and more neutrally oriented ones. A recommended sequence of reduction strategies is depicted in Figure 14.4. As teachers consider reductive strategies, they are cautioned to keep records, develop plans of action, and follow state and local guidelines.

The use of *natural* and *logical consequences* can help children and adolescents learn to be more responsible for their behaviors (West, 1986, 1994). These principles are particularly important for students with special needs who often have difficulty seeing the link between their behavior and the resulting consequences.

With **natural consequences,** the situation itself provides the contingencies for a certain behavior. For example, if a student forgets to return a permission slip to attend an off-campus event, the natural consequence is that the student is not allowed to go and must remain at school. Thus, rather than intervening in a given situation, the teacher allows the situation to teach the students. Natural consequences are an effective means to teach common sense and responsibility (West, 1994).

In **logical consequences,** there is a logical connection between inappropriate behavior and the consequences that follow. If a student forgets lunch money, a logical consequence might be that money must be borrowed from someone else. The uncomfortable consequence is the hassle or embarrassment of requesting financial assistance. These tactics can

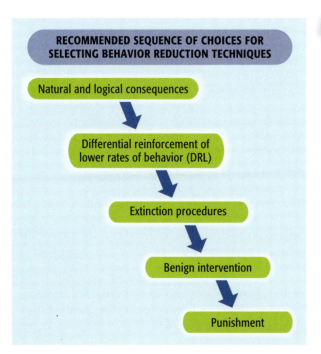

FIGURE 14.4

Recommended Sequence of Selected Behavior Reduction Techniques

help students recognize that their own behavior has created the discomfort and not something the teacher has done to them. When using this approach, teachers should clarify to students that they are responsible for their own behaviors. Logical consequences relate the disciplinary response directly to the inappropriate behavior.

As noted earlier in the chapter, an important, recently developed approach to behavioral reduction is through the use of positive behavioral supports. As Horner (2000) notes, "Positive behavior support involves the assessment and reengineering of environments so people with problem behaviors experience reductions in (these behaviors) and increased social [and] personal quality in their lives. . . . It is an approach that blends values about the rights of people with disabilities with the practical science about how learning and behavior change occur" (p. 181).

The essential element of positive behavior support is the emphasis on fixing environments rather than focusing just on changing the behavior of individuals. Thus, the key element is to design schools and curricula to prevent problem behaviors from occurring and thus make them "irrelevant, inefficient, and ineffective" (Horner, 2000, p. 182). As discussed in Chapter 7, the basis for effective positive behavior support programs is the use of functional behavior assessment which identifies classroom events that serve to predict the occurrence of problem behaviors and function to maintain positive behaviors (Horner, 2000). Thus, the reader is encouraged to consider the remaining behavioral reduction strategies discussed in this chapter in light of the need to balance the focus on the individual with the more significant focus on designing a curriculum and operating a classroom in ways in which behavioral disturbances are minimized and students with special needs are more accepted members of the classroom.

The next option on the continuum is the use of *differential reinforcement of lower (DRL) rates of behavior.* This technique uses positive reinforcement strategies as a behavior reduction tool. A teacher using this procedure provides appropriate reinforcement to students for displaying lower rates of a certain behavior that has been targeted for reduction. It is important to remember that the goal should be to decrease the frequency or duration of the unwanted behavior.

An example of this technique used with groups of students is the "good behavior game" (originally developed by Barrish, Saunders, & Wolf, 1969), in which student teams receive reinforcement if the number of occurrences of inappropriate behaviors remains under a preset criterion. Tankersley (1995) provides a good overview of the use of the good behavior game:

> First, teachers should define target behaviors that they would like to see improved and determine when these behaviors are most problematic in their classrooms. Criteria for winning must be set and reinforcers established; the students should be taught the rules for playing. Next, the classroom is divided into teams and team names are written on the chalkboard. If any student breaks a rule when the game is in effect, the teacher makes a mark by the name of the team of which the disruptive student is a member. At the end of the time in which the game is played, any team that has fewer marks than the preestablished criterion wins. Members of the winning team(s) receive reinforcers daily. In addition, teams that meet weekly criterion receive reinforcers at the end of the week. (p. 20)

Here are additional considerations:

▶ Understand that undesirable behaviors will still occur and must be tolerated until target levels are reached.
▶ Reduce the criterion level after students have demonstrated stability at the present level.
▶ Avoid making too great a jump between respective criterion levels to ensure that students are able to meet the new demands.

Tankersley (1995, p. 23) stresses the value of this strategy in noting that it "can be very effective in changing students' behaviors, can lead to improved levels of academic skills . . . , can reduce the teacher's burden of incorporating several individual contingency systems

CONSIDER THIS

What are some advantages of using a DRL approach when working on a complex behavior, rather than simply reinforcing the student only after a targeted behavior has completely disappeared?

for managing behavior, . . . [makes] use of natural supports available in the classroom, [and] can help promote generalization" (p. 26).

The next reduction option involves **extinction** procedures. In this technique, the teacher withholds reinforcement for a behavior. Over time, such action, in combination with the positive reinforcement of related desirable behaviors, should extinguish the inappropriate behavior. One example is for the teacher to cease responding to student misbehavior. For some situations, it will be necessary to involve a student's peers in the extinction process to eliminate a behavior because the peers' actions are controlling the relevant reinforcers. The following are additional suggestions:

▶ Analyze what is reinforcing the undesirable behavior, and isolate the reinforcer(s) before initiating this procedure.
▶ Understand that the extinction technique is desirable because it does not involve punishment, but it will take time to be effective.
▶ Do not use this technique with behaviors that require immediate intervention (e.g., fighting).
▶ Recognize that the withholding of reinforcement (1) is likely to induce an increase ("spiking" effect) in the occurrence of the undesirable behavior, as students intensify their efforts to receive the reinforcement they are used to getting, and (2) may produce an initial aggressive response.
▶ Provide reinforcement to students who demonstrate appropriate incompatible behaviors (e.g., taking turns versus interrupting).

The fourth option is the use of techniques that border on being punishment but are so unobtrusive that they can be considered *benign tactics*. These suggestions are consistent with a concept developed by Cummings (1983) called the "law of least intervention" and that of Evertson and colleagues (2003) called "minor interventions." The main idea is to eliminate disruptive behaviors quickly with a minimum of disruption to the classroom or instructional routine. The following suggestions can be organized into physical, gestural, visual, and verbal prompts:

▶ Position yourself physically near students who are likely to create problems.
▶ Redirect behavior in unobtrusive ways (i.e., not embarrassing to an individual student) that are directed to the whole class or through the use of humor.

TEACHING TIP

When attempting to reduce an inappropriate behavior by ignoring it, teachers must remember to positively reinforce behaviors that are desired.

TEACHING TIP

Being physically close to students who often display behavior problems is a powerful method of reducing inappropriate behaviors.

Positioning yourself by a student who is disruptive is often a powerful management technique.

▶ Touch a student's shoulder gently to convey your awareness that the student is behaving in some inappropriate (albeit previously identified) way.

▶ Use subtle and not-so-subtle gestures to stop undesirable behaviors (e.g., pointing, head shaking, finger spelling).

▶ Establish eye contact and maintain it for a while with a student who is behaving inappropriately. This results in no disruption to the instructional routine.

▶ Stop talking for a noticeable length of time to redirect student attention.

▶ Call on students who are not attending, but ask them questions that they can answer successfully.

▶ Give the student a choice.

▶ Use an "I-Message."

▶ Minimize "dead" time.

▶ Avoid sarcasm and confrontation.

The last option in this reduction hierarchy and the one that is most intrusive is the use of **punishment.** It is the least preferable option because it involves the presentation of something unpleasant or the removal of something pleasant as a consequence of the performance of an undesirable behavior. This option should be considered only as a last resort. However, in situations in which a more immediate cessation of undesirable behaviors is required, punishment may be necessary. Because of their potency, punishment strategies should be weighed carefully; they can interfere with the learning process if not used sparingly and appropriately. Given that all teachers are likely to use punishment at some point, the key is to ensure that it is used appropriately.

Three punishment techniques are commonly used in classrooms: **reprimands, time out,** and **response cost.** For these forms of punishment to work, it is critical that they be applied immediately after the occurrence of the undesirable behavior and that students understand why they are being applied. A overview of these techniques is provided in Table 14.5.

TEACHING TIP

To ensure proper compliance, teachers must always be aware of state or local guidelines when using time out for reducing student behavior.

TABLE 14.5   **Three Commonly Used Punishment Techniques**

Type	Definition	Advantages	Disadvantages
Reprimand	A verbal statement or nonverbal gesture that expresses disapproval	Easily applied with little or no preparation required No physical discomfort to students	Sometimes not effective Can serve as positive reinforcement if this is a major source of attention.
Response Cost	A formal system of penalties in which a reinforcer is removed contingent upon the occurrence of an inappropriate behavior	Easily applied with quick results Does not disrupt class activities No physical discomfort to students	Not effective once student has "lost" all reinforcers Can initially result in some students being more disruptive
Time Out	Limited or complete loss of access to positive reinforcers for a set amount of time	Fast-acting and powerful No physical discomfort to students	Difficult to find secluded areas where students would not be reinforced inadvertently May require physical assistance to the time-out area Overuse can interfere with educational and prosocial efforts

From *Student Teacher to Master Teacher* (p. 149) by M. S. Rosenberg, L. O'Shea, and D. J. O'Shea, 1991, New York: Macmillan. Reprinted by permission.

A reprimand represents a type of punishment in which an unpleasant condition (verbal reprimand from the teacher) is presented to the student. The following are some specific suggestions:

▶ Do not let this type of interchange dominate your interactions with students.
▶ Look at the student and talk in a composed way.
▶ Do not verbally reprimand a student from across the room. Get close to the student, maintain a degree of privacy, and minimize embarrassment.
▶ Let the student know exactly why you are concerned.
▶ Convey to the student that it is the behavior that is the problem and not him or her.

With time out a student is removed from a situation in which he or she typically receives positive reinforcement, thus being prevented from enjoying something pleasurable. Different ways are available to remove a student from a reinforcing setting: (1) students are allowed to observe the situation from which they have been removed (contingent observation); (2) students are excluded from the ongoing proceedings entirely (exclusion time out); and (3) students are secluded in a separate room (seclusion time out). The first two versions are most likely to be considered for use in general education classrooms. The following suggestions are extremely important if time out is to succeed.

▶ Confirm that the ongoing situation from which a student is going to be removed is indeed reinforcing; if not, this technique will not serve as a punisher and rather may be a form of positive reinforcement.
▶ Ensure that the time-out area is devoid of reinforcing elements. If it is not a neutral setting, this procedure will fail.
▶ Do not keep students in time out for long periods of time (i.e., more than ten minutes) or use it frequently (e.g., daily), as students will miss significant amounts of instructional time.
▶ As a rule of thumb with younger children, never allow time-out periods to extend beyond one minute for every year of the child's age (up to a maximum of ten minutes).
▶ Use a timer to ensure accuracy in the length of time out.
▶ Incorporate this procedure as one of the classroom procedures explained and taught at the beginning of the school year.
▶ Consider using a time-out system in which students are given one warning before being removed.
▶ Signal to the student when it is appropriate to return.
▶ Do not use this technique with certain sensitive students.
▶ Keep records on frequency, reason for using, and amount of time placed when using seclusion time-out procedures.

Response cost involves the loss of something the student values, such as privileges or points. It is a system in which a penalty or fine is levied for occurrences of inappropriate behavior. The following are some specific suggestions:

▶ Explain clearly to students how the system works and how much one will be fined for a given offense.
▶ Make sure all penalties are presented in a nonpersonal manner.
▶ Confirm that privileges that are lost are indeed reinforcing to students.
▶ Make sure that all privileges are not lost quickly, resulting in a situation in which a student may have little or no incentive to behave appropriately.
▶ Tie this procedure in with positive reinforcement at all times.

Generalization and Maintenance   After behaviors have been established at acceptable levels, the next stages involve transferring what has been learned to new contexts and maintaining established levels of performance. Teachers often succeed in teaching students certain behaviors but fail to help them apply the skills to new situations or to retain them over time. Teaching appropriate behaviors and then hoping that students will be able to use various skills at some later time is detrimental to many students with special needs because a core difficulty they experience is performing independently in the classroom.

Teachers need to program for generalization, the wider application of a behavior skill, by giving students opportunities to use new skills in different settings, with different people, and at different times. Students often need help in identifying the cues that should trigger the performance of an acquired behavior, action, or skill.

Students also need to practice what they have learned previously, in order to maintain their skills. Instructional planning should allow time for students to determine how well they have retained what they have learned. This time usually can be provided during seatwork activities or other arrangements.

Suggestions for generalization and maintenance include the following:

◗ Create opportunities for students to practice in different situations what they have learned.
◗ Work with other teachers to provide additional opportunities.
◗ Place students in situations that simulate those that they will encounter in the near and distant future, both within school and in other areas of life.
◗ Show students how these skills or behaviors will be useful to them in the future.
◗ Prompt students to use recently acquired skills in a variety of contexts.
◗ Maintain previously taught skills by providing ongoing practice or review.

As noted previously, the use of positive behavior supports has become more popular in working with students with special needs, particularly because of its effectiveness and its emphasis on the environment rather than the individual. A key to behavioral generalization and maintenance, therefore, is to focus beyond the student and ensure that the learning environment is designed in such a way that students can use their newly acquired skills effectively to become accepted and active members of the classroom while enhancing their learning opportunities. In addition, key elements of generalization and maintenance relate to self-management strategies, which become essential in work with adolescents.

Self-Management   Ultimately, we want all students to be able to manage their own behaviors without external direction because this ability is a requirement of functioning independently in life. Special attention needs to be given to those who do not display independent behavioral control and thus must develop *student-regulated strategies*—interventions that, though initially taught by the teacher, are intended to be implemented independently by the student. Bender (2003) refers to this end state as the "self-discipline" phase.

The concept is an outgrowth of cognitive behavior modification, a type of educational intervention for students with disabilities in use since the 1980s, that stresses active thinking about behavior. Shapiro, DuPaul, and Bradley-Klug (1998) provide a good overview of self-management. They state:

> It is helpful to conceptualize self-management interventions as existing on a continuum. At one end, the intervention is completely controlled by the teacher . . . ; this individual provides feedback regarding whether the student's behavior met the desired criteria and administers the appropriate consequences for the behavior. At the other end, the student engages in evaluating his or her own behavior against the criteria for performance, without benefit of teacher . . . input. The student also self-administers the appropriate consequences. In working with students with behavior problems, the objective should be to move a student as far toward the self-management side of the continuum as possible. Although some of these students may not be capable of reaching levels of independent self-management, most are certainly capable of approximating this goal. (p. 545)

Fiore, Becker, and Nerro (1993) state the rationale for such interventions: "Cognitive-behavioral [intervention] is . . . intuitively appealing because it combines behavioral techniques with cognitive strategies designed to directly address core problems of impulse control, higher order problem solving, and self-regulation" (p. 166). Whereas traditional behavioral interventions most often stress the importance of teacher monitoring of student behavior, extrinsic reinforcement, and teacher-directed learning, cognitive inter-

CONSIDER THIS

Why is it so important to teach students to manage their own behaviors without external guidance from teachers? How can self-management assist students with disabilities in their inclusion in the community?

ventions instead focus on teaching students to monitor their own behavior, to engage in self-reinforcement, and to direct their own learning in strategic fashion (Dowdy, Patton, Smith, & Polloway, 1997).

Such approaches have become particularly popular with students with learning and attentional difficulties because they offer the promise of

- increasing focus on selective attention.
- modifying impulsive responding.
- providing verbal mediators to assist in academic and social problem-solving situations.
- teaching effective self-instructional statements to enable students to "talk through" tasks and problems.
- providing strategies that may lead to improvement in peer relations. (Rooney, 1993)

While using self-management strategies with students with special needs in inclusive settings has been far more limited than studies of using them in pull-out programs, the moderate to strong positive outcomes reported in research are encouraging (McDougall, 1998).

Student-regulated strategies form the essence of self-management. Although variations exist in how these are defined and described, the components listed in Figure 14.5 represent the central aspects of self-management.

Two components with particular utility for general education teachers are self-monitoring and self-instruction. **Self-monitoring,** a technique in which students observe and record their own behavior, has been commonly employed with students with learning problems. Lloyd, Landrum, and Hallahan (1991) note that self-monitoring was initially seen as an assessment technique, but as individuals observed their own behavior, the process also resulted in a change in behavior. Self-monitoring of behavior, such as attention, is a relatively simple technique that has been validated with children who have learning disabilities, mental retardation, multiple disabilities, attention deficits, and behavior disorders; it has also been profitable for nondisabled students (McDougall, 1998; Lloyd et al., 1991; Prater, Joy, Chilman, Temple, & Miller, 1991). Increased attention, beneficial to academic achievement, has been reported as a result.

A common mechanism for self-monitoring was developed by Hallahan, Lloyd, and Stoller (1982). It involves using a tape-recorded tone, which sounds at random intervals (e.g., every 45 seconds), and a self-recording sheet. Each time the tone sounds, children ask themselves whether they are paying attention and then mark the *yes* or the *no* box on the tally sheet. While students are often not accurate in their recording, nevertheless

CONSIDER THIS

Do you engage in any self-monitoring techniques? If so, how do you use them, and how effective are they?

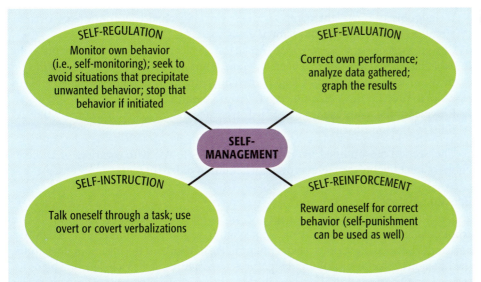

FIGURE **14.5**

Components of Self-Management

From *Guide to Attention Deficits in the Classroom* (p. 162) by C. A. Dowdy, J. R. Patton, E. A. Polloway, and T. E. C. Smith, 1998, Austin, TX: Pro-Ed. Used by permission.

positive changes in behavior have been observed in many research studies. While self-monitoring procedures may prove problematic for one teacher to implement alone, a collaborative approach within a cooperative teaching arrangement offers much promise.

Teachers should consider ways to creatively use self-monitoring in their classrooms as an adjunct to other ongoing management strategies. McDougall (1998) offered this unique suggestion:

> Practitioners . . . could train students to use tactile cues to mediate self-management in much the same manner that students use visually cued, audio-cued, or covert self-monitoring. Tactile cues such as those produced by vibrating pagers might be a functional option for (a) students who have difficulty responding to visual and auditory cues, (b) students with multiple, profound, or sensory disabilities, (c) situations in which audio or visual cues might distract other students, and (d) students who wish to maintain privacy when self-monitoring. (p. 317)

Self-instruction represents another useful intervention. Pfiffner and Barkley (1991) describe components of a self-instruction program as follows:

> Self-instructions include defining and understanding the task or problem, planning a general strategy to approach the problem, focusing attention on the task, selecting an answer or solution, and evaluating performance. In the case of successful performance, self-reinforcement (usually in the form of a positive self-statement, such as "I really did a good job") is provided. In the case of an unsuccessful performance, a coping statement is made (e.g., "Next time I'll do better if I slow down") and errors are corrected. At first, an adult trainer typically models the self-instructions while performing a task. The child then performs the same task while the trainer provides the self-instructions. Next, the child performs the task while self-instructing aloud. These overt verbalizations are then faded to covert self-instructions. (p. 525)

Clear, simple self-instruction strategies form an appropriate beginning for interventions with students with learning or attentional difficulties in the general education classroom. Such approaches are likely to enhance success. Pfiffner and Barkley (1991) recommend the STAR program, in which "children learn to *Stop, Think* ahead about what they have to do, *Act* or do the requested task while talking to themselves about the task, and *Review* their results" (p. 529).

Detailed and systematic procedures have been developed for implementing self-management strategies. Some basic recommendations follow:

▶ Allocate sufficient instructional time to teach self-management to students who need it.
▶ Establish a sequence of activities that move by degrees from teacher direction to student direction and self-control.
▶ Include objectives relevant to improved behavior and enhanced learning (e.g., increased attention yields reading achievement gains).
▶ Provide strategies and assistive materials (e.g., self-recording forms) for students to use.
▶ Model how effective self-managers operate. Point out actual applications of the elements of self-management (as highlighted in Figure 14.5), and give students opportunities to practice these techniques with your guidance.
▶ Provide for the maintenance of learned strategies and for generalization to other settings in and out of school.

This section has outlined management strategies to use with a variety of students. Table 14.6 highlights strategies especially helpful to older students.

Behavioral Intervention Plans (BIPs)   The concept of BIPs was introduced in Chapter 4 and explored in more detail in Chapter 7 for its particular relevance to students with emotional and behavioral problems. This planning process, mandated under IDEA for any student displaying serious behavioral problems, is built on the idea of understanding the functions of behavior prior to designing ways to address it. Most behavioral plans will include intervention ideas discussed in this section. A detailed analysis of this federal

CROSS-REFERENCE

Review Chapter 6 on learning disabilities to see how self-monitoring and self-instructional techniques are used with students with learning disabilities.

CROSS-REFERENCE

Refer back to Chapter 4 for a thorough discussion of behavioral intervention plans.

T ABLE 14.6	**Considerations for Working with Adolescents**

Anticipate the likely consequences of any intervention strategy being considered.

Emphasize self-management strategies.

Stress the application of natural and logical consequences.

Use group-oriented contingencies to involve peers in a comprehensive plan for change.

Select only age-appropriate reinforcers.

Avoid response cost procedures that are likely to result in confrontation.

Collaborate with other professionals and parents in designing effective programs.

Select strategies that will not exacerbate problem situations.

requirement for BIPs and functional behavioral assessment is presented by Fad, Patton, and Polloway (1998/2000) and also is discussed by McConnell, Hivitz, and Cox (1998); Simpson (1998); and Zurkowski, Kelly, and Griswold (1998). See the Rights & Responsibilities feature for a discussion of disciplinary issues and federal law.

Instructional Dimension

All of the dimensions discussed in this chapter relate to the broad concern for instructional outcomes. However, certain aspects of instruction are closely related to sound

Rights & Responsibilities

Disciplinary Issues and Federal Law

Under PL 94–142, relevant state statues, and IDEA, students with disabilities were protected from arbitrary suspension or expulsion in instances in which their behavioral difficulty is determined to be related to their disability. This provision was promoted as a major victory for the rights of students with disabilities because it decreased the likelihood that they could be denied a free, appropriate public education. The unforeseen side effect was that the protection of the rights of an individual came to be perceived as a potential threat to school discipline in general and to the safety and security of other students, teachers, and staff by creating a two-tiered system of discipline.

The extent of serious behavioral problems associated with students with disabilities has been a controversial issue. Nevertheless, a distinct minority of such students may present troublesome behaviors that challenge a school's ability to effectively educate all children and youth. As a result, it is not surprising that when possible amendments to the IDEA were discussed, concern was determining the balance between the rights of students with disabilities and the needs for an orderly learning environment in the schools.

The legal resolution of this debate was the incorporation of a requirement for specific practices within the new regulations under PL 105–17 (1997 amendments to IDEA). Foremost among these were the establishment of clearer guidelines for the removal of students with disabilities from the regular school setting, the need for a functional behavioral assessment, and the establishment of a requirement for the development of a behavioral intervention plan for individual students who present challenging behaviors within the school setting. The final regulations issued in March 1999 reaffirmed the use of these procedures.

For follow-up questions about disciplinary issues and federal law, go to Chapter 14 of the Companion Website (ablongman.com/sppd4e) and click Rights & Responsibilities.

Adapted from *Behavioral Intervention Planning* (p. 27) by K. Fad, J. R. Patton, E. A. Polloway, 2000, Austin, TX: Pro-Ed. Used by permission.

organizational and management practices, such as scheduling, transitions, grouping, lesson planning, and technology and can have a significant impact on quality of instruction.

Scheduling involves the general temporal arrangement of events for both (1) the entire day (i.e., master schedule) and (2) a specific class period. This section focuses on the latter. The importance of a carefully planned schedule cannot be overemphasized. This is particularly true in classrooms that include students with special needs.

The thoughtful scheduling of a class period can contribute greatly to the amount of time that students can spend actively engaged in learning. It can also add to the quality of what is learned. For instance, a science lesson might include the following components:

▶ Transitional activities (into the classroom)
▶ Attention-getting and motivating techniques
▶ Data-gathering techniques
▶ Data-processing techniques
▶ Closure activities
▶ Transitional activities (to the next class period)

All components support the instructional goal for the day. Reminders or cues from the teacher can augment such a system. The following are some specific suggestions:

▶ Provide time reminders (visual and audible) for students during the class period so that they know how much time is available.
▶ Plan for transitions (see next section).
▶ Require students to complete one activity or task before moving on to the next.
▶ Vary the nature of class activities to keep students engaged and to create a stimulating instructional tempo and pace.
▶ Minimize noninstructional time when students are not academically engaged.

Scheduling involves planning for class period *transitions.* Efficient transitions can minimize disruptions, maximize the amount of time allocated to instructional tasks, and maintain desired conditions of learning. Structured approaches to transitions will be particularly helpful to students with special needs. Several ways to ease transitions follow:

▶ Model appropriate transitions between activities (Rosenberg et al., 1991).
▶ Let students practice appropriate transition skills.
▶ Use specific cues (e.g., blink lights, a buzzer, teacher signal) to signal students that it is time to change instructional routine.

Several other examples of strategies for transitions are listed in Table 14.7.

Grouping refers to how students are organized for instructional purposes. The need to place students into smaller group arrangements depends on the nature of the curricular area or the goal of a specific lesson. For students with special needs, the main concern within a group setting is attention to individual needs. Using innovative grouping arrangements and providing different cooperative learning opportunities allow for variety in the instructional routine for students with special needs. Some specific suggestions follow:

CROSS-REFERENCE

See Chapter 15 for more information on using grouping strategies for students with disabilities.

▶ Give careful consideration to the makeup of groups.
▶ Make sure that group composition is not constant. Vary membership as a function of having different reasons for grouping students.
▶ Use different grouping arrangements that are based on interest or for research purposes (Wood, 1996).
▶ Use cooperative learning arrangements on a regular basis, as this approach, if structured properly, facilitates successful learning and socialization.
▶ Determine the size of groups based on ability levels: the lower the ability, the smaller the size of the group (Rosenberg et al., 1991).
▶ Use mixed-ability groups when cooperative learning strategies are implemented to promote the active involvement of all students.

TABLE 14.7 **Potential Transition Problems and Suggested Solutions**

Transition Problem	Suggested Solution
Students talk loudly at the beginning of the day. The teacher is interrupted while checking attendance, and the start of content activities is delayed.	Establish a beginning-of-day routine, and clearly state your expectations for student behavior at the beginning of the day.
Students talk too much during transitions, especially after a seatwork assignment has been given but before they have begun working on it. Many students do not start their seatwork activity for several minutes.	Be sure students know what the assignment is; post it where they can easily see it. Work as a whole class on the first several seatwork exercises so that all students begin the lesson successfully and at the same time. Watch what students do during the transition, and urge them along when needed.
Students who go for supplemental instruction stop work early and leave the room noisily while rest of the class is working. When these students return to the room, they disturb others as they come in and take their seats. They interrupt others by asking for directions for assignments.	Have a designated signal that tells these students when they are to get ready to leave, such as a special time on the clock. Have them practice leaving and returning to the room quietly. Reward appropriate behavior. Leave special instructions for what they are to do, when they return, in a folder, on the chalkboard, or on a special sheet at their desks. Or for younger students, establish a special place and activity (e.g., the reading rug) for returning students to wait until you can give them personal attention.
During the late afternoon activity students quit working well before the end; they then begin playing around and leave the room in a mess.	Establish an end-of-day routine so that students continue their work until the teacher gives a signal to begin preparations to leave; then instruct students to help straighten up the room.
Whenever the teacher attempts to move the students from one activity into another, a number of students don't make the transition, but continue working on the preceding activity. This delays the start of the next activity or results in confusion.	Give students a few minutes' notice before an activity is scheduled to end. At the end of the activity students should put all the materials from it away and get out any needed materials for the next activity. Monitor the transition to make sure that all students complete it; do not start the next activity until students are ready.

From *Classroom Management for Elementary Teachers* (2nd ed., pp. 127–128) by C. M. Evertson, E. T. Emmer, B. J. Clements, J. P. Sanford, and M. E. Worsham, 1989, Englewood Cliffs, NJ: Prentice-Hall. Used by permission.

Lesson plans help teachers prepare for instruction. Many teachers start out writing very detailed lesson plans and eventually move to less comprehensive formats. However, some teachers continue to use detailed plans throughout their teaching careers, as they find the detail helpful in providing effective instruction. Detailed planning is frequently needed for lessons that must be modified to be appropriate for gifted students or students

Lesson planning helps teachers prepare for instruction and aids in managing classrooms.

with disabilities. Typical components include objectives, anticipatory set, materials, guided practice, independent practice, closure, options for early finishers, specific accommodations, and evaluation. Suggestions for developing lesson plans follow:

▶ Create interest in and clarify the purpose of lessons. This concern is particularly important for students with special needs.
▶ Consider the importance of direct instruction to help students acquire an initial grasp of new material.
▶ Assign independent practice, some of which can be accomplished in class and some of which should be done as homework.
▶ Plan activities for students who finish early. Such planning might be particularly useful for gifted students.
▶ Anticipate problems that might arise during the course of the lesson, and identify techniques for dealing with them.

Evertson and colleagues (2003) have developed a checklist for planning for instruction—see Table 14.8. The checklist provides a nice way of ensuring that key issues related to an instructional lesson are considered prior to actual instruction. This type of reminder is extremely useful for beginning teachers.

The application of *technology* to curriculum and instruction is widespread today. From a management perspective, teachers must consider a number of variables when deciding to use technology. While more software choices are available commercially these days, the selection of software that is appropriate for students and that relates to instructional objectives requires effort and knowledge. Some suggestions follow:

▶ Consider accessibility needs of students with disabilities.
▶ Obtain necessary input and output devices for students who require such hardware.
▶ Determine whether websites are considerate of students with disabilities.
▶ Make sure that websites are appropriate for usage.
▶ Consider the use of Internet filters.
▶ Design lessons that utilize computers in ways that are engaging.
▶ Teach students dos and don'ts of using e-mail and the Internet (e.g., giving out private information).

Organizational Dimension

The increased diversity in today's general education classrooms has created numerous new challenges for the teacher. Some have likened the current classroom to a "one-room schoolhouse," in which the classroom teacher must respond to the unique needs of many students. This section acknowledges how time management in the areas of personnel interactions, the work environment, administrative duties, instructional applications, and personal applications can promote success. The nearby Personal Spotlight describes how one teacher uses time management techniques.

In the typical education classroom, teachers regularly interact with special education teachers, other classroom teachers, professional support staff (e.g., speech–language pathologists, psychologists), paraeducators, teacher trainees, volunteers, and peer tutors. To enhance *personnel interactions,* teachers should consider these recommendations:

CONSIDER THIS

What are some of the key issues associated with having educational assistants (i.e., paraeducators) working with students with special needs in general education classrooms?

▶ Establish good initial working relationships with support personnel.
▶ Clarify the supports professional personnel are providing to students in your class. See the nearby Inclusion Strategies feature for more ideas.
▶ Clarify the roles of these persons and the classroom teachers as collaborators for instructional and behavioral interventions.
▶ Establish the roles and responsibilities of aides, volunteers, and trainees.
▶ Determine the level of expertise of paraeducators, and discuss with them specific activities that they can perform and supports they can provide to students.

| ABLE 14.8 | **Planning for Instruction Checklist** | |

Check When Complete	Before the Lesson Ask Yourself	Notes
❏	A. What are the most important concepts or skills to be learned?	_____
❏	B. What kind of learning is your goal (memorization, application)?	_____
❏	C. Are there difficult words or concepts that need extra explanation?	_____
❏	D. How will you help students make connections to previous learning?	_____
❏	E. What activities will you plan to create interest in the lesson?	_____
❏	F. How will you make transitions between activities?	_____
❏	G. What materials will be needed? Will students need to learn how to use them?	_____
❏	H. What procedures will students need to know to complete the activities?	_____
❏	I. How much time will you allocate for the lesson? For different parts of the lesson?	_____
❏	J. If activities require that students work togeteher, how will groups be formed? How will you encourage productive work in groups?	_____
❏	K. What examples and questioning strategies will you use? Prepare a list of examples for explanations and list higher-order questions.	_____
❏	L. How will you know during and after the lesson what students understand?	_____
❏	M. What are some presentation alternatives if students have trouble with concepts? Peer explanation, media, etc.?	_____
❏	N. Are there extra- or special-need students?	_____
❏	O. How will you make sure that all students participate?	_____
❏	P. How will you adjust the lesson if time is too short or long?	_____
❏	Q. What kind of product, if any, will you expect from students at the end of the lesson?	_____
❏	R. What will students do when they finish?	_____
❏	S. How will you evaluate students' work and give them feedback?	_____
❏	T. How will the concepts you present be used by students in future lessons?	_____

From *Classroom Management for Elementary Teachers* (pp. 109–110) by C. M. Evertson, E. T. Emmer, and M. E. Worsham, 2003, Boston: Allyn and Bacon. Copyright 2003 by Pearson Education. Reprinted by permission.

▶ Delegate noninstructional (and, as appropriate, instructional) duties to classroom aides when these assistants are available.
▶ In cases in which a paraeducator accompanies a child with a disability in the general education classroom, develop a comprehensive plan with the special education teacher for involving this assistant appropriately.

Personal Spotlight

Third-Grade Teacher

Karen Weeks Canfield is a third grade teacher. As such, she has to deal with a very heterogeneous group of children. Some children in Karen's room have identified disabilities and receive special education for part of the day, some appear to be at risk for developing problems, and others seem to be your "typical nine-year-old." Karen notes that "with so many types of teaching, and with parents involved in the classroom in various ways, attention to organization is critical."

Karen uses several methods to help herself stay organized. Without a certain level of organization, she believes that teaching would be an impossible task. Some of Karen's methods for staying organized are these:

1. Completing forms as soon as she receives them so they do not get lost "in the shuffle"
2. Not taking part in conversations during the school day that do not benefit herself or her students in some way
3. Grading all papers the same day that they are turned in

Karen
Weeks
Canfield

Lynchburg Public Schools, Lynchburg, VA

4. Using a correspondence file for all students so she has a record of all of her communications with parents—both good communication and negative communication
5. Using a "to do" list for her planning periods

These organizational tips help Karen manage her classroom more efficiently. Without such strategies, she believes that she would have to spend a great deal of time at home doing schoolwork, which would take away time from her family.

Karen notes that "being a well-organized teacher affects not only my job performance, but the students' performance as well. The days that I am less organized are the days that the students seem to be 'crazy.' I don't think it's a coincidence. I am constantly looking for ways to make the most out of a priceless commodity—time."

For follow-up questions about this Personal Spotlight, go to Chapter 14 of the Companion Website (ablongman.com/sppd4e) and click Personal Spotlight.

The **work environment** refers to the immediate work area used by teachers—usually the desk and files. Teachers must consider how to utilize work areas and how to organize them. For instance, a teacher's desk may be designated as off-limits to all students or may be used for storage only or as a work area. Suggestions for establishing a work environment are listed here:

▶ Keep the teacher's desk organized and free of stacks of papers.
▶ Organize files so that documents and information can be retrieved easily and quickly.
▶ Use color-coded systems for filing, if possible.

Along with instructional duties, teaching includes numerous *administrative duties*. Two of the most time-demanding activities are participating in meetings and handling paperwork, including various forms of correspondence. The presence of students with special needs will increase such demands. The following are some strategies for handling paperwork:

▶ Prepare form letters for all necessary events (e.g., permissions, notifications, status reports, memo formats, reimbursement requests).
▶ Prepare master copies of various forms that are used regularly (e.g., certificates and awards, record sheets, phone conversation sheets).
▶ Keep notes of all school-related phone conversations with parents, teachers, support staff, administrators, or any other person.
▶ Handle most paperwork only once.
▶ Make the most of meetings—request an agenda and ask that meetings be time-limited and be scheduled at times that are convenient.

TEACHING TIP

Teachers must develop their own time-management strategies; however, adopting strategies that are effective for other teachers may or may not be effective for you.

Collaboration: Ways to Involve Other Personnel in Management

1. The school principal or administrator can
   - supply any necessary equipment or materials.
   - provide flexibility in staffing patterns.
   - show support for the teacher's actions.
2. The school guidance counselor can
   - provide individual counseling sessions.
   - work with other students who may be reinforcing the inappropriate behavior of the disruptive student.
   - offer the teacher information about what may be upsetting to the student.
3. The school nurse can
   - review the student's medical history for possible causes of difficulties.
   - recommend the possibility and practicality of medical or dietary intervention.
   - explain the effects and side effects of any medication the student is taking or may take in the future.
4. The school psychologist can
   - review the teacher's behavior management plan and make recommendations for changes.
   - observe the student in the classroom and in other settings to collect behavioral data and note possible environmental instigators.
   - provide any useful data on the student that may have been recently collected, e.g., test scores, behavioral observations, etc.
5. The social worker can
   - provide additional information about the home environment.
   - schedule regular visits to the home.
   - identify other public agencies that may be of assistance.
6. Other teachers can
   - provide curricular and behavior management suggestions that work for them.
   - offer material resources.
   - provide carryover and consistency for the tactics used.

For follow-up questions about collaboration, go to Chapter 14 of the Companion Website (ablongman.com/sppd4e) and click Inclusion Strategies.

Adapted from *The Special Educator's Handbook* (p. 119) by D. L. Westling and M. A. Koorland, 1989, Boston: Allyn and Bacon. Used by permission.

Some additional *instructional applications* of time-management techniques are provided here, focusing on materials and technology that can make the job of teaching easier. The most attractive piece of equipment available to teachers is the microcomputer. With the appropriate software, teachers can greatly reduce the amount of time spent on test generation, graphic organizers, IEP development, and so on. The following are some specific suggestions:

- Use self-correcting materials with students to reduce the amount of time required to correct student work.
- Use grade-book programs for recording student scores and determining grades.
- Use computers to generate a variety of instructionally related materials (tests, graphic organizers, puzzles).
- Give students computer-generated calendars that include important dates.

Since it is impossible to completely divorce the management of one's personal time from management of professional time, it is worthwhile considering various time-management tactics that have a more *personal application* but can affect one's efficiency and effectiveness in the classroom as well. Some basic recommendations are provided here:

- Use a daily to-do list.
- Break down major tasks into smaller pieces and work on them.
- Avoid getting overcommitted.

▶ Work during work time. This might mean avoiding situations at school in which long social conversations will cut into on-task time.

▶ Avoid dealing with trivial activities if important ones must be addressed.

▶ Use idle time (e.g., waiting in lines) well. Always be prepared for these situations by having reading material or other portable work available.

The efficient management of one's professional and personal time can pay off in making day-to-day demands less overwhelming. Thus, the efforts to become a better time manager are certainly worthwhile.

Summary

Basic Concepts About Classroom Management and Organization

▶ Classroom management includes all teacher-directed activities that support the efficient operations of the classroom and establish optimal conditions for learning.

▶ The key elements of the classroom environment that have a significant effect on instruction and learning include multidimensionality, simultaneity, immediacy, unpredictability, publicness, and history, while the key principles of successful management are careful planning, proactive strategies, consistency, awareness, and overlapping.

Components of Effective Classroom Organization and Management

▶ Classroom rules provide a general sense of what is expected of students.

▶ Rules chosen should be essential for classroom functioning and for the development of a positive learning environment.

▶ Classroom procedures should include the specific ways in which certain activities or situations will be performed.

▶ Effective physical management includes classroom arrangement, accessibility, seating, and the use of specialized equipment.

▶ Desirable behaviors are increased through the use of positive reinforcement.

▶ Undesirable behaviors can be reduced through a variety of reduction strategies.

▶ Hierarchy of options would include (from least to most restrictive) natural and logical consequences, differential reinforcement, extinction, benign tactics, reprimands, response costs, and time out.

▶ Successful educational programs help students develop self-management strategies.

▶ Instructional management includes careful attention to scheduling, transitions, grouping, and lesson plans.

▶ Successful teachers are organized and engage in the careful management of time. Technology can assist teachers in time management.

▶ Teachers need to take the student's culture into consideration when dealing with management issues.

Further Readings

Christian, B. T. (1999). *Outrageous behavior modification.* Austin, TX: Pro-Ed.

Everston, C., Emmer, E. T., & Worsham, M. E. (2003). *Classroom management for elementary teachers* (6th ed.). Boston: Allyn and Bacon.

Everston, C., Emmer, E. T., & Worsham, M. E. (2003). *Classroom management for secondary teachers* (6th ed.). Boston: Allyn and Bacon.

Fad, K. M., Patton, J. R., & Polloway, E. A. (2000). *Behavioral intervention planning* (rev. ed.). Austin, TX: Pro-Ed.

Hammill, D. D., & Bartel, N. R. (1995). *Teaching students with learning and behavior problems.* Austin, TX: Pro-Ed.

Jones, V. F., & Jones, L. S. (2001). *Comprehensive classroom management: Creating positive learning environments for all students* (6th ed.). Boston: Allyn and Bacon.

Kaplan, J. S., & Carter, J. (1999). *Beyond behavior modification: A cognitive-behavioral approach to behavior management in the school* (3rd ed.). Austin, TX: Pro-Ed.

Koegel, L. K., Koegel, R. L., & Dunlap, G. (Eds.). (1996). *Positive behavioral support.* Baltimore: Brookes.

Lavelle, L. (1998). *Practical charts for managing behavior.* Austin, TX: Pro-Ed.

Levin, J., & Nolan, J. F. (2000). *Principles of classroom management* (3rd ed.). Boston: Allyn and Bacon.

McConnell, K., Reyser, G., & Patton, J. R. (2002). *Practical ideas that really work for disruptive, defiant, and difficult students: Preschool through grade 4.* Austin, TX: Pro-Ed.

McConnell, K., Reyser, G., & Patton, J. R. (2002). *Practical ideas that really work for disruptive, defiant, and difficult students: Grades 5 through 12.* Austin, TX: Pro-Ed.

Scotti, J. R., & Meyer, L. H. (Eds.). (1999). *Behavioral intervention: Principles, models, and practices.* Baltimore: Brookes.

VideoWorkshop Extra!

If the VideoWorkshop package was included with your textbook, go to Chapter 14 of the Companion Website (www.ablongman.com/sppd4e) and click on the VideoWorkshop button. Follow the instructions for viewing video clips 5 and 10. Then consider this information along with what you've read in Chapter 14 while answering the following questions.

1. The two video clips show several students with significant behavioral problems. This chapter offers a number of interventions and strategies for helping children achieve age-appropriate classroom behavior.

   a. What interventions and/or strategies would you use with Eric?
   b. What interventions and/or strategies would you use with Nick?

2. Most public schools have support staff to help with students who have special needs, such as a school psychologist, social worker, or nurse. How will you involve these specialists in your classroom efforts to instruct students with special needs?

15 Teaching Students with Special Needs in Elementary Schools

After reading this chapter, you should be able to

1. describe the impact of inclusion on elementary students with disabilities.
2. define the concept of comprehensive curriculum for students at the elementary level.
3. identify curricular content considerations for academic, social skills, and transitional instruction.
4. describe ways that collaboration can enhance inclusion in elementary schools.
5. identify appropriate instructional adaptations.

Asha Kim was told by one of her college professors that the elementary classrooms of the new millennium were becoming increasingly similar to the "one-room schoolhouses of the turn of the twentieth century," encompassing a diversity of learning needs that had never been greater. Asha was excited by this challenge and, in her first year of teaching, often reflected on this comment.

Asha is teaching a class of second graders in a self-contained general education class. She has responsibility for 22 eager students for all subjects except art, music, health, and physical education. She has found their diversity to be exciting and somewhat overwhelming.

Naturally, one of her greatest concerns has been in the area of language arts. After doing some informal observations and after reading the records of her students, she realized during the second week of the academic year that the ability levels of her students ranged greatly; two students were virtual nonreaders, whereas five pupils were functioning significantly above grade level in terms of their academic achievement.

It has become apparent to Asha that these students do not all learn in the same way, but she continues to struggle to find approaches that will meet the needs of this diverse classroom. She is fortunate to be working two hours a day during her language arts instructional block with Elise Ramirez, a special education teacher who is certified in learning disabilities.

QUESTIONS TO CONSIDER

1. How can Asha and Elise develop effective collaboration strategies that will take advantage of their own talents and meet the needs of their students?
2. How can they resolve their ongoing questions about approaches for instruction for beginning readers in general and for those with learning difficulties?
3. What curriculum adaptations can be made to more effectively meet the needs of students with special needs in this classroom?

This opening vignette illustrates a point that is consistent with the discussion in the early chapters of the book: elementary school presents unique challenges and unique opportunities for young students with special needs who are included in general education. Although the learning needs of the students are frequently quite diverse and challenging, the degree of curricular differentiation (i.e., the need for alternative curricular focuses) is typically much more limited than it will be at the secondary level. In elementary school, the relative similarity of educational content for all students is at its greatest. Thus, in terms of curricular content there is an excellent opportunity for students with special needs to prosper in general education with the appropriate supports in place.

Elementary school also offers an important beginning point for students with disabilities to profit from positive interactions with their peers who are not disabled. Preparation for successful lives beyond the school setting requires the ability to learn, live, and work with a diversity of individuals. Thus, inclusion offers benefits both to students who are disabled and to their peers. There is clearly no better time for school interaction to commence than in early childhood and throughout the primary and elementary grades.

The advent of the inclusion movement has increased the likelihood that many young students with disabilities will receive a significant portion, or all, of their instruction in the general education classroom. According to the *23rd Annual Report to Congress,* 57.2% of all students with disabilities (ages 6–11) were served in general education for at least 79% of the school day, while an additional 23.6% were in regular classes for 40–79% of the day during 1998–1999. These data reflect a clear trend (U.S. Department of Education, 2001). Thus, beginning at the elementary level, careful attention must be given to these students' educational needs.

This chapter provides an overview of curricular and instructional accommodations for elementary-age students with special needs. The initial section outlines core curriculum considerations. The discussion that follows emphasizes instructional accommodations and modifications that provide the means for achieving curricular goals.

General Curricular Considerations

Curriculum has been defined in varied ways. For example, Armstrong (1990) refers to it as a "master plan for selecting content and organizing learning experiences for the purpose of changing and developing learners' behaviors and insights" (p. 4). For all students, any consideration of curriculum should include an outcomes orientation; our concept of curriculum thus must embrace consideration for the preparation of students for life after the completion of K–12 schooling.

Although curriculum design often is preordained in general education programs, it is nevertheless important to consider the concept of *comprehensive curriculum.* The concept takes into account the reality that students are enrolled in school on a time-limited basis. Educators must consider what will happen to their students in the future and consider the environments that students will need to adapt to in order to function successfully. Thus, curriculum design should be predicated on a focus on these **subsequent environments** (e.g., middle school, high school, college, community). The degree to which this subsequent-environments attitude permeates general education will significantly affect the ultimate success of students with disabilities taught in such settings.

An elementary-level comprehensive curriculum therefore would reflect the following qualities:

▸ Responsive to the needs of the individual at the current time
▸ Reflective of the need to balance maximum interaction with peers against critical curricular needs

---

CONSIDER THIS

Inclusive classrooms are more common at the elementary level than at the secondary. Why do you think this statement is true?

) Derived from a realistic appraisal of potential long-term outcomes for individual students

) Consistent with relevant forthcoming transitional needs (e.g., transition from elementary to middle school) (adapted from Polloway, Patton, Epstein, & Smith, 1989)

As mentioned before, the curricular needs of the vast majority of students at the elementary level, both those with and those without special needs, are quite consistent. Thus, with appropriate modification in instruction and with collaborative arrangements, most students' needs can be met entirely, or to a significant extent, in the general education classroom.

Curricular Content

Academic Instruction

Elementary students in general, and certainly most students with disabilities, primarily need sound instruction in reading, writing, and mathematics to maximize their academic achievement. These needs can typically be met by a developmental approach to instruction, supplemented as needed by a remedial focus for students who experience difficulty. In the sections that follow, an overview of principles and practices is provided.

Reading Instruction   Reading problems are a foremost concern for all elementary teachers working in inclusive classrooms. Young students with special needs commonly experience difficulties in both the decoding processes inherent in word recognition as well as in reading comprehension. In a general sense, educators have responded to the need for quality instruction by selecting one (or a combination) of the three common approaches in elementary-level reading and language arts programs: (1) **basal series,** (2) **direct instruction,** and (3) **whole language.**

Basal Series   Basal series, or graded class-reading texts, are the most typical means of teaching reading and, for that matter, other curricular domains including spelling and math, in the elementary school. Most reading basals are intended to meet developmental needs in reading. However, there is a multiplicity of programs, and it would be impossible to typify the focus of all basal series. Although basals are routinely criticized, Polloway, Smith, and Miller (2003) indicated that such series have both advantages and disadvantages. They noted that on the positive side, basals contain inherent structure and sequence, a controlled vocabulary, a wide variety of teaching activities, and materials that provide preparation for the teacher. Weaknesses, on the other hand, include possible inappropriate pacing for an individual child, a common concern for certain skills to the exclusion of others, and the encouragement of group instructional orientation.

Direct Instruction   Direct instruction (i.e., the directive teaching of skills) has often been associated with a remedial perspective, although it clearly has played a significant preventive role as well. Often it has been tied to a focus on basic skills, which has typically constituted the core of most elementary special education curricula. In the area of reading, direct instruction programs are most often associated with an emphasis on decoding skills.

Basic skills programs typically are built on the development of phonological awareness (i.e., a sensitivity to the sounds inherent in our language system) and subsequently phonetic analysis instruction. Research on beginning reading emphasizes the critical importance of children developing sound-symbol correspondences as a basis for subsequent reading success (Center for Future of Teaching and Learning, 1996; Mather, Bos, & Babur, 2001; National Reading Panel, 2000; Pressley & Rankin, 1994; Shaywitz & Shaywitz, 1997).

CONSIDER THIS

Although general educators can rarely offer a truly "comprehensive curriculum," collaborative efforts with special educators can effect a more broad-based program. How can this work?

CONSIDER THIS

Basal programs vary significantly in terms of emphasis. How does this variability affect students with special needs?

Fletcher, Francis, and Schatschneider (1998) noted:

> Underlying both success and failure in word recognition is the development of phonological awareness. . . . When children learn how print represents the internal structure of words, they become accurate at word recognition; when they learn to recognize words quickly and automatically, they become fluent. . . . For some children . . . learning these skills is not straightforward. In the absence of explicit instruction in word recognition and phonological awareness skills, our research suggests that many [high risk] children are destined to a life of reading failure. (pp. 3–4)

Basic skills programs typically have a long-term orientation based on the assumption that such skills ultimately will increase students' academic achievement and enable all to reach at least a minimal level of functional literacy. Not all skills programs are equally effective; those that incorporate effective instructional practice have most often empirically demonstrated substantial gains in achievement (e.g., Kavale & Forness, 1999). The characteristic features of successful direct instruction programs which mirror research on effective instruction include high levels of academic engaged time, signals for attention, ongoing feedback to learners, group-based instruction, fast pacing, and error-free learning.

Whole Language   Whole language approaches (i.e., programs that primarily emphasize meaning in the beginning of the reading process) at the primary and elementary level dramatically increased in popularity in the 1990s. They embrace a more holistic view of learning than direct instruction, which tends to be oriented much more to specific skills acquisition. Whole language programs attempt to break down barriers within the area of language arts between reading, writing, and speaking, as well as barriers between reading and other curricular areas, by stressing an integrated approach to learning.

Polloway, Patton, and Serna (2001) provide a series of examples of whole language:

> . . . orally sharing stories by the teacher; sustained silent reading; silent reading time segments in which students write responses to what they are reading and share this with other students or with the teacher in individual conferences; language experience activities in which children write stories in a group or individually to be used for future reading experiences; time set aside for large group writing instruction followed by students' writing, revising, editing, and sharing their own writing; and finally reading and writing activities that involve a content area theme such as science or social studies. (p. 241)

Whole language programs rely on authentic reading sources (e.g., literature) as the main source of content for reading opportunities. The use of literature (e.g., novels, stories, magazine articles) has the following advantages: it is varied; it is current, since it reaches the market quickly; it provides a basis for meeting diverse student needs and interests; and it offers alternative views on topics and issues as well as opportunities to study them in depth. In addition, with the broad spectrum of choices in literature, students can be given more opportunity to select their own reading material (Mandlebaum, Lightbourne, & VardenBrock, 1994).

Though holistic programs remain popular, questions arose in the late 1990s about their use, particularly with students who are at risk or have identified disabilities. Mastropieri and Scruggs (1997) pointed to the issue of validation:

> In part, experimental research is lacking because of the position taken by many advocates of whole language that traditional, quantitative research, including quantitative measures of reading achievement, is not valid. However, qualitative research to date has failed to demonstrate the superiority of whole language methods in facilitating reading comprehension of students with learning disabilities over direct, skill-based teaching. . . . Until more empirical evidence . . . becomes available, teachers should be advised to proceed with caution. Nevertheless, some aspects of whole language, such as students making choices about their reading, having time for private reading, and taking ownership for their own learning, appear positive. (pp. 208–209)

The emphasis on meaning inherent in holistic approaches takes on greater emphasis as students move through the elementary grades. Comprehension thus becomes "arguably, the most important academic skill learned in school" (Mastropieri & Scruggs, 1997, p. 197).

Reading Perspectives   These reading methods can each enhance the inclusion of students with disabilities in general academic programs. However, teachers must review progress on a regular basis and make modifications as needed, because it is unlikely that a single program can meet all of a student's needs. Mather (1992), in her review of the literature, argued persuasively that students who are not good readers need specific skill instruction to achieve satisfactory progress. The challenge for classroom teachers is to balance the needs of able readers (for whom explicit instruction in phonics may prove unnecessary and for whom meaning-based instruction is clearly most appropriate) with the needs of students who require more systematic instruction to unlock the alphabetic relationships within our written language.

Inclusion presents a complex challenge in the area of curriculum design. Teachers who adhere solely to one position concerning reading instruction may inadvertently neglect the learning needs of individual children who experience difficulties in school. Outstanding teachers, in contrast, draw eclectically from a variety of approaches to design reading programs (Pressley & Rankin, 1994).

Mather, Bos, and Babur (2001) noted in their research review that it was critical that general education teachers be aware that

> early, systematic instruction in phonological awareness provided in the general education classroom improves children's early reading and spelling skills and results in a reduction of the number of students who are reading below grade level and are identified as having learning disabilities. . . . Children who continue to fail at reading require instructional approaches that focus on phonemic awareness, phonic skills, and the application of these skills to real words in text. (p. 492)

A broader view of reading needs for children was reflected by Foorman and Torgeson (2001), who summarized the foci of programs needed to foster reading success in children. They concluded:

> Effective classroom reading instruction on phonemic awareness, phonemic decoding, fluency in word recognition and text processing, construction of meaning, vocabulary, spelling, and writing can maximize the probability that all but a very small percentage of children can learn to read on grade level. To address the needs of this small percentage we need to provide additional instruction on the same components in a small-group or one-on-one format. . . . [It] will need to be more explicit and comprehensive, more intensive, and more supportive than that typically provided by schools. (p. 210)

Recent research has also provided guidance regarding the teaching of reading comprehension. The National Reading Panel (2000) summarized the results of more than 200 studies and concluded that eight instructional strategies were most effective:

1. Comprehension monitoring: readers learn how to be conscious of their understanding during reading and learn procedures to deal with problems in understanding as they arise.
2. Cooperative learning: readers work together to learn strategies in the context of reading.
3. Graphic and semantic organizers: readers learn to present graphically the meanings and relationships of the ideas that underlie the words in the text.
4. Story structure: readers learn to ask and answer who, what, where, when, and why questions about the plot and map out the timeline, characters, and events in stories.
5. Question answering: readers answer questions posed by the teacher and are given feedback on the correctness of their answers.
6. Question generation: readers ask what, when, were, why, what will happen, how, and who questions.
7. Summarization: readers attempt to identify and write the main idea that integrates the other meanings of the text into a coherent whole.

CONSIDER THIS

The emphasis on meaning and the integration of the language arts make whole language approaches particularly attractive for use with students with special needs. Why do you think these approaches are effective?

8. Multiple-strategy teaching: readers use several of these procedures and interact with the teacher over the text (adapted from pp. 4–6).

One program for elementary reading instruction developed by Englert, Mariage, Garmon, and Tarrant (1998) illustrates how an approach that blends holistic and skills-based reading foci can be established within the context of effective instructional principles. Their Early Literacy Project has been used effectively with students with special needs in inclusive classrooms and involves a combination of instructional activities. Table 15.1 summarizes these elements.

Writing   Elementary-age children with special needs commonly experience problems with writing, especially with written expression. It is essential that they be given ample opportunities to write and that appropriate attention be given to handwriting and spelling (see Polloway, Miller, & Smith, 2003, for a fuller discussion of writing instruction).

TABLE 15.1   Early Literacy Project

Activity	Description	Purpose
Thematic Unit	▶ Teacher and students brainstorm, organize, write drafts, read texts, or interview people to get additional information about a topic or theme from multiple sources ▶ Students use reading/writing strategies flexibly to develop and communicate their knowledge ▶ Theme is used as basis for selecting expository and narrative texts, and to organize and relate all activities ▶ Reading and writing are continuously connected as students participate in discussions and read for information as a basis for writing, comprehending and responding to texts	Model learning-to-learn strategies; introduce language, genres, and strategies; model reading/writing processes and connections; provide interrelated and meaningful contexts for acquisition and application of literacy knowledge; conventionalize and develop shared knowledge about the purpose, meaning, and self-regulation of literacy acts
Choral Reading	▶ Teachers and students chorally read poems, predictable books, class stories, literature, student-authored texts ▶ Teachers model and teach a number of reading strategies, including predicting, organizing, summarizing, asking questions, rereading, locating information, and clarifying meaning	Develop word recognition, phonic skills, context clues, and voice-print match Provide experience reading whole texts and talking about literature Develop literacy success immediately Develop comprehension and personal response to texts
Undisturbed Silent Reading	Students engage in reading under several conditions: ▶ Reading alone ▶ Reading to an adult or peer ▶ Listening to new story at listening center	Develop fluency; provide practice in preparation for author's chair; provide experience with varied genres; read texts related to thematic unit Students ask and answer questions; prepare to make comments about or interpretations of the stories
Partner Reading/Writing	▶ Students read books or poems; or write stories with partner or small group ▶ Students listen to taped stories with partner ▶ Students make personal responses to texts, complete story maps, or construct maps with partners that will be shared with whole class	Work on fluency for author's chair; provide opportunities for students to fluently read and write connected texts; provide opportunities for students to use literacy language and knowledge; develop reading/writing vocabulary and enjoyment of reading
Sharing Chair	▶ Students share books, poems, or their own personal writing ▶ Students control discourse and support each other ▶ Students ask questions, answer questions and act as informants to peers and teacher	Promote reading/writing connection; empower students as members of the community; allow students to make public their literacy knowledge and performance and develop shared knowledge; develop students' notions of "community"

In a recent research review, Vaughn, Gersten, and Chard (2000) summarized findings in research with students in third through ninth grades. They concluded that best practices in expressive writing instruction included the following:

▸ *Explicit teaching of the critical steps in the writing process.* This was often supported by a "think sheet," prompt card, or mnemonic. However, the teacher invariably modeled how to use these steps by writing several samples.
▸ *Explicit teaching of the conventions of a writing genre.* These "text structures" provided a guide for undertaking the writing task at hand, whether it was a persuasive essay, a personal narrative, or an essay comparing and contrasting two phenomena.
▸ *Guided feedback.* Teachers or peers provided frequent feedback to students on the quality of their work, elements missing from their work, and the strengths of their work. (p. 103)

▸ Activity	▸ Description	▸ Purpose
Morning News	▸ Students dictate personal-experience stories for newspaper publication—group composition of story ▸ Teacher acts as a scribe in recording ideas and as a coach in modeling, guiding, and prompting literacy strategies in text composition and comprehension ▸ Students interact with authors to ask questions which elicit information from that author in order to shape and edit the language and content of the news story	Model and conventionalize writing and self-monitoring strategies; demonstrate writing conventions and skills; provide additional reading and comprehension experiences; make connections between oral and written texts; promote sense of community; empower students; provide meaningful and purposeful contexts for literacy strategies
Story Response/ Discussion	▸ Students read narrative stories and respond to them in various ways (e.g., sequence or illustrate story events, map story events or informamation, summarize story, make personal response, etc.) ▸ Students work with partners or small groups to develop response	Promote students' application of literacy strategies; present varied genres to students; promote students' ownership of the discourse about texts; further students' enjoyment of texts; make text structures visible to students
Journal Writing	▸ Students write entries in a journal ▸ Teachers may assign topic related to thematic unit which requires students to write, or they may ask students to write freely about any self-selected topic ▸ Teacher reads and responds to journal, or asks students to share journal entry in sharing chair	Promote writing fluency; provide opportunities for students to write varied genres and about personal topics; provide an opportunity for students to write stories that they can share with other members of the classroom during sharing chair; provide specific occasions for students to experience and develop specific writing strategies (e.g., generate written retellings about a narrative or expository text)
Author's Center	▸ Process writing approach (students plan, organize, gather information from sources, draft, edit, and publish texts) ▸ Students write and work collaboratively to brainstorm ideas, gather additional information from texts, write drafts, share drafts, receive questions, and write final draft ▸ Students use literacy and learning-to-learn strategies modeled in thematic center	Develop sense of community; develop shared knowledge; provide opportunities for students to rehearse literacy strategies; empower students in the appropriation and transformation of strategies
Project Read	▸ Sound–symbol correspondences are emphasized ▸ Students are taught how to perform phonemic segmentation and sound blending in order to read and spell words ▸ Students learn "red words" which represent sight words that are not phonetically regular	Develop basic skills for recognizing and spelling printed words

From "Accelerating Reading Progress in Early Literacy Project Classrooms: Three Exploratory Studies" (pp. 144–145) by C. S. Englert, T. B. Mariage, M. A. Garman, and K. L. Tarrant, 1998, *Remedial and Special Education, 19.* Used by permission.

A key concern is to provide sufficient opportunities to write that are seen as meaningful tasks (e.g., writing for an authentic audience, or treating a topic that is important or interesting to the student). Graham (1992) suggests the following ideas for providing frequent and meaningful writing opportunities:

▶ Assist students in thinking about what they will write.
▶ Ask students to establish goals for what they hope to achieve.
▶ Arrange the writing environment so that the teacher is not the sole audience for students' writing.
▶ Provide opportunities for students to work on the same project across days or even weeks.
▶ Incorporate writing into broad-based curricular activities (e.g., integrated curriculum). (p. 137)

Portfolios represent a positive approach to enhancing the development of writing. They involve students in the evaluation of their own writing samples by allowing them to select samples to be kept and letting them compare changes in their writing over time.

Mathematics   Mathematics represents a third potentially challenging academic area for students with disabilities. Development of both computational skills and problem-solving abilities forms the foundation of successful math instruction and learning.

Computation   In the area of computation, teachers should focus first on the students' conceptual understanding of a particular skill and then on the achievement of automaticity with the skill. Cawley's (1984) interactive unit and Miller, Mercer, and Dillon's (1992) concrete/semiconcrete/abstract systems afford excellent options to the teacher (Figure 15.1). The interactive unit gives teachers 16 options for teaching math skills, based on four teacher input variables and four student output variables. The resulting 4 × 4 matrix provides a variety of instructional approaches that can be customized to assist learners who experience difficulties. The interactive unit also reflects a logical process that begins with the important emphasis on the concrete instructional activities (manipulate/manipulate) to build mathematical concepts, moves to a semiconcrete focus (display/identify) to enhance concept development, and arrives at the abstract (say/say, write/write), which focuses on achieving automaticity (e.g., automatic responses to math facts). These emphases offer two proven benefits in the general education classroom: they have been used successfully with students with disabilities, and they offer alternative teaching strategies for all learners—a particularly significant advantage, given that math is the most common area of failure in schools.

Problem Solving   Problem solving can be particularly difficult for students with disabilities and thus warrants special attention. For learners with special needs, and for many other students as well, instruction in specific problem-solving strategies can greatly enhance math understanding. After a problem-solving strategy has been selected or designed, the strategy's steps should be taught and followed systematically so that students learn to reason through problems and understand problem-solving processes. One such example is the SOLVE-IT strategy (Figure 15.2). Inherent in each step is a focus on an area of difficulty common to students with special needs (e.g., "O"—learning to identify distracting information in real-life problems and omitting it from problem solutions). The use of learning strategies in general and their value for students with and without disabilities are discussed further in Chapter 16.

The potential benefits of including students with special needs in general education classrooms to study core academic areas also extend to *other academic areas*. Subjects such as science, social studies, health and family life, and the arts offer excellent opportunities for social integration, while effective instructional strategies can lead to academic achievement. These subjects also lend themselves well to integrated curricular approaches (discussed later in the chapter). **Cooperative teaching** (also discussed later in the chapter) presents an excellent instructional alternative in these areas because it combines the

FIGURE 15.1   **Interactive Unit Model**

Group A: Geometry (8 students)	Group B: Fractions (10 students)	Group C: Addition (5 students)
Manipulate/Manipulate* *Input:* Teacher walks the perimeter of a geometric shape. *Output:* Learner does the same.	**Display/Write** *Input:* Write the fraction that names the shaded part. 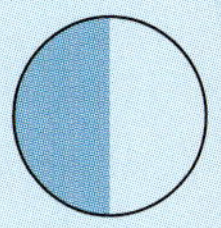 *Output:* Learner writes $\frac{1}{2}$	**Write/Write** *Input:* $\begin{array}{r} 3 \\ +2 \\ \hline \end{array}$ Write the answer. *Output:* Learner writes 5
Display/Identify *Input:* 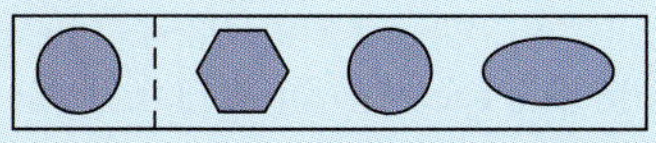 From the choices, mark the shape that is the same as the first shape. *Output:* Learner marks 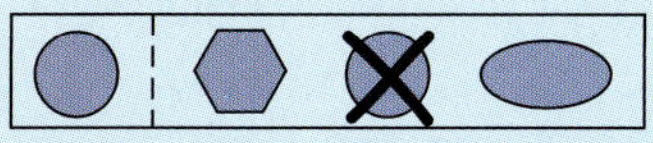	**Manipulate/Say*** *Input:* 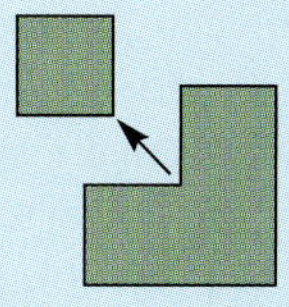 Teacher removes portion of shape and asks learner to name the part. *Output:* Learner says, "One fourth"	**Display/Write** *Input:* 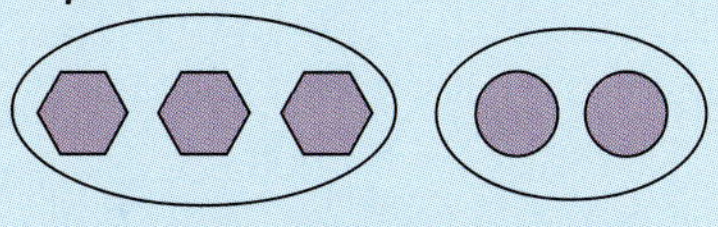 Write the number there is in all. *Output:* Learner writes 5
Write/Identify *Input:* 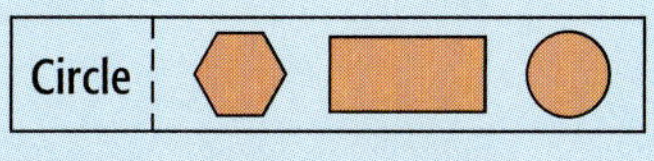 Circle Mark the shape that shows the word. *Output:* Learner marks 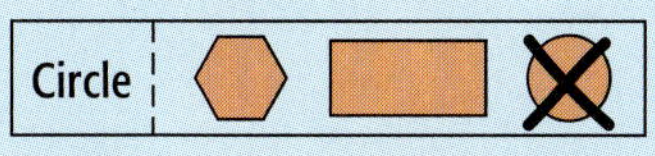 Circle	**Write/Write** *Input:* one half Write this word statement as a numeral. *Output:* Learner writes $\frac{1}{2}$	**Say/Say*** *Input:* Teacher says, "I am going to say some addition items. Six plus six. Tell me the answer." *Output:* Learner says, "Twelve"

Row time labels (left margin): 15 minutes / 15 minutes / 15 minutes

*Teacher present in group

From *Developmental Teaching of Mathematics for the Learning Disabled* (p. 246) by J. F. Cawley (Ed.), 1984, Austin, TX: Pro-Ed. Copyright 1984 by Pro-Ed, Inc. Used by permission.

FIGURE 15.2

**Problem-Solving Strategy
for Mathematics**

From *Strategies for Teaching Learners with
Special Needs* (7th ed., p. 328) by E. A.
Polloway, J. R. Patton, and L. Serna, 2001,
Columbus, OH: Merrill. Used by permission.

S	**SAY**	the problem to yourself (repeat).
O	**OMIT**	any unnecessary information from the problem.
L	**LISTEN**	for key vocabulary indicators.
V	**VOCABULARY**	Change vocabulary to math concepts.
E	**EQUATION**	Translate problem into a math equation.
I	**INDICATE**	the answer.
T	**TRANSLATE**	the answer back into the context of the word problem.

expertise and resources of the classroom teacher with the talents of the special education teacher, rather than requiring them each to develop separate curricula in these respective curricular areas.

Social Skills Instruction

As discussed in earlier chapters, virtually all students identified with mental retardation or emotional and behavioral disorders, and many with learning disabilities, have difficulties related to the development of *social skills* (Cullinan & Epstein, 1985). The challenge for classroom teachers is to find ways to incorporate this focus in their classes. Seeking assistance from a special education teacher or a counselor is a good idea. Because performance in the social domain is often predictive of success or failure in inclusive settings, the development of social skills should not be neglected. Gresham (1984) noted some years ago that students with disabilities interact infrequently and, to a large extent, negatively with their peers because many lack the social skills that would enable them to gain acceptance by their peers. This observation remains valid.

Polloway et al. (2001) identified four approaches to educating students about appropriate social behavior: (1) direct social skills training, (2) behavioral change, (3) affective

Science class offers an excellent opportunity for social integration of students with special needs.

education, and (4) cognitive interventions. **Direct social skills training** focuses on attaining skills that help students overcome situations in classrooms and elsewhere that prevent assimilation. A **behavioral change strategy** typically targets a behavior that needs modification and creates a reinforcement system that will lead to a behavior change. Steps in such programs typically include selecting the target behavior, collecting baseline data, identifying reinforcers, implementing a procedure for reinforcing appropriate behaviors, and evaluating the intervention (see Chapter 14). **Affective education** typically emphasizes the relationship between self and others in the environment. The emotional, rather than only the behavioral, aspects of social adjustment figure prominently in this approach. Finally, **cognitive interventions** (see Chapter 14) have proved fruitful (Kavale & Forness, 1999) in effecting behavioral change and social skills acquisition; they involve teaching students to monitor their own behavior, engage in self-instruction, and design and implement their own reinforcement programs. The four programs offer options for social adjustment programming in the future. However, teachers should carefully evaluate their success and modify programs accordingly. All educators agree about the importance of social competence, but, as discussed in Chapter 7, concern remains about the modest effects that social skills instruction has had, according to research (Kavale, 2001).

Korinek and Polloway (1993) note several key considerations related to instruction for students who have difficulties in the social area. First, priority should be given to skills most needed for immediate interactions in the classroom, thus enhancing the likelihood of a student's successful inclusion. Teachers can begin by teaching behaviors that will "naturally elicit desired responses from peers and adults" (Nelson, 1988, p. 21), such as sharing, smiling, asking for help, attending, taking turns, following directions, and solving problems (McConnell, 1987). These skills will promote social acceptance and can be applied across many settings.

A second consideration involves selecting a social adjustment program that promotes both social skills and social competence. Whereas social skills facilitate individual interpersonal interactions, **social competence** involves the broader ability to use skills at the right times and places, showing social perception, cognition, and judgment of how to act in different situations (Sargent, 1991). A focus limited to specific skill training may make it difficult for the child to maintain the specific social skills or transfer them to various settings. Table 15.2 outlines a typical sequence within a social skills curriculum.

Third, a decision must be made as to who will teach social skills. Often initial instruction occurs in pull-out programs (e.g., resource rooms) with generalization plans developed for transfer to the general education classroom. For inclusive classrooms, a useful strategy is the use of the complementary instructional model of cooperative teaching (see Chapter 2).

Finally, there is a need to consider those who have significant learning needs, as the placement of students with severe disabilities in inclusive classes has clear implications for the social environment. Research provides little assurance that the social skills of these students will develop simply because they are physically integrated into such classes. McEnvoy, Shores, Wehby, Johnson, and Fox's (1990) research review reveals that the more that teachers provide specific instruction, physical prompts, modeling, and praise directed to the acquisition and maintenance of social skills, the more these students succeed in learning appropriate patterns of interaction.

Transitional Needs

In addition to the academic and social components of the curriculum, career education and transition form an important emphasis even for younger children. For all elementary students, career awareness and a focus on facilitating movement between levels of schooling (i.e., vertical transitions) are curricular essentials. Figure 15.3 outlines key vertical transitions and also illustrates the concept of horizontal transitions (i.e., from more to less restrictive settings).

T ABLE 15.2   **Sample Social Skills Curriculum Sequence**

Session I	**Session IV**
Listening	Suggesting an activity to others
Meeting people—introducing self, introducing others	Working cooperatively
Beginning a conversation	Offering help
Listening during a conversation	**Session V**
Ending a conversation	Saying thank you
Joining an ongoing activity	Giving and accepting a compliment
Session II	Rewarding self
Asking questions appropriately	**Session VI**
Asking favors appropriately	Apologizing
Seeking help from peers and adults	Understanding the impact your behavior has on others
Following directions	Understanding others' behavior
Session III	
Sharing	
Interpreting body language	
Playing a game successfully	

From *Managing Attention Disorders in Children: A Guide for Practitioners* (pp. 342–343) by S. Goldstein and M. Goldstein, 1990, New York: John Wiley. Used by permission.

Transition from Preschool to Primary School   Research on students moving from preschool programs into school settings has identified variables that predict success in school. Four such variables include early academic (i.e., readiness) skills, social skills, responsiveness to instructional styles, and responsiveness to the structure of the school environment (Polloway et al., 1992). Analyzing the new school environment can help a teacher determine the skills a student will need to make this crucial adjustment.

Academic readiness skills have traditionally been cited as good predictors of success at the primary school level. Examples include the ability to recognize numbers and letters, grasp a writing utensil, count to ten, and write letters and numbers. Yet a clear delineation between academic readiness and academic skills is not warranted. Rather, to use reading as an example, it is much more productive to consider readiness as inclusive of examples of early reading skills, or what has been termed *emergent literacy*. Programming in this area should focus on academic activities that advance the processes of learning to read, write, or calculate.

Social skills consistent with the developmental attributes of other five- and six-year-olds are clearly important to success in the elementary school. It is particularly critical that students be able to function in a group. Thus, introducing small group instructional activities in preschool programs prepares students to function in future school situations.

Developing responsiveness to instructional styles is another challenge for the young child. Since the instructional arrangement in the preschool program may vary significantly from that of the kindergarten or first grade school program, providing instructional experiences that the student can generalize to the new school setting will be helpful; some learning activities in the preschool class should approximate those of kindergarten to provide the preparation.

Responsiveness to the daily learning environment is a fourth concern. Changes may include new transportation arrangements, extended instructional time, increased expectations of individual independence, and increased class size resulting in a reduction in in-

T EACHING TIP

Teachers should accept responsibility to prepare students for their next school-life challenge or transition (e.g., preschool to elementary school, middle school to secondary school).

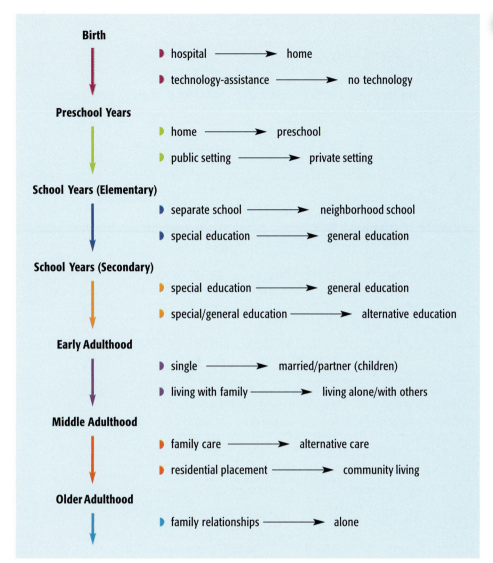

FIGURE 15.3

Vertical and Horizontal Transitions

From *Transition from School to Young Adulthood: Basic Concepts and Recommended Practices* (p. 2) by J. R. Patton and C. Dunn, 1998, Austin, TX: Pro-Ed. Used by permission.

dividual attention. Teachers may set up opportunities for the preschoolers to visit kindergarten classes to familiarize them with the future environment.

Increasingly, public schools have provided prekindergarten programs for young children, particularly those deemed at risk for later school difficulties. In addition, federal law requires that young children identified as having disabilities be provided special education programs, with the actual years of eligibility and the nature of the service delivery program determined by individual state guidelines. The discussion, herein, does not focus on the needs of preschoolers with disabilities or those at risk, but the particular discussions on areas such as listening, following directions, and cooperative learning are equally applicable for young children as they are for those at the elementary school level.

Transition Curricular Considerations   *Career education* in general, and *life skills* education in particular, have become major emphases among secondary school teachers, especially those who work with students who have disabilities. Yet life skills concepts should also be incorporated into elementary and middle school programs (Patton & Cronin, 1993; Patton & Dunn, 1998). Table 15.3 provides a matrix of topics that may be incorporated into an elementary-level life skills curriculum. Even programs for young children should be designed to encourage positive long-term outcomes for all students.

TABLE 15.3   Life Skills in the Elementary School Curriculum

	Consumer Economics	Occupational Knowledge	Health	Community Resources	Government and Law
Reading	Look for ads in the newspaper for toys.	Read books from library on various occupations.	Read the school lunch menu.	Find television listing in the *TV Guide*.	Read road signs and understand what they mean.
Writing	Write prices of items to be purchased.	Write the specific tasks involved in performing one of the classroom jobs.	Keep a diary of food you eat in each food group each day.	Complete an application to play on a Little League team.	Write a letter to the mayor inviting him/her to visit your school.
Speaking, Writing, Viewing	Listen to bank official talk about savings accounts.	Call newspaper in town to inquire about delivering papers in your neighborhood.	View a film on brushing teeth.	Practice the use of the 911 emergency number.	Discuss park playground improvements with the mayor.
Problem Solving	Decide if you have enough coins to make a purchase from a vending machine.	Decide which job in the classroom you do best.	Role-play what you should do if you have a stomachache.	Role-play the times you would use the 911 emergency number.	Find the city hall on the map. Decide whether you will walk or drive to it.
Interpersonal Relations	Ask for help finding items in a grocery store.	Ask a student in the class to assist you with a classroom job.	Ask the school nurse how to take care of mosquito bites.	Call the movie theater and ask the show times of a movie.	Role-play being lost and asking a police officer for help.
Computation	Compute the cost of a box of cereal with a discount coupon.	Calculate how much you would make on a paper route at $3 per hour for 5 hours per week.	Compute the price of one tube of toothpaste if they are on sale at 3 for $1.	Compute the complete cost of going to the movie (admission, food, transportation).	Compute tax on a candy bar.

From "Curricular Considerations: A Life Skills Orientation" (p. 31) by J. R. Patton, M. E. Cronin, E. A. Polloway, D. R. Hutchison, and G. A. Robinson, in *Best Practices in Mild Mental Retardation,* edited by G. A. Robinson, J. R. Patton, E. A. Polloway, and L. Sargent, 1989. Reston, VA: CEC-MR. Used by permission.

TEACHING TIP

Integrated curricular approaches also can enable gifted students to extend their learning beyond the curriculum.

Concepts and topics related to life skills can be integrated into existing subject areas, thus broadening the curriculum without the necessity of creating a new subject. This purpose can be accomplished in three ways. The first approach, *augmentation,* uses career-education–oriented materials to supplement the existing curriculum. The second approach *infuses* relevant career-education topics into the lessons laid out in the existing curriculum.

The third approach employs an *integrated curriculum,* similar to the unit approach traditionally used in many education programs. An integrated curriculum addresses a topic by drawing together content related to it from various academic areas, enabling students to apply academic skills across these areas. Life skills related to the broad topic can be woven into the curriculum. Using a matrix format (Table 15.4 on pages 458 and 459), reading, math, and language skills, as well as career topics and life skills, can be tied together. This curriculum can also help primary- and elementary-age students understand that different academic subjects have important interrelationships.

Transition to Middle School   Elementary students with disabilities need to be prepared for movement to middle school or junior high school. To make this vertical transition successfully, students need an organized approach to their work, time-management and study skills, note-taking strategies, homework strategies, and the ability to use lockers. Robinson, Braxdale, and Colson (1988) observed that the demands faced by students in junior high school fall into three categories: academic skills, self-management and study skills, and social-adaptive skills. Problems in any of these three areas may cause significant difficulties for students.

Wenz-Gross and Siperstein (1998) similarly focused on transitional issues relative to students' success at the middle school level. They concluded that interventions for students in middle school should emphasize developing coping skills for academic demands, peer stress, and relationships with teachers. Helping students develop time-management and organizational skills should also be a focus. To do so, teachers and parents should help these students prioritize multiple tasks and integrate and master the information needed at the middle school level.

Students need to strengthen interpersonal skills so that they can build more positive peer relationships. To assist students in these areas, schools should start before middle school and add emphasis in this area in middle school, when peer relationships become so important. Students also need to be empowered to better deal with the problems experienced by adolescence.

A variety of instructional strategies may assist in the transition process: having middle school faculty visit elementary classes to discuss programs and expectations, viewing videotaped middle school classes, and taking field trips to the middle school to get a sense of the physical layout, the changing of classes, and environmental and pedagogical factors (Jaquish & Stella, 1986). Cooperative planning and follow-up between both general and special education teachers at the two school levels will smooth the transition. Further attention to transition is provided in Chapter 16.

Professional Collaboration

As noted in Chapters 1 and 2, professional collaboration is a key component of effective elementary schools and a necessity for successful inclusion. Collaboration can occur in IEP meetings (see Chapter 4), through cooperative teaching (see Chapter 2), and within the prereferral (or child study) process (see Chapter 4).

Cooperative teaching is essential to implementing the prereferral interventions discussed in Chapter 4; it potentially can help prevent or correct the learning problems of any student while effecting the remediation of identified deficits for students with disabilities. Perhaps the best vehicle for attaining successful inclusive classrooms, it truly provides **supported education,** the school-based equivalent of supported work in which students are placed in the least restrictive environment and provided with the necessary support

Team teaching involving a general classroom teacher and special education teacher works well in inclusive settings.

TABLE 15.4   **Integrated Curriculum**

Science Subtopics	Science Activities	Related Subject/Skill Areas	
		Math	Social Studies
Introductory lesson	Attraction of ants Collection Observation Research ant anatomy	Measurement of distance traveled as a function of time	Relationship of population demographics for ants and humans
Ant farms	Individual set-ups Daily observation Development of collection procedures	Linear measurement Frequency counts	Roles in the community Relationship to human situations
Food preferences chart	Research and predict Construct apparatus for determining preference Design data collection procedures Collect/record data Experiment with food substance positions	Frequency counts Graphs of daily results	Discussion of human food preferences Cultural differences
Ant races	Conduct races with and without food Data collection Predictive activities	Temporal measurement Averages	History of racing Sports and competition
Closing	Analyze information	Tabulate data	

From "Integrated Curriculum" (pp. 52–58) by J. C. Kataoka and J. R. Patton, *Science and Children, 16.* Reprinted with permission from NSTA Publications, copyright 1989 from *Science and Children,* National Science Teachers Association, 1840 Wilson Boulevard, Arlington, VA 22201-3000.

(e.g., by the special educator) to be successful. The nearby Personal Spotlight describes one approach to helping new teachers learn how to collaborate with other professionals.

Prereferral Interventions

Another key area for collaboration is through the prereferral process (also referred to as child study or teacher assistance teams). According to Buck, Patton, Fad, and Polloway (2002), prereferral is best conceptualized as a problem-solving process aimed at meeting the needs of students who exhibit learning or behavioral problems.[1] The process is typically carried out within a school by a team made up of various school personnel and sometimes joined by parents.

The objective of the prereferral process is to meet the challenges presented by students within the context of their classrooms. Teams review student cases and develop instructional and/or behavioral strategies to resolve problems. Several assumptions are inherent in this team approach:

▶ Problems can be solved more effectively when they are clearly defined.
▶ Members of a team often can objectively perceive a student problem better than the referring teacher, who may be emotionally involved in the situation.

---

[1]This section is adapted in part from Buck, G. H., Patton, J. R., Fad, K. M., & Polloway, E. A. (2002). *Prereferral intervention resource guide* (pp. 6–8). Austin, TX: Pro-Ed, and is used with permission.

Related Subject/Skill Areas			
▶ *Arts*	▶ *Computer Application*	▶ *Life Skills*	▶ *Language Arts*
Drawings of ant anatomy Ant mobiles Creative exploration	Graphic drawings of ants	Picnic planning Food storage and protection	Oral sharing of observations
Diagram of farm Diorama Ant models Role-playing of ant behavior	Spreadsheets for calculations Graphing Database storing observations	Relate to engineers, architects, sociologists, geographers	Library skills Creative writing Spelling Research involving note taking, outlining, and reading Vocabulary development Oral reports
Design data collection forms Role-play ant eating behavior		Graphic designer Food services Researchers	
Film making Rewrite lyrics to "The Ants Go Marching In" based on activities	Graphic animation	Athletics Coaches	
Finalize visual aids	Printout	Guest speakers	Presentation

▶ A team of professionals is better able to develop intervention strategies than one or two professionals.

▶ Many of the problems students have are complex and require the expertise of professionals from varied backgrounds and disciplines.

▶ Most learning and behavior problems are not indicative of a disability. With environmental manipulations, such problems can be reduced and eliminated without the need for special education services.

Since its beginnings, the prereferral process has been perceived in part to be intended as a means of reducing the number of students being evaluated for, and placed into, special education. The process has the potential to affect special education evaluation, eligibility, and placement rates. In addition, the prereferral process may not only improve student outcomes but also enhance the professional competencies of staff.

The prereferral process usually occurs in three stages:

1. A teacher or other school staff notices that a student is having difficulty in one or more areas (e.g., academics, social behavior, truancy).
2. The prereferral team attempts to analyze the student's difficulties.
3. Once the problem has been clearly defined, the prereferral team develops strategies to resolve the student's difficulties. In some cases, the team members may provide assistance to the teacher as he or she attempts to implement these strategies in the classroom.

Personal Spotlight

Teacher Educator

Over the past 26 years, **Val Sharpe** has taught in many educational settings. She notes: "It is the ongoing process of change in order to meet the needs of students with disabilities that has afforded me the opportunity for diversification as an educator." As a teacher educator, Val and her colleagues (e.g., Roberta Strosnider) have developed a "hands-on" approach to teaching methods courses in a professional development school (PDS) setting at Hood College.

During the teacher-training process, the future special educator is exposed to a variety of learning theories, adaptations, and modifications designed to facilitate instruction and enhance concept mastery. Within the PDS, the student is provided with multiple opportunities to practice these theories, adaptations, and modifications with children in the classroom setting. Initially, the Hood faculty teach a concept through modeling and incorporating the necessary adaptations and strategies that facilitate learning. The next step is for the student to practice teaching this concept to other future educators. Once the student acquires mastery of the concept, the student teaches this concept to children. This is the stage when the future educator is introduced to the collaborative process.

Val Sharpe
Teacher Educator

Hood College, Frederick, MD

In teaching the collaborative process, Val feels it necessary for future educators to be afforded the opportunity to become acquainted with this process through the implementation of various reality-based activities. After teaching the prerequisite skills and successful ingredients involved in the collaborative process, Val has her students actively participate in this process using the following vehicles:

1. Students become knowledgeable about a variety of learning theories, adaptations, and modifications and their implementation.
2. Students complete a collaborative work sheet.
3. Students are given an assignment to teach a lesson to a group of children within an inclusive setting. Using the

collaboration process, decisions are made regarding appropriate topics for the lesson, as well as the necessary adaptations needed to facilitate the learning process. Via the collaborative process, the students then decide upon the topic and develop a lesson plan. The lesson is then taught to the children. The implemented lesson is evaluated by the children, the students, the PDS teachers, and the college supervisor.

4. Students reflect upon this venture by referring back to their collaborative work sheet as well as discussing this experience with their classmates.

Throughout the student teaching practicum, Val enables the students to utilize the collaborative process. These future educators are required to collaborate with parents in the form of a conference, collaborate with other teachers with regard to lesson development and implementation, collaborate with administrators in terms of scheduling and school policy, and collaborate with the multidisciplinary team in developing an IEP.

This hands-on approach to the collaborative process enables the future teacher to practice this process in a variety of settings. It is beneficial because it helps them make connections about the collaborative process. This approach incorporates the elements of good instructional practices through the use of modeling, repetition, guided practice, independent practice, and reflection. Future educators become familiar with the collaborative process and become comfortable using this process.

For follow-up questions about this Personal Spotlight, go to Chapter 15 of the Companion Website (ablongman.com/sppd4e) and click Personal Spotlight.

Instructional Adaptations

In general, students with disabilities profit directly from the same types of teaching strategies that benefit all students. However, in particular, certain research-validated interventions are associated with successful learning outcomes for students with learning disabilities and other special needs. Vaughn et al. (2000) identified three instructional features that stand out as producing the most significant impact on learning:

▶ Control of task difficulty (i.e., sequencing examples and problems to maintain high levels of student success).
▶ Teaching students in small interactive groups of six or fewer students.

▶ Directed response questioning (i.e., involves the use of procedures . . . that promote "thinking aloud" about text being read, mathematical problems to be solved, or about the process of composing a written essay or story). (p. 101)

Vaughn et al. (2000) further noted that *all students* benefit when best practices for students with learning disabilities, such as these, are used.

With these basic principles reflected in instruction, adaptations made to instructional programs in the general education classroom then form the keys to successful inclusion. As the traditional saying goes, special education is not necessarily special, it is just good teaching, and good teaching often means making appropriate modifications and accommodations. Assuming the curricular content is appropriate for individual students who have disabilities, the challenge is to adapt it to facilitate learning.

It is useful to have a common set of definitions to build upon in discussing classroom adaptations. Polloway, Epstein, and Bursuck (2002) provide the following differentiation between two types of adaptations. **Accommodations** refer to changes in input and output processes in teaching and assessment, such as in the format of instructional presentations, as well as test practice and preparation activities. The concept of **modifications** refers to changes in content or standards. In curricular areas, modifications could involve changes in content or skill expectations for different groups of students. As a general pattern, Polloway, Epstein, and Bursuck (2002) reported that teachers indicate a greater willingness to consider accommodations, while they express more reluctance to consider the implementation of modifications.

Thus, a key component of successful inclusion is the treatment (or teacher) acceptability of specific interventions to accommodate the needs of students with disabilities. The term *treatment acceptability* has been used in a variety of ways. Polloway, Bursuck, Jayanthi, Epstein, and Nelson (1996) used the term in a broad sense to refer to the likelihood that certain specific classroom interventions will be acceptable to the general education teacher. Thus it may include, for example, the helpfulness, desirability, feasibility, and fairness of the intervention, as well as how other students will perceive it in a particular setting. As Witt and Elliott (1985) noted, the "attractiveness" of an intervention is important: if the treatment is not deemed acceptable, it is unlikely to be implemented.

In a review of research on adaptations, Scott, Vitale, and Masten (1998) summarized the types of adaptations that have been researched for their effectiveness. They use the qualifier *typical* to refer to specific examples that are routine, minor, or applicable to an entire class, and *substantial* to refer to those that are tailored to the needs of individual students. Their categories (as adapted) are as follows:

▶ *Adapting instruction:* typical (concrete classroom demonstrations, monitoring classroom understanding); substantial (adjusting the pace to individual learners, giving immediate individual feedback, using multiple modalities)
▶ *Adapting assignments:* typical (providing models); substantial (breaking tasks into small steps, shortening assignments, lowering difficulty levels)
▶ *Teaching learning skills:* typical (study skills, note-taking techniques); substantial (learning strategies, test-taking skills)
▶ *Altering instructional materials:* substantial (using alternative materials, taping textbooks, using supplementary aids)
▶ *Modifying curriculum:* substantial (lowering difficulty of course content)
▶ *Varying instructional grouping:* substantial (using peer tutoring, using cooperative groups)
▶ *Enhancing behavior:* typical (praise, offering encouragement); substantial (using behavioral contracts, using token economies, frequent parental contact)
▶ *Facilitating progress monitoring:* typical (read tests orally; give extended test-taking time; give frequent, short quizzes; provide study guides); substantial (retaking tests, obtaining direct daily measures of academic progress, modifying grading criteria) (p. 107)

In Table 15.5, the findings of Scott et al. (1998) relative to research on specific accommodations and modifications are presented.

TABLE 15.5   **Representative Examples of Instructional Adaptations**

Munson, 1986–1987 (elementary)	1. Simplify/supplement the curriculum 2. Provide concrete materials 3. Change papers, worksheets 4. Shorten assignments 5. Provide peers for individual instruction
Johnson & Pugach, 1990 (elementary)	1. Adjust performance expectations in the student's problem area to increase the likelihood that the student will succeed 2. Use peer tutors, volunteers, or aides to work with student physically 3. Use alternative textbook or materials 4. Talk with school psychologist, special education teachers, counselor, or other special education personnel about ways to work on the student's academic problem 5. Give additional explicit oral or written instructions to the student
Ysseldyke, Thurlow, Wotruba, & Nania, 1990 (K–12)	1. Alter instruction so student can experience success 2. Use different materials to instruct failing student 3. Adjust lesson pace to meet student's rate of mastery 4. Inform student frequently of his/her instructional needs 5. Use alternative methods to instruct failing student
Bacon & Schulz, 1991 (K–12)	1. Use lower-level workbooks or worksheets 2. Provide volunteer tutor (adult) 3. Provide note takers 4. Use taped lectures 5. Provide hands-on activities, manipulatives
Schumm & Vaughn, 1991 (K–12)	1. Establish personal relationship with mainstreamed student 2. Adapt daily plans 3. Use alternative materials 4. Pair with classmate 5. Modify long-term curriculum goals
Whinnery, Fuchs, & Fuchs, 1991 (1–6)	1. Regroup students for language arts across grades into homogeneous groups 2. Regroup students for language arts within grades into homogeneous groups 3. Use resource staff in classroom for the lowest language arts groups 4. Establish mixed-ability student partners with low- and high-ability pairs 5. Cover the same basic instructional activities each day with the lowest language arts group
Fuchs, Fuchs, & Bishop, 1992 (elementary)	1. Vary goals 2. Use alternative materials 3. Alter teaching activities 4. Vary groupings 5. Adjust schedule
Schumm & Vaughn, 1992 (K–12)	1. Plan or make adaptations in the curriculum 2. Plan or make adaptations to tests 3. Make adaptations while the student is working
Blanton, Blanton, & Cross, 1994 (elementary)	1. Provide extra time for the student's reading instruction 2. Provide instruction for the student in smaller steps 3. Use computer-assisted instruction 4. Make use of teacher-directed reading instruction 5. Use peer tutors, volunteers, or aides to work with student physically
Schumm, Vaughn, & Saumell, 1994 (K–12)	1. Preview textbook with students 2. Read textbook aloud to students 3. Write abridged versions of textbooks 4. Provide questions to guide reading 5. Model effective reading strategies

Table 15.5 continued

Polloway, Epstein, Bursuck, Jayanthi, & Cumblad, 1994 (K–12)	1. Adjust length of assignment 2. Evaluate on the basis of effort, not performance 3. Provide extra credit opportunities 4. Check more frequently with student about assignments and expectations 5. Allow alternative response formats
Schumm, Vaughn, Gordon, & Rothlein, 1994 (K–12)	1. Vary group composition (e.g., small group, large group, whole class) for main-streamed students 2. Adapt daily planning for mainstreamed students 3. Use frequent checks with individual students to monitor the progress of main-streamed students
Bender, Vail, & Scott, 1995 (elementary-middle)	1. Suggest particular methods of remembering 2. Provide peer tutoring to assist slow learners 3. Use reading materials that highlight the topic sentence and main idea for slow learners 4. Use several test administration options, such as oral tests or extended-time tests 5. Use advance organizers to assist students in comprehension of difficult concepts
Schumm, Vaughn, Haager, McDowell, Rothlein, & Saumell, 1995 (K–12)	1. Preplan lesson(s) experiences for students with LD 2. Monitor a lesson and make adaptations in response to the progress of students with LD 3. Postplan for later lessons (e.g., reteach a lesson)
Jayanthi, Epstein, Polloway, & Bursuck, 1996 (K–12)	1. Prepare tests that are typewritten rather than handwritten 2. Give shorter, more frequent tests rather than fewer, more comprehensive tests 3. Change the setting in which the student takes the test 4. Allow students to dictate their responses 5. Limit the number of matching items to 10
Bursuck, Polloway, Plante, Epstein, Jayanthi, & McConeghy, 1996 (K–12)	1. Base grades on amount of improvement an individual makes 2. Award separate grades for process (e.g., effort) and product (e.g., tests) 3. Adjust grades according to student's ability 4. Base grades on less content than for the rest of the class 5. Base grades on a modified grading scale (e.g., from 93–100 = A to 90–100 = A)

From "Implementing Instructional Adaptations for Students with Disabilities in Inclusive Classrooms: A Literature Review" (pp. 111–112) by B. J. Scott, M. R. Vitale, and W. G. Masten, 1998, *Remedial and Special Education, 19.* Used by permission.

The specific modifications and accommodations for students with disabilities in elementary classes discussed next vary in nature and in terms of teacher acceptability. Many of the suggested adaptations will prove beneficial to all students, not only to those with special needs. Teachers are encouraged to select strategies that appear applicable to a given situation and then evaluate their effectiveness. Tips for Adapting an Elementary Lesson Plan shows a sample lesson plan incorporating instructional adaptations.

Enhancing Content Learning Through Listening

Many children will not listen carefully just because they are told to do so. Rather, they often need oral presentations provided in ways that promote successful listening. Students who struggle with selective attention (i.e., focus) or sustained attention (i.e., attention maintained over a period of time) respond more easily to speaking that supports the listener. Wallace, Cohen, and Polloway (1987) note that listeners attend more when

- content is [emphasized] through repetition, vocal emphasis, and cuing.
- the message is meaningful, logical, and well organized.
- messages are given in short units.

TEACHING TIP

For many students with disabilities, the skill of listening must be directly targeted if academic success is to occur in inclusive settings.

Tips for Adapting an Elementary Lesson Plan

Topic: Oral dictation of story endings

Objective: Given one story read orally, the students will dictate a new story ending with 80% mastery.

1. **Review of previous lesson:** "Yesterday we completed orally reading the story *My Friend Bear* by Jez Alborough."

2. **Advance organizer:** "Today we will dictate our own story endings for the story that I will read to the class. We will first play a game with partners, and then we will orally retell the new story endings."

3. **Motivator, introduction, command for attention, and obtaining commitment to learn:** "Have you ever been listening to a story being read to you, and the ending of the story was not the one you wanted? You can change that problem! Today, we will practice making up our own story endings. I am going to read a story to you, and you will tell me how you think the story should end."

4. **Direct instruction:** Reread the story *My Friend Bear.* Stop before reading the end. Tell the students that they will now make up their own ending instead of reading the ending of the book. Be sure and "think out loud" when modeling. For example—"I do not like the way that story ends. Instead of having the bear and the boy both walking away from each other, I am going to have the bear go home with the boy. Can you think of anything else?" Brainstorm with the students, and provide feedback when they give answers. Orally model the ending of the story.

5. **Guided practice and feedback:** "We will now practice orally dictating our own story endings." Put the students into groups of two, and give each group a game board, dice, tape recorder, pennies for playing pieces, and short story cards. Have them brainstorm for possible new story endings for the stories (previously read) listed on the cards. Closely supervise each group. Have each student orally dictate a new story ending. Use tape recorder to record responses.

6. **Independent practice and feedback:** Have each student pick the name of a story out of a box. Instruct each student to think of a new ending to the story that he or she picked. Have the students orally tell the teacher their new story endings.

7. **Adaptations to lesson:** To successfully include students with special needs in the lesson, use the following strategies:
   - Stop periodically while giving instruction to ensure understanding; ask questions to verify.
   - Provide prompts about possible points to consider in developing endings.
   - Establish dyads in which the student with a disability is paired with a supportive peer.
   - After the pair creates a story, be sure that the child with special needs has a chance to dictate a portion of the story.
   - Add pictures to the story cards to cue meaning.

8. **Techniques for student evaluation:** The teacher will read one story orally. The students will dictate new story endings (can be done with the use of a tape recorder). The teacher will use a checklist to check for student understanding.

9. **Summary and transition to next lesson:** "Today we learned that we can change the endings of stories by making our own endings. We orally dictated new story endings. Tomorrow, we will review oral dictation of story endings. We will then begin work on making new story endings that can be orally presented to the entire class."

The authors thank Stacy Roberts of the University of Alabama, Birmingham, for contributing this sample lesson plan, which we have adapted.

- the speaker allows for listener participation in the form of clarification, feedback, or responding.
- reinforcement for attending is given in the form of participation, praise, or increased ability to perform.
- the listener knows there will be an opportunity to reflect upon and integrate the message before having to formulate a response. (p. 75)

To facilitate learning, teachers must consider vehicles for the effective presentation of content to enhance successful listening and learning. Adaptations in this area typically prove beneficial to all students. Some specific considerations follow:

- Use concrete concepts before teaching abstractions (e.g., teach the concept of freedom by discussing specific rights to which students are entitled).
- Relate information to students' prior experiences and provide an overview before beginning.
- Reduce the number of concepts introduced at a given time.
- Encourage children to detect errors in messages and report what they could not understand.
- Review lessons before additional content is introduced.
- Keep oral directions short and direct, and supplement them with written directions as needed.
- Provide repetition, review, and additional examples.
- Provide further guided practice by requiring more responses, lengthening practice sessions, or scheduling extra sessions.
- Clarify directions for follow-up activities so that tasks can be completed successfully. (Adapted from Chalmers, 1991; Cheney, 1989; Dowdy, 1990; McDevitt, 1990.)

Adapting Reading Tasks

In many instances, instructional tasks, assignments, or materials may be relevant and appropriate for children with disabilities, but may present problematic reading demands. Teachers should consider options for adapting the task or the textual materials. The following suggestions address problems that may arise in processing reading content:

- Establish an assignment's purpose and importance.
- Highlight key words and phrases (e.g., color coding of text) and concepts (e.g., providing outlines, study guides).
- Encourage periodic feedback from students to check their understanding.
- Preview reading material with students to assist them in establishing purpose, activating prior knowledge, budgeting time, and focusing attention.
- Preteach vocabulary words to ensure that students can use them rather than simply recognize them.
- Locate lower-level content material on the same topic to adapt tasks for students with reading difficulties.
- Utilize advance organizers and visual aids (e.g., charts, graphs) to provide an orientation to reading tasks or to supplement them.
- Demonstrate how new content relates to content previously learned.
- Encourage students to facilitate their comprehension by raising questions about a text's content.
- Teach students to consider K-W-L as a technique to focus attention. "K" represents prior knowledge, "W" what the student wants to know, and "L" what has been learned as a result.
- Teach the use of active comprehension strategies in which students periodically pause to ask themselves questions about what they have read.
- Use reciprocal teaching in which students take turns leading discussions that raise questions about the content read, summarize the most important information, clarify

TEACHING TIP

Few students at the elementary level, disabled or not, can attend to a lengthy lecture. Although learning to focus for 20 minutes is a useful skill to acquire for upper elementary students, teachers should plan for variety within a given instructional period.

CROSS-REFERENCE

Ultimately, students will need to learn to adapt reading tasks themselves, through the use of learning strategies, in order to become independent learners. Chapter 16 shows how this process plays out at the secondary level.

concepts that are unclear, and predict what will occur next. (Adapted from *CEC Today,* 1997; Chalmers, 1991; Cheney, 1989; Gartland, 1994; Hoover, 1990; Reynolds & Salend, 1990; Schumm & Strickler, 1991.)

Another key element to successful reading is the strategies acquired by students to promote independence. Consistent with the earlier observation about the role of "thinking aloud," students need to develop approaches that enable them to engage in the following:

▶ *Comprehension Monitoring* (i.e., teaching students to monitor their comprehension and use "repair strategies" when they begin to lose understanding of the text).
▶ *Text Structuring* (i.e., providing students with ways to ask themselves questions about what they read). (Vaughn et al., 2000, p. 104)

Enhancing Written Responses

The adaptations noted here may assist students who have difficulty with responding in written form. The suggestions will enhance the ability of children to meet the written language demands of the inclusive classroom.

▶ When appropriate, allow children to select the most comfortable method of writing (i.e., cursive or manuscript).
▶ Change the response mode to oral when appropriate.
▶ Set realistic, mutually agreed upon expectations for neatness.
▶ Allow children to circle or underline responses.
▶ Let students type or tape-record answers.
▶ Provide the student with a copy of lecture notes produced by the teacher or a peer.
▶ Reduce amounts of board copying or text copying; provide the written information itself or an outline of the main content.
▶ Allow sufficient space for answering problems.
▶ Allow group-written responses (by means of projects or reports). (Adapted from Chalmers, 1991; Cheney, 1989; Dowdy, 1990)

Promoting Following Instructions and Completing Assignments

Another key area is enhancing children's ability to follow instructions and complete work assignments. The following suggestions are adapted from *CEC Today* (1997, p. 15):

▶ Get the student's attention before giving directions.
▶ Use alerting cues.
▶ Give one direction at a time.
▶ Quietly repeat the directions to the student after they have been given to the entire class.
▶ Check for understanding by having the student repeat the directions.
▶ Break up tasks into workable and obtainable steps, and include due dates.
▶ Provide examples and specific steps to accomplish the task.
▶ List or post requirements necessary to complete each assignment.
▶ Check assignments frequently.
▶ Arrange for the student to have a study buddy.

Involving Peers Through Cooperative Learning

Cooperative learning (CL) is a key means of facilitating the successful inclusion of students with disabilities in general education classrooms. It is categorized by classroom techniques that involve students in group learning activities, in which recognition and reinforcement are based on group, rather than individual, performance. Heterogeneous small groups work together to achieve a group goal, and an individual student's success directly affects the success of other students (Slavin, 1987).

A variety of formats can be used to implement cooperative learning. These include peer tutoring and group projects of various types.

Peer Tutoring   Peer teaching, or peer tutoring, is a relatively easy-to-manage system of cooperative learning. It can benefit both the student being tutored and the tutor. Specific activities that lend themselves to peer tutoring include reviewing task directions, drill and practice, recording material dictated by a peer, modeling of acceptable or appropriate responses, and providing pretest practice (such as in spelling).

One effective tutoring program is *classwide peer tutoring* (CWPT). As summarized by Seeley (1995), CWPT involves the following arrangements:

▶ Classes are divided into two teams, which engage in competitions typically of 1–2 weeks' duration.
▶ Students work in pairs, both tutoring and being tutored on the same material in a given instructional session.
▶ Partners reverse roles after 15 minutes.
▶ Typical subjects tutored include math, spelling, vocabulary, science, and social studies.
▶ Teachers break down the curriculum into manageable subunits.
▶ Students accumulate points for their team by giving correct answers and by using correct procedures, and they receive partial credit for corrected answers.
▶ Individual scores on master tests are added to the team's total.

CWPT is a promising approach for inclusive settings. It has been positively evaluated in terms of enhancing content learning, promoting diversity and integration, and freeing teachers to prepare for other instructional activities (King-Sears & Bradley, 1995; Simmons, Fuchs, Hodge, & Mathes, 1994).

Another example of a successful peer tutoring approach is Peer Assisted Learning Strategies (PALS), described by Mathes and Torgesen (1998). In PALS, beginning readers are assisted in learning through paired instruction in which each member of the pair takes turns serving as a coach and a reader. The first coach is the reader who is at a higher achievement level who listens to, comments on, and reinforces the other student before the roles are reversed. These researchers found that the use of this approach enhanced students' reading by promoting careful attention to saying and hearing sounds, sounding

Classwide peer tutoring is one peer tutoring program that is effective in inclusive settings.

out words, and reading stories. They recommended using the approach three times a week for approximately 16 weeks with each session lasting 35 minutes. The PALS program complements general education instruction by enhancing the academic engaged time of each student.

Group Projects   Group projects allow students to pool their knowledge and skills to complete an assignment. The task is assigned to the entire group, and the goal is to develop a single product reflecting the contributions of all members. For example, in social studies, a report on one of the 50 states might involve making individual students responsible for particular tasks: drawing a map, sketching an outline of state history, collecting photos of scenic attractions, and developing a display of products from that state. The benefits of groups are enhanced when they include high, average, and low achievers.

The *jigsaw format* is an approach that involves giving all group members individual tasks to be completed before the group can reach its goal. Each individual studies a portion of the material and then shares it with other members of the team. For example, Salend (1990) discussed an assignment related to the life of Dr. Martin Luther King, Jr., in which each student was given a segment of his life to research (e.g., religious beliefs, protest marches, opposition to the war). The students then had to teach others in their group the information from the segment they had mastered. In using this approach, teachers are cautioned to oversee the individual assignments within the group project and keep in mind the importance of distributing student expertise over aspects of the assignment.

Cooperative learning strategies offer much promise as inclusive practices. These approaches have been used successfully with low, average, and high achievers to promote the acquisition of academic and social skills and to enhance independence. The fact that CL appears to be effective in general education and special education classrooms would seem to support the benefits of its use with heterogeneous populations (McMaster & Fuchs, 2002). Cooperative learning also can enhance the social adjustment of students with special needs by helping to create natural support networks involving nondisabled peers, such as within the "circle of friends" approach discussed in Chapter 8.

At the same time, teachers should keep in mind that cooperative learning approaches are not the single solution for resolving the academic challenges faced by students with special needs. As McMaster and Fuchs (2002) concluded, the state of research in this area is such that CL is best seen as a "promising instructional strategy (rather than as) an unqualified effective approach" (p. 116). Thus, as with many classroom interventions, teachers are encouraged to assess the effectiveness of CL if they use it as a tool to promote the successful inclusion of students with special needs.

Multicultural Issues in Curriculum and Instruction

Educators need to consider issues related to cultural diversity when working with elementary-age students with special needs. Students who come from different language backgrounds and whose families reflect values that differ from those of the majority culture must be treated with sensitivity and respect.

Considerations of linguistic and cultural diversity must inform all aspects of curriculum design and should be reflected in instructional practices. The continued overrepresentation of minority children in high-incidence special education categories underscores the importance of this focus (e.g., Oswald et al., 1999). Because students with special needs benefit from direct, hands-on approaches to such topics, teachers should introduce specific activities which promote cultural awareness and sensitivity to develop students' appreciation of diversity at the elementary level and then lay the foundation for subsequent programming at the middle and secondary school level.

An excellent resource for building a multicultural focus in the curriculum is through the use of the Internet. Technology Today presents an innovative approach to web usage.

TrackStar

Trackstar (http://trackstar.hprtec.org) is an online resource that helps teachers and students organize and annotate websites (more specifically, the addresses or URLs to the websites) for lessons, presentations, assignments, or instructional resources. TrackStar allows users to organize favorite websites into tracks under a specific topic and make them accessible to anyone with Internet access.

Tracks are created by teachers or students and are stored on servers. All the tracks (approximately 63,000) are organized and cataloged by grade level. Users can select from tracks created for early childhood, primary grades (K–2), intermediate grades (3–4), middle school (5–9), high school (9–12), college/adult, or all grades. Likewise, users can select tracks organized by keyword (i.e., special education), by author, or by themes and standards. If you are interested in the most popular tracks, users have access to the month's "Track-A-Day," a list of all "Top Tracks," and tracks by subject or category. For the user uncertain of how to begin locating a track, TrackStar has a "How to Find a Track" tutorial.

Developed to help teachers and parents address some of the challenges the World Wide Web offers, TrackStar features a variety of tools. These tools attempt to eliminate these Internet hurdles and allow teachers to focus on instruction, access resources that will enhance classroom activities, and hopefully further individualize the general curriculum. More important, TrackStar saves time. For the novice or experienced user, TrackStar offers an environment where a learning community has already organized relevant information in a format that can be immediately shared with others.

 For follow-up questions about online resources, go to Chapter 15 of the Companion Website (ablongman.com/sppd4e) and click Technology Today.

Adapted from "Technology for Organizing and Presenting Digital Information" (pp. 306–310) by S. J. Smith & S. B. Smith, 2002, *Intervention in School and Clinic, 37.*

Adapting the Temporal Environment

Time is a critical element in classroom assignments and can be associated with special challenges for students with disabilities. Thus, adapting deadlines and other requirements can help promote success. When handled properly, these adaptations need not impinge on the integrity of the assignments or place undue burdens on the classroom teacher. Some suggestions follow:

▶ Develop schedules that balance routines (to establish predictability) with novelty (to sustain excitement).
▶ Review class schedules with students to reinforce routines.
▶ Provide each student with a copy of the schedule.
▶ Increase the amount of time allowed to complete assignments or tests.
▶ Contract with students concerning time allotment, and tie reinforcement to a reasonable schedule of completion.
▶ Allow extra practice time for students who understand content but need additional time to achieve mastery.
▶ Teach time-management skills (use of time lines, checklists, and prioritizing time and assignments).
▶ Space short work periods with breaks or changes of task (thus using the Premack principle for scheduling: making desirable events contingent on completion of less desirable events). (Adapted from Chalmers, 1991; Guernsey, 1989; Polloway et al., 2001.)

Adapting the Classroom Arrangement

Changes in the classroom arrangement can also help in accommodating children with special needs. Some specific examples include these:

▶ Establish a climate that fosters positive social interactions between students.
▶ Balance structure, organization, and regimentation with opportunities for freedom and exploration.
▶ Use study carrels.

CROSS-REFERENCE

See also the discussion on classroom arrangement in Chapter 14.

▶ Locate student seats and learning activities in areas free from distractions.
▶ Allow students to decide where it is best for them to work and study.
▶ Provide opportunities for approved movement within the class.
▶ Establish high- and low-frequency areas for class work (thus using the Premack principle to allow students to move to "fun" areas contingent on work completion in more academically rigorous areas).
▶ Set aside space for group work, individual seatwork, and free-time activities. (Adapted from Cheney, 1989; Guernsey, 1989; Hoover, 1990; Minner & Prater, 1989; Polloway et al., 2001.)

Enhancing Motivation

Given the failure often experienced by students with disabilities, as well as the boredom experienced by gifted students, motivational problems can seriously undermine the learning process. Although student motivation typically becomes more problematic at the secondary level, young students should be taught in a way that prevents motivational problems. Attention to both the motivational qualities of the material and the characteristics of the student can develop and sustain a positive attitude toward learning. The following suggestions can help spark motivation:

▶ Have students set personal goals and graph their progress.
▶ Use contingency contracts in which a certain amount of work at a specified degree of accuracy earns the student a desired activity or privilege.
▶ Allow students to choose where to work, what tools to use, and what to do first, as long as their work is being completed.
▶ Provide immediate feedback (e.g., through teacher monitoring or self-correcting materials) on the correctness of work.
▶ Camouflage instructional materials that are at a lower instructional level (using folders, covers).
▶ Use high-status materials for instructional activities (e.g., magazines, catalogs, newspapers).
▶ Allow students to earn points or tokens to exchange for a valued activity or privilege.
▶ Provide experiences that ensure success, and offer positive feedback when students are successful. (Adapted from Cheney, 1989, p. 29.)

Developing Effective Homework Programs

CONSIDER THIS

The importance of homework adaptations to the successful inclusion of students with special needs has been confirmed in numerous research studies. How important do you think they are? Why?

Homework has always been an essential element of education, but educational reform led to its increased use by elementary general education teachers. In a national survey, teachers reported that they most commonly assigned homework from two to four times per week (Polloway, Epstein, Bursuck, Jayanthi, & Cumblad, 1994). Research on the effectiveness of homework as an instructional tool suggests that it leads to increased school achievement for students in general, with particular benefits in the area of habit formation for elementary students (Cooper, 1989; Walberg, 1991). However, students with disabilities experience significant problems in this area because of difficulties in attention, independence, organization, and motivation (Epstein, Polloway, Foley, & Patton, 1993; Gajria & Salend, 1995).

Homework for students with disabilities presents several dilemmas for general education teachers. Epstein et al. (1996) recognized that communication concerning homework is often negatively affected by the inadequate knowledge base of general education teachers. Figure 15.4 presents typical problems (ordered from most to least serious by teachers) in this area.

Polloway and colleagues (1994) asked teachers to rate specific strategies that were most helpful to students with disabilities. Table 15.6 summarizes these responses; each column reflects teachers' ratings from most to least helpful.

1. Do not know enough about the abilities of students with disabilities who are mainstreamed in their classes.

2. Do not know how to use special education support services or teachers to assist students with disabilities about homework.

3. Lack knowledge about the adaptations that can be made to homework.

4. Are not clear about their responsibility to communicate with special education teachers about the homework of students with disabilities.

5. Are not aware of their responsibility to communicate with parents of students with disabilities about homework.

FIGURE 15.4

Homework Communication Problems Noted by Elementary Teachers

Note: Items were ranked by general education teachers from *most* to *least* serious.

From "Homework Communication Problems: Perspectives of General Education Teachers" by M. H. Epstein, E. A. Polloway, G. H. Buck, W. D. Bursuck, L. M. Wissinger, F. Whitehause, and M. Jayanthi, 1997. In *Learning Disabilities Research and Practice 12,* pp. 221–227. Used by permission.

TABLE 15.6   Teachers' Ratings of Helpfulness of Homework Adaptations and Practices

| Types of Homework | Consequences | | | |
	Teacher-Directed Activities	Failure to Complete	Complete Assignments	Adaptations
Practice of skills already taught	Communicate clear consequences about successfully completing homework.	Assist students in completing the assignment.	Give praise for completion.	Provide additional teacher assistance.
Preparation for tests	Begin assignment in class, and check for understanding.	Make adaptations in assignment.	Provide corrective feedback in class.	Check more frequently with student about assignments and expectations.
Unfinished class work	Communicate clear expectations about the quality of homework completion.	Talk to them about why the assignment was not completed.	Give rewards for completion.	Allow alternative response formats (e.g., oral or other than written).
Makeup work due to absences	Use a homework assignment sheet or notebook.	Require corrections and resubmission.	Monitor students by charting performance.	Adjust length of assignment.
Enrichment activities	Communicate clear consequences about failure to complete homework.	Call students' parents.	Record performance in grade book.	Provide a peer tutor for assistance.
Preparation for future class work	Give assignments that are completed entirely at school. Begin assignment in class without checking for understanding	Keep students in at recess to complete the assignment. Keep students after school to complete the assignment. Lower their grade. Put students' names on board.	Call students' parents.	Provide auxiliary learning aids (e.g., calculator, computer). Assign work that student can do independently. Provide a study group. Provide extra credit opportunities. Adjust (i.e., lower) evaluation standards. Adjust due dates. Give fewer assignments.

Note: Arranged from most helpful to least helpful.

From "A National Survey of Homework Practices of General Education Teachers" (p. 504) by E. A. Polloway, M. H. Epstein, W. Bursuck, M. Jayanthi, and C. Cumblad, *Journal of Learning Disabilities, 27.* Used by permission.

Most recently, Patton et al. (2001) reviewed the research on collaboration concerning homework and identified recommended practices that are respectively school-based, teacher-directed, parent-initiated, and student-regulated. These are listed in Table 15.7.

Developing Responsive Grading Practices

The assignment of grades is an integral aspect of education. Grading serves multiple purposes in contemporary education, as summarized in Table 15.8. Thus, grading practices have been subject to frequent evaluation and review, generating a number of problematic issues.

Grading students with special needs received little attention prior to the increased inclusion of students with disabilities. However, beginning in the mid-1990s, research attention to various aspects of grading increased significantly. In a study of school district policies, Polloway et al. (1994) reported that over 60% of districts with grading policies had one related to students with disabilities; most common was the inclusion of stated accommodations within the IEP. Bursuck et al. (1996) found that approximately 40% of general educators shared responsibilities for grading with special education teachers. Thus, the trend toward collaboration and, in many cases, these key components of cooperative teaching, has had an impact on this important area.

CROSS-REFERENCE

See Chapter 3 for in-depth discussion of parental involvement in homework.

TABLE 15.7   **Recommended Homework Practices**

School-Based
▶ Require frequent written communication from teachers to parents
▶ Schedule parent-teacher meetings in the evening
▶ Provide release time for teachers to communicate with parents
▶ Establish telephone hotlines
▶ Establish after school sessions to provide extra help
▶ Institute peer tutoring programs

Teacher-Directed
▶ Require and teach students to use homework assignment books
▶ Assess students' skills related to homework completion
▶ Involve parents and students in the homework process from the beginning of the school year
▶ Establish an ongoing communication system with parents to convey information related to homework assignments
▶ Coordinate homework assignments with other teachers
▶ Present assignments clearly and provide timely feedback
▶ Teach students techniques for managing their time more effectively

Parent-Initiated
▶ Discuss homework assignments with their children daily
▶ Attend regularly parent-teacher conferences
▶ Communicate views, concerns, and observations about homework to teacher(s) or other school personnel
▶ Provide support to their child when doing homework by creating and maintaining an appropriate homework environment

Student-Regulated
▶ Demonstrate a range of self-advocacy skills including the ability to ask for help when needed
▶ Become an interdependent learner
▶ Manage time more effectively

From "Home-School Collaboration About Homework: What Do We Know and What Should We Do?" (p. 233) by J. R. Patton, M. Jayanthi, & E. A. Polloway, 2001, *Reading & Writing Quarterly, 17.*

TABLE 15.8   **Purposes of Grading**

1. *Achievements:* To certify and measure mastery of curricular goals and specific skills (e.g., learning standards).
2. *Progress:* To indicate progress in learning over a specific period of time.
3. *Effort:* To acknowledge and indicate the effort a student puts forth in learning.
4. *Comparison:* To compare students in terms of their competence, progress, and effort.
5. *Instructional planning:* To identify students' learning strengths and needs, and to group students for instruction.
6. *Program effectiveness:* To examine the efficacy of the instructional program.
7. *Motivation:* To motivate students to learn, to reward learning, and to promote self-esteem.
8. *Communication:* To provide feedback to students, families, and others.
9. *Educational and career planning:* To aid students, families, and school districts in determining the courses and educational services needed by students, placing students who enter the school district from another school district, and planning for the future (e.g., facilitate student advisement and career planning).
10. *Eligibility:* To determine eligibility for graduation and promotion, and rank students in terms of their eligibility for certain programs and awards (e.g., honors programs, participation in extracurricular activities, grants, scholarships, rankings for college admission).
11. *Accountability:* To provide measures of student achievement to the community, employers, legislators, and educational policymakers (e.g., grades provide employers with a point of reference concerning the aptitude and job skills of prospective employees).

Adapted from "Grading Students in Inclusive Settings" (pp. 13–14) by S. Salend & L. Garrick Duhaney, 2002, *Teaching Exceptional Children, 34.*

This collaboration is timely because existing grading systems make success challenging for students who are disabled. Prior studies on grading patterns documented generally poor grades for students with disabilities in general education (e.g., Donahue & Zigmond, 1990; Valdes, Williamson, & Wagner, 1990). Further, although general education teachers reported that written comments and checklists are most helpful with these individuals, the most common systems in use at the elementary level are letter grades (Bursuck et al., 1996).

In the Bursuck et al. (1996) study, elementary teachers evaluated adaptations and indicated that adaptations allowing for separate grades for process and product and grades indexed against student improvement were particularly helpful, whereas passing students "no matter what" or basing grades on effort alone was not; this finding is consistent with the distinction of accommodations versus modifications made by Polloway, Epstein, and Bursuck (2002) noted earlier in this chapter. Figure 15.5 presents Bursuck et al.'s (1996) ranking of grading adaptations.

A related issue is the feasibility of specific adaptations in general education. Bursuck et al. (1996) assessed this question by determining whether teachers actually use these same adaptations with students without disabilities. As implied by Figure 15.5, three of the four adaptations deemed most helpful for students with disabilities (i.e., grading on improvement, adjusting grades, giving separate grades for process and product) were also seen as feasible because they were used by 50% or more of the teachers (regardless of grade level) with nondisabled students. Basing grades on less content and passing students no matter what are frowned upon in both general and special education.

Questions of fairness also influence the discussion on grading (e.g., Are adaptations in grading made only for students with disabilities really fair to other students?). Bursuck et al. (1996) report that only 25% of general education teachers thought such adaptations were fair. Those who believed they were fair noted that students should "not be punished" for an inherent problem such as a disability, that adaptations for effort are appropriate

CROSS-REFERENCE

Grading issues become more problematic at the secondary level; see Chapter 16 for more information.

FIGURE 15.5

Elementary Teachers' Ratings of Helpfulness of Grading Adaptations for Students with Disabilities

Note: Items ranked from most helpful to least helpful by general education teachers. Numbers in parentheses refer to general education rankings of adaptations from most likely to least likely to be used with nondisabled students.

Adapted from "Report Card Grading Practices and Adaptations" by W. Bursuck, E. A. Polloway, L. Plante, M. H. Epstein, M. Jayanthi, and J. McConeghy, 1996, *Exceptional Children, 62,* pp. 301–318. Used by permission.

1. Grades are based on the amount of improvement an individual makes. (#1)
2. Separate grades are given for process (e.g., effort) and product (e.g., tests). (#3)
3. Grades are based on meeting IEP objectives. (#9)
4. Grades are adjusted according to student ability. (#2)
5. Grading weights are adjusted (e.g., efforts on projects count more than tests). (#4)
6. Grades are based on meeting the requirements of academic or behavioral contracts. (#5)
7. Grades are based on less content than the rest of the class. (#7)
8. Students are passed if they make an effort to pass. (#6)
9. Grades are based on a modified grading scale (e.g., from 93 – 100 = A, 90 – 100 = A). (#8)
10. Students are passed no matter what. (#10)

because the students are "fighting uphill battles," and that adaptations allow students to "be successful like other kids."

Those teachers who thought adaptations unfair indicated that other students experience significant learning problems even though they have not been formally identified, that some students have extenuating circumstances (e.g., divorce, illness) that necessitate adaptations, and that all students are unique and deserve individual consideration (i.e., students both with and without disabilities may need specific adaptations). Finally, a significant minority of general educators believe that because classes have standards to uphold, all students need to meet those standards without adaptations (Bursuck et al., 1996).

One additional perspective on fairness is provided by Bursuck, Munk, and Olsen (1999) who reported that a majority of all students without disabilities felt that no adaptations were fair; while some were perceived as relatively more fair, the researchers concluded that equity was the greatest concern of these students.

Polloway et al. (2001) suggest these overall considerations about grading:

▶ Plan for special and general education teachers to meet regularly to discuss student progress.
▶ Emphasize the acquisition of new skills as a basis for grades assigned, thus providing a perspective on the student's relative gains.
▶ Investigate alternatives for evaluating content that has been learned (e.g., oral examinations for poor readers in a science class).
▶ Engage in cooperative grading agreements (e.g., grades for language arts might reflect performance both in the classroom and the resource room).
▶ Use narrative reports as a key portion of, or adjunct to, the report card. These reports can include comments on specific objectives within the student's IEP.
▶ Develop personalized grading plans for students (see Munk and Bursuck, 2001).

The nearby Inclusion Strategies feature on grading provides additional perspectives.

Effective Grading Practices

Grading is a critical element of successful inclusion. Salend and Garrick Duhaney (2002) provided a series of recommendations, which include the following:

▶ **Communicating Expectations and Grading Guidelines.** Student performance is enhanced when teachers clearly communicate their expectations to students and families and share their grading guidelines and criteria with them.

▶ **Informing Students and Families Regarding Grading Progress on a Regular Basis.** Providing students and their families with ongoing information concerning current performance and grades helps all involved parties understand the grading guidelines. Ongoing sharing of students' grading progress facilitates the modifications of instructional programs so that students and families are not surprised by the grades received at the end of the grading period. It also prompts students to examine their effort, motivation, and attitudes and their impact on their performance and grades.

▶ **Using a Range of Assignments That Address Students' Varied Learning Needs, Strengths, and Styles.** Rather than assigning grades based solely on test performance or a limited number of assignments, many teachers determine students' grades by weighing a variety of student assignments (e.g., tests, homework, projects, extra credit, class participation, attendance, behavior, and other factors).

▶ **Employing Classroom-Based Assessment Alternatives to Traditional Testing.** Whereas grades are frequently determined by students' performance on tests, they also can be based on classroom-based assessment techniques, such as performance assessment, portfolio assessment, and curriculum-based measurement. By using performance assessment, teachers grade students on authentic products (e.g., creating and making things, solving problems, responding to stimulations) that demonstrate their skills, problem-solving abilities, knowledge, and understanding of the learning standards. Similarly, student portfolios and curriculum-based measurements that are linked to the learning standards serve as tools for grading students and guiding the teaching and learning process.

▶ **Providing Feedback on Assignments and Grading Students After They Have Learned Something Rather Than While They Are Learning It.** Before grading students on an assignment or a test, teachers should provide a range of appropriate learning activities and give nongraded assignments that help students practice and develop their skills. As students work on these assignments, teachers should give them feedback and additional instructional experiences to improve their learning of the material, which is then assessed when they have completed the learning cycle.

▶ **Avoiding Competition and Promoting Collaboration.** While grading on a curve results in a consistent grade distribution, it hinders the teaching and learning process by promoting competition among students. Therefore, educators minimize competition by grading students in reference to specific learning criteria and refraining from posting grades. Teachers also promote collaboration among students by structuring learning and assessments activities so that students work together and are graded cooperatively.

▶ **Designing Valid Tests and Providing Students with Appropriate Testing Accommodations.** Teachers enhance the value of their tests and promote student performance by developing valid tests and providing students with appropriate testing accommodations. In designing valid tests, teachers select the content of the test so that it relates to the learning standards, the manner in which the content was taught, and the amount of class time devoted to the topics on the test. Teachers also carefully examine the format and readability of their tests, and provide students with the testing accommodations outlined on their IEPs.

▶ **Teaching Test-Taking to Students.** Instruction in test-taking skills helps students perform at their optimal levels by reducing testing anxiety and assisting them in feeling comfortable with the format of the test.

For follow-up questions about effective grading practices, go to Chapter 15 of the Companion Website (ablongman.com/sppd4e) and click Inclusion Strategies.

Adapted from "Grading Students in Inclusive Settings" (pp. 13–14) by S. Salend & L. Garrick Duhaney, 2002, *Teaching Exceptional Children, 34*(3).

Summary

General Curricular Considerations

▶ The curriculum for elementary students with disabilities should meet their current and long-term needs, facilitate their interactions with nondisabled peers, and facilitate their transition into middle school.

Curricular Content

▶ Reading instruction should reflect emphases on both decoding skills and whole language to provide a comprehensive, balanced program.

▶ Math instruction should provide students with concrete and abstract learning opportunities and should stress the development of problem-solving skills.

▶ Teachers should select programs and strategies that focus on the social skills most needed by students in their classrooms.

▶ Life skills instruction should be a part of the elementary curriculum through the use of augmentation, infusion, or an integrated curriculum.

Professional Collaboration

▶ Cooperative teaching involves a team approach in which teachers share their talents in providing class instruction to all students. This requires a commitment to planning, time, and administrative support to reach its potential for success.

Instructional Adaptations

▶ Instructional adaptations should be evaluated against their "treatment acceptability" (e.g., their helpfulness, feasibility, desirability, and fairness).

▶ Listening is a skill that requires conscious effort on the part of students and planned intervention strategies on the part of teachers.

▶ Reading tasks can be adapted through a variety of instructional strategies such as clarifying intent, highlighting content, modifying difficulty level, and using visual aids.

▶ Written responses can be facilitated through modification of the response requirement.

▶ Cooperative learning affords teachers a unique opportunity to involve students with disabilities in classroom activities.

▶ Adaptations in class schedules or classroom arrangements should be considered in order to enhance the learning of students with disabilities.

▶ Educational programs should be designed to reflect the importance of motivation.

▶ Homework creates significant challenges for students with special needs; these should be addressed by using intervention strategies.

▶ Classroom grading practices should be flexible enough to facilitate inclusion.

Further Readings

Bashan, A., Appleton, V. E., & Dykeman, C. (2000). *Team building in education: A how-to guidebook.* Denver: Love.

Bauwens, J., & Hourcade, J. (1995). *Cooperative teaching.* Austin, TX: Pro-Ed.

Buck, G. H., Patton, J. R., Fad, K. M., & Polloway, E. A. (in press). *Prereferral intervention resource guide.* Austin, TX: Pro-Ed.

Coutinho, M. J., & Repp, A. C. (1999). *Inclusion: The integration of students with disabilities.* Belmont, CA: Wadsworth.

Fulk, B. M., & King, K. (2001). Classwide peer tutoring at work. *Teaching Exceptional Children, 34*(2), 49–53.

Mastropieri, M. A., & Scruggs, T. E. (2000). *The inclusive classroom: Strategies for effective instruction.* Columbus, OH: Merrill

Polloway, E. A., Patton, J. R., & Serna, L. (2001). *Strategies for teaching learners with special needs* (7th ed.). Columbus, OH: Merrill.

VideoWorkshop Extra!

If the VideoWorkshop package was included with your textbook, go to Chapter 15 of the Companion Website (www.ablongman.com/sppd4e) and click on the VideoWorkshop button. Follow the instructions for viewing video clip 4. Then consider this information along with what you've read in Chapter 15 while answering the following question:

The narrator of this video clip suggests that the specific teaching strategies of direct instruction, coaching, feedback, mediation, and modeling are appropriate for students whose are not native English speakers. Explain how each of these strategies might benefit such students.

16 Teaching Students with Special Needs in Secondary Schools

After reading this chapter, you should be able to

1. define the concept of a comprehensive curriculum and discuss curricular alternatives for students with disabilities.
2. discuss ways to determine the curricular needs of secondary school students.
3. discuss the transition planning process for students with disabilities.
4. identify and describe the key elements of effective instruction.
5. discuss the role of general education and special education teachers in ensuring successful secondary school programs for students with special needs.
6. identify accommodations and adaptations that can facilitate learning for secondary school students.
7. identify and give examples of study skills and learning strategies that can enhance school performance for adolescent learners.
8. define transition and describe how school personnel should implement transition planning and services.

Mike just turned 17 years old. While extremely happy about reaching this milestone in his life, he feels very frustrated in school. Mike was identified as having a learning disability in reading and written expression in the third grade; due to his slow reading rate, he has difficulty finishing in-class assignments and homework, and taking tests with peers. Since third grade, he has spent time in resource room programs every year, ranging from one hour daily in the elementary grades to three hours last year as a ninth grader in middle school. Now, as a junior in high school, Mike is embarrassed when he has to go to the resource room. His classmates have begun to call him "dummy" and "retard." While he knows that a learning disability has nothing to do with intelligence, he wants to stop going to the resource room so his friends will stop calling him names. He has told his parents about these feelings. They are meeting this afternoon with the high school counselor, special education teacher, and assistant principal. As the high school special education resource room teacher, you have been asked by the principal to conduct the meeting and be prepared to make some specific recommendations about Mike's program. You are weighing the benefits of the resource room versus the negatives associated with peer rejection.

QUESTIONS TO CONSIDER

1. What are the benefits of continuing to serve Mike in the resource room?
2. How can Mike be provided with support services without experiencing peer ridicule and rejection?
3. How might the changes Mike is requesting in his IEP affect the outcome of his transitional goal of attending college?
4. What is your final recommendation for Mike? What is this recommendation based on?

CONSIDER THIS

Do special education support staff need different skills at the secondary level than they need in elementary schools? If so, what are some of the differences?

TEACHING TIP

Special education teachers might want to provide a staff development session to general classroom teachers outlining the purposes of an inclusive program and provide some success stories. Ensure that classroom teachers know that they have some supports.

Important differences exist between elementary and secondary settings in terms of organizational structure, curricula, and learner characteristics. These differences create special challenges for successful inclusion. Certainly one concern is the gap found between the demands of the classroom setting and academics and the ability of many students with disabilities. Academically, this gap widens; many students with disabilities exhibit limited basic skills and therefore experience difficulty in performing higher-level cognitive tasks.

A second concern is that teachers are often trained primarily as content specialists, yet are expected to present complex material in such a way that a diverse group of students can master the information (Masters, Mori, & Mori, 1999). Secondary teachers are more likely to focus on teaching the content than on individualizing instruction to meet the unique needs of each student. Further, because there may be reluctance to change grading systems or make other accommodations, it may become difficult for students with disabilities to experience success in general education settings.

A third challenge is the general nature of adolescence. Adolescence is a difficult and trying time for all young people. For students with disabilities, the developmental period is even more challenging. Problems such as a lack of motivation associated with adolescence are exacerbated by the presence of a disability (Masters et al., 1999). A fourth problem in including students with disabilities at the secondary level is the current movement to reform schools. For example, these changes may mean that all students will have to take more math and science courses or achieve a passing grade on a minimum competency test; such requirements may prove difficult to meet for many students who experience learning and behavior problems.

Perhaps, given these concerns, it is not surprising to find that secondary teachers have been less positive overall toward efforts at inclusion (Scruggs & Mastropieri, 1996). However, regardless of the difficulties associated with placing adolescents with special needs in general education programs, more students with disabilities are going to depend on classroom teachers to help develop and provide appropriate educational programs. Therefore, classroom teachers in secondary schools must be prepared to offer specialized instruction and modified curricula to facilitate success for these special students.

Secondary School Curricula

More curricular differentiation has been advocated at the secondary level to accommodate the individual needs and interests of the wide variety of students attending comprehensive high schools in the United States. At the same time, most high schools have a general curriculum that all students must complete. This curriculum, generally prescribed by the state education agency, includes science, math, social studies, and English. Often, state and local education agencies add such areas such as art education, sexuality, drug education, and foreign languages to the required general curriculum.

Students have opportunities to choose curricular alternatives, which are usually related to postschool goals. For example, students planning to go to college choose a college preparatory focus that builds on the general curriculum with higher-level academic courses and often the study of a language. This college preparatory option helps prepare students for the rigorous courses found at college. Other students choose a vocational program, designed to help prepare them for specific job opportunities after high school. Still other students choose a general curriculum, with some course choices for students who do not plan to go to college and who are not interested in a specific vocational choice (Smith, 1990).

Although the specific curricula offered in different secondary schools vary, they generally follow state guidelines. Individual schools, however, offer unique curricular options that appeal to particular students. The curricular focus that students choose should be an important consideration because the decision could have long-term implications after the student exits school.

The educational reform movements of the 1980s and 1990s have had a direct impact on the secondary curriculum. Schools have begun to offer, and in some cases require, more science and math courses. Also, in many states and districts, students must successfully complete high school competency examinations before they are eligible for graduation. Students not passing these exams may receive a certificate of attendance or completion instead of a diploma. These changes seem to have had a positive effect on students in general education, since their graduation rate continues to climb. Newburger and Curry (1999) report that the national high school completion rate, including those earning the General Education Development (GED) certificate and those completing an adult education program, is 90%. Unfortunately, these changes have not resulted in more positive outcomes for students with special needs.

Special Education Curriculum in Secondary Schools

The curriculum for students with disabilities is the most critical programming consideration in secondary schools. Even if students have excellent teachers, if the curriculum is inappropriate to meet their needs, then the teaching may be ineffective. The high school curriculum for students with disabilities must be comprehensive; that is, it must

▶ be responsive to the needs of individual students.
▶ facilitate maximum integration with nondisabled peers.
▶ facilitate socialization.
▶ focus on the students' transition to postsecondary settings.

Determining Curricular Needs of Students

The curriculum for any student should be based on an appraisal of desired long-term outcomes and an assessment of current needs and selected to meet the individual needs of students. The *22nd Annual Report to Congress on the Implementation of IDEA* (U.S. Department of Education, 2000) reported that only 32.8% of all students with disabilities, aged 14 and above, who left special education during the 1998–1999 year, graduated with a diploma or certificate. The drop-out rate for these students was 26.8%. Unlike their nondisabled peers, data suggests that individuals with disabilities who drop out of school seldom obtain their GED or attend an adult program (Center for Adult Learning and Educational Credentials, 1999). Unfortunately, school dropout rate is also tied to negative adult outcomes. Only 15% of individuals with disabilities who do not have a high school diploma are in the labor force; that number doubles with a high school diploma and continues to increase with the years of postsecondary training (Yelin & Katz, 1994).

Several follow-up studies have shown that adults with disabilities are significantly more likely to be employed part-time, underemployed, or unemployed than their nondisabled peers (Blackerby & Wagner, 1996). Only 32% of individuals with disabilities (ages 18–64) work part-time or full-time, compared to 81% of their nondisabled peers (National Organization on Disability, 2000). Therefore, regardless of the efforts made in secondary schools to meet the individual needs of students with disabilities, many of these students seem unprepared to achieve success as young adults, despite the fact that more than twice as much is spent on a student in special education than on his or her general education peer (Chambers, Parrish, Lieberman, & Woman, 1998).

To ensure that students have the optimum chance at success in their lives after high school, transition planning is an essential responsibility and legal requirement (see the Rights & Responsibility feature). The transition IEP helps individuals and their families focus on the future, most often choosing vocational training, a two- or four-year college education, or obtaining a job, and living as independently as possible in a community. A

CONSIDER THIS

Describe some of the reforms made in secondary schools and their impact on providing services to students with special needs. For example, how does increasing graduation requirements affect students with special needs?

TEACHING TIP

Teachers must remember that students with disabilities can be successful in an academic curriculum. The curricular needs of each student should be assessed before any conclusions are drawn about the student's program of study.

CONSIDER THIS

What are some things that schools could do to increase the number of students with disabilities who stay in school and graduate? Should schools do these things?

Legal Requirements Related to Transition

In 1990, with the reauthorization of the Individuals with Disabilities Education Act (IDEA Amendments of 1997; Public Law 105–17), transition became a critical mandate and component of the law. This mandate requires that schools provide a process for planning for students' attainment of future postschool outcomes through the development of an appropriate educational course of study. This process is defined as "an outcome-oriented process that promotes movement from school to postschool activities" (PL 101–476, Section 300.29).

Further IDEA goes on to clarify that transition planning must be "based on the individual student's needs, taking into account the student's preferences and interests" (PL 101–476,

Section 300.29). The adult postschool outcomes that are described in transition IEPs focus on the areas of employment, postsecondary education and training, and community living.

For follow-up questions about legal requirements and transition, go to Chapter 16 of the Companion Website (ablongman.com/sppd4e) and click Rights & Responsibilities.

Adapted from "Connecting Outcomes, Goals, and Objectives in Transition Planning" by D. E. Steere & D. Cavaiuolo, 2002, *Teaching Exceptional Children, 34*(6), 54–59.

team of professionals will participate in developing the plan, but the student should be an active participant. His or her role might include planning the meeting, sending invitations, preparing the room, presenting his or her interests and goals, proposing activities and interacting with parents and other team members to identify the objectives and activities that will most likely lead to the desired outcome (Steere & Cavaioulo, 2002). Recent studies suggest that many states have been too slow in implementing transition service requirements and have failed to meet minimal levels of compliance (Johnson, Stodden, Emanuel, Lluecking, & Mack, 2002). Many challenges face educators as they try to implement methods to meet transition service needs of students with disabilities. High expectations must be maintained and students must remain on a "full curriculum track," with additional opportunities as appropriate in vocational education, community work experience, service learning, and adult living skills (Johnson, 2002).

One method of facilitating the transition planning for students is to use a person-centered approach, which is based on the premise that the student is the central part of the planning process. Using this model, school personnel acknowledge that all students, regardless of their disability, have certain strengths and capacities and interweave these with formal and informal community supports. Table 16.1 compares the use of a personal futures planning model to the more traditional transition planning model that many schools use. As you can see, the futures planning approach is based on a circle of support that is available for the student (Everson, 1998).

Everson (1998) notes that mapping can be used as one approach in transition planning. This approach requires the development of a personal profile of the student, which consists of the following maps:

▶ Background map
▶ Relationship map
▶ Setting map
▶ Choice map
▶ Preference map

These maps can then be used to develop a transition plan. Table 16.2 on page 484 shows how transition mapping information can be translated into transition goals and objectives. For students with disabilities, these goals should be delineated in the IEP and also reflected in individual transition plans (ITPs), according to IDEA, for students over the

TEACHING TIP

Teachers and other school personnel must include students with disabilities and their family members in planning for the future.

TABLE 16.1   **Comparison of Personal Futures Planning and Traditional Transition Planning Concepts**

Traditional Transition Planning	*Personal Futures Planning*
A team of service providers meets annually with parents to develop a plan for educational and related services.	A circle of support made up of the focus person with a disability, parents, and other family members meets with service providers and other community members monthly or as frequently as needed to develop and implement a future vision for the focus individual.
A transdisciplinary team conducts and interprets assessment data using standardized and nonstandardized assessment mechanisms.	A circle of support gathers, organizes, and manages assessment information into a personal profile and future vision using highly visual and graphic maps.
The student with a disability is invited to participate in the team meeting as appropriate.	The circle defines a role for every focus person and assists the person in assuming the role in a respected and competent manner.
Parents are invited to participate in the development of the individualized service plan.	Parents, other family members, friends, and general community members define the personal profile and future vision and look to service providers for support.
An IEP with a statement of needed transition services is mandated to guide services.	A future vision and action plan guide the circle's activities and should be used to drive IEP/transition plan content.
Implementation of the plan is ensured through provision of entitlement services, due process, and professional services.	Implementation of the plan depends upon the commitment and energy of the circle of support and their connections with the focus person and family.

From *Transition Services for Youths Who Are Deaf–Blind: A "Best Practices" Guide for Educators* (p. 27), edited by J. M. Everson, 1995, Sands Point, NY: Helen Keller National Center–Technical Assistance Center. Used by permission.

age of 14. But such planning should commence even earlier (Battle, Dickens-Wright, & Murphy, 1998), as discussed in Chapter 15.

The overriding goal of the IEP and ITP for secondary students is to achieve personal fulfillment as an adult. To be successful, students need to identify and use all services and supports available to them. These steps lead to the acquisition of usable skills and knowledge and to the identification of adult service agencies that will help them meet the demands of adulthood at their maximum potential (Patton & Dunn, 1998). Figure 16.1 on page 485 depicts this process.

The ITP shown in Figure 16.2 on pages 486 and 487 displays the transition plan for John, who wants to go to work after high school. Notice the involvement of the adult agencies in John's plan.

The most commonly accessed adult agencies and their potential contributions for students going to postsecondary education or employment, as well as those needing assistance with independent living, are shown in Table 16.3 on page 488.

Programs for Students in Secondary Schools

Most secondary students with disabilities are currently included in general education classrooms for at least a portion of each school day. *The 22nd Annual Report to Congress* indicated that 70% of students with disabilities, aged 12–17, were served in either resource rooms or regular classrooms (U.S. Department of Education, 2000). Therefore, the responsibility for these students becomes a joint effort between general education classroom teachers and special education personnel (Walther-Thomas et al., 2000). Unfortunately, many of these students do not experience success in the general classroom setting. They frequently fail classes, become frustrated and act out, and may even drop out of school because they are not prepared to meet the demands placed on them by secondary

TABLE 16.2   **Translating Mapping "Data" into Transition Planning Goals and Objectives**

Step #1:	Create personal profile and future vision maps for all transition-age youth. These maps may be created as part of personal futures planning team activities, as units in high school self-advocacy or career exploration activities, as youth group or church activities, or as family activities.
Step #2:	Bring maps to IEP/transition planning meetings. Use them to open the meeting and establish a more person-centered environment for discussion. Post the original copies on the wall during the meetings. Staple reduced-sized copies of the maps to the youth's educational file. Ask the youth and his or her family members to summarize the maps.
Step #3:	Discuss themes, things that work, and things that don't work in the personal profile maps. Think about people, places, materials, activities, schedules, and communication patterns. Discuss the implications of these findings for the youth's current educational programming. Discuss the implications of these findings for the youth's future educational program.
Step #4:	Discuss the future vision map. What services and supports currently exist to support the youth's future dreams? What gaps exist? What opportunities, experiences, and environments does the youth need to fulfill his or her future dreams? If a local community or regional transition planning team exist, share both future vision and service gap information with them. If the youth has a personal future planning team, ensure that some members serve as members of both teams.
Step #5:	Discuss each transition planning area along with associated mapping data. For example, employment goals can be clarified by reviewing the future vision map, preferences map, and setting map. The optional communication and health maps may also yield important employment planning information.
Step #6:	Select educational environments and activities for instruction based upon mapping information, other assessment information, demographics of community, and school logistics. For example, if the relationship map indicates that the youth has little opportunity to interact with typical peers and non-paid adults, look for environments and activities that will expand the number and type of people in the youth's life.
Step #7:	Develop IEP/transition planning goals. Use the future vision map as a checkpoint. Will the articulated goals move the focus individual toward his or her desired future? Will mastery of these goals assist the individual in leading a more community-inclusive adult life? If the answer is no or if there is uncertainty, the team should discuss and possibly reconsider the goals.
Step #8:	For each goal, determine necessary IEP/transition planning components. Create an "obstacles and opportunities" map to identify existing services as well as service gaps needed to achieve the individual's future vision. Identify interagency linkages and responsibilities. When service gaps exist, brainstorm potential solutions—are some team members willing to engage in personal futures planning activities? Is there a local community or regional team willing to assist in the necessary systems change?
Step #9:	Repeat this process each year, refining the future vision and obstacles and opportunities map each year. Celebrate small and large successes.

From *Transition Services for Youths Who Are Deaf–Blind: A "Best-Practices" Guide for Educators* (p. 31), edited by J. M. Everson, 1995, Sands Point, NY: Helen Keller National Center–Technical Assistance Center. Used by permission.

teachers. There are numerous reasons why many students with disabilities fail in secondary classes:

▶ Lack of communication between special education personnel and classroom teachers
▶ Discrepancies between the expectations of classroom teachers and the abilities of students
▶ Students' lack of understanding about the demands of the classroom
▶ Classroom teachers' lack of understanding about students with disabilities

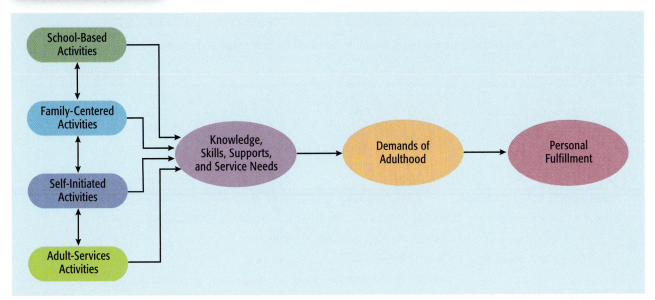

FIGURE 16.1   **Adulthood Implications of the Transition Process**

From *Transition from School to Young Adulthood: Basic Concepts and Recommended Practices* (p. 521) by J. R. Patton & C. Dunn, 1998, Austin, TX: Pro-Ed.

▶ Special education personnel's lack of knowledge about working with classroom teachers
▶ School policies that are inflexible

Regardless of the reasons why some students with disabilities do not achieve success in general education settings, the fact remains that the majority will be taught in inclusive settings. Therefore, classroom teachers and special education personnel must work together to increase the chances that these students will be successful. Figure 16.3 on page 489 displays the mismatch between the characteristics of students with disabilities and the academic and setting demands of high school, as well as the need for instructional interventions that will be described later in the chapter.

Roles of Personnel

As noted, the responsibility for educating students with disabilities in public schools is shared by general classroom teachers and special education personnel. Therefore, educators must improve their skills at working together to help students with various learning and behavior problems.

General Education Teachers   The primary role of general classroom teachers is to assume the responsibility for students with disabilities in particular classes or subject areas. Most classroom teachers present information using one general technique, but they will probably have to expand their instructional activities when dealing with students with disabilities. Various accommodations and modifications in instructional techniques and materials will be discussed later in the chapter.

Classroom teachers have general responsibilities that apply to students with and without disabilities. These include managing the classroom environment, providing instruction at an appropriate level and pace, using an appropriate curriculum, and evaluating student success and modifying instruction as appropriate. For students with disabilities, general classroom teachers have the added responsibility of participating on an interdisciplinary team (Masters et al., 1999).

In addition, teachers should ensure that all students have an opportunity to answer questions and a good chance of achieving at least moderate success in classroom activities.

General education teachers are primarily responsible for students with special needs in their classrooms.

FIGURE 16.2   An Individualized Transition Plan

ITP for Student with an Emotional Disability Enrolled in a 10th Grade Diploma-Bound Program

Student Profile. *John is a 16-year-old student. He is currently attending his neighborhood high school for four periods a day since returning to his family's home after a year-long stay in a group home for youth with emotional disabilities. John enjoys his class in auto mechanics, but has difficulty accepting responsibility for regular attendance and project completions. His academic skills are at grade level. John has signed up for a job skills class at the adult education night school to build his confidence in job interview skills. John wants to work full time after graduation.*

Individualized Transition Plan

Name *John T.*   **Birth Date** *01/31/81*   **Age** *16*   **Social Security**

Graduation Status   *X* Diploma   Special Diploma   Certificate of Completion   **Expects to Graduate:** *1999*

Describe Post-School Outcomes: Employment: *Full-time independent* **Residential:** *Semi-independent*

Education: *No additional school*   **Other:**

Work Experience Completed: **Vocational Classes:** *Woodshop; auto mechanics*

Community-Based Instruction: *3 hrs/school day training at Sea World — Custodial*

Work Experience: *8 hrs/week paid work at Sea World for 6 months*

Other:

Preparation for Adulthood:

Does student have	Yes	No	When?	In Process	Adult Agency Referral	Date to be referred	A–Active I–Inactive
Social Security Card	X				*Vocational Rehabilitation*	*3/99*	*I*
Driver's Education		X	*12th gr*		*Health & Human Services*	*N/A*	
Driver's License		X	*12th gr*		*Comm. College Dist. (Dis Stu Svcs)*	*N/A*	
State Identification Card	X		X		*Social Security (SSI)*		*A*
Bus Identification Card	X		X		*Employment Development Dept.*	*10/97*	
Birth Certificate	X				*County Mental Health Services*	*5/97*	*A*
Resume Completed		X	*11th gr*	X	*Dept. of Social Services (Dev/Dis)*	*N/A*	
Other					*Other*	*N/A*	

Continued on next page

This is not a call for teachers to "give" students with disabilities passing grades, only a requirement that students with disabilities receive an equal chance at being successful.

Classroom teachers should also do all they can to work effectively with special education professionals. Open communication and dialogue between classroom teachers and special education personnel is crucial if inclusion is to be successful. Communication among all individuals providing services to students with disabilities is the most important factor related to the success of inclusion (Walther-Thomas et al., 2000).

When working with students with disabilities, classroom teachers must realize that no single method always works; teachers have to individualize their efforts, constantly evaluating the effectiveness of their teaching efforts. The Inclusion Strategies on page 490 offers a guide for these reflections.

When teaching content courses, such as history and science, teachers should give students with disabilities the same opportunities to learn that they give all other students, remembering that the students with special needs would not be placed in the general classroom setting if an interdisciplinary team had not determined that they could benefit from that environment.

Prioritize issues to Be Addressed for This ITP

	Post-secondary	1	Employment/Training		Adult Agency Linkages
	Residential		Community Recreation/Leisure	2	Personal/Domestic Management
	Health and Medical		Financial and Income		Family Life and Social
3	Self-Advocacy		Mobility/Transportation		Other

Transition Domain	Transition Goals	Time-line	Agency/Person Responsible	Evaluation
Employment/Training	John will enroll in evening job-seeking skills class.	6/97	John, Counselor	___ Met ___ Modify ___ Continue
Employment/Training	John will apply for two jobs in areas of interest.	6/97	John, Teacher, Counselor	___ Met ___ Modify ___ Continue
Employment/Training	John will complete application and participate in summer Hire-A-Youth program.	5/96 & 5/97	John, Counselor	___ Met ___ Modify ___ Continue
Personal Management	John will attend weekly counseling meetings at County Mental Health and continue working on meeting personal goals and independent living goals.	6/97 — ongoing	John, Counselor	___ Met ___ Modify ___ Continue
Self-Advocacy	John will identify future lifestyle goals within each domain (i.e., employment, rec/leisure, etc.) and create a list describing his desires for each area.	9/97	John, Teacher, Parents	___ Met ___ Modify ___ Continue
Self-Advocacy	John will attend and participate in his ITP meetings and be able to communicate his employment and personal goals.	9/97– 6/98	John, Parents, Teachers	___ Met ___ Modify ___ Continue

Prioritize issues to Be Addressed at Next ITP Meeting:

	Post-secondary	3	Employment/Training	4	Adult Agency Linkages
1	Residential		Community Recreation/Leisure		Personal/Domestic Management
	Health and Medical	2	Financial and Income		Family Life and Social
	Self-Advocacy		Mobility/Transportation		Other

Additional Participants at Next ITP Meeting:
Name _Ms. Smith_____   Agency _County Mental Health_____
Signatures: Student _____   Parent(s) _____
Teacher _____   Adult agency _____
Transition Specialist _____   Principal _____
Counselor _____   Other _____

Adapted from *Teaching Children and Adolescents with Special Needs* (2nd ed., pp. 386–387) by J. L. Olson and J. M. Platt, 1996, Upper Saddle River, NJ: Merrill Prentice Hall, pp. 573–574. Copyright 1996 by Prentice Hall Publishing Company. Reprinted by permission.

Within the classroom, teachers can do several things that will facilitate the success of students with disabilities. They can modify the environment, alter the task presentation, vary the student requirements, and make the grading procedures more flexible (Finson & Ormsbee, 1998; Munsk et al., 1998; Salend, 1998). They must remember that students with disabilities, as well as those without disabilities, have different learning styles and needs and therefore require, from time to time, some alteration of instruction.

Teachers must think carefully about how realistic their expectations are of students. Schumm, Vaughn, and Leavell (1994) developed the planning pyramid that allows teachers to identify different degrees of learning to address individual needs and abilities; the philosophy is that all students will learn something but not all students will learn everything.

TABLE 16.3   **Common Community Agencies and the Transition Services They May Offer**

Agency/Program* (Purpose and Funding Source)	Examples of Employment Services	Examples of Postsecondary Education Services	Examples of Adult and Independent Living Services
Vocational Rehabilitation Agency assists persons with cognitive, sensory, physical, or emotional disabilities to attain employment and increased independence. Funded by federal and state money, VR agencies typically operate regional and local offices. VR services typically last for a limited period of time and are based on an individual's rehabilitation plan. If needed, an individual with disabilities can request services at a later time, and a new rehabilitation plan will be developed.	▶ Vocational guidance and counseling ▶ Medical, psychological, vocational, and other types of assessments to determine vocational potential ▶ Job development, placement, and follow-up services ▶ Rehabilitation, technological services and adaptive devices, tools, equipment, and supplies	▶ Apprenticeship programs, usually in conjunction with Department of Labor ▶ Vocational training ▶ College training toward a vocational goal as part of an eligible student's financial aid package	▶ Housing or transportation supports needed to maintain employment ▶ Interpreter services ▶ Orientation and mobility services
Mental Health and Mental Retardation Agencies provide a comprehensive system of services responsive to the needs of individuals with mental illness or mental retardation. Federal, state, and local funding are used to operate regional offices; local funding is often the primary source. Services are provided on a sliding payment scale.	▶ Supported and sheltered employment ▶ Competitive employment support for those who need minimal assistance		▶ Case management services to access and obtain local services ▶ Therapeutic recreation, including day activities, clubs, and programs ▶ Respite care ▶ Residential services (group homes and supervised apartments)
Independent Living Centers help people with disabilities to achieve and maintain self-sufficient lives within the community. Operated locally, ILCs serve a particular region. ILCs may charge for classes, but advocacy services are typically available at no cost.	▶ Information and referral services ▶ Connecting students with mentors with disabilities	▶ Advocacy training ▶ Connecting students with mentors with disabilities	▶ Advocacy training ▶ Auxiliary social services (e.g., maintaining a list of personal care attendants) ▶ Peer counseling services ▶ Housing assistance ▶ Training in skills of independent living (attendant management, housing, transportation, career development) ▶ Information and referral services ▶ Connecting with mentors
Social Security Administration operates the federally funded program that provides benefits for people of any age who are unable to do substantial work and have a severe mental or physical disability. Several programs are offered for people with disabilities, including Social Security Disability Insurance (SSDI), Supplemental Security Income (SSI), Plans to Achieve Self-Support (PASS), Medicaid, and Medicare.	Work incentive programs which may include: ▶ Cash benefits while working (e.g., student-earned income) ▶ Medicare or Medicaid while working ▶ Help with any extra work expenses the individual has as a result of the disability ▶ Assistance to start a new line of work	▶ Financial incentives for further education and training	▶ Medical benefits ▶ Can use income as basis for purchase or rental of housing

*Names of agencies or programs may differ slightly from state to state.

From *Transition Planning: A Team Effort* (pp. 4–5) by S. H. de Fur, 1999, Washington, DC: NICHCY.

INSTRUCTIONAL CONDITIONS

Learning Characteristics

▶ Academic deficits
▶ Learning strategy deficits
▶ Study skill deficits
▶ Thinking deficits
▶ Social interaction problems
▶ Motivation problems

Academic Demands

▶ Acquire information written at secondary level
▶ Gain information through lectures
▶ Demonstrate knowledge through tests
▶ Express information in writing
▶ Use problem-solving strategies
▶ Work independently
▶ Be motivated to learn

Setting Realities

▶ Coverage of large amounts of content
▶ Use of difficult texts
▶ Limited opportunities for academic interactions
▶ Classes of diverse learners
▶ Emphasis on achieving students
▶ Limited planning and teaching time

ESSENTIAL SERVICES

Learning Strategies

▶ Techniques, principles, or rules that enable students to learn, to solve problems, and to complete tasks independently

Content Enhancements

▶ Devices and teaching routines that help teachers present content in a learner-friendly manner to help students identify, organize, comprehend, and recall critical information.

Study Skills Techniques

▶ Specific techniques and devices to help students acquire, retain, and express knowledge

FIGURE 16.3

Instructional Conditions and Essential Services for Students with Learning Problems

From *Teaching Students with Learning Problems* (6th ed., p. 532) by C. D. Mercer & A. R. Mercer, 2001, Upper Saddle River, NJ: Merrill.

In Figure 16.4 on page 491, you see a learning pyramid developed for a science class by Watson and Houtz (2002) for culturally and linguistically diverse students. This process works equally as well for students with disabilities.

Collaborative Role of the Special Education Teacher

The special education teacher plays an important role in the successful inclusion of students with disabilities in secondary schools. In addition to collaborating with general educators, the special education teacher must prepare students for the challenges that occur daily in the general education environment and equip them for future challenges in independent living and employment. Above all, special education teachers play a major support role for general classroom teachers. They should communicate regularly with classroom teachers and provide assistance through consultation or through direct instruction (Masters et al., 1999).

The specific roles of the special education teacher include counseling students for the personal crises that may occur daily and preparing students for content classes, the high school graduation exam, postsecondary training, independent living, and, ultimately, employment (Smith, Finn, & Dowdy, 1993). Special education teachers and general teachers often collaborate in performing these roles.

Counseling for Daily Crises   Adolescence is a difficult time of change for all children; for children with disabilities, the period is even more challenging. In American society, students are constantly trying to grasp the subtle changes in roles for males and females. They experience more exposure to drugs and alcohol, and pregnancy and AIDS are common issues.

CROSS-REFERENCE

Review Chapters 5–11 and reflect on how different disabilities influence preparation for high school content courses.

Questions for Evaluating the Instructional Process

▶ *Student motivation* Am I creating a context in which learning is valued?

▶ *Student attention* Am I creating an environment in which students can and are encouraged to attend to the learning task?

▶ *Encouragement* Am I creating a setting in which students are encouraged to take risks and be challenged by learning?

▶ *Modeling* Are the students given the opportunity to watch, listen, and talk to others so that they can see how the knowledge or skill is learned?

▶ *Activating prior knowledge* Am I getting the students to think about what they already know about a skill or topic, and are they given the opportunity to build upon that information in an organized fashion?

▶ *Rate, amount, and manner of presentation* Are the new skills and knowledge

being presented at a rate and amount that allows the students time to learn, and in a manner that gives them enough information yet does not overload them?

▶ *Practice* Are the students given ample opportunity to practice?

▶ *Feedback* Are the students given feedback on their work so they know how and what they are learning?

▶ *Acquisition* Are the students given the opportunity to learn skills and knowledge until they feel comfortable with them and to the point they do or know something almost automatically?

▶ *Maintenance* Are the students given the opportunity to continue to use their skills and knowledge so that they can serve as tools for further learning?

▶ *Generalization* Are the students generalizing the skills and knowledge to other

tasks, settings, and situations? Are the students, other teachers, or parents seeing the learning?

▶ *Application* Are the students given the opportunity to apply their skills and knowledge in new and novel situations, thereby adapting their skills to meet the new learning experiences?

 For follow-up questions about evaluating the instructional process, go to Chapter 16 of the Companion Website (ablongman.com/sppd4e) and click Inclusion Strategies.

From *Strategies for Teaching Students with Learning and Behavior Problems* (5th ed., p. 26) by C. S. Bos & S. Vaughn, 2002, Boston: Allyn and Bacon.

The increased tension, frustration, and depression can lead to suicide, the second leading cause of death among adolescents (Spirito, Hart, Overholser, & Halverson, 1990; Smith et al., 1993), or a variety of behavior and emotional problems. Special education teachers need to collaborate with general educators to help students deal with these problems.

Preparing for High School Content Classes The special education teacher should be aware of factors such as classroom teacher expectations, teaching styles, and the demands of the learning environment (Welch & Link, 1991). One way special education teachers can help students deal with the "general education world" is to teach them how to self-advocate. In order to do so, students need to understand their specific learning problems. Therefore, special education teachers may need to have a discussion with their students about the nature of specific disabilities.

Deshler, Ellis, and Lenz (1996) suggest that the primary role of special education teachers should be to teach their students effective strategies to compensate for their learning deficits and therefore increase the likelihood of success in general education classes. They suggest teaching numerous strategies for memorizing, test taking, listening, note taking, proofreading, time management, and organization. Specific techniques for several of these are discussed later in the chapter. If students with learning problems know how to use these kinds of strategies, they will have a better chance of achieving success in general classrooms.

When working with students with disabilities in general education classrooms, the role of the special educator expands to include informing the general educator as to the unique abilities and challenges presented by each student, providing ongoing support and collaboration for the student and teacher, and frequent monitoring to ensure that the arrangement is satisfactory for both the student and the teacher.

Preparing for the High School Graduation Exam Passing a high school graduation exam as a requirement for receiving a regular diploma began in many states in the 1980s as part

TEACHING TIP

Teachers need to evaluate each student to determine the level of skills necessary for success in post-secondary settings and develop plans to improve weak areas.

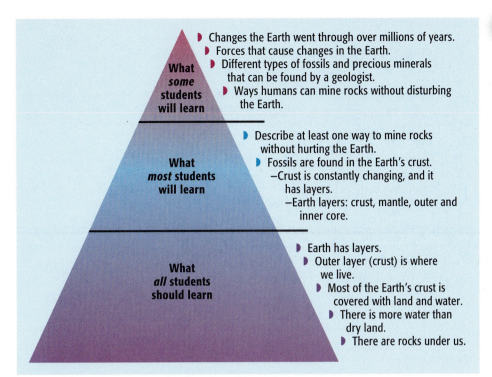

FIGURE 16.4

A Learning Pyramid for a Science Class

From "Teaching Science: Meeting the Academic Needs of Culturally and Linguistically Diverse Students" (p. 270) by S. M. R. Watson & L. E. Houtz, 2002, *Intervention in School and Clinic, 37*(5).

of the national reform movements in education. Students with disabilities may or may not be required to take the exam, depending on state regulations and local school district policies. In some states, students with disabilities are granted a regular high school diploma without having to complete the examination; in others, students with disabilities who do not pass the graduation exam are given a certification of attendance or completion.

Special education teachers, in conjunction with classroom teachers, have two roles regarding the high school graduation exam. On one hand, they are obligated to help the student prepare for the exam if it is the decision of the IEP team that the student should be prepared to take the exam. On the other hand, the special education teacher and classroom teachers may choose to focus on convincing the student and parents that time could more appropriately be spent on developing functional skills rather than on preparing for the graduation exam. Information on testing is discussed later in the chapter.

Preparing for Postsecondary Training   Students with disabilities absolutely should aim for postsecondary education if they have the ability and motivation. Postsecondary education does not have to mean attending a four-year institution. A community college, vocational-technical school, trade school, or some other form of postsecondary education and training are other possibilities. Teachers, both general and special education, need to inform students about future employment trends and help them select a realistic career with employment potential. A variety of reports regarding the importance of education in the future for students with and without disabilities have concluded the following:

1. Higher levels of academic achievement will be required, and very few jobs will be appropriate for individuals deficient in reading, writing, and math.
2. There will be an increase in service industry jobs and a decrease in manufacturing jobs.
3. More than half of the new jobs created in the 1990s required education beyond high school, and more than a third were filled by college graduates.
4. Technology will play an increasing role for all individuals.

Preparing for Independent Living   Independent living is a realistic goal for the vast majority of individuals with disabilities; however, for them to live successfully in today's complex, automated world, direct instruction in certain independent living skills may be required. This is also important in a student's transition program. The following areas may be problematic for persons with disabilities:

▶ Sexuality
▶ Managing personal finances
▶ Developing and maintaining social networks
▶ Maintaining a home
▶ Managing food
▶ Employment
▶ Transportation
▶ Self-confidence and self-esteem
▶ Organization
▶ Time management

Special education teachers must help students with disabilities achieve competence in these areas. Several curricular guides are available to structure intervention in these areas. Two excellent resources are the Life-Centered Career Education Program (Brolin, 1989) and Cronin and Patton's (1993) life skills program. The former presents a comprehensive curriculum for teaching life skills, whereas the latter is a resource guide for program development. Cronin and Patton (1993) present particularly useful models and strategies for infusing life skills into the regular curriculum. In addition, creative teachers can use community resources, gathering real materials from banks, restaurants, the local court house, and so forth, for developing their own program.

Preparing for Employment   The ultimate goal of all education is the employment of graduates at their maximum vocational potential. The passage of the Americans with Disabilities Act (ADA) in 1990 has made that dream a reality for millions of people with disabilities. Encompassing areas of employment, transportation, public accommodations, and telecommunications, the law prohibits discrimination against individuals with disabilities. ADA requires employers to make "reasonable accommodations" to assist persons with disabilities in performing their jobs. Supported employment initiatives (i.e., providing job coaches to support workers on the job) have emerged as particularly powerful tools. Teachers need to help students prepare for employment by teaching them the necessary skills for vocational success.

Inclusive vocational and technical programs present a unique opportunity to offer students both a functional curriculum and integration with nondisabled peers. These programs can provide appropriate entry into work-study programs, business apprenticeships, and technical and trade school programs.

Teachers must be sure that students with disabilities can communicate their strengths and limitations to persons in postsecondary and future employment settings. These self-advocacy skills will empower individuals to seek employment and independent living opportunities on their own. Field, Hoffman, and Spezia (1998) suggest the following to assist students with disabilities in developing self-determination skills:

▶ Encourage students to take risks through participating in an approved Adventure Challenge Program. Higher level challenges include scaling a 40-foot wall, traveling across a high ropes course, and using a map and compass to find your way back to a campsite. Students should always be asked, "What do you have to lose?" and "What can you gain from this experience?" A key component of Adventure Challenge Education is the firm commitment that all group members act in a manner that keeps themselves and their classmates safe. This encourages trust and emphasizes responsibility.
▶ While watching a tape with the sound turned off, instruct students to analyze the nonverbal communication of characters through their facial expressions, hand gestures, and body language. Discuss what the class believes the characters are communicating. Replay the tape with the sound on and evaluate how accurate they were in

CONSIDER THIS

In what ways can self-advocacy and self-determination affect young adults with disabilities? Should schools teach self-advocacy skills to adolescents with disabilities? Why or why not?

the translation. This is especially effective with tapes of the daily soap operas. Students enjoy the opportunity to view their favorite soap while analyzing the non-verbal communication signals.

▶ Use small groups to identify characteristics of the ideal or "dream" mentor. Give each group a large piece of paper and marking pens. Ask them to draw a person or an outline of one and fill in the characteristics of their ideal mentor on the drawing. To make the outline of a person, one student can lie on the paper and another can draw an outline around him or her.

▶ Demonstrate to students the concept of active listening by role-playing how to actively listen and how not to actively listen. Review the following steps of active listening with students:

• Listen carefully.
• Ask clarifying questions.
• State back to the speaker what you heard.
• Accept what the speaker says; do not challenge.

▶ Have students practice verbal communication skills through memorizing and reciting poetry. This process takes time and practice. Students quickly learn the value of "practice makes perfect." Record the students' recitations on individual cassette tapes. Encourage students to analyze their tapes for the quality of tone, volume, and pitch. Save the tapes and record often to measure progress.

▶ Emphasize the importance of not giving in or giving up! Identify support resources early and assist students as they plan how and when they will access support.

▶ Provide students with opportunities to interact with individuals who have personally experienced goal setting and self-determination. Design a single-page interview form. Select a sample group and instruct students to complete the interview with a representative of the sample group. Examples of sample groups include parents, grandparents, individuals with disabilities or illnesses, businesspeople or entrepreneurs, athletes, and teachers. Students should be encouraged to openly share the results of their interview and to look for common elements of self-determination among all of the interviews. Another variation of this activity includes using books or magazines to research famous people such as politicians, actors and actresses, television personalities, authors, and musicians. Create a collection of these reports organized by topic. Encourage students to write personally to their favorite celebrity. It is likely many will receive personal responses.

▶ Provide the entire class with the opportunity to be trained in Conflict Management and Peer Mediation. These courses not only provide individuals with important survival skills but equip all students with the skills necessary to resolve conflicts with their peers. Often, students who experience the most difficulty in resolving personal conflicts do very well at helping others resolve theirs.

▶ Provide a variety of games for the class. Select games that simulate life experiences. Many of these games are available through teacher supply catalogs and stores, but many are also available at local toy stores. Purchase four or five copies of each game and set up for tournaments. Suggest that students rate the games they play to determine their effectiveness. Value student opinions as they rate the games. Play games with the students to get a feel for the level of difficulty.

▶ Find an appropriate simulation kit at a teacher supply store or in an education catalog. Simulations can last for as little as one hour or as long as a full semester. Students work their way through the simulation and evaluate themselves on their effectiveness. Simulations provide an opportunity for students to practice skills prior to real life application. Examples of simulations that seem most effective include job search, independent living, interviewing, and entrepreneurship.

▶ Explore computer software stores and catalogs for materials that provide practice and simulation in the skills of negotiation and conflict resolution. Groups of students can be assigned a computer task for resolution. Numerous software programs are also available to support the development of all the self-determination skills, including self-esteem, job skills, problem solving, and goal setting.

▶ Create "Self-Determination Portfolios." Have students maintain their own portfolios, providing examples of their efforts in self-determination. Review the portfolios with the individual students often. This strategy encourages ongoing review of the action plan and discourages the tendency to give up.

TEACHING TIP

Use role-playing situations to help students understand how to utilize conflict management strategies. When situations occur where such strategies are not used, initiate a class discussion to talk about how things could have been handled better.

Personal Spotlight

Student and Football Player

Bill **Flowers** is a winner on and off the football field! "Some people get academic gifts; my gift is athletics," he said. Bill's goal is to be a professional football player like his dad and brother, but he knows he must work hard to attain that goal. Hard work is not new to Bill. In high school he practiced football before and after school; his coach talked about his impressive work ethic, noting that Bill was always looking for someone to throw to him. As a result, he was named Player of the Year for his area, Back of the Year by the Sports Writers Association, and Alabama's Player of the Year by Gatorade.

With learning disabilities, Bill has had to work as hard off the field as on. He attended a special school in Miami for children with special needs, where his fellow students were learning disabled, mentally retarded, and physically challenged. In high school, he went to tutors for two years to help him "pass math" and prepare for the graduation exam and the ACT. He didn't want the academic challenges to stand in his way. His high school teachers provided testing in distraction-reduced settings and with extended time.

Currently in college, Bill says college has been easier in some ways because of the note-taker that has been provided as

Bill Flowers

Student, University of Mississippi

an accommodation. His ADHD makes it really hard to listen and take notes; plus, he said his notes looked like "chicken scratch" when he tried to read them later! With the note-taker he can keep his mind on the lecture and learn while the professor talks. As a result, he now takes most of his tests with the class. College is still a real challenge, but Bill is confident that things will turn out for the best.

When asked about his successes, Bill always gives credit to others—his family, teachers, tutors, coaches, and other players. He is also very religious, and he feels that he was given a learning disability in order to make him a better person. He uses his setbacks as challenges to conquer, and he wants his story to help others who may not see their disability as a gift and to help those who haven't learned to see the gifts in every person.

For follow-up questions about this Personal Spotlight, go to Chapter 16 of the Companion Website (ablongman.com/sppd4e) and click Personal Spotlight.

▸ Help students learn about the effectiveness of various communication styles by asking them to describe the type of communication they used in different situations during the week (i.e., passive, assertive, or aggressive). Then have them tell what the outcome of that communication was.

▸ Have students generate a list of the pros and cons of avoiding conflict and of confronting conflict. Then discuss the pros and cons and when they might want to avoid conflict and when they would want to confront it. (pp. 29–31)

The nearby Personal Spotlight highlights a young adult with a learning disability who has become a strong self-advocate.

Methods to Facilitate Students' Success in General Education Classes

Students with disabilities traditionally have been placed in general education classrooms for instruction when they were determined to have the requisite academic ability necessary for success. With the advent of the inclusion movement, however, students with disabilities are often placed in such classes for other reasons. For most of these students, there is no need to dilute the curriculum; however, teachers will probably need to make accommodations, and students will need to use special learning strategies in order to achieve success.

Accommodations and Adaptations

In most instances, general education teachers are responsible for making accommodations or adaptations to help students with disabilities achieve in the secondary school.

This process is hampered by the fact that typically only one-fourth to one-half of secondary teachers have either taken a class or participated in in-service training in this area (e.g., Bursuck et al., 1996; Struyk et al., 1995, 1996). Unfortunately, even though most general education teachers view accommodations as desirable and reasonable, they often do not implement them. After reviewing numerous studies on this topic, Scott, Vitale, and Masten (1998) reported that the main reasons given by teachers for not implementing accommodations were a lack of training and school support.

Accommodations, or instructional adaptations, can either be typical/routine or substantial/specialized. "Typical/routine adaptations are either strategies directed toward the class as a whole or relatively minor adaptations that a teacher might make for any student. In contrast, substantial/specialized adaptations refer to individually tailored adjustments intended to address the needs of individual students with disabilities" (Scott et al., 1998, p. 107).

The following are examples of major categories of teacher adaptations (previously cited in Chapter 15 for elementary students) that have been modified for application with secondary students (Scott et al., 1998):

▶ Modify instruction by using different instructional approaches, focusing on different learning styles, and relating instruction to activities engaged in by adolescents.
▶ Modify assignments in ways to facilitate success for adolescents with disabilities and basic skill deficits.
▶ Teach study skills such as note taking, test taking, reading for content, and memory strategies that can be applied in content classes.
▶ Use alternative instructional materials that are interesting to adolescents and that can be accessed easily by adolescents with basic skill deficits.
▶ Alter curricula by providing adolescents with life skills, study skills, and prevocational opportunities.
▶ Vary instructional grouping to take advantage of cooperative learning and peer support systems.
▶ Enhance behavior by using age-appropriate reinforcement for adolescents.
▶ Facilitate progress monitoring by using a wide variety of methods to evaluate progress that meets the individual needs of students.

Accommodations should be designed to offer the least amount of alteration of the regular programming that will still allow the student to benefit from instruction. This approach is fair to nondisabled students and provides the students with disabilities with a realistic sense of their abilities and limitations. If too many accommodations are made, some students may be set up for failure in college or in other academically demanding environments. Students with too many accommodations may also begin to feel that they bring very little to the class; this feeling can further damage an already fragile self-concept. Modifications used in settings or classes designed to prepare an individual for a future job or postsecondary training program should reflect real conditions present in these future environments.

Many different accommodations can be used effectively with students with disabilities. Often, a great deal of a student's grade may be determined by the quality of work on assignments; yet sometimes students with disabilities may not understand an assignment or may lack the ability or time to complete it. Therefore, teachers may need to make some accommodations in the area of assignments. Chalmers (1991) suggests the following:

1. *Preteach vocabulary and preview major concepts:* Students must have the vocabulary necessary to complete an assignment. If they do not know a particular word, they may not know how to find its definition, causing them to possibly fail the assignment. Similarly, students need to understand the major concepts required to complete the assignment.
2. *State a purpose for reading:* Students need to know why they have to do things. Helping them understand the context of the assignment may aid in motivating them.

CROSS-REFERENCE

Review Chapters 5–11 to determine specific accommodations suggested for children with different disabilities.

CONSIDER THIS

Should teachers who refuse to make accommodations for students in their classes with different learning needs be required to make such efforts? What are the consequences for students included in classrooms where teachers refuse to make accommodations?

3. *Provide repetition of instruction:* Choral responding, group work, and hands-on activities are examples of providing students with disabilities with the opportunities necessary for learning. One instance of instruction may simply not be sufficient to ensure learning.

4. *Provide clear directions and examples:* "I didn't understand" is a common response from students when they fail. For many students, this response may simply be an effort to evade negative consequences. For many students with disabilities, however, the statement may reflect a true misunderstanding of the assignment. Therefore, teachers need to make every effort to explain all assignments in such a way that they are understandable to all students.

5. *Make time adjustments:* Teachers should individualize the time requirements associated with assignments. Some students may be capable of performing the work successfully, only to become frustrated with time restraints. Teachers should make adjustments for students who simply need more time or who may become overwhelmed by the volume of work required in a particular time period.

6. *Provide feedback:* All individuals need feedback; they need to know how they are doing. For students with disabilities and a history of failure, the feedback, especially positive feedback, is even more critical. Teachers should provide feedback for every assignment as soon as possible after the assignment is completed.

7. *Have students keep an assignment notebook:* Often, students with disabilities are disorganized; they may need some organization imposed upon them externally. Requiring students to keep an assignment notebook is an example. The assignment notebook not only negates the excuse "I did not have my assignment" or "I lost my assignment," but it also helps some students maintain a semblance of order in their assignments and facilitates their completion of all required work.

8. *Provide an alternate assignment:* Provide opportunities for students to complete an assignment differently. For example, if a student has difficulty with oral language, the teacher could accept a written book report rather than an oral one. Videotaped, tape-recorded, and oral presentations can be used in conjunction with written presentations.

9. *Allow manipulatives:* Cue cards, charts, and number lines are examples of manipulatives that can help some students comprehend information. Some students prefer to learn visually, whereas others prefer the auditory mode. Manipulatives can facilitate the learning of all students.

10. *Highlight textbooks:* Highlight the important facts in textbooks. These books can be passed on to other students with similar reading problems next year. Highlighting material enables students to focus on the important content.

> **TEACHING TIP**
>
> These accommodations are helpful for all students, including those without disabilities who do not need specialized instruction.

Another important accommodation that teachers can make is the alteration of materials. Deshler, Ellis, and Lenz (1996) describe a way to reduce the content in textbooks. Students may be given chapter summaries or outlines, or important sections in a chapter may be highlighted. Some students, while capable of reading and understanding, often take significantly longer to read than their peers. Therefore, teachers may wish to reduce the amount of content without altering the nature of the content. When selecting materials, teachers should consider cultural diversity issues.

In addition to significant curricular modifications, teachers can make numerous simple adjustments to teach specific information to students:

▶ Repeat important information several times.
▶ Write important facts on the board.
▶ Repeat the same information about a particular topic over several days.
▶ Distribute handouts that contain only the most important information about a particular topic.

Figure 16.5 provides a checklist teachers can use for further ideas, documentation, and evaluation of options implemented for accommodating learning needs.

FIGURE 16.5   **Checklist of Options for Accommodating Learning Needs**

Student _____ Teacher _____ Date(s) _____

[Circle accommodations attempted; mark successful accommodations with plus (+), unsuccessful with minus (–)]

Classroom
Design constructive learning environment.

Preferential seating (specifiy): _____

Group size:	___ 1–1 w/teacher	___ 1–1 w/peer	___ Small group	___ Large group
Need for movement:	___ Little	___ Average	___ High	
Distraction management:	___ Carrels	___ Headsets	___ Seating	___ Other
Noise:	___ None	___ Quiet	___ Moderate	
Lighting:	___ Dim	___ Average	___ Bright	
Temperature:	___ Warm	___ Average	___ Cool	

Other (specify): _____

Schedule
Arrange productive learning schedule.

Peak time:	___ Early morning	___ Late morning	___ Midday	___ Afternoon
Lesson length:	___ 5–10 min.	___ 15–20 min.	___ 25–30 min.	___ 30+ min.
Variation needed:	___ Little	___ Some	___ Average	___ Much
Extra time needed:	___ Little	___ Some	___ Average	___ Much

Other (specify): _____

Lessons
Use best stimulus/ response format.

Stimulus Format			*Response Format*		
Visual:	___ Observe	___ Read	Choose:	___ Point	___ Mark
Auditory:	___ Oral	___ Discuss	Tell:	___ Restate	___ Explain
Touch:	___ Hold	___ Feel	Write:	___ Short answer	___ Essay
Model:	___ Coach	___ Demonstrate	Word process:	___ Some	___ All
Multisensory:	___ Combination		Show:	___ Demonstrate	___ Make

Other (specify): _____

Materials
Make constructive material adjustments.

___ Vary stimulus/response	___ Vary directions	___ Vary sequence
___ Highlight essential content	___ Use partial content	___ Add steps
___ Expand practice	___ Add self-checking	___ Add Supplements
___ Segment	___ State key concepts in margins	(see below)

Other (specify): _____

Supplements
Provide supplementary aids to facilitate learning.

Instructional Strategies	*Materials*	*Assignments*	*Human Resources*
___ Advance organizers	___ Adaptive/assistive devise	___ Adapted testing	___ Co-teacher
___ Charted progress	___ Autiotapes of text	___ Advance assignment	___ Cooperative group
___ Checklist of steps	___ Calculator	___ Alternate assignments	___ Instructional coach
___ Computer activities	___ Captioned films	___ Extended time	___ Interpreter
___ Evaluation checklists	___ Coded text	___ Extra practice	___ Peer advocate
___ Graphic organizers	___ Computer programs	___ Outlined tasks	___ Peer notetaker
___ Modeling	___ Games for practice	___ Partial outlines	___ Peer prompter
___ Mnemonic guides	___ Highlighted text	___ Question guides	___ Peer tutor
___ Multisensory techniques	___ Key term definitions	___ Reference access	___ Personal attendant
___ Organization charts	___ Large print texts	___ Scripted practice	___ Study buddy
___ Repeated readings	___ Manipulatives	___ Segmented tasks	___ Volunteer tutor
___ Scripted demonstrations	___ Math number charts	___ Shortened assignments	
___ Self-questioning	___ Multiple text	___ Simplified directions	*Management Strategies*
___ Strategy posters	___ Parallel text	___ Simplified tasks	___ Charted performance
___ Verbal rehearsal	___ Simplified text	___ Structured notes	___ Checklists
___ Video modeling	___ Summaries	___ Study guides	___ Contracts
___ Visual imagery	___ Video enactments	___ Timed practice	___ Extra reinforcement
___ Other	___ Other	___ Other	___ Other
_____	_____	_____	_____

From Choate, J. S. (2002) *Successful inclusive teaching: Proven ways to detect and correct special needs* (3rd ed.) Boston, Allyn and Bacon, p. 38.

Homework, Grading, and Testing

CONSIDER THIS

Should standardized tests play such an important role in public schools? How does the expansion of these tests affect students with disabilities?

Homework, grading, and testing stand out as important considerations in students' success within secondary school classrooms. They have become more significant in light of trends toward making academic standards more rigorous and toward accountability in general education classrooms. Higher expectations for student performance in general education classes and the emphasis on national achievement tests affect testing and grading. This section explores these problem areas, focusing on adaptations to facilitate student success.

Homework   Problems in homework often become more pronounced at the secondary level. The trend has been to require more homework of students, which has become an issue in raising the standards of public education (Bryan & Sullivan-Burstein, 1998). Roderique et al. (1994) report that for school districts with a homework policy, the average amount of homework assigned at the high school level was over 1 hour and 40 minutes per daily assignment, and the frequency was 4.28 nights per week. Struyk et al. (1995) report that 70% of the teachers assigned homework two to four times per week; 11% assigned it five times per week. The time period needed to complete the homework varied from less than 30 minutes to 1.5 hours per day; 43% of the teachers assigned at least 30 minutes of homework per night. Given that students typically have 4–6 teachers, assignments represent a significant hurdle for middle and high school students with disabilities. While the amount of homework assigned provides a challenge, the unique difficulties of students with disabilities are underscored by the types of problems they are likely to have. Figure 16.6 lists the highest-rated homework problems of adolescents. Yet each problem carries implicit potential remedies.

Given that students with special needs experience problems with homework, a number of strategies can be pursued. For example, Struyk et al. (1995) found that, with regard to the helpfulness of specific *types of homework,* teachers rated preparation for tests and practice of skills already taught as moderately helpful, whereas enrichment activities and preparation for future class work were seen as least helpful. They rated in-class structures such as checking the level of the students' understanding when beginning an in-class assignment and using a homework assignment sheet or notebook as the most helpful *procedures.* Finally, teachers also rated the helpfulness of specific *adaptations* for students with disabilities. Their responses are summarized in Figure 16.7

Collaboration among general and special education teachers and parents will encourage successful completion of homework. Teachers should attend to communication problems that can evolve regarding homework. Struyk et al. (1996) cite communication prob-

FIGURE 16.6

Homework Problems of Adolescents with Behavior Disorders

Note: These are the highest rated problems noted by special educators.

From "A Comparison of Homework Problems of Secondary School Students with Behavior Disorders and Nondisabled Peers" (p. 152) by J. Soderlund, W. Bursuck, E. A. Polloway, and R. A. Foley, 1995, *Journal of Emotional and Behavioral Disorders, 3.* Used by permission.

1. Easily distracted by noises or activities of others.
2. Responds poorly when told by parent to correct homework.
3. Procrastinates, puts off doing homework.
4. Fails to complete homework.
5. Whines or complains about homework.
6. Easily frustrated by homework assignment.
7. Must be reminded to sit down and start homework.
8. Fails to bring home assignment and necessary materials.
9. Daydreams or plays with objects during homework session.
10. Refuses to do homework assignment.
11. Takes unusually long time to do homework.
12. Produces messy or sloppy homework.
13. Hurries through homework and makes careless mistakes.

1. Provide additional teacher assistance.
2. Check more frequently with student about assignments and expectations.
3. Provide a peer tutor for assistance.
4. Allow alternative response formats (e.g., oral or other than written).
5. Provide auxiliary learning aids (e.g., calculator, computer).
6. Adjust length of assignment.
7. Assign work that student can do independently.
8. Provide a study group.
9. Provide extra credit opportunities.
10. Evaluate based on effort, not on performance.
11. Adjust (i.e., lower) evaluation standards.
12. Adjust due dates.
13. Give fewer assignments.

FIGURE 16.7

Homework Adaptations for Adolescents with Disabilities

Note: Items are ranked from most helpful to least helpful.

From "Homework, Grading, and Testing Practices Used by Teachers with Students with and without Disabilities" (p. 52) by L. R. Struyk, M. H. Epstein, W. Bursuck, E. A. Polloway, J. McConeghy, and K. B. Cole, 1995, *The Clearing House, 69.* Used by permission.

lems as experienced by parents, special education teachers, and general education teachers. Parents' highest-ranked problems were frequency of communication, early initiation of communication, and follow-through. Similar concerns were voiced by special education teachers (i.e., early initiation, frequency, follow-through). Finally, general education teachers cited the following challenges to regular communication: the competing demands of record keeping and paperwork, difficulty in coordinating schedules to set up time to talk with parents, and the large number of students with disabilities in their classes.

Certain policies and procedures can increase students' success with homework. The following ideas have proved effective for general education teachers:

▶ Schedule after-school sessions at which students can get extra help on their homework.
▶ Provide peer tutoring programs that concentrate on homework.
▶ Provide sufficient study hall time during school hours for students to complete their homework.
▶ Use community volunteers to assist students in completing homework. (Epstein et al., 1996)

Students can also get help with their homework through the Internet. Secondary teachers need to become familiar with this new source of support and make this information available to students. Finally, a little reinforcement always helps. Figure 16.8 shows a homework pass that can be given for turning in homework. When the specified number are collected, they can be used to skip a homework assignment.

CONSIDER THIS

Should school policies regarding homework be altered to increase the likelihood of success for students with disabilities, or should these students be required to follow a rigid policy designed for all students? Why or why not?

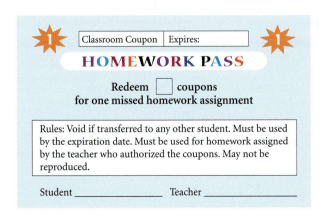

FIGURE 16.8

Example of a Homework Pass Used for Reinforcement

From *Successful Inclusive Teaching* (3rd ed., p. 389) by J. S. Choate, 2000, Boston: Allyn and Bacon.

Grading The challenges of inclusion of adolescents with disabilities are perhaps most clearly reflected in the area of grading. School systems should develop a diverse committee to study the best practices in grading that support mastery of academic standards and meet legal guidelines to develop a policy for the entire system (Salend & Duhaney, 2002). Figure 16.9 provides optional grading systems that might be adopted for different purposes.

The research in this area has not shown positive results. For example, Zigmond and her associates (Donahue & Zigmond, 1990; Zigmond, Levin, & Laurie, 1985) report that approximately 60% to 75% of high school students with learning disabilities received passing grades in their general education classes, but they consistently received below-average grade-point averages (GPAs) (i.e., an overall GPA of 0.99 on a 4.0 scale, or D work). These patterns seem to reflect a persistent lack of academic success for students with disabilities who are also found to receive lower grades than their peers in general education (Munk & Bursuck, 2001).

FIGURE 16.9   **Grading Systems**

✓ **Numeric/Letter Grades:** Teachers assign numeric or letter grades based on students' performance on tests or specific learning activities.

✓ **Checklists/Rating Scales:** Teachers develop checklists and rating scales that delineate the benchmarks associated with their courses and evaluate each student according to mastery of these benchmarks. Some school districts have revised their grading systems by creating rating scales for different grade levels. Teachers rate students on each skill, using a scale that includes "not yet evident," "beginning," "developing," and "independent."

✓ **Anecdotal/Descriptive and Portfolio Grading:** Teachers write descriptive comments regarding students' skills, learning styles, effort, attitudes, and growth, and strategies to improve student performance. These comments can be included with examples of students' work as part of portfolio grading.

✓ **Pass/Fail Systems:** Minimum course competencies are specified and students who demonstrate mastery receive a "P" grade, while those who fail to meet the minimum standards are given an "F" grade. Some schools have modified the traditional pass/fail grading system to include such distinctions as honors (HonorP), high pass (HP), pass (P), and low pass (LP).

✓ **Mastery Level/Criterion Systems:** Students and teachers meet to divide the material into a hierarchy of skills and activities, based on an assessment of individual needs and abilities. After completing the learning activities, students take a post-test or perform an activity to demonstrate mastery of the content. When students demonstrate mastery, they receive credit for that accomplishment and repeat the process with the next skill to be mastered.

✓ **Progressive Improvement Grading:** Students take exams and engage in learning activities, and receive feedback and instruction based on their performance throughout the grading period. Only performance on cumulative tests and learning activities during the final weeks of the grading period, however, are used to determine students' grades.

✓ **Multiple Grading:** Teachers grade students in the areas of ability, effort, and achievement. Students' report cards can then include a listing of the three grades for each content area, or grades can be computed by weighting the three areas.

✓ **Level Grading:** Teachers use a numeric subscript to indicate the level of difficulty at which the students' grades are based. For example, a grade of B6 can be used to note that a student is working in the B range at the sixth-grade level. Subscript systems can also be devised to indicate whether students are working at grade level, above grade level, or below grade level.

✓ **Contract Grading:** Teachers and students agree on a contract outlining the learning objectives; the amount, nature, and quality of the products students must complete; and the procedures for evaluating student products and assigning a grade.

✓ **Individualized Education Program (IEP) Grading:** Teachers assign grades that acknowledge students' progress in meeting the students' IEP goals and performance criteria.

From "Grading Students in Inclusive Settings" (p. 11) by S. J. Salend & L. M. G. Duhaney, 2002, *Teaching Exceptional Children,* January/February.

1. Separate grades are given for process (e.g., effort) and product (e.g., tests).
2. Grades are based on the amount of improvement an individual makes.
3. Grading weights are adjusted (e.g., effort or projects count more than tests).
4. Grades are based on meeting the requirements of academic or behavioral contracts.
5. Grades are based on meeting IEP objectives.
6. Grades are adjusted according to student ability.
7. Grades are based on a modified grading scale (e.g., change 93–100 = A to 90–100 = A).
8. Grades are based on less content than required for the rest of the class.
9. Students are passed if they make an effort to pass.
10. Students are passed no matter what.

FIGURE 16.10

Grading Adaptations for Adolescents with Disabilities

Note: Items are ranked from most to least helpful.

From "Homework, Grading, and Testing Practices Used by Teachers with Students with and without Disabilities" (p. 53) by L. R. Struyk, M. H. Epstein, W. Bursuck, E. A. Polloway, J. McConeghy, and K. B. Cole, 1995, *The Clearing House, 69.* Used by permission.

In researching classroom report card practices, Struyk et al. (1995) found that, in determining grades, teachers weighed tests and quizzes highest, and in-class work and homework second highest. Teachers reported that checklists indicating level of competence and skills, supplemented by written comments, were the most helpful apparatus for reporting grades for students with disabilities.

Teachers' responses for grading adaptations for students with disabilities are summarized in Figure 16.10. This list provides a basis for designing grading practices that help adolescents with disabilities succeed in school.

In addition, teachers should carefully evaluate the fairness of their grading patterns for students with special needs. Bursuck, Munk, and Olson (1999) asked students with and without disabilities their opinions about report card and grading accommodations. The majority of students, both those with and those without disabilities, considered most of the accommodations to be unfair. Both groups were more supportive of adaptations that gave students with disabilities credit for effort and showing improvement. They both felt it was unfair to grade equally when the student with a disability had been given less material to learn or to pass those students no matter how poorly they did even if they were trying hard. The Office for Civil Rights has specified that legally school districts cannot treat students with and without disabilities differently in regard to grades. A modified grading system may be used if it is available for all students, or if a student with a disability is taking a class for no credit or the purpose of participation is not for content mastery. In these cases, the IEP objectives may be used to evaluate (LRP Productions, 1997).

Testing   The inclusion movement has raised concerns regarding how students with special needs will be assessed. Simple adaptations can make the difference between taking a test successfully or poorly. For example, reading a test to a student who is a very poor reader gives the student a chance to display knowledge or skills. If such students have to read the questions themselves, test results will reflect students' poor reading skills and fail to assess knowledge of a particular content area. Teachers can address this situation in the following ways:

▶ Have another student read the test to the student.
▶ Have the special education teacher or aide read the test to the student.
▶ Give the student additional time to complete the test.
▶ Reword the test to include only words that are within the student's reading vocabulary.

A full consideration of adaptations in testing, however, extends beyond the consideration of reading ability. Smith et al. (1993) list ways in which teachers can make tests more accessible to students: generous spacing between items on the pages, adequate space allowed for responses, generous margins, readability of text, appropriate test length, logical organization, and clear instructions. The following examples are techniques to adapt measurement instruments:

▶ Using information about performance outside of school in making evaluations
▶ Administering frequent short tests, rather than a few long tests

CROSS-REFERENCE

Review Chapters 5–11 and determine specific testing adaptations that might be necessary with students with different types of disabilities.

▶ Dividing tests or tasks into smaller, simpler sections or steps

▶ Developing practice items or pretest trials using the same response format as the test

▶ Considering the appropriateness of the instrument or procedure in terms of age or maturity

▶ Giving open-book tests

▶ Reducing the number of test items or removing items that require more abstract reasoning or have high levels of difficulty

▶ Using different levels of questions for different students

▶ Having a student develop a product or packet of materials that show knowledge and understanding of the content of a unit (portfolio assessment)

▶ Providing alternative projects or assignments

▶ Having peers administer tests

▶ Allowing students to make up tests

▶ Videotaping a student performing a task and then playing it back to him or her to show skills learned and areas needing improvement

▶ Using a panel of students to evaluate one another on task performance

▶ Allowing students to type answers

▶ Allowing students to use a computer during testing

▶ Allowing small groups to work together on a task to be evaluated (such as a project or test)

▶ Using short written or verbal measures on a daily or weekly basis to provide more feedback on student progress

▶ Increasing the amount of time allowed to complete the test

▶ Altering the presentation (written, oral, visual) of tests

▶ Altering the types of responses to match a student's strengths (written, oral, short answer, or simple marking)

▶ Having a student review the course or unit content verbally so that he or she is not limited to test item recall

▶ Limiting the number of formal tests by using checklists to observe and record learning

▶ Assessing participation in discussions

▶ Giving extra credit for correction of mistakes

CROSS-REFERENCE

Refer to Chapter 15 for information regarding treatment acceptability.

Testing adaptations raise questions of treatment acceptability. Relative to this concern, Struyk et al. (1995) report that adaptations commonly used for students without disabilities include extending the time students have for completing the test (92%), giving feedback to individual students during the test (94%), and allowing students to take open-book or open-notes tests (96%). Since these techniques already are commonly in use, they should be considered as the initial adaptation options for students with disabilities. General education teachers' preferences in testing adaptations for adolescent students with

General education teachers can make many different adaptations to successfully test students with special needs.

1. Give extended time to finish tests.
2. Give extra help preparing for tests.
3. Simplify wording of test questions.
4. Give individual help with directions during tests.
5. Give practice questions as a study guide.
6. Use black and white copies (rather than ditto).
7. Read test questions to students.
8. Allow use of learning aids during tests (e.g., calculators).
9. Highlight key words in questions.
10. Use tests with enlarged print.
11. Give the actual test as a study guide.
12. Give feedback to individual students during test.
13. Change question type (e.g., essay to multiple choice).
14. Give open-book/note tests.
15. Allow students to answer fewer questions.
16. Teach students test-taking skills.
17. Allow oral instead of written answers (e.g., tape recorders).
18. Test on less content than rest of the class.
19. Provide extra space on tests for answering.
20. Allow word processors.
21. Allow answers in outline format.
22. Give tests to small groups.
23. Give take-home tests.

FIGURE 16.11

Testing Adaptations for Adolescents with Disabilities

Note: Items are ranked from most to least helpful.

From "Homework, Grading, and Testing Practices Used by Teachers with Students with and without Disabilities" (p. 54) by L. R. Struyk, M. H. Epstein, W. Bursuck, E. A. Polloway, J. McConeghy, and K. B. Cole, 1995, *The Clearing House, 69.* Used by permission.

disabilities are summarized in Figure 16.11. A survey of middle school students' opinions found that preferred modifications were open-notes or open-book tests, practice questions for study, and multiple choice instead of essay. Their least preferred modifications were having the teacher read the test, tests with fewer questions, and tests covering less material (Nelson, Jayanthi, Epstein, & Bursuck, 2000).

For students to perform successfully on tests, they will need to learn individual test-taking and organizational strategies, which are often difficult for students with disabilities. Such strategies are typically subsumed within the area of study skills, discussed in the next section.

Study Skills and Learning Strategies

Teachers' accommodations are insufficient to guarantee that students with special needs will be successful. Students must develop their own skills and strategies to help them overcome, or compensate for, a disability. Understanding how to use study skills will greatly enhance their chances for being successful in future academic, vocational, or social activities. Classroom teachers can help students acquire a repertoire of study skills. Study skills are tools that students can use to assist them with their learning. They include listening, note taking, reading rate, test taking, remembering information, managing time, managing behavior, motivation, and goal setting (Hoover & Patton, 1995).

Many students have an innate ability in these areas. For example, some students are good readers, adept at comprehension and able to read quickly; other students find it easy to memorize facts. These students may not need instruction in study skills. For other students, however, study skills represent an "invisible curriculum" that must be taught directly if they are to be successful. For example, the study skill of listening is critical in most educational settings because teachers provide so much information verbally. If students are not able to attend to auditory information, they will miss a great deal of content. Table 16.4 summarizes key study skills and their significance for learning.

TABLE 16.4   Study Skills and Their Significance for Learning

Study Skill	Significance for Learning
Reading rate	Rates vary with type and length of reading materials; students need to adjust rate to content.
Listening	Ability to listen is critical in most educational tasks and throughout life.
Note taking/outlining	Ability to take notes and develop outlines is critical in content courses and essential for future study.
Report writing	Written reports are frequently required in content courses.
Oral presentations	Some teachers require extensive oral reporting.
Graphic aids	Visual aids can help students who have reading deficits understand complex material.
Test taking	Students must be able to do well on tests if they are to succeed in content courses.
Reference material/dictionary usage	Using reference materials makes learners more independent.
Time management	Ability to manage and allocate time is critical for success in secondary settings.
Self-management of behavior	Self-management assists students in assuming responsibility and leads to independence.

Adapted from *Teaching Students with Learning Problems to Use Study Skills: A Teacher's Guide* (p. 7) by J. J. Hoover and J. R. Patton, 1995, Austin, TX: Pro-Ed.

Closely related to study skills are learning strategies—ways to use active learning to acquire and use new information and solve problems ("learning to learn") (Table 16.5). Teachers should be alert not only to ways to teach content but also to ways to learn and use the content. The nearby Technology Today lists computer programs and websites to reinforce skills and provide multiple opportunities to practice.

Reading comprehension, error monitoring in writing, problem solving in math, and test preparation are also important skills that can be developed and strengthened through strategy training. A comprehensive source on numerous strategies for learning (and their use) is provided by Masters et al. (1999). Teachers may have to instruct students how to use a given learning strategy. Alley and Deshler (1979) described an eight-step procedure for teaching strategies to students. While this model has been modified from time to time, the general approach still remains effective. The following steps are included in the approach (Masters et al., 1999):

1. Testing the student's current level of functioning
2. Describing the steps of the strategy and providing a rationale for each step
3. Modeling the strategy so the student can observe all of the processes involved
4. Verbally rehearsing the steps of the strategy to criterion
5. Practicing controlled materials written at the student's reading ability level
6. Practicing content materials from the student's grade placement level
7. Giving positive and corrective feedback
8. Giving the post test (p. 119)

The following are examples of learning strategies:

▶ **SCROL** (Grant, 1993) is a strategy that helps students learn how to use textbook headings to improve comprehension. There are five steps in the strategy (Scholes, 1998):
1. **S**urvey the heading. Read each heading and subheading and answer the following questions: What do I already know about this topic? What do I expect the author to include in this section?

CONSIDER THIS

What would it be like if all students were provided with instructional strategies that made them more effective learners? How would this affect the number and types of children needing special education?

TABLE 16.5　　Learning Strategies

Acquisition Strategies

Word identification strategy: teaches students a problem-solving procedure for quickly attacking and decoding unknown words in reading materials allowing them to move on quickly for the purpose of comprehending the passage.

Paraphrasing strategy: directs students to read a limited section of material, ask themselves the main idea and the details of the section, and put that information in their own words. This strategy is designed to improve comprehension by focusing attention on the important information of a passage and by stimulating active involvement with the passage.

Self-questioning strategy: aids reading comprehension by having students actively ask questions about key pieces of information in a passage and then read to find the answers for these questions.

Visual imagery strategy: improves students' acquisition, storage, and recall of prose material. Students improve reading comprehension by reading short passages and visualizing the scene which is described, incorporating actors, action, and details.

Interpreting visuals strategy: aids students in the use and interpretation of visuals such as maps, graphs, pictures, and tables to increase their ability to extract needed information from written materials.

Multipass strategy: involves making three passes through a passage for the purpose of focusing attention on key details and main ideas. Students survey a chapter or passage to get an overview, size up sections of the chapter by systematically scanning to locate relevant information which they note, and sort out important information in the chapter by locating answers to specific questions.

Storage Strategies

FIRST–Letter mnemonic strategy: aids students in memorizing lists of information by teaching them to design mnemonics or memorization aids, and in finding and making lists of crucial information. (Published by Edge Enterprises)

Paired associates strategy: aids students in memorizing pairs of small groups of information by using visual imagery, matching pertinent information with familiar objects, coding important dates, and a first-syllable technique.

Listening and note-taking strategy: teaches students to develop skills that enhance their ability to learn from listening experiences by identifying the speaker's verbal cues or mannerisms which signal that important information is about to be given, noting key words, and organizing their notes into an outline for future reference or study.

Expression and Demonstration of Competence Strategies

Sentence writing strategy: teaches students how to recognize and generate four types of sentences: simple, compound, complex, and compound-complex.

Paragraph writing strategy: teaches students how to write well-organized, complete paragraphs by outlining ideas, selecting a point-of-view and tense for the paragraph, sequencing ideas, and checking their work.

Error monitoring strategy: teaches students a process for detecting and correcting errors in their writing and for producing a neater written product. Students are taught to locate errors in paragraph organization, sentence structure, capitalization, overall editing and appearance, punctuation, and spelling by asking themselves a series of questions. Students correct their errors and rewrite the passage before submitting it to their teacher.

Theme writing strategy: teaches students to write a five-paragraph theme. They learn how to generate ideas for themes and how to organize these ideas into a logical sequence. Then the student learns how to write the paragraphs, monitor errors, and rewrite the theme.

Assignment completion strategy: teaches students to monitor their assignments from the time an assignment is given until it is completed and submitted to the teacher. Students write down assignments; analyze the assignments; schedule various subtasks; complete the subtasks, and ultimately, the entire task; and submit the completed assignment.

Test taking strategy: aids students during test taking. Students are taught to allocate time and read instructions and questions carefully. A question is either answered or abandoned for later consideration. The obviously wrong answers are eliminated from the abandoned questions and a reasonable guess is made. The last step is to survey the entire test for unanswered questions.

From "The Strategic Intervention Model" (p. 206) by R. Tralli, B. Colombo, D. D. Deshler, and J. B. Schumaker, 1996, *Remedial and Special Education, 17.* Used by permission.

2. **C**onnect. How are the headings related to each other? Write down words from the headings that provide connections between them.
3. **R**ead the text. As you read, look for words or phrases that provide important information about the headings. Stop and make sure you understand the major ideas and supporting details at the end of each section. Reread if you don't understand.
4. **O**utline. Outline the major ideas and supporting details in the section. Try to do this without looking back.
5. **L**ook back. Look back at the text to check the accuracy of your outline. Correct your outline as needed. (p. 111)

Multimedia Programs and Websites That Complement Instructional Principles

Instructional Principles	Implementation with Multimedia	
	Multimedia Context	*Programs and Websites*
Automaticity and Overlearning	Provides a context for application of basic facts, anchors instruction in visual context, uses auditory feedback.	Spell It Deluxe, Davidson (Grades 1–5) Simon Sounds It Out, Don Johnston (Grades I–4) Simon Spells, Don Johnston (Grades K–4) SuperSonic Phonics, Curriculum Associates (Grades 1–12) Wild World of Words Challenge, Web Page
Mastery Learning	Arranges instruction so that all students learn objectives to mastery.	Net Frog: Web Page (high school) WebQuests, Matrix of Examples, Web Page
Mnemonics	Uses visual and auditory stimuli to assist the memorization and retention of important information and skills.	Curious Creatures, Curriculum Associates (Grades 2–8) BioSci, Videodiscovery (Grades 3–12) A World Alive, St. Louis Zoo (all grades) Inspiration, Inspiration Software (Grades 3–12)
Direct Instruction	Structures educational environment with specific objectives, rapid pacing, frequent feedback, and opportunities to answer.	Mastering Series Systems Impact (Grades 5–12) Windows on Science, Optical Data (Grades 1–8) Windows on Math, Optical Data (Grades 1–8) Earobics, Cognitive Concepts (Grades K–6)
Situated Cognition	Provides situations from which students can generate their own questions within authentic situations.	Adventures of Jasper Woodbury, Optical Data (Grades 4–8) Science Sleuths, Videodiscovery (Grades 3–9) The Real Scoop on Tobacco, WebQuest
Cooperative Learning	Provides students opportunities to work together to solve problems and assist one another in learning new information.	Decisions, Decisions, Tom Snyder (Grades 5–10) Choices, Choices, Tom Snyder (Grades K–6) Cultural Debates, Tom Snyder (Grades 6–12) Great Solar System and Ocean Rescue (Grades 5–8)
Writing Instruction	Incorporates visual and auditory prompts to assist with creating writing.	Write OutLoud & Co: Writer, Don Johnston (Grades K–12) Imagination Express, Edmark (Grades 2–8) Student Writing Center, Learning Company (Grades 5–12) Storybook Weaver, Learning Company (Grades 1–6) Postcards, Curriculum Associates (Grades 5–8) The Read to Write Project, Web Page
Reading Comprehension	Encourages student research, provides models for management and searching of data.	Living Books, Broderbund (Grades K–3) Little Planet, Little Planet Software (Grades K–3) Start-to-Finish Books, Don Johnston (Grades 5–8) Rainbow, Curriculum Associates (Grades 1–3) Online story, Web Page

continued

Instructional Principles	Implementation with Multimedia	
	Multimedia Context	Programs and Websites
Study Skills	Presents text with visual and auditory clues to enhance comprehension.	TrackStar, Web Page Yahooligans, Web Directory & Search Engine The Traveling Tutor from the Alphabet Superhighway, Web Inspiration, Inspiration Software (Grades 3–12) My First Amazing Incredible Dictionary, DK (Grades K–4) Multimedia Encyclopedias

For follow-up questions about multimedia and websites that complement instructional practices, go to Chapter 15 of the Companion Website (ablongman.com/sppd4e) and click Technology Today.

From "Multimedia or Not to Multimedia? That Is the Question with Learning Disabilities" (p. 36) by C. A. Wissick & J. E. Gardner, 2000, *Teaching Exceptional Children, 32*(4).

▸ The **COPS** strategy (Schumaker et al., 1981) is an error-monitoring strategy for writing. The acronym stands for four tasks:
  1. **C**apitalization,
  2. **O**verall appearance (e.g., neatness, appropriate margins),
  3. **P**unctuation, and
  4. **S**pelling. (p. 11)

These strategies have proved effective for use with students with learning problems at the upper elementary, middle, and secondary school levels (Shannon & Polloway, 1993).

Efforts to validate the use of specific strategies within inclusive classrooms continue. An exciting aspect of instruction in strategies is its potential to benefit students with and without disabilities (Fisher, Schumaker, & Deshler, 1995).

Summary

Secondary School Curricula
▸ Important differences exist between elementary and secondary settings in terms of organizational structure, curriculum, and learner characteristics.
▸ From a curricular perspective, integrating students with disabilities into general classes is more challenging at the secondary level than at the elementary level.
▸ The period of adolescence adds to the problems experienced by students with disabilities.

Programs for Students in Secondary Schools
▸ Curricular options for students at the secondary level with particular relevance for students with disabilities include basic skills, social skills, tutoring, learning strategies, vocational skills, and life skills.
▸ Individualized Transition Plans are required by law, and their effectiveness is critical for successful lives after high school for individuals with disabilities.

▸ Classroom teachers and special education teachers must collaborate to ensure effective secondary school programs.
▸ Special education teachers must help prepare students for academic content classes.
▸ Transition to the secondary level is a major endeavor for students with disabilities.

Methods to Facilitate Students' Success in General Education Classes
▸ Accommodations are changes that teachers can make to facilitate the success of students with disabilities.
▸ Specific challenges for successful inclusion occur in the areas of homework, grading, and testing.
▸ Study skills are skills that students with disabilities can use to help them achieve success in general and special education classes.
▸ Learning strategies enable students to achieve independence as they "learn how to learn."

Further Readings

Baker, B. L., Brightman, A. J., Blacher, J. B., Heifetz, L. J., Hinshaw, S. P., & Murphy, D. M. (1997). *Steps to independence: Teaching everyday skills to children with special needs.* Baltimore: Brookes.

Choate, J. S. (2000). *Successful inclusive teaching: Proven ways to detect and correct special needs* (3rd ed.). Boston: Allyn and Bacon.

Hoover, J. J., & Patton, J. R. (1995). *Teaching students with learning problems to use study skills.* Austin, TX: Pro-Ed.

Hoover, J. J., & Patton, J. R. (1997). *Curriculum adaptations for students with learning and behavior problems* (2nd ed.) Austin, TX: Pro-Ed.

Hughes, C., & Carter, E. W. (1999). *The transition handbook: Strategies high school teachers use that work.* Baltimore: Brookes.

Johnson, D., Stodden, R., Emanuel, E. J., Luecking, R., & Mack, M. (2002). Current challenges facing secondary education and transition services: What research tells us. *Exceptional Children, 68*(4), 519–531.

Kame'enui, E. J., Carnine, D. W., Dixon, R. C., Simmons, D. C., & Coyne, M. D. (2002). *Effective teaching strategies that accommodate diverse learners* (2nd ed.). Upper Saddle River, NJ: Merrill.

LRP Publications. (1997). Grading. *Individuals with Disabilities Education Law Report, 25*(2), 387–391.

Lyndsey, J. D. (Ed.). (1999). *Technology and exceptional individuals* (3rd ed.). Austin, TX: Pro-Ed.

Masters, L. F., Mori, B. A., & Mori, A. A. (1999). *Teaching secondary students with mild learning and behavior problems.* Austin, TX: Pro-Ed.

Mastropieri, M. A., & Scruggs, T. E. (2000). *The inclusive classroom: Strategies for effective instruction.* Upper Saddle River, NJ: Merrill.

Miller, S. P. (2001). *Validated practices for teaching students with diverse needs and abilities.* Boston: Allyn and Bacon.

Olson, J. L., & Platt, J. M. (2000). *Teaching children and adolescents with special needs* (3rd ed.). Upper Saddle River, NJ: Merrill.

Prater, M. A. (2000). Using juvenile literature with portrayals of disabilities in your classroom. *Intervention in School and Clinic, 35*(3), 167–176.

Scott, B. J., Vitale, M. R., & Masten, W. G. (1998). Implementing instructional adaptations for students with disabilities in inclusive classrooms. *Remedial and Special Education, 19*(2), 106–119.

Wehman, P. (1996). *Life beyond the classroom: Transition strategies for young people with disabilities* (2nd ed.). Baltimore: Brookes.

Wehman, P. (Ed.). (1997). *Exceptional individuals in school, community, and work.* Austin, TX: Pro-Ed.

Wehman, P., & Kregel, J. (Eds.) (1998). *More than a job: Securing satisfying careers for people with disabilities.* Baltimore: Brookes.

VideoWorkshop Extra!

If the VideoWorkshop package was included with your textbook, go to Chapter 16 of the Companion Website (www.ablongman.com/sppd4e) and click on the VideoWorkshop button. Follow the instructions for viewing video clip 6. Then consider this information along with what you've read in Chapter 16 while answering the following questions.

1. Using the information in this chapter and in the video clip, suggest a curricular program that would be appropriate to meet Bridget's goal for going to college. How could her high school program choices help her overcome the fear that she will never be able to get or keep a job?

2. Based on the inclusion strategies provided in your text, what would you suggest for Bridget? Compile a list to meet each of her deficits or areas of difficulty as noted in the video clip.

Appendixes A and B

Appendixes A and B present sample IEPs. In Appendix A the IEP is for Brooke Jones, an eight-year-old third grader classified as having a learning disability. The IEP in Appendix B is for Diana Camp, an eighth grader also classified as having a learning disability. The majority of children with disabilities included in general education classrooms will be classified as having a learning disability. Therefore, these two examples present the most likely scenario that you will find in schools today. As a secondary student, Diana's IEP includes information related to her transition from school to postschool activities. Remember, when students with disabilities reach the age of 14, IEPs must include information related to transition.

In both IEPs, general assessment information is provided. Teachers developing and implementing IEPs usually have access to this sort of assessment information. When reviewing the IEPs, take note of the relationship between the assessment information, including the stated strengths and weaknesses of the student, and the student's IEP goals and objectives. Current functioning levels of the student should directly relate to the goals and objectives included in the IEP.

When reviewing the IEPs in the appendixes, pay attention to the margin notes that point out specific components of the IEPs and cross-references to places in the text where more information about specific topics can be found. Also, note the role that general classroom teachers and special education teachers play in implementing the IEPs. When dealing with students with these types of disabilities, a great deal of a student's IEP is implemented in the general education classroom by the regular teacher.

Sample IEP for an Elementary Student

Arcadia Public Schools
Individual Educational Program

Name _Brooke Jones_   Grade _3_   Age _8_   DOB _8-24-94_

School Attending _Arcadia Elementary_   Resides in _Arcadia_   Attendance Area

Disability _Learning Disability_   Related Services _____   New IEP ✓

IEP Revision _____

Parent/Guardian/Surrogate _Donna Jones_

Most Recent Eligibility Date _6-11-02_   Project Triennial Date _6-03_

Meeting Date	Signature of Persons Present	Relationship to Student
5-23-02	Bob Roberts	LEA Administrator or Designee
5-23-02	Jennifer Lee	Special Education Teacher
5-23-02	Patty Lopez	Regular Education Teacher
5-23-02	Donna Jones	Parent/Guardian/Surrogate

> **TAKE NOTE**
> Ensure that individuals involved in the development of the IEP sign the form.

Present Level of Performance (Part A)

K-TEA

	Age SS
Reading	91
Spelling	93
Math	84

Date _4-22-02_

Woodcock-Johnson

	Age SS		Age SS
broad Reading	___	calculations	___
broad Math	___	app. prob.	___
broad wr. lang.	___	dictation	___
broad knowledge	___	wr. samples	___
letter wr. id.	___	science	___
passage comp.	___	s. studies	___
		humanities	___

Date _____

Other Test Results

WISC- III	Age SS
Full scale IQ	92
Performance IQ	95
Verbal IQ	89

> **TAKE NOTE**
> Present level of functioning is a required component of the IEP.

> **CROSS-REFERENCE**
> Refer to Chapter 4 to review the required components of the IEP.

Analysis of Evaluation/Re-Evaluation Results/Strengths and Weaknesses:
Weaknesses are noted in visual processing, nonverbal processing, organizational skills and ability to concentrate and attend. Strengths are noted in social comprehension and auditory long-term memory.

Involvement in General Curriculum:
The most recent eligibility results suggest that this student's intellectual abilities fall in the
low average to average range and may be one predictor of progress in the general curriculum. The student's disability may have further impact on involvement and progress in age/grade-appropriate general curriculum.

	No Impact	Mild/Moderate Impact	Significant Impact
Reading	____	✔	____
Written Language	____	✔	____
Math	____	____	____
Content Areas	✔	____	____
Other _Spelling_____	____	✔	____

TAKE NOTE
A requirement is to include the involvement of the student in the general education curriculum.

Area Affected by Disability: *Written Language and Spelling*
Present Level of Performance (Part B): *Brooke can write up to 3 sentences remaining on topic. She can orally recognize the 4 types of sentences but does not always punctuate correctly when writing. Capitalization skills are weak. Brooke can spell phonetically on a 2nd grade level.*

Annual Goals: *Brooke will write a paragraph remaining on topic using correct mechanics, spelling and grammar with 85% accuracy.*

Procedures Used to Assess Goal:

✔ classroom participation   ____ checklists   ✔ classwork   ✔ tests and quizzes

____ observation   ____ special projects   ✔ written reports

____ other _____

TAKE NOTE
Criteria for evaluating the success of goals and objectives must be included in the IEP.

Key to Progress Notes:
Progress Notes (to be completed at the end of each 6 weeks)

1	2	3	4	5	6

S – sufficient progress being made to achieve goal with this IEP's duration
M – minimal progress being made; goal may not be achieved within this IEP's duration
C – goal has been completed
NT – instruction has not been provided on this goal during this marking period
O – other _____

Short-Term Objectives:
Brooke will

1. *punctuate sentences correctly in written language.*
2. *capitalize words correctly in written language.*
3. *identify and use subject and verb correctly.*
4. *write 2 detail sentences about a given topic.*
5. *pass weekly spelling tests.*
6. *use weekly spelling list words correctly in sentences with correct mechanics and grammar.*
7. *identify and use nouns, verbs, adjectives, and adverbs.*

TAKE NOTE
Short-term objectives are always related to goals.

Services: Special Education/Related Services/Supplementary Aids and Services

Placement	Amount of Time	Projected Beginning	Anticipated Completion	Personnel	Location
P.E. (regular, modified, adaptive)	1 hr/wk	8-26-02	6-6-03	PE Tchr	Reg PE Class
SpEd Direct	8 hrs/wk	8-26-02	6-6-03	SpEd Tchr	SpEd Class
RegED	22hrs/wk	8-26-02	6-6-03	RegEd Tchr	Reg Class

Environment for:
	sp. ed.	reg. ed.	NA
music	____	✔	____
P.E.	____	✔	____
library	____	✔	____
lunch/recess	____	✔	____
school programs	____	✔	____
other _____	____	✔	____

CROSS-REFERENCE
Refer to Chapter 1 to review the requirements for least restrictive environment.

Program Accommodations/Modifications/Supports

This student will be provided access to general education, special education, other school services and activities (including nonacademic activities and extracurricular activities), and education-related settings:

____ with no accommodations/modifications

✔ with the following accommodations/modifications

Accommodations/modifications provided as part of the instructional and testing/assessment process will allow the student equal opportunity to access the curriculum and demonstrate achievement. Accommodations/modifications also provide access to nonacademic and extracurricular activities and educationally related settings. Accommodations/modifications based solely on the potential to enhance performance beyond providing equal access are inappropriate.

Accommodations may be in, but not limited to, the areas of time, scheduling, setting, presentation, and response. The impact of any modifications listed should be discussed. This includes the earning of credits for graduation.

Accommodation/Modification/Support	Frequency	Location	Duration Projected Beginning	Anticipated Completion
Brooke will				
• repeat directions to ensure understanding	as needed	all settings	8-26-02	6-6-03
• have tests read aloud	as tests are given	all classes	8-26-02	6-6-03
• be given a legible copy of class notes	daily	content area classes	8-26-02	6-6-03
• write answers only, not questions and statements	daily	all classes	8-26-02	6-6-03
• have a reduction in the amt. of required math problems	as needed	math class	8-26-02	6-6-03
• have modifications in the amt. of required written work	as needed	all classes	8-26-02	6-6-03
• not be penalized for handwriting	daily	all classes	8-26-02	6-6-03

TAKE NOTE
Projected dates for services must be included in the IEP.

Sample IEP for a Secondary Student

Briarwood CITY SCHOOLS
INDIVIDUALIZED EDUCATION PROGRAM

	IEP INITIATION/DURATION DATES
STUDENT'S NAME Diana Camp	
DOB 5/6/88 SCHOOL YR 2002-2003 GRADE 8th	From 8/14/02 to 5/29/03

THIS IEP WILL BE IMPLEMENTED DURING THE REGULAR SCHOOL TERM UNLESS NOTED IN EXTENDED SCHOOL YEAR SERVICES.

STUDENT PROFILE

Diana Camp is completing 7th grade at Briarwood Middle School. Diana is outgoing, artistic, and popular among her peers. She has maintained passing grades this year as a result of her work ethic and motivation to do well. All teachers note that Diana has great difficulty with reading, but tries very hard to compensate in various ways. She asks her teachers for assistance, comes for extra help after school, is diligent about completing make-up work or extra credit, and uses her class time productively. All of these positive behaviors and a cooperative attitude make Diana well liked by teachers.

Math is a relative strength for Diana. She has average mastery of basic operations with whole and decimal numbers. She knows her math facts. Diana has improved in her problem-solving skills, but continues to lack confidence when confronted with word problems. Equations, expressions, integers, formulas, and graphing functions are all skills that were new for her this year. She has a beginning understanding of them. Diana usually requires additional individual examples and explanations before working on her own. She benefits from checking her work as she practices so she gets feedback on whether she is doing the work correctly.

Language Arts, specifically reading decoding and written expression, are areas of significant weakness for Diana. She can read basic sight words but is unable to apply phonetic rules to decode unfamiliar words. She often is frustrated when trying to read aloud. Her listening comprehension exceeds her ability to decode text. Her writing is repetitive and simplistic, lacking focus. Diana's written products are often difficult to transcribe because of extremely poor spelling. Grammar skills are inconsistent. She has frequent word usage problems in her writing. She has worked from grade level vocabulary text this year with modifications. It is recommended that reading decoding be the priority focus for Diana's Language Arts program in 8th grade, followed by writing.

Both Science and Social Studies are very challenging because Diana can not read grade level text. She requires considerable accommodations and modifications to be successful. Diana has difficulty understanding abstract concepts like forms of government or transfer of energy/heat. Graphics help her "see" relationships and key points. She has been given study guides to focus her study time as she prepares for tests. Alternative forms of assessment like creating models or posters may be effective ways to help Diana learn and focus on "core" concepts.

It is recommended that in 8th grade Diana be placed in regular classes for all subjects. She should receive daily support in her pre-algebra classroom. She will require daily time in a resource room for part of Language Arts to meet her IEP benchmarks. Content areas will require accommodations and modifications in the regular classroom to ensure success.

TAKE NOTE
A narrative of the student's strengths and weaknesses is a better way of describing the student than simply listing test scores.

Items checked "YES" will be addressed in this IEP:

CROSS-
REFERENCE
Review Chapters
4 and 15 to de-
termine when
transition serv-
ices must be ad-
dressed in IEPs.

SPECIAL INSTRUCTIONAL FACTORS:	YES	NO
• Does the student have behavior which impedes his/her learning or the learning of others?	____	✓
• Does the student have limited English proficiency?	____	✓
• Does the student need instruction in Braille and the use of Braille?	____	✓
• Does the student have communication needs (deaf or hearing impaired only)?	____	✓
• Does the student need assistive technology devices and/or services?	____	✓
• Does the student need special transportation?	____	✓
• Are transition services addressed in this IEP?	✓	____

NONACADEMIC and EXTRACURRICULAR ACTIVITIES

The student will have the opportunity to participate in nonacademic/extracurricular activities with his/her nondisabled peers.

☑ YES   ☐ YES, with supports. Describe: _____

☐ NO.   Explanation must be provided: _____

METHOD/FREQUENCY FOR REPORTING PROGRESS OF ATTAINING GOALS TO PARENTS

TAKE NOTE
Parents must be
notified of the
progress being
made by their
children on the
same schedule
that parents of
nondisabled
children receive
notification.

Progress reports (indicating whether the progress, if continued, is sufficient to meet the annual goal) will be sent to parents each grading period as scheduled by the school system every __9 weeks.__
Other __Progress 4½ weeks__

Page ____ of ____

Student Name: Diana

AREA: Reading

Present Level of Performance:

Diana confuses her letters—b's and d's, d's and t's. She has difficulty hearing sounds—ending and vowel sounds particularly. When confronted with unknown words, Diana will attempt the beginning sound and, if the word doesn't come easily, will give up. She recognizes most of the Dolch basic sight words. Diana decoded the QRI first-level word list this spring. On a third-level QRI narrative story, her comprehension was strong. When reading, Diana expends so much energy decoding that she doesn't question whether what she is reading makes sense.

	Date of Mastery
ANNUAL GOAL to be measured by achievement of benchmarks: Diana will use improved reading decoding skills to read phonetically predictable text. Progress will be measured by program assessments or teacher-constructed probes.	

For transition benchmark(s), person(s)/agency(ies) responsible:

Special Education, Related Services, Supplementary Aids & Services, Assistive Technology, Program Accommodations/Modifications and Support for Personnel *(including frequency, duration, & location)*

- Diana will receive a minimum of 45 minutes each day of direct reading instruction in a resource room or other designated setting.
- Diana's reading benchmarks will be the primary focus of her Language Arts curriculum.
- Regular and special education teachers will work together to modify assignments for the remainder of Diana's time in the regular classroom.
- Regular and special education teachers will collaborate to determine Diana's grades.

Benchmarks

After receiving direct instruction in a reading decoding program (like, but not limited to, Fast Forward, Scottish Rite, or MegaWords),

By the end of:

Benchmark	Transition Area	Date of Mastery
1st 9 weeks, when given 20 words with cvc syllable patterns, Diana will read the words with 80% accuracy.		
2nd 9 weeks, when given 20 words with **ccvc, cvcc,** and **cvce** syllable patterns, Diana will read the words with 80% accuracy		
3rd 9 weeks, when given 20 words with vowel syllable patterns (**vv, vr,** etc.), Diana will read the words with 80% accuracy.		
4th 9 weeks, when given 20 words with **cle** patterns, **tion,** and common suffixes (**ly, ful, ment, some, ness**), Diana will read the words with 80% accuracy.		

Circle Type(s) Of Evaluation For Annual Goal

a. Data Collection	f. See Benchmarks
b. Teacher/Text Test	g. Diagnostic Test
c. Work Samples	h. Other _____
d. Teacher Observation	i. Other _____
e. Grades	

Student Name: Diana

AREA: Written Expression

Present Level of Performance:
While Diana may initially balk at having to write, once she starts she's very serious about it, and usually must be reminded to stop. Diana, when prompted, will utilize graphic organizers to order her thoughts before she begins writing. She has a tendency to repeat herself (e.g., words, ideas) as she writes. Diana's sentence structure is poor with many of the sentences beginning with conjunctions. She confuses verb tenses and often has subject/verb disagreements and improper word usage. Diana's dyslexia severely affects her spelling and makes her writing difficult to decipher at times. Her handwriting is neat and legible.

	Date of Mastery
ANNUAL GOAL to be measured by achievement of benchmarks: Diana will demonstrate the ability to plan and write a multiparagraph response directly related to a specific prompt.	

TAKE NOTE
Person(s) responsible for addressing goals and objectives should be included in the IEP.

For transition benchmark(s), person(s)/agency(ies) responsible:

Special Education, Related Services, Supplementary Aids & Services, Assistive Technology, Program Accommodations/Modifications and Support for Personnel (including frequency, duration, & location)
* Diana will receive direct instruction in written expression from a Special Education teacher 2–3 times per week in a resource setting
* Regular and Special Education teachers will modify writing assignments in the regular class to align with IEP objectives
* Writing will be evaluated based on relevant content and writing mechanics will be graded separately.
* Writing benchmarks will take the place of regular classroom writing assignments

CROSS-REFERENCE
Refer to Chapter 4 on the IEP process.

Benchmarks	Transition Area	Date of Mastery
1st 9 weeks, Diana • when given a prompt, will write a topic sentence directly related to the prompt 3 out of 4 times. • will define 4 genres of writing: narrative, descriptive, expository, persuasive. • when shown an example of writing, will correctly identify the genre 6 of 8 times. • will edit writing for capitalization, punctuation, and spelling*.		
Benchmarks	Transition Area	Date of Mastery
2nd 9 weeks, Diana • when given a prompt, will write a paragraph with a topic sentence, three supporting details, and a concluding sentence directly related to the prompt. • will write a minimum of 2 paragraphs in each of the 4 targeted genres. • will edit for above* and word usage*.		
Benchmarks	Transition Area	Date of Mastery
3rd 9 weeks, Diana • when given a prompt, will use a graphic organizer to plan 2–3 related paragraphs on the topic. • using a graphic organizer, will write 2–3 paragraphs directly related to a topic/prompt. • will edit for above* and sentence complexity.		
Benchmarks	Transition Area	Date of Mastery
4th 9 weeks, Diana • when given a genre-specific prompt, will plan (using graphic organizer) and write a 2–3 paragraph response for the prompt in a minimum of 3 genres.		

Circle Type(s) Of Evaluation For Annual Goal

a. Data Collection   f. See Benchmarks
b. Teacher/Text Test   g. Diagnostic Test
c. Work Samples   h. Other _____
d. Teacher Observation   i. Other _____
e. Grades

Student Name: Diana

AREA: Content Areas: Science and Social Studies

Present Level of Performance:

Diana tries very hard in the content area classes. Both Science and Social Studies are very challenging because she cannot read grade level text. She requires considerable accommodations and modifications to be successful. Diana has difficulty understanding abstract concepts like forms of government or transfer of energy/heat. Graphics help her "see" relationships and key points. She has been given study guides to focus her study time as she prepares for tests. Alternative forms of assessment like creating models or posters may be effective ways to help Diana learn and focus on "core" concepts.

TAKE NOTE
Accommodations and modifications in general education classrooms are common components of IEPs for secondary students.

ANNUAL GOAL to be measured by achievement of benchmarks:
Diana will demonstrate understanding of core curriculum in the areas of Science and Social Studies as demonstrated by passing grades.

	Date of Mastery

For transition benchmark(s), person(s)/agency(ies) responsible:

Special Education, Related Services, Supplementary Aids & Services, Assistive Technology, Program Accommodations/Modifications and Support for Personnel *(including frequency, duration, & location)*

- Content areas will be taught in the regular classroom.
- Special education teacher will monitor progress on a regular basis.
- Special education teachers will assist regular teachers in identifying core curriculum, finding appropriate materials, and modifying assignments.
- Regular teachers and special education teachers will collaborate to provide copies of notes, study guides, or pertinent study tools prior to assessments.
- Read tests to Diana.
- Allow testing in an alternative setting if needed.
- Provide modified assessments.
- Encourage Diana to systematically record assignments in a daily planner.
- Seat and/or group Diana with positive role models.
- Regular teacher will communicate with special education teacher and parents about Diana's progress and any concerns.

CROSS-REFERENCE
Review Chapter 2 for the roles of special education and general education teachers in inclusive settings.

Benchmarks

By the end of each semester course, Diana

- will have demonstrated an understanding* of 5–10 essential concepts from each unit/topic/chapter of the curriculum.
- will have demonstrated an understanding* of 10–15 vocabulary words from each unit/topic/chapter of the curriculum.

*Demonstration of understanding can include, but is not limited to

- recitation of information.
- creation of a visual product.
- development of study tools.
- group project.
- modified test.
- completed assignments.
- technology task.
- graphic organizers.

- will be observed by the regular education teacher to exhibit behavior that supports learning* 4 of 5 days.

*Behavior to Support Learning including, but not limited to

- listening in class.
- taking notes when appropriate.
- following directions.
- using time wisely to complete work.
- turning in work on time.

Transition Area	Date of Mastery

Circle Type(s) Of Evaluation For Annual Goal

a. Data Collection	f. See Benchmarks
b. Teacher/Text Test	g. Diagnostic Test
c. Work Samples	h. Other _____
d. Teacher Observation	i. Other _____
e. Grades	

TAKE NOTE

The transition of students from high school to post high school must be addressed in the IEPs of students 14 years of age and older.

Transition Goal (Beginning at age 14, or younger if appropriate):

Employment outcome: Professional employment
Postsecondary training/education outcome: Four-year college or university
Community living outcome: Independent living

Statement of Transition Service Needs That Focuses on Student's Course of Study (Beginning at age 14, or younger if appropriate):

Diana is currently enrolled in a precollege curriculum that focuses on preparation for enrollment in a four-year college or university program. She should be prepared to successfully pass the High School Graduation Examination.

Meeting Date(s)/Signatures of Attendees:

Attendee: _____   Date: _____

Attendee: _____   Date: _____

Attendee: _____   Date: _____

Attendee: _____   Date: _____

Attendee: _____   Date: _____

Attendee: _____   Date: _____

References

Abbott, M. W., Walton, C., & Greenwood, C. R. (2002). Phonemic awareness in kindergarten and first grade. *Teaching Exceptional Children, 34*(4), 20–26.

Ad Hoc Committee on Terminology and Classification. (2001, September-October). Request for comments on proposed new edition of *Mental Retardation: Definition, Classification, and Systems of Supports. American Association on Mental Retardation News and Notes, 14*(5), 1, 9–12.

Affleck, J. Q., Edgar, E., Levine, P., & Kortering, L. (1990). Postschool status of students classified as mildly mentally retarded, learning disabled, or non-handicapped: Does it get better with time? *Education and Training in Mental Retardation, 25,* 315–324.

Agnew, C. M., Nystul, B., & Conner, L. A. (1998). Seizure disorders: An alternative explanation for students' inattention. *Professional School Counselor, 2,* 54–59.

Agosta, J., & Melda, K. (1996). Supporting families who provide care at home for children with disabilities. *Exceptional Children, 62,* 271–282.

Agrawal, A. (2001). The stammering brain. *Science Now.* American Association for the Advancement of Science. Washington, DC.

Alber, S. R., Heward, W. L., & Hippler, B. J. (1999). Teaching middle school students with learning disabilities to recruit positive teacher attention. *Exceptional Children, 65,* 253–270.

Alberto, P. A., & Troutman, A. C. (1995). *Applied behavior analysis for teachers* (4th ed.). Englewood Cliffs, NJ: Merrill.

Alexander, K., & Alexander, M. D. (2001). *American public school law* (5th ed.). Belmont, CA: Wadsworth/Thomson Learning.

Algozzine, B. (2001). Effects of interventions to promote self determination for individuals with disabilities. *Review of Educational Research, 71,* 219–277.

Algozzine, R., Serna, L., & Patton, J. R. (2001). *Childhood behavior disorders: Applied research and educational practices* (2nd ed.). Austin, TX: Pro Ed.

Allen, K. E. (1992). *The exceptional child: Mainstreaming in early childhood education* (2nd ed.). Albany, NY: Delmar.

Alley, G. R., & Deshler, D. D. (1979). *Teaching the learning disabled adolescent: Strategies and methods.* Denver: Love.

Allsopp, D. H., Santos, K. E., & Linn, R. (2000). Collaborating to teach pro-social skills. *Intervention in School and Clinic, 33,* 142–147.

American Academy of Allergy and Immunology. (1991). *Asthma and the school child (Tip #19).* Milwaukee, WI: Author.

American Academy of Ophthalmology. (1984). Policy statement. *Learning disabilities, dyslexia, and vision.* San Francisco: Author.

American Academy of Pediatrics. (1988). *Learning disabilities and children: What parents need to know.* Elk Grove Village, IL: Author.

American Association on Mental Retardation. (1992). *Mental retardation: Definition, classification, and systems of supports* (9th ed.). Washington, DC: Author.

American Association on Mental Retardation. (2002). *Mental retardation: Definition, classification, and systems of supports* (10th ed.). Washington, DC: Author.

American Foundation for the Blind. (1998). *AFB directory of services for blind and visually impaired persons in the United States and Canada* (27th ed.). New York: Author.

American Psychiatric Association. (1994). *Diagnostic and statistical manual of mental disorders (DSM-IV)* (5th ed.). Washington, DC: Author.

American Psychiatric Association. (2000). *Diagnostic and statistical manual of mental disorders (DSM-IV-TR)* (4th ed. rev.). Washington, DC: Author.

American Speech-Language-Hearing Association. (1982). Definitions: Communicative disorders and variations, *ASHA, 24,* 949–950.

American Speech-Language-Hearing Association. (1995, March). Position statement—Facilitated communication. *Asha, 37* (Suppl. 14), p. 12.

American Speech-Language-Hearing Association. (1996, May). *Cultural differences in communication and learning styles.* Accessed on September 23, 2002, at http://professional.asha.org/resources/multicultural/reading_2.cfm. Compiled by the Multicultural Issues Board, Rockville, MD: Author

American Speech-Language-Hearing Association. (1999). *Terminology pertinent to fluency and fluency disorders: Guidelines, 41,* 29–36.

American Speech-Language-Hearing Association. (2000). *What's language? What's speech?* Rockville, MD: Author.

American Speech-Language-Hearing Association. (2002a). *Communication facts: Incidence and prevalence of communication disorders and hearing loss in children—2002 edition.* Accessed on June 29, 2002 at http://professional.asha.org/resources/factsheets/children.cfm. Rockville, MD: Author.

American Speech-Language-Hearing Association. (2002b). *Roles and responsibilities of speech-language pathologists with respect to reading and writing.* Rockville, MD: Author.

Amerson, M. J. (1999). Helping children with visual and motor impairments make the most of their visual abilities. *Review, 31,* 17–20.

Anastopoulos, A. D., Smith, J. M., & Wien, E. E. (1998). Counseling and training parents. In R. A. Barkley (Ed.), *Attention-deficit/hyperactivity disorder: A handbook for diagnosis and treatment* (2nd ed.). New York: Guilford Press.

Anderson, J. A., Kutash, K., & Duchnowski, A. J. (2001). A comparison of the academic progress of students with ED and students with LD. *Journal of Emotional and Behavioral Disorders, 9,* 106–115.

Andrews, J. F., & Jordan, D. C. (1998). Multimedia stories for deaf children. *Teaching Exceptional Children, 30,* 28-33.

Angold, A., Erkali, A., Egger, H. L., & Costell, J. E. (2000). Stimulant treatment for children: A community perspective. *Journal of the American Academy of Child and Adolescent Psychiatry, 39*(8), 975–987.

Anhalt, K., McNeil, C. B., & Bahl, A. B. (1998). The ADHD classroom kit: A whole-classroom approach for managing disruptive behavior. *Psychology in the Schools, 35*(1), 67–79.

Annie E. Casey Foundation. (1998). *1998 kids count data book: Overview.* Baltimore: Author.

Anthony, S. (1972). *The discovery of death in childhood and after.* New York: Basic Books.

Arc (1993, November/December). Second national status report on inclusion reveals slow progress. *ARC Newsletter,* p. 5.

Arc (1995). Report finds nation's schools still failing at inclusion. *The Arc Today, 44*(4), 1, 4.

Armstrong, D. G. (1990). *Developing and documenting the curriculum.* Boston: Allyn and Bacon.

Arnold, L. E. (1999). Treatment alternative for attention-deficit/hyperactivity disorder (ADHD). *Journal of Attention Disorders, 3*(1), 30–48.

Arnos, K. S., Israel, J., Devlin, L., & Wilson, M. P. (1996). Genetic aspects of hearing loss in childhood. In F. N. Martin & J. G. Clark (Eds.), *Hearing care for children* (pp. 20–44). Boston: Allyn and Bacon.

Association for Supervision and Curriculum Development (1997, November). Homework: A new look at an age-old practice. *Education Update, 39*(7), 1, 5, 8.

At-risk youth in crisis: A handbook for collaboration between schools and social services. (1991). Albany, OR: Linn-Benton Education Service Digest.

Austin, J. F. (1992). Involving noncustodial parents in their student's education. *NASSP Bulletin, 76,* 49–54.

Austin, V. L. (2001). Teachers' beliefs about co-teaching. *Remedial and Special Education, 22,* 245–255.

Autism Society of America (2000). *Advocate, 33,* 3

Autism Society of America (2002). *Advocate, 35,* 2

Babkie, A. M., & Provost, M. C. (2002). Select, write, and use metacognition strategies in the classroom. *Intervention, 37,* 172–175.

Baker, B. L., Brightman, A. J., Blacher, J. B., Heifetz, L. J., Hinshaw, S. P., & Murphy, D. M. (1997). *Steps to independence: Teaching everyday skills to children with special needs.* Baltimore: Brookes.

Baker, S. B., & Rogosky-Grassi, M. A. (1993). Access to school. In F. L. Rowlley-Kelly & D. H. Reigel (Eds.), *Teaching the students with spina bifida* (pp. 31–70). Baltimore: Brookes.

Banks, J. (1992). A comment on "Teacher perceptions of the Regular Education Initiative." *Exceptional Children, 58,* 564.

Baren, M. (2000). *Hyperactivity and attention disorders in children: A guide for parents.* San Ramon, CA: Health Information Network.

Barkley, R. A. (1990). *Attention deficit hyperactivity disorder: A handbook for diagnosis and treatment.* New York: Guilford Press.

Barkley, R. A. (1991). *Attention deficit hyperactivity disorder: A clinical workbook.* New York: Guilford Press.

Barkley, R. A. (1997). *Defiant children: A clinician's manual for assessment and parent training.* New York: Guildord Press.

Barkley, R. A. (1998). *Attention-deficit/hyperactivity disorder: A handbook for diagnosis and treatment* (2nd ed.). New York: Guilford Press.

Barkley, R. A. (1999–2000). *ADHD in children and adolescents.* Fairhope, AL: Institute for Continuing Education.

Barnes, K. E. (1982). *Preschool screening: The measurement and prediction of children at risk.* Springfield, IL: Thomas.

Barr, R. D., & Parrett, W. H. (1995). *Hope at last for at-risk youth.* Boston: Allyn and Bacon.

Barr, R. D., & Parrett, W. H. (2001). *Hope fulfilled for at-risk and violent youth: K–12 programs that work* (2nd ed.). Boston: Allyn and Bacon.

Barraga, N. C., & Erin, J. N. (1992). *Visual handicaps and learning* (3rd ed.). Austin, TX: Pro-Ed.

Barrish, H. H., Saunders, M., & Wolf, M. M. (1969). Good-behavior game: Effects of individual contingencies for group consequences on disruptive behavior in a classroom. *Journal of Applied Behavior Analysis, 2,* 119–124.

Batshaw, M. L., & Parret, Y. M. (1986). *Children with handicaps: A medical primer.* Baltimore: Brookes.

Battle, D. A., Dickens-Wright, L., & Murphy, S. C. (1998). How to employ adolescents. *Teaching Exceptional Children, 30,* 28–33.

Bau, A. M. (1999). Providing culturally competent services to visually impaired persons. *Journal of Visual Impairment & Blindness, 93,* 291–297.

Bauer, E. J., Lurie, N., Yeh, C., & Grant, E. N. (1999). Screening for asthma in an inner city elementary school in Minneapolis, MN. *Journal of School Health, 69,* 12–16.

Bauwens, J., & Hourcade, J. J. (1995). *Cooperative teaching: Rebuilding the schoolhouse for all students.* Austin, TX: Pro-Ed.

Bauwens, J., Hourcade, J., & Friend, M. (1989). Cooperative teaching: A model for general and special education integration. *Remedial and Special Education, 10*(2), 17–22.

Beigel, A.R. (2000). Assistive technology assessment: More than a device. *Intervention in School and Clinic, 55*(4), 237–243.

Beirne-Smith, M. (1989a). A systematic approach for teaching note-taking skills to students with mild learning handicaps. *Academic Therapy, 24,* 425–437.

Beirne-Smith, M. (1989b). Teaching note-taking skills. *Academic Therapy, 24,* 452–458.

Beirne-Smith, M., Ittenbach, R. F., & Patton, J. R. (1998). *Mental retardation* (5th ed.). Upper Saddle River, NJ: Prentice-Hall/Merrill.

Beirne-Smith, M., Ittenbach, R. F., & Patton, J. R. (2000). *Mental retardation* (6th ed.). Upper Saddle River, NJ: Prentice-Hall/Merrill.

Belcher, R. N., & Fletcher-Carter, R. (1999). Growing gifted students in the desert: Using alternative, community-based assessment and an enriched curriculum. *Teaching Exceptional Children, 32*(1), 17–24.

Bender, W. N. (1995). *Learning disabilities: Characteristics, identification, and teaching strategies* (2nd ed.). Boston: Allyn and Bacon.

Bender, W. N. (2001a). *Learning disabilities: Characteristics, identification, and teaching strategies* (4th ed.). Boston: Allyn and Bacon.

Bender, W. N. (2001b). Previous school violence by identified kids in trouble. *Intervention, 37,* 105–111.

Bender, W. N. (2003). *Relational discipline: Strategies for in-your-face kids.* Boston: Allyn and Bacon.

Bender, W. N., Rosenkrans, C. B., & Crane, M. K. (1999). Stress, depression and suicide among students with learning disabilities: Assessing the risk. *Learning Disability Quarterly, 42*(2), 143–156.

Bennett, T., Rowe, V., & DeLuca, D. (1996). Getting to know Abby. *Focus on Autism and Developmental Disabilities, 11,* 183–188.

Bergland, M., & Hoffbauer, D. (1996). New opportunities for students with traumatic brain injury: Transition to postsecondary education. *Teaching Exceptional Children, 28,* 54–57.

Berres, M. S., & Knoblock, P. (1987). Introduction and perspective. In M. S. Berres & P. Knoblock (Eds.), *Program models for mainstreaming* (pp. 1–18). Austin, TX: Pro-Ed.

Beukelman, D. R., & Mirenda, P. (1998). *Augmentative and alternative communication* (2nd ed.). Baltimore: Brookes.

Biederman, J., Faraone, S. V., Mick, E., Spencer, T., Wilens, T., Kiely, K. I., Guite, J., Ablone, J. S., Reed, E., & Warbufton, R. (1995). High risk for attention-deficit/hyperactivity disorder of parents with childhood onset of the disorder: A pilot study. *American Journal of Psychiatry, 152,* 431–435.

Bigge, J. L. (1991). *Teaching individuals with physical and multiple disabilities* (3rd ed.). New York: Macmillan.

Biklen, D. (1990). Communication unbound: Autism and praxis. *Harvard Educational Review, 60*(3), 291–314.

Biklen, D., Morton, M. W., Gold, D., Berrigan, C., & Swaminathan, S. (1992). Facilitated communication: Implications for individuals with autism. *Topics in Language Disorders, 2,* 23.

Blackerby, J., & Wagner, M. (1996). Longitudinal post school outcomes of youth with disabilities: Findings from the national longitudinal study. *Exceptional Children, 62,* 399–413.

Blackman, H. P. (1989). Special education placement: Is it what you know or where you live? *Exceptional Children, 55,* 459–462.

Blackman, J. A. (1990). *Medical aspects of developmental disabilities in children birth to three* (2nd ed.). Rockville, MD: Aspen.

Blackman, J. A. (Ed.). (1984). *Medical aspects of developmental disabilities in children birth to three.* Rockville, MD: Aspen.

Blalock, G., & Patton, J. R. (1996). Transition in students with learning disabilities: Creating sound futures. In J. R. Patton & G. Blalock (Eds.), *Transition in students with learning disabilities: Facilitating the movement from school to adult life* (pp. 1–18). Austin, TX: Pro-Ed.

Blasi, M. J., & Priestly, L. (1998). A child with severe hearing loss joins our learning community. *Young Children, 22,* 44–49.

Blatt, B. (1987). *The conquest of mental retardation.* Austin, TX: Pro-Ed.

Blenk, K. (1995). *Making school inclusion work: A guide to everyday practices.* Cambridge, MA: Brookline Books.

Bloom, T. (1996). Assistive listening devices. *The Hearing Journal, 49,* 20–23.

Bowman, B. T. (1994). The challenge of diversity. *Phi Delta Kappa, 76,* 218–224.

Brackett, D. (1990). Communication management of the mainstreamed hearing-impaired student. In M. Ross (Ed.), *Hearing-impaired children in the mainstream* (pp. 119–130). Parkton, MD: York Press.

Brackett, D. (1997). Intervention for children with hearing impairment in general education settings. *Language, Speech, and Hearing Services in Schools, 28,* 355–361.

Breeding, M., Stone, C., & Riley, K. (n.d.) *LINC: Language in the classroom.* Unpublished manuscript. Abilene, TX: Abilene Independent School District.

Brice, A. E. (2002). *The Hispanic child: Speech, language, culture, and education.* Boston: Allyn and Bacon.

Brody, J., & Good, T. (1986). Teacher behavior and student achievement. In M.C. Wittrock (Ed.), *Handbook of research on teaching* (pp. 328–375). New York: Macmillan.

Brolin, D. E. (1989). *Life-centered career education.* Reston, VA: CEC.

Browder, D., & Snell, M. E. (1988). Assessment of individuals with severe disabilities. In M. E. Snell (Ed.), *Severe disabilities.* Columbus, OH: Merrill.

Brown, D. L., & Moore, L. (1992). The Bama bookworm program: Motivating remedial readers to read at home with their parents. *Teaching Exceptional Children, 24,* 17–20.

Brown, J., Cohen, P., Johnson, J. G., & Salzinger, S. (1998). A longitudinal analysis of risk factors for child maltreatment: Findings of a 17-year prospective study of officially recorded and self-reported child abuse and neglect. *Child Abuse & Neglect, 22,* 1065–1078.

Bruce, B.A., et al. (1993). *Developing phonological awareness through alphabet books.* Paper presented at the annual meeting, National Reading Conference, Charleston, SC, December.

Bryan, T. (1999). Reflections on a research career: It ain't over til it's over. *Exceptional Children, 65*(4), 438–447.

Bryan, T., Bay, M., & Donahue, M. (1988). Implications of the learning disabilities definition for the regular education initiative. *Journal of Learning Disabilities, 21*(1), 23–27.

Bryan, T., Bay, M., Lopez-Reyna, N., & Donahue, M. (1991). Characteristics of students with learning disabilities: A summary of the extant data base and its implications for educational programs. In. J. W. Lloyd, N. N. Singh, & A. C. Repp (Eds.), *The regular education initiative: Alternative perspectives* (pp. 121–131). Sycamore, IL: Sycamore.

Bryan, T. A., & Sullivan-Burstein, K. (1998). Teacher selected strategies for improving homework completion. *Remedial and Special Education, 19,* 263–273.

Bryant, D. P., Patton, J. R., & Vaughn, S. (2002). *Step by step guide for including students with disabilities in state-wide assessment.* Austin, TX: Pro-Ed.

Bryant, D. P., Ugel, N., Thompson, S., & Hamff, A. (1999). Instructional strategies for content-area reading instruction. *Intervention in School and Clinic, 34*(5), 293.

Buck, G. H., Bursuck, W. D., Polloway, E. A., Nelson, J., Jayanthi, M., & Whitehouse, F. A. (1996). Homework-related communication problems: Perspectives of special educators. *Journal of Emotional and Behavioral Disorders, 4,* 105–113.

Buck, G. H., Fad, K., Patton, J. R., & Polloway, E. A. (2003). *Prereferral intervention resource guide.* Austin, TX: Pro-Ed.

Buck, G. H., Polloway, E. A., Kirkpatrick, M. A., Patton, J. R., & Fad, K. (1999). Developing intervention plans: A sequential approach. *Intervention, 36,* 3–9.

Buck, G. H., Polloway, E. A., Patton, J. R., & McConnell, K. (2002). *The pre-referral guide.* Austin, TX: Pro-Ed. In press.

Buck, G. H., Wilcox-Cook, K., Polloway, E. A., & Smith-Thomas, A. (2002). *Preferral intervention processes: A survey of practices.* Manuscript submitted for publication.

Budgar, L. (2001). Say again: Stuttering may be more than a case of nerves. *Psychology Today, 34*(6): 16. Sussex Publishers, Inc.

Bullock, L. (1992). *Exceptionalities in children and youth.* Boston: Allyn and Bacon.

Bullock, L. M., Zagar, E. L., Donahue, C. A., & Pelton, G. B. (1985). Teachers' perceptions of behaviorally disordered students in a variety of settings. *Exceptional Children, 52,* 123–130.

Burnley, G. D. (1993). A team approach for identification for an attention deficit hyperactivity disorder child. *The School Counselor, 40,* 228–230.

Burns, B. J., Hoagwood, K., & Maultsby, L. T. (1999). Improving outcomes for children and adolescents with serious emotional and behavioral disorders: Current and future directions. In M. H. Epstein, K. Kutash, & A. Duchnowski (Eds.), *Outcomes for children and youth with behavioral and emotional disorders in their families: Programs and evaluation of best practices* (pp. 685–707). Austin, TX: Pro-Ed.

Bursuck, W., Harniss, M. K., Epstein, M. H., Polloway, E. A., Jayanthi, M., & Wissinger, L. M. (in press). Solving communication problems about homework: Recommendations of special education teachers. *Learning Disabilities Research & Practice.*

Bursuck, W., Munk, D., & Olson, M. (1999). The fairness of report card grading adaptations: What do students with and without disabilities think? *Remedial and Special Education, 20,* 84–92, 105.

Bursuck, W., Polloway, E., Epstein, M., & Jayanthi, M. (n.d.). Recommendations of general education teachers regarding communication problems about homework and students with disabilities. (Manuscript in preparation.)

Bursuck, W. D., Polloway, E. A., Plante, L., Epstein, M. H., Jayanthi, M., & McConeghy, J. (1996). Report card grading and adaptations: A national survey of classroom practices. *Exceptional Children, 62,* 301–318.

Bussing, R., Zima, B., Perwien, A. R., Belin, T. R., & Widawski, M. (1998). Children in special education programs: Attention deficit hyperactivity disorder, use of services, and unmet needs. *American Journal of Public Health 88*(6), 880–886.

Butera, G., Klein, H., McMullen, L., & Wilson, B. (1998). A statewide study of FAPE and school discipline policies. *The Journal of Special Education, 32,* 108–114.

Callahan, C. M., & McIntire, J. A. (1994). *Identifying outstanding talent in American Indian and Alaska native students.* Washington, DC: Office of Educational Research and Improvement.

Callahan, K., Redemacher, R., & Hildreth, T. A. (1998). The effectiveness of parent participation in strategies to improve homework performance of students at risk. *Remedial and Special Education, 19,* 131–141.

Calloway, C. (1999). Promote friendship in the inclusive classroom. *Intervention in School and Clinic, 34*(3), 176–177.

Candler, A. C., & Hildreth, B. L. (1990). Characteristics of language disorders in learning disabled students. *Academic Therapy, 25*(3), 333–343.

Cantrell, M. L. (1992). Guest editorial. *Journal of Emotional and Behavioral Problems, 1,* 4.

Cantu, N. (1993). OCR clarifies evaluation requirements for ADD. *The Special Educator, 9*(1), 11–12.

Carbone, E. (2001). Arranging the classroom with an eye (and ear) to students with ADHD. *Teaching Exceptional Children, 34,* 72-81.

Carnegie Council on Adolescent Development. (1989). *Turning point: Preparing American youth for the 21st century.* New York: Carnegie.

Carnine, D., Silbert J., & Kameenui, E. J. (1990). *Direct instruction reading* (2nd ed.). Columbus, OH: Merrill.

Caroley, J. F., & Foley, T. E. (2001). Enhancing the quality of mathematics for students with learning disabilities: Illustrations from subtraction learning disabilities. *Learning Disabilities: A Multidisciplinary Journal, 12*(2), 47–59.

Carpenter, S. L., & McKee-Higgins, E. (1996). Behavior management in inclusive classrooms. *Remedial and Special Education, 17,* 195–203.

Carr, E. G., Dozier, C. L., Patel, M. R. (2002). Treatment of automatic resistance to extinction. *Research in Developmental Disabilities, 23,* 61–78.

Carroll, D. (2001). Consider paraeducator training roles and responsibilities. *Teaching Exceptional Children, 34,* 60–64.

Cartledge, G., & Milburn, J. F. (1996). *Cultural diversity and social skills instruction: Understanding ethnic and gender differences.* Champaign, IL: Research Press.

Cawley, J. (1984). *Developmental teaching of mathematics for the learning disabled.* Austin, TX: Pro-Ed.

Cawley, J., & Foley, J. F. (2001). Enhancing the quality of math for students with learning disabilities. *Learning Disabilities: A Multidisciplinary Journal, 11,* 47–59.

Center, D. B. (1985). PL 94-142 as applied to *DSM-III* diagnosis: A book review. *Behavioral Disorders, 10,* 305–306.

Center, D. B., & Eden, A. (1989–1990). A search for variables affecting under-identification of students with behavior disorders: II. *National Forum of Special Education Journal, 1,* 12–18.

Center, D. B., & Obringer, J. (1987). A search for variables affecting underidentification of behaviorally disordered students. *Behavioral Disorders, 12,* 169–174.

Center for Future of Teaching and Learning. (1996). Overview of reading research. Washington DC: Author.

Center for Teaching and Learning. (1986). Thirty years of NICHD research: What we now know about how children learn to read. *Effective School Practices, 15*(3), 33–46.

Centers for Disease Control. (1988). *AIDS surveillance report.* Atlanta, GA: Author.

Centers for Disease Control. (1997). AIDS among children—United States, 1996. *Journal of School Health, 67,* 175–177.

Chalfant, J. C., & Pysh, M. V. (1989). Teacher assistance teams: Five descriptive studies on 96 teams. *Remedial and Special Education, 10*(6), 49–58.

Chalfant, J. C., Pysh, M. V., & Moultrie, R. (1979). Teacher assistance teams: A model for within-building problem solving. *Learning Disability Quarterly, 2*(3), 85–96.

Chalfant, J. C., & Van Dusen Pysh, R. L. (1993). Teacher assistance teams: Implications for the gifted. In C. J. Maker (Ed.), *Critical issues in gifted education: Vol 3. Programs for the gifted in regular classrooms* (pp. 32–48). Austin, TX: Pro-Ed.

Chalmers, L. (1991). Classroom modifications for the mainstreamed student with mild handicaps. *Intervention in School and Clinic, 27*(1), 40–42, 51.

Chambers, J. G., Parrish, T. B., Lieberman, J. C., & Woman, J. M. (1999). *What are we spending on special education in the U.S.? CSEF brief.* Palo Alto, CA: Center for Special Education Finance.

Chase, P. A., Hall, J. W., & Werkhaven, J. A. (1996). Sensorineural hearing loss in children: Etiology and pathology. In F. N. Martin & J. G. Clark (Eds.), *Hearing care for children* (pp. 73–88). Boston: Allyn and Bacon.

Cheney, C. O. (1989). The systematic adaptation of instructional materials and techniques for problem learners. *Academic Therapy, 25,* 25–30.

Chiriboga, D. A., & Catron, L. S. (1991). *Divorce.* New York: University Press.

Choate, J.S. (2002). *Successful inclusive teaching: Proven ways to determine and correct special needs* (3rd ed.). Boston: Allyn and Bacon.

Christensen, K. M., & Delgado, G. L. (1993). *Multicultural issues in deafness.* White Plains, NY: Longman.

Christenson, S. L., Ysseldyke, J. E., & Thurlow, M. L. (1989). Critical instructional factors for students with mild handicaps: An integrative review. *Remedial and Special Education, 10*(5), 21–31.

Christian, B. T. (1999). *Outrageous behavior model.* Austin, TX: Pro-Ed.

Christiansen, J., & Vogel, J. R. (1998). A decision model for grading students with disabilities. *Teaching Exceptional Children, 31*(2), 30–35.

Clark, B. (1997). *Growing up gifted: Developing the potential of children at home and at school* (5th ed.). Upper Saddle River, NJ: Merrill/Prentice-Hall.

Clark, B. (2002). *Growing up gifted: Developing the potential of children at home and at school* (6th ed.). Upper Saddle River, NJ: Merrill/Prentice-Hall.

Clark, G. M., Field, S., Patton, J. R., Brolin, D. E., & Sitlington, P. L. (1994). Life skills and instruction: A necessary component for all students with disabilities: A position statement of the Division on Career Development and Transition. *Career Development for Exceptional Individuals, 17,* 125–134.

Clark, J. G., & Jaindl, M. (1996). Conductive hearing loss in children: Etiology and pathology. In F. N. Martin & J. G. Clark (Eds.), *Hearing care for children* (pp. 45–72). Boston: Allyn and Bacon.

Clark, S. G. (2000). The IEP process as a tool for collaboration. *Teaching Exceptional Children, 33,* 56–66.

Clary, D. L., & Edwards, S. (1992). Spoken language. In E. A. Polloway, J. R. Patton, J. S. Payne, & R. A. Payne (Eds.), *Strategies for teaching learners with special needs* (4th ed., pp. 185–285). Columbus, OH: Merrill.

Cline, S., & Schwartz, D. (1999). *Diverse populations of gifted children.* Boston: Allyn and Bacon.

Clinkenbeard, P. R. (1991). Unfair expectations: A pilot study of middle school students' comparisons of gifted and regular classes. *Journal for the Education of the Gifted, 15,* 56–63.

Cochran, P. S., & Bull, G. L. (1993). Computers and individuals with speech and language disorders. In J. D. Kindsey (Ed.), *Computers and exceptional individuals* (pp. 211–242). Austin, TX: Pro-Ed.

Cognitive-behavioral intervention. (2001). In R. Algozzine, L. Serna, & J. R. Patton (Eds.), *Childhood behavior disorders: Applied research and educational practices* (2nd ed.) (pp. 207–228). Austin, TX: Pro-Ed.

Colangelo, N., & Davis, G. A. (Eds.). (1997). *Handbook of gifted education* (2nd ed.). Boston: Allyn and Bacon.

Colangelo, N., & Davis, G. A. (Eds.). (2003). *Handbook of gifted education* (3rd ed.). Boston: Allyn and Bacon.

Colarusso, R. P., & Kana, T. G. (1991). Public Law 99-457, Part H, infant and toddler programs: Status and implications. *Focus on Exceptional Children, 23,* 1–12.

Colarusso, R. P., Keel, M. C., & Dangel, H. L. (2001). A comparison of eligibility criteria and their impact on minority representation in learning disabilities programs. *Learning Disabilities Research and Practice, 16*(1), 1–17.

Coleman, E. B. (1998). Using explanatory knowledge during problem solving in science. *Journal of Learning Science, 1,* 387–427.

Coleman, L. J., & Cross, T. L. (2001). *Being gifted in school: An introduction to developing, guidance, and teaching.* Austin, TX: Pro-Ed.

Coleman, M. C., & Webber, J. (2002). *Emotional and behavioral disorders: Theory and practice* (4th ed.). Boston: Allyn and Bacon.

Collins, B. C., Hendricks, T. B., Fetko, K., & Land, L. A. (2002). Student-2-student learning in inclusive classrooms. *Teaching Exceptional Children, 34,* 56–61.

Conderman, G., Ikan, P. A., & Hatcher, R. E. (2000). Student-led conferences in inclusive settings. *Intervention in School and Clinic, 36,* 22–26.

Conderman, G., & Katsiyannis, A. (1995). *Intervention in School and Clinic, 31*(1), 44.

Condition of education. (1990). Washington, DC: Office of Educational Research and Improvement.

Conoley, J. C., & Kramer, J. J. (1989). *Tenth mental measurements yearbook.* Lincoln, NE: Buros Institute.

Conroy, E. (1993). Strategies for counseling with parents. *Elementary School Guidance and Counseling, 29,* 60–66.

Conte, R. (1991). Attention disorders. In B. Y. L. Wong (Ed.), *Learning about learning disabilities* (pp. 55–101). New York: Academic Press.

Cooke, N. L., Heron, T. E., & Heward, W. L. (1983). *Peer tutoring: Implementing classroom-wide programs.* Columbus, OH: Special Press.

Cooper, H. (1989). *Homework.* White Plains, NY: Longman.

Corn, A. L., Hatlen, P., Huebner, K. M., Ryan, F., & Siller, M. A. (1995). *The national agenda for the education of children and youths with visual impairments, including those with multiple disabilities.* New York: American Foundation for the Blind.

Corn, A. L., & Koening, A. J. (Eds.). (1996). *Foundations of low vision: Clinical and functional perspectives.* New York: American Foundation for the Blind.

Cotler, S. (1986). Epidemiology and outcome. In J. M. Reisman (Ed.), *Behavior disorders in infants, children, and adolescents* (pp. 196–211). New York: Random House.

Cottier, C., Doyle, M., & Gilworth, K. (1997). *Functional AAC intervention: A team approach.* Austin, TX: Pro-Ed.

Council for Exceptional Children. (1992). *Children with ADD: A shared responsibility.* Reston, VA: Author.

Council for Exceptional Children. (1997a). A disability or a gift? *CEC Today, 4*(3), 7.

Council for Exceptional Children. (1997b). Effective accommodations for students with exceptionalities. *CEC Today, 4*(3), 1, 9, 15.

Council for Exceptional Children. (1999). The hidden problem among students with exceptionalities—depression. *CEC Today, 5*(5), 1, 5, 15.

Council of Administrators in Special Education. (1992). *Student access: Section 504 of the rehabilitation act of 1973.* Reston, VA: Author.

Coutinho, M. J., & Repp, A. C. (1999). *Inclusion: The integration of students with disabilities.* Belmont, CA: Wadsworth.

Cozzins, G., Dowdy, C. A., & Smith, T. E. C. (1999). *Adult agencies.* Austin: TX: Pro-Ed.

Craig, C., Hough, D.L., & Churchwell, C. (2001). A statewide study on the literacy of students with visual impairments. *Journal of Visual Impairments and Blindness, 96,* 452–455.

Craig, S., Hull, K., Haggart, A. G., & Crowder, E. (2001). Storytelling addressing the literacy needs of diverse learners. *Teaching Exceptional Children, 33*(5), 46–51.

Cramer, S. (1998). *Collaboration: A successful strategy for special education.* Boston: Allyn and Bacon.

Cramer, S., Erzkus, A., Mayweather, K., Pope, K., Roeder, J., & Tone, T. (1997). Connecting with siblings. *Teaching Exceptional Children, 30*(1), 46–51.

Crane, L. (2002). *Mental retardation: A community integration approach.* Belmont, CA: Thomson Publishing.

Crawford, H. (1998). Classroom acoustics: Creating favorable environments for learning. *ADVANCE for Speech-Language Pathologists & Audiologists, 36,* 25–27.

Creekmore, W. N. (1988). Family–classroom: A critical balance. *Academic Therapy, 24,* 207–220.

Crews, W. D., Bonaventura, S., Hay, C. L., Steele, W. K., & Rowe, F. B. (1993). Gilles de la Tourette disorder among individuals with severe or profound mental retardation. *Mental Retardation, 31,* 25–28.

Cronin, J. F. (1993). Four misconceptions about authentic learning. *Educational Leadership, 50*(7), 78–80.

Cronin, M. E., & Patton, J. R. (1993). *Life skills instruction for all students with special needs.* Austin, TX: Pro-Ed.

Cross, T. L. (1999). Psychological and sociological aspects of educating gifted students. *Peabody Journal of Education, 72,* 180–200.

Csikszentmihalyi, M., Rathunde, K., & Whalen, S. (1997). *Talented teenagers. The roots of success and failure.* Cambridge, UK: Cambridge University Press.

Cullinan, D., & Epstein, M. (1985). Teacher related adjustment problems. *Remedial and Special Education, 6,* 5–11.

Cummings, C. (1983). *Managing to teach.* Edmonds, WA: Teaching Inc.

Cunningham, A. E., & Stanovich, K. E. (1997). Early reading acquisition and its relationship to reading ability ten years later. *Developmental Psychology, 33,* 934–945.

Dagenais, P. A., Critz-Crosby, P., Fletcher, S. G., & McCutcheon, M. J. (1994). Comparing abilities of children with profound hearing impairments to learn consonants using electropalatography or traditional aural–oral techniques. *Journal of Speech and Hearing Research, 37,* 687–699.

Daly, D. A. (1991, April). *Multi-modal therapy for fluency clients: Strategies that work.* Paper presented at the Spring Convention of the Texas Speech-Language-Hearing Association, Houston, TX.

Davis, G.A., & Rimm, S.B. (1998). *Education of the gifted and talented* (4th ed.). Boston: Allyn and Bacon.

Davis, J. (1996). Two different flight plans: Advanced placement and gifted programs—different and necessary. *Gifted Child Today, 19*(2), 32–36, 50.

Davis, W. E. (1993). *At-risk children and educational reform: Implications for educators and schools in the year 2000 and beyond.* Orono, ME: College of Education, University of Maine.

Davis, W. E. (1995). Students at risk: Common myths and misconceptions. *The Journal of At-Risk Issues, 2,* 5–10.

deBettencourt, L. U. (1987). How to develop parent relationships. *Teaching Exceptional Children, 19,* 26–27.

Deiner, P. L. (1993). *Resources for teaching children with diverse abilities: Birth through eight.* Ft. Worth, TX: Harcourt Brace Jovanovich.

DeLong, R. (1995). Medical and pharmacological treatment of learning disabilities. *Journal of Child Neurology, 10*(suppl. 1), 92–95.

Del Prete, T. (1996). Asset or albatross? The education and socialization of gifted students. *Gifted Child Today, 19*(2), 24–25, 44–49.

Denning, C. B., Chamberlain, J. A., & Polloway, E. A. (2000). An evaluation of state guidelines for mental retardation: Focus on definition and classification practices. *Education and Training in Mental Retardation and Developmental Disabilities, 35,* 135–144.

Denbo, S. J., & Beaulieu, L. M. (2002). *Improving schools for African Americans: A reader for educational leaders.* Springfield, IL: Charles C Thomas.

Deno, E. (1970). Special education as development capital. *Exceptional Children, 55,* 440–447.

Deno, S. L., Foegen, A., Robinson, S., & Espin, C. (1996). Commentary: Facing the realities of inclusion for students with mild disabilities. *Journal of Special Education, 30,* 345–357.

Deno, S. L., & Fuchs, L. S. (1987). Developing curriculum-based measurement systems for data-based special education problem-solving. *Focus on Exceptional Children, 19*(8), 1–16.

Deshler, D. D., Ellis, E. S., & Lenz, B. K. (1996). *Teaching adolescents with learning disabilities: Strategies and methods* (2nd ed.). Denver: Love.

Deshler, D. D., & Lenz, B. K. (1989). The strategies instructional approach. *International Journal of Disability, Development and Education, 36*(3), 203–224.

Deshler, D., & Schumaker, J. B. (1988). Learning strategies: An instructional alternative for low-achieving adolescents. *Exceptional Children, 52,* 83–89.

Desrochers, J. (1999). Vision problems—How teachers can help. *Young Children, 54,* 36–38.

Deyhle, D., & LeCompte, M. (1999). Cultural differences in child development: Navajo adolescents in middle schools. In R. H. Sheets & E. R. Hollins (Eds.), *Racial and ethnic identity in school practices: Aspects of human development* (pp. 123–139). Mahwah, NJ: Erlbaum.

Diana v. State Board of Education, C-70-37 R.F.P. (N.D., California, Jan. 7, 1970, and June 18, 1972).

Diefendorf, A. O. (1996). Hearing loss and its effects. In F. N. Martin & J. G. Clark (Eds.), *Hearing care for children* (pp. 3–18). Boston: Allyn and Bacon.

Dobbs, R. F., Primm, E. B., & Primm, B. (1991). Mediation: A common sense approach for resolving conflicts in education. *Focus on Exceptional Children, 24,* 1–12.

Donahue, K., & Zigmond, N. (1990). Academic grades of ninth-grade urban learning disabled students and low-achieving peers. *Exceptionality, 1,* 17–27.

Dorn, L., & Allen, A. (1995). Helping low-achieving first-grade readers: A program combining reading recovery tutoring and small-group instruction. *Journal of School Research and Information, 13,* 16–24.

Dowdy, C. A. (1998). Strengths and limitations inventory: School version. In C. A. Dowdy, J. R. Patton, T. E. C. Smith, & E. A. Polloway (Eds.), *Attention deficit/hyperactivity disorder in the classroom: A practical guide for teachers.* Austin, TX: Pro-Ed.

Dowdy, C. A., Carter, J., & Smith, T. E. C. (1990). Differences in transitional needs of high school students with and without learning disabilities. *Journal of Learning Disabilities, 23*(6), 343–348.

Dowdy, C. A., Patton, J. R., Smith, T. E. C., & Polloway, E. A. (1998). *Attention deficit/hyperactivity disorders in the classroom.* Austin, TX: Pro-Ed.

Dowdy, C. A., & Smith, T. E. C. (1991). Future-based assessment and intervention. *Intervention in School and Clinic, 27*(2), 101–106.

Downing, J. A. (2002). Individualized behavior contracts. *Intervention, 37,* 164-172.

Doyle, W. (1986). Classroom organization and management. In M. C. Wittrock (Ed.), *Handbook of research and teaching* (3rd ed., pp. 392–431). New York: Macmillan.

Drasgow, E., Yell, M.L., & Robinson, T. (2001). Developing legally correct and educationally appropriate IEPs. *Remedial and Special Education, 22*, 359–373.

Drug use increasing. (1992). *Youth Today, 1*, 27–29.

Duane, D. D., & Gray, D. B. (Eds.) (1991). *The reading brain: The biological basis of dyslexia.* Parkton, MD: York.

Duhaney, L. M. G., & Salend, S. J. (2000). Parental perceptions of inclusive educational placements. *Remedial and Special Education, 21*, 121–128.

Dunn, L. M. (1968). Special education for the mildly handicapped: Is much of it justifiable? *Exceptional Children, 35*, 5–22.

Dunst, C. J., Johanson, C., Trivette, C. M., & Hamby, D. (1991). Family-oriented early intervention policies and practices: Family-centered or not? *Exceptional Children, 58*, 115–126.

DuPaul, G. J., & Eckert, T. L. (1998). Academic interventions for students with attention-deficit/hyperactivity disorder: A review of the literature. *Reading and Writing Quarterly, 14*(1), 59–83.

Dyches, T. (1998). The effectiveness of switch training on communication of children with autism and severe disabilities. *Focus on Autism and Other Developmental Disabilities, 13*, 151–162.

Easterbrooks, S. R. (1999). *Adapting regular classrooms for children who are deaf/hard of hearing.* Paper presented to the Council for Exceptional Children convention, Minneapolis, MN.

Eaves, R. C. (1992). Autism. In P. J. McLaughlin & P. Wehman (Eds.), *Developmental disabilities* (pp. 68–80). Boston: Andover Medical.

Edgar, E. (1987). Secondary programs in special education: Are many of them justifiable? *Exceptional Children, 53*, 555–561.

Edgar, E. (1988). Employment as an outcome for mildly handicapped students: Current status and future directions. *Focus on Exceptional Children, 21*(1), 1–8.

Edgar, E. (1990, Winter). Is it time to change our view of the world? *Beyond Behavior*, 9–13.

Edgar, E., & Polloway, E. A. (1994). Education for adolescents with disabilities: Curriculum and placement issues. *Journal of Special Education, 27*, 438–452.

Edmunds, A. L. (1999). Cognitive credit cards: Acquiring learning strategies. *Teaching Exceptional Children.* March/April, 68–73.

Edwards, C. (1996). Educational management of children with hearing loss. In F. N. Martin & J. G. Clark (Eds.), *Hearing care for children* (pp. 303–315). Boston: Allyn and Bacon.

Egel, A. L. (1989). Finding the right educational program. In M. D. Powers (Ed.), *Children with autism: A parent's guide.* New York: Woodbine House.

Eggert, L. L., & Herting, J. R. (1993). Drug involvement among potential dropouts and "typical" youth. *Journal of Drug Education, 23*, 31–55.

Ehlers, V. L., & Ruffin, M. (1990). The Missouri project—Parents as teachers. *Focus on Exceptional Children, 23*, 1–14.

Elam, S. M., & Rose, L. C. (1995). The 22nd annual poll of the public's attitudes toward the public schools. *Phi Delta Kappan, 77*, 41–56.

Elam, S. M., Rose, L. C., & Gallup, A. M. (1996). The 23rd annual Gallup poll of the public's attitudes toward the public schools. *Phi Delta Kappan, 73*, 41–55.

Elders, J. (2002). Keynote address. *57th Annual Conference of the Association for Supervision and Curriculum Development.* San Antonio, TX.

Elizer, E., & Kauffman, M. (1983). Factors influencing the severity of childhood bereavement reactions. *American Journal of Orthopsychiatry, 53*, 393–415.

Elksnin, L. K., Bryant, D. P., Gartland, D., King-Sears, M., Rosenberg, M. S., Scanlon, D., Strosnider, R., & Wilson, R. (2001). LD summit: Important issues for the field of learning disabilities. *Learning Disability Quarterly, 24*, 297–305.

Elksnin, L. K., & Elksnin, N. (1998). Teaching social skills to students with learning and behavioral problems. *Intervention in School and Clinic, 33*, 131–140.

Ellenwood, A. E., & Felt, D. (1989). Attention-deficit/hyperactivity disorder: Management and intervention approaches for the classroom teacher. *LD Forum, 15*, 15–17.

Ellis, E. S., & Lenz, B. K. (1990). Techniques for mediating content-area learning: Issues and research. *Focus on Exceptional Children, 22*, 1–16.

Emerick, L. L., & Haynes, W. O. (1986). *Diagnosis and evaluation in speech pathology* (3rd ed.). Englewood Cliffs, NJ: Prentice-Hall.

Emery, R. E. (1989). Family violence. *American Psychologist, 44*, 321–327.

Engelmann, S., & Carnine, D. (1982). *Theory of instruction.* New York: Irvington.

Englert, C. S., Mariage, T. B., Garman, M. A., & Tarrant, K. L. (1998). Accelerating reading progress in early literacy project classrooms: Three exploratory studies. *Remedial and Special Education, 19*, 142–159, 180.

Epilepsy Foundation of America. (1992). *Seizure recognition and observation: A guide for allied health professionals.* Landover, MD: Author.

Epstein, M. H. (1999). The development and the validation of a scale to assess the emotional and behavioral strengths of children–adolescents. *Remedial and Special Education, 20*, 258–262.

Epstein, M. H., & Charma, J. (1998). *Behavioral and emotional rating scale: A strength-based approach to assessment.* Austin, TX: Pro-Ed.

Epstein, M. H., Kutash, K., & Duchnowski, A. (1998). *Outcomes for children and youth with behavioral and emotional disorders and their families: Programs and evaluation of best practices.* Austin, TX: Pro-Ed.

Epstein, M. H., Munk, D. D., Bursuck, W. D., Polloway, E. A., & Jayanthi, M. M. (1999). Strategies for improving home-school communication problems about homework for students with disabilities: Perceptions of general educators. *Journal of Special Education, 33*, 166–176.

Epstein, M. H., Patton, J. R., Polloway, E. A., & Foley, R. (1992). Educational services for students with behavior disorders: A review of individualized education programs. *Teacher Education and Special Education, 15*, 41–48.

Epstein, M. H., Polloway, E. A., Buck, G. H., Bursuck, W. D., Wissinger, L. M., Whitehouse, F., & Jayanthi, M. Homework-related communication problems: Perspectives of general education teachers. *Learning Disabilities Research and Practice, 12*, 221–227.

Epstein, M. H., Polloway, E. A., Bursuck, W., Jayanthi, M., & McConeghy, J. (1996). Recommendations for effective homework practices. (Manuscript in preparation.)

Epstein, M. H., Polloway, E. A., Foley, R. M., & Patton, J. R. (1993). Homework: A comparison of teachers' and parents' perceptions of the problems experienced by students identified as having behavioral disorders, learning disabilities, or no disabilities. *Remedial and Special Education, 14*(5), 40–50.

Erickson, J. G. (1992, April). *Communication disorders in multicultural populations.* Paper presented at the Texas Speech-Language-Hearing Association Annual Convention, San Antonio, TX.

Erwin, E. J. (1993). The philosophy and status of inclusion. *The Lighthouse,* 1–4.

Etscheidt, S. K., & Bartlett, L. (1999). The IDEA amendments: A four-step approach for determining supplementary aids and services. *Exceptional Children, 65,* 163–174.

Everson, J. M. (1998). *Transition for youths who are deaf-blind: A best practices guide for educators.* Sands Point, NY: Helen Keller National Center-Technical Assistance Center.

Evertson, C., Emmer, E. T., & Worsham, M. E. (2000). *Classroom management for elementary teachers* (5th ed.). Boston: Allyn and Bacon.

Evertson, C. M., Emmer, E. T., Clements, B. J., Sanford, J. P., & Worsham, M. E. (1989). *Classroom management for elementary teachers* (2nd ed.). Englewood Cliffs, NJ: Prentice-Hall.

Evertson, C. M., Emmer, E. T., Clements, B. J., Sanford, J. P., & Worsham, M. E. (2003). *Classroom management for elementary teachers* (6th ed.). Englewood Cliffs, NJ: Prentice-Hall.

Fad, K., Patton, J. R., & Polloway, E. A. (2000). *Behavioral intervention planning: Completing a functional behavioral assessment and developing a behavioral intervention plan* (2nd ed.). Austin, TX: Pro-Ed.

Favazza, P. C., Phillipsen, L., Kumar, P. (2000). Measuring and promoting acceptance of young children with disabilities. *Exceptional Children, 66,* 491–508.

Federal Register, 42, 42478.

Federal Register, 58, 48952.

Fedorowitz, C., Benezra, E., MacDonald, W., McElgunn, B., Wilson, A., & Kaplan, B. (2001). Neurological brains of learning disabilities: An update. *Learning Disabilities Association Multidisciplinary Journal, 11,* 1–74.

Fehling, R. H. (1993). *Weekday speech activities to promote carryover.* Austin, TX: Pro-Ed.

Feingold, B. F. (1975). *Why your child is hyperactive.* New York: Random House.

Feiring, C., Taska, L., & Lewis, M. (1999). Age and gender differences in children's and adolescents' adaptation to sexual abuse. *Child Abuse & Neglect, 23,* 115–126.

Feldhusen, H. J. (1993a). Individualized teaching of the gifted in regular classrooms. In C. J. Maker (Ed.), *Critical issues in gifted education: Vol. 3. Programs for the gifted in regular classrooms* (pp. 263–273). Austin, TX: Pro-Ed.

Feldhusen, H. J. (1993b). Synthesis of research on gifted youth. *Educational Leadership, 22,* 6–11.

Feldhusen, J. F. (1999). Programs for the gifted few or talent development for the many. *Phi Delta Kappan, 79,* 735–738.

Felner, R., Ginter, M., Boike, M., & Cowan, E. (1981). Parental death or divorce and the school adjustment of young children. *American Journal of Community Psychology, 9,* 181–191.

Ferguson, D. L. (1995). The real challenge of inclusion: Confessions of a "rabid inclusionist." *Phi Delta Kappan, 77,* 281–287.

Ficker-Terrill, C. (2001, May-June). Perhaps the time has come to change our name. *American Association on Mental Retardation News and Notes, 14*(3), 3.

Field, S., Hoffman, A., & Spezia, S. (1998). *Self determination strategies for adolescents in transition.* Austin, TX: Pro-Ed.

Filipek, P. A. (1999). Neuroimaging in the developmental disorders: The state of the science. *Journal of Child Psychology and Psychiatry, 40,* 113–128.

Final regulations for IDEA. (1999). Washington, DC: U.S. Printing Office.

Finn, C. E., Rotherham, A. J., Hokanson, C. R. (2002). *Rethinking special education for a new century.* Washington, DC: Fordham Foundation.

Finson, K. D., & Ormsbee, C. R. (1998). Rubrics and their use in inclusion science. *Intervention in School and Clinic, 34,* 79–88.

Fiore, T. A., Becker, E. A., & Nerro, R. C. (1993). Educational interventions for students with attention deficit disorder. *Exceptional Children, 60,* 163–173.

Fisher, D., Pumpian, I., & Sax, C. (1998). Parent and caregiver impressions of different educational models. *Remedial and Special Education, 19,* 173–180.

Fisher, J. B., Schumaker, J., & Deshler, D. D. (1995). Searching for validated inclusive practices: A review of the literature. *Focus on Exceptional Children, 28,* 1–20.

Fisher, S., Clark, G.M., & Patton, J.R. (in press). *Understanding occupational vocabulary.* Austin, TX: Pro-Ed.

Fleming, J.L., Monda-Amaya, L.E., (2001). Process variables critical for team effectiveness. *Remedial and Special Education, 22,* 158–171.

Fletcher, J. M., Lyon, G. R., Barnes, M., Stuebing, K. K., Francis, D. J., Olson, R. K., Shaywitz, S. E., & Shaywitz, B. A. (2001). *Classification of learning disabilities: An evidence-based evaluation.* Paper presented at the LD Summit, Washington, D.C.

Flick, G. L. (1998). Managing AD/HD in the classroom minus medication. *Education Digest, 63*(9), 50–56.

Foley, R. M., & Kittleson, M. J. (1993). Special educators' knowledge of HIV transmission: Implications for teacher education programs. *Teacher Education and Special Education, 16,* 342–350.

Foorman, B. R., & Torgeson, J. (2001). Critical elements of classroom and small group instruction promoting reading success in all children. *Research and Practice, 16,* 203–212.

Ford, A., Pugach, M. C., & Otis-Wilborn, A. (2001). Preparing general educators to work well with students who have disabilities: What's reasonable at the preservice level? *Learning Disability Quarterly, 24,* 275–285.

Forness, S. R. (2001). Special education and related services: What have we learned from meta-analysis? *Exceptionality, 9,* 185–197.

Forness, S. R. (1999). Stimulant medication revisited: Effective treatment of children with attention deficit disorder. *Journal of Emotional and Behavior Problems, 7,* 230–233.

Forness, S. R., & Kavale, K. A. (1988). Planning for the needs of children with serious emotional disturbance: The National Mental Health and Special Education Coalition. *Behavior Disorders, 13,* 127–133.

Forness, S. R., & Polloway, E. A. (1987). Physical and psychiatric diagnoses of pupils with mild mental retardation currently being referred for related services. *Education and Training in Mental Retardation, 22,* 221–228.

Forness, S. R., Sweeney, D. P., & Toy, K. (1996). Psychopharmacologic medication: What teachers need to know. *Beyond Behavior, 7*(2) 4–11.

Foster-Johnson, L., & Dunlap, G. (1993). Using functional assessment to develop effective, individualized interventions for challenging behaviors. *Teaching Exceptional Children, 56,* 44–52.

Fowler, M. (1992a). *Attention deficit disorder*. NICHY briefing paper. Washington, DC: National Information Center for Children and Youth with Disabilities.

Fowler, M. (1992b). *C.H.A.D.D. educators manual: An in-depth look at attention deficit disorder for an educational perspective*. Fairfax, VA: CASET Associates, Ltd.

Fox, P., & Emerson, E. (2001). Socially valid outcomes of intervention for people with MR and challenging behavior: Views of different stakeholders. *Journal of Positive Behavior Interventions, 3*(3), 183–189.

Frankenberger, W., & Harper, J. (1988). States' definitions and procedures for identifying children with mental retardation: Comparison of 1981–82 and 1985–86 guidelines. *Mental Retardation, 26*, 133–136.

Frederico, M. A., Herrold, W. G., Venn, J. (1999). Helpful tips for successful inclusion: A checklist for educators. *Teaching Exceptional Children, 32*, 76–82.

French, N., & Gerlach, K. (1999). Paraeducators: Who are they and what do they do? *Teaching Exceptional Children, 32*, 65–69.

Friedman, D., & Scaduto, J. J. (1995). Let's do lunch. *Teaching Exceptional Children, 28*, 22–26.

Friend, M. (2000). Myths and misunderstandings about professional collaboration. *Remedial and Special Education, 21*, 130–132.

Friend, M. F., & Bursuck, W. D. (1999). *Including students with special needs: A practical guide for classroom teachers*. Boston: Allyn and Bacon.

Friend, M. F., & Bursuck, W. D. (2002). *Including students with special needs: A practical guide for classroom teachers* (3rd ed.) Boston: Allyn and Bacon.

Frymier, J., & Gansneder, B. (1989). *The Phi Delta Kappan study of students at risk*. Washington, DC: Author.

Fuchs, D., Fernston, P., Scott, S., Fuchs, L., & Vandermeer, E. (1994). Classroom ecological inventory. *Teaching Exceptional Children, 26*, 13–16.

Fuchs, D., & Fuchs, L. S. (1994–1995). Sometimes separate is better. *Educational Leadership, 52*, 22–24.

Fuchs, L. S., & Fuchs, D. (1986). Effects of systematic formative evaluation: A meta-analysis. *Exceptional Children, 53*, 199–208.

Fuchs, L. S., & Fuchs, D. (2001). Helping teachers formulate sound test accommodation decisions for students with learning disabilities. *Learning Disability Research and Practice, 16*(3), 174–181.

Fulk, B. M., & King, K. (2001). Classwide peer tutoring at work. *Teaching Exceptional Children, 34*, 49–54.

Fulk, B. M., & Montgomery-Grymes, D. J. (1994). Strategies to improve student motivation. *Intervention in School and Clinic, 30*(1), 28–33.

Gable, R. A., Arllen, N. L., & Hendrickson, J. M. (1994). Use of students with emotional/behavioral disorders as behavior change agents. *Education and Treatment of Children, 17*, 267–276.

Gajria, M., & Salend, S. J. (1995). Homework practices of students with and without learning disabilities: A comparison. In W. Bursuck (Ed.), *Homework: Issues and practices for students with learning disabilities* (pp. 97–106). Austin, TX: Pro-Ed.

Gallagher, J. J. (1979). *Issues in gifted education*. Ventura, CA: Ventura County Superintendent of Schools Office.

Gallagher, J. J. (1997). Least restrictive environment and gifted students. *Peabody Journal of Education, 13*, 153–165.

Gallagher, J. J., & Gallagher, S. A. (1994). *Teaching the gifted child* (4th ed.). Boston: Allyn and Bacon.

Gallegos, A. Y., & Gallegos, M. L. (1990). A student's perspective on good teaching: Michael. *Intervention in School and Clinic, 26*, 14–15.

Garcia, J. G., Krankowski, T. K., & Jones, L. L. (1998). Collaboration intervention for assisting students with acquired brain injury. *Professional School Counselor, 2*, 33–38.

Garcia, S. B., Wilkinson, C. Y., & Ortiz, A. A. (1995). Enhancing achievement for language minority students: Classroom, school, and family contexts. *Education and Urban Society, 27*(4), 441–462.

Gardner, H. (1983). *Frames of mind: The theory of multiple intelligences*. New York: Basic Books.

Gardner, H. (1993). *Multiple intelligences: The theory in practice*. New York: Basic Books.

Gardner, H., & Hatch, T. (1989). Multiple intelligences go to school: Educational implications of the theory of multiple intelligences. *Educational Researcher, 18*(8), 4–9.

Gargiulo, R. M. (1990). Child abuse and neglect: An overview. In R. L. Goldman & R. M. Gargiulo (Eds.), *Children at risk* (pp. 1–35). Austin, TX: Pro-Ed.

Gargiulo, R. M. (2003). *Special education in contemporary society*. Belmont, CA: Wadsworth.

Gargiulo, R. S., O'Sullivan, P., Stephens, D. G., & Goldman, R. (1989–1990). Sibling relationships in mildly handicapped children: A preliminary investigation. *National Forum of Special Education Journal, 1*, 20–28.

Gartin, B. C., & Murdick, N. L. (2001). A new IDEA mandate: The use of functional assessment of behavior and positive behavior supports. *Remedial and Special Education, 22*, 344–349.

Gartland, D. (1994). Content area reading: Lessons from the specialists. *LD Forum, 19*(3), 19–22.

Gay, Lesbian, and Straight Education Network. (1999). *GLSEN's national school climate survey*. Washington, DC: Author.

Gearheart, B. R., Weishahn, M. W., & Gearheart, C. J. (1996). *The exceptional student in the regular classroom* (6th ed.). Columbus, OH: Merrill.

Geisthardt, C., & Munsch, J. (1996). Coping with school stress: A comparison of adolescents with and without learning disabilities. *Journal of Learning Disabilities, 29*(3), 287–296.

Gerber, P. J., & Reiff, H. B. (1998). Reframing the learning disabilities experience. *Journal of Learning Disabilities, 29*(1), 98–102.

Gersh, E. S. (1991). What is cerebral palsy? In E. Geralis (Ed.), *Children with cerebral palsy: A parents' guide*. New York: Woodbine House.

Gerstein, R., Brengleman, S., & Jimenez, R. (1994). Effective instruction for culturally and linguistically diverse students: A reconceptualization. *Focus on Exceptional Children, 27*(1), 1–6.

Gerstein, R., & Woodward, J. (1994). The language-minority student and special education: Issues, trends, and paradoxes. *Exceptional Children, 60*(4), 310–322.

Gersten, R. (1994). Effective instruction for culturally and linguistically diverse students. *Focus on Exceptional Children, 27*, 1–16.

Gersten, R., & Chard, D. (1999). Number sense: Rethinking arithmetic instruction for students with math disorders. *Journal of Special Education, 33*, 18–28.

Getch, Y. Q., Neuhart-Pritchett, S. (1999). Children with asthma: Strategies for educators. *Teaching Exceptional Children, 31*, 30–36.

Giangreco, M. F., Dennis, R., Cloninger, C., Edelman, S., & Schattman, R. (1993). I've counted Jon: Transformational experiences of teachers educating students with disabilities. *Exceptional Children, 59,* 359–372.

Giangreco, M. F., Edelman, S. W., Broer, S. M., & Doyle, M. B. (2001). Paraprofessional support of students with disabilities: Literature from the past decade. *Exceptional Children, 68,* 45–63.

Gibb, G. S., & Dykes, T. T. (2000). *Guide to writing quality individualized educational programs.* Boston: Allyn and Bacon.

Gillberg, C. (Ed.). (1989). *Diagnosis and treatment of autism.* New York: Plenum Press.

Ginsberg, R., Gerber, P. J., & Reiff, H. B. (1994). Employment success for adults with learning disabilities. In P. Gerber & H. Reiff (Eds.), *Learning disabilities in adulthood* (pp. 204–213). Stoneham, MA: Andover Medical Publishers.

Ginsburg, H. P. (1989). *Children's arithmetic: How they learn it and how you teach it* (2nd ed.). Austin, TX: Pro-Ed.

Glazer, S. M. (1998). At risk students: No instant solutions. *Teaching Pre–K–8, 28*(7), 84–86.

Goldman, S., & Rueda, R. S. (1988). Developing writing skills in bilingual exceptional children. *Exceptional Children, 56*(2), 121–129.

Goldstein, S., & Goldstein, M. (1990). *Managing attention disorder in children: A guide for practitioners.* New York: John Wiley & Sons.

Goldstein, S., & Turnbull, A. P. (1981). Strategies to increase parent participation in IEP conferences. *Exceptional Children, 48,* 360–361.

Gonzalez, V., Brusca-Vega, R., & Yawkey, T. (1997). *Assessment and instruction of culturally diverse students.* Boston: Allyn and Bacon.

Goodwin, M. W. (1999). Cooperative learning and social skills: What skills to teach and how to teach them. *Intervention in School and Clinic, 35,* 29–32.

Gorman, J. C. (1999, January/February). Understanding children's hearts and minds. *Teaching Exceptional Children, 31,* 72–77.

Graham, S. (1992). Helping students with LD progress as writers. *Intervention in School and Clinic, 27,* 134–144.

Graham, S., & Harris, K. R. (1997). Whole language and process writing: Does one approach fit all? In I. W. Lloyd, E. J. Kameenui, & D. Chard (Eds.), *Issues in educating students with disabilities* (pp. 239–258). Mahwah, NJ: Erlbaum.

Greenbaum, P. E., Dedrick, R. F., Friedman, R. M., Kutash, K., Brown, E. C., Lardieri, S. P., & Pugh, A. M. (1998). National adolescent and child treatment study (NACTS): Outcomes for children with serious emotional behavioral disturbance. In M. H. Epstein, K. Kutash, & A. Duchnowski (Eds.), *Outcomes for children and youth with emotional and behavioral disorders and their families: Programs and evaluation of best practices* (pp. 21–54). Austin, TX: Pro-Ed.

Greenspan, S. (1996, October 11). *Everyday intelligence and a new definition of mental retardation.* Fifth Annual MRDD Conference, Austin, TX.

Greenwood, C. R., Arrega-Mayer, C., Utley, C. A., Gavin, B., & Terry, L. (2001). Classwide peer tutoring management system: Application with elementary-level English language learners. *Remedial and Special Education, 22,* 34–47.

Greer, J. V. (1991). At-risk students in the fast lanes: Let them through. *Exceptional Children, 57,* 390–391.

Gregory, C., & Katsiyannis, A. (1995). Section 504 accommodation plans. *Intervention in School and Clinic, 31*(1), 42–45.

Gresham, F. M. (1982). Misguided mainstreaming: The case for social skills training with handicapped children. *Exceptional Children, 48*(5), 422–431.

Gresham, F. M. (1984). Social skills and self-efficacy for exceptional children. *Exceptional Children, 51,* 253–261.

Griswold, D.E., Barnhill, G.P., Myles, B.S. (2002). Asperger's syndrome and academic achievement. *Focus on Autism and Other Developmental Disabilities, 17,* 94-102.

Grosenick, J. K., George, N. L., George, M. P., & Lewis, T. J. (1991). Public school services for behaviorally disordered students: Program practices in the 1980s. *Behavioral Disorders, 16,* 87–96.

Grossman, H. J. (1983). *Classification in mental retardation.* Washington, DC: American Association on Mental Deficiency.

Guernsey, M. A. (1989). Classroom organization: A key to successful management. *Academic Therapy, 25,* 55–58.

Guetzloe, E. (1988). Suicide and depression: Special education's responsibility. *Teaching Exceptional Children, 20,* 25–28.

Guterman, B. R. (1995). The validity of categorical learning disabilities services: The consumer's view. *Exceptional Children, 62,* 111–124.

Guyer, B. (2000). Reaching and teaching the adolescent. In B. D. Guyer (Ed.), *ADHD: Achieving success in school and in life.* Boston: Allyn and Bacon.

Guyer B. D. (2002). So you have a learning disability: Do you have what it takes to succeed in college? *LDA Newsbriefs,* May/June, 3–5.

Haight, S. L., Patricia, L. A., Burns, M. K. (2001). A statewide analysis of the eligibility criteria and procedures for determining learning disabilities. *Learning Disabilities, 11,* 39–46.

Hallahan, D. P., & Kauffman, J. M. (1995). *The illusion of full inclusion.* Austin, TX: Pro-Ed.

Hallahan, D. P., & Kauffman, J. M. (1997). *Exceptional learners: Introduction to special education* (7th ed.). Boston: Allyn and Bacon.

Hallahan, D. P., & Kauffman, J. M. (2000). *Exceptional children: Introduction to special education* (8th ed.). Boston: Allyn and Bacon.

Hallahan, D. P., & Kauffman, J. M. (2003). *Exceptional children: Introduction to special education* (9th ed.). Boston: Allyn and Bacon.

Hallahan, D. P., Kauffman, J. M., & Lloyd, J. W. (1996). *Introduction to learning disabilities.* Boston: Allyn and Bacon.

Hallahan, D. P., Kauffman, J. M., & Lloyd, J. W. (1999). *Introduction to learning disabilities* (2nd ed.). Boston: Allyn and Bacon.

Hallahan, D. P., & Keogh, D. P. (2001). *Research and global perspectives in learning disabilities: Essays in honor of William M. Cruickshank.* Mahwah, NJ: Lawrence Erlbaum Associates.

Hallahan, D. P., & Mercer, C. D. (2001). *Learning disabilities: Historical perspectives.* Paper presented at the 2001 LD Summit: Building a Foundation for the Future. Available on-line from www.air.org/ldsummit.

Hallahan, D. P., Lloyd, J. W., & Stoller, L. (1982). *Improving attention with self-monitoring: A manual for teachers.* Charlottesville, VA: University of Virginia Press.

Halvorsen, A. T., & Neary, T. (2001). *Building inclusive schools: Tools and strategies for success.* Boston: Allyn and Bacon.

Hamaguchi, P. A. (2002). *It's time to listen: Metacognitive activities for improving auditory processing in the classroom* (2nd ed.) Austin, TX: Pro-Ed.

Hammill, D. D., & Bartel, N. R. (1995). *Teaching students with learning and behavior problems.* Austin, TX: Pro-Ed.

Hammill, D. D., & Bryant, B. R. (1991). The role of standardized tests in planning academic instruction. In H. L. Swanson (Ed.). *Handbook on the assessment of learning disabilities.* Austin, TX: Pro-Ed.

Hamre-Nietupski, S., Ayres, B., Nietupski, J., Savage, M., Mitchell, B., & Bramman, H. (1989). Enhancing integration of students with severe disabilities through curricular infusion: A general/special educator partnership. *Education and Training in Mental Retardation, 24,* 78–88.

Hansen, C. R. (1992). What is Tourette syndrome? In T. Haerle (Ed.), *Children with Tourette syndrome: A parents' guide* (pp. 1–25). Rockville, MD: Woodbine House.

Hansen, J. B., & Feldhusen, J. F. (1994). Comparison of trained and untrained teachers of gifted students. *Gifted Child Quarterly, 38*(3), 115–121.

Hanson, M. J., & Carta, J. J. (1996). Addressing the challenges of families with multiple risks. *Exceptional Children, 62,* 201–212.

Hanson, M.J., Horn, E., & Sandall, S. (2001). After pre-school inclusion: Children's educational pathways over the early school years. *Exceptional Children, 68,* 65–83.

Hardman, M. L., Drew, C. J., Egan, M. W., & Wolf, B. (1993). *Human exceptionality: Society, school, and family* (4th ed.). Boston: Allyn and Bacon.

Harn, W. E., Bradshaw, M. L., & Ogletree, B. T. (1999). The speech–language pathologist in the schools: Changing roles. *Intervention in School and Clinic, 34*(3), 163–170. Austin, TX: Pro-Ed.

Harris, D., & Vanderheiden, G. C. (1980). Augmentative communication techniques. In R. L. Schiefelbusch (Ed.), *Nonspeech language and communication: Analysis and intervention* (pp. 259–302). Austin, TX: Pro-Ed.

Harris, K. C. (1998). *Collaborative elementary teaching: A casebook for elementary special and general educators.* Austin, TX: Pro-Ed.

Harwell, J. M. (1989). *Learning disabilities handbook.* West Nyack, NY: Center for Applied Research in Education.

Hasselbring, T., & Goin, L. (1993). Integrated media and technology. In E. A. Polloway & J. R. Patton (Eds.), *Strategies for teaching learners with special needs* (5th ed., pp. 145–162). Columbus, OH: Macmillan.

Healthy People 2000. (1992). Washington, DC: U.S. Government Printing Office.

Heaton, S., & O'Shea, D. J. (1995). Using mnemonics to make mnemonics. *Teaching Exceptional Children, 28*(1), 34–36.

Heflin, L. J., & Simpson, R. (1998). The interventions for children and youth with autism: Prudent choices in a world of extraordinary claims and promises: Part II. *Focus on Autism and Other Developmental Disabilities, 13,* 212–220.

Heinrich, S.R. (1999). Visually impaired students can use the internet. *NASSP Bulletin, 83,* 26–29.

Heller, K., Monks, F., & Passow, A. H. (Eds.). (1993). *International handbook of research and development of giftedness and talent.* Oxford: Pergamon Press.

Heller, K. W., Alberto, P. A., Forney, P. E., & Schwartzman, M. N. (1996). *Understanding physical, sensory, and health impairments.* Pacific Grove, CA: Brooks/Cole.

Helmsetter, E., Curry, C. A., Brennan, M., & Sampson-Saul, M. (1998). Comparison of general and special education classrooms of students with severe disabilities. *Education and Training in Mental Retardation and Developmental Disabilities, 33,* 216–226.

Henry, N. A., & Flynt, E. S. (1990). Rethinking special education referral: A procedural model. *Intervention in School and Clinic, 26,* 22–24.

Herer, G., & Reilly, M. (1999). Pediatric audiology: Poised for the future. *ASHA, 13,* 24–30.

Hetfield, P. (1994). Using a student newspaper to motivate students with behavior disorders. *Teaching Exceptional Children, 26,* 6–9.

Heward, W. L. (1995). *Exceptional children: An introductory survey of special education* (4th ed.). New York: Macmillan.

Heward, W. L. (2000). *Exceptional children: An introduction to special education* (7th ed.). Englewood Cliffs, NJ: Prentice-Hall.

Hietsch, D. G. (1986). Father involvement: No moms allowed. *Teaching Exceptional Children, 18,* 258–260.

Higgins, E. L., Raskind, M. H., Goldberg, R. J., & Herman, K. L. (2002). Stages of acceptance of learning disabilities: The impact of labeling. *Learning Disability Quarterly, 25,* 3–18.

Hill, D. (1991). Tasting failure: Thoughts of an at-risk learner. *Phi Delta Kappan, 73,* 308–310.

Hill, M., Szefler, S. J., & Larsen, G. L. (1998). Asthma pathogenesis and the implications for therapy in children. *Pediatric Clinics of North America, 39,* 1205–1222.

Hiller, J. F. (1990). Setting up a classroom-based language instruction program: One clinician's experience. *Texas Journal of Audiology and Speech Pathology, 16*(2), 12–13.

Hilton, A. (1990). *Parental reactions to having a disabled child.* Paper presented at annual International Conference of the Council for Exceptional Children.

Hoagwood, K., Kelleher, K. J., Feil, M., & Comer, D. M. (2000). Treatment services for children with ADHD: A national perspective. *Journal of the American Academy of Child and Adolescent Psychiatry, 39*(2), 198–206.

Hobbs, T., & Westling, D. L. (1998). Promoting successful inclusion. *Teaching Exceptional Children, 34,* 10–14.

Hobson v. *Hansen,* 269 F. Supp. 401 (D.DC), 1967.

Hoida, J. A., & McDougal, S. E. (1998). Fostering a positive school environment for students with cancer. *NASSP Bulletin, 82,* 59–72.

Holcomb, D., Lira, J., Kingery, P. M., Smith, D. W., Lane, D., & Goodway, J. (1998). Evaluation of jump into action: A program to reduce the risk of non–insulin-dependent diabetes mellitus in school children on the Texas–Mexico border. *Journal of School Health, 68,* 282–287.

Hollingsworth, H. L. (2001). We need to talk: Communication strategies for effective collaboration. *Teaching Exceptional Children, 33,* 4–8.

Homme, L. (1969). *How to use contingency contracting in the classroom.* Champaign, IL: Research Press.

Hoover, J. J. (1988). Implementing a study skills program in the classroom. *Academic Therapy, 24,* 471–476.

Hoover, J. J. (1990). Curriculum adaptations: A five-step process for classroom implementation. *Academic Therapy, 25,* 407–416.

Hoover, J. J., & Patton, J. R. (1995). *Teaching students with learning problems to use study skills: A teacher's guide.* Austin, TX: Pro-Ed.

Hoover, J. J., & Patton, J. R. (1997). *Curriculum adaptations for students with learning and behavior problems* (2nd ed.). Austin, TX: Pro-Ed.

Horner, R. H. (2000). Positive behavior supports. In M. L. Wehmeyer & J. R. Patton (Eds.), *Mental retardation in the 21st century* (pp. 181–196). Austin, TX: Pro-Ed.

How you can help. (2001, December 14). *Time for Kids, 7*(11), 5.

Howell, R. W., Evans, C. T., Gardiner, R. W. (1997). Medication in the classroom: A hard pill to swallow? *Teaching Exceptional Children, 29,* 58–61.

Hoy, C., & Gregg, N. (1994). *Assessment: The special educator's role.* Pacific Grove, CA: Brooks/Cole.

Huff, C. R. (1999). *Comparison of criminal behaviors of youth gangs and at-risk youth*. Washington, DC: Department of Justice National Institute of Justice.

Hughes, C., & Carter, E. W. (1999). *The transition handbook: Strategies high school teachers use that work*. Baltimore: Brookes.

Hughes, C., Copeland, S. R., Guth, C., Rung, L. L., Hwang, B., Kleeb, G., & Strong, M. (2001). General education students' perspectives on their involvement in a high school peer buddy program. *Education and Training in Mental Retardation and Developmental Disabilities, 36*, 343–355.

Hunt, P., Doering, K., Hirose-Hatae, A. (2001). Across-program collaboration to support students with and without disabilities in general education classrooms. *Journal of the Association for Persons with Severe Handicaps, 26*, 240–256.

Hunt, P., Hirose-Hatae, A., Doering, K. (2000). "Communication" is what I think everyone is talking about. *Remedial and Special Education, 21*, 305–317.

Huure, T. M., Komulainen, E. J., & Aro, H. M. (1999). Social support and self-esteem among adolescents with visual impairments. *Journal of Visual Impairment & Blindness, 93*, 326–337.

Hux, K., & Hackley, C. (1996). Mild traumatic brain injury. *Intervention in School and Clinic, 31,* 158–165.

ICD-10: International statistical classification of diseases and related health problems (1992). (10th rev. ed.). Geneva, Switzerland: World Health Organization.

Individuals with Disabilities Education Act. (1997). Washington, DC: U.S. Government Printing Office.

Infusini, M. (1994). From the patient's point of view. *The Journal of Cognitive Rehabilitation, 12*, 4–5.

Inge, K. J. (1992). Cerebral palsy. In P. J. McLaughlin & P. Wehman (Eds.), *Developmental disabilities* (pp. 30–53). Boston: Andover Press.

Iskowitz, M. (1998). Psychosocial issues. *ADVANCE for Speech-Language Pathologists and Audiologists, 36*, 14–15.

Jan, J. E., Ziegler, R. G., & Erba, G. (1991). *Does your child have epilepsy?* (2nd ed.) Austin, TX: Pro-Ed.

Janover, C. (1997). *Zipper: The kid with ADHD*. Bethesda, MD: Woodbine House.

Jaquish, C., & Stella, M. A. (1986). Helping special students move from elementary to secondary school. *Counterpoint, 7*(1), 1.

Jayanthi, M., Bursuck, W., Epstein, M. H., & Polloway, E. A. (1997). Strategies for successful homework. *Teaching Exceptional Children, 30*(1), 4–7.

Jayanthi, M., Bursuck, W. D., Polloway, E., & Epstein, M. (1996). Testing adaptations for students with disabilities: A national survey of classroom practices. *Journal of Special Education, 30,* 99–115.

Jayanthi, M., Nelson, J. S., Sawyer, V., Bursuck, W. D., & Epstein, M. H. (1994). Homework-communication problems among parents, general education, and special education teachers: An exploratory study. *Remedial and Special Education, 16*(2), 102–116.

Jenkins, J. R., & Heinen, A. (1989). Students' preferences for service delivery: Pull-out, in-class, or integrated models. *Exceptional Children, 55*, 516–523.

Jenkins, J., & O'Connor, R. (2001). *Early identification and intervention for young children with reading/learning disabilities*. Paper presented at the 2001 LD Summit: Building a Foundation for the Future. Available on-line from www.air.org/ldsummit.

Jensen, P. S. (2000). Commentary: The NIH ADHD consensus statement: Win, lose, or draw? *Journal of the American Academy of Child and Adolescent Psychiatry, 39*(2), 194–197.

Jensen, P. S., Kettler, L., Roper, M., Sloan, M. T., Dulcan, M. K., Hoven, C., Bird, H. R., Bauermeister, J. J., & Payne, J. (1999). Are stimulants over prescribed? Treatment of ADHD in four US communities. *Journal of the American Academy of Child and Adolescent Psychiatry, 38*(7), 797–804.

Johnson, A. (2001). How to use thinking skills to differentiate curricula for gifted and highly creative students. *Gifted Child Today, 24*(4), 58–63.

Johnson, D. J. (1999). The language of instruction. *Learning Disabilities: A Multidisciplinary Journal 9*(2), 1–7.

Johnson, D. R., Stodden, R. A., & Emanuel, E. J. (2002). Curricular challenges facing secondary education and transition services. *Exceptional Children, 68*, 519–531.

Johnson, G., & Jefferson-Aker, C. R. (2001). HIV/AIDS prevention: Effective instructional strategies for adolescents with mild mental retardation. *Teaching Exceptional Children, 33*, 28–32.

Johnson, L. F., & Dunlap, G. (1993). Using functional assessment to develop individual interventions. *Teaching Exceptional Children, 25*, 44–47.

Johnson, L. J., Pugach, M. C., & Devlin, S. (1990). Professional collaboration. *Teaching Exceptional Children, 22*, 9–11.

Johnson, L. R., & Johnson, C. E. (1999, March/April). Teaching students to regulate their own behavior. *Teaching Exceptional Children,* 6–10.

Jones, V. F., & Jones, L. S. (1995). *Comprehensive classroom management* (4th ed.). Boston: Allyn and Bacon.

Jones, V. F., & Jones, L. S. (2001). *Comprehensive classroom management* (6th ed.). Boston: Allyn and Bacon.

Kaderavek, J. N., & Pakulski, L. A. (2002). Minimal hearing loss is not minimal. *Teaching Exceptional Children, 34*, 14–18.

Kalyanpur, M., & Harry, B. (1999). *Cultural reciprocity: Building reciprocal family-professional relationships.* Baltimore: Brookes.

Kamps, D. B., Leonard, B. R., Vernon, S., Dugan, E. P., Delquadri, J. C., Gershon, B., Wade, L., & Folk, L. (1992). Teaching social skills to students with autism to increase peer interactions in an integrated first-grade classroom. *Journal of Applied Behavior Analysis, 25*, 281–288.

Kaplan, J. S., & Carter, J. (1999). *Beyond behavior modification: A cognitive-behavioral approach to behavior management in the school* (3rd ed.). Austin, TX: Pro-Ed.

Kaplan, P. S. (1996). *Pathways for exceptional children: School, home, and culture.* St. Paul, MN: West.

Kataoka, J. C. (1987). *An example of integrating literature.* (Unpublished manuscript.)

Kataoka, J. C., & Patton, J. R. (1989). Integrated curriculum. *Science and Children, 16*, 52–58.

Katims, D. S. (2001). Literacy assessment of students with mental retardation: An exploratory investigation. *Education and Training in Mental Retardation and Developmental Disabilities, 36*(4), 363–372.

Katsiyannis, A., Hodge, J., & Lanford, A. (2000). Paraeducators: Legal and practice considerations. *Remedial and Special Education, 21*, 297–304.

Katsiyannis, A., Landrum, T. J., & Vinton, L. (1997). Practical guidelines for monitoring treatment of Attention-Deficit/Hyperactivity Disorder. *Prevention of School Failure, 41*(3) 132–136.

Katsiyannis, A., & Maag, J. W. (2001). Manifestation determination as a golden fleece. *Exceptional Children, 68*, 89–96.

Katsiyannis, A., Yell, M. L., & Bradley, R. (2001). Reflections on the 25th anniversary of the Individuals with Disabilities Education Act. *Remedial and Special Education, 22*, 324–334.

Katsiyannis, A., Zhang, D., & Zhang, H. (2002). Placement and exit patterns for students with mental retardation: An analysis of national trends. *Education and Training in Mental Retardation and Developmental Disabilities, 37*, 134–145.

Kauffman, J. M. (1993). *Characteristics of emotional and behavioral disorders of children and youth.* Columbus, OH: Merrill.

Kauffman, J. M., Lloyd, J. W., Baker, J., & Riedel, T. M. (1995). Inclusion of all students with emotional or behavioral disorders? Let's think again. *Phi Delta Kappan,* 542–546.

Kauffman, J. M., & Wong, K. L. H. (1991). Effective teachers of students with behavioral disorders: Are generic teaching skills enough? *Behavioral Disorders, 16*, 225–237.

Kavale, K. A., (2001a). *Discovering models in the identification of learning disabilities. Executive summary.* Washington, DC: LD Summit.

Kavale, K. A. (2001b). Decision making in special education: The function of meta-analysis. *Exceptionality, 9*, 245–268.

Kavale, K. A., & Forness, S. R. (1996a). *Efficacy of special education and related services.* Washington, DC: American Association on Mental Retardation.

Kavale, K. A., & Forness, S. R. (1996b). Treating social skill deficits in children with learning disabilities: A meta-analysis of the research. *Learning Disability Quarterly, 19*(1), 2–13.

Kavale, K. A., & Forness, S. R. (1999). The future of research and practice in behavior disorders. *Journal of Behavior Disorders, 24*, 305–318.

Kavale, K. A., & Forness, S. R. (2000). History, rhetoric, and reality: Analysis of the inclusion debate. *Remedial and Special Educaiton, 21*, 279–296.

Kerr, L., Delaney, B., Clarke, S., Dunlap, G, & Childs, K. (2001). Improving the classroom behavior of students with emotional and behavioral disorders using individualized curricular modifications. *Journal of Emotional and Behavioral Disorders, 9*, 239–247.

Kerrin, R. G. (1996). Collaboration: Working with the speech–language pathologist. *Intervention in School and Clinic, 32*(1), 56–59.

Keyser-Marcus, L., et al. (2002). Enhancing the schooling of students with traumatic brain injury. *Teaching Exceptional Children, 34*, 62–65.

Killoran, J., Templeman, T. P., Peters, J., & Udell, T. (2001). Identifying paraprofessional competencies for early intervention and early childhood special education. *Teaching Exceptional Children, 34*, 68–73.

King-Sears, M. E. (2001a). Institutionalizing peer-mediated instruction and interventions in schools. *Remedial and Special Education, 22*, 89–101.

King-Sears, M. E. (2001b). Three steps for gaining access to the general education curriculum for learners with disabilities. *Intervention in School and Clinic, 37*, 67–76.

King-Sears, M. E., & Bradley, D. (1995). Classwide peer tutoring: Heterogeneous instruction in general education classrooms. *Preventing School Failure, 40*, 29–36.

King-Sears, M. E., & Cummings, C. S. (1996). Inclusive practices of classroom teachers. *Remedial and Special Education, 17*, 217–225.

Kingsley, E. P. (1987). Welcome to Holland. Retrieved from http://www.nas.com/downsyn/holland.html on June 20, 2002.

Kirk, R., & Even, B. (2001). Disability or difference: Reflections on learning. *New Teacher Advocate.* Indianapolis, IN: Kappa Delta Pi.

Kirk, S. A. (1962). *Educating exceptional children.* Boston: Houghton Mifflin.

Kirk, S. A., Gallagher, J. J., & Anastasiow, A. (2000). *Educating exceptional children* (8th ed.). Boston: Houghton Mifflin.

Kirsten, I. (1981). *The Oakland picture dictionary.* Wauconda, IL: Don Johnston.

Kitano, M. K. (1993). Critique of Feldhusen's "individualized teaching of the gifted in regular classrooms." In C. J. Maker (Ed.), *Critical issues in gifted education: Vol. 3. Programs for the gifted in regular classrooms* (pp. 274–281). Austin, TX: Pro-Ed.

Klassen, R. (2002). A question of calibration: A review of the self-efficacy beliefs of students with learning disabilities. *Learning Disabilities Quarterly, 25*, 88–102.

Kluwin, T. N. (1996). Getting hearing and deaf students to write to each other through dialogue journals. *Teaching Exceptional Children, 28*, 50–53.

Kluwin, T. N., Moores, D. F., & Gaustad, M. G. (Eds.). (1998). *Toward effective public school programs for deaf students: Context, process, and outcomes.* New York: Teachers College Press.

Knitzer, J., Steinberg, Z., & Fleisch, B. (1990). *At the schoolhouse door.* New York: Bank Street College of Education.

Knowles, M. (1984). *The adult learner: A neglected species* (3rd ed.). Houston: Gulf.

Koegel, L. K., Koegel, R. L., & Dunlap, G. (Eds.). (1996). *Positive behavioral support.* Baltimore: Brookes.

Koegel, L. K., Koegel, R. L., Hurley, C., & Frea, W. D. (1992). Improving social skills and disruptive behavior in children with autism through self-management. *Journal of Applied Behavior Analysis, 25*, 341–353.

Koegel, R. L., & Koegel, L. K. (1995). *Teaching children with autism.* Baltimore: Brookes.

Koenig, A. J., & Holbrook, M. C. (1995). *Learning media assessment of students with visual impairments: A resource guide for teachers* (2nd ed.). Austin, TX: Pro-Ed.

Kohn, A. (1996a). *Beyond discipline: From compliance to community.* Washington, DC: Association for Supervision and Curriculum Development.

Kohn, A. (1996b). What to look for in the classroom. *Educational Leadership, 54*, 54–55.

Korinek, L., & Polloway, E. A. (1993). Social skills: Review and implications for instruction for students with mild mental retardation. In R. A. Gable & S. F. Warren (Eds.), *Advances in mental retardation and developmental disabilities* (Vol. 5, pp. 71–97). London: Jessica Kingsley.

Korinek, L., Walther-Thomas, C., McLaughlin, V. L., Williams, B. T. (1999). *Intervention in School and Clinic, 35*, 3–8.

Kounin, J. (1970). *Discipline and group management in classrooms.* New York: Holt, Rinehart & Winston.

Krauss, M. W. (1990). New precedent in family policy: Individualized family service plan. *Exceptional Children, 56*, 388–395.

Kravolek, E., & Buell, J. (2000). *The end of homework: How homework disrupts families, overburdens children, and limits learning.* Boston: Beacon Press.

Kruczek, T., & Vitanza, S. (1999). Treatment effects with an adolescent abuse survivor's group. *Child Abuse & Neglect, 23*, 477–485.

Kubler-Ross, E. (1969). *On death and dying.* New York: Macmillan.

Lahey, M. (1988). *Language disorders and language development.* New York: Macmillan.

Lambros, K. M., Ward, S. L., Bocian, K. M., MacMillan, D. L., & Gresham, F. M. (1998). Behavioral profiles of children at-risk for emotional and behavioral disorders: Implications for assessment and classification. *Focus on Exceptional Children, 30*(5), 1–16.

Landau, S., Milich, R., & Diener, M. B. (1998). Peer relations of children with attention-deficit hyperactivity disorders. *Reading and Writing Quarterly, 14*(1) 83–106.

Lang, L. (1998). Allergy linked to common ear infection. *ADVANCE for Speech-Language Pathologists and Audioligists, 36*, 8–9.

Lange, C. M., Ysseldyke, J. E., & Lehr, C. A. (1997). Parents' perspectives on school choice. *Teaching Exceptional Children, 30*(1), 14–19.

Langerock, N.L. (2000). A passion for action research. *Teaching Exceptional Children, 33*, 26–34.

Larry P. v. *Riles,* C-71-2270 (RFP, District Court for Northern California), 1972.

Larson, S. A. Lakin, K. C., Anderson, L., Kwak, N., Lee, J. H., & Anderson, D. (2001). Prevalence of mental retardation and developmental disabilities: Estimates from the 1994/1995 National Health Interview Survey Disability Supplements. *American Journal on Mental Retardation, 106*, 231–252.

Latham, P. S., & Latham, P. H. (1999). ADHD views from the courthouse. *The ADHD Report, 7*(4), 9–11, 14.

Lavelle, L. (1998). *Practical charts for managing behavior.* Austin, TX: Pro-Ed.

LDA Newsbriefs. (1996). Toll free access to adult services. *LDA Newsbriefs, 31*(3), 22, 24.

Lerner, J. W. (1993). *Learning disabilities: Theories, diagnosis, and teaching strategies.* Boston: Houghton Mifflin.

Lerner, J. W. (2000). *Learning disabilities: Theories, diagnosis, and teaching strategies* (4th ed.) Boston: Houghton Mifflin.

Lesar, S., Gerber, M. M., & Semmel, M. (1996). HIV infection in children: Family stress, social support, and adaptations. *Exceptional Children, 62*, 224–236.

Leverett, R. G., & Diefendorf, A. O. (1992). Suggestions for frustrated teachers. *Teaching Exceptional Children, 24*, 30–35.

Levin, J., & Nolan, J. F. (2000). *Principles of classroom management* (3rd ed.). Boston: Allyn and Bacon.

Lewis, T. J., & Sugai, G. (1999). Effective behavior support: A systems approach to proactive school-wide management. *Focus on Exceptional Children, 31*(6), 1–24.

Lipsky, D. K., & Gartner, A. (1996). The evaluation of inclusive programs. *NCERI Bulletin, 2*, 1–7.

Lisnov, L., Harding, C. G., Safer, L. A., & Kavanagh, J. (1998). Adolescents' perceptions of substance abuse prevention strategies. *Adolescence, 33*, 301–312.

Lloyd, J. (1988). Academic instruction and cognitive techniques: The need for attack strategy training. *Exceptional Education Quarterly, 1*, 53–63.

Lloyd, J. W., Forness, S. R., & Kavale, K. A. (1998). Some methods are more effective than others. *Intervention in School and Clinic, 33*, 195–200.

Lloyd, J. W., Kauffman, J. M., Landrum, T. J., & Roe, D. L. (1991). Why do teachers refer pupils for special education? An analysis of referral records. *Exceptionality, 2*, 115–126.

Lloyd, J. W., Landrum, T., & Hallahan, D. P. (1991). Self-monitoring applications for classroom intervention. In G. Stoner, M. R. Shinn, & H. M. Walker (Eds.), *Interventions for achievement and behavior problems* (pp. 201–213). Washington, DC: NASP.

Locke, M. N., Banken, L. L., & Mahone, T. E. (1994). *Adapting early childhood curriculum for children with special needs.* New York: Merrill.

Loehr, J. (2002). *Read the picture stories for articulation* (2nd ed.). Austin, TX: Pro-Ed.

Logan, K.R., Hansen, C.D., Nieminen, P.K., Wright, E.H. (2001). Student support teams: Helping students succeed in general education classrooms or working to place students in special education? *Education and Training in Mental Retardation and Developmental Disabilities, 36*, 280–292.

Lopez, R., & MacKenzie, J. (1993). A learning center approach to individualized instruction for gifted students. In C. J. Maker (Ed.), *Critical issues in gifted education: Vol. 3. Programs for the gifted in regular classrooms* (pp. 282–295). Austin, TX: Pro-Ed.

Lovitt, T. C., Cushing, S. S., & Stump, C. S. (1994). High school students rate their IEPs: Low opinions and lack of ownership. *Intervention in School and Clinic, 30*(1), 34–37.

Lucas, C. (Ed.). (1990). *Sign language research.* Washington, DC: Gallaudet University Press.

Luckasson, R. (1992). *Mental retardation: Definition, classification and systems of supports.* Washington, DC: American Association on Mental Retardation.

Luckasson, R. (2002). *Mental retardation: Definition, classification and systems of supports.* Washington, DC: American Association on Mental Retardation.

Luckasson, R., Coulter, D., Polloway, E. A., Reis, S., Schalock, R., Snell, M., Spitalnik, D., & Stark, J. (1992). *Mental retardation: Definition, classification and systems of supports.* Washington, DC: American Association on Mental Retardation.

Luckasson, R., Schalock, R., Snell, M., & Spitalnik, D. (1996). The 1992 AAMR definition and preschool children: Response from the committee on terminology and classification. *Mental Retardation, 34*, 247–253.

Luckner, J. (1994). Developing independent and responsible behaviors in students who are deaf or hard of hearing. *Teaching Exceptional Children, 26*, 13–17.

Luckner, J. (1999). An example of two coteaching classrooms. *American Annals of the Deaf, 44*, 24–34.

Luckner, J., & Denzin, D. (1998). In the mainstream: Adaptions for students who are deaf or hard of hearing. *Perspectives in Education and Deafness, 17*, 8–11.

Lueck, A. H. (1999). Setting curricular priorities for students with visual impairments. *Review, 31*, 54–63.

Lynch, E. W., & Hanson, M. J. (1998). *Developing cross-cultural competence: A guide for working with children and their families* (2nd ed.). Baltimore: Brookes.

Lyndsey, J. D. (Ed.). (1999). *Technology and exceptional individuals* (3rd ed.). Austin, TX: Pro-Ed.

Lyon, G. R. (1995). Research initiatives in learning disabilities: Contributions from scientists supported by the National Institutes of Child Health and Human Development. *Journal of Child Neurology, 10*(1), 5120–5126.

Lyon, G. R., Fletcher, J. M., Shaywitz, S. E., Shaywitz, B. A., Torgesen, J. K., Wood, F. B., Schulte, A., & Olson, R. (2001). Rethinking learning disabilities. In C. E. Finn, A. J. Rotherham, & C. R. Hokanson, Jr. (Eds.), *Rethinking special education for a new century* (pp. 259–287). Washington, DC: Thomas B. Fordham Foundation.

Lytle, R. K., & Bordin, J.(2001). Enhancing the IEP team: Strategies for parents and professionals. *Teaching Exceptional Children, 33,* 40–44.

Maag, J. W., & Katsiyannis, A. (1998). Challenges facing successful transition for youths with E/BD. *Behavioral Disorders, 23,* 209–221.

MacArthur, C. A. (1998, July/August). From illegible to understandable. *Teaching Exceptional Children,* 66–71.

Mackie, E. (1996). *Oral-motor activities for school aged-children.* Austin, TX: Pro-Ed.

MacMillan, D. L. (1989). Mild mental retardation: Emerging issues. In G. Robinson, J. R. Patton, E. A. Polloway, & L. R. Sargent (Eds.), *Best practices in mild mental retardation* (pp. 1–20). Reston, VA: CEC-MR.

MacMillan, D. L., & Forness, S. R. (1998). The role of IQ in special education placement decisions: Primary and determinative or peripheral and inconsequential? *Remedial and Special Education, 19,* 239–253.

MacMillan, D. L., Gresham, F. M., & Siperstein, G. N. (1993). Conceptual and psychometric concerns about the 1992 AAMR definition of mental retardation. *American Journal of Mental Retardation, 98,* 325–335.

MacMillan, D. L., & Siperstein, G. N. (2001). *Learning disabilities as operationally defined by schools.* Paper presented at the 2001 LD Summit: Building a Foundation for the Future. Washington, DC.

Maheady, L., Harper, G. F., & Mallette, B. (2001). Peer-mediated instruction and interventions and students with mild disabilities. *Remedial and Special Education, 22,* 4–14.

Maker, C. J. (1993). Gifted students in the regular education classroom: What practices are defensible and feasible? In C. J. Maker (Ed.), *Critical issues in gifted education: Vol. 3. Programs for the gifted in regular classrooms* (pp. 413–436). Austin, TX: Pro-Ed.

Malott, R. W., Whaley, D. L., & Malott, M. E. (1997). *Elementary principles of behavior* (3rd ed.). Upper Saddle River, NJ: Prentice-Hall.

Mandlebaum, L. H. (1989). Reading. In J. R. Patton, E. A. Polloway, & L. R. Sargent (Eds.), *Best practices in mild retardation.* Reston, VA: CEC-MR.

Mandlebaum, L. H., Lightbourne, L., & VardenBrock, J. (1994). Teaching with literature. *Intervention in School and Clinic, 29,* 134–150.

Mandlebaum, L. H., & Wilson, R. (1989). Teaching listening skills in the special education classroom. *Academic Therapy, 24,* 449–459.

Mangold, S. S., & Roessing, L. J. (1982). Instructional needs of students with low vision. In S. S. Mangold (Ed.), *A teacher's guide to the special educational needs of blind and visually handicapped children.* New York: American Foundation for the Blind.

Marchant, J. M. (1992). Deaf-blind handicapping conditions. In P. J. McLaughlin & P. Wehman (Eds.), *Developmental disabilities* (pp. 113–123). Boston: Andover Press.

Marcotte, D., Fortin, L., Potvin, P., & Papillon, M. (2002). Gender differences in depressive symptoms during adolescence: Role of gender-typed characteristics, self-esteem, body image, stressful life events, and pubertal status. *Journal of Emotional and Behavioral Disorders, 10,* 29–42.

Markwardt, F. C. (1989). *Peabody individual achievement test—Revised.* Circle Pines, MN: American Guidance Service.

Marland, S. P. (1992). *Education of the gifted and talented: Report to the Congress by the U.S. Commissioner of Education and background papers submitted to the U.S. Office of Education* (2 volumes, pp. 79–118). Washington, DC: U.S. Government Printing Office.

Marston, D., & Magnusson, D. (1985). Implementing curriculum-based measurement in special and regular education settings. *Exceptional Children, 52,* 266–276.

Masi, G., Mucci, M., & Favilla, L. (1999). Depressive symptoms in adolescents with mild mental retardation. *Education and Training in Mental Retardation and Developmental Disabilities, 34,* 223–226.

Masters, L. F., Mori, B. A., & Mori, A. A. (1999). *Teaching secondary students with mild learning and behavior problems.* Austin, TX: Pro-Ed.

Mastropieri, M. A., & Scruggs, T. E. (1993). *A practical guide for teaching science to students with special needs in inclusive settings.* Austin, TX: Pro-Ed.

Mastropieri, M. A., & Scruggs, T. E. (1994). *Effective instruction for special education* (2nd ed.). Austin, TX: Pro-Ed.

Mastropieri, M. A., & Scruggs, T. E. (1997). Best practices in promoting reading comprehension in students with learning disabilities: 1976 to 1996. *Remedial and Special Education, 18,* 197–218.

Mastropieri, M. A., & Scruggs, T. E. (2001). Promoting inclusion in secondary classrooms. *Learning Disability Quarterly, 24,* 265–274.

Mastropieri, M. A., & Scruggs, T. E. (2000). *The inclusive classroom: Strategies for effective instruction.* Columbus, OH: Merrill.

Mastropieri, M. A., Sweda, J., & Scruggs, T. E. (2000). Putting mnemonic strategies to work in an inclusive classroom. *Learning Disabilities Research and Practice, 15*(2), 69–74.

Mather, N. (1992). Whole language reading instruction for students with learning disabilities: Caught in the crossfire. *Learning Disabilities Research and Practice, 7,* 87–95.

Mather, N., Bos, C., & Babur, N. (2001). Perceptions and knowledge of preservice and inservice teachers about early literacy instruction. *Journal of Learning Disabilities, 34,* 472–482.

Mathes, P., & Torgesen, J. (1998, November). *Early reading basics: Strategies for teaching reading to primary-grade students who are at risk for reading and learning disabilities.* Paper presented at the Annual Council for Learning Disabilities Conference, Albuquerque, NM.

Mayer-Johnson, R. (1986). *The picture communications symbols* (Book 1). Solana Beach, CA: Mayer-Johnson.

McAnally, P. L., Rose, S., & Quigley, S. P. (1999). *Reading practices with deaf learners.* Austin, TX: Pro-Ed.

McBurnett, K., Lahey, B., & Pfiffner, L. (1993). Diagnosis of attention deficit disorders in *DSM-IV:* Scientific basis and implications for education. *Exceptional Children, 60*(2), 108–117.

McCarney, S. B., & Wunderlich, K. K. (1988). *The pre-referral intervention manual.* Columbia, MO: Hawthorne Educational Services.

McConaughy, S. H., & Wadsworth, M. E. (2000). Life history reports of young adults previously referred for mental health services. *Journal of Emotional and Behavioral Disorders, 8,* 202–215.

McConnell, J. (1987). Entrapment effects and generalization. *Teaching Exceptional Children, 17,* 267–273.

McConnell, J. (1999). Parents, adolescents, and career planning for visually impaired students. *Journal of Visual Impairment and Blindness, 93,* 498–515.

McConnell, K. (2001). Placement. In R. Algozzine, L. Serna, & J. R. Patton (Eds.), *Childhood behavior disorders: Applied research and educational practice* (pp. 309–330). Austin, TX: Pro-Ed.

McConnell, K., Ryser, G., & Patton, J. R. (2002a). *Practical ideas that really work for disruptive, defiant, and difficult students: Preschool through grade 4.* Austin, TX: Pro-Ed.

McConnell, K., Ryser, G., & Patton, J. R. (2002b). *Practical ideas that really work for disruptive, defiant, and difficult students: Grades 5 through 12.* Austin, TX: Pro-Ed.

McConnell, M. E., Hilvitz, P. B., & Cox, C. J. (1998). Functional assessment: A systematic process for assessment and intervention in general and special education classrooms. *Intervention in School and Clinic, 34,* 10–20.

McCordle, P., Cooper, J., Houle, G. R., Karp, N., & Paul-Brown, D. (2001). Next steps in research and practice. *Learning Disabilities Research and Practice, 16*(4), 250–254.

McCormick, L., Noonan, M. J., Ogata, V., & Heck, R. (2001). Co-teaching relationship and program quality: Implications for preparing teachers for inclusive preschool settings. *Education and Training in Mental Retardation and Developmental Disabilities, 36,* 119–132.

McDevitt, T. M. (1990). Encouraging young children's listening. *Academic Therapy, 25,* 569–577.

McDonnell, J. J., Hardman, M. L., McDonnell, A. P., & Kiefer-O'Donnell, R. (1995). *An introduction to persons with severe disabilities.* Boston: Allyn and Bacon.

McDougall, D. (1998). Research on self-management techniques used by students with disabilities in general education settings: A descriptive review. *Remedial and Special Education, 19,* 310–320.

McEachlin, J. J., Smith, T., & Lovaas, O. I. (1993). Long-term outcome for children with autism who received early intensive behavioral treatment. *American Journal on Mental Retardation, 97,* 359–372.

McEnvoy, M. A., Shores, R. E., Wehby, J. H., Johnson, S. M., & Fox, J. J. (1990). Special education teachers' implementation of procedures to promote social interaction among children in integrated settings. *Education and Training in Mental Retardation, 25,* 267–276.

McEvoy, A., & Welker, R. (2000). Antisocial behavior and academic failures and school climate: A critical review. *Journal of Emotional and Behavior Disorders, 8,* 24–33.

McEwen, M., Johnson, P., Neatherlin, J., Millard, M. W., & Lawrence, G. (1998). School-based management of chronic asthma among inner city African American school children in Dallas, Texas. *Journal of School Health, 68,* 196–201.

McGrail, L. (1998). Modifying regular classroom curricula for high ability students. *Gifted Child Today, 21,* 36–39.

McIntosh, R., Vaughn, S., Bennerson, B., (1995). FAST social skills with a SLAM. *Teaching Exceptional Children, 28,* 37–41.

McKamey, E. S. (1991). Storytelling for children with learning disabilities: A first-hand account. *Teaching Exceptional Children, 23,* 46–48.

McKeever, P. (1983). Siblings of chronically ill children: A literature review with implications for research and practice. *American Journal of Orthopsychiatry, 53,* 209–217.

McKenzie, J. (1998). Creating technology enhanced student-centered learning environments. *From Now On, 7*(6), 1–14.

McLaughlin-Cheng, E., (1998). The Asperger syndrome and autism: A literature review and meta-analysis. *Focus on Autism and Other Developmental Disabilities, 13,* 234–245.

McLesky, J., Henry, D., & Hedges, D. (1999). Inclusion: What progress is being made across disability categories? *Teaching Exceptional Children, 31,* 60–64.

McLoughlin, J. A., & Lewis, R. B. (1999). *Assessing special students* (3rd ed.). Columbus, OH: Merrill.

McMaster, K.N., & Fuchs, D. (2002). Effects of cooperative learning on the academic achievement of students with learning disabilities. *Learning Disabilities Research and Practice, 17,* 107–117.

McNeill, J. H., & Fowler, S. A. (1996). Using story reading to encourage children's conversations. *Teaching Exceptional Children, 28*(2), 43–47.

McReynolds, L. (1990). Functional articulation disorders. In G. H. Shames & E. H. Wiig (Eds.), *Human communication disorders: An introduction* (2nd ed., pp. 139–182). Columbus, OH: Merrill.

Mercer, C. D. (1997). *Students with learning disabilities.* (5th ed.). New York: Merrill.

Meyer, D. (2001). Meeting the unique concerns of brothers and sisters of children with special needs. *Insight, 51,* 28–32.

Meyer, M. S. (2000). The ability achievement discrepancy: Does it contribute to an understanding of learning disability? *Educational Psychology Review Special Issue: Intelligence Part II, 12,* 319–337.

Michaels, C. (1994). *Transition strategies for persons with learning disabilities.* San Diego: Singular.

Miller, R. J. (1995). Preparing for adult life: Teaching students their rights and responsibilities. *CEC Today, 1*(7), 12.

Miller, S. P., Mercer, C. D., & Dillon, A. S. (1992). CSA: Acquiring and retaining math skills. *Intervention in School and Clinic, 28,* 105–110.

Minner, S., & Prater, G. (1989). Arranging the physical environment of special education classrooms. *Academic Therapy, 25,* 91–96.

Mira, M. P., Tucker, B. F., & Tyler, J. S. (1992). *Traumatic brain injury in children and adolescents: A sourcebook for teachers and other school personnel.* Austin, TX: Pro-Ed.

Miracle, S. A., Collins, B. C., Schuster, J. W., Grisham-Brown, J. (2001). Peer- versus teacher-delivered instruction: Effects on acquisition and maintenance. *Education and Training in Mental Retardation and Developmental Disabilities, 36,* 373–384.

Mirman, N. J. (1991). Reflections on educating the gifted child. *G/C/T, 14,* 57–60.

Moats, L. C., & Lyon, G. R. (1993). Learning disabilities in the United States: Advocacy, science, and the future of the field. *Journal of Learning Disabilities, 26*(5), 282–294.

Moecker, D. L. (1992, November). Special education decision process: For Anglo and Hispanic students. Paper presented at the *Council for Exceptional Children* Topical Conference on Culturally and Linguistically Diverse Exceptional Children, Minneapolis.

Montague, M., McKinney, J. D., & Hocutt, L. (1994). Assessing students for attention deficit disorder. *Intervention in School and Clinic, 29*(4), 212–218.

Montgomery, J. R., & Herer, G. R. (1994). Future watch: Our schools in the 21st century. *Language, Speech, and Hearing Services in the Schools, 25,* 130–135. American Speech-Language-Hearing Association.

Moores, D. (1999). *Educating the deaf: Psychology, principles, and practices* (5th ed.). Columbus, OH: Merrill.

Moores, D. (2001). *Educating the deaf: Psychology, principles, and practices* (6th ed.). Columbus, OH: Merrill.

Morgan, S. (1985). *Children in crisis: A team approach in the schools.* Austin, TX: Pro-Ed.

Morgan, S. R. (1994a). *At-risk youth in crises: A team approach in the schools* (2nd ed.). Austin, TX: Pro-Ed.

Morgan, S. (1994b). *Children in crisis: A team approach in the schools* (2nd ed.). Austin, TX: Pro-Ed.

Moriarty, D. (1967). *The loss of loved ones.* Springfield, IL: Charles C Thomas.

Morris, S. (2002). Promoting social skills among students with non-verbal learning disabilities. *Teaching Exceptional Children, 34,* 66–70.

Morrison, G. S. (1997). *Teaching in America.* Boston: Allyn and Bacon.

Munden, A. C., & Archelus, J. (2001). *The ADHD Handbook: A guide for parents and professionals.* New York: Jessica Kingsley.

Mundschenk, N. A., & Foley, R. M. (1997). Collaborative activities and competencies of secondary schools special educators: A national survey. *Teacher Education in Special Education, 20,* 47–60.

Munger, R., & Morse, W. C. (1992). When divorce rocks a child's world. *The Educational Forum, 43,* 100–103.

Munk, D. D., & Bursuck, W. D. (2001). Preliminary findings on personalized grading plans for middle school students with learning disabilities. *Exceptional Children, 67,* 211–234.

Munk, D. D., Bursuck, W. D., Epstein, M. H., Jayanthi, M., Nelson, J., & Polloway, E. A. (2001). Homework communication problems: Perspectives of special and general education parents. *Reading and Writing Quarterly, 17,* 189–203.

Murawski, W. W., & Swanson, H. L. (2001). A meta-analysis of co-teaching research. *Remedial and Special Education, 22,* 258–267.

Musselwhite, C. R. (1987). Augmentative communication. In E. T. McDonald (Ed.), *Treating cerebral palsy: For clinicians by clinicians* (pp. 209–238). Austin, TX: Pro-Ed.

Myles, B. S., & Simpson, R. L. (1998). Aggression and violence by school-age children and youth: Under the aggression cycle and prevention/intervention strategies. *Intervention in School and Clinic, 33,* 259–264.

Nagel, L., McDougall, D., & Granby, C. (1996). Students' self-reported substance use by grade level and gender. *Journal of Drug Education, 26,* 49–56.

Naremore, R. C. (1980). Language disorders in children. In T. J. Hixon, L. D. Shriberg, & J. H. Saxman (Eds.), *Introduction to communication disorders* (pp. 111–132). Englewood Cliffs, NJ: Prentice-Hall.

National Association for the Deaf. (2002). *Information center.* Retrieved on September 20, 2002, from http://www.nad.org.

National Cancer Foundation. (1997). Cancer risk report. Washington, DC: Author.

National Center for Education Statistics. (1989). *Digest of educational statistics, 1989.* Washington, DC: U.S. Department of Education, Office of Research and Improvement.

National Center for Education Statistics. (1991). *The condition of education, 1991 edition.* Washington, DC: Author.

National Center on Child Abuse and Neglect. (1986). *Status of child abuse in the United States.* Washington, DC: Author.

National Coalition for the Homeless. (1999). *Homeless families with children* (Fact Sheet 7). Washington, DC: Author.

National Education Goals Panel. (1998). *Ready schools.* Washington, DC: Author.

National Head Injury Foundation. (1988). *An educator's manual: What educators need to know about students with traumatic brain injury.* Southborough, MA: Author.

National Heart, Lung, and Blood Institute. (1998). How asthma friendly is your school? *Journal of School Health, 68,* 167–168.

National Information Center for Children and Youth with Handicaps. (1990). *Children with autism.* Washington, DC: Author.

National Information Center for Children and Youth with Handicaps. (1991). *The education of children and youth with special needs: What do the laws say?* Washington, DC: Author.

National Institutes of Health. (2000). Consensus and development conference statement: Diagnosis and treatment of attention-deficit/hyperactivity disorder. *Journal of the American Academy of Child and Adolescent Psychiatry, 39*(2), 182–193.

National Joint Committee on Learning Disabilities. (1988). Letter to NJCLD member organizations.

National Law Center on Homelessness and Poverty. (1990). *Shut out: Denial of education to homeless children.* Washington, DC: Author.

National Minority AIDS Education and Training Center. (1999). Cultural competency resources. Retrieved October 30, 2002, from http://www.nmaetc.org

National Reading Panel. (2000). *Report of the National Reading Panel: Teaching children to read.* Washington, DC: National Institute of Child Health and Human Development.

National Study on Inclusion: Overview and summary report. *National Center on Educational Restructuring Inclusion, 2,* 1–8.

Neito, S. (1996). *Affirming diversity* (2nd ed.). White Plains, NY: Longman.

Nelson, K. C., & Prindle, N. (1992). Gifted teacher competencies: Ratings by rural principals and teachers. *Journal of the Education of the Gifted, 15,* 357–369.

Nelson, N. W. (1988). Curriculum-based language assessment and intervention. *Language, Speech and Hearing Services in School, 20,* 170–183.

Ness, J., & Price, L. A. (1990). Meeting the psychosocial needs of adolescents and adults with LD. *Intervention, 26,* 16–21.

Newburger, E. C., & Curry, A. (1999). *Educational attainment in the United States.* Washington, DC: U.S. Department of Commerce.

No Child Left Behind Act. 34 CFR Part 200 (2001).

Nolan, E. E., Volpe, R. J., Gadow, K. D., & Sprafkin, J. (1999). Developmental, gender, and co-morbidity differences in clinically referred children with ADHD. *Journal of Emotional & Behavioral Disorders, 7*(1), 11–21.

Nowacek, E. J., & McShane, E. (1993). Spoken language. In E. A. Polloway & J. R. Patton (Eds.), *Strategies for teaching learners with special needs* (5th ed., pp. 183–205). Columbus, OH: Merrill.

Nyman McMaster, K., & Fuchs, D. (2002). Effects of cooperative learning on the academic achievement of students with learning disabilities: An update of Tateyama-Sniezek's review. *Learning Disabilities Research and Practice, 17,* 107–117.

Office of Education Research and Improvement. (1988). *Youth indicators, 1988: Trends in the well-being of American youth.* Washington, DC: U.S. Department of Education.

Office of Educational Research. (1998). *Tools for schools: From at-risk to excellence.* Washington, DC: Office of Educational Research.

Office of Juvenile Justice and Delinquency Prevention. (1995). *Juvenile offenders and victims: A national report.* Pittsburgh, PA: National Center for Juvenile Justice.

Olson, J. L., & Platt, J. M. (1996). *Teaching children and adolescents with special needs* (2nd ed). Englewood Cliffs, NJ: Merrill.

Orr, T. J., Myles, B. S., & Carlson, J. R. (1998). The impact of rhythmic entertainment on a person with autism. *Focus on Autism and Other Developmental Disabilities, 13,* 163–166.

Ortiz, A. A. (1997). Learning disabilities occurring concomitantly with linguistic differences. *Journal of Learning Disabilities, 30*(3), 321–332.

O'Shaughnessy, T. E. & Swanson, H. L. (1998). Do immediate memory deficits in students with learning disabilities in reading reflect a developmental lag or deficit? *Learning Disability Quarterly, 21,* 123–148.

Oswald, D. P., Coutinho, M. J., Best, A. M., & Singh, N. N. (1999). Ethnic representation in special education: The influence of school-related economic and demographic values. *The Journal of Special Education, 32,* 194–206.

Owens, R. E., Jr. (1984). *Language development: An introduction.* Columbus, OH: Merrill.

Oyer, H. J., Crowe, B., & Haas, W. H. (1987). *Speech, language, and hearing disorders: A guide for the teacher.* Boston: Little, Brown.

Palinscar, A., & Klenk, L. (1992). Fostering literacy learning in supportive contexts. *Journal of Learning Disabilities, 25,* 211–225.

Palmer, D. S., Borthwick-Duffy, S. A., & Widaman, K. (1998). Parents perceptions of inclusive practices for their children with significant cognitive disabilities. *Exceptional Children, 64,* 271–279.

Palmer, D. S., Fuller, K., Arora, T., & Nelson, M. (2001). Taking sides: Parent views on inclusion for their children with severe disabilities. *Exceptional Children, 67,* 467–484.

Pancheri, C., & Prater, M. A. (1999, March/April). What teachers and parents should know about Ritalin. *Teaching Exceptional Children,* 20–26.

Pandiani, J. A., Schacht, L. M., & Banks, S. M. (2001). After children's services: A longitudinal study of significant life events. *Journal of Emotional and Behavioral Disorders, 9,* 131–138.

Parke, B. N. (1989). *Gifted students in regular classrooms.* Boston: Allyn and Bacon.

Parker, H. G. (1992). *The ADD hyperactivity handbook for schools.* Santa Barbara, CA: Special Needs Project.

Patton, J. R. (1994). Practical recommendations for using homework with students with learning disabilities. *Journal of Learning Disabilities, 27,* 570–578.

Patton, J. R., Blackburn, J., & Fad, K. (2001). *Focus on exceptional children* (8th ed.). Columbus, OH: Merrill.

Patton, J. R., & Cronin, M. E. (1993). *Life skills instruction for all students with disabilities.* Austin, TX: Pro-Ed.

Patton, J. R., Cronin, M. E., & Wood, J. D. (1999). *Infusing real-life topics into extra-curriculuar activities.* Austin, TX: Pro-Ed.

Patton, J. R., & Dunn, C. R. (1998). *Transition from school to adult life for students with special needs: Basic concepts and recommended practices.* Austin, TX: Pro-Ed.

Patton, J. R., Jayanthi, M. & Polloway, E. A. (2001). Home-school collaboration about homework. *Reading and Writing Quarterly, 17,* 230–236.

Patton, J. R., Polloway, E. A., & Smith, T. E. C. (2000). Educating students with mild mental retardation. In M. L. Wehmeyer & J. R. Patton (Eds.), *Mental retardation in the 21st century.* Austin, TX: Pro-Ed.

Patton, J. R., Polloway, E. A., Smith, T. E. C., Edgar, E., Clark, G. M., & Lee, S. (1996). Individuals with mild mental retardation: Postsecondary outcomes and implications for educational policy. *Education and Training in Mental Retardation and Developmental Disabilities, 31,* 77–85.

Paul, P. V. (1998). *Literacy and deafness: The development of reading, writing, and literate thought.* Boston: Allyn and Bacon.

Pearpoint, J., Forest, M., & O'Brien, J. (1996). MAPs, circles of friends, and PATH. In S. Stainback & W. Stainback (Eds.), *Inclusion: A guide for educators* (pp. 67–86). Baltimore: Brookes.

Pentecost, D. (1999). *Parenting the ADD child: Can't do? Won't do? Practical strategies for managing behavior problems in children with ADD and ADHD.* New York: Jessica Kingsley.

Pfiffner, L., & Barkley, R. (1991). Educational placement and classroom management. In R. Barkley (Ed.), *Attention deficit hyperactivity disorder: A handbook for diagnosis and treatment* (pp. 498–539). New York: Guilford.

Physicians' Desk Reference (1994). Oravell, NJ: Medical Economics Company.

Physicians' Desk Reference (1999). Oravell, NJ: Medical Economics Company.

Pickett, A. L., & Gerlach, K. (1997). *Paraeducators.* Austin, TX: Pro-Ed.

Pierce, C. (1994). Importance of classroom climate for at-risk learners. *Journal of Educational Research, 88,* 37–44.

Pless, I. B. (Ed.) (1997). *The epidemiology of childhood disorders.* New York: Oxford Press.

Plummer, D. L. (1995). Serving the needs of gifted children from a multicultural perspective. In J. L. Genshaft, M. Bireley, & C. L. Hollinger (Eds.), *Serving gifted and talented students: A resource for school personnel* (pp. 285–300). Austin, TX: Pro-Ed.

Pocock, A., Lambros, S., Karvonen, M., Test, D. W., Algozzine, B., Wood, W., & Martin, J. S. (2002). Successful strategies for promoting self-advocacy among students with learning disabilities: The LEAD Group. *Intervention in School and Clinic, 37*(4), 209–216.

Podemski, R. S., Marsh, G. E., Smith, T. E. C., & Price, B. J. (1995). *Comprehensive administration of special education.* Columbus, OH: Merrill.

Polloway, E. A. (1984). The integration of mildly retarded students in the schools: A historical review. *Remedial and Special Education, 5*(4), 18–28.

Polloway, E. A. (1997). Developmental principles of the Luckasson et al. AAMR definition: A retrospective. *Education and Training in Mental Retardation and Developmental Disabilities, 32,* 174–178.

Polloway, E. A. (2002). The profession of learning disabilities: Progress and promises. *Learning Disability Quarterly, 25,* 103–112.

Polloway, E. A., Bursuck, W., & Epstein, M. H. (1999). Testing adaptations in the general education classroom. *Reading and Writing Quarterly.*

Polloway, E. A., Bursuck, W. D., & Epstein, M. H. (2001). Homework for students with learning disabilities: The challenge of home-school communication. *Reading and Writing Quarterly, 17,* 181–187.

Polloway, E. A., Bursuck, W., Jayanthi, M., Epstein, M., & Nelson, J. (1996). Treatment acceptability: Determining appropriate interventions within inclusive classrooms. *Intervention in School and Clinic, 31,* 133–144.

Polloway, E. A., Epstein, M. H., Bursuck, W. D. (2002). Homework for students with learning disabilities. *Reading and Writing Quarterly, 17,* 181–187.

Polloway, E. A., Epstein, M. H., Bursuck, W. D., Jayanthi, M., & Cumblad, C. (1994). Homework practices of general education teachers. *Journal of Learning Disabilities, 27,* 500–509.

Polloway, E. A., Epstein, M. H., Bursuck, W. D., Roderique, T. W., McConeghy, J., & Jayanthi, M. (1994). Classroom grading: A national survey of policies. *Remedial and Special Education, 15*(2), 162–170.

Polloway, E. A., & Jones-Wilson, L. (1992). Principles of assessment and instruction. In E. A. Polloway & T. E. C. Smith (Eds.), *Language instruction for students with disabilities* (pp. 87–120). Denver: Love.

Polloway, E. A., Miller, L., & Smith, T. E. C. (2003). *Language instruction for students with disabilities* (3rd ed.). Denver: Love.

Polloway, E. A., Patton, J. R., Epstein, M. H., & Smith, T. E. C. (1989). Comprehensive curriculum: Program design for students with mild handicaps. *Focus on Exceptional Children, 21*(8), 1–12.

Polloway, E. A., Patton, J. R., Payne, J. S., & Payne, R. A. (1989). *Strategies for teaching learners with special needs* (5th ed). Columbus, OH: Merrill.

Polloway, E. A., Patton, J. R., & Serna, L. (2001). *Strategies for teaching learners with special needs* (7th ed.). Columbus, OH: Merrill.

Polloway, E. A., Patton, J. R., Smith, J. D., & Roderique, T. W. (1992). Issues in program design for elementary students with mild retardation: Emphasis on curriculum development. *Education and Training in Mental Retardation, 27,* 142–150.

Polloway, E. A., Patton, J. R., Smith, T. E. C., & Buck, G. H. (1997). Mental retardation and learning disabilities: Conceptual issues. *Journal of Learning Disabilities, 30,* 219–231.

Polloway, E. A., & Smith, J. D. (1988). Current status of the mild mental retardation construct: Identification, placement, and programs. In M. C. Wang, M. C. Reynolds, & H. J. Walberg (Eds.), *The handbook of special education: Research and practice* (Vol. II, pp. 1–22). Oxford, UK: Pergamon Press.

Polloway, E. A., & Smith, J. D. (2001). Biological sources of mental retardation and efforts for prevention. In *Mental Retardation* (6th ed.) (pp. 150–195). Upper Saddle River, NJ: Merrill Prentice Hall.

Polloway, E. A., Smith, J. D., Chamberlain, J., Denning, C., & Smith, T. E. C. (1999). Levels of deficit vs. levels of support in mental retardation classification. *Education and Training in Mental Retardation and Development Disabilities, 34,* 48–59.

Polloway, E. A., Smith, J. D., Patton, J. R., & Smith, T. E. C. (1996). Historic changes in mental retardation and developmental disabilities. *Education and Training in Mental Retardation and Developmental Disabilities, 31,* 3–12.

Polloway, E. A., & Smith, J. E. (1982). *Teaching language skills to exceptional learners.* Denver: Love.

Polloway, E. A., & Smith, T. E. C. (2000). *Language instruction for students with disabilities.* Denver: Love.

Popp, R. A. (1983, Winter). Learning about disabilities. *Teaching Exceptional Children,* 78–81.

Powers, M. D. (1989). *Children with autism: A parent's guide.* New York: Woodbine House.

Prater, M. A. (1992). Increasing time-on-task in the classroom. *Intervention in School and Clinic, 28*(1), 22–27.

Prater, M. A., Joy, R., Chilman, B., Temple, J., & Miller, S. R. (1991). Self-monitoring of on-task behavior by adolescents with learning disabilities. *Learning Disability Quarterly, 14,* 164–177.

Premack, D. (1959). Toward empirical behavior laws: 1. Positive reinforcement. *Psychological Review, 66,* 219–233.

Pressley, M., & Rankin, J. (1994). More about whole language methods of reading instruction for students at risk for early reading failure. *Learning Disabilities Research & Practice, 9,* 157–168.

Public Law 94-142 (1975). *Federal Register, 42,* 42474–42518.

Public Law 101-476 (1990). *Federal Register, 54,* 35210–35271.

Pugach, M. C., & Warger, C. L. (2001). Curriculum matters. *Remedial and Special Education, 22,* 194–196.

Pugh, K. R., Mencl, W. E., Jenner, A. R., Lee, J. R., Katz, L., Frost, S. J., Shaywitz, S. E., & Shaywitz, B. A. (2001). Neuroimaging studies of reading development and reading disability. *Learning Disabilities Research and Practice, 16*(4), 240–249.

Pugh, S. (1999). Working with families of individual students. *Gifted Children Today, 22,* 26–31.

Quay, H., & Peterson, D. (1987). *Revised behavior problem checklist.* Coral Gables, FL: University of Miami.

Quinn, M. M., Kavale, K. A., Mathur, S. R., Rutherford, R. B., Jr., & Forness, S. R. (1999). A meta-analysis of social skill interventions for students with emotional and behavioral disorders. *Journal of Emotional and Behavioral Disorders, 7,* 54–64.

Ramos-Ford, V., & Gardner, H. (1997). Giftedness from a multiple intelligences perspective. In N. Colangelo & G. A. Davis (Eds.), *Handbook of gifted education* (2nd ed., pp. 54–66). Boston: Allyn and Bacon.

Rankin-Erickson, J. L., & Pressley, M. (2000). A survey of instructional practices of special education teachers nominated as effective teachers of literacy. *Learning Disabilities Research and Practice, 15*(4), 206–225.

Raskind, M. H., Goldberg, R. J., Higgins, E. L., & Herman, K. L. (2002). Teaching life success to students with learning disabilities: Lessons learned from a 20-year study. *Intervention in Schools and Clinic, 37*(4), 201–208.

Raskind, W. W. (2001). Current understanding of the genetic basis of reading and spelling differences. *Learning Disabilities Quarterly, 24,* 141–157.

Ratner, V. L., & Harris, L. R. (1994). *Understanding language disabilities: The impact of language.* Eau Claire, WI: Thinking Publications.

Raza, S. Y. (1997). Enhance your chances for success with students with ADHD. *Intervention in School and Clinics, 33*(1), 56–58.

Rea, P. J., McLaughlin, V. L., & Walther-Thomas, C. (2002). Outcomes for students with learning disabilities in inclusive and pullout programs. *Exceptional Children, 68,* 203–222.

Reeve, R. E. (1990). ADHD: Facts and fallacies. *Intervention in School and Clinic, 26,* 71–78.

Reid, R. (1999). Attention deficit hyperactivity disorder: Effective methods for the classroom. *Focus on Exceptional Children, 32,* 1–19.

Reid, R., Maag, J. W., Vasa, S. F., & Wright, C. (1994). Who are the children with attention-deficit-hyperactivity disorder? A school-based study. *The Journal of Special Education, 28,* 117–137.

Reid, R., & Nelson, J. R. (2002). The utility, acceptability, and practicality of functional behavioral assessment for students with high-incidence problem behaviors. *Remedial and Special Education, 23,* 15–23.

Reid, R. E. (1986). Practicing effective instruction: The exemplary center for reading. *Exceptional Children, 52,* 510–519.

Reis, S. M. (1989). Reflections on policy affecting the education of gifted and talented students. *American Psychologist, 44,* 399–408.

Reis, S. M. (2001). External barriers experienced by gifted and talented girls. *Gifted Children Today, 24,* 31–36.

Reis, S. M., & Schack, G. D. (1993). Differentiating products for the gifted and talented: The encouragement of independent learning. In C. J. Maker (Ed.), *Critical issues in gifted education: Vol. 3. Programs for the gifted in regular classrooms* (pp. 161–186). Austin, TX: Pro-Ed.

Renzulli, J. S. (1979). *What makes giftedness: A reexamination of the definition of the gifted and talented.* Ventura, CA: Ventura County Superintendent of Schools Office.

Renzulli, J. S., & Reis, S. M. (1985). *The schoolwide enrichment model: A comprehensive plan for educational excellence.* Mansfield Center, CT: Creative Learning Press.

Renzulli, J. S., & Reis, S. M. (1997). The schoolwide enrichment model: New directions for developing high-end learning. In N. Colangelo & G. A. Davis (Eds.), *Handbook of gifted education* (2nd ed.). Boston: Allyn and Bacon.

Renzulli, J. S., Reis, S. M., & Smith, L. M. (1981). *The revolving door identification model.* Wethersfield, CT: Creative Learning Press.

Repp, A. C., & Horner, R. H. (Eds.). (1999). *Functional analysis of problem behavior: From effective assessment to effective support.* Pacific Grove, CA: Brooks/Cole.

Research identifies opportunities and offers solutions for improving family involvement. (2001, Fall). *Research Connections, 9,* 2–5.

Reschly, D. (1988). Incorporating adaptive behavior deficits into instructional programs. In G. A. Robinson, J. R. Patton, E. A. Polloway, & L. R. Sargent (Eds.), *Best practices in mental disabilities* (Vol. 2, pp. 53–80). Des Moines, IA: Iowa State Department of Education.

Reynolds, C. T., & Salend, S. J. (1990). Teacher-directed and student-mediated textbook comprehension strategies. *Academic Therapy, 25,* 417–427.

Rhodes, L., & Dudley-Marling, C. (1996). *Readers and writers with a difference.* Portsmouth, NH: Heinemann.

Riccio, C. A., Hynd, G. W., Cohen, M., & Gonzales, T. (1994). Attention deficit hyperactivity disorder (ADHD) and learning disabilities. *Learning Disabilities Quarterly, 17,* 113–122.

Rich, H. L., & Ross, S. M. (1989). Students' time on learning tasks in special education. *Exceptional Children, 55,* 508–515.

Rich, H. L., & Ross, S. M. (1991). Regular class or resource room for students with disabilities? A direct response to "Rich and Ross, A Mixed Message." *Exceptional Children, 57,* 476–477.

Richards, T. L. (2001). Functional magnetic resonance imaging and spectroscopic imaging of the brain: Application of fMRI and fMRS to reading disabilities and education. *Learning Disabilities Quarterly, 24*(3), 189–203.

Rieck, W. A., & Wadsworth, D. E. (1999). Foreign exchange: An inclusion strategy. *Intervention, 35,* 22–28.

Riley, T. (1999). The role of advocacy: Creating change for gifted children throughout the world. *Gifted Child Today, 22,* 44–47.

Riggs, C. G. (2001). Work effectively with paraeducators in inclusive settings. *Intervention in School and Clinic, 37,* 114–117.

Roach, V. (1995). Supporting inclusion: Beyond the rhetoric. *Phi Delta Kappan, 77,* 295–299.

Robertson, J., Alper, S., Schloss, P. J., & Wisniewski, L. (1992). Teaching self-catheterization skills to a child with myelomeningocele in a preschool setting. *Journal of Early Intervention, 16,* 20–30.

Robin, S. S., & Johnson, E. O. (1996). Attitude and peer cross pressure: Adolescent drug and alcohol use. *Journal of Drug Education, 26,* 69–99.

Robinson, C. S., Manchetti, B. M.& Torgesen, J. K. (2002). Toward a two-factor theory of one type of mathematics disability. *Learning Disabilities Research and Practice, 17,* 81–89.

Robinson, S. M., Braxdale, C. T., & Colson, S. E. (1988). Preparing dysfunctional learners to enter junior high school: A transitional curriculum. *Focus on Exceptional Children, 18*(4), 1–12.

Rock, E. E., Rosenberg, M. S., & Carran, D. T. (1995). Variables affecting the reintegration rate of students with serious emotional disturbance. *Exceptional Children, 6,* 254–268.

Roderique, T. W., Polloway, E. A., Cumblad, C., Epstein, M. H., & Bursuck, W. (1994). Homework: A study of policies in the United States. *Journal of Learning Disabilities, 22,* 417–427.

Rogers, J. (1993). The inclusion revolution. *Research Bulletin.* Washington, DC: Phi Delta Kappa Center for Evaluation, Development, and Research.

Rogers, K. B. (1989). Training teachers of the gifted. *Roeper Review, 11,* 142–151.

Roller, C. (1996). *Variability not disability: Struggling readers in a workshop class.* Newark, DE: International Reading Association.

Rooney, K. (1993). *Attention deficit hyperactivity disorder: A videotape program.* Richmond, VA: State Department of Education.

Rooney, K. J. (1995). Dyslexia revisited: History, educational philosophy, and clinical assessment applications. *Intervention in School and Clinic, 31*(1), 6–15.

Roseberry-McKibbins, C. & Brice, A. (2002). Choice of language instruction: One or two? *Teaching Exceptional Children, 33,* 10–16.

Rosenberg, M. S., O'Shea, L., & O'Shea, D. J. (1991). *Student teacher to master teacher: A handbook for preservice and beginning teachers of students with mild and moderate handicaps.* New York: Macmillan.

Rosenberg, M. S., Wilson, R., Maheady, L., & Sindelar, P. (1992). *Educating students with behavior disorders.* Boston: Allyn and Bacon.

Rosenshine, B., & Stevens, R. (1986). The use of scaffolds for teaching higher-level cognitive strategies. *Educational Leadership, 49,* 26–33.

Ross, S. M., Smith, L. J., Casey, J., & Slavin, R. E. (1995). Increasing the academic success of disadvantaged children: An examination of alternative early intervention programs. *American Educational Research Journal, 32,* 773–800.

Rosselli, H. (1993). Process differentiation for gifted learners in the regular classroom: Teaching to everyone's needs. In C. J. Maker (Ed.), *Critical issues in gifted education: Vol. 3. Programs for the gifted in regular classrooms* (pp. 139–155). Austin, TX: Pro-Ed.

Rossow, A., & Hess, C. (2001). Engaging students in meaningful reading: A professional development journey. *Teaching Exceptional Children, 33,* 15–20.

Ruble, L. A., & Dalrymple, M. J. (2002). COMPASS: A parent-teacher collaboration model for students with autism. *Focus on Autism and Other Developmental Disabilities, 17,* 76–83.

Ryan, A. G., & Price, L. (1992). Adults with learning disabilities in the 1990s. *Intervention in School and Clinic, 28,* 18–20.

Rylance, B. J. (1998). Predictors of post-high school employment for youth identified as severely emotionally disturbed. *The Journal of Special Education, 32,* 184–192.

Sabatino, D. A. (1987). Preventive discipline as a practice in special education. *Teaching Exceptional Children, 19,* 8–11.

Sacks, S., Wolffe, B. A., & Tierney, F. (1998). Lifestyles of students with visual impairments: Preliminary studies of social networks. *Exceptional Children, 64,* 63–78.

Sacks, S. Z., & Silberman, R. K. (1998). *Educating students who have visual impairments with other disabilities.* Baltimore: Brookes.

Safer, D. J., & Krager, J. M. (1988). A survey of medication treatment for hyperactive/inattentive students. *Journal of the American Medical Association, 260,* 2256–2258.

Safford, P. L., & Safford, E. J. (1998). Visions of the special class. *Remedial and Special Education, 19,* 229–238.

Safran, J. S. (2002). A practical guide to research on Asperger's syndrome. *Intervention in School and Clinic, 37*, 283–293.

Safran, S. P., & Safran, J. S. (1996). Intervention assessment programs and pre-referrential teams: Directions for the twenty-first century. *Remedial and Special Education, 17*, 363–369.

Saintonge, S., Achille, P. A., & Lachance, L. (1998). The influence of big brothers on the separation-individuation of adolescents from single-parent families. *Adolescence, 33*, 343–352.

Salend, S. J. (1994). *Effective mainstreaming: Creating inclusive classrooms* (2nd ed.). Columbus, OH: Merrill/Prentice-Hall.

Salend, S. J. (1999). Facilitating friendships among diverse students. *Intervention in School and Clinic, 35*, 9–15.

Salend, S. J. (2000). Parental perceptions of inclusive placement. *Remedial and Special Education, 21*, 121–128.

Salend, S. J. (2001). *Creating inclusive classrooms: Effective and reflective practices* (4th ed.). Columbus, OH: Merrill/Prentice Hall.

Salend, S., & Duhaney, L. G. (1999). The impact of inclusion on students with and without disabilities and their education. *Remedial and Special Education, 20*, 114–126.

Salend, S., & Duhaney, L. G. (2002). Grading students in inclusive settings. *Teaching Exceptional Children, 34*, 13–14.

Salend, S. J., Gordon, J., & Lopez-Vona, K. (2002). Evaluating cooperative teaching teams. *Intervention in School and Clinic, 37*, 195–200.

Salend, S. J. & Melland, J. (2002). Evaluating cooperative teaching teams. *Intervention in School and Clinic, 37*, 195–200.

Salvia, J., & Ysseldyke, J. E. (1998). *Assessment* (8th ed.). Boston: Houghton Mifflin.

Sander, E. K. (1972). When are speech sounds learned? *Journal of Speech and Hearing Disorders, 37*, 62.

Sanders, R., Colton, M., & Roberts, S. (1999). Child abuse fatalities and cases of extreme concern: Lessons from reviews. *Child Abuse and Neglect, 23*, 257–273.

Sandieson, R. (1998). A survey on terminology that refers to people with mental retardation/developmental disabilities. *Education and Training in Mental Retardation and Developmental Disabilities, 33*, 290–295.

Santrock, J. W., & Warshak, R. A. (1979). Father custody and social development in boys and girls. *Journal of Social Issues, 35*, 112–125.

Sargent, L. R. (1991). *Social skills for school and community.* Reston, VA: CEC-MR.

Savage, R. C. (1997). Integrating the rehabilitation and education services for school–age children. *Journal of Head Trauma Rehabilitation, 12*, 11–20.

Savage, R. C., & Wolcott, G. F. (Eds.) (1994). *Educational dimensions of acquired brain injury.* Austin, TX: Pro-Ed.

Scanlon, D., & Melland, D. F. (2002). Academic and participant profiles of school-age drop outs with and without disabilities. *Exceptional Children, 68*, 239–258.

Schaffner, C. B., & Buswell, B. E. (1996). Ten critical elements for creating inclusive and effective school communities. In S. Stainback & W. Stainback (Eds.), *Inclusion: A guide for educators* (pp. 49–65). Baltimore: Brookes.

Schalock, R. (2001, May-June). Consortium on language presents phase one report. *American Association on Mental Retardation News and Notes, 14*(3), 1, 4–6.

Schalock, R. L., Stark, J. A., Snell, M. E., Coulter, D. L., Polloway, E. A., Luckasson, R., Reiss, S., & Spitalnik, D. M. (1994). Changing conceptualizations of and definition of mental retardation: Implications for the field. *Mental Retardation, 32*, 181–193.

Schaughency, E. A., & Rothlind, J. (1991). Assessment and classification of attention deficit hyperactivity disorders. *School Psychology Review, 20*(2), 197–202.

Scheuerman, B., Jacobs, W. R., McCall, C., & Knies, W. (1994). The personal spelling dictionary: An adoptive approach to reducing the spelling hurdle in written language. *Intervention in School and Clinic, 29*(5), 292–299.

Scheuerman, B., & Webber, J. (2002). *Autism: Teaching does make a difference.* Belmont, CA: Wadsworth.

Schiever, S. W. (1993). Differentiating the learning environment for gifted students. In C. J. Maker (Ed.), *Critical issues in gifted education: Vol. 3. Programs for the gifted in regular classrooms* (pp. 201–214). Austin, TX: Pro-Ed.

Schleichkorn, J. (1993). *Coping with cerebral palsy: Answers to questions parents often ask* (2nd ed.). Austin, TX: Pro-Ed.

Schulte, A., & Olson, R. (2001). Rethinking learning disabilities. In C. E. Finn, A. J. Rotherham, & C. R. Hokanson, Jr. (Eds.), *Rethinking special education for a new century.* Washington, DC: Thomas B. Fordham Foundation.

Schulz, E. (1994, October 5). Beyond behaviorism. *Education Week, 14*(5), 19–21, 24.

Schulz, J. B., & Carpenter, C. D. (1995). *Mainstreaming exceptional students: A guide for classroom teachers.* Boston: Allyn and Bacon.

Schumm, J. S., & Strickler, K. (1991). Guidelines for adapting content area textbooks: Keeping teachers and students content. *Intervention in School and Clinic, 27*, 79–84.

Schwartz, S. E., & Karge, B. D. (1996). *Human diversity: A guide for understanding* (2nd ed.). New York: McGraw-Hill.

Scott, A. (1997). Education and acceptance. *ADVANCE for Speech-Language Pathologists and Audiologists, 36*, 10–12.

Scott, B. J., Vitale, M. R., & Masten, W. G. (1998). Implementing instructional adaptations for students with disabilities in inclusive classrooms: A literature review. *Remedial and Special Education, 19*, 106–119.

Scott, T. M., & Nelson, M. C. (1998). Confusion and failure in facilitating generalized social responding in the school setting: Sometimes 2+2=5. *Behavioral Disorders, 23*, 264–275.

Scotti, J. R., & Meyer, L. H. (Eds.). (1999). *Behavioral intervention: Principles, models, and practices.* Baltimore: Brookes.

Scruggs, T. E. (1997). *Advances in learning and behaviors disorders, vol. 11.* Greenwich, CT: JAI Press.

Scruggs, T. E., & Mastropieri, M. A. (1994). Successful mainstreaming in elementary science classes: A qualitative study of three reputational cases. *American Educational Research Journal, 31*, 785–811.

Scruggs, T. E., & Mastropieri, M. A. (1996). Teacher perceptions of mainstreaming/inclusion, 1958–1995: A research synthesis. *Exceptional Children, 63*, 59–74.

Searcy, S., & Meadows, N. B. (1994). The impact of social structures on friendship development for children with behavior disorders. *Education and Treatment of Children, 17*, 255–268.

Sears, P. S. (1978). The Terman genetic studies of genius, 1922–1972. In A. H. Passow (Ed.), *The gifted and the talented: Their education and development* (Vol. 78, pp. 75–96). Chicago: University of Chicago Press.

Seeley, K. (1995). Classwide peer tutoring. Unpublished manuscript, Lynchburg College (VA).

Seery, M. E., Davis, P. M., & Johnson, L. J. (2000). Seeing eye to eye: Are parents and professionals in agreement about the benefits of preschool inclusion? *Remedial and Special Education, 21*, 368–378.

Semrul-Clikerman, M., Steingard, R. J., Filipek, P., Biederman, J., Bekken, K., and Renshaw, P. F. (2000). Using MRI to examine brain-behavior relationships in males with attention-deficit hyperactivity disorder. *Journal of the American Academy of Child and Adolescent Psychiatry, 39*(4), 477–484.

Sevcik, R. A., & Romski, M. (2000). *AAC: More than three decades of growth and development.* American Speech-Language-Hearing Association. Washington, D.C.

Sexton, D., Snyder, P., Wolfe, B., Lobman, M., Stricklin, S., & Akers, P. (1996). Early intervention inservice training strategies: Perceptions and suggestions from the field. *Exceptional Children, 62,* 485–496.

Shames, G. H., & Wiig, E. H. (1990). *Human communication disorders* (3rd ed.). New York: MacMillan.

Shane, H. C., & Sauer, M. (1986). *Augmentative and alternative communication.* Austin, TX: Pro-Ed.

Shaner, M. Y. (1991). Talented teachers for talented students. *G/C/T, 22,* 14–15.

Shanker, A. (1994–1995). Educating students in special programs. *Educational Leadership, 52,* 43–47.

Shapiro, E. S., DuPaul, G. J., & Bradley-Klug, K. L. (1998). Self-management as a strategy to improve the classroom behavior of adolescents with ADHD. *Journal of Learning Disabilities, 31,* 545–555.

Shaywitz, S., & Shaywitz, B. (1997, November). *The science of reading: Implications for children and adults with learning disabilities.* Paper presented at the 13th Annual Harvard University Institute on Learning Disorders, Cambridge, MA.

Shea, T. M., & Bauer, A. M. (1991). *Parents and teachers of children with exceptionalities: A handbook for collaboration.* Boston: Allyn and Bacon.

Shields, J. M., & Heron, T. E. (1989). Teaching organizational skills to students with learning disabilities. *Teaching Exceptional Children, 20,* 8–13.

Shimon, D. A. (1992). *Coping with hearing loss and hearing aids.* San Diego: Singular.

Siccone, F. (1995). *Celebrating diversity: Building self-esteem in today's multicultural classrooms.* Boston: Allyn and Bacon.

Sileo, T. W., Sileo, A. P., & Prater, M. A. (1996). Parent and professional partnerships in special education: Multicultural considerations. *Intervention in School & Clinic, 31,* 145–153.

Silver, L. B. (1995). Controversial therapies. *Journal of Child Neurology, 10*(1), 96–100.

Silver, L. B. (1999). *Attention deficit hyperactivity disorder: A clinical guide to diagnosis and treatment for health and mental health.* Washington, DC: American Psychiatric Press.

Silver, L. B. (2000). Alternative treatment for ADHD. In B. P. Guyer (Ed.), *ADHD: Achieving success in school and in life.* Boston: Allyn and Bacon.

Silverman, A. B., Reinherz, H. Z., & Giaconia, R. M. (1996). The long-term sequelae of child and adolescent abuse: A longitudinal community study. *Child Abuse and Neglect, 20,* 709–723.

Silverman, L. K. (1986). What happens to the gifted girl? In C. J. Maker (Ed.), *Critical issues in gifted education: Defensible programs for the gifted* (Vol. 1, pp. 43–89). Austin, TX: Pro-Ed.

Simmons, D., Fuchs, D., Hodge, J., & Mathes, P. (1994). Importance of instructional complexity and role reciprocity to classwide peer tutoring. *Learning Disabilities Research and Practice, 9,* 203–212.

Simpson, R. (1996). *Working with parents and families of exceptional children and youth* (3rd ed.). Austin, TX: Pro-Ed.

Simpson, R. (1998). Behavior modification for children and adolescents with exceptionalities. *Intervention in School and Clinic, 33,* 219–226.

Simpson, R. (2001). ABA and studentswith autism spectrum disorders. *Focus on Autism and Developmental Disabilities, 16,* 68–71.

Sitlingon, P. L., & Frank. A. C. (1998). *Follow-up studies: A practical handbook.* Austin, TX: Pro-Ed.

Skiba, R., Grizzle, K., & Minke, K. M. (1994). Opening the floodgates? The social maladjustment exclusion and state SED prevalence rates. *Journal of School Psychology, 32,* 267–283.

Slicker, E. K., & Palmer, D. J. (1993). Mentoring at-risk high school students: Evaluation of a school-based program. *The School Counselor, 40,* 327–334.

Smith, C. R. (1994). *Learning disabilities: The interaction of learner, task, and setting* (3rd ed.). Boston: Allyn and Bacon.

Smith, C. R. (1998). From gibberish to phoneme awareness: Effective decoding instruction. *Teaching Exceptional Children, 30,* 20–25.

Smith, D. D., & Luckasson, R. (1995/1998). *Introduction to special education: Teaching in an age of challenge.* Boston: Allyn and Bacon.

Smith, D. D., & Rivera, D. (1993). *Effective discipline* (2nd ed.). Austin, TX: Pro-Ed.

Smith, D. D., & Rivera, D. P. (1995). Discipline in special and regular education. *Focus on Exceptional Children, 27*(5), 1–14.

Smith, J. D. (1994). The revised AAMR definition of mental retardation: The MRDD position. *Education and Training in Mental Retardation and Developmental Disabilities, 29,* 179–183.

Smith, J. D. (1995). Inclusive school environments and students with disabilities in South Carolina: The issues, the status, the needs. *Occasional Papers, 1,* 1–5.

Smith, J. W., & Smith, S. B. (2002). Technology for organizing and presenting digital information. *Intervention in School and Clinic, 37,* 306–310.

Smith, M. D., Belcher, R. G., & Juhrs, P. D. (1995). *A guide to successful employment for individuals with autism.* Baltimore: Brookes.

Smith, P. M. (1997). You are not alone: For parents when they learn that their child has a disability. *NICHY News Digest, 2,* 2–5.

Smith, S. W. (1990a). A comparison of individualized education programs (IEPs) of students with behavioral disorders and learning disabilities. *Journal of Special Education, 24,* 85–100.

Smith, S. W. (1990b). Individualized education programs (IEPs) in special education: From intent to acquiescence. *Exceptional Children, 57,* 6–14.

Smith, S. W., & Simpson, R. L. (1989). An analysis of individualized education programs (IEPs) for students with behavior disorders. *Behavioral Disorders, 14,* 107–116.

Smith, T. E. C. (1990). *Introduction to education* (2nd ed.). St. Paul, MN: West.

Smith, T. E. C. (2001). Section 504, the ADA, and public schools: What educators need to know. *Remedial and Special Education, 21,* 335–343.

Smith, T. E. C. (2002). Section 504: Basic requirements for schools. *Intervention in School and Clinic, 37,* 2–6.

Smith, T. E. C., & Dowdy, C. A. (1992). Future-based assessment and intervention and mental retardation. *Education and Training in Mental Retardation, 27,* 23–31.

Smith, T. E. C., Dowdy, C. A., Polloway, E. A., & Blalock, G. (1997). *Children and adults with learning disabilities.* Boston: Allyn and Bacon.

Smith, T. E. C., Finn, D. M., & Dowdy, C. A. (1993). *Teaching students with mild disabilities.* Ft. Worth, TX: Harcourt Brace Jovanovich.

Smith, T. E. C., & Hendricks, M. D. (1995). *Prader-Willi syndrome: Practical considerations for educators.* Little Rock, AR: Ozark Learning.

Smith, T. E. C., & Hilton, A. (1994). Program design for students with mental retardation. *Education and Training in Mental Retardation and Developmental Disabilities, 29,* 3–8.

Smith, T. E. C., & Patton, J. R. (1998). *Section 504 and public schools.* Austin, TX: Pro-Ed.

Smith, T. E. C., Price, B. J., & Marsh, G. E. (1986). *Mildly handicapped children and adults.* St. Paul, MN: West.

Smutny, J. F., Walker, S. Y., & Meckstroth, E. A. (1997). *Teaching young gifted children in the regular classroom: Identifying, nurturing, and challenging ages 4–9.* Minneapolis, MN: Free Spirit.

Snell, M., & Drake, G. P. (1994). Replacing cascades with supported education. *Journal of Special Education, 27,* 393–409.

Solomon, C. R., & Serres, F. (1999). Effects of parental verbal aggression on children's self-esteem and school marks. *Child Abuse & Neglect, 23,* 339–351.

Soto, G., Muller, E., Hunt, P., and Goetz, L. (2001). Professional skills for serving students who use AAC in general education classrooms: A team perspective. *Language, Speech, and Hearing Services in the Schools, 32,* 51–56.

Southern, W. T., & Jones, E. D. (1991). Academic acceleration: Background and issues. In W. T. Southern & E. D. Jones (Eds.), *Academic acceleration of gifted children* (pp. 1–17). New York: Teachers College Press.

Spirito, A., Hart, K. I., Overholser, J., & Halverson, J. (1990). Social skills and depression in adolescent suicide attempters. *Adolescence, 25,* 543–552.

Squires, E. C., & Reetz, L. J. (1989). Vocabulary acquisition activities. *Academic Therapy, 14,* 589–592.

Stainback, S., Stainback, W., East, K., & Sapon-Shevin, M. (1994). A commentary on inclusion and the development of a positive self-identity by people with disabilities. *Exceptional Children, 60,* 486–490.

Stainback, W., & Stainback, S. (1984). A rationale for the merger of special and regular education. *Exceptional Children, 51,* 102–111.

Stainback, W. C., Stainback, S., & Wehman, P. (1997). Toward full inclusion into general education. In P. Wehman (Ed.), *Exceptional individuals in school, community, and work* (pp. 531–557). Austin, TX: Pro-Ed.

Stephien, S., & Gallagher, S. (1993). Problem-based learning: As authentic as it gets. *Educational Leadership, 50*(7), pp. 25–28.

Sternberg, R. J. (1991). Giftedness according to the triarchic theory of human intelligence. In N. Colangelo & G. A. Davis (Eds.), *Handbook of gifted education* (pp. 45–54). Boston: Allyn and Bacon.

Stewart, D. A., & Kluwin, T. N. (2001). *Teaching deaf and hard of hearing students.* Boston: Allyn and Bacon.

Storey, K. (1993). A proposal for assessing integration. *Education and Training in Mental Retardation and Developmental Disabilities, 28,* 279–286.

Stormont-Spurgin, J. (1997). I lost my homework: Strategies for improving organization in students with ADHD. *Intervention in School and Clinic, 32*(5), 270–274.

Stover, D. (1992, May). The at-risk students schools continue to ignore. *The Education Digest,* 37–40.

Streeter, C. E., & Grant, C. A. (1993). *Making choices for multicultural education.* New York: Macmillan.

Struyk, L. R., Cole, K. B., Epstein, M. H., Bursuck, W. D., & Polloway, E. A. (1996). Homework communication: Problems involving high school teachers and parents of students with disabilities. (Manuscript submitted for publication.)

Struyk, L. R., Epstein, M. H., Bursuck, W., Polloway, E. A., McConeghy, J., & Cole, K. B. (1995). Homework, grading, and testing practices used by teachers with students with and without disabilities. *The Clearing House, 69,* 50–55.

Swanson, H. L. (1994). Short-term memory and working memory: Do both contribute to our understanding of academic achievement in children and adults with learning disabilities? *Journal of Learning Disabilities, 27,* 34–50.

Swanson, H. L. (1999). Cognition and learning disabilities. In W. N. Bender (Ed.), *Professional Issues in Learning Disabilities.* Austin, TX: Pro-Ed.

Swanson, H. L. (2000). Are working memory differences in readings with learning disabilities hard to change? *Journal of Learning Disabilities, 33,* 551–566.

Summers, M., Bridge, J., & Summers, C. R. (1991). Sibling support groups. *Teaching Exceptional Children, 23,* 20–25.

Tabassam, W., & Grainger, J. (2002). Self-concept, attributional style, and self-efficacy beliefs of students with learning disabilities with and without ADHD. *Learning Disabilities Quarterly, 25,* 141–151.

Tankersley, M. (1995). A group-oriented management program: A review of research on the good behavior game and implications for teachers. *Preventing School Failure, 40,* 19–28.

Tannenbaum, A. J. (1997). The meaning and making of giftedness. In N. Colangelo & G. A. Davis (Eds.), *Handbook of gifted education* (2nd ed.). Boston: Allyn and Bacon.

Tavzel, C. S., & Staff of LinguiSystems. (1987). *Blooming recipes.* East Moline, IL: LinguiSystems.

Taylor, R. L. (2000). *Assessment of individuals with mental retardation.* San Diego: Singular.

Teen drug use is on the rise again. (1996). *Executive Educator, 18,* 7–8.

Templeton, R. A. (1995). ADHD: A teacher's guide. *The Oregon Conference Monograph, 7,* 2–11.

Tennant, C., Bebbington, P. R., & Hurry, J. (1980). Parental death in childhood and risk of adult depressive disorders: A review. *Psychological Medicine, 10,* 289–299.

Terman, L. M. (1925). *Genetic studies of genius* (Vol. 1: *Mental and physical traits of a thousand gifted children*). Stanford, CA: Stanford University Press.

Terman, L. M., & Oden, M. H. (1959). *Genetic studies of genius* (Vol. 5: *The gifted group at mid-life*). Stanford, CA: Stanford University Press.

Tests in Print. (1989). Austin, TX: Pro-Ed.

Thomas, P. J., & Carmack, F. F. (1993). Language: The foundation of learning. In J. S. Choate (Ed.), *Successful mainstreaming: Proven ways to detect and correct special needs* (pp. 148–173). Boston: Allyn and Bacon.

Thompson, A. E., & Kaplan, C. A. (1999). Emotionally abused children presenting to child psychiatry clinics. *Child Abuse & Neglect, 23,* 191–196.

Thousand, J. S., & Villa, R. A. (1990). Strategies for educating learners with severe disabilities within their local home schools and communities. *Focus on Exceptional Children, 23,* 1–24.

Tirosh, E., & Canby, J. (1993). Autism with hyperlexia: A distinct syndrome? *American Journal on Mental Retardation, 98,* 84–92.

Tomlinson-Keasey, C., & Little, T. D. (1990). Predicting educational attainment, occupational achievement, intellectual skill, and personal adjustment among gifted men and women. *Journal of Educational Psychology, 82,* 442–455.

Torres, I., & Corn, A. L. (1990). *When you have a visually handicapped child in your classroom: Suggestions for teachers.* New York: American Foundation for the Blind.

Tovey, R. (1995). Awareness programs help change students' attitudes towards their disabled peers. *Harvard Educational Letter, 11*(6), 7–8.

Trad, P. V. (1999). Assessing the patterns that prevent teenage pregnancy. *Adolescence, 34,* 221–238.

Turnbull, A. P., Strickland, B., & Hammer, S. E. (1978). IEPs: Presenting guidelines for development and implementation. *Journal of Learning Disabilities, 11,* 40–46.

Turnbull, A. P., & Turnbull, H. R. (1997). *Families, professionals, and exceptionality: A special partnership.* Columbus, OH: Merrill.

Turnbull, H. R. (1993). *Free appropriate public education: The law and children with disabilities.* (4th ed.). Denver: Love.

Turnbull, H. R. (1998). *Free appropriate public education: The law and children with disabilities* (5th ed.). Denver: Love.

Turnbull, H. R. Pereira, L., & Blue-Banning, M. (2000). Teachers as friendship facilitators. *Teaching Exceptional Children, 32,* 66-70.

Turnbull, H. R., & Turnbull, A. P., (1986). *Families, professionals, and exceptionality: A special partnership.* Columbus, OH: Merrill.

Turnbull, H. R., & Turnbull, A. P. (2000). *Free appropriate public education* (6th ed.). Denver: Love.

Turnbull, H. R., Turnbull, A. P., Shank, S., Smith, S., & Lead, D. (2002). *Exceptional lives: Special education in today's schools* (3rd ed.). Upper Saddle, NJ: Merrill.

Update to the membership concerning a division name change proposal. (Winter 2001). *MRDD Express, 12*(2), 3.

U.S. Department of Commerce. (1993). *Poverty in the United States: 1992.* Washington, DC: Author.

U.S. Department of Commerce. (1995). *Population Profile of the United States, 1995.* Washington, DC: Author.

U.S. Department of Education. (1989). *11th annual report to Congress on the implementation of IDEA.* Washington, DC: Author.

U.S. Department of Education. (1990). *12th annual report to Congress on the implementation of the Education of the Handicapped Act.* Washington, DC: Author.

U.S. Department of Education. (1990, January 9). Reading and writing proficiency remains low. *Daily Education News,* pp. 1–7.

U.S. Department of Education. (1991, September 16). Memorandum: Clarification of policy to address the needs of children with attention deficit disorders within general and/or special education. Washington, DC: Author.

U.S. Department of Education. (1993). *15th annual report to Congress on the implementation of IDEA.* Washington, DC: Author.

U.S. Department of Education. (1994). *16th annual report to Congress on the Implementation of the Individuals with Disabilities Education Act.* Washington, DC: U.S. Government Printing Office.

U.S. Department of Education. (1996). *18th annual report to Congress on the implementation of IDEA.* Washington, DC: Author.

U.S. Department of Education. (1997). New report links fathers' involvement with children's success. *Community Update, 52,* 3.

U. S. Department of Education. (1998a). *Safe and smart: Making the after-school hours work for kids.* Washington, DC: Author.

U.S. Department of Education. (1998b). *20th annual report to Congress on the implementation of the Individuals with Disabilities Education Act.* Washington, DC: Author.

U. S. Department of Education. (1999). *The condition of education, 1998.* Washington, DC: Author.

U.S. Department of Education. (2002). *23rd annual report to Congress on the implementation of the Individuals with Disabilities Education Act.* Washington, DC: Author.

U.S. Office of Education (USOE). (1977). Assistance to states for education of handicapped children: Procedures for evaluating specific learning disabilities. *Federal Register, 42,* 65082–65085.

U.S. Office of Education (USOE). (1999, March 12). Assistance to the states for the education of children with disabilities and the early intervention program for infants and toddlers with disabilities; final regulations. *Federal Register, 64*(48) 12406–12458. Washington, DC: U.S. Government Printing Office.

Valdes, K. A., Williamson, C. L., & Wagner, M. M. (1990). *The national longitudinal transition study of special education students* (Vol. 1). Menlo Park, CA: SRI International.

Van Eerdewegh, M. M., Bieri, M. D., Parrilla, R. H., & Clayton, P. J. (1982). The bereaved child. *British Journal of Psychiatry, 140,* 23–29.

Van Laarhoven, T., Coutinho, M., Van Laarhoven-Myers, T., & Repp, A. C. (1999). Assessment of the student instructional setting, and curriculum to support successful integration. In M. J. Coutinho & A. C. Repp (Eds.), *Inclusion: The integration of students with disabilities.* Belmont, CA: Wadsworth Publishing.

Van Riper, C., & Emerick, L. (1984). *Speech correction: An introduction to speech pathology and audiology* (7th ed.). Englewood Cliffs, NJ: Prentice-Hall.

VanTassel-Baska, J. (1989). Appropriate curriculum for gifted learners. *Educational Leadership, 47,* 13–15.

VanTassel-Baska, J. (1998). *Gifted and talented learners.* Denver: Love.

VanTassel-Baska, J., Patton, J., & Prillaman, D. (1989). Disadvantaged gifted learners at-risk for educational attention. *Focus on Exceptional Children, 22*(3), 1–16.

Vaughn, C., & Long, W. (1999). Surrender to win: How adolescent drug and alcohol users change their lives. *Adolescence, 34,* 9–22.

Vaughn, S., Bos, C. S., & Schumm, J. S. (2000). *Teaching exceptional, diverse, and at-risk students in the general education classroom* (2nd ed.). Boston: Allyn and Bacon.

Vaughn, S., Gersten, R., & Chard, D. J. (2000). The underlying message in learning disabilities intervention research: Findings from research synthesis. *Exceptional Children, 67,* 99–114.

Vaughn, S., & Kinger, J. (1999). Teaching reading comprehensive skills to students with learning disabilities in general education classrooms. *Learning Disabilities, 9,* 6–11.

Vaughn, S., Schumm, J. S., & Arguelles, M. E. (1997). The ABCDEs of co-teaching. *Teaching Exceptional Children, 30*(2), 4–10.

Victory in landmark "full inclusion" case. (1994). *Disability Rights Education and Defense Fund News, 1,* 6.

Vogeltanz, N. D., Wilsnack, S. C., Harris, T. R., Wilsnack, R. W., Wonderlich, S. A., & Kristjanson, A. F. (1999). Prevalence and risk factors for childhood sexual abuse in women: National survey findings. *Child Abuse & Neglect, 23,* 579–592.

Voltz, D., Brazil, N., & Ford, A. (2001). What matters most in inclusive education. *Intervention in School and Clinic, 37,* 23-30.

Wadsworth, D. E., & Knight, D. (1999). Preparing the classroom for students with speech, physical, and health needs. *Intervention in School and Clinic, 34,* 170–175.

Walberg, H. J. (1991). Does homework help? *School Community Journal, 1*(1), 13–15.

Waldon, N. L., & McLusky, J. (1998). The effects of an inclusive school program on students with mild and severe learning disabilities. *Exceptional Children, 64,* 395–405.

Walker, B. (1993, January). *Multicultural issues in education: An introduction.* Paper presented at Cypress–Fairbanks Independent School District In-Service, Cypress, TX.

Walker, J. E., & Shea, T. M. (1988). *Behavior management: A practical approach for educators* (4th ed.). New York: Merrill/Macmillan.

Walker, J. E., & Shea, T. M. (1995). *Behavior management: A practical approach for educators* (6th ed.). Columbus, OH: Merrill.

Wallace, G., Cohen, S., & Polloway, E. A. (1987). *Language arts: Teaching exceptional children.* Austin, TX: Pro-Ed.

Wallace, G., Larsen, S. C., & Elksnin, L. K. (1992). *Educational assessment of learning problems.* Boston: Allyn and Bacon.

Walther-Thomas, C., Korinek, L., McLaughlin, V. L., & Williams, B. T. (2000). *Collaboration for inclusive education.* Boston: Allyn and Bacon.

Wanat, C. L. (1992). Meeting the needs of single-parent children: School and parent views differ. *NASSP Bulletin, 76,* 43–48.

Wang, M. C., & Gordon, E. W. (Eds.). (1994). *Educational resilience in inner-city America.* Hillsdale, NJ: Erlbaum.

Wang, M. C., Reynolds, M. C., & Walberg, H. J. (1994–1995). Serving students at the margins. *Educational Leadership, 52,* 12–17.

Warren, D. (1994). *Blindness in children.* Cambridge, MA: Cambridge University Press.

Warren, S. F. (2000). The future of early communication in language intervention. *Topics in Early Childhood Special Education, 20,* 33–37.

Warren, S. F. (2000, May-June). Mental retardation: Curse, characteristic, or coin of the realm? *American Association on Mental Retardation News and Notes, 13*(3), 1, 10–11.

Waterman, B. B. (1994). Assessing children for the presence of a disability. *NICHY News Digest, 4*(1), Washington, DC: U.S. Government Printing Office.

Watson, S. M., & Houtz, L. E. (2002). Teaching science: Meeting academic and cultural needs of students. *Intervention in School and Clinic, 37,* 268–278.

Wayman, K., Lynch, E., & Hanson, M. (1990). Home-based early childhood services: Cultural sensitivity in a family systems approach. *Topics in Early Childhood Special Education, 10*(4), 65–66.

Webber, J. (1997). Responsible inclusion: Key components for success. In P. Zionts (Ed.), *Effective inclusion of students with behavior and learning problems.* Austin, TX: Pro-Ed.

Webber, J., & Scheuermann, B. (1991). Accentuate the positive . . . Eliminate the negative! *Teaching Exceptional Children, 24,* 14–17.

Wehby, J. H., Symons, F. J., Canale, J. A., & Go, F. J. (1998). Teaching practices in classrooms for students with emotional and behavioral disorders: Discrepancies between recommendations and observations. *Behavioral Disorders, 24,* 51–56.

Wehman, P. (1996). *Life beyond the classroom: Transition strategies for young people with disabilities* (2nd ed.). Baltimore: Brookes.

Wehman, P. (Ed.). (1997). *Exceptional individuals in school, community, and work.* Austin, TX: Pro-Ed.

Wehman, P., & Kregel, J. (Eds.). (1998). *More than a job: Securing satisfying careers for people with disabilities.* Baltimore: Brookes.

Wehmeyer, M. (1993). Self-determination as an educational outcome. *Impact, 6*(4), 16–17, 26.

Wehmeyer, M. (1994). Perceptions of self-determination and psychological empowerment of adolescents with mental retardation. *Education and Training in Mental Retardation and Developmental Disabilities, 29,* 9–21.

Wehmeyer, M. L., Lattin, D., & Agram, M. (2001). Achieving access to the general education curriculum for students with mental retardation: A curriculum decision-making model. *Education and Training in Mental Retardation and Developmental Disabilities, 36,* 327–342.

Wehmeyer, M. L., Morningstar, M., & Husted, D. (1999). *Family involvement in transition planning and implementation.* Austin, TX: Pro-Ed.

Wehmeyer, M. L., & Patton, J. R. (2000). *Mental retardation in the 21st century.* Austin, TX: Pro-Ed.

Weinbender, M. L. M., & Rossignol, A. M. (1996). Lifestyle and risk of premature sexual activity in a high school population of Seventh-Day Adventists: Valuegenesis 1989. *Adolescence, 31,* 265–275.

Wenz-Gross, M., & Siperstein, G. N. (1998). Students with learning problems at risk in middle school: Stress, social support, and adjustment. *Exceptional Children, 65,* 91–100.

Wesson, C. L., & Deno, S. L. (1989). An analysis of long-term instructional plans in reading for elementary resource room students. *Remedial and Special Education, 10*(1), 21–28.

West, G. K. (1986). *Parenting without guilt.* Springfield, IL: Thomas.

West, G. K. (1994, Nov. 10). Discipline that works: Part 1. *The News and Daily Advance.*

West, G. K. (2000). *The Shelbys need help: A choose-your-own-solutions guidebook for parents.* Atascadero, CA: Impact.

West, G. K. (2002). Parent education programs and benefits for parents of children with disabilities. Unpublished manuscript, Lynchburg College in Lynchburg, VA.

Westling, D. L., & Koorland, M. A. (1988). *The special educator's handbook.* Boston: Allyn and Bacon.

Wetherby, A. M., & Prizant, B. M. (Eds.). (2000). *Autism spectrum disorders: A transactional developmental perspective.* Baltimore: Brookes.

Weyandt, L. L. (2001). *An ADHD primer.* Boston: Allyn and Bacon.

White, C. C., Lakin, K. C., Bruininks, R. H., & Li, X. (1991). *Persons with mental retardation and related conditions in state-operated residential facilities: Year ending June 30, 1989, with longitudinal trends from 1950 to 1989.* Minneapolis, MN: University of Minnesota, Institute on Community Integration.

Wicks-Nelson, R., & Israel, A. C. (1991). *Behavior disorders of childhood.* Englewood Cliffs, NJ: Prentice-Hall.

Wiedemeyer, D., & Lehman, J. (1991). House plan: Approach to collaborative teaching and consultation. *Teaching Exceptional Children, 23*(3), 6–10.

Wiederholt, J. L., & Bryant, B. (1986). *Gray oral reading test—Revised.* Austin, TX: Pro-Ed.

Wiig, E. H. (1986). Language disabilities in school-age children and youth. In G. H. Shames & E. H. Wiig (Eds.), *Human communication disorders* (2nd ed., pp. 331–383). Columbus, OH: Merrill.

Wiig, E. H., & Semel, E. (1984). *Language assessment and intervention for the learning disabled* (2nd ed.). Columbus, OH: Merrill.

Will, M. C. (1984). Educating children with learning problems: A shared responsibility. *Exceptional Children, 52,* 411–415.

Williamson, J. M., Borduin, C. M., & Howe, B. A. (1991). The ecology of adolescent maltreatment: A multilevel examination of adolescent physical abuse, sexual abuse, and neglect. *Journal of Consulting and Clinical Psychology, 59,* 449–457.

Wilson, C. L. (1995). Parents and teachers: Can we talk? *LD Forum, 20*(2), 31–33.

Winebrenner, S. (1992). Teaching gifted kids in the regular classroom: Strategies and techniques every teacher can use to meet the academic needs of the gifted and talented. Minneapolis, MN: Free Spirit.

Winocur, S. L., & Mauer, P. A. (1997). Critical thinking and gifted students: Using IMPACT to improve teaching and learning. In N. Colangelo and G. A. Davis (Eds.), *Handbook of gifted education* (2nd ed., pp. 308–317). Boston: Allyn and Bacon.

Winzer, M. A., & Mazurek, K. (1998). *Special education in multicultural contexts.* Upper Saddle River, NJ: Prentice Hall.

Witt, J. C., & Elliott, S. N. (1985). Acceptability of classroom management strategies. In T. R. Kratochwill (Ed.), *Advances in school psychology* (Vol. 4, pp. 251–288). Hillsdale, NJ: Erlbaum.

Wolfe, P. S. (1997). Deaf-blindness. In P. Wehman (Ed.), *Exceptional individuals* (pp. 357–381). Austin, TX: Pro-Ed.

Wood, D. K., & Frank, A. R. (2000). Using memory-enhancing strategies to learn multiplication facts. *Teaching Exceptional Children, 32*, 78–82.

Wood, J. W. (1984). *Adapting instruction for the mainstream.* Columbus, OH: Merrill.

Wood, J. W. (1996). *Adapting instruction for mainstreamed and at-risk students* (3rd ed.). New York: Merrill.

Wood, M. (1998). Whose job is it anyway? Educational roles in inclusion. *Exceptional Children, 64*, 181–196.

Woodrich, D. L. (1994). *What every parent wants to know: Attention deficit hyperactivity disorder.* Baltimore: Brookes.

Woodrich, D. L. (1998). Managing AD/HD in the classroom minus medication. *Education Digest, 63*, 50–56.

Worthington, L. A., Patterson, D., Elliott, E., & Linkous, L. (1993). *Assessment of children with ADHD: An inservice education program for educator and parents.* Unpublished manuscript. University of Alabama, Department of Special Education, Tuscaloosa.

Wright, J. V. (1995). Multicultural issues and attention deficit disorders. *Learning Disabilities Research and Practice, 10*(3), 153–159.

Wright-Strawderman, C., & Watson, B. L. (1992). The prevalence of depressive symptoms in children with learning disabilities. *Journal of Learning Disabilities, 25*, 258–264.

Yamaguchi, B. J., Strawser, S., & Higgins, K. (1997). Children who are homeless: Implications for educators. *Intervention in School and Clinic, 33*, 90–98.

Yates, J. R., & Ortiz, A. A. (1995). Linguistically and culturally diverse students. In R. Podemski, G. E. Marsh II, T. E. Smith, & B. J. Price, *Comprehensive administration of special education* (2nd ed.) (pp. 129–155). Englewood Cliffs, NJ: Prentice Hall.

Yehle, A. K., & Wambold, C. (1998, July/August). An ADHD success story: Strategies for teachers and students. *Teaching Exceptional Children,* 8–13.

Yelin, E., & Katz, P. P. (1994). Labor force trends of persons with and without disabilities. *Monthly Labor Review, 117*, 36–42.

Yell, M. L., Rogers, D., & Rogers, E. L. (1998). The legal history of special education: What a long, strange trip it's been! *Remedial and Special Education, 19*, 219–228.

Yell, M. L., & Shriner, J. G. (1997). The IDEA amendments of 1997: Implications for special and general education teachers, administrators, and teacher trainers. *Focus on Exceptional Children, 30*, 1–12.

Yess, M. L., Rogers, D., & Rogers, E. (1998). The legal history of special education: What a long strange trip it's been. *Remedial and Special Education, 19*, 219–228.

Ylvisaker, M., Hartwick, P., & Stevens, M. (1991). School reentry following head injury. *Journal of Head Trauma Rehabilitation, 6*, 10–22.

Ylvisaker, T., Szekeres, N., Hartwick, R., & Tworek, L. L. (1994). Collaboration in preparation for personal injury suits after TBI. *Topics in Language Disorders, 15*, 1–20.

York, J., & Vandercook, T. (1991). Designing an integrated program for learners with severe disabilities. *Teaching Exceptional Children, 23*, 22–28.

York, J., Vandercook, T., MacDonald, C., Heise-Neff, C., & Caughey, E. (1992). Feedback about integrating middle-school students with severe disabilities in general education classes. *Exceptional Children, 58*, 244–258.

Young, G., & Gerber, P. J. (1998). Learning disabilities and poverty: Moving towards a new understanding of learning disabilities as a public health and economic-risk issue. *Learning Disabilities, 9*, 1–6.

Young, M. E., Kersten, L., & Werch, T. (1996). Evaluation of patient-child drug education program. *Journal of Drug Education, 26*, 57–68.

Ysseldyke, J. E., & Olsen, K. (1999). Putting alternative assessments into practice: What to measure and possible sources of data. *Exceptional Children, 65*, 175–185.

Ysseldyke, J. E., Algozzine, B., & Thurlow, M. L. (2000). *Critical issues in special education* (3rd ed.). Boston: Houghton Mifflin.

Zabel, R. H., & Zabel, M. K. (1996). *Classroom management in context.* Boston: Houghton Mifflin.

Zargoza, N., Vaughn, S., & McIntosh, R. (1991). Social skills instruction and children with behavior problems: A review. *Behavior Disorders, 16*, 260–275.

Zhang, D. (2001a). The effectiveness of "Next STEP" on the self-determination skills of students with learning disabilities. *Career Development for Exceptional Individuals, 24*, 121-132.

Zhang, D. (2001b). Self-determination and inclusion: Are students with mild mental retardation more self-determined in regular classrooms? *Education and Training in Mental Retardation and Developmental Disabilities, 36*(4), 357–362.

Zigmond, N., Levin, E., & Laurie, T. (1985). Managing the mainstream: An analysis for teacher attitudes and student performance in mainstream high school programs. *Journal of Learning Disabilities, 18*, 535–541.

Zionts, P. (1997). *Inclusion strategies for students with learning and behavior problems.* Austin, TX: Pro-Ed.

Zirkell, P. (1999). Districts should use caution in determing substantive obligation for services to Section 504 students. *Section 504 Compliance Advisor, 3*, 3–4.

Zirpoli, T., & Melloy, G. (1993). *Behavior management: Applications for teachers and parents.* Columbus, OH: Merrill.

Zucker, S. H., & Polloway, E. A. (1987). Issues in identification and assessment in mental retardation. *Education and Training in Mental Retardation, 22*, 69–76.

Zurkowski, J. K., Kelly, P. S., & Griswold, D. E. (1998). Discipline and IDEA 1997: Instituting a new balance. *Intervention in School and Clinic, 34*, 3–9.

Name Index

Page numbers followed by *f* or *t* indicate figures or tables, respectively.

Subject Index

Page numbers followed by the letters *f* or *t* indicate figures or tables, respectively.

Photo Credits

Pages 2, 3, 32, 33, 90, 91, 128, 228, 229, 246, 250, 286, 287, 296 (both), 340, 457, 478, 479, Will Hart; **pages 9, 320,** Robert Harbison; **page 10,** courtesy of John Colbert; **pages 23, 139, 150, 159, 160, 178, 193, 235, 360, 377, 378, 417,** Will Hart/PhotoEdit; **pages 39, 56, 167, 175, 310, 323, 384, 385, 502,** Brian Smith; **pages 46, 70, 80, 116, 253, 277, 412, 413,** Will Faller; **page 48,** courtesy of Debi Smith and Betty Bolte; **pages 64, 65,** Rosalie Winard; **page 71,** courtesy of Tracey Corriveau; **page 74,** Will & Deni McIntyre/Photo Researchers; **page 77,** Robert E. Daemmrich/Getty Images; **page 96,** Stephen Marks; **page 102,** courtesy of Susan Parrish; **page 105,** Laura Dwight Photography; **pages 124, 125, 153,** Vickie D. King/The Clarion-Ledger; **page 148,** courtesy of Dave Birt; **pages 185, 435, 442, 443, 464,** Mary Kate Denny/PhotoEdit; **page 196,** courtesy of Larry Silver; **pages 200, 201, 217, 224,** Dennis MacDonald/PhotoEdit; **page 206,** Nancy Richmond/The Image Works; **page 215,** courtesy of Mike Kelly; **page 221,** Dana White/PhotoEdit; **page 242,** courtesy of Max Lewis; **pages 247, 467,** Ellen Senisi/The Image Works; **pages 256, 257, 268, 276, 406, 427,** Michael Newman/PhotoEdit; **page 282,** Amy Etra/PhotoEdit; **page 283,** courtesy of Bonnie Lawrence; **page 294** (top), courtesy of Kim Carper; **page 294** (bottom), Paul Conklin/PhotoEdit; **page 303,** Richard Hutchings/PhotoEdit; **pages 314, 315, 325, 328,** Robin Sachs/PhotoEdit; **page 338,** courtesy of Martha Drennan; **pages 348, 349,** Jay Malonson/Metrowest Daily News; **page 375,** courtesy of Joy Kataoka; **page 391,** courtesy of Sara Gillison; **page 395,** T. Lindfors/Lindfors Photography; **page 408,** Skojld Photographs; **page 438,** courtesy of Karen Weeks Canfield; **page 452,** Jeff Greenberg/PhotoEdit; **page 460,** courtesy of Val Sharpe; **page 485,** Jose L. Pelaez/Corbis Stock Market; **page 494,** courtesy of the Flowers family.